DECODING DOMESDAY

DECODING DOMESDAY

David Roffe

THE BOYDELL PRESS

First published 2007
The Boydell Press, Woodbridge

ISBN 978 1 84383 307 9

The Boydell Press is an imprint of Boydell & Brewer Ltd
PO Box 9, Woodbridge, Suffolk IP12 3DF, UK
and of Boydell & Brewer Inc.
668 Mt Hope Avenue, Rochester, NY 14620, USA
website: www.boydellandbrewer.com

A catalogue record of this publication is available from the British Library

This publication is printed on acid-free paper

Typeset by Carnegie Book Production, Lancaster
Printed in Great Britain by Antony Rowe Ltd, Chippenham, Wiltshire

Contents

Tables

For my mother

Preface

In *Domesday: the Inquest and the Book* (*DIB*) I challenged a consensus of 800 years standing that the production of Domesday Book was the aim of the Domesday inquest. Through a radical re-examination of the Domesday texts and the nature of the inquest, I argued that the inquiry of 1086 was a different enterprise from that of the book, the one being a communal information gathering exercise, the other a private administrative process. As is the way of the modern world, a complex argument was soon translated into tabloid terms: 'It was Bill Wot Didn't Do it!' In what was little more than an aside, I had tentatively suggested that the aftermath of the revolt against William Rufus in 1088 was a possible context for the production of the book and that Rannulf Flambard, the Peter Mandelson of his day, was the probable moving spirit behind it. The sometimes furious debate that followed publication in 2000 concentrated almost exclusively on the date of Domesday Book.

The debate goes on; I contribute a further pennyworth myself in the discussion of the date of Domesday Book below. The point, however, is subordinate to a much wider and important one. Of none of the inquests of the later Middle Ages is it possible to say that it had *a* purpose; articles of enquiry were always diverse, were often changed, and not infrequently abandoned for completely new ones as the participants responded to circumstances. It is clear from contemporary accounts and the surviving texts that the Domesday inquest was no different. Domesday Book was undoubtedly conceived as a register of one kind or another, but, regardless of its date – whether it be 1086–7 or later – its concerns were not necessarily those of the process that gathered the data. My examination of the documentation of the inquest led me to suggest that its subjects were indeed otherwise. They were broadly two. The first was a drive to maximize royal income as manifest in an audit of the king's estates and regalia, most notably a review of the geld. The second was a reassessment of the military service owed by the tenants-in-chief.

The geld and knight service are still purposes that dare not speak their name and have thus been studiously ignored by critics. However, the principle has been accepted: it is not possible to squeeze the Domesday process into a single bottle. That perception is the conceptual starting point of this book. The notion of a seamless

Domesday process, from inception in 1085 to completion of Great Domesday Book in 1087, has had a profound effect on how Domesday data have been viewed and interpreted at all levels of analysis. Examination of the physical forms of the texts should, it might be supposed, be entirely empirical. And yet palaeographical and codicological studies have been largely concerned with demonstrating the application of a fully formed purpose. There was only one game, it is presumed, and each player kept his eye on the goal. The examination of every item of Domesday data has been, to a greater or lesser degree, similarly confined. Mutually exclusive perceptions of a single purpose have led to reductionist arguments and contradictory conclusions. The upshot has been the singular lack of consensus that is apparent in almost all areas of Domesday studies.

Teleology can be fun, but in the study of history it is incompatible with rigorous enquiry. *Decoding Domesday* proposes a radical reappraisal of Domesday data in terms of the aims of the various processes that amassed them. From the start the texts are examined as artefacts in their own right – no satellites here: all texts are equal – and their sources and concerns are explored. Some of the results are surprising. A hitherto unsuspected survey of royal churches, for example, is identified for the first time and the missing account of Winchester is uncovered. Other processes like the geld inquest are better known, but are accorded their own integrity as concerns. The method in its turn leads to new insights into hoary old controversies such as the nature of ploughlands and the meaning of waste and leads to reassessment of the limits of Domesday data. Above all, it results in a new appraisal of the scope of the Domesday texts. Domesday Book came to be perceived as an exhaustive survey of land, but it cannot be what its sources were not: it was compiled from inquest records in which the focus was less lordship and land than the more limited service and soke.

The structure of the book largely reflects this programme. By way of introduction, it commences in 'Domesday Past and Present' with an account of changing views of the Domesday processes over the centuries, with especial emphasis on the underlying assumptions of analysis in the last hundred years. The book continues in chapters 2 and 3 with an examination of the Domesday texts and their interpretative possibilities and then an overview of the inquest process and the production of Domesday Book. The interrelationship between the forms of the texts and the procedures of the inquest provide the background to the detailed discussion of content that follows. Here the organizing principle is that of Domesday Book itself. The borough and county customs are often the first item of information in each county. They are accordingly examined first in chapter 4. Rural estates follow. There is no entry form that is common to every county surveyed, but the types of information recorded fall into a small number of categories. These have been grouped in chapters 5 to 8 in an order that approximates to that found in the Prologue to the Inquisitio Eliensis that purports to record the questions asked by the commissioners, thus:

Lordship, Land, and Service

y [the pre-Conquest holder] held	Pre-Conquest lordship
a [the tenant-in-chief] and b [his tenant]	Post-Conquest lordship
hold for a manor	The manor and service

The Vill and Taxation

In x [the place]	Names and places
z hides/carucates of land	The hides, the geld, and local government
it has never gelded	The forest and inland
There is land for p^1 ploughs there	The ploughland

The Economy and Society

In demesne	The demesne
there are p^2 ploughs and l livestock	Ploughs
There are v villagers there	Population
c cattle, s sheep, and g goats	Livestock
There is pasture and a church	Manorial appurtenances
It was and is worth w pounds	Value
It is waste	Waste

The Communities of the Shire

The vill/manor measures f^1 x f^2 furlongs	The vill
In h hundred	The hundred
The men of the shire say	The shire
c claims this land	Disputes

There follows a chapter on the 'beyond' of Domesday, the use of its data to reconstruct the fabric of English society before the Conquest. The book concludes with an overview of the nature of the Domesday enterprise and its legacy.

Throughout reference has been made to the manuscripts of Domesday Book, available in facsimile in the Alecto edition, citing the recto or verso of the relevant folio. To this has been added the unique entry identifications of the Phillimore edition of the text. The Alecto translation has been used unless otherwise stated. For the other Domesday texts the standard editions have been used, although the various manuscripts have been consulted where appropriate. I have acknowledged translations where they are available and I have used them, but otherwise I have silently translated myself, transcribing significant words and phrases where the meaning is obscure or the import technical.

The reading of texts is the most important exercise for the historian. The secondary literature on Domesday Book is immense and I have not been able, nor indeed willing, to review the historiography in detail. Nevertheless, I have not been able to ignore pioneering works by the likes of Round and Maitland in the late nineteenth century, and reference will frequently be found to earlier analyses that have defined the shape of the debate. Inevitably, some of the arguments presented here have been pre-figured by earlier writers. Round, for example, thought that

Little Domesday Book was a dry run for Great Domesday (I would, of course, suggest another context) and Douglas was convinced that Domesday Book was, if not an afterthought, then certainly *post hoc*. I have noted these concurrences where they have come to my attention. However, most of the secondary sources cited have appeared in the last forty years or so. In part this reflects current debates and fashions, but mostly it is a function of a recent renaissance in Domesday studies. The novocentenary of the Battle of Hastings in 1966 and of the Domesday inquest in 1986 stimulated a renewed appetite in the subject that the completion of the Phillimore edition of Domesday Book and, above all, the publication of the Alecto facsimile were able amply to satisfy. The outcome has been a plethora of new insights which command close attention and consideration.

Domesday studies have been likened to one of the more abstruse branches of nuclear physics. In an age in which television historians decry the small-mindedness of academic history, it is salutary to remember that Einstein did not publish either his Special or General Theory of Relativity in a twelve part prime-time series. Domesday studies may not be so earth-shattering (and some will say a good thing too), but they demand equally technical discussion. In what follows, I have tried as much as possible to relegate the hard-core anorak material to the footnotes where it can be safely ignored if so desired. But there is no denying that many of the concepts employed are complex. Some stem from method. In rejecting a single Domesday process, I have had to jettison simple reductionist arguments. Where scholars have seen the ploughland, for example, as either a tax assessment or a measure of land, I have had to accept it as both within a wider concept of a process of assessment. Inevitably a moving target is more difficult to hit than a sitting one. Other difficult ideas are simply inherent in eleventh-century society. From a modern, as indeed from a thirteenth-century, perspective, lordship was identified with land. There was no such simple equation in 1086. Domesday England was still an essentially tributary society (albeit one which Domesday Book was soon to change for ever). There the familiar poles of the public and the private, of taxation and service, of freedom and thraldom can no longer be clearly discerned. Reconstructing something of that world in its own image rather than our own is a difficult task by any standards; it is the ultimate aim of this book.

Acknowledgements

Decoding Domesday was in large part drafted in parallel with my monograph *Domesday: the Inquest and the Book* published in 2000. The fact that it has taken a further six years to complete is not just testimony to a busy life. The work was originally conceived as a more accessible account of Domesday studies in the last thirty years. In the event *Decoding* turned into something else: it developed a thesis of its own. Casting the Domesday inquest adrift from the Book, and postulating taxation and service as its overarching concerns, I became increasingly aware that the significance of Domesday data not only could be reassessed but had to be. Inevitably in a book which touches on so many areas of expertise, I have had to consult widely. My debt to recent scholarship in all areas of Domesday studies will be apparent from the footnotes and books and articles cited in the bibliography. Less apparent, but no less significant, have been the various contributions to the debate that *DIB* engendered. Numerous references will be found in the following pages to critics of my understanding of the Domesday process. I am grateful to them all for sometimes penetrating comments and for always concentrating my mind on the further implications of my thesis.

Two sections have already been presented to academic audiences in one form or another. The discussion of ploughlands is derived from a paper read to the Haskins Society conference at Cornell University in November 2002, and the final chapter is based on a paper prepared for the postgraduate seminar series in the (then) Department of English Local History, University of Leicester, in December of the same year, and then subsequently read at the Battle Conference in 2005 and published in *Anglo-Norman Studies*, 28 (2006). Ideas on the nature and purpose of abbreviations of inquest records were developed in papers given at Kumamoto University, Kyoto University, and Keio University in Tokyo in April 2001. I am grateful for the opportunity to try out the various ideas in these forums and for the comments of the participants on all these occasions. Thanks are due to Christine Roffe and Kate Wilde of the Department of Geriatric Medicine at Keele University for reviewing my comments on cliometric methodologies and statistical analysis in general. Above all I owe a debt of gratitude to Ann Williams, Valentine Fallan, and Christine Mahany for reading and commenting on earlier versions of the book. Any errors of fact or interpretation remain, of course, entirely my own responsibility.

Book production will never be my favourite occupation, and so I am grateful to Caroline Palmer and Vanda Andrews for making the experience if not entirely pain free, then as tolerable as is possible in the circumstances. Finally, I have to thank my wife Christine for her love and support throughout the writing of this book and to apologize to my sons Joschka and Theo. *Decoding Domesday* cannot compete in the bedtime reading stakes with Harry Potter, and I promise not to read it to them. I hope, however, that it will find a place on the bookshelves of those who do choose to read Domesday Book and wish to understand more.

Abbreviations

Many of the Domesday texts are cursory lists of lands or brief descriptions of manors. The abbreviations given below refer to the standard editions of these texts. For a full discussion of the nature of the sources, see Chapter 2.

Abingdon A	D. C. Douglas, 'Some Early Surveys from the Abbey of Abingdon', *EHR*, 44 (1929), 623.
Abingdon B	D. C. Douglas, 'Some Early Surveys from the Abbey of Abingdon', *EHR*, 44 (1929), 623–25.
ANS	*Anglo-Norman Studies.*
ASC	*The Anglo-Saxon Chronicle: A Revised Translation*, eds D. Whitelock, D. C. Douglas and S. I. Tucker, 2nd edn (London, 1963).
Attenborough	*The Laws of the Earliest English Kings*, ed. F. L. Attenborough (Cambridge, 1922).
Bath A	*Two Chartularies of the Priory of St Peter at Bath*, ed. W. Hunt, Somerset Record Society, 7 (1893), 67–8.
Bath B	*Two Chartularies of the Priory of St Peter at Bath*, ed. W. Hunt, Somerset Record Society, 7 (1893), 35–6.
Braybrooke Cartulary	G. H. Fowler, 'An Early Cambridgeshire Feodary', *EHR*, 46 (1931), 422–3.
Burton B	J. F. R. Walmsley, 'Another Domesday Text', *Medieval Studies* 39 (1977), 116.
Bury A	*Feudal Documents from the Abbey of Bury St Edmunds*, ed. D. C. Douglas (London, 1932), 1–15.
Bury B	*Feudal Documents from the Abbey of Bury St Edmunds*, ed. D. C. Douglas (London, 1932), 15–24.
Bury C	*Feudal Documents from the Abbey of Bury St Edmunds*, ed. D. C. Douglas (London, 1932), 25–44.
COEL	*The Continental Origins of English Landholders 1066–1166 database and the COEL Database System on CD-ROM*, K. S. B. Keats-Rohan, Coel Enterprises Ltd, 2002.
Crowland DB	*Rerum Anglicarum Scriptores Veteres*, ed. W. Fulman (Oxford, 1684), i, 80–2.

DB Beds	*Domesday Book: Bedfordshire*, ed. J. Morris (Chichester, 1977).
DB Berks	*Domesday Book: Berkshire*, ed. P. Morgan (Chichester, 1979).
DB Bucks	*Domesday Book: Buckinghamshire*, ed. J. Morris (Chichester, 1978).
DB Cambs	*Domesday Book: Cambridgeshire*, ed. A. Rumble (Chichester, 1981).
DB Cheshire	*Domesday Book: Cheshire*, ed. P. Morgan (Chichester, 1978).
DB Cornwall	*Domesday Book: Cornwall*, eds C. Thorn and F. Thorn (Chichester, 1979).
DB Derby	*Domesday Book: Derbyshire*, ed. P. Morgan (Chichester, 1978).
DB Devon	*Domesday Book: Devon*, eds C. Thorn and F. Thorn (Chichester, 1985).
DB Dorset	*Domesday Book: Dorset*, eds C. Thorn and F. Thorn (Chichester, 1983).
DB Essex	*Domesday Book: Essex*, ed. A. Rumble (Chichester, 1983).
DB Gloucs	*Domesday Book: Gloucestershire*, ed. J. S. Moore (Chichester, 1982).
DB Hants	*Domesday Book: Hampshire*, ed. J. Munby (Chichester, 1982).
DB Hereford	*Domesday Book: Herefordshire*, eds F. Thorn and C. Thorn (Chichester, 1983).
DB Herts	*Domesday Book: Hertfordshire*, ed. J. Morris (Chichester, 1976).
DB Hunts	*Domesday Book: Huntingdonshire*, ed. S. Harvey (Chichester, 1975).
DB Kent	*Domesday Book: Kent*, ed. P. Morgan (Chichester, 1983).
DB Leics	*Domesday Book: Leicestershire*, ed. P. Morgan (Chichester, 1979).
DB Lincs	*Domesday Book: Lincolnshire*, eds P. Morgan and C. Thorn (Chichester, 1986).
DB Middlesex	*Domesday Book: Middlesex*, ed. J. Morris (Chichester, 1975).
DB Norfolk	*Domesday Book: Norfolk*, ed. P. Brown (Chichester, 1984).
DB Northants	*Domesday Book: Northamptonshire*, eds F. Thorn and C. Thorn (Chichester, 1979).
DB Notts	*Domesday Book: Nottinghamshire*, ed. J. Morris (Chichester, 1977).
DB Oxon	*Domesday Book: Oxfordshire*, ed. J. Morris (Chichester, 1978).
DB Rutland	*Domesday Book: Rutland*, ed. F. Thorn (Chichester, 1980).
DB Salop	*Domesday Book: Shropshire*, eds F. Thorn and C. Thorn (Chichester, 1986).
DB Somerset	*Domesday Book: Somerset*, eds C. Thorn and F. Thorn (Chichester, 1980).
DB Staffs	*Domesday Book: Staffordshire*, ed. J. Morris (Chichester, 1976).
DB Suffolk	*Domesday Book: Suffolk*, ed. A. Rumble (Chichester, 1986).
DB Surrey	*Domesday Book: Surrey*, ed. J. Morris (Chichester, 1975).
DB Sussex	*Domesday Book: Sussex*, ed. J. Morris (Chichester, 1976).
DB Warks	*Domesday Book: Warwickshire*, ed. J. Morris (Chichester, 1976).

DB Wilts	*Domesday Book: Wiltshire*, eds C. Thorn and F. Thorn (Chichester, 1979).
DB Worcs	*Domesday Book: Worcestershire*, eds F. Thorn and C. Thorn (Chichester, 1982).
DB Yorks	*Domesday Book: Yorkshire*, eds M. L. Faull and M. Stinson (Chichester, 1986).
Descriptio Terrarum	D. R. Roffe, 'The Descriptio Terrarum of Peterborough Abbey', *Historical Research*, 65 (1992), 15–16.
DIB	D. R. Roffe, Domesday: *The Inquest and the Book* (Oxford, 2000).
Domesday Monachorum A	*The Domesday Monachorum of Christ Church Canterbury*, ed. D. C. Douglas (London, 1944), 80–1.
Domesday Monachorum B	*The Domesday Monachorum of Christ Church Canterbury*, ed. D. C. Douglas (London, 1944), 81–98.
Domesday Monachorum D	*The Domesday Monachorum of Christ Church Canterbury*, ed. D. C. Douglas (London, 1944), 98–9.
Domesday Monachorum E	*The Domesday Monachorum of Christ Church Canterbury*, ed. D. C. Douglas (London, 1944), 99–104.
EcHR	*Economic History Review.*
EHD	*English Historical Documents, i: c.500–1042*, ed. D. Whitelock, 2nd edn (London and New York, 1979), ii: 1042–1189, eds D. C. Douglas and G. W. Greenaway, 2nd edn (London, 1981).
EHR	*English Historical Review.*
Ely A	*Inquisitio Comitatus Cantabrigiensis*, ed. N. E. S. A. Hamilton (London, 1876), 168–73.
Ely B	*Inquisitio Comitatus Cantabrigiensis*, ed. N. E. S. A. Hamilton (London, 1876), 174–5.
Ely C	*Inquisitio Comitatus Cantabrigiensis*, ed. N. E. S. A. Hamilton (London, 1876), 175–83.
Ely D	*Inquisitio Comitatus Cantabrigiensis*, ed. N. E. S. A. Hamilton (London, 1876), 184–89.
Evesham A	P. H. Sawyer, 'Evesham A, a Domesday Text', *Miscellany 1*, Worcestershire Historical Society (1960), 22–36.
Evesham F	London, British Library, Cotton MS Vespasian B xxiv, fol. 11r.
Evesham K	London, British Library, Cotton MS Vespasian B xxiv, fols 57r–62r.
Evesham M	London, British Library, Cotton MS Vespasian B xxiv, fols 62r–63v.
Evesham P	London, British Library, Harleian MS 3763, fol. 71v.
Evesham Q	London, British Library, Harleian MS 3763, fol. 82r.
Excerpta	*An Eleventh-Century Inquisition of St Augustine's, Canterbury*, ed. A. Ballard, Records of the Social and Economic History of England, 4 (London, 1920), 1–33.
Exon	*Libri Censualis, vocati Domesday Book, Additamenta ex Codic. Antiquiss. Exon Domesday; Inquisitio Eliensis; Liber Winton; Boldon Book*, ed. H. Ellis (London, 1816).

GDB	*Great Domesday*, ed. R. W. H. Erskine (London, 1986)
Hemingi Chartularium	*Hemingi Chartularium Ecclesiae Wigorniensis*, ed. T. Hearne, 2 vols (Oxford, 1723)
ICC	*Inquisitio Comitatus Cantabrigiensis*, ed. N. E. S. A. Hamilton (London, 1876), 1–96.
IE	*Inquisitio Comitatus Cantabrigiensis*, ed. N. E. S. A. Hamilton (London, 1876), 97–167.
Kentish Assessment List	R. S. Hoyt, 'A Pre-Domesday Kentish Assessment List', *A Medieval Miscellany for Doris Mary Stenton*, eds P. M. Barnes and C. F. Slade, Pipe Roll Society, new series, 36 (1960), 199–202.
LDB	Little Domesday Book.
OE	Old English.
Robertson	*The Laws of the Kings of England from Edmund to Henry I*, ed. A. J. Robertson (Cambridge, 1925).
S	P. H. Sawyer, *Anglo-Saxon Charters: an Annotated List and Bibliography*, Royal Historical Society Guides and Handbooks, 8 (1968).
TRE	*Tempore Regis Edwardi*, 'in the time of King Edward', i.e. 1066 or before.
TRHS	*Transactions of the Royal Historical Society.*
TRW	*Tempore Regis Willelmi*, 'in the time of King William', i.e. between 1066 and 1086.
VCH	*Victoria History of the Counties of England.*
Worcester A	*Hemingi Chartularium Ecclesiae Wigornensis*, ed. T. Hearne (Oxford, 1723), 83–4.
Worcester B	*Hemingi Chartularium Ecclesiae Wigornensis*, ed. T. Hearne (Oxford, 1723), 298–313.

1

Domesday Past and Present

I T IS UNLIKELY that Domesday Book will ever join the Bible and Shakespeare as an indispensable companion of the castaway marooned on a desert island. Nonetheless in one way or another it is a cultural icon of equal power in English consciousness. For many today that power is all but subliminal. 'Domesday' is nowadays most often used as a tabloid term for any comprehensive list with pretensions to permanent record. We have had the BBC Domesday of 1986 (sadly unreadable after twenty years of technological advance),[1] a Domesday of the government art collection, a Domesday of village greens, even a Domesday of rap. No one has to read on to find out the nature of the enterprise in question. *The* Domesday Book may often be dimly perceived. Its most common outing is in estate agents' descriptions as an imprimatur of heritage. The very name, though, conjures up ideas that lie at the heart of the Christian inheritance. Domesday Book is the embodiment of final authority.

Apart from its obvious antiquity, the reality might disappoint the more apocalyptically minded. Domesday Book is preserved in the National Archives in Kew, London, where it is on display in the museum as the oldest and most precious of the English public records.[2] It is an abstract of a survey of lords, lands, and taxes ordered by William the Conqueror at the Christmas court at Gloucester in 1085. In fact, it is not one book but two. Volume one, known as Great Domesday Book (GDB), is an account of thirty-one of the thirty-four shires of Norman England; volume two, Little Domesday Book (LDB), is concerned with the remaining three. The language of both is Latin and it is highly contracted into a business-like shorthand. GDB is an accomplished production. It is written in two columns in neat Carolingian minuscules, the current form of writing in the eleventh century, on 382 folios (764 pages) fifteen by eight inches, and attention is drawn to important

---

[1] A team from Leeds University has now recovered the data from the original laser discs for storage on more accessible media (http://news.bbc.co.uk/1/hi/technology/2534391.stm). Will the CD-ROM technology and the like to which it is to be transferred survive to allow easy access as long as the eleventh-century equivalent?

[2] It has the call number E31, but is not generally available for inspection. Readers are referred to the facsimiles or translations. For editions, see below, pp.32–6.

items of information such as the names of manors by capitalization and through-lining[3] or shading (rubrication) in red ink. LDB extends to 450 folios eleven by eight inches, but is smaller in format and written in one column; it too is rubricated, although by no means so thoroughly as GDB, but is altogether a less neatly ordered production. The whole work was rebound in five parts in 1984 to facilitate reference.

Domesday Book does not stand alone as a witness to the Domesday process. There are a number of documents which emanate from earlier stages in the enter-prise. Two of these, the Liber Exoniensis (Exon) and the Inquisitio Comitatus Cantabrigiensis (ICC), are extensive sources covering a county or series of counties. Several others, notably Bath A, the Crowland Domesday, and the Inquisitio Eliensis (IE), contain accounts of individual fees; the remainder are mostly summary texts which amount to little more than a list of place-names and assessments to taxation. None of these texts, however, can compare in breadth and accomplishment with either volume of Domesday Book. Furthermore, they were not widely known or disseminated in the medieval period. Domesday Book, GDB and LDB, dazzled administrators and historians alike and it has continued to do so down to the modern day.

The first notice of the work probably occurs in a charter of 1099–1101 where reference is made to the *liber regis*, 'the king's book'. In a passage written in about 1120 at the end of Yorkshire folios of GDB a note refers to it as the *Liber de Wintonia*, 'the book of Winchester'. Elsewhere in the twelfth and thirteenth centuries it was variously called 'the king's register', 'the king's rolls', and the like.[4] However, it was accorded its popular name at an early date. Richard fitzNigel, writing *c.*1179 in the Dialogue of the Exchequer, explained that the book was commonly known by the native English as Domesday, that is, the Day of Judgement:

> for as the sentence of that strict and terrible last account cannot be evaded by any skilful subterfuge, so when this book is appealed to on those matters which it contains, its sentence cannot be quashed or set aside with impunity. That is why we have called the book 'the Book of Judgement', not because it contains decisions on various difficult points, but because its decisions, like those of the Last Judgement, are unalterable.[5]

---

[3] To the uninitiated the rubrication of place-names looks like crossing out. In fact, the scribe *underlined* in black ink to indicate words erroneously entered into the record. For scribal practices and conventions, see below, pp. 47–53.

[4] V. H. Galbraith, 'Royal Charters to Winchester', *EHR*, 35 (1920), 389; GDB, 332v: *DB Yorks*, 31,1. For early references, see E. M. Hallam, *Domesday Book through Nine Centuries* (London, 1986), 32–51.

[5] *Dialogus de Scaccario, the Course of the Exchequer, and Constitutio Domus Regis, the King's Household*, ed. C. Johnson (London, 1950), 64.

From the thirteenth century it was known officially as 'the book called Domesday'.[6]

Such popular awareness of a document was probably unique in the twelfth century. Indeed, it would be difficult to find parallels at any time in the Middle Ages.[7] Wherein lay its power in popular perception is not clear in fitzNigel's account. The symbolism of its form was no doubt potent. To the medieval mind the book was immediately associated with authority with a force that is difficult to appreciate today. In England administrative and business records took the form of rolls throughout the Middle Ages. The book was reserved for very special texts, most notably the Gospels.[8] The eschatological referents of the name Domesday Book, then, were evidently no mere whimsy. Domesday was an object of authority not least because it was a *book*, and the fact that it was an old one only added to its mystique.

Of its talismanic status from the thirteenth century there can be no doubt. The subject matter of Domesday Book is exclusively the land of the tenants-in-chief and the honorial barony (the chief tenants of the tenants-in-chief). Its effectiveness in legal terms for the man in the furrow was largely confined to proof of tenure in ancient demesne. If land had once been held by the king its unfree tenants were entitled to exemption from arbitrary taxation by their lord: Domesday Book was the touchstone of such pleas. However, this limited efficacy did not diminish expectation. Throughout the Middle Ages and beyond all manner of men saw in Domesday Book the remedy for their ills. Time and again appeal was made to the record in the forlorn hope of demonstrating freedom in the face of seigneurial oppression where it could never have been of help.[9]

Nevertheless, the lesson was not lost upon everyone. Awe was paralleled by outrage. Richard fitzNigel perceived a high political programme in Domesday Book:

> [It] … is the inseparable companion in the Treasury of the royal seal. The reason for its compilation was told to me by Henry, bishop of Winchester, as follows. When the famous William 'the Conqueror' of England, the Bishop's near kinsman, had brought under his sway the farthest limits of the island, and had tamed the minds of the rebels by awful examples, to prevent error from having free course in the future, he decided to bring the conquered people under the rule of written law. So, setting out before him the English

---

[6] Hallam, *Domesday through Nine Centuries*, 34.

[7] The Ragman inquest of 1274–75 is the closest parallel. Its name was also a popular one, but enthusiasm for the process was short-lived: as the Dunstable chronicler said, 'nothing came of it' (*Annales Monastici*, ed. H. R. Luard, Rolls Series, 36, 5 vols (1864–69), iii, 263).

[8] M. T. Clanchy, *From Memory to Written Record* (London, 1979), 102–5.

[9] For a list of known exemplifications, see Hallam, *Domesday through Nine Centuries*, 199–214.

laws in their threefold versions, namely Mercian law, Dane law, and Wessex law, he repudiated some of them, approved others and added those Norman laws from overseas which seemed to him most effective in preserving the peace. Lastly, to give the finishing touch to all this forethought, after taking counsel he sent his most skilful councillors in circuit throughout the realm. By these a careful survey of the whole country was made, of its woods, its pastures and meadows, as well of arable land, and was set down in common language and drawn up into a book; in order, that is, that every man may be content with his own rights, and not encroach unpunished on those of others.[10]

Writing in the mid thirteenth century, Matthew Paris transformed the notion of such a purpose into a critique; it was, he averred, with the compilation of Domesday Book that 'the manifest oppression of England began'.[11] This was a sentiment that was to inform radical political thought into the modern period; it was the common currency of the Levellers in the Civil War and it coloured the debate between Whigs and Tories in the eighteenth and nineteenth centuries.[12] It is even current today. Reviewing the BSE inquiry report, Professor Hugh Pennington wrote in December 2000:

> The [BSE] inquiry joins a long English tradition of detailed government-commissioned reports compiled with state-of-the-art technology. The *Domesday Book* was the first and BSE might be thought of as a tardy riposte to that Norman intrusion – the disease, after all, has crossed the Channel in the opposite direction.[13]

As we shall see,[14] the sentiment uncannily echoes the reaction of an English monk writing in 1086.

Domesday Book was nothing if not ideological, and herein lay its real staying power. It documented the origins of the English landed classes and validated their title. Compiled within thirty or so years of the Norman Conquest, Domesday Book was a tangible representation of the tenurial revolution that had seen the all-but-complete eclipse of the Old English aristocracy by the companions of William the Conqueror. Domesday stood at the beginning of family history. Likewise, it marked, if not always the origins, then a supremely decisive stage in the history of religious institutions. Domesday Book was an icon of an order and was constantly in the public gaze as such for the first two hundred years of its

---

[10] *Dialogus de Scaccario*, 62–3.

[11] *Matthei Parisiensis, Monachi Sancti Albani, Historia Anglorum*, ed. F. Madden, 3 vols, Rolls Series, 44 (1866–68), iii, 172.

[12] Hallam, *Domesday Book through Nine Centuries*, 37, 132–4.

[13] Hugh Pennington, review of *The BSE Inquiry: Vols I–XVI*, in *The London Review of Books*, 14 December 2000.

[14] Below, p. 6.

existence. Although associated with the Treasury at Winchester, it regularly moved with that department as successive kings travelled through their kingdom. We are fortunate that it was not with King John's treasure when his baggage train was lost to the sea crossing the Wash in 1216. How it was used is largely unknown,[15] but it must have been a constant presence in royal administration and justice. Its value to the lord, however, is well attested. From at least the late twelfth century no archive was complete without a copy of the Domesday entries for the estate.[16] There could be no more powerful an argument for a claim on land or service than that it appeared in Domesday Book.

From the very start of its recorded history Domesday Book has, then, lain at the heart of diverse notions of Englishness. As such, of course, it is not unique. Magna Carta and the Bill of Rights each have a similar iconic status. What does distinguish Domesday Book, however, is that unlike these documents, it also stands all-but-alone as an historical source. Without it our knowledge of Anglo-Saxon England would be so much the poorer as to be unintelligible, the Norman Conquest and settlement would be unmapped, and the foundations of feudal society invisible. More so than for any other source, it is therefore important to determine what Domesday Book is describing. Hitherto the answer has seemed simple enough. With contemporary accounts of the wide scope of the survey, historians have fixed on the formidable reputation of Domesday Book and its use in royal administration from the late twelfth century to characterize the whole of the Domesday process. In so doing, they have adopted three basic propositions derived from its forms and content. First, the production of Domesday Book was the aim of the Domesday inquest; second, its contents are authoritative; third, it embodies a comprehensive survey of land. It is concluded that Domesday data are about lordship and land, real estates and real economies.

[15] A handful of charters from the reign of Henry I are often cited as evidence of the use of Domesday Book in the early twelfth century; see, for example, V. H. Galbraith, *Domesday Book: its Place in Administrative History* (Oxford, 1974), 103–6. Hallam, *Domesday through Nine Centuries*, 32–51, is more cautious. For a critique of the charters, see below, pp. 24–5.
[16] The point is nicely made by an entry in a fourteenth-century register of Waltham Abbey: 'Many advantages may arise from the possession of the copy [of Domesday], because it shows how the manors of this Church were held before the Conquest and at the Conquest. It also shows how many hides there are in each manor, and, if the king should wish to tallage his realm by hides, by how many hides our manors are taxed, even though this Church is free by charter of the tallage of hidage. It also shows what status the tenants of our manors have by right ... If, God forbid, any malicious pleas should ever in future be raised by any one to take away the possessions of this Church, the extract shows which words in the books or rolls should be used as evidence, and likewise any advantages or gains which may be brought to this Church. Many other uses may be found for such a copy; and let it be known that these things which are here noted from the Book of Domesday are written word for word.' Cited in Hallam, *Domesday through Nine Centuries*, 52. There has been no systematic survey of such copies of Domesday entries. Such an exercise would be useful in determining knowledge of Domesday sources and ease of access to them.

The conclusion appears to gain irrefutable support from modern statistical analysis. Economic and social historians are now confident in the use of Domesday data to reconstruct the economy and society of late eleventh-century England. Nevertheless, the whole structure is less secure than it seems. Despite this confidence in the use of Domesday data, there has been no general agreement on the purpose of the enterprise and as a result the import of just about every item of Domesday data is disputed. The historians who use Domesday to reconstruct eleventh-century society are rather like the man who protests that he knows nothing about art but knows what he likes. An examination of the development of the modern consensus reveals a number of inconsistencies and lapses in method at the heart of Domesday studies. In its turn it suggests the need for a radical re-appraisal of Domesday data. The problem begins with the contemporary accounts of the Domesday process. It is their eloquence on the how and what of the enterprise that has contrived to conceal the more important question of why.

From content to purpose: the mystique of the book

On Christmas Day 1085 William, duke of Normandy and conqueror and king of England, had much thought and deep discussion with his council at Gloucester about England:

> how it was occupied or with what sort of people. Then he sent his men over all England into every shire and had them find out how many hundred hides there were in the shire, or what land and cattle the king himself had in the country, or what dues he ought to have in twelve months from the shire. Also he had a record made of how much land his archbishops had, and his bishops and his abbots and his earls – and though I relate it at too great a length – what or how much everyone had who was occupying land in England, in land or cattle, and how much money it was worth. So very narrowly did he have it investigated, that there was no single hide nor virgate of land, nor indeed (it is a shame to relate but it seemed no shame for him to do) one ox nor one cow nor one pig which was there left out, and not put down in his record; and all these records were brought to him afterwards.[17]

So wrote the English author of the E version of the Anglo-Saxon Chronicle within a year of what is now known as the Domesday inquest. A second contemporary account, penned by Bishop Robert Losinga of Hereford, is appended to a treatise on chronology based on a passage in the chronicle of Marianus Scotus.

> [In the] twentieth year of his reign by order of William, king of the English, there was made a survey (*descriptio*) of the whole of England; of the lands in each of the counties; of the possessions of each of the magnates, their

---

[17] *ASC*, 161–2.

lands, their manors (*mansionibus*), their men both bond and free, living in cottages or with their own houses and lands; of ploughs, horses, and other animals; of the services and payments due from all the men in the whole land. Other investigators followed the first and were sent to counties that they did not know, and where they themselves were unknown, to check the first description and to denounce any wrongdoers to the king. And the land was vexed with much violence arising from the collection of the king's taxes.[18]

Both are extraordinary accounts of the procedure of the inquest that manage to convey a sense of remarkable events. A third reference, a letter written by Lanfranc, archbishop of Canterbury, sometime in the course of the survey, to a royal official identified as 'S', is more prosaic:

I confirm that in those counties in which you have been assigned the duty of making an inquest I have no demesne land; all the lands of our church in those parts are entirely given over to providing food for the monks. The brother who is bringing you this letter has told me a great deal in your favour, too much to be set out here in the brief limits of a letter. May almighty God, whose memory nothing escapes, recompense you according to his knowledge many times over, and be your vigilant helper at all times to defend you from every evil machination.[19]

LDB preserves a record of what use 'S' made of this information.[20]

There is nothing exactly comparable with these three first-hand witnesses of the Domesday inquest for any of the surveys of the later Middle Ages,[21] but none of the passages indicates why William initiated the inquest in the first place, much less

---

[18] W. H. Stevenson, 'A Contemporary Description of the Domesday Survey', *EHR*, 22 (1907), 74. This passage is echoed in a copy of Marianus' History probably from Worcester (BL, Cotton MS, Nero C v). It reads: 'William, king of the English, ordered all of the possessions of the whole of England to be described, in fields, in men, in all animals, in all manors from the greatest to the smallest, and in all payments which could be rendered from the land of all. And the land was vexed with much violence proceeding therefrom.' See Stevenson, 'A Contemporary Description of the Domesday Survey', 77.

[19] *The Letters of Lanfranc Archbishop of Canterbury*, eds and trans. H. Glover and M. Gibson (Oxford, 1979), no. 56; F. Barlow, 'Domesday Book: A Letter of Lanfranc', *EHR*, 78 (1963), 289. Translation from Hallam, *Domesday Book through Nine Centuries*, 23.

[20] In Essex it is Holy Trinity, that is presumably the monks, that is accordingly listed as holding in chief at the beginning of the county folios. In Suffolk, by contrast, Archbishop Lanfranc is credited with the lands both in the list and at the head of the appropriate chapter, although there 'for the monks' supplies' is added (LDB, 1, 12v, 281, 372v: *DB Essex*, L. 5,1; *DB Suffolk*, L. 15,1). This might imply that Essex was written after Suffolk (P. Taylor, 'Introduction', *Little Domesday Book, Essex*, eds A. Williams and G. H. Martin (London, 2000), 10–11), but equally the discrepancy may have existed in the scribes' sources.

[21] Most inquests go largely unremarked in chronicles. The hundred roll inquiry of 1279–80 was the most ambitious ever undertaken, Domesday notwithstanding, and yet there are

makes explicit reference to Domesday Book. It was certainly a time of momentous events. 1085 was a year of crisis. The Anglo-Saxon Chronicle records that:

> people said and declared for a fact, that Cnut, king of Denmark, son of King Swein, was setting out in this direction and meant to conquer this country with the help of Robert, count of Flanders, because Cnut was married to Robert's daughter. When William, king of England, who was then in Normandy – for he was in possession of both England and Normandy – found out about this, he went to England with a larger force of mounted men and infantry from France and Brittany than had ever come to this country, so that people wondered how this country could maintain all that army. And the king had all the army dispersed all over the country among his vassals, and they provisioned the army each in proportion to his land. And people had much oppression that year, and the king had the land near the sea laid waste, so that if his enemies landed, they should have nothing to seize on so quickly. But when the king found out for a fact that his enemies had been hindered and could not carry out their expedition – then he let some of the army go to their own country, and some he kept in this country over winter.[22]

There was good reason why William took this threat so seriously. Large fleets had invaded England in 1069, 1070, and 1075 and all three invasions had been accompanied by serious revolts of the English, and, latterly, disaffected Norman lords. Cnut's claim to the throne by inheritance from King Cnut was as good as William's, and an alliance with Count Robert of Flanders enabled him to marshal his forces and recruit reinforcements in Flemish ports before the short crossing to England.[23] William, already assailed on all sides by enemies, was forced to leave Normandy to defend the wealthier half of his dominion.

Again, there were great events afoot in the following year. 'Then [King William] travelled about so as to come to Salisbury at Lammas [1 August]; and there his councillors came to him, and all the people occupying land who were of any account over all England, no matter whose vassals they might be; and they all submitted to him and became his vassals, and swore oaths of allegiance to him, that they would be loyal to him against all other men.'[24] Mass homage on this scale, clearly performed in return for land, is only otherwise paralleled by coronation. And yet neither the 'oath of Salisbury' of mid 1086 nor the crisis of defence in 1085 is explicitly related to the Domesday inquest in the first-hand sources.

---

just two passing notices of it (S. Raban, *A Second Domesday?: The Hundred Rolls of 1279–80* (Oxford, 2004), 45–6).
[22] *ASC*, 161.
[23] N. Higham, 'The Domesday Survey: Context and Purpose', *History*, 78 (1993), 11–16.
[24] *ASC*, 162.

Writing some ten years later in the cartulary of the church of Worcester, Hemming emphasizes that the inquest was about the lands of 'the king and the leading men'; he describes the session in Worcestershire in the following terms:

> The whole shire of Worcester confirmed this evidence through a sworn oath, with the exhortation and encouragement of the most holy and wise father, lord Bishop Wulfstan, in the time of the elder King William, before the same King's leading men, that is Bishop Remigius of Lincoln, Earl Walter Giffard, Henry de Ferrers, and Adam, brother of Eudo the king's steward. They had been sent by the king himself to seek out and set down in writing the possessions and customs, both of the king and of his leading men, in this province and in several others, at the time when the said king had (details of) the whole of England set down in writing.[25]

This account provides an important record of the names of the commissioners who conducted the inquest in Worcestershire, but, oddly if Domesday Book was central to the process, no account of the estates of the church of Worcester are appended, and again there is no indication of the purpose of the inquest.

We have to wait until the 1120s before any such statement is made. It occurs in the Ecclesiastical History of Orderic Vitalis. For the year 1086 Orderic writes:

> King William carefully surveyed his whole kingdom, and had an exact description made of all the dues in the time of King Edward. Also he allocated land to knights and arranged their contingents in such a way that the kingdom of England should always have 60,000 knights, ready to be mustered at a moment's notice in the king's service whenever necessary.[26]

The Domesday inquest was, according to Orderic, about the definition of knight service. In a later passage he provides a context. He states that

> At this time King William had a record made of the military strength of England, and found that there were sixty thousand knights, all of whom he commended to be ready for service if need arose. For Cnut the younger, king of Denmark was then preparing a great fleet, and making arrangements to invade England, conquered in earlier times by his ancestors Swein and Cnut, and claim his right.[27]

Orderic goes on to say that the threat caused much consternation, but that Cnut was prevented by various circumstances from carrying it out.

---

[25] *Hemingi Chartularium*, 287–8. Translation from *DB Worcs*, appendix V, Worc F.

[26] *The Ecclesiastical History of Orderic Vitalis*, ed. M. Chibnall, 6 vols (Oxford, 1969–80), ii, 267.

[27] *The Ecclesiastical History of Orderic Vitalis*, iv, 52–3. Chibnall considered the mustering of military resources a separate enterprise from the Domesday inquest (*ibid.*, 52n).

Orderic's understanding of the Domesday inquest is otherwise unparalleled.[28] Like the authors of the Anglo-Saxon Chronicle, twelfth-century writers did not make the connection between the crisis of 1085 and the Domesday inquest. Not knowing Orderic's History, or discounting it, they copied or précised the annalist or Bishop Robert until attention became focused on Domesday *Book*. From the late twelfth century its production was widely perceived as the purpose of the Domesday inquest.

The notion first surfaces in the work of a Worcester monk writing in the mid twelfth century. Paraphrasing the 1085 annal of the Anglo-Saxon Chronicle, he subtly changes its import with an explicit reference to the volume:

A.D. 1086. William, king of the English, sent through all the provinces of England, and caused it to be inquired how many hides were held in the whole of England, and how much the king had in lands and cattle and live-stock in each province, and what customary dues each year. This he caused to be done in respect of the lands and dues both of all the churches and of all his barons. He inquired what these were worth, and how much they then rendered, and how much they were able to render in the time of King Edward. And so thoroughly was all this carried out that there did not remain in the whole of England a single hide or a virgate of land or an ox or a cow or a pig which was not written in that return. And all the writings of all these things were brought back to the king. And the king ordered that all should be written in one volume (*volumen*), and that that volume should be placed in his Treasury at Winchester and kept there.[29]

Whether the Worcester annalist understood this to be William's intention all along is unclear. It is Richard fitzNigel who first explicitly states that the production of Domesday Book was the purpose of the inquest, and it was he who gave the notion currency. His understanding has conditioned analysis ever since. Its implications for method are considerable. With the advent of critical studies of the Domesday texts in the nineteenth century, an important corollary was formulated to supplement the notion. If there is no contemporary statement of the purpose of the Domesday inquest, then the documents to which the process gave birth will provide the answer. In the last hundred years or so much of Domesday studies has been devoted to textual criticism on the assumption that form and content are related to intent. Purpose is derived from content.

John Horace Round was the first Domesday scholar to argue in this way. For him 'the key to Domesday' was ICC, published for the first time by N. E. S. A. Hamilton

---

[28] John of Worcester asserts that one of the questions asked was '*quot feudatos milites?*', 'how many enfeoffed knights?' (*The Chronicle of John of Worcester, 3: The Annals from 1067 to 1140 with the Gloucester Interpolations and the Continuation to 1141*, ed. and trans. P. McGurk (Oxford, 1998), 44–5), but goes no further.

[29] *EHD*, ii, 853.

in 1876.[30] ICC is a full Domesday account of the county of Cambridge (less the demesne lands of the king) that contains considerably more detail than its GDB counterpart. Notably it preserves a full account of the livestock belonging to the lord. Its most significant characteristics, though, are its record of the jurors empan-elled in each hundred and arrangement by hundred and by vill. According to IE, a sister text to ICC, the inquest was made 'by the oath of the sheriff of the shire and of all the barons and their Frenchmen and of the whole hundred, of the priest, the reeve, and six villagers of each village'.[31] Round established that the exemplar of ICC (it survives only in a late twelfth-century copy) was earlier than the GDB text, and so drew what appeared the obvious conclusion: ICC was the record of the Domesday inquest in Cambridgeshire. Since tax was levied hundred by hundred, its purpose could only be the reassessment of the geld in the light of the resources in land and livestock recorded.

Round argued that similar documents were produced throughout the country and these, 'the original returns', were sent to Winchester where Domesday Book was compiled from them. Just why there was a change of format is not explained. It was left to Frederic William Maitland to explain its function. In *Domesday Book and Beyond*, published in 1897, the second and still the greatest critical book on Domesday, Maitland accepted Round's analysis and extended its logic to Domesday Book:

> All the lands, all the land-holders of England may be brought before us, but we are told only of such facts, such rights, such legal relationships as bear on the actual or potential payment of geld. True, that some minor purposes may be achieved by the king's commissioners, though the quest for geld is their one main object. About the rents and renders due from his own demesne manors the king may thus obtain some valuable information. Also he may learn, as it were by the way, whether any of his barons or other men have presumed to occupy, to 'invade', lands which he has reserved for himself. Again, if several persons are in dispute about a tract of ground, the contest may be appeased by the testimony of shire and hundred, or may be reserved for the king's audience; at any rate the existence of an outstanding claim may be recorded by the royal commissioners. Here and there the peculiar customs of a shire or a borough will be stated, and incidentally the services that certain tenants owe to their lords may be noticed. But all this is done sporadically and unsystematically. Our record is no register of title, it is no feodary, it is no customal, it is no rent roll; it is a tax book, a geld book.
>
> We say this, not by way of vain complaint against its meagreness, but because in our belief a care for geld and for all that concerns the assess-ment and payment of geld colours far more deeply than commentators have

---

[30] J. H. Round, *Feudal England* (London, 1895), 3ff.
[31] IE, 96.

usually supposed the information that is given to us about other matters. We should not be surprised if definitions and distinctions which at first sight have little enough to do with fiscal arrangements, for example the definition of a manor and the distinction between a villein and a 'free man', involved references to the apportionment and the levy of the land-tax. Often enough it happens that legal ideas of a very general kind are defined by fiscal rules; for example, our modern English idea of 'occupation' has become so much part and parcel of a system of assessment that lawyers are always ready to argue that a certain man must be an 'occupier' because such men as he are rated to the relief of the poor. It seems then a fair supposition that any line that Domesday Book draws systematically and sharply, whether it be between various classes of men or between various classes of tenements, is somehow or another connected with the main theme of that book – geldability, actual or potential.[32]

In short the purpose of the Domesday inquest was the collection of data 'which would enable the royal officers to decide what changes were necessary in order that all England might be taxed in accordance with a just and uniform plan'.

Such was the remorselessness of Round's argument, and the insight and eloquence of Maitland's application of it, that it remained largely unchallenged for almost fifty years. But when it came, the criticism was devastating. In an article published in 1942 and more fully in *The Making of Domesday Book* of 1961, V. H. Galbraith tore apart Round's thesis and replaced it with an alternative analysis which was to prove equally influential.[33] Galbraith came to Domesday studies relatively late in his career. His interest was stimulated by his discovery of the Herefordshire Domesday, a twelfth-century copy of the GDB account of Herefordshire which had been partially up-dated to the 1160s.[34] There geld assessments are entered in the margin for easy reference, but the fact merely underlined for him how difficult it was to use Domesday Book as a taxation record. What it was most immediately about was tenure and title. This was his starting point. Exon, the full Domesday-like account of the south-western counties arranged by lordships (as opposed to shires) and anterior to the corresponding sections of the GDB text, became his key to the making of Domesday and its purpose. In 1912 Baring had already drawn attention to the fact that the text hardly fitted into Round's thesis;[35] Round had, in fact, studiously ignored it. It now became the cornerstone of the Galbraith thesis. The production of GDB was the aim of the Domesday inquest and from early on in the process the data were arranged by

---

[32] F. W. Maitland, *Domesday Book and Beyond* (Cambridge, 1897), 27–8.
[33] V. H. Galbraith, 'Making of Domesday Book', *EHR*, 57 (1942), 161–77; *The Making of Domesday Book* (London, 1961).
[34] *Herefordshire Domesday, circa 1160–1170*, eds V. H. Galbraith and J. Tait, Pipe Roll Society, 63, new series, 25 (1950); Hallam, *Domesday through Nine Centuries*, 166.
[35] F. H. Baring, 'The Exeter Domesday', *EHR*, 27 (1912), 309–18.

lordship. ICC represented one stage of production in the eastern counties, but Exon was the more normal form and it was the return from the south-western shire, or at least its immediate predecessor, from which GDB was compiled. LDB represents a second return that was never abbreviated. From beginning to end the Domesday process was about lordship.

It seemed common sense to assume that documents say what they mean and mean what they say. It followed that the purpose of Domesday Book was no less than a feodary of the new Norman order.

> The all-important fact about Domesday is that it is our earliest public record, carefully preserved by the officers of the king's household for more than eight centuries, and so to be found today at the Public Record Office, Chancery Lane, where it can be seen in the Museum. There must be some good reason to explain this lone survivor of the Conqueror's no doubt considerable archives. And it is not far to seek; for, in striking contrast with later official surveys, the prudent Norman clerks at Winchester, subordinating completeness to practical utility, deliberately jettisoned more than half the information gathered by the king's *legati*, commissioners or justices, compressing the mass of statistics into a single volume, albeit a large one. It was, in short, a forward-looking handy summary, made to last. And so it proved, having served ever since as the blueprint of the new society created after 1066.[36]

In the aftermath of the tenurial revolution that the Conquest had seen, William the Conqueror had inaugurated military tenures, and Domesday Book was to act as both a guide to the Norman settlement and an administrative instrument for the management of the new dues to which the king had become entitled.

Galbraith's insights almost immediately superseded Round's analysis and had the effect of reinvigorating Domesday studies. The emphasis on an integrated Domesday process – the explicit wedding of the inquest to the book – stimulated renewed interest in the Domesday texts. They ceased to be mere sources and became 'satellites' that could be put in order to indicate the intricacies of procedure.[37] In the process Galbraith's idea of successive versions more nearly approximating to the ideal of GDB was significantly modified by Sally Harvey.[38] Confronted with an ever-more elaborate taxonomy and inherent contradictions in the sources, she hypothesized the use of the routine documentation of local administration in the early stages of the inquest. At a stroke the tight timetable postulated by Galbraith for the completion of GDB by the death of King William in September 1087 became feasible.

Galbraith's concept of Domesday Book as the representation of a new order was also elaborated. Paul Hyams took issue with Maitland's assertion that Domesday

---

[36] Galbraith, *Domesday Book*, 18–19.
[37] See chapter 2.
[38] S. P. J. Harvey, 'Domesday Book and its Predecessors', *EHR*, 86 (1971), 753–73.

Book was 'no register of title'. The Domesday inquest was clearly about right as well as tenure, and, however imperfectly, Domesday Book strove to establish a legal basis for landholding.[39] Sir James Holt linked the production of Domesday to the oath of Salisbury and further postulated a new social contract:

> Domesday Book seems to embody a hard-headed deal. William got a survey of his own and his tenants' resources; he was strengthened in the exercise of his feudal rights. His tenants got a record of their tenure, in effect a confirmation of their enfeoffment. In short, as regards the tenant-in-chief, Domesday Book was a vast land book which put a final seal on the Norman occupation.[40]

Domesday Book afforded secure title to what had been precariously held.

In 1986 Henry Loyn famously announced that 'we are all Galbraithians now'.[41] There was a new consensus on the making of Domesday Book. Its purpose, however, remained a matter of debate. Why 1086? The 'new order' school did not seem to have a convincing answer to this question.[42] Surely the crisis of 1085 must have had some impact on the decision to instigate the Domesday inquest at Christmas. There developed in response to this line of thought a 'neo-fiscal' interpretation of Domesday Book. Sally Harvey has been the main proponent. She has accepted that there were feudal concerns in the inquest, but for her the main rationale was the need to raise cash to pay mercenaries:

> A coherent assembly of the evidence accumulated suggests the following picture. In or following the military crisis of 1084–5, William started a reappraisal of fiscal liability in the south-west. It seems to have been unsuccessful. It was certainly short-lived: further abbreviations of DB by the Exchequer omitted it altogether and preserved the 1066 rating in them. William had in 1084 already extorted a huge geld of 6s on the hide which was not completely collected, so there was little possibility of increasing the levy on the existing rating. Moreover, on that rating many of the wealthiest lands lay untapped and exempt. It seems likely that the abortive attempt at reappraisal formed a motive for the searching enquiry into assets and possibilities (and

---

[39] P. Hyams, '"No Register of Title": The Domesday Inquest and Land Adjudication', *ANS*, 9 (1986), 127–41.

[40] J. C. Holt, '1086', *Domesday Studies*, ed. J. C. Holt (Woodbridge, 1987), 56

[41] Thus in a lecture he delivered at Sutton Bonington in Nottinghamshire, one in a series he gave throughout the country in that novocentenary year. For his espousal of Galbraith's thesis, see H. R. Loyn, 'A General Introduction to Domesday Book', *Domesday Book Studies*, eds A. Williams and R. W. H. Erskine (London, 1987), 1–21. For a radical restatement of the Galbraithian view, see C. Flight, *The Survey of the Whole of England: Studies of the Documentation Resulting from the Survey Conducted in 1086*, British Archaeological Reports, British Series, 405 (Oxford, 2006).

[42] Holt relates it to William the Conqueror's departure for France in late 1086 to counter threats to Normandy. This, of course, just begs the question.

by inference into exemptions and their validity) called Domesday Book, with the ploughland representing a completely new assessment ...[43]

For Harvey Domesday Book was primarily a tax book, but one in a tradition of seigneurially arranged lists.[44]

Nicholas Higham has rejected this interpretation and developed an alternative neo-fiscal view. He points out that there is no sign of a reassessment of the geld in the twelfth century. Where evidence survives, gelds were generally levied on the Domesday hide rather than the ploughland. For him the statement 'there is land for so many hides' is merely a measure of extent.[45] Again, however, he puts the Domesday inquest firmly in the context of the crisis of 1085 and sees it as an attempt to placate the under-baronage, that is the men of the tenants-in-chief:

> If [Domesday Book] was not directed at the distribution of geld, it follows that it was concerned with the billeting which had been imposed during 1085, in which case Domesday Book was a novel solution to a novel imposition. It created a register capable of a fairer allocation of this burden than had been possible using existing geld lists, by including the near geld-free *terra regis* and all those estates of the great vassals that enjoyed beneficial hidation. This was perhaps the only major concession which William could make, given his urgent need of renewed taxation and the necessity of billeting mercenaries over what must have seemed an indefinite period. By commissioning the Domesday Book, William was conceding an equality of misery to his baronage and agreeing to shoulder an equivalent share of that misery himself. The new system was demonstrably fairer than the geld lists as a basis for the quartering of troops.[46]

For Higham Domesday Book was a quartermaster's manual.

Finally, A. R. Bridbury has placed the Domesday inquest in the context of the need to tax more efficiently.[47] For him the ploughland is neither land nor fiscal assessment. Rather it is a measure of the supply of ploughs to the lord's demesne and to what extent it was exploited. The Domesday commissioners took no interest in the land of the peasant and only noticed his assets in so far as they were burdened to service. It was the net income of the lord that was the focus of the survey and the king's interest was in determining whether he was maximizing it.

---

[43] S. P. J. Harvey, 'Taxation and the Ploughland in Domesday Book', *Domesday Book: A Reassessment*, ed. P. H. Sawyer (London, 1985), 103.

[44] S. P. J. Harvey, 'Taxation and the Economy', *Domesday Studies*, ed. J. C. Holt (Woodbridge, 1987), 249–64; 'Taxation and the Ploughland in Domesday Book', *Domesday Book: A Reassessment*, ed. P. H. Sawyer (London, 1985), 86–103.

[45] N. Higham, 'Settlement, Land Use and Domesday Ploughlands', *Landscape History*, 12 (1990), 33–44.

[46] Higham, 'Domesday Survey', 17–18.

[47] A. R. Bridbury, 'Domesday Book: A Re-interpretation', *EHR*, 105 (1990), 284–309.

[The commissioners'] task was to convey to the king the most exact account they could compile of the truth about manorial income and its sources, leaving it to him to settle problems connected with future revisions of codings [assessments to the geld] and allowances.[48]

Bridbury's Domesday Book was an annual tax return.

From genealogy and topography to society and economy

Such a variety of interpretations for a source, and such an important one, is extraordinary. The nearest parallel is perhaps the Bible. Nevertheless, there has been no doubt that Domesday Book was likewise authoritative and, in its own terms, comprehensive. Common to the views of all these modern commentators is the notion that Domesday data were the product of a process of recognition, that is of formal legal determination: its contents are what contemporary society would have accepted as attested fact.[49] Matters of title, then, come to the fore and it therefore follows that the Domesday inquest was a complete survey or at least it aimed at being so. The perception has enabled those who wish to use Domesday data to ignore the issue of purpose. In this, the use of Domesday data to reconstruct the society and economy of eleventh-century England, Domesday studies have changed little since the seventeenth century when the source was first widely used for historical purposes.

Domesday was first examined as an historical source for genealogical and topographical studies, and these probably still remain the most common reasons for consulting the text. Domesday Book is stuffed with names.[50] Antiquarians were usually content merely to quote: Domesday provided the first written notice of most families and places, but references are often difficult to put in context since they occur in isolation. Typically, early histories dutifully cite the Domesday evidence quickly to pass on to the thirteenth and fourteenth centuries when the continuous history begins. There were exceptions, however. Dugdale, for example, often tried to bridge the gap.[51] Analysis of the source as a whole was precluded by

[48] Bridbury, 'Domesday Book: A Re-interpretation', 305
[49] It will be noticed that time and again the word 'recognition', the medieval term for legal determination, a judgement, comes up in the historiography.
[50] For indices, see J. McN. Dodgson and J. J. N. Palmer, *Domesday Book: Index of Places* (Chichester, 1992); J. McN. Dodgson and J. J. N. Palmer, *Domesday Book: Index of Persons* (Chichester, 1992); K. S. B. Keats-Rohan, *Domesday People: A Prosopography of Persons Occurring in English Documents, 1066–1166: 1. Domesday Book* (Woodbridge, 1998). H. Ellis, *A General Introduction to Domesday Book* (London, 1833), still remains useful for Latin forms of personal names. A comprehensive list of place-names with identifications can be found in H. C. Darby and G. R. Versey, *A Domesday Gazetteer* (Cambridge, 1975). Place-name forms are also conveniently listed in the indexed search section of the *Digital Domesday* database (Alecto Historical Editions, London, 2002) with identifications updated to 2002.
[51] W. Dugdale, *The Antiquities of Warwickshire*, 2 vols (London, 1656).

its availability. There is some evidence that readers could browse at an early period,[52] but from the late thirteenth century access to the manuscript was restricted and a charge was made for exemplification of each entry (that is, the making of an official copy of a passage). Reflecting the authority of the text, each extract had to be written up by an Exchequer clerk in a Domesday hand.[53] It was not until 1783 and the publication of an edition by Abraham Farley that the text became more freely accessible.[54]

For many Domesday remains a simple datum in the history of one family or place.[55] From the early nineteenth century, however, historians attempted to go beyond the raw data to reconstruct the fabric of eleventh-century society and the economy. John Clarke, John Thompson, and Sir Henry Ellis were early pioneers in the analysis of Domesday data. They produced the first indices of people, places, and subjects, along with summary tables of population, and began the process of counting that has been the lot of Domesday scholars, computerization notwithstanding, ever since.[56] Subsequent analysis was initially founded in the belief that Domesday Book was a complete and transparent survey of England: it meant what it said and said what it meant and, like census returns or royal commission reports, it was amenable to straightforward numerical analysis. It followed that Domesday Book provided a complete picture of the Norman settlement and was equally eloquent in its portrayal of its administrative and landscape backdrops; the area of the hide was as determinable as the extent of arable, pasture, or woodland.[57]

[52] See, for example, the Basset Cartulary and the Historia Croylandensis (Northampton Record Office, ZB347; *Rerum Anglicarum Scriptores Veteres*, i, ed. W. Fulman (Oxford, 1684), 80–2). The scribe of the Bassett cartulary copied from a number of GDB Nottinghamshire *breves* and, in the process, managed to confuse Colston Bassett with Car Colston. The compiler of the Crowland Domesday copied widely from GDB and also from a series of contemporary 'hundred rolls'. I am grateful to Dr Trevor Foulds for the reference to the Basset Cartulary and a transcript of the Domesday entry.

[53] Hallam, *Domesday Book through Nine Centuries*, 56–7. Similarly, final concords, solemn settlements of disputes, were written up in an antique hand into the nineteenth century. Copper Plate, of course, is still used for certificates and the like.

[54] *Domesday Book; Seu Liber Censualis Willelmi Primi ...*, ed. A. Farley (London, 1783). Hallam, *Domesday Book through Nine Centuries*, 132–40, provides a useful account of the genesis of this famous edition. See also, G. H. Martin, 'Abraham Farley's Transcription of Domesday Book', *The Digital Domesday*.

[55] A search of the internet throws up many thousands of pages devoted to individuals, families, and specific people and locations. Discussion group searches suggest that most family historians have abandoned the text in favour of Katherine Keats-Rohan's, *Domesday People*.

[56] *Domesday Book; seu Liber Censualis Vocati Domesday Book, Indices*, ed. H. Ellis (London, 1816); H. Ellis, *A General Introduction to Domesday Book*; Hallam, *Domesday Book through Nine Centuries*, 147–8; A. Prescott, 'Sir Henry Ellis and Domesday Book', *Domesday Book*, eds E. Hallam and D. Bates (Stroud, 2001), 159–90.

[57] The approach is exemplified by the contents of the two volumes that came out of the octocentenary celebrations of Domesday Book of 1886 (*Domesday Studies: being the Papers*

This was an age of innocence in Domesday studies. It was brought to an abrupt end in the late nineteenth century by Round.[58] Round honed his historical skills in the field of genealogy. The romantic yearnings of Victorian gentlemen for ancestry were an easy target for a sharp and critical mind that was aware of the importance of sources and was equipped to interpret them. Round seems to have always revelled in diatribe. Writing for *The Complete Peerage*, he took great delight in putting down and vilifying his rivals at *Burke's Peerage* and *Burke's Landed Gentry*. Domesday Book soon became a famous battleground. In combating the wishful thinking of most of his peers, he brought a hitherto unprecedented rigour to the study of families, and that in its turn led him on to wider areas of concern: studies of knights and tenants-in-chief inspired analyses of honours, the introduction of knight service, and much else.[59]

Hand in hand with the realization of the possibilities of family history came an awareness of its limitations. Round, as well-versed in post-Conquest charters as in Domesday, knew full well that Domesday Book provided a far from full account of tenure in 1086. There was many a vassal who is nowhere to be found in its folios. This is a characteristic that has stimulated too little research into the status of those who are recorded.[60] For Round it seems to have pointed to a wider understanding of the nature of Domesday data. Domesday is not always what you want it to be. Round's epiphany was the geld. His examination of the distribution of hides, the unit of tax assessment throughout much of England in the eleventh century, led him to the conclusion that assessment was imposed from above; the hidage of Domesday manors was derived from a distribution of a tax quota imposed on the shire and the hundred rather than from measured survey.[61] The hide is an artefact. It was an important realization, for Domesday data were no longer transparent. Ever since Domesday studies have had to grapple with what is 'real' and what is formal in the Domesday corpus. Ploughlands, population figures, and resources all became more or less 'suspect'. Nominalists still vie with realists to demonstrate to what extent these data represent eleventh-century society.

No overall consensus has emerged. There are still some radical realists out there. Nevertheless, most historians and geographers would agree that, while the data need interpretation, they are by and large representative. This was a notion that informed H. C. Darby's *Domesday Geographies* series. As a geographer Darby recognized that one of the easiest ways of representing Domesday information,

---

Read at the Meetings of the Domesday Commemoration 1886, ed. P. E. Dove, 2 vols (London, 1888–91)).

[58] W. R. Powell, *John Horace Round, Historian and Gentleman of Essex*, Essex Record Office Publications (Chelmsford, 2001).

[59] For a bibliography of his Domesday studies, see D. R. Bates, *A Bibliography of Domesday Book* (Woodbridge, 1985).

[60] See below, pp. 163–4.

[61] Round, *Feudal England*.

and more importantly making sense of it, was the distribution map. He began by plotting Domesday woodland in eastern England, and then in 1935 published a 'Domesday geography' of Cambridgeshire.[62] This early work revealed the potential of the approach. From 1952 he mapped as much of the Domesday data as he could, county by county, in five regional volumes.[63] Discrete data like settlements, fisheries, mills etc. are represented by dots, but other types are aggregated in various ways. Where size matters, circles of varying diameter are used. Population, ploughs, ploughlands, woodland, meadow, and value are represented in this way. Additionally, some items are mapped as densities per square mile on the basis of modern land use. Throughout Darby recognized the complexities of the data, as then understood, and did not map where he considered the results would be misleading. Throughout, however, his analytical criteria were derived from the 'scientific' methodology of geographical studies rather than from history. Units, for example, might be defined by surface geology or arbitrary measures like the square mile as opposed to the manor or Domesday hundred. Darby averred that his maps were a more or less accurate representation of the society, economy, and landscape of eleventh-century England.

By the time he came to write his concluding volume, *Domesday England* published in 1977,[64] Darby had begun to retreat somewhat from this position. Hitherto he, in common with most Domesday scholars, had tended to perceive the deficiencies in the data as defects in the survey. A new perspective was emerging. In the wake of a renewed interest in the historical landscape and the sources for its study,[65] it was becoming increasingly clear that Domesday Book was primarily about lordship. Commodities and land, it was argued, were described because they contributed to the lord's income.[66]

Economists, demographers, and geographers now accept this fact as a limitation of their data. And, oddly enough, in so doing they have found renewed authority

---

[62] H. C. Darby, 'Domesday Woodland in Huntingdonshire', *Transactions of the Cambridgeshire and Huntingdonshire Archaeological Society*, 5 (1931–36), 269–73; 'Domesday Woodland in East Anglia', *Antiquity*, 8 (1934), 211–15; 'The Domesday Geography of Cambridgeshire', *Proceedings of the Cambridge Antiquarian Society*, 36 (1934–35), 35–57.

[63] *The Domesday Geography of Eastern England* (Cambridge, 1952; 2nd edn, 1957; 3rd edn, 1971); H. C. Darby and L. B. Terrett, *The Domesday Geography of Midland England* (Cambridge, 1954; 2nd edn, 1971); H. C. Darby and I. S. Maxwell, *The Domesday Geography of Northern England* (Cambridge, 1962); H. C. Darby and E. M. J. Campbell, *The Domesday Geography of South-East England* (Cambridge, 1962); H. C. Darby and R. Welldon Finn, *The Domesday Geography of South-west England* (Cambridge, 1967).

[64] H. C. Darby, *Domesday England* (Cambridge, 1977).

[65] See, for example, the papers in *Medieval Settlement*, ed. P. H. Sawyer (London, 1976). Much of the stimulation came from a new generation of historical geographers and archaeologists. Landscape history had arrived.

[66] The view has been most recently summarized, and indeed developed, in A. R. Bridbury, 'Domesday Book: A Re-interpretation', *EHR*, 105 (1990), 284–309.

in Domesday statistics. In the last twenty years sophisticated statistical tools have been brought to bear on the Domesday data, notably by Professors McDonald and Snooks,[67] and the results have been held to be significant (both in the statistical as well as in the everyday sense). High correlations are found between almost all the variables of Domesday Book. Thus, it has been shown that manorial resources increase in proportion to the assessment of estates and that values accurately reflect this reality. The record of less important resources like churches, mills, and fisheries, is often eccentric, but in the essentials of the manorial economy Domesday is consistent and thorough. Criticism there has been of statistical method,[68] but it is still widely concluded that Domesday Book is about real estate and real economies. Andrew Wareham has stated the case most eloquently in a recent statistical analysis of the Norfolk and Suffolk folios of LDB:

> LDB can be compared to the *Feudal Book of Bury Saint Edmunds* and the *Inquisitio Eliensis*. The latter two sources respectively list the resources and assets of the abbots of Bury St Edmunds and Ely, and they generally correlate with evidence of LDB. The folios of all three texts are characterised by a comprehensive itemisation of all assets and resources ... Landlords itemised the number and state of their assets because they were frightened that their capital assets would be run down or misused by lessees, and this concern influenced the contents of LDB.[69]

Some historians still debate whether Domesday values represent net incomes (that is the lord's profit after all expenses such as the subsistence of his dependent labour

---

[67] J. McDonald and G. D. Snooks, *Domesday Economy: A New Approach to Anglo-Norman History* (Oxford, 1986); J. McDonald and G. D. Snooks, 'The Determinants of Manorial Income in Domesday England: Evidence from Essex', *Journal of Economic History*, 45 (1985), 541–56; J. McDonald and G. D. Snooks, 'Were the Tax Assessments of Domesday England Artificial? The Case of Essex', *EcHR*, 2nd series, 38 (1985), 353–73.

[68] McDonald and Snooks, for example, have been taken to task for using a parametric analysis where most statisticians would agree that a non-parametric methodology is more appropriate. In simple terms that is as if they have drawn a line graph where a bar chart is what is needed. More devastating still has been Dr J. D. Hamshere's observation that high correlations mean very little where there are so many variables (J. D. Hamshere, 'Regressing Domesday Book: Tax Assessments in Norman England', *EcHR*, 2nd ser., 40 (1987), 247–51, at 248). In some areas of Lincolnshire I found a high correlation between Domesday assessment to the geld and the number of pubs marked on the modern 1:50000 Ordnance Survey map. All sorts of data may correlate, but they may not therefore be related in any straightforward way.

[69] A. Wareham, 'The "Feudal Revolution" in Eleventh-Century East Anglia', *ANS*, 22 (2000), 296. The notion of accountability has been further developed, albeit from a royal perspective, by A. Godfrey and K. Hooper, 'Accountability and Decision-Making in Feudal England: Domesday Book Revisited', *Accounting History*, 1 (1996), 35–54.

force are accounted for) or rents.[70] But for Wareham, as for most, either way the Domesday inquest was an inventory survey of a well-established type and Domesday Book preserves much of its data.

With the definition of the limits of the dataset, economists and geographers have felt more confident in drawing wider conclusions. Adjustments can thus be made to convert the figures into absolute values to produce, say, a figure for the population of England in 1086 or the productivity of the kingdom.[71] Various strategies, depending on the type of data, have been adopted for determining conversion factors. Domesday itself has been used as a control. Exceptionally detailed sections of the text, like LDB for example, have been taken as reliable raw data. More usually appeal has been made to contemporary or later documentation.[72] It is widely assumed that early twelfth-century estate and shire surveys are directly comparable to Domesday Book and their more expansive data can be used to 'correct' its figures. Economic modelling of estates also becomes a possibility. Numerous studies, for example, have claimed to define the extent of demesne exploitation by manipulating various items of Domesday data; an attempt has even been made to quantify productive efficiency.[73] It is now held as axiomatic that Domesday Book is about real estates and real economies and that, with a bit of ingenuity, its data provide us with a host of indicators of wealth and how it was exploited.

Of statistics and shopping lists

Founded in impeccable twelfth-century sources, the three assumptions of modern Domesday historiography – the primacy of the Book, its authoritative content, and its comprehensive range – seem to gain unassailable support from these studies of Domesday data. Those less familiar with quantitative statistical methods may feel suspicious of approaches to historical data that they do not understand – the jargon bandied about in Domesday studies is indeed very much the preserve of the statistician rather than the historian – but any attempt to argue on the same

[70] G. D. Snooks, 'A Note on the Calculation of GDP and GDP per capita in 1086 and 1300', *A Commercialising Society*, eds R. H. Britnell and B. M. S. Campbell (Manchester, 1995), appendix 1; N. Mayhew, 'The Calculation of GDP from Domesday Book', *ibid.*, appendix 2; C. Dyer, 'A Note on Calculating GDP in 1086 and 1399', *ibid.*, appendix 3.
[71] See below, chapter 7.
[72] See, for example, J. F. R. Walmsley, 'The Censarii of Burton Abbey and the Domesday Population', *North Staffordshire Journal of Field Studies*, 8 (1968), 73–80, and J. S. Moore, '"Quot homines?": The Population of Domesday England', *ANS*, 19 (1997), 307–34; J. S. Moore, *From Anglo-Saxon to Anglo-Norman: North Gloucestershire in Domesday Book*, Deerhurst Lecture 1998, The Friends of Deerhurst Church (Bristol, 2000), 15–17.
[73] J. McDonald, 'Using William the Conqueror's Accounting Record to Assess Manorial Efficiency', *Accounting History*, 10 (2005), 125–45.

grounds comes up with more or less the same correlations. There appears to be no gainsaying of the hard facts: the figures add up as accounts of real estates.

The structure, however, is much less robust than it superficially appears. First, the statistical argument is not the knock-out blow that social and economic historians would like it to be. In arguing thus they ignore the limits of statistical analysis, what the statisticians would no doubt call 'the parameters' of the method. D. G. Altman has succinctly expressed the problem in a medical context:

> Interpretation of association is often problematic because **causation cannot be directly inferred.** If we observe an association between two variables A and B there are several possible interpretations. Excluding the possibility that it is a chance finding, it may be because
>
> 1.   A influences (or 'causes') B;
> 2.   B influences A; or
> 3.   both A and B are influenced by one or more other variables.
>
> Where data are available for some suspected common cause C, it is possible to see if the observed association between A and B remains for C when allowing for C by calculating the partial correlation. With this exception, it is not in general possible to distinguish statistically between the three possibilities above, and interferences must be based on other knowledge. **When looking at variables where there is no background knowledge, inferring a causal link is not justified.** This applies regardless of the strength of the observed association. [Emboldened text is the author's.][74]

Historical data are no different. In spite of popular perception, statistical analysis is about testing hypotheses; it is not about generating them (or at least it should not be).[75] The fact that there is a correlation between data indicates that they are related, but it does not prove causality. The hypothesis must be coherent. The assertion that God presses a light switch twice a day is not proved by the highly significant correlation of daylight and time of day ($p=<0.0000$).[76] To borrow a computer cliché, garbage in, garbage out.

The correlation of Domesday statistics is a fact. Maitland, indeed, came to the conclusion over a hundred years ago without the paraphernalia of regression analysis

---

[74] D. G. Altman, *Practical Statistics for Medical Research* (London, 1991), 297.

[75] Producing hypotheses from the data is known in the trade as 'data-dredging'.

[76] The point seems to be taken by J. McDonald and G. D. Snooks, *Domesday Economy: A New Approach to Anglo-Norman History* (Oxford, 1986), 127: 'In most sciences, the principal method used to assess whether numerical evidence supports or contradicts a theory is statistical method. Often a theory can be represented in terms of a relationship between variables, an example being the relationship between manorial tax assessments and annual values. Given a set of data on manorial assessments and values, statistical analysis can be applied to determine whether or not a relationship exists and, if so, to quantify that relationship.'

and computers.[77] However, to prove that Domesday Book is about estates, a further question must be posed: how sound is the hypothesis? The signs have never been good. It should have raised a query in the statisticians' minds long ago that historians have singularly failed to identify anything in Domesday Book that looks like a perception of an economic unit. The contemporary sources conveniently tell us that King William was interested in manors, but what was the beast? The manor of the text has proved remarkably elusive. Outside the Lincolnshire, Nottinghamshire, and Derbyshire folios, its various elements are not generally described together and much of the time it is not even identified. Most historians have been inclined to believe that the Domesday manor has no meaningful content.[78]

In the absence of hard and compelling evidence for 'estates' in the economic sense, no conclusions can be sensibly drawn from the correlations of Domesday variables *per se*. A real economy is just one among a number of possibilities. Many historians have argued that Domesday statistics are essentially fiscal units and no amount of correspondence between those figures and 'real' items can on its own prove otherwise. Domesday data are emphatically not self-verifying. Even less so is the baroque structure that now underpins modern Domesday studies. At the outset, there is a glaring lapse of method at the heart of the matter. In an age of written law, record and burgeoning bureaucracy, it is perhaps understandable that Richard fitzNigel saw Domesday Book in terms of its content. Nevertheless, it was a categorical error then and remains so today. Content is no infallible guide to purpose. A list of names and figures, for example, takes on entirely different perspectives depending on whether it relates to a ballot or an opinion poll. In itself there is not enough data to decide either way. Indeed, in some processes the purpose of a record might be completely different from its content. A royal commission on street crime might collect data on levels of school drop-out and unemployment, but without the context we could easily assume that it was all about job creation. Paradoxically, the subject matter of an inquiry is often what its documents are not about.

Purpose cannot be infallibly derived from content. The contents and forms of Domesday Book tell us, at best, what the *book* was compiled for; they do not necessarily reveal why the data were collected in the first place. From a broader medieval perspective it might be surprising if they did. At the very beginning of his analysis Galbraith states that the notion of Domesday Book as an after-thought is 'a contingency unlikely in itself, and one for which there is no earlier or later precedent'.[79] Well, his premise is simply wrong. Although there is no earlier evidence since substantial inquest records do not survive, later practice is quite clear. Abbreviations of inquest records were always later, and usually *post hoc*, often

[77] F. W. Maitland, *Domesday Book and Beyond* (Cambridge, 1897), 532–45.
[78] For the historiography and comment, see below, pp. 176–82.
[79] *Making of Domesday Book*, 19.

as much as a hundred years after the event.[80] The reasons for compilation were various, but the aim was to preserve data that were considered of permanent value. Most strikingly of all, such abbreviations never embody the decisions that were derived from the inquest records. They were entirely contingent to the purpose of the inquiry in which the data were collected.

We have no such explicit evidence for the compilation of Domesday Book, neither GDB nor LDB. Nor do we have accounts of attitudes to it before the 1140s. Nevertheless, there is evidence that the Book did not figure large in consciousness in the first fifty years of its existence. All the extant cartularies and registers compiled between 1086 and 1135, namely those of St Augustine's, Canterbury, Peterborough, Rochester, Shaftesbury, and Worcester, quote extensively from inquest records. None, however, originally contained extracts from Domesday Book.[81] Early twelfth-century charters show some awareness of the work in royal circles, but again inquest records seem to figure larger in a broader context. The writ of c.1100 in which Domesday Book is probably first noticed is often cited as evidence that it was in the forefront of public consciousness.[82] In reality the document tends to suggest the opposite. It does indeed refer to the gift of Hayling Island to the priory of Winchester by Queen Emma 'as the king's book testifies'. But this is not quite accurate. More precisely the Domesday entry reads that 'the monks of the bishopric of Winchester *claim* this manor, because Queen Emma gave it to the Church of St Peter and St Swithun', and the manor is enrolled in the lands of the abbey of Jumièges.[83] Would the monks have cited the text had they known that it ascribes the land to another religious house? It seems more

---

[80] *DIB*, 186–7.

[81] Canterbury, Dean and Chapter, MS Lit. E28; London, Society of Antiquaries, MS 60 (the Black Book of Peterborough); *Textus Roffensis: Rochester Cathedral Library Manuscript A.3.5. Pt 1*, ed. P. Sawyer, Early English MSS in Facsimiles, 7 (Copenhagen, 1957); London, British Library, Harl. MS 61; *Hemingi Chartularium*. Claims have been made that sections of Hemming's cartulary were extracted from GDB (*DB Worcs*, appendix V). Only one copy of the privileges of Oswaldlow Hundred is identical with the entry at the beginning of the bishop of Worcester's Worcestershire *breve* (GDB, 172c: *DB Worcs*, 2,1; App. V, Worcs F). It must be remembered, however, that the bishop's *breve* appears not to have been compiled by the GDB scribe but to have been copied from a cathedral source. See below, p. 212. Worcester D, a schedule of geld liability of 28 tenants-in-chief in Worcestershire, exhibits the same order of fees as GDB, but is clearly not directly derived from it since it contains information on exemptions that is not found there (*DB Worcs*, Worc D). The account of the church of Wolverhampton is apparently taken word for word from GDB, but it is postscriptal (N. R. Ker, 'Hemming's Cartulary: A Description of the Two Worcester Cartularies in Cotton Tiberius A. xiii', *Studies in Medieval History Presented to Frederick Maurice Powicke*, eds R. W. Hunt, W. A. Pantin, and R. W. Southern (Oxford, 1948), 61). Ker dates the hand of the addition as 'xi/xii' century.

[82] Following V. H. Galbraith, 'Royal Charters to Winchester', *EHR*, 35 (1920), 389; *Making of Domesday Book*, 209.

[83] GDB, 43v: *DB Hants*, 10.1.

likely that they were using documents that emanated from the Domesday inquest. The same is evidently true of Faritius, abbot of Abingdon, who, according to a writ of Queen Matilda of 1108–1113, demonstrated that his manor of Lewknor in Oxfordshire owed suit to Lewknor Hundred rather than Pyrton by reference to 'the book of the Treasury'.[84] The work cited was presumably GDB,[85] perhaps reflecting the usage of Chancery in a royal context, but the claim was apparently based on a different source since neither hundred nor suit to it is mentioned in the Oxfordshire folios. All other charter references before 1130 are best interpreted as derived from local sources.[86]

The production of Domesday Book is not self-evidently the purpose of the Domesday inquest. Nor are its data necessarily authoritative. Much was presented by juries of one kind and another and all were undoubtedly sworn to tell the truth. It is true that in the post-Conquest period (although apparently not before) this procedure was used in royal courts to 'recognize' right; it was the standard method by which a legal determination was made. In accepting the twelfth-century version of the genesis of Domesday Book, historians have unquestioningly assumed that the Domesday inquest was an executive and/or judicial process of this kind. However, in 1086 as throughout the Middle Ages not all verdicts were such. Indeed, juries were most often called to give evidence as opposed to judgements. This was no more so than in inquests or inquiries and there the data collected were less decisions than more or less commonly agreed fact that could inform future decisions.

That much of Domesday evidence is of this kind should be evident from the contradictory verdicts that are recorded throughout the texts. Even those 'judgements' that stand in glorious isolation have been shown to be remarkably insubstantial, few proving to be effective in the long run. Recognitions were made in some sessions in Lincolnshire, but they were separate and later than the main Domesday inquest; others can be shown to have been deferred to the routine meetings of the shire. Domesday Book is not a repository of unalloyed truth.

Finally, the scope of Domesday Book. The Anglo-Saxon chronicler was at pains to indicate the unprecedented scale of the inquiry, but his assertion that 'no single hide nor virgate of land, nor indeed ... one ox nor one cow nor one pig which was there left out, and not put down in his record' cannot be taken literally. The record

[84] *Historia Ecclesie Abbendonensis: The History of the Church of Abingdon*, vol. 2, edited and translated by John Hudson, Oxford Medieval Texts (Oxford, 2002), 170–1.
[85] S. P. J. Harvey, 'Domesday Book and Anglo-Norman Governance', *TRHS*, 5th series, 25 (1975), 179, argues that 'the book of the treasury' must have been a different work since it did contain the information.
[86] *Regesta Regum Anglo-Normannorum 1066–1154*, eds H. W. C. Davis, C. Johnson, H. A. Cronne, and R. H. C. Davis, 4 vols (Oxford, 1913–69), ii, nos 468, 976, 1000, 1488, 1500, 1515, 1887; *The Cartulary of Worcester Cathedral*, ed. R. R. Darlington, Pipe Roll Society, new series, 38 (1968), 26–7.

of livestock, at least, is patently partial – the lord's animals alone are recorded – and we must conclude that the chronicler was indulging a taste for hyperbole that was characteristic of his genre. Rather, if we reject the primacy of content, then the scope of the Domesday survey must clearly be a function of its purpose. It should be axiomatic in historical studies that the content of a document, the nature of its data, is determined by its purpose. A comprehensive list of household items found in a supermarket may appear to be a thorough stock-taking indicative of retail trends in the early twenty-first century, that is until you realize you have lost your weekly shopping list. As Max Weber rightly observed many years ago in a different context, *verstehen* is everything.[87] In assuming that Domesday Book was a complete survey and deriving purpose from that, historians have put the cart before the horse.

There are, then, serious objections to the modern consensus on the purpose, making, and scope of Domesday Book. If any more proof were needed of the fragility of the foundations of modern Domesday studies, it is to be found in the conclusions drawn. 'By their fruits ye shall know them': the greatest indictment of students of Domesday is their signal failure to explain. None of the interpretations of the purpose of the Domesday process has commanded consensus since loose ends stick out from every tightly wrapped concept. The exponents of the new order hypothesis have signally failed to explain why the inquest was undertaken some nineteen years after the Conquest, while the neo-fiscalists have been unable to point to any tangible change in the system of taxation.[88] Inexorably, the lack of agreement on purpose has led in its turn to radically opposed views on almost every item of Domesday data. The hide, the ploughland or teamland, population figures, manorial stock, value, waste, and just about everything else, are less battlefields than campaigns in on-going Domesday Wars.[89] The Domesday inquest records and Domesday Book have resolutely refused to be stuffed into a single bottle.

From purpose to content: the primacy of the inquest

The failure to explain suggests that the basic assumptions of Domesday studies are misconceived. In *Domesday: the Inquest and the Book* I questioned the centrality and authority of the Book. Throughout the Middle Ages a clear distinction can be found between the inquest and the subsequent abbreviation of its records. The one, the inquest, never was a glorified court of law that decided matters; rather

---

[87] R. Swedberg, *The Max Weber Dictionary: Keys Words and Central Concepts* (Stanford, 2005), 279–81.

[88] For reviews, see W. E. Kapelle, 'Domesday Book: F. W. Maitland and his Successors', *Speculum*, 64 (1989), 620–40; 'The Purpose of Domesday Book: A Quandary', *Essays in Medieval Studies*, Proceedings of the Illinois Medieval Association, 9 (1992), 55–65.

[89] The salient points of each debate are dissected below.

it collected information to inform decisions yet to be made. Before the advent of parliaments in the second half of the thirteenth century, it was the chief means by which kings found out about their realm and took the political temperature of their subjects. The other, the abbreviation of verdicts, by contrast, was a purely administrative process designed to preserve potentially useful information for use in routine governance.

Domesday conforms, I have argued, to this pattern. The threat of invasion from Denmark in 1085 had brought to light shortcomings in the system of taxation and defence. The inquest was a response to the crisis. Its concerns were many and varied, but fall into two broad areas of interest. First, there was an audit of royal income which involved a survey of royal estates, shire customs, and sundry dues, and a geld inquest. Second, there was a survey of the lands and services of the king's principal tenants. The outcome, agreed and formalized by the oath at Salisbury in August 1086, was an extension of the geld to formerly exempt demesne and a rene-gotiation of knight service. In the face of a threat to the commonweal, the inquest was an exercise in consultation which resulted in a new social contract. None of this, however, was embodied in Domesday Book. It appears to have originally been a private document compiled for the management of the royal demesne and regalia. The tenurial chaos after the rebellion against William Rufus in 1088 is a possible context, although it is not impossible that it was written at any time up to the early years of the reign of Henry I.

The debate that followed the publication of *Domesday: the Inquest and the Book* centred largely on the interpretation of the various passages adduced in support of a late date for Domesday Book.[90] Special pleading apart, however, the notion of the distinct identity of inquest records and abbreviations made from them has been tacitly accepted. The centrality of service has been studiously ignored, but never-theless a multiplicity of purposes, albeit with the production of Domesday Book as one of them, has been recognized. The parameters of Domesday studies have changed. The liberation of inquest from book, and purpose from content, demands a reconsideration of the third assumption of Domesday studies, the comprehensive scope of Domesday Book as a survey of landed estates. In its turn it provides a framework in which to undertake it.

The aim of this book is a radical re-assessment of Domesday data in these terms. In chapters two and three the nature of the surviving documentation, the processes of the inquest, and the compilation of the book are reprised. It might be thought that the study of Domesday texts, from palaeography and diplomatic to forms and interrelationship, ought to be entirely empirical. And yet almost all

---

[90] F. R. Thorn and C. Thorn, 'Writing of Great Domesday Book', *Domesday*, eds Hallam and Bates, 71; J. C. Holt, 'Domesday Studies 2000', *Domesday*, eds Hallam and Bates, 24; S. Baxter, review of *Domesday: The Inquest and the Book*, http://www.history.ac.uk/reviews/paper/baxterStephen.html.

studies have been concerned with demonstrating the application of a fully formed purpose from the beginning of the Domesday process. If content is a function of purpose, then the rejection of a one-dimensional Domesday process opens up a multitude of new interpretative possibilities. Anomalous forms become less an embarrassment than valuable evidence of separate sources and concerns. It is these, the activities identified, that inform the rest of the book. Chapter by chapter each item of Domesday information is re-examined in order to assess its sources and thereby interpret its nature and purpose within the Domesday process. The book concludes with a new characterization of Domesday Book and Domesday data. The validity of the conclusions drawn must be judged from their ability to explain the often apparently contradictory data.

2

The Domesday Texts

I T IS no doubt the iconic status of Domesday Book in the medieval period that has ensured the survival of a mass of documentation from the Domesday process. No fewer than thirty-three texts can be directly related to the enterprise. Of these the three largest are contemporary manuscripts. Exon is a composite document. The bulk of it is a series of accounts, fee by fee, of the lands of the king and his tenants-in-chief in Somerset, Dorset, Devon, and Cornwall with a single Wiltshire entry. Interspersed are geld accounts, related to an *inquisitio geldi*, lists of *terre occupate*, that is lands that had been illegally seized, and summaries of fees detailing total geld assessments, ploughs, population for the demesne and enfeoffed lands, values, a ploughland total for the whole fee, and a figure for its increase in value since acquired.[1] LDB and GDB, by contrast, are self-evidently compilations that follow a programme. LDB is confined to the three counties of Essex, Norfolk, and Suffolk which form the major divisions of the text. Within each county section the account proceeds by fees and concludes with a list of *invasiones*, illegal seizures of land.[2] GDB exhibits much the same form. It covers the rest of England county by county and within each fee by fee. The only materials extraneous to the programme are intermittent accounts of boroughs and royal dues that precede these accounts in many counties, a series of claims relating to lands in Yorkshire, Lincolnshire, and Huntingdonshire, and a summary list of vills and manors in Yorkshire.[3]

---

[1] For a detailed list of the contents of Exon, see V. H. Galbraith, *Domesday Book: its Place in Administrative History* (Oxford, 1974), 184–8.

[2] LDB, 99–103v, 273–280, 447v–450: *DB Essex*, 90; *DB Norfolk*, 66; *DB Suffolk*, 76–7. The *invasiones* of Bishop William [of Thetford] in Norfolk, however, are appended to his chapter in the body of the text (LDB, 197v–201: *DB Norfolk*, 10,48–93), for which, see below, pp. 273–9.

[3] In Huntingdonshire the claims (there entered without a rubric) are appended to the end of the county Domesday in the body of the text without explanatory rubric, but those of Yorkshire and Lincolnshire are entered together in a separate quire at the end of the volume after the Lincolnshire folios. The Yorkshire series is a compilation from various sources and is demonstrably incomplete; those of Huntingdonshire and Lincolnshire are fair copies (D. R. Roffe, 'Domesday and Northern Society: A Reappraisal', *EHR*, 105 (1992), 325–6).

The remaining documentation survives in later copies. Four texts are full Domesday-like compilations. ICC is the widest in scope, covering all the land in thirteen out of sixteen of the Cambridgeshire hundreds except for the demesne estates of the king. In marked contrast to the parallel account of the county in GDB, however, it is arranged by hundred and vill as opposed to fee. IE is a composite source. Surviving in three manuscripts, much of it is an account of the estates of Ely Abbey in the six counties in which it held land in a form that is very close to LDB and ICC. Additionally, however, it preserves what have been called the articles of inquiry in the prologue, lists of jurors for the counties of Cambridgeshire and Hertfordshire, summaries identical in form and content to those of Exon for a number of fees in Cambridgeshire and for Ely in Hertfordshire, Huntingdonshire, Norfolk, Suffolk, and Essex, and a schedule of Ely claims. Bath A is an Exon-like account of the lands of Bath Abbey in Somerset. The Crowland Domesday is a composite account of the lands of Crowland Abbey which draws upon the GDB account and an independent geographically arranged list of vills and hundreds and possibly records of presentments of juries.[4]

Excluding obviously straightforward copies or extracts of Domesday, like the Domesday breviates (later copies),[5] the rest of the corpus consists of some twenty-six texts that, with varying degrees of detail, fall short of full Domesday descriptions but contain similar or related material. Apart from their relative brevity, there is nothing that characterizes these documents as a coherent group. Nevertheless, for

The Yorkshire Summary is entered in the same quire as the Yorkshire and Lincolnshire *clamores* (D. R. Roffe, 'The Yorkshire Summary: A Domesday Satellite', *Northern History*, 27 (1991), 242–60).

[4] Claims have been made for a document known as 'Rights and Laws of the Archbishop Thomas in York' as a Domesday 'satellite' (D. W. Rollason, *Sources for York History to AD 1100*, The Archaeology of York, i (1998), 210–13; D. M. Palliser, *Domesday York*, Borthwick Paper no. 78, University of York (York, 1990), 25). Witnessed by twelve Englishmen of York, the archbishop and six Normans, it survives in English and French versions. The date of the document can be determined no more precisely that between *c.*1070 and sometime in the 1080s. Nevertheless, Palliser suggested a Domesday context on the ground that the jurors were composed of English and French. This remains possible but, perhaps, not probable. According to IE four English and four French men were called from each hundred in the Domesday inquest; whatever the status of York as a unit of local government, we might therefore have expected equal numbers of native and foreign jurors in the Rights and Laws if it was a product of the same process. Presentments to inquests written in the vernacular are known in the thirteenth century (PRO SC5 Chapter House/Essex/1–3), but are unparalleled in the Domesday corpus. There is little in the Domesday account of York that can be firmly said to be derived from the source, and at the moment it therefore seems more prudent to be agnostic. 'Rights and Laws' remains an important early source for the history of the City.

[5] Easier said than done. For the problems of identifying the nature of various documents, and those that have been excluded, see below.

convenience we shall call these sources 'schedules' (in the sense of a tabulated inventory). Their salient features are summarized in Table 2.1.

Table 2.1 *The Domesday schedules*

	Content								Forms						
	Assessment to the geld	Demesne/tenanted	Ploughlands	Ploughs	Population	Value	Presentments	Claims	Order as GDB/LDB	Order not as GDB/LDB	English orthography	Arrangement by fee	Arrangement by 100	Extract/schedule of fee	Extract from 100 roll
Abingdon A	✓	✓							✓		✓				✓
Bath B	✓	✓							✓		✓				
Braybrooke	✓	✓	✓		✓				✓						✓
Burton B	✓	✓	✓		✓				✓		✓			✓	
Bury A	✓	✓		✓			✓		✓		✓				
Bury B	✓	✓		✓			✓		✓		✓				
Bury C	✓	✓			✓										
Des. Ter.	✓	✓								✓	✓			?	
DM A	✓									✓	✓			?	
DM B	✓	✓			✓					✓	✓				✓
DM D					✓					✓	✓			✓	
DM E	✓	✓			✓				✓		✓				
Ely A		✓	✓	✓					✓		✓				
Ely B		✓	✓	✓						✓	✓				
Ely C	✓	✓		✓	✓				✓		✓				
Ely D	✓		✓	✓	✓		✓			✓	✓				
Evesham A	✓	✓		✓	✓	✓			✓		✓		✓		
Evesham F	✓	✓								✓	✓			✓	
Evesham K	✓						?		✓		✓	✓			
Evesham M	✓	✓					✓		✓		✓	✓			
Evesham P	✓	✓					?		✓		✓	✓			
Evesham Q	✓						?		✓		✓				
Excerpta	✓	✓				✓	✓		✓		✓				
Kentish Ass. List	✓								✓		✓	✓			
Worcester A	✓	✓								✓	✓				
Worcester B	✓	✓							✓		✓				

With such a wealth of surviving documentation, it is tempting to weigh in straightaway to mine the content. That is precisely what many antiquaries did in the past and some local historians do today. To succumb to the temptation, however, is to ignore what is implicit and fail to appreciate the context of what is explicit. The Domesday texts are first and foremost artefacts and their study starts with their appearance, production, and relationship to each other. This, of course, is hardly a revolutionary agenda. As we have seen, the nature of the texts has been a leitmotif of Domesday studies for the last hundred years. And indeed, with the publication of new editions and translations, it is an area that has been studied with gathering pace in recent years. In the process, new insights have been gained. The appreciation of the stratigraphy of the texts, for example, their different stages of composition, have been of fundamental importance to almost all areas of Domesday studies. However, wider analyses, especially of date and relationship, have rarely been as dispassionate. In this chapter basic assumptions about the Domesday texts are re-examined and an attempt is made to distinguish what can be said about them and what cannot.

Translations and editions

All the texts are written in an abbreviated Latin which is difficult for the uniniti-ated to read. GDB and LDB, however, are now widely available in translation. The Victoria County Histories provide texts for every shire except Lincolnshire,[6] and these have recently been standardized and completely revised in the light of modern scholarship for the Alecto Domesday County Edition (now available in one volume published by Penguin Books and on a fully searchable CD-ROM as *The Digital Domesday*).[7] Phillimore & Co. has also published a complete trans-lation.[8] Here John Morris, the founding editor of the series, opted for a rendering of the text in an English which would have been used today rather than retaining technical terms. The result is not entirely happy. 'Villager' is an acceptable trans-lation of 'villein' (although the 'villan' of the Alecto edition is perhaps better), but the attempt to translate technical terms is plain misleading. 'Jurisdiction' for *soca*, 'full jurisdiction' for *saca et soca*, 'lordship' for *dominium*, and the like oversimplify to the point of absurdity.[9] What can the ordinary reader make of the distinction

---

[6] *VCH Lincs* volume 1 is still awaited. The translation intended for it was published as *The Lincolnshire Domesday and Lindsey Survey*, eds C. W. Foster and T. Longley, Lincoln Record Society, 19 (1921).

[7] *VCH; Domesday Book*, eds R. W. H. Erskine, A. Williams, and G. H. Martin (London: Alecto Historical Editions, 1986–2000); *Domesday Book: A Complete Translation*, eds A. Williams and G. H. Martin (London: Penguin Books, 2002); Alecto Historical Editions, *The Digital Domesday*, CD-ROM (London, 2002). The Penguin edition has a place-name index, but, inexplicably, no personal name index.

[8] *Domesday Book*, History from the Sources, gen. ed. J. Morris (Chichester, 1975–86).

[9] Since the Latin text is given in parallel, the referents of the terms can be readily identi-fied. For a useful word list with the Phillimore equivalents, see J. D. Foy, *Domesday Book: Index of Subjects* (Chichester, 1992), 283–91.

between 'free man' and 'freeman'?[10] Furthermore, the text is not standardized. In the early volumes the opening clauses of entries were not reproduced where repetitive and some way through the series personal name forms were changed to conform to those of von Feilitzen.[11] Nevertheless, it would be churlish to cavil too much. The Phillimore edition is cheap and cheerful, and, most importantly, readily available in most public libraries. Moreover, it provides the most useful and precise system of referencing[12] and an unparalleled critical apparatus.[13] John Palmer has produced an electronic version of the GDB counties, *The Domesday Explorer*, with innovative search and mapping utilities.[14]

More recently, collections of what classical scholars used to call 'gobbets', have made their appearance. Robin Fleming has filleted Domesday Book for all information that has a bearing on legal status and actions.[15] She identifies and translates no fewer than 3217 passages that cast light on all manner of relationships in late eleventh-century England. The indices appended to the volume set a new standard in providing access to a rich but often difficult corpus.[16] Katharine Keats-Rohan has extracted every entry of a prosopographical import for her Continental Origins of English Landholders (COEL) database.[17] She also provides data from

[10] The one translates *liber homo*, 'free man', and the other *sochmannus*, 'sokeman'. Or is it vice versa? At least the literal translation has the merit of maintaining the distinction.

[11] O. von Feilitzen, *Pre-Conquest Personal Names of Domesday Book* (Uppsala, 1937).

[12] The entries, largely defined by content and usually signalled in the MSS by place-names and rubrication, are numbered consecutively by section (boroughs etc.) or chapter within each county. Thus, *DB Oxon*, 25,6 refers to the sixth entry in the 25th chapter of the Oxfordshire folios, that is Henry de Ferrers' manor of 'Ash' in Oxfordshire. The system was pioneered by Foster and Longley in their edition of the Lincolnshire Domesday and Lindsey Survey of 1921, although they tended to restore material to the place where the scribe indicated it should be read rather than the place where he actually wrote it. Otherwise, reference has usually been made to the folio of the MS with or without indication of the column. For a concordance of the various referencing systems, see Foy, *Domesday Book: Index of Subjects*, 293–317. Both folio numbers and Phillimore references are given here.

[13] Entry by entry the notes are an invaluable commentary which became fuller as the series developed. Similarly, there are also innumerable appendices in which contemporary sources, 'satellites' as they are called, are compared with the Domesday text.

[14] J. J. N. Palmer, M. Palmer, and G. Slater, *Domesday Explorer* (Phillimore, 2000). LDB will be added in due course and a standardization of names is promised. Almost any combination of data items can be pulled out of this database. However, executing anything other than a simple search requires extensive coding. For a review of version 1.0, see D. R. Roffe, *The Medieval Review*, December 2003, at http://www.hti.umich.edu/cgi/t/text/text-idx?c=t mr;idno=baj9928.0312.011;rgn=main;view=text.

[15] R. Fleming, *Domesday Book and the Law: Society and Legal Custom in Early Medieval England* (Cambridge, 1998).

[16] For the limitations of the list, see the review by E. Z. Tabuteau in H-Law, August 2000, at http://www2.h-net.msu.edu/reviews/showrev.cgi?path=24363965413295.

[17] *The Continental Origins of English Landholders 1066–1166 Database and the COEL Database System on CD-ROM*, K.S.B. Keats-Rohan, Coel Enterprises Ltd, 2002. The Domesday

all the ancillary texts and a sophisticated computer program to manipulate it all.[18] Palmer's *Domesday Explorer* goes even further in promising the mechanization of such 'custom Domesdays'. With its exhaustive tagging of the Phillimore translation it is now as easy to produce a Domesday of mills as of hawk eyries or any other item of Domesday data.[19] For bedtime readers and technophobes, more conventional finding aids are available. Ellis' *General Introduction to Domesday Book* is now superseded by the place-name, personal name, and subject indices for the whole of the two volumes of Domesday Book published in the Phillimore series[20] and a consolidated place-name index to the Alecto edition.[21]

All of these are invaluable tools for navigating the Domesday text. Never again will students of Domesday be completely reliant on the card index. Older historians might suspect that new technology makes the whole process too easy: in future thesis generation cannot help but be simpler. There are, however, dangers.[22] In history context is all. Extracting legal material from Domesday Book does not make it a legal treatise,[23] and to treat it as such is to run the risk of mistaking the exceptional for the routine.[24] All the editors have formulated stringent criteria of inclusion and exclusion. Indeed, COEL minimizes interpretation by citing the exact Latin form of each name every time it occurs. Nevertheless, it remains true that all divorce their data from their context.[25] Here Alecto's *Digital Domesday* comes into its own. It provides the complete Alecto translation with the minimal amount of tagging: it is largely confined to place-names and personal names. But the program is provided with a string search facility that not only enables the identification of individual items of information, but also phrases, and all can be viewed within the context of the folio in which it occurs.[26]

---

names are also available in print as K.S.B. Keats-Rohan, *Domesday People: A Prosopography of Persons Occurring in English Documents, 1066–1166: I. Domesday Book* (Woodbridge, 1998).
[18] For a review, see D. R. Roffe, 'The Continental Origins of English Landholders 1066–1166 database and the COEL Database System on CD-ROM', *Nottingham Medieval Studies*, 45 (2001), 234–7.
[19] J. J. N. Palmer, 'Great Domesday on CD-ROM', *Domesday Book*, eds E. Hallam and D. Bates (Stroud, 2001), 141–50.
[20] *Domesday Book: Index of Places*, eds J. McN Dodgson and J. J. N. Palmer (Chichester, 1992); *Domesday Book: Index of Persons*, eds J. McN Dodgson and J. J. N. Palmer (Chichester, 1992); *Domesday Book: Index of Subjects*. Although often difficult to use, the Subject Index is an indispensable tool for the Domesday historian.
[21] *Domesday Book: A Complete Translation*.
[22] D. R. Roffe, 'Domesday Databases', http://www.roffe.co.uk/dbdatabases.htm.
[23] *Pace* Fleming, *Domesday and the Law*, 5–6.
[24] See below, pp. 278–9.
[25] For this reason attempts to introduce other systems of reference, like Fleming's 'F' numbers, should be resisted.
[26] D. R. Roffe, 'The Digital Domesday', http://www.roffe.co.uk/ddb.htm. *Domesday Explorer* also provides string searches, although not by default in context, but there on a less satisfactory text from which, as far as I can see, editorial additions cannot be excluded.

Translations and collections of extracts aid accessibility for the general public, but there is no substitute for the Latin text. Domesday Book was first edited by Abraham Farley in the late eighteenth century and published by the government in two volumes in 1783.[27] The work is now rare, but we must be grateful to Phillimore for reproducing it parallel to the translation in their edition and to Alecto for republishing it with *The Digital Domesday*. It was set in a specially designed font called Record Type that was intended to reproduce as far as possible the forms of the manuscript. The font has the advantage of being relatively non-interpretative, but it could not represent all the variations of the hand and is therefore no substitute for the manuscript. The two volumes of Domesday Book are now bound in five parts (LDB three, GDB two) to aid consultation. Access, however, is restricted. Excessive handling would be injurious but, fortunately, facsimiles are available. The text was photographed by the Ordnance Survey Office between 1861 and 1863 in a monotone process called 'photozincography'.[28] The result is a silhouette, with some retouching in places where the process could not distinguish blurred images, but rubrication was overprinted from a second plate that was prepared by hand. A technically more accomplished facsimile is the Editions Alecto edition of 1985 and 2000.[29] Using a specially built camera and a four-colour continuous tone printing process for GDB and stochastic lithography for LDB, it provides an image that reproduces the density of the ink and the numerous rulings and prickings that lay bare the processes of writing and production. It is important to realize, however, that it does not supersede the earlier facsimile. Different aspects of the text are revealed by each so that it is possible to see things in the one that are not visible in the other. For example, the addition of *et lx acre prati* added to the end of the account of Ainsty Wapentake in the Yorkshire Summary is only apparent in the OS facsimile.[30] Both are now available on CD-ROM and should be used together.[31]

The other major texts have not been served so well. Parts of Exon are available in translation in the relevant *VCH* volumes and an edition can be found in the fourth volume of the Record Commission edition of Domesday.[32] Its data have been usefully collated with GDB by Caroline Thorn and Frank Thorn in the Phillimore edition of the relevant Domesday counties. However, there is no facsimile. One

[27] *Domesday Book*, ed. A. Farley (London, 1783). For the circumstances of printing, see M. M. Condon and E. Hallam, 'Government Printing of the Public Records in the Eighteenth Century', *Journal of the Society of Archivists*, 7 (1984), 348–88.
[28] E. Hallam, *Domesday Book through Nine Centuries* (London, 1986), 154–6.
[29] H. Pearson, 'The Alecto Domesday Project', *Domesday Book*, eds E. Hallam and D. Bates (Stroud, 2001), 151–8.
[30] GDB, 379v: *DB Yorks*, SW, An18. A comparison of the two facsimiles would be desirable.
[31] *DIB*, 72.
[32] *Libri Censualis, vocati Domesday Book, Additamenta ex Codic. Antiquiss. Exon Domesday; Inquisitio Eliensis; Liber Winton; Boldon Book*, ed. H. Ellis (London, 1816).

is urgently needed. The exact nature of the compilation will not be elucidated until the manuscript is made more generally available in facsimile. IE was also published in *Domesday Book* iv, but Hamilton's edition of 1876 provides a better text with variant readings. ICC was edited for the first time in the same volume. Both texts are again set in Record Type and are thus difficult to read. A new critical edition is badly needed. Many of the Domesday schedules have attracted attention of this kind. Frank and Caroline Thorn have provided translations of many of the Evesham and Worcester sources in appendices to the volumes they edited for Phillimore, and a full text of the Evesham corpus is promised by Howard Clarke.[33] Various scholars have edited other fragmentary sources with a greater or lesser degree of success. The COEL database allows access to much of this material, but its use would be greatly facilitated if all the texts were collected together. Although there is less of a rationale to produce facsimiles of copies, the option should not be automatically rejected. The layout of some texts may perpetuate that of their exemplars and editions may therefore sacrifice some of the evidence.[34]

Manuscripts, scribes, and scribal practices

The study of the Domesday texts begins with the manuscripts themselves. More than in most documents physical composition, characteristics of the hands, scribal techniques, the identification of additions and corrections, and the like are essential preliminaries to a full understanding of the data that they contain. The point is a truism, but it has so often been missed. The most cursory examination of the LDB manuscript, for example, will show that it was the hundred that was the primary division of each chapter of that work rather than the individual manor or vill. And yet this is an observation that has been lost on most students of Domesday. Despite the availability of the more than adequate Ordnance Survey facsimile from 1863, historians have preferred to use the Farley edition of the text or a trans-lation where the physical layout of the LDB text is simply lost.[35] The rebinding of Domesday Book in 1953 and 1984, however, has stimulated important studies of the manuscripts – GDB, LDB, and Exon – that have gone a long way to restore the balance. Nevertheless, it remains a fact that there are still no entry by entry studies of the three Domesday manuscripts.[36] The report on the 1953 rebinding produced only summary accounts of rulings, numbers of lines, compression, the

---

[33] To be published by the Worcestershire Historical Society.

[34] See, below, p. 46.

[35] D. R. Roffe, 'Introduction', *Little Domesday Book, Norfolk*, eds A. Williams and G. H. Martin (London, 2000), 12. LDB is quintessentially a seigneurially arranged circuit return in the Galbraithian schema. For its composition from ICC-like sources, see below, p. 88–91.

[36] One is promised by Caroline Thorn and Michael Gullick.

incidence of additions and interlineations,[37] and the misunderstandings that this produced misled more than one historian.[38] Boring as lists are to produce and read, we cannot be confident of the import of any entry until we are apprised of its full palaeographical details.

If we still await such an invaluable reference work, much has been achieved, especially in the last twenty years or so. The composition and binding history of the three manuscripts is now well understood. As early as 1816 an attempt was made to reconstruct the original order of the quires of Exon when the manuscript was rebound in two volumes. Ker revisited the problem in the 1970s and was able tentatively to suggest a possible order of about a third of the quires at the time when they were first bound.[39] However, each quire was generally devoted to the land of a single individual, and it seems clear that the collection was originally used as a series of unbound pamphlets.[40] In LDB and GDB quires, or more often groups of quires, were similarly discrete entities, there devoted not to the land of a single lord but to all the land in a shire.[41] The order in which they are bound in both volumes almost certainly reflects that of the first bindings probably in the late eleventh or early twelfth century. A series of quire signatures (letters written on the outer sheets to guide the binder) in a contemporary English hand, indicates that the last ten gatherings of GDB are ordered as intended,[42] and the dating colophon at the end of the Suffolk folios in LDB was probably always at the end of the volume since it refers to the three counties therein described.[43] Nevertheless, rubbing on the outer sheets of most of the quires indicates that they too were originally used as separate pamphlets. However, despite this similarity Exon is a very different type of work from LDB and GDB.

Exon was written by at least fifteen main scribes. Both Welldon Finn and Tessa Webber have attempted to identify a coherent pattern of work, but neither could find one.[44] Scribes seem to have written in a haphazard sort of way, starting off in the middle of sections, even at times half way through sentences. Nor is there

---

[37] Public Record Office, *Domesday Book Rebound* (London, 1954).
[38] See, for example, V. H. Galbraith, *The Making of Domesday Book* (Oxford, 1961), 203–4.
[39] N. R. Ker, *Medieval Manuscripts in British Libraries II, Abbotsford-Keele* (Oxford, 1977), 800–7.
[40] A. R., Rumble, 'The Palaeography of the Domesday Manuscripts', *Domesday Book: A Reassessment*, ed. P. H. Sawyer (London, 1985), 29–32.
[41] For the quires of the Domesday MSS, see *Domesday Book Rebound*, end pull-outs, and M. Gullick, 'The Great and Little Domesday Manuscripts', *Domesday Studies*, eds A. Williams and R. W. H. Erskine (London, 987), 93–112 and Appendix III.
[42] C. Thorn, 'Marginal Notes and Signs in Domesday Book', *Domesday Studies*, eds A. Williams and R. W. H. Erskine (London, 987), 133.
[43] LDB, 450: *DB Suffolk*, 77,5.
[44] R. Welldon Finn, 'The Exeter Domesday and its Construction', *Bulletin of the John Rylands Library*, 41 (1958–59), 360–87; T. Webber, 'Salisbury and the Exon Domesday: Some

any apparent underlying rationale, such as the extent of the hundred; that is, no one scribe was responsible for entering the estates for any particular hundred. Webber, following up observations made by Ker,[45] has identified three of the hands in Salisbury sources where a similar pattern of copying is well attested. She concludes that the Exon scribes were probably also copying with one scribe taking over from another on an *ad hoc* basis as and when. Further research may modify this picture in its detail. There has been little study of the organizing principles of the Exon text; a starting point might be the account of the lands of the Count of Mortain in Cornwall which seems to be arranged geographically.[46] However, Webber's conclusion probably stands. Nevertheless, if the scribes were copying, the task was clearly not a mechanical one. Numerous emendations, additions, glosses, and interpolations suggest that the scribes were also responsible for a degree of formulation from disparate sources.[47]

LDB was also written by a number of scribes. Seven in all have been identified, although the last did not contribute to the body of the text, being responsible only for the colophon and possibly the rubrication (Table 2.2).[48] Nevertheless, LDB is a more co-ordinated work than Exon. In its entirety it was written from folio to folio, that is the quire does not feature as a significant division within its three major divisions. Lists of tenants-in-chief are found at the beginning of each county, but were probably drafted after the text was written (their numberings do not regularly appear in the text and there are few disparities). The king's lands appear first in each county, and in Essex churchmen follow, then lay tenants-in-chief, and finally sergeants, thegns, and free men. In Norfolk and Suffolk ecclesiastics are grouped together but appear in the middle of the sequence of lay lands. Within chapters the hundred is the major division, with prominence given to the hundred

Observations Concerning the Origins of Exeter Cathedral MS 3500', *English Manuscript Studies 1100–1700*, I, eds P. Beal and J. Griffiths (Oxford, 1989), 1–18.

[45] N. R. Ker, 'The Beginnings of Salisbury Cathedral Library', *Medieval Learning and Literature: Essays Presented to Richard Hunt*, eds J. J. G. Alexander, M. T. Gibson (Oxford, 1976), 34–8.

[46] Exon, 224–64. Colin Flight, *The Survey of the Whole of England: Studies of the Documentation Resulting from the Survey Conducted in 1086*, British Archaeological Reports, British Series, 405 (Oxford, 2006), 45–7, assumes that ICC-like sources lay behind the whole of the text. Hypothesizing that the sources were divided into a number of pamphlets and the scribes copied from them as they became free, he has produced an algorithm to account for changes in hands. However, a widespread geographical substructure to the text remains unproven: his algorithm should produce a regular hundredal sequence in Exon and the corresponding parts of GDB which is not regularly there (R. Welldon Finn, *Domesday Studies: The Liber Exoniensis* (London, 1964), 36–9).

[47] R. Welldon Finn, *The Domesday Inquest and the Making of Domesday Book* (London, 1961), 164–6; *DB Devon*, Exon Introduction.

[48] A. R. Rumble, 'The Domesday Manuscripts: Scribes and *Scriptoria*', *Domesday Studies*, ed. J. C. Holt (Woodbridge, 1987), 99–100.

Table 2.2 *The scribes of LDB*
(after Rumble, 'Domesday MSS: Scribes and Scriptoria')

Section		Scribe	Text	
DB Essex	L–2,9	1	ESSEX:	list of tenants, caps 1–2
		2		partial list of tenants
	3,1–8,11	1		caps 3–8
		2		partial list of tenants
	9,1–90,1	1		caps 9–90 (part)
	90,2–3	3		cap 90 (part)
	90,5–87	1		cap 90 (part)
	B	3		Colchester
DB Norfolk	L–1,7	2	NORFOLK:	list of tenants, cap 1 (pt)
	1,8–9	4		cap 1 (part)
	1,9–7,21	2		caps 1 (part) –7
	8,1–14	3		cap 8 (part)
	8,15–138	5		cap 8 (part)
	9,1–5	1		cap 9 (part)
	9,6–37	2		cap 9 (part)
	9,38–45	5		cap 9 (part)
	9,46–78	2		cap 9 (part)
	9,78–87	5		cap 9 (part)
	9,88–104	2		cap 9 (part)
	9,104–115	1		cap 9 (part)
	9,115–234	6		cap 9 (part)
	10,1–16	1		cap 10 (part)
	10,16–13,24	5		caps 10 (part)–13
	14,1–19,8	1		caps 14–19 (part)
	19,9–65,17	6		caps 19 (part)–65
	66,1–91	1		cap 66 (part)
	66,91–99	2		cap 66 (part)
	66,99–108	1		cap 66 (part)
DB Suffolk	L	2,1	SUFFOLK:	list of tenants
	1,1–115	2		cap 1 (part)
	1,115–121	1		cap 1 (part)
	1,122a-g	5		cap 1 (part)
	2,1–20	2		cap 2
		1		partial list of tenants
	3,1–56	2		cap 3 (part)
	3,56–9	1		cap 3 (part)
	3,59–95	2		cap 3 (part)
	3,95	1		cap 3 (part)
	3,96–4,1	2		cap 3 (part)–4 (part)
	4,1–3	1		cap 4 (part)

Section	Scribe	Text
4,3–9,3	2	caps 4 (part)–9 (part)
9,4	1	cap 9 (part)
10,1–13,7	2	caps 10–13
14,1–167	5	cap 14
	2	partial list of tenants
15,1–16,48	5	caps 15–16
17,1	1	cap 17
18,1–21,105	5	caps 18–21
22,1–3	1	cap 22
23,1–76,23	5	caps 23–76
77,1–4	2	Malet/Bayeux dispute
	7	COLOPHON

headings. Entries do not always appear on a new line, especially in Norfolk and Suffolk, being signalled by a *paragraphos*, that is a gallows sign.[49]

There is a degree of co-ordination here that is absent from Exon. Scribe 1, who wrote most of the Essex folios, probably had a supervisory role in the production of the volume since he corrected the work of the other scribes in Norfolk and Suffolk. However, it was probably scribe no. 2 who was in overall charge. The form of words of the sections that he wrote departs from that of the others (he omits the otherwise general statement that land was held 'for a manor (*pro manerio*)' and 'for so many carucates (*pro x carucatis*)'), suggesting perhaps a greater degree of independence. More significantly, he wrote indices to the contents of individual quires, and drafted the lists of tenants-in-chief at the head of the accounts of Norfolk and Suffolk.[50] The scribal practices of the other scribes have not been studied in detail.[51]

All the hands are business-like, that is, they are clear but not unnecessarily ornate. There are, however, relatively few additions, and it would seem that the manuscript is in some sense a 'fair copy'. This, though, does not preclude the possibility that the scribes were abstracting from a document of a different form.[52] The order of chapters seems to be more or less haphazard. Little is known of the scribes. Linguistic quirks like the use of *Ph* for initial *F* are unparalleled, but the unvoicing of final *d* to *t* hints at a continental influence. Generally, nevertheless, LDB exhibits both personal and place-name forms that are often closer to OE usage than equivalents in GDB. The scribes were clearly not ignorant of the

[49] C. Thorn, 'Marginal Notes and Signs in Domesday Book', 123. The use of the gallows sign is not consistent.
[50] D. R. Roffe, 'Introduction', *Little Domesday, Norfolk*, 11–12.
[51] For some general comments, see Rumble, 'The Domesday Manuscripts: Scribes and *Scriptoria*', 86–93.
[52] See below, pp. 88–92.

English language.[53] Unfortunately, none has been recognized in other manuscripts. Many of the problems of Domesday studies would be solved if the scriptorium in which LDB was written could be identified. Now, there's a challenge.

GDB is by far the most accomplished of the Domesday manuscripts. It is largely the work of a single scribe (the main scribe or scribe A, who will be called 'the GDB scribe' here) who drafted and rubricated the whole manuscript. A second scribe, known somewhat misleadingly as 'the correcting scribe'[54] or, less prejudiciously as scribe B, subsequently added about twenty additional entries, some hundreds of words, and the odd emendation throughout the text (Table 2.3). Some four other scribes contributed the occasional word or phrase here and there, and a fifth the quire signatures.[55] The GDB scribe brought a decided programme to his work, albeit a developing one. From the start he drafted with easy reference in mind. With some important exceptions, each shire begins with an account of the county town or towns and various miscellaneous items of information relating to the rights of the king. These sections are not particularly uniform, and their composition would seem to be often driven by what material was available.[56] Thereafter, however, there is a common format. First, there is a finding list of holders of land. The king is invariably the first to be listed and is followed by the ecclesiastics, tenants-in-chief, and then sundry extras like sergeants and king's thegns (*taini regis*). Within each section the order of entries is determined by precedence weighted for local prominence; a second-rate baron is promoted to the first division if he is one of the main landholders in the county. All things being equal, lords are then grouped by the initial letter of their names; thus all Richards are listed together and might be followed by Rogers and Roberts. Women, however, even the Queen, are invariably relegated to a position just above the salt before the king's thegns.[57]

[53] P. H. Sawyer, 'Place-Names of the Domesday Manuscripts', *Bulletin of the John Rylands Library*, 38 (1955–56), 497; Feilitzen, *Pre-Conquest Personal Names of Domesday Book*, 6.

[54] Misleadingly, since of course the vast majority of the corrections were made by the main scribe. Scribe B clearly worked at some point with A, for at the end of the Berkshire folios B wrote an entry relating to the land held by Robert fitzRolf which was followed by A who wrote a further two entries; none was rubricated (GDB, 63v: *DB Berks*, 65,20–2). Nevertheless, GDB is the work of one man with a bit of tinkering by others.

[55] F. R. Thorn and C. Thorn, 'Writing of Great Domesday Book', *Domesday Book*, eds E. Hallam and D. Bates (Stroud, 2001), 37–73. For scribes C–F, see *eidem*, 41; the entries occur on fols 37v, 121, 121, 235.

[56] See below, pp. 113–32.

[57] For the status of women in Domesday Book, see P. Stafford, 'Women in Domesday', *Reading Medieval Studies*, 15 (1989), 75–94; M. Meyer, 'Women's Estates in Later Anglo-Saxon England', *Haskins Society Journal*, 3 (1991), 111–29; M. Meyer, 'The Queen's Demesne in Later Anglo-Saxon England', *The Culture of Christendom: Essays in Medieval History in Commemoration of Denis T. Bethell*, ed. M. Meyer (London and Rio Grande, 1993), 75–113.

Table 2.3 *The main contributions of scribe B to GDB*

County	Folio	Line
Berkshire	63d	42–5
Devon	117d	49
Gloucestershire	166b	24
Herefordshire	180b	2
Cambridgeshire	190a	42–5
Cambridgeshire	191b	23
Cambridgeshire	191c	1–2
Nottinghamshire	281c	3, 46
Nottinghamshire	283b	13
Nottinghamshire	286b	18
Nottinghamshire	287b	38
Nottinghamshire	288a	16
Lincolnshire	357a	2

Although disparities between the list and the text are not unknown (manifestly lists were often drawn up before the drafting of the text),[58] it was easy enough to find the lands of any particular lord in any particular county. Within chapters it was the manor that was flagged up as of importance. The devices used varied from area to area. The names identifying manors are almost always written in upper case 'rustic' letters and are ruled through in red. They immediately draw the eye. Initial letters of such entries, however, were also emphasized. They are larger than the rest of the text and often 'square' in form whether they be the name of the place itself, the tenant, the tenant-in-chief, or the preposition 'In'. All of this is in contrast to the treatment of subordinate land where names and initial letters are not differentiated.

All this aided use of the GDB at a time when the concept of a real index did not exist. Despite our computer-driven databases, it is also of use to the historian today. The various devices drew attention to what the scribe thought was important. It was not simply land but the manor or, to be more specific, the manor house or hall. Equally the devices concentrate our mind on the deviations from the norm. From time to time the scribe corrected himself by changing one letter form to another.[59] So, what do we make of, say, sokeland that is written up in a 'manorial'

[58] Galbraith, *The Making of Domesday Book*. See, for example, Shropshire where tenants-in-chief I to IV were written first and V to IX subsequently. The additional material was added to the first folio of a new quire and may have come to light after the drafting of the first part of the Shropshire text (C. P. Lewis, 'Introduction to the Shropshire Domesday', *The Shropshire Domesday*, eds A. Williams and R. W. H. Erskine (London, 1990), 7–8).
[59] In the account of Eudo son of Hubert's manor of Gamlingay in Cambridgeshire the scribe originally wrote a rustic I to introduce the entry, but he appears to have subsequently

form? Or a manor that is in a 'subordinate' form? We cannot assume that they are all mistakes or insignificant. Sometimes the import may be merely local. A manor in Oakham (Rutland) held by Leofnoth opens with a rustic I which seems to indicate that it was subordinate to Queen Edith's estate in the same place: its assessment is otherwise included in that of the main manor.[60] Important, to a degree, in the history of Oakham, but hardly earth-shattering unless we be surprised that one manor could belong to another. But what of a series of rustic initial letters in the account of the lands of the canons of Hereford in Herefordshire?[61] Manors are included aplenty, so we can hardly think in terms of manorial dependence. A rubric signalling that 'these lands which follow belong to the canons of Hereford' suggests a more interesting alternative. The anomalous forms seem to indicate that what follows is a list and we can perhaps conclude that the information was taken from a separate schedule. A deviation in form here indicates something of the scribe's sources.[62]

This is equally true of deviations in method. With the exception of counties like Yorkshire, the GDB scribe worked with remarkable confidence.[63] Content and expression, of course, vary from county to county, reflecting his source material, but, by and large, he wrote fluently. Nevertheless, there is a sufficient number of additions, corrections, emendations, and glosses to indicate that he was not simply copying from an exemplar. Mapping the stratigraphy of the text is, then, one of the most importance analyses for the recovery of his sources, and here we enter serious anorak country.[64] First, two general principles. Additions can be (a) foreseen or unforeseen and (b) current, that is part of the initial drafting, or postscriptal, that is after. On occasion the scribe knew that he had additional material to add and left a space. Such instances can be difficult to spot if he estimated

---

found that the land was a capital manor and changed the initial letter to a square I (GDB, 197v: *DB Cambs*, 25,9). In Bedfordshire the scribe was less careful where a marginal M signalled a manor, but in the case of Stevington he similarly felt the need to amend his text (GDB, 211: *DB Beds*, 15,2).

[60] GDB, 293v: *DB Rutland*, R18. Martinsley Wapentake was assessed at twelve carucates according to a note at the top of the account of Rutland, and yet the total assessment of the manors described in the account of the wapentake, including Leofnoth's, is thirteen carucates.

[61] GDB, 181v–182v: *DB Hereford*, 2,4–54.

[62] *DIB*, 219.

[63] Roffe, 'Domesday Book and Northern Society: A Reassessment', 323–4: D. M. Palliser, 'An Introduction to the Yorkshire Domesday', *The Yorkshire Domesday*, eds A. Williams and G. H. Martin (London, 1992), 1–38.

[64] For guides, see Rumble, 'The Domesday Manuscripts: Scribes and *Scriptoria*'; Rumble, 'The Palaeography of the Domesday Manuscripts'; C. Thorn, 'Marginal Notes and Signs in Domesday Book'; M. Gullick, 'The Great and Little Domesday Manuscripts', *Domesday Book: Studies*, eds A. Williams and R. W. H. Erskine (London, 1987), 93–112. The most succinct account is that of Thorn and Thorn, 'Writing of Great Domesday Book'.

the space accurately and the entry is current.[65] Sometimes it is only the almost imperceptible misalignment of the margin or a slight difference in pressure on the quill that hints at the change. Postscriptal additions are generally more obvious, but they may or may not fill the space allocated to them. In both instances the range of interpretation is, relatively speaking, limited. Foreseen additions tend to suggest that the scribe either had to check details in another source or derive the whole of the account from it. Neither necessarily indicates that the inquest was still in progress.[66] Conversely, they indicate that he had references in his main source that pointed implicitly or explicitly to those other sources (unless, of course, he had an impressive memory).

So far, so good. It must be borne in mind, however, that not all additions to spaces will necessarily be foreseen. Spaces in the text were left for a number of different reasons and were only subsequently employed to enter material. In Lincolnshire blank lines were left to distinguish sections of the text and were on occasion used for material that subsequently came to light.[67] So it is that current and foreseen additions fade into current and postscriptal unforeseen additions. Generally, however, these latter are easy to identify. Extensive passages may be written on a separate sheet that is inserted into a quire.[68] Otherwise, additions are interlined, that is written between two lines; added to an incomplete line; entered in the side, top, or bottom margin; or appended to the end of a column, section, or chapter. Only in the last context are they easily overlooked if current and the scribe has not employed signs to indicate where they should be read (a common but by no means an invariable device).[69] Here in broad terms additions attest a process of checking. Those that are current tend to suggest that a scribe overlooked an item while copying; his eye may, for example, have jumped from one entry to another similar one (haplography), and he only realized that he had missed out material some entries later. Postscriptal additions may, of course, often suggest the same, but it is also possible that other sources were consulted too. Nuances to the

[65] See, for example, the insertion of sokeland into the account of some royal manors in Yorkshire.
[66] This is a widespread notion, recently re-stated by F. and C. Thorn, 'Writing of Great Domesday Book', 48, 54, who assert that the estimation of ploughland was probably on-going. This is but one explanation for missing information. In the absence of other evidence, all that can be said is that other materials were as yet to be assembled when the main scribe embarked on his task.
[67] For the clearest example, and in many ways the most mysterious, see Count Alan's chapter in which all of the wapentake rubrics have been skilfully inserted from the beginning of the account of his lands in Kesteven to the end of the *breve* (GDB, 347–348v: *DB Lincs*, 12).
[68] Such sheets are indicated on the quire map in *Domesday Rebound*, end foldout, reprinted in *Great Domesday Studies*, 164–5, and animated in *The Digital Domesday*.
[69] Where there are no perceptible differences in the hand or pen, other characteristics must be examined. Line counts, disruption in hundredal sequence, aberrant subject matter may all be indicative.

interpretation are afforded by the place where an addition is made. Thus, soke of A in B which is entered after a further manor in B might well imply that the scribe's source was geographically arranged.

Checking was an on-going process both before and after the manuscript was rubricated. Caroline Thorn has identified a number of campaigns, not only involving the main scribe but also scribe B who may or may not have had a supervisory role.[70] There are instances where corrections have themselves been corrected.[71] What it all means, though, will probably never be entirely resolved. How, for example, does one interpret the insertion of an entry in the Lincolnshire folios where sokeland of Walcot in Haithby is entered, perhaps currently in a space left for another purpose, after the account of Peterborough Abbey's manor of Walcot?[72] Walcot had soke in Haithby all right, but the scribe got the wrong Walcot. What was intended was a second manor of Walcot some forty miles away on the Humber.[73] Was this incidental? Or do we conclude that sokelands were not enrolled with the manorial centres in the scribe's source but that he had a list indicating which should go with which? There are too many imponderables.

Analysis of stratigraphy is not for the faint-hearted. Often its interpretation will come down to a fine judgement and intuition. There are, indeed, many variations in the hand that cannot always be quantified and yet they attest the workings of the scribe. Sometimes a slight deviation from the norm will merely point to nothing more than a temporary break. Others, where they coincide with a change in form or material, may suggest that the scribe had paused to consult another source. Is this not what we must interpret by the fainter hand of the account of Richmond-shire in the Yorkshire folios?[74] Again, on similar grounds surely the account of Chester must be derived from a number of sources. There can be no doubt that it was written by the GDB scribe at more or less one sitting. But differences in alignment, the 'feel' of the hand, and the use of differently sized initial letters leave one with the unmistakable impression that there are three sections. It is difficult not to conclude that the account of the City proper, on the one hand, was distinct from 'the laws of the City' and the county customs on the other.[75]

The GDB scribe was a consummate craftsman as well as an administrative genius. He is, of course, anonymous, but something of his personal history can be gleaned from his writing. He wrote in a simple book hand with insular characteristics, that

---

[70] F. and C. Thorn, 'Writing of Great Domesday Book', 52. Scribe B only appears after drafting, extensive checking, and rubrication. If he was involved at an earlier stage, he has left no trace.

[71] F. and C. Thorn, 'Writing of Great Domesday Book', 52. See, for example, the account of Upchurch and Stuppington in Kent (GDB,9: *DB Kent*, 5,116–17).

[72] GDB, 345v: *DB Lincs*, 8,10.

[73] GDB, 346: *DB Lincs*, 8,28.

[74] GDB, 381: *DB Yorks*, SN,CtA.

[75] GDB, 262v: *DB Cheshire*, C. See below, p. 115 n30, for a detailed analysis of the entry.

is he was probably trained in an English scriptorium. His Latin is varied but still formulaic, but his knowledge of place-names is revealing. Part of his programme was to Latinize English phonology, but he still reveals a knowledge of English pronunciation which suggests that he was bilingual.[76] His hand is found in three postscriptal entries in Exon and three other manuscripts that may have Durham affinities.[77] It would seem that he was a northerner of English descent. Scribe B wrote in a decidedly Norman hand; he has not been identified elsewhere.

Where scribal practices reveal much about the contemporary texts, it might be expected that we have no such depth of evidence where documents survive only in later copies. Copies, abstracts, and abbreviations tended to serve their own purposes. Fortunately, however, this is not entirely true. Sometimes the form of a text was so integral to its content that it could not be easily suppressed. Evesham K, for example, preserved in a late twelfth-century cartulary, provides a list of estates and their assessments with the hundred in which each was situated interlined above.[78] This table-like structure is reminiscent of the section of GDB known (somewhat misleadingly) as the Yorkshire Summary, and it almost certainly preserves something of the form of the original text from which it was copied.[79] Even more surprising is the apparent survival of textual forms in the Crowland Domesday. This text is a compilation from GDB itself and a 'hundred roll' which emanated from the Domesday inquest. It now survives in two printed editions of 1596 and 1684, as well as a late sixteenth-century transcript, themselves based upon early fifteenth-century manuscripts. Nevertheless, the printers of both editions have used black letters and the like to indicate the form of initial capitals and place-names which, at several removes, seemingly perpetuate the forms of the eleventh-century originals.[80] All the texts that are extant in later manuscripts would repay an examination of their layout and calligraphy. It is likely, however, that

[76] Sawyer, 'The Place-Names of the Domesday Manuscripts', 483–506; C. Clark, 'Domesday Book – a Great Red-herring; Thoughts on some Eleventh-Century Orthographies', *England in the Eleventh Century*, ed. C. Hicks, Harlaxton Medieval Studies, 2 (1992), 317–31.

[77] P. Chaplais, 'William of Saint-Calais and the Domesday Survey', *Domesday Studies*, ed. J. C. Holt (Woodbridge, 1987), 65–78. Caroline Thorn doubts that the Durham affinities pre-date 1090; she considers that it is unlikely that Durham was the place where Domesday Book was written because it was too remote for the efficient transmission of the data (F. and C. Thorn, 'Writing of Great Domesday Book', 71 and note). The later date poses no problem if the writing of Domesday Book is put into the reign of Rufus, and, of course, there is no necessity to believe that it was written in the scriptorium of the main scribe.

[78] London, British Library, Cotton MS Vespasian B xxiv, fols 57r–62r; translation *DB Gloucs*, appendix.

[79] H. B. Clarke, 'The Domesday Satellites', *Domesday Book: A Reassessment*, ed. P. H. Sawyer (London, 1985), 62–3.

[80] *Scriptores Post Bedam*, ed. H. Savile (London, 1596); *Rerum Anglicarum Scriptorum Veterum* i, ed. W. Fulman (Oxford, 1684), 80–2; D. R. Roffe, 'The Historia Croylandensis: A Plea for Reassessment', *EHR*, 110 (1995), 96n.

the gleanings will be slender. Scribes copied for their own purposes, and so they produced an edition rather than a copy. Generally, they must have felt no need to reproduce the emendations of their sources, unless the meaning was unclear. A postscript, then, may be silently incorporated into the text. Of such elisions we will forever remain ignorant. The evidence is lost.

Diplomatic and forms

Where the working practices of the scribes cannot always be reconstructed, their forms of expression are inherent in the texts. The usages of the Domesday scribes are here called 'diplomatic' by analogy with the standard forms used in the drafting of legal instruments of one kind or another from an early period.[81] The importance of Domesday diplomatic has been appreciated for over a hundred years. Far from being random, differences in the record of woodland, pasture, and the like are regionally distributed. Eyton, Baring, Ballard, and Stephenson argued that such patterns were a function of the way in which individual groups of commissioners went about their work, and local communities responded to them, and concluded that they effectively identified Domesday circuits.[82]

Their method, if not the circuits they identified, has remained largely unquestioned. They did not exhaust its potential, though. Some forms and items of data are peculiar to specific counties. A record of *taillia*, tallage, for example, is all but unique to Lincolnshire.[83] All sorts of forms change from county to county. Some of these variations must represent selection processes at the level of the shire. The hundred and vill also shaped the texts. From chapter to chapter and document to document a common sequence of hundreds and vills is often apparent. The phenomenon is best illustrated in a county like Norfolk where the hundreds are consistently indicated in the text (Table 2.4). Tenements in Clackclose are entered first (if the tenant-in-chief held in that hundred), and then the account proceeds in a sequence of hundreds which is common to all chapters through to Clavering. In the chapters of Ralph de Tosny, Hugh de Montfort, and Walter Giffard the sequence is broken, that is, it starts halfway through and then returns to the beginning. Otherwise, it is only the chapters of the king, Count Alan, William de Warenne, Roger Bigod, the bishop of Thetford, and Ralph Baynard that deviate

---

[81] Professor Holt has objected to the use of the term 'diplomatic' because 'this gives scribal conventions a much more official standing than in fact that they had' (J. C. Holt, 'Domesday Studies 2000', *Domesday*, eds E. M. Hallam and D. Bates, 23). It will, of course, be understood that no such implication is intended.
[82] R. W. Eyton, *Domesday Studies: An Analysis and Digest of the Staffordshire Survey* (London, 1881), 1–2; A. Ballard, *The Domesday Inquest* (London, 1906), 12–13; C. Stephenson, 'Notes on the Composition and Interpretation of Domesday', *Speculum*, 22 (1947), 1–15.
[83] There are 268 references in the Lincolnshire folios but otherwise only one each in Nottinghamshire and Yorkshire (GDB, 285v, 321: *DB Notts*, 9,74; *DB Yorks*, 12W28).

from this pattern: there a number of sections are found, but in each the common sequence is repeated one or more times, as it is in each of the subsections of the *invasiones*.[84]

Table 2.4 *The order of hundreds in Norfolk*

1. Clackclose	13. Gallow	25. Eynesford
2. Freebridge	14. Brothercross	26. Taverham
3. Docking	15. Holt (v)	27. South Erpingham
4. Smethdon	16. North Greenhoe	28. Tunstead
5. South Greenhoe	17. North Erpingham	29. Happing
6. Grimshoe	18. Walsham	30. East Flegg
7. Wayland	19. Blofield	31. Norwich
8. Shropham	20. West Flegg	32. Thetford
9. Guiltcross	21. Henstead	33. Humbleyard
10. Launditch	22. Earsham	34. Depwade
11. Forehoe	23. Diss	35. Clavering
12. Mitford	24. Loddon	

Again, within each hundred a common sequence of vills can be found. Freebridge Hundred and a Half in the north-west of Norfolk has a highly fragmented tenurial and settlement structure, and yet almost every entry conforms to a neat organizing principle that proceeds from vill to vill (Table 2.5).

Only for Buckinghamshire, Shropshire, and Suffolk are hundred rubrics anywhere near as complete as in the Norfolk folios, and there similar structures can be identified. The phenomenon is, however, widespread. It is found in Yorkshire and Cambridgeshire where the area of the hundreds is known from the Yorkshire Summary and ICC respectively.[85] Elsewhere it can be identified only by using later evidence in combination with whatever rubrication Domesday affords.[86] Comprehensive records of the constituent vills of each hundred usually begin to appear in the early fourteenth century, but often they preserve a state of affairs from an earlier period. The fragmentary rubrication and order of entries of the Derbyshire folios of GDB bear no relation to the twelfth- and thirteenth-century structure

---

[84] Count Alan's chapter may be an exception. There the order of hundreds is 5, 10, 11, 12, 14, 15, 16, 17, 20, 25, 26, 27, 28, 29, 25, 1, 2, 8, 9, 23, 29, 31, 32, 33, a sequence that could represent a fractured single sequence.

[85] The evidence of the Yorkshire Summary is particularly impressive: with important exceptions, it is the formal archetype of the Domesday text (Roffe, 'The Yorkshire Summary', 242–60, esp. at 250–1). For Cambridgeshire, see C. R. Hart, *The Hidation of Cambridgeshire* Department of English Local History, University of Leicester, Occasional Papers, 2nd series, 6 (1974).

[86] Hundred headings are not always correct. See F. R. Thorn in the series of 'Hundreds and Wapentakes' articles in the County Edition of Domesday Book (London, Alecto, 1986–2001).

Table 2.5 *Sequence of vills in Freebridge Hundred and a Half*

	1	2	4	5	7	8	9	10	13	14	15	16	18	19	20	21	22	23	29	31	34	35	49	51	66	66
Lynn									4						19		32								17	55
Winch, West														9											18	
Wiggenhall																	24								19	
Walton, West					21					4			4													
Terrington								12									31									
Walsoken												3														
Walpole																							9			
Islington		44							13	4	6			1		10										56
Clenchwarton														2												
Middleton		45					5							4		11										
Runcton, North									14					5												
Bilney, West																12										
Pentney						2																				
Walton, East		45				2									15										21	
Acre, Castle					22						5				16											
Gayton Thorpe	1					3									17										22	
Winch, East	131					3									20										20	
Gayton					23								7			13									23	
Ashwicken		45												10												
Glosthorpe				1																						
Bawsey		45		2																						
Well													1													
Leziate																									58	
Gaywood							1																			
Mintlyn						50																				
Wootton	132																									
Grimston		2			25																				1	
Congham					26																				2	
Hillington					28													1							3	
Massingham	1			1	29	5							8	11				2								
Babingley																		3	1							
Dersingham																		4	2							
Sandringham																					1					
Harpley		3			30																					
Anmer				2	31																					
Snettisham		4																								
Flitcham		4			32	4, 6																				
Appleton						7														3						
Newton, West		4																								
Rising, Castle		4																								
Roydon		4																								

Numbers in *italics* at the head of columns refer to chapters in the Norfolk section of LDB. The remaining numbers refer to the order of entries within each chapter.

of hundreds/wapentakes. And yet they make complete sense in terms of the 1334 Lay Subsidy.[87] This subsidy was the first to be levied on the vill (as opposed to the individual) and it would seem that an early twelfth-century list was employed which preserves the Domesday hundreds. The Derbyshire folios exhibit an almost perfect hundred and villar sequence.

Much of this type of evidence has been gathered by Frank Thorn in the course of reconstructing the Domesday hundreds of England for the Alecto edition of Domesday Book. The Hampshire folios alone appear to betray no sign of geographical substructures.[88] Even here, however, further work may reveal the complex interrelations of a number of sequences rather than a random pattern. In the Cambridgeshire folios the hundredal sequence is identical with the order of hundreds in ICC. Sawyer, who reviewed the evidence in 1955,[89] argued that the widespread occurrence of sequences elsewhere must indicate that there were ICC-like documents behind the Domesday accounts of many other counties. He believed that the disjunctions in sequence were a function of how the accounts were written down: where a regular sequence suggests that the accounts of all the hundreds were sewn together in some way, broken and inverted sequences point to a number of separate quires. In fact lists of hundreds and vills drawn up at any point in the proceedings may have imposed an order on the GDB text without the necessity of there being a full hundredally arranged recension. There are indications, for example, that the Yorkshire text derived its order directly from the exemplar of the Yorkshire Summary.[90] Certainly in the Count of Mortain's chapter that source was consulted a number of times with matters of lordship in mind. It is unlikely that it was directly derived from a Yorkshire ICC (although that is not to say that there was not one).[91]

More indicative of the form of such sources are the diplomatic and data associated with each hundred. Variations can be considerable. Some may have been derived from schedules like the Yorkshire Summary. In South Greenhoe Hundred in Norfolk, for example, values are given for *quando recepit* or *quando invenit*, when the land was acquired, where elsewhere the term *post*, later, is used, while in Docking, Smethdon, and South Greenhoe carucates to the geld are frequently omitted. Other variations, by contrast, must have come from fuller sources. In

[87] D. R. Roffe, 'The Origins of Derbyshire', *The Derbyshire Archaeological Journal*, 106 (1986), 102–22.
[88] F. R. Thorn, 'Hundreds and Wapentakes', *The Hampshire Domesday*, eds A. Williams and R. W. H. Erskine (London, 1989), 28–39.
[89] P. H. Sawyer, 'The "Original Returns" and Domesday Book', *EHR*, 70 (1955), 177–97.
[90] See, for example, the account of the king's manor of Northallerton where the order of enrolment of its eleven berewicks is determined by an interlineation in the Summary: vills 7 to 12 – Great Smeaton, Little Smeaton, Cowton, Borrowby, Romanby, and Yafforth – were interlined above 2 to 6 – Birkby, Sowerby, Kirby, Landmoth, and Thornton – and the order in the king's *breve* is 2,7,38,49,5,10,6,11,12 (GDB, 299, 381: *DB Yorks*, 1Y2; SN,A1).
[91] Roffe, 'The Yorkshire Summary: A Domesday Satellite', 242–60; *DIB*, 84–6.

North Greenhoe, Eynesford, Earsham, Henstead, and Loddon, again in Norfolk, the unusual formulation *inter omnes*, or *inter homines* is used of the total number of ploughs, and in the hundreds in central Norfolk *sochemannus* is preferred to *liber homo*, where the opposite obtains in the south-east. Most tellingly of all, in the same county foldsoke is only mentioned in the hundreds of Clavering, Loddon, Humbleyard, Henstead, Depwade, Walsham, Clackclose, and Smethdon.[92]

In parallel to the geographical is the seigneurial. Lordship is a dominant theme of all documents, determining overall form in all but ICC and Abingdon A. It should not be surprising, then, that there are variations in expression from fee to fee. Roger de Lacy's lands in Shropshire, for example, are distinguished by a number of different expressions and forms.[93] Uniquely, half villeins appear, as do the only miller, beekeeper, and female cottars in the county; the cottars generally are called cotsets (*cozets*) rather than the standard Shropshire term cottar (*cotarius*); those who owed riding service appear as radknights where radmen is the form used elsewhere; female and male slaves are listed together where they are otherwise usually itemized. Other characteristics are common to some groups of fees but not to others. In Leicestershire, for example, TRE ploughs appear on some fees as opposed to ploughlands on others.[94] Such forms clearly indicate that lords and tenants had a considerable input into the sources of the texts.

Sometimes diplomatic directly identifies them. We have already noted that the distinctive use of the *In X…* formula in the account of the lands of the canons of Hereford in Herefordshire probably points to the use of a separate schedule.[95] In Devon the use of similar documents is hinted at in the *terra regis*. The king's demesne manors, which had been held by Edward the Confessor TRE, begin with the formula 'The king holds *X*', but the formula changes to '*X* gelded for *y* hides' for manors formerly held by Queen Edith, Earl Harold, Earl Leofwin, and Beorhtric and later Queen Edith which are each signalled by an explanatory rubric and entered in a separate sequence.[96] In Norfolk similar subdivisions, duly marked, are found of the king's *breve*, Roger Bigod's, and the bishop of Thetford's. Here there is no distinctive form of words, but significantly each section repeats the common sequence of hundreds as if it were a separate chapter. Repetition of this kind is common, although rarely defined by a rubric, and it must often point to different source materials.

---

[92] C. Johnson, 'Introduction to the Norfolk Domesday', *VCH Norfolk*, ii, ed. W. Page (London, 1906), 31.

[93] C. P. Lewis, 'Introduction to the Shropshire Domesday', *The Shropshire Domesday*, eds A. Williams and R. W. H. Erskine (London, 1990), 8–9.

[94] H. C. Darby, *Domesday England* (Cambridge, 1977), 348–9. This distribution contrasts with that in Shropshire where ploughlands are largely absent until GDB, 257a: *DB Salop*, 4,11,17. See *DIB*, 163.

[95] Above, p. 43.

[96] GDB, 100–101v: *DB Devon*, 1,1–72.

From the Domesday scribes' perspective, all these variations were the given of their sources and can be termed the vertical element in diplomatic, that is they were present in their sources and they incorporated them into their texts. The extent of this type of influence on the texts cannot be gauged until a systematic examination of the Domesday data has been undertaken hundred by hundred and chapter by chapter.[97] More recently it has been recognized that there is also a horizontal element, that is the forms that compilers brought to their work.[98] This is a vitally important area of study, for it provides insights into how the compilers perceived the data they were enrolling and, by extension, the nature of those data. And yet it is a source that has hardly been tapped. The Exon scribes have been characterized as copyists, and yet emendations suggest that they were responsible for some formulation and a study of their language may well determine to what degree. It is yet to be attempted. Likewise, we have noted that the language of scribe 2 in LDB suggests that he was in charge of the co-operative writing process, but there has been no analysis of the contribution of the other five scribes who worked on the body of the text. GDB has been served somewhat better.[99] The minutiae of language have been used to identify no fewer than forty-four basic forms that reveal a sequence of writing (see Appendix).

This sequence can be recognized only because the postscriptal passages in the GDB text have been identified. There can be no doubt that the autograph manuscript facilitates this type of analysis. However, it is not essential. If there is one source that has been pored over more intensely than Domesday Book it is the Bible. No 'original' manuscripts, of course, exist for any of its constituent books, and yet the fact has not precluded elucidation of its sources through its language. Close reading of the Pentateuch, for example, has identified a number of elements. E and J betray their presence by the distinctive use of Elohim and Yahweh for God, P and D by their interest in priestly matters and the law. Additional material was added by an editor to bring the disparate elements together in a coherent programme.[100]

All the Domesday texts can be read in the same way. Of especial interest to the analysis are apparent duplicate entries.[101] Throughout the Domesday corpus there are numerous instances in which the same piece of land is described in two,

---

[97] This type of study is not exactly a riveting exercise but can be productive. I have undertaken it for all the Danelaw shires from Yorkshire to Suffolk; many of the results appear in the following pages. *Domesday Explorer* should facilitate the process.

[98] Roffe, 'Domesday Book and Northern Society'; *DIB*, chapter 8.

[99] *DIB*, chapter 8.

[100] For a popular introduction, see R. E. Friedman, *Who Wrote the Bible?* (London, 1988).

[101] For a general account, see A. Williams, 'Apparent Repetitions in Domesday Book', *Domesday Book Studies*, eds A. Williams and R. W. H. Erskine (London, 1987), 90–2; for Exon, Welldon Finn, *Domesday Studies: The Liber Exoniensis*, 78–81; for GDB, Galbraith, *Making of Domesday Book*, 162–5; for LDB, W. Welldon Finn, *Domesday Studies: The Eastern Counties* (London, 1967), 49–51.

sometimes even three or more, different contexts. On occasion the scribe simply nodded and entered the same land twice. A note concerning the assessment of Hinxton is found twice in the Cambridgeshire folios, and in the second instance it is marked for deletion.[102] More usually the phenomenon attests more interesting processes. Sometimes rival claims to the tenement are responsible; aggrieved parties in disputes were often loath to concede and had their former estate entered in their chapter. Both Robert d'Oilly and Robert Dispenser claimed Barston in Warwickshire and, with entries in each of their chapters, it is not clear who actually held it.[103] Different sources lie behind others. Eight parcels of land are described with the City of York in the Yorkshire folios which also appear in the chapters of their respective lords.[104] Finally, multiple interests in the same land may lead to repetition. In the North land was frequently held by one lord and its soke by another and both of them might contrive to enter their respective interests. Likewise, in the South West land is entered in the king's chapter as well as the actual tenant's. In all cases, however, the parallel entries are but rarely identical. Differences in content and expression are invaluable clues to the contrasting forms of vertical and horizontal diplomatic.

Once the warp and weft of the sources has been determined, it is possible to begin to examine the referents of the various terms. Round was one of the first to realize the significance of this approach. Comparing the use of language in ICC and the parallel passages in GDB he was able to demonstrate that phrases like 'he could recede', 'he could go with his lands', 'he could sell', and the like were equivalents (although in other cases what he thought were variations on a single theme have subsequently proved to be significant).[105] Stephen Baxter is now examining the different terms for relationships of this kind in order to assess to what extent they represent differences in lordship throughout the country. The early results are promising.[106] The manor has been examined in similar terms. The fact that land may be said to be 'held for a manor' is apparently dependent on the duty scribe in LDB suggests that the term does not mark out the entries so distinguished. It may be suspected, then, that the intermittent use of the formula in GDB is only significant in relation to tenements that were not manors rather than those that clearly were but are not explicitly stated to be so.

[102] GDB, 189v, 190: *DB Cambs*, 1,10;22. The second instance is postscriptal.
[103] GDB, 242, 242v: *DB Warks*, 17,15.23,4.
[104] GDB, 298, 298v, 301, 313, 328: *DB Yorks*, 1W1–2.6W,2;4–6;8.23N36.
[105] Round, *Feudal England*, 23–6.
[106] S. Baxter, 'The Representation of Lordship and Land Tenure in Domesday Book', *Domesday Book*, eds E. Hallam and D. Bates (London, 2001), 73–102.

Texts, taxonomies, and dates

Palaeographical and diplomatic analysis informs a wider examination of the texts. Much of recent Domesday scholarship has been concerned with producing a taxonomy of the sources. All the texts in the Domesday corpus are in some way related to the Domesday inquest, but the problem has been to determine the nature of the relationship in each case. The most comprehensive examination of the corpus as a whole was undertaken by Howard Clarke in 1985.[107] He drew together analyses of individual schedules by a number of scholars, notably Galbraith, Sawyer, Harvey, and himself, to produce an account of the genesis of Domesday Book. He accepted that documents like Abingdon A and the Kentish Assessment List were pre-Domesday sources pressed into service in the inquest to inform the initial collection of evidence from the tenants-in-chief. Evesham A represents the sort of schedule that was then drawn up for validation by hundred jurors, and seigneurially arranged Bath A and geographically arranged ICC are representatives of the two types of source that their presentments took. From these county drafts regional returns, exemplified by Exon and LDB, were produced with the use of 'conversion tables', like Evesham K and Q, which facilitated the transformation of a hundredal to a seigneurial form where necessary. Finally, GDB was produced by abbreviating the regional returns.

This analysis accepts a number of assumptions that must be tested. The first relates to techniques of dating texts. That the Domesday inquest was conducted in 1086 is clear, but none of the Domesday texts is unambiguously dated. The colophon at the end of LDB states categorically that 'this survey (*ista descriptio*) was made in the year one thousand and eighty six from the incarnation of the lord and the twentieth of the reign of William, not only throughout these three counties but also throughout the others'.[108] It must be noted, however, that this is a postscriptal comment written by scribe 7, who did not otherwise participate in the production of the volume, and he almost certainly understood *ista* ('this there') *descriptio*, as the survey itself rather than LDB.[109] None of the remaining texts is explicitly dated, the best indication being a statement that a text or schedule was drawn up 'when England was described' or the like. The problem is a common one with medieval records and the normal way of tackling it is to narrow down a date range from the known history of individuals and institutions. 'Dead dating' works well with charters; people cannot grant land or witness transactions when they themselves are dead or not in office, and if they do a fishy smell hangs over

---

[107] Clarke, 'The Domesday Satellites', 50–70. For an independent but similar analysis, see A. Freason, 'Domesday Book: The Evidence Reviewed', *History*, 71 (1986), 375–93.

[108] LDB, 450.

[109] Rumble, 'The Domesday Manuscripts: Scribes and *Scriptoria*', 100. For the use of *descriptio* as the survey, as opposed to its records, see F. and C. Thorn, 'Writing of Great Domesday Book', 69 and note 109.

the document. Unfortunately, however, the Domesday documents are not always amenable to this type of analysis. It has been asserted that the Kentish Assessment List must pre-date Domesday, inter alia because in one entry GDB records a successor to the tenant.[110] At best this can only prove that the document is earlier than GDB, a different matter from demonstrating that it precedes the Domesday inquest. At best, for Domesday texts are often imprecise in their record. Queen Matilda appears as a tenant-in-chief in the Buckinghamshire folios and yet at the beginning of 1086 she had been dead for over two years.[111] The problem is even more acute with holders of land before 1086. The assize (the temporal limit of the inquiry) was set at 'the day on which King Edward was alive and dead' at an early stage in the process, although this had been amended to the more realistic 'in the time of King Edward' by the time GDB came to be written. Thus, it is often assumed that a past tense in a Domesday text can be safely translated as 'before 1066'. In fact, the referent might be to any predecessor in the previous thirty years. Earl Siward appears regularly in the Northern folios and yet he died in 1055[112] and Earl Waltheof more widely, although he was still in possession of his lands within a decade of the inquest.[113] Domesday was dependent on its sources and these were various.

On these grounds content is an equally treacherous anchor. Bath B might seem to be earlier than the acquisition of Tidenham by Earl William fitzOsbern between 1066 and 1069, for it ascribes the manor to the demesne of the abbey of Bath. And yet Ely D shows that schedules of claims were drawn up at an early stage of the inquest and the common enrolment of such lands in the *breves* of the claimants shows that they influenced the composition of the texts. Bath Abbey, then, may have simply been making a pitch for land formerly lost.[114] Its otherwise close agreement with the parallel section of GDB suggests that Bath B is closely associated with the Domesday inquest.[115] Again, Sally Harvey dates Abingdon A as pre-Domesday because it records TRE geld assessments where GDB has TRW figures.[116] Inherent in her argument is the assumption that the purpose of the geld inquest, which she saw as a contemporary but independent initiative, was to reassess tax liability. This is in itself questionable, but even within its own terms the argument does not work. In many counties TRE assessments are given and there is no indication that a reassessment was ever intended; Domesday hidation survived

[110] R. S. Hoyt, 'A Pre-Domesday Kentish Assessment List', *A Medieval Miscellany for Doris Mary Stenton*, eds P. M. Barnes and C. F. Slade, Pipe Roll Society, new series, 36 (1962 for 1960); S. P. J. Harvey, 'Domesday Book and its Predecessors', *EHR*, 86 (1971), 755–9.

[111] GDB, 152v; *ASC*, 160.

[112] *ASC*, 130.

[113] *ASC*, 158.

[114] *DIB*, 166–7. 'Lost' lands are entered on a regular basis in the various Ely *breves*.

[115] *DB Somerset*, appendix II, Bath B.

[116] Harvey, 'Domesday and its Predecessors', 755–61.

in many cases into the thirteenth century and occasionally beyond. But, more to the point, in Cambridgeshire there was a reduction in liability between 1066 and 1086 and yet both assessments are used in different contexts throughout the Cambridgeshire text.[117] Abingdon Abbey seems to have maintained two different assessments, one for acquitting service to the king and one for its own tenants.[118] It would seem that the burden of the Danegeld might be reduced but by necessity other dues continued to be calculated on the older assessments.[119]

Dead dating is, then, of dubious value. Given the manifold sources of the Domesday texts, it will probably always be misleading in providing a *terminus ante quem*; a reference to a person or place will not be an adequate ground for fixing a date before which a text was written. It can be of more positive use in determining a *terminus post quem*. It is self-evident that a document that makes reference to King William must have been written after 1066. On these grounds Christopher Lewis was able to argue that GDB must post-date the death of William the Conqueror, if only in part, because in the Huntingdonshire and Surrey folios William de Warenne is called Earl William, a title he was granted by William Rufus.[120] In this case, however, the deduction can only be made because it is apparent from the manuscript that *comes*, 'earl', is an integral part of the text. Where such a reference is postscriptal certainty dissolves. Claims have long been made that the Surrey section must already have been written when William the Conqueror issued a writ, 'after the description of the whole of England', which set the assessment of Westminster Abbey's manor of Pyrford in Surrey at 8 hides, for in GDB the scribe originally recorded its liability as 16 hides only subsequently to

[117] *DIB*, 110.
[118] N. Hooper, 'An Introduction to the Berkshire Domesday', *The Berkshire Domesday*, eds A. Williams and R. W. H. Erskine (London, 1988), 11.
[119] For dual assessments before the Conquest, see S1409; E. John, *Land Tenure in Early England* (Leicester, 1964), 147.
[120] C. P. Lewis, 'The Earldom of Surrey and the Date of Domesday Book', *Historical Research*, 63 (1990), 327–36. Proponents for an early date for Domesday have fought a fierce rearguard action to demonstrate that the scribe was confused in both contexts, the writing of '*comes*' being prompted by the proximity of entries noticing other earls (F. and C. Thorn, 'Writing of Great Domesday Book', 71; Holt, 'Domesday Studies 2000', 24; S. Baxter, review of *Domesday: The Inquest and the Book*, Institute of Historical Research, Reviews in History, http://www.history.ac.uk/reviews/paper/baxterStephen.html). Well, both references are unambiguously there and, special pleading apart, the most substantial objection seems to be that William de Warenne is not called earl elsewhere in the many hundreds of entries in which reference is made to him; if Domesday Book were later, it would have been updated. This is simply not so. Abbreviations of inquest records were always that: they stuck to the sources. If the GDB scribe nodded, it was in inadvertently adding later material. It should be noted that, *pace* Holt, the dating of GDB is not just based on this entry. (D. R. Roffe, reply to Stephen Baxter, Institute of Historical Research, Reviews in History, http://www.history.ac.uk/reviews/paper/roffeDavid.html). See below, pp. 104–6.

add postscriptally that 'it now gelds for 8 hides'.[121] The assumption, however, is unwarranted. The writ clearly sets a *terminus post quem* for the addition, but can hardly provide a *terminus ante quem* for the text itself.[122] At most it can be said that the information was not in the scribe's original source.

Here we must substitute a positive with a qualified negative. Where we have original working documents this is often possible. Even qualified negatives, though, can become meaningless when we have texts only in later copies, for there is generally no way of knowing whether a reference is integral. Evesham K contains surveys of Gloucester and Winchcombe with information that dates parts of them to *c.*1100, but this hardly dates the whole text. Rather it merely provides a *terminus post quem* for that part and may or may not provide a *terminus post quem*, or indeed a *terminus ante quem*, for the rest of the text. Place-name forms, it is true, can sometimes hint at different strata in compound documents, but it can never be assumed that a scribe always copied what was before him. In the Crowland Domesday place-names were modernized to fourteenth-century forms except for those of places in which the abbey no longer had interests at the time of writing, and it would seem that the scribe accurately copied only those that were unfamiliar to him.[123]

If precise dating is elusive, textual forms promise the possibility of constructing a relative chronology. Frank and Caroline Thorn have eloquently demonstrated how the language and layout of Exon have directly influenced the production of GDB.[124] The GDB scribe's repeated transcription of textual peculiarities and misunderstandings of emendations indicate beyond doubt that the Exeter text was his principal source for the account of the south-western counties. Where one or both texts are later copies, this sort of analysis is rarely possible,[125] but diplomatic may betray a relationship. The geographically arranged ICC is a case in point. The account of each vill commences with the statement 'X [the place] defended itself for y hides, A^1 holds …' while other fees in the same vill have the form 'In the same vill A^2 holds …' These forms are consistently translated into GDB as 'X defended itself for y hides …' and 'In X A holds …' and it is thus clear that ICC precedes the account and was probably a principal source.[126]

[121] *Facsimiles of English Royal Writs to A.D. 1100 Presented to Vivian Hunter Galbraith*, eds T. A. M. Bishop and P. Chaplais (Oxford, 1957), no. 24; Galbraith, T*he Making of Domesday Book*, 206; J. C. Holt, '1086', *Domesday Studies*, ed. J. C. Holt (Woodbridge, 1987), 52n.

[122] Otherwise it could be claimed that this (postscriptal) note dates the above text to 1086 since it notices the Pyrford charter.

[123] Roffe, 'The Historia Croylandensis', 98.

[124] *DB Devon*, Exon Introduction.

[125] For an exception, see the Crowland Domesday where some attempt has been made to represent the MS in one version of the text.

[126] J. J. N. Palmer, 'The Domesday Manor', *Domesday Studies*, ed. J. C. Holt (Woodbridge, 1987), 144.

More subtle are editorial reorganizations of material. The GDB scribe is consistently more concise and organized than the scribes of Exon with only the occasional
slip hinting at his more expansive source. They in their turn had imposed their
own concept of what was required upon their material and the process indicates
that Bath A was one of their sources. In content this document varies little from
Exon, but where the one lists demesne and villagers' hides followed by demesne
and villagers' ploughs, the other regroups the information so that the demesne
assessment and ploughs come first. Furthermore, its language is somewhat looser.
All in all, it seems clear that it was slightly earlier than Exon.[127]

The organization of texts may also hint at a relationship. Common sequences of
vills and hundreds are ubiquitous in the Domesday corpus and in themselves prove
little beyond a common identity in a process: many a schedule exhibits a structure
that is identical with that of LDB or GDB, but it may as easily be a precursor of
the engrossed texts as an abstract or extract thereof. Evesham K and Q are difficult to interpret on these grounds. Rather it is in the disruption of sequences that
relationships become apparent. The Suffolk section of IE shares a villar sequence
with its LDB counterpart, but the order of hundreds is completely different.[128]
It would thus seem that it was extracted from a geographically arranged source in
which each hundred was entered in a separate quire and as such it represents a
precursor of the LDB text. Again, however, the phenomenon is not always easy to
interpret. It has been commonly assumed that the sequences are ultimately derived
from the order in which hundred juries were called to make their presentments,
and it therefore follows that aberrant forms must precede that stage in the inquiry.
On these grounds Sawyer has claimed that Evesham A stands at the very beginning
of the Domesday process, representing a geographical arrangement of seigneurial
returns preparatory to validation by the hundred juries.[129] In reality, however,
changes could be made at later stages in the process. The bishop of Worcester's
breve in the Worcestershire folios of GDB is radically different in organization from
the rest of the Worcestershire text, but it manifestly postdates the presentments
of the hundred juries.[130] Similarly, the Yorkshire Summary appears to postdate
hundredal presentments, for it is the formal archetype of much of the Yorkshire
text, but in the account of the lands of the Count of Mortain there is a disruption
of that order occasioned by a scanning of the Summary exemplar a number of
times.[131]

From these techniques of dating sources a few firm conclusions can be drawn.
GDB was conceived as an abbreviation of its sources which drew directly on Exon

---

[127] R. Lennard, 'A Neglected Domesday Satellite', *EHR*, 58 (1943), 32–41.

[128] Sawyer, 'The "Original Returns" and Domesday Book', 189.

[129] P. H. Sawyer, 'Evesham A, a Domesday Text', *Worcestershire Historical Society Miscellany
1* (Worcester and London, 1960), 3–36.

[130] GDB, 172v–174. The bishop probably wrote the account himself (*DIB*, 143, 220–8).

[131] Roffe, 'The Yorkshire Summary: A Domesday Satellite', 251–2.

and ICC, and in Yorkshire was preceded by a document that had the same form as the Yorkshire Summary, while Exon in its turn drew upon Bath A, and LDB was preceded, in part at least, by IE. These are precious conclusions. They are, nevertheless, a meagre harvest from such a volume of material. There is scarcely enough material to produce a complete taxonomy.

A way forward seems to be offered by analogy, but in reality it is a method fraught with pitfalls for the unwary. The placing of LDB in the Domesday corpus illustrates the dangers. V. H. Galbraith, and most subsequent writers, have equated it with Exon.[132] The argument put forward, however, is essentially a classic syllogism. Exon is earlier than GDB and records demesne livestock where GDB does not; LDB records demesne livestock and therefore it is contemporary with Exon and earlier than GDB. In fact the differences between Exon and LDB are greater than the similarities.[133] Exon is a working document, in effect a series of office files, which is arranged by regional fee. LDB, by contrast, is a fully compiled fair copy in which the shire is the basic organizing principle. As such, its affinities are nearer to ICC than Exon, but its closest analogue is GDB itself, the record of demesne livestock notwithstanding.

The problem here is not only one of choosing the right characteristics to compare, it is also one of perception. All too often the production of the Domesday texts has been seen in rigid, mutually exclusive stages, witness the table produced by Clarke.[134] Symptomatic of this attitude is the assumption that, like chronicles, all documents have a single stemma, that is a straight line of transmission from a single original. The upshot has been to elaborate the taxonomy. Time and again it is asserted that if two documents share material but each contains data that are not found in the other, then they must be independently derived from a third source. So the Braybrooke Cartulary schedule has given birth to an ur-ICC and Exon to an intermediary before GDB.[135] In reality, there is no necessity for documents to be copied from one source: many are patently compilations from a number of sources.[136]

The concept of a stemma is, then, an unhelpful one, for it applies a model of authorship to a process that is of necessity other. The neat taxonomy that Clarke produces is less a function of what the texts themselves tell us than of a preconceived notion of what the Domesday process was about. What other reason is there for putting Evesham A at the head of the queue than a conviction that Domesday Book was from the outset the aim of the Domesday inquest? We

[132] Galbraith, *The Making of Domesday Book*, 30–2.
[133] For the following, see *DIB*, 89–98, 220–3.
[134] Clarke, 'Domesday Satellites', 52.
[135] G. H. Fowler, 'An Early Cambridgeshire Feodary', *EHR*, 46 (1931), 422–3; Galbraith, *The Making of Domesday Book*, 30–2.
[136] I have suggested that Braybrooke is essentially a copy of ICC with the addition of local knowledge (*DIB*, 109).

are repeatedly told that all the Domesday texts with the exception of GDB are 'satellites', they are merely a means to an end. Only thus has it been possible to put them into an order.

It seems to me that the authority for this concept is dubious. The so-called 'articles of inquiry' preserved in the prologue to IE have frequently been adduced as evidence of the purpose of the inquest at its earliest stage. They are, however, bad evidence. The articles are undoubtedly in a form that is very like that of Domesday Book:

> Here follows the inquest of lands, as the king's barons made it, to wit: by the oath of the sheriff of the shire and of all the barons and their Frenchmen and of the whole hundred, of the priest, the reeve, and six villagers of each village. In order, what is the manor called? Who held it in the time of King Edward? Who now holds it? How many hides? How many ploughs on the demesne? How many men? How many villagers? How many cottars? How many slaves? How many free men? How many sokemen? How much wood? How much meadow? How much pasture? How many mills? How many fish ponds? How much has been added or taken away? How much, taken together, it was worth and how much now? How much each free man or sokeman had or has. All this at three dates, to wit in the time of King Edward and when King William gave it and as it is now. And if it is possible for more to be had than is had.[137]

But this list of questions does not necessarily imply a feudal survey. No mention is made of the fee and it could as easily have informed the account of each holding within the vills of ICC as a GDB-like source. In fact, the list is almost certainly very late in the Domesday process. Its very similarity to GDB should long ago have cast suspicion upon it. With no notice made of demesne livestock, it seems hardly possible that it could have informed the process that produced Exon, ICC, IE, or LDB. If not a literary conceit of the late twelfth century, when IE was compiled, the list was probably drawn up as an abbreviation guide for the GDB scribe.[138]

The form of Exon has been cited as further evidence that the production of Domesday Book was the aim of the Domesday inquest. Galbraith took issue with Round who believed that ICC was the typical product of the inquest.[139] His objections, however, were misconceived. Whereas ICC was compiled from various sources to a conscious plan, Exon was a working record. Its form, then, is contingent to the aim of the inquest since it was a function of its sources. As Galbraith himself rightly divined,[140] much of the Domesday data could come only from the

---

[137] IE, 97
[138] *DIB*, 114–17. The use of *mansio* for 'manor' perhaps tips the scales in favour of an eleventh-century context for its drafting.
[139] Galbraith, *The Making of Domesday Book*; Round, *Feudal England*, 1–95.
[140] Galbraith, *The Making of Domesday Book*, 82.

tenant-in-chief and it was therefore inevitable that it should be first written down in a 'seigneurial' form. On its own the form of Exon is no conclusive evidence for the aim of the survey.

No more so is the form of ICC. In reality, what evidence the Domesday sources afford suggests that there was no one single enterprise. The Anglo-Saxon annalist pointedly contrasts an audit of 'how many hundred hides there were in the shire, or what land and cattle the king himself had in the country, or what dues he ought to have in twelve months from the shire' with a survey of the lands and resources of his tenants-in-chief in the words 'also he had a record made of how much land his archbishops had, and his bishops, and his abbots and his earls'. At least some of the Domesday texts may relate to the former process. Abingdon A is said in the apology that introduces it to have been derived from a hundredally arranged source which was kept in the Exchequer with Domesday Book, and the compiler of the Crowland Domesday refers to hundred rolls likewise kept with Domesday which he had consulted. Several other records make reference, more or less unambiguously, to similar records.

There is, then, no overall taxonomy of the Domesday texts. Clarke's inductive approach to Domesday must be rejected. It seems clear enough that any examination of the processes of the Domesday inquest can only be founded in those documents that are directly related to each other, that is, Bath A, Exon, ICC, IE, and above all LDB and GDB. Devoid of any clue as to their provenance and function, the remaining texts are useless as guides. The origins of some will probably always remain uncertain. For most the best that can be hoped for is a suggested function once different processes have been identified in the principal Domesday texts.

3

The Inquest and the Book

D OMESDAY BOOK was clearly abbreviated from the documentation of the Domesday inquest, but it is another matter to claim that inquest and book were conceived of as an integrated process. There is nothing in the texts themselves that necessarily demands such a conclusion. It is as well, then, first to consider what an inquest of the Domesday type was and what sorts of records it commonly produced. This is easier said than done. In the last fifty years or so it has become increasingly clear that the inquest was not a Norman importation. Something like the jury of presentment is attested in the late tenth-century Danelaw and it is highly likely that there was a similar institution elsewhere in England.[1] Nevertheless, Domesday is the first extensive document of its kind that survives. If there was anything vaguely comparable before the Conquest we have no idea of its form.[2] By necessity, we have to look to the twelfth century and later. From that time with a quickening pace the general inquest became an integral part of the governance of England until it was superseded by parliament in the fourteenth century.[3] In consequence there survives a large body of material, from simple

---

[1] In III Æthelræd, 3.1, it is declared that 'a meeting is to be held in each wapentake, and the twelve leading thegns, and with them the reeve, are to come forward and swear on the relics which are put into their hands that they will accuse no innocent man nor conceal any guilty one' (Robertson, III Æthelræd, 3.1; *EHD*, i, 403). What has become known as Athelstan's IV law code (*ibid.*) is almost certainly the record of an inquest into tolls undertaken in London (P. Wormald, 'Ethelred the Lawmaker', *Ethelred the Unready*, ed. D. Hill (Oxford, 1978), 62; P. Wormald, *The Making of English Law: King Alfred to the Twelfth Century – Volume I, Legislation and its Limits* (Oxford, 1999), 17–18; R. C. Van Caenigem, *Royal Writs in England from the Conquest to Glanvill: Studies in the Early History of the Common Law*, Selden Society, 77 (1959), 67–103.

[2] According to the author of the Historia Croylandensis, King Alfred commissioned a survey that was arranged by hundred. The excerpts given, however, clearly emanate from the Domesday process (*Rerum Anglicarum Scriptores Veteres*, ed. W. Fulman (Oxford, 1684), i, 80).

[3] J. C. Holt, 'The Prehistory of Parliament', *The English Parliament in the Middle Ages*, eds R. G. Davies and J. H. Denton (Manchester, 1981), 1–28.

presentments, through compiled verdicts, to abstracts and abbreviations.[4] What
emerges as striking from this vast corpus is the central role that the verdict of
the hundred played. The jurors whose names are recorded at the top of each roll
and whose seals were appended to the bottom spoke for the community at large.
However, they did not take it upon themselves to interpret its concerns. The
presentments of individuals and vills were sought and then incorporated into their
verdicts: it is clear from those that survive that these verdicts were compilations
drawn up before the formal court sessions.[5] Thereafter, abstracts and abbreviations
might be compiled from these sources, but they never superseded them. The point
is nicely made in a note on the flysheet of the Book of Fees, apparently written
when that work was compiled from a series of thirteenth-century inquest records in
1302: 'Remember that this book was composed and compiled from several official
inquests ... and therefore the contents of this book are to be used for evidence
here in the Exchequer and not for the record'.[6] Abstracts and abbreviations were
extensively used for reference purposes by the Chancery or Exchequer in the course
of routine administration, but it would seem that, at least initially, they did not
assume any legal force. It was always the original verdicts that were cited in actions
that came out of the inquests.[7]

These are characteristics of the inquest that are at variance with much of recent
thinking about Domesday. And yet there are indications that they lie at the heart of
the inquest as a procedure. The realization has a considerable bearing on the way in
which the evidence of the workings of the Domesday inquest is interpreted. It also
places the Domesday inquest in context. There can be no doubt that the enterprise
was considered to be extraordinary at the time, but it is clear that surprise was
occasioned by its extent rather than the fact in itself.

[4] There has been no general discussion of this material, but see H. Hall, *Studies in Offi-
cial English Historical Documents* (London, 1908), 281–306; H. M. Cam, *The Hundred and
the Hundred Rolls* (London, 1930); D. E. Greenway, 'A Newly Discovered Fragment of the
Hundred Rolls of 1279–80', *Journal of the Society of Archivists*, 7 (1982), 73–8; S. Raban, 'The
Making of the 1279–80 Hundred Rolls', *Historical Research*, 70 (1997), 123–45; S. Raban, *A
Second Domesday? The Hundred Rolls of 1279–80* (Oxford, 2004); D. R. Roffe, 'The Hundred
Rolls of 1255', *Historical Research*, 69 (1996), 201–10; D. R. Roffe, 'The Hundred Rolls and
their Antecedents: Some Thoughts on the Inquisition in Thirteenth-Century England',
Haskins Society Journal, 7 (1996), 179–87.
[5] *Stamford in the Thirteenth Century: Two Inquisitions from the Reign of Edward I*, ed.
D. R. Roffe (Stamford, 1994), 12–19.
[6] *The Book of Fees*, Public Record Office, 2 vols in 3 (London, 1920–31), i, xx.
[7] The Ragman Rolls of 1274–5, for example, are annotated in the court proceedings
resulting from them where the extract rolls of the same are not (*Rotuli Hundredorum*, ed.
W. Illingworth, Record Commission (1812–18), *passim*.

The Domesday inquest and its organization

Scattered through the Domesday texts are a thousand or so references to evidence given by jurors representing the various strata of local society.[8] Juries of Englishmen, Frenchmen, vill, hundred, wapentake, riding, and shire are all found, usually alone but not infrequently in combination. There are, however, few clues as to their workings in the texts themselves, for their opinions are recorded only where controversy was overt or anticipated. But the IE prologue tells us that six men were called from each vill along with the priest and reeve, and eight men from each hundred, four French, four English, the names of whom it records for the whole of Cambridgeshire and Hertfordshire.[9] Here was a procedure that underlies the Domesday process.

To Round's generation it was axiomatic that they provided all the Domesday data, but no one would espouse such a populist view nowadays. There are a number of references to evidence provided by tenants-in-chief and their men, both individually and collectively,[10] and, as Galbraith pointed out forty or so years ago, it is clear that most of the manorial data were beyond the competence of the representatives of the local community.[11] Jurors confined themselves to matters within the public domain, namely to questions of title, assessment, and tenure.[12] So much is uncontroversial. There has still survived from the nineteenth century, however, the perception that that evidence was in some way uniquely authoritative. Christopher Lewis and Robin Fleming, it is true, have been at pains to point out just how partial jurors might be.[13] The hundredmen were drawn from a middling class of tenant, somewhere above the common free man but below the honorial tenant, that is not widely recorded in the Domesday texts. But it is clear from the limited evidence available that they were commended to local lords who make an appearance therein, and it would seem clear that they must have often represented these their lords' interests. Many of those lords themselves were evidently jurors of the shire.[14] The jury was no unbiased fount of truth. This was the reality of inquests throughout the Middle Ages. Nevertheless, such jurors embodied the free communities of the shire and the sworn verdicts (*veredictum*, true statement)

---

[8] For the most succinct categorization of the various references, see R. Fleming, *Domesday Book and the Law: Society and Legal Custom in Early Medieval England* (Cambridge, 1998), Index IX/3, Those who gave testimony, pp. 540–4.

[9] IE, 97–101.

[10] Fleming, *Domesday Book and the Law*, Index IX/3, Those who gave testimony, pp. 540–4.

[11] V. H. Galbraith, *The Making of Domesday Book* (Oxford, 1961), 82.

[12] For presentments on value, see below, pp. 243–4.

[13] C. P. Lewis, 'Domesday Jurors', *The Haskins Society Journal*, 5 (1993), 17–44; Fleming, *Domesday Book and the Law*, 17–28.

[14] See below, pp. 271–3.

that they pronounced, it is argued, constituted judgements in the oral society of eleventh-century England. By definition, Fleming concludes, the Domesday jurors informed a process of determination.[15]

Two disparate notions come together in this perception of the role of the jury. From the past, possibly historical, certainly historiographical, are echoes of a free Anglo-Saxon society which determined its own affairs within autonomous local assemblies.[16] From the future is the use of the jury in the bureaucratic processes of the common law.[17] Neither encapsulates the essence of the inquest. That is best sought in the use of the device both before and after the Conquest. The inquest is conspicuous by its absence in the Old English law codes. For Pollock and Maitland it was thus clear that the device was a Norman importation.[18] This, however, is to miss the point. The law codes are concerned (where the matters are aired) with the processes of proof and in pre-Conquest society this was determined by compurgation, the enlistment of oath-helpers to swear to the truth of a cause.[19] Something like the inquest is, however, evidenced in other pre-Conquest sources. Local men were regularly consulted in the fenland, it would seem, and their place in the legal process is illustrated by perhaps the most famous of these cases.[20] In the late tenth century unnamed sons of a certain Boga of Hemingford laid claim to Ely Abbey's estate of Bluntisham in Huntingdonshire. They claimed it by right of their maternal uncle Tope who, they asserted, ought to have had it by inheritance from his grandmother. However, it had been unjustly forfeited to the king even though before her marriage the grandmother had made the requisite submission to Edward the Elder at Cambridge. This plea was contradicted by 'the wise old men of the shire (*sapientes illius provincie et senes*)'. They declared that Edward the Elder had acquired Huntingdon before Cambridge and therefore any submission made at the latter could not have indemnified the grandmother in her tenure of lands in Huntingdonshire. The jurors found in favour of Wulfnoth who had granted Bluntisham to Ely. A shire court was then convened and the plea was again aired. Wulfnoth gathered in his support all the best men of six hundreds and

---

[15] 'Oral testimony was central to the purpose of the inquest, and it provided the means by which neighbours of all social classes and peoples witnessed and recognised the permanence of the Norman settlement; and the inquest rather than the book became the means through which the whole of the tenurial revolution (much of which had been accomplished without written order or public sanction) came clearly and finally into every man's view, and it was the way in which the Conquest was at last fit snugly and publicly within the law' (R. Fleming, 'Oral Testimony and the Domesday Inquest', *ANS*, 17 (1994), 120).

[16] See, for example, *Anglo-Saxonism and the Construction of Social Identity*, eds A. J. Frantzen and J. D. Niles (Gainesville, 1997).

[17] F. Pollock and F. W. Maitland, *The History of English Law*, 2nd edn, 2 vols (Cambridge, 1923), i, 143–4.

[18] Pollock and Maitland, *The History of English Law*, i, 140–2.

[19] Pollock and Maitland, *The History of English Law*, ii, 633–7.

[20] *Liber Eliensis*, ed. E. O. Blake, Camden Society, 3rd series, 92 (1962), 98–9.

over a thousand men undertook to swear on his behalf. The sons of Boga were then unwilling to proceed, and all declared their support for Wulfnoth's title and right to grant the land.

This was no royal process; it was a popular and communal device.[21] Nevertheless, here we see what is in effect a jury supplying evidence, and that evidence was a verdict in the sense that they were expected to tell the truth. But it did not determine the matter; that was afforded by the due processes of compurgation in the shire court.[22] The inquest provided authoritative evidence on which decisions could be based. And so it continued to function into the later Middle Ages. From the twelfth century it was harnessed to the developing procedures of the common law and in time the jury was called upon to make a second pronouncement, a recognition, that effectively determined causes in procedures by writ.[23] But the inquest itself was never an executive instrument. Thus it was that the major surveys of the thirteenth century brought to light matters which were pursued through the courts for years after, often until the parties died.[24]

To state the obvious, the inquest was an investigative process.[25] At a local level it informed the day-to-day workings of government and administration. In the inquisition *post mortem*, for example, it was used to establish basic facts about the tenure of the deceased in order to determine the rights of the king. Nationally, the inquest might also be used in the same way: the surveys of regalia of 1212 and 1255 and the scutage of 1242 were of this order.[26] But even in these more or less routine administrative contexts, the inquest represented something more. By defining the

---

[21] For Maitland, as others, the inquisition was a royal privilege that was granted to individuals who could therefore benefit from the delegation of the royal right to judge (Pollock and Maitland, *The History of English Law*, i, 140–2; J. Glénisson, 'Les Enquêtes Administratives en Europe Occidentale aux XIIIe et XIVe Siècles', *Histoire Comparée de l'Administration*, ed. W. Paravicini and K. F. Werner (Munich, 1980), 17–25). In consequence inquests are defined in relation to kingship. The device becomes less problematic when divorced from judgement (S. Reynolds, *Kingdoms and Communities in Western Europe 900–1300* (Oxford, 1984), 33–4).

[22] According to Ramsey and Thorney memoranda, a dispute between the two abbeys over King's Delph Fen appears to have been settled by a local jury. Van Caenigem accepts this as a recognition (*Royal Writs*, 69–71). However, the text is corrupt (*Anglo-Saxon Writs*, ed. F. E. Harmer (Manchester, 1952), 252–6). The procedure is more reminiscent of post-Conquest witness by the twelve-carucate hundred in boundary disputes (*Documents Illustrative of the Social and Economic History of the Danelaw from Various Collections*, ed. F. M. Stenton, British Academy Records of Social and Economic History, 5 (1920), lxviii–lxix).

[23] Van Caenigem, *Royal Writs*, 51–3.

[24] In the Extract Rolls of the Ragman inquest, probably compiled in the 1290s, those participants who had died are noted.

[25] Roffe, 'The Hundred Rolls and their Antecedents'.

[26] *Book of Fees*. See also, Roffe, 'The Inquest of 1255' for the verdicts that survive in the Hundred Rolls series (London, PRO, SC5).

rights of the king, it also effectively confirmed the title of the tenant. The inquest was, in effect, an occasion for negotiation.[27] Indeed, in times of crisis, it mediated the relationships between the king and his subjects by providing a body of agreed fact on which decisions could be made: it often informed a conscious dialectic of investigation, legislation, and enforcement as in 1258 and 1275.[28] The inquest was to remain the main forum of consultation between ruler and ruled until it was superseded by parliaments in the early fourteenth century.[29]

The Domesday jurors' verdicts were of this order: they set up hares but did not catch them. The inquest which they informed was of a piece with the character of late Anglo-Saxon government and society.[30] On the eve of the Conquest England south of the Tees was divided into a series of shires. Each was generally in the charge of an earl, a military leader who commanded the county's levies on the king's behalf, and a king's shire reeve or sheriff, the representative of the crown who executed writs, collected taxation, and supervised the maintenance of the king's peace. Between them earl and sheriff oversaw an integrated system of local government. The primary forum in which they operated was the shire court, to which the greatest landholders of the shire paid suit. Held in the county town, it was there that the king's pleas were heard, felonies tried, and weighty matters that affected the interests of the king, such as the right to bookland, were determined. More mundane business, both judicial and administrative, however, was delegated to local courts. In hidated England these were known as hundreds; substantially the same institution in the carucated Northern Danelaw was called the wapentake. As communal meeting places and areas of land, many hundreds predate the shrieval system, others were apparently a function of it. Varying origins are reflected in different forms. Some hundreds were confined to a single estate which encompassed a small number of settlements, others were assigned large groups of vills, units of local government at its lowest level, which in themselves were often composed of several settlements and communities, and they could be constituted as compact blocks of land or widely scattered estates. However, the responsibilities of the hundred were uniform. Each was competent to determine minor trespasses and pleas of customary land, and its officers supervised the policing of the area and the muster of its levies through its network of vills. From vill to shire court

---

[27] D. R. Roffe, 'Talking to Others: The Domesday Inquest', *Worlds Apart Together: Documents and Society in Medieval England and Japan*, eds H. Tsurushima and D. R. Roffe (forthcoming); http://www.roffe.co.uk/talking.htm.

[28] J. R. Maddicott, 'Edward I and the Lessons of Baronial Reform: Local Government 1258–93', *Thirteenth Century England i: Proceedings of the Newcastle upon Tyne Conference*, eds P. R. Coss, S. D. Lloyd (Woodbridge, 1986), 1–30.

[29] Holt, 'Pre-history of Parliament'.

[30] For succinct accounts, see H. R. Loyn, *The Governance of Anglo-Saxon England 500–1087* (London, 1984), especially chapter 6, and A. Williams, *Kingship and Government in Pre-Conquest England c.500–1066* (London, 1999), 107–22.

the sheriff oversaw the running of a coherent system of government that prevented the fragmentation of power that saw the emergence of territorialized feudalism throughout much of continental Europe.

Not all shires had the same origins as territorial units, but the main stages in the development of the shrieval system *qua* institution are well understood. From the eighth century kings had insisted on the reservation of the *trinoda necessitas*, that is, the three common burdens of army service, borough defence, and bridge building. In the face of Danish conquest and settlement King Alfred of Wessex fashioned these duties, through an assessment to the geld in hides, into the first co-ordinated system of local defence that prefigured the shire. In the course of the tenth century the system was extended to the lands conquered by the kings of Wessex and its responsibilities were extended until by the late tenth century it had largely attained the form that it exhibited at the time of the Domesday inquest.

The chronology is clear, but the dynamics of the system have not always been so clearly comprehended. The shire emerged in a period of conquest and reconquest and in consequence historians have tended to view it as a species of military government. The king commanded respect because kingship was strong. This, of course, begs the question: Wherein lay the strength of monarchy? The answer is mundane. The genius of King Alfred and his successors lay not just in conquest. More importantly, they fostered stability and this they achieved by appealing to the various free communities of the shire. King and subject made common cause against disruptive forces, be they invaders, felons, or over-mighty lords. The inquest as a means of communication, then, fits nicely into this context. There is only one record of its use in this way before the Conquest: the document known as Athelstan's fourth law code is in fact the records of an inquiry into the collection of tolls and the like in London.[31] But it must be suspected that it was regularly used to provide information, notably the extent of land to inform assessment to the geld, on which negotiations could be based and decisions made.

By its nature, then, the Domesday enterprise was a communal one.[32] For the process to be effective channels of communication had to be unimpeded. In the later Middle Ages the inquest was often preceded by a purge of local government personnel. In 1170, for example, an inquest into the workings of local government

---

[31] Robertson, IV Athelstan.

[32] For a contrary view, see Cooper, 'Protestations of Ignorance in Domesday Book'. *The Experience of Power in Medieval Europe, 950–1350*, eds R. Berkhofer, A. Cooper, and A. Kosto (Aldershot, 2005), 169–82. There, it should be noted, the juries are assumed to have been natives who were unequal to the job of refereeing the disputes that arose in the inquest: they were the creatures of the various predatory lords on whom they depended. In reality, the jurors were more broadly representative, indeed including tenants-in-chief, and, as we shall see, disputed tenure was not their only or main concern.

started with the arrest of some two-thirds of the sheriffs.[33] New faces had no debts to call in and in consequence local juries were free to dish the dirt. Although there is evidence aplenty in the Domesday corpus of bent sheriffs (and there is some indication that complaints against them may have been invited),[34] there is simply not enough evidence to indicate whether a similar expedient was resorted to in 1086.[35] What is clear, however, is that local administrations played a key role in the organization of the inquest. The activities of the sheriff are largely invisible, but as the king's representative, he must have shouldered much of the responsibility for the smooth running of the process.[36]

Not the least of his tasks was the marshalling of informants and jurors. A conservative estimate suggests that at least 60,000 people gave evidence in one form or another.[37] It seems that every tenant-in-chief had to be present at key sessions and numerous passages in the Domesday corpus indicate that he was accompanied by his principal tenants, the honorial barons, bailiffs, and reeves.[38] Bishops and abbots frequently brought all their communities with them,[39] and sundry thegns, free men, Frenchmen, and divers others seem to have represented themselves and their interests.[40] The community for its part was variously represented by juries of shire, riding, division, lathe, rape, and borough, as well as the

---

[33] *EHD*, ii, 437–48; W. L. Warren, *The Governance of Norman and Angevin England 1086–1272* (London, 1987), 120–1.

[34] There were numerous complaints against the three most notorious sheriffs, Eustace of Huntingdon, Picot of Cambridge, and Urse d'Abetot (R. P. Abels, 'Sheriffs, Lord-Seeking and the Norman Settlement of the South-East Midlands', *ANS*, 19 (1997), 19–50). In Lincoln the following is recorded: 'Of the aforesaid waste messuages, 166 had been destroyed on account of the castle. The remaining 74 have been destroyed outside the castle boundary, not because of the oppression of the sheriffs and officers, but because of misfortune and poverty and the ravages of fire' (GDB, 336v: *DB Lincs*, C26). Burgesses of Yarmouth are said to have rendered £4 to the sheriff 'gladly and in friendship' (LDB, 118v: *DB Norfolk*, 1,68). In Gloucestershire there is an explicit complaint: 'Urse the sheriff oppressed the men [of Sodbury] to such an extent that now they cannot render the salt' (GDB, 163v: *DB Gloucs*, 1,48).

[35] J. A. Green, *English Sheriffs to 1154*, Public Record Office Handbooks no. 24 (London, 1990); J. A. Green, 'The Sheriffs of William the Conqueror', *Proceedings of the Battle Conference*, [*ANS*] 5 (1982), 129–45. Many of the difficulties that Professor Green experienced in identifying sheriffs in 1086 may reflect that fact that there was a purge.

[36] For the sheriff's role in the post-Conquest period, see W. A. Morris, *The Medieval English Sheriff to 1300* (Oxford, 1927).

[37] *DIB*, 122–3. Fleming suggests seven or eight thousand ('Oral Testimony', 105), but does not seem to have considered the villagers. The writer of the preface to Bury A claimed that 'almost all the inhabitants of the land' swore.

[38] For a convenient list, see Fleming, *Domesday Book and the Law*, 543.

[39] The monks of Chertsey, Abingdon, and St Augustine's, Canterbury, attended en masse in Surrey, Berkshire, and Kent (GDB, 34, 59, 47: *DB Surrey*, 8,30. *DB Berks*, 7,38. *DB Kent*, 5,149. *DB Worcs*, 2).

[40] Fleming, *Domesday Book and the Law*, 540–5.

hundred and vill.[41] Unlike these latter, the composition of the juries of higher courts remains an unknown (unless 'the thegns of the shire' who gave evidence in Wiltshire appeared for one or other),[42] but it seems likely that they were of higher status than the relatively lowly hundred jurors. By the early twelfth century the suitors to the shire, the *barones*, were the tenants-in-chief, and there is no reason to believe that they were not so in 1086.[43]

Then there were all the servants of the court to organize. Bailiffs, reeves, and messengers, all vital in summoning the respondents to attend, must have worked overtime. Other tasks were equally vital. All the evidence provided had to be translated and written down. Various references to individuals styled *latimer* and *interpres* are probably to translators in the service of lords. But others must have been regularly employed in local courts and presumably the sheriff had to ensure that enough were on hand for each of the Domesday sessions.[44] It is unlikely that local courts had scribes attached to them as a matter of course. It is not inconceivable, however, that the sheriff employed one in his own household. Such figures have left no trace in the Domesday texts.

The sheriff and his officers mustered the free communities of the shire. The king for his part was represented by commissioners. As *barones* or *legati*,[45] they are noticed from time to time in the text and the identity of several is known from other sources. As we have seen, Bishop Remigius of Lincoln (accompanied by a clerk and two monks), Earl Walter Giffard, Henry de Ferrers, and Adam, the brother of Eudo the king's steward, officiated in Worcestershire, and 'S', possibly Samson, in East Anglia, while William de St Calais, the bishop of Durham, was probably active in the South West and Bishop Osmund of Salisbury in the East Midlands.[46]

---

[41] Fleming, *Domesday Book and the Law*, 540–5.

[42] GDB, 69, 70v, 71: *DB Wilts*, 23,7.26,19.28,10.

[43] See below, pp. 271–3, for indications that the tenant-in-chief was a regular suitor. The emergence of the knights of the shire, who were to replace them, was a late twelfth-century development.

[44] H. Tsurushima, 'Domesday Interpreters', *ANS*, 18 (1996), 201–22.

[45] Not all references to *legati* and *barones* are to Domesday commissioners. See, for example, LDB, 7: *DB Essex*, 1,28. The hundred of Uttlesford in Essex witnessed that Robert Gernon held two free men with 2½ hides of land, but it 'knows not how he had them, since there came into the Hundred neither writ nor officer on the king's behalf [to say] that the king had given him that land (*hundredum nescit quo modo eos habuerit quia neque breve neque legatus venit ex parte regis in hundredro quod rex sibi dedisset illam terram*)'. The *legatus* here is clearly not a DB commissioner and was probably a royal reeve or the sheriff. The same is probably true of the *legatus* of GDB, 262v: *DB Cheshire*, C3. For lists of earlier 'pleas', see Fleming, *Domesday Book and the Law*, 544–5; P. Wormald, 'Domesday Lawsuits: A Provisional List and Preliminary Comments', *England in the Eleventh Century*, ed. C. Hicks Harlaxton Medieval Studies, 2 (Stamford, 1992), 95–8.

[46] *Hemingi Chartularium*, 287–8; F. Barlow, 'Domesday Book: A Letter of Lanfranc', *EHR*, 78 (1963), 284–9; R. Welldon Finn, *Domesday Studies: The Liber Exoniensis* (London, 1964), 101; GDB, 87v: *DB Somerset*, 2,9; *Regesta Regum Anglo-Normannorum: The Acta of William*

It is usually assumed that commissioners like these supervised the inquest from beginning to end.[47] In reality they seem to have been absent in its early stages. Bishop Robert of Hereford's statement that 'other investigators followed the first and were sent to counties that they did not know, and where they themselves were unknown, to check the first description and to denounce any wrongdoers to the king'[48] clearly implies that initial data collection was a local matter. This is consonant with later practice. In the normal course of events evidence was gathered by *milites inquisitores*, knights of the shire who were appointed or elected for the purpose, from individuals and juries of vill, hundred, and shire and they drew up the composite verdict for the hundred to present to the commissioners.[49] This was almost certainly the procedure in Cambridgeshire in 1086; the names of the jurors of each hundred are recorded at the head of each (composite) presentment in ICC. The various references to thegns of the shire, the Frenchmen, and the like in Domesday may be indicative of a similar process of drafting.

The location of sessions has become a controversial issue of late. No one would now espouse the nineteenth-century view that each hundred met locally in its traditional meeting place. There are frequent references to different juries pronouncing on the same issue on apparently the same occasion; jurors clearly repaired to a central court.[50] It is the identity of that forum that is at issue. In their discussion of the Cheshire folios of GDB, Peter Sawyer and Alan Thacker have pointed to the great differences in the information collected in each shire to argue that

---

I 1066–1087, ed. D. Bates (Oxford, 1998), no. 189. For a speculative assignation of William's bishops to circuits, see H. R. Loyn, 'William's Bishops: Some Further Thoughts', *ANS*, 10 (1988), 229.

[47] For a recent statement of the consensus view, see H. R. Loyn, 'A General Introduction to Domesday Book', *Domesday Book Studies*, eds A. Williams and R. W. H. Erskine (London, 1987), 1–21, especially at 4–5.

[48] W. H. Stevenson, 'A Contemporary Description of the Domesday Survey', *EHR*, 22 (1907), 74.

[49] See, for example, the survey of 1212 where the Lancashire roll was sealed by seventeen knights of the shire although their account was derived from the presentments of juries of borough and hundred (*Book of Fees*, i, 206, 221). More extensive rolls survive for the Ragman inquest in Norfolk (London, PRO, SC5/Tower/Norfolk).

[50] See, for example, GDB, 44v: *DB Hants*, 23,3 where something like a free-for-all erupted in the sessions: 'William de Chernet claims this land, saying that it belongs to the manor of South Charford, [in] Hugh de Port's fief, through inheritance from his predecessor; and he has brought as his testimony to this the better men and the old men of the whole shire and hundred; and Picot has brought against it as his testimony villeins and common people and reeves, who are willing to maintain by oath, or by the judgement of God, that he who held the land was a free man, and could go with his land where he would. But the witnesses of William refuse to accept [any] law except that of King Edward until it be determined by the king. It was worth 15s; and afterwards 8s; now 10s.' Debate must have been acrimonious on many an occasion. Fleming cites 104 instances in which there are multiple presentments (*Domesday Book and the Law*, 543).

all the data were collected in the shire court.[51] Robin Fleming, emphasizing the similarities between the account of groups of counties and adducing pre-Conquest precedents, has urged the case for extraordinary regional courts.[52] Both possibilities would appear to be true.[53] Multiple sessions are indicated by parallel entries for complexes of land in GDB and Exon. The account of Rutland is particularly instructive. The main entry is appended to the Nottinghamshire folios (it was an estate that was administered by the sheriff of Nottingham in 1086) and is, anomalously, geographical in form.[54] The royal estates therein are otherwise unparalleled, but the lands of the tenants-in-chief also appear, in slightly different terms, in the Lincolnshire folios where they are fully integrated into the seigneurially arranged text with their own place in the common sequence of Lincolnshire wapentakes.[55] If the shrieval administration conducted the earliest stages of the inquest, then the shire court must have been the context. Here, however, we have clear evidence of a second session in which Rutland, and therefore presumably Nottinghamshire of which it was an administrative part, met with Lincolnshire.

Thacker and Sawyer's contention that similarities in the accounts of different counties are a function of compilation rather than data collection is clearly incorrect. Lanfranc's letter refers to the 'counties (*comitatus*)' assigned to the commissioner 'S' and Hemming reports that the Worcester commissioners also worked in other counties.[56] We can safely conclude that the groups of shires defined by common forms and content were circuits in which common sessions were held. Seven circuits in all have been identified (Table 3.1). This reconstruction follows that of Stephenson in 1944 with the exception of assigning Staffordshire to Circuit IV rather than Circuit V.[57] Stephenson does not seem to have noticed, or at least did

---

[51] A. Thacker and P. H. Sawyer, 'Domesday Survey', *VCH Cheshire*, i, ed. B. E. Harris (London, 1987), 293–7. C. Flight, *The Survey of the Whole of England: Studies of the Documentation Resulting from the Survey Conducted in 1086*, British Archaeological Reports, British Series, 405 (Oxford, 2006), 1, seems to agree, asserting that circuits are 'a silly conjecture which has done a great deal of damage. Words of this sort are idols. We need not waste time subverting them; it is enough just to ignore them.'

[52] Fleming, 'Oral Testimony'.

[53] *DIB*, 125–8.

[54] GDB, 293v–294: *DB Rutland*, R.

[55] GDB, 349v, 355v, 358v, 366, 367: *DB Lincs*, 13,38.24,78.27,46–8.51,10.56,11–18, 20–2. The sequence of wapentakes in Lincolnshire, see D. R. Roffe, 'Hundreds and Wapentakes', *The Lincolnshire Domesday*, eds A. Williams and G. H. Martin (London, 1992), 36. Rutland appears as no. 29 in the sequence between Aveland and Threo Wapentakes.

[56] Barlow, 'Domesday Book: A Letter of Lanfranc', 289; *Hemingi Chartularium*, 287–8.

[57] C. Stephenson, 'Notes on the Composition and Interpretation of Domesday', *Speculum*, 22 (1947), 1–15. Some of the formulas that define the circuits are mapped in H. C. Darby, 'Domesday Book and the Geographer', *Domesday Studies*, ed. J. C. Holt (Woodbridge, 1987), 103–8. Exon, the main source for the South West in GDB, interweaves the accounts of Wiltshire, Dorset, Somerset, Devon, and Cornwall, and it thereby suggests that those five counties constituted one such. Much of the form of the corresponding GDB folios is

Table 3.1 *Domesday circuits*

I	South East	Kent, Sussex, Surrey, Hampshire, Berkshire
II	South West	Wiltshire, Somerset, Dorset, Devon, Cornwall
III	East Midlands	Middlesex, Cambridgeshire, Bedfordshire, Buckinghamshire, Hertfordshire
IV	Midlands	Staffordshire, Warwickshire, Northamptonshire, Oxfordshire, Leicestershire
V	West	Gloucestershire, Worcestershire, Herefordshire, Shropshire, Cheshire
VI	North	Yorkshire, Lincolnshire, Nottinghamshire, Derbyshire Huntingdonshire
VII	East Anglia	Essex, Norfolk, Suffolk

not attach much importance to, the phenomenon of cross-enrolment, that is the entry of estates in one county in the folios of another.[58] Staffordshire estates are entered in Warwickshire and Northamptonshire and vice versa, and it therefore seems best to group the shire with those counties.[59] The analysis suggests that five counties were assigned to each of six groups of commissioners with the remaining three counties of East Anglia and Essex constituting the seventh circuit.[60]

derived from the scribe's well-realized concept of structure and expression, but peculiarities crept in from his sources. In the Wiltshire and Dorset folios, for example, the assessment of the demesne is consistently recorded, a rarity elsewhere in GDB, ICC, and IE, but the norm in Exon. Quirks of form and content of this kind indicate five further groups of counties. The distinctive opening formula '*In* X habuit Y ...' of group VI is found in the Huntingdonshire section of IE but not consistently elsewhere, while the forms of III are directly related to ICC, a source of the Cambridgeshire folios, and common to all five counties is the otherwise unique admeasurement of meadow in ploughlands. Group I is characterized by the record of the TRE tenant at the beginning of the entry, as in the Domesday Monachorum B, a precursor of the Kent text, and the likewise unique admeasurement of woodland in swine renders. Groups IV and V are more difficult to distinguish from each other, but are ultimately defined by the placing of the record of TRE tenure at the end or the beginning of entries. Finally, group VII is defined by the many peculiarities of LDB which are also found in one of its precursors, the Essex section of IE.

[58] *DIB*, 126.

[59] The stray entries are appended to the county texts in *DB Staffs*, E; *DB Warks*, E; *DB Northants*, E. The relevant hundred rubric is often attached to individual entries, indicating that the estates truly belonged to the county concerned. For a list of all 'cross-enrolments' of this king, see *DIB*, 126.

[60] It is possible that some of the circuits were subdivided. Yorkshire and Lincolnshire were more closely identified with each other than with the other three shires of Circuit VI in GDB. The *clamores* for both shires, for example, are enrolled together in a separate quire at the end of GDB. Against this, however, it should be remembered that there was apparently a session for Lincolnshire, Rutland, and presumably Nottinghamshire. Wiltshire and Dorset, on the one hand, and Somerset, Devon, and Cornwall, on the other, were more clearly sub-groups of Circuit II: in Exon each chapter is supra-comital within those two

There was probably nothing particularly novel about these circuits *per se*. Before the Conquest joint shire courts were convened as and when business required.[61] However, by and large they were *ad hoc*. Some counties were indeed regularly associated. In the late tenth century the Five Boroughs (Lincoln, Stamford, Nottingham, Derby, Leicester) and their associated territories had a common meeting place, probably in Nottingham.[62] The shires of Mercia were grouped at a similar time. There was a Mercian council,[63] and Oxfordshire, Warwickshire, Gloucestershire, and Worcestershire are known to have met together at *Gildberg* where their boundaries march.[64] Cambridgeshire, Bedfordshire, and Hertfordshire in Circuit III may have long been associated in 1086, for their meeting place at Guilden Morden where their boundaries march has every appearance of antiquity.[65] But, as can be readily seen, these associations did not dictate the constitution of the Domesday circuits. Circuit VI has a possible rationale in the extent of the earldom of Northumbria,[66] but if it did so, it stands alone.

Data collection

The account of Rutland in the Nottinghamshire folios is a full description of all the lands there. However, recording the geld quotas for the area and the soke dues owed to the crown, its focus is the rights of the king. In essence it represents the business of the first, local, stage of the inquiry in the shire.[67] That the survey of the king's demesne lands (but not manors held directly of the king by his tenants, be they thegns or ministers) was in some way separate from that of his tenants-in-chief has long been recognized. It is a fact that is difficult to escape. When

divisions (T. Webber, 'Salisbury and the Exon Domesday: Some Observations Concerning the Origins of Exeter Cathedral MS 3500', *English Manuscript Studies 1100–1700*, I, eds P. Beal and J. Griffiths (Oxford, 1989), 1–18). There seems little doubt, however, about the integrity of the suggested circuits. It must be supposed that separate sessions were instituted, under the auspices of the same commissioners, as circumstances dictated.

[61] Fleming, 'Oral Testimony'.

[62] Robertson, III Æthelræd, 1.1; D. R. Roffe, 'The Origins of Derbyshire', *The Derbyshire Archaeological Journal*, 106 (1986), 102–22; D. R. Roffe, 'Anglo-Saxon Nottingham and the Norman Conquest', *A Centenary History of Nottingham*, ed. J. V. Beckett (Manchester, 1997), 24–42. Nottingham and Derby met in joint sessions after the Conquest, but there is no evidence that the other shires met with them.

[63] A. Williams, '*Princeps Merciorum Gentis*: The Family, Career and Connections of Ælfhere, Ealdorman of Mercia 956–83', *Anglo-Saxon England*, 10 (1982), 161–6.

[64] GDB, 238c: *DB Warks*, 3,4 and note.

[65] *DB Warks*, 3,4n.

[66] *DIB*, 127. But the earldom ceased to exist after the forfeiture of Earl Waltheof in 1075. Common documentation, however, may have influenced the grouping of its constituent counties in a circuit.

[67] Some of the information must have been derived from the second stage in which the tenants-in-chief gave details of their estates.

ICC was drawn up there was already an account of the *terra regis*, referred to in three places as the *breve regis* in ICC and GDB,[68] and it seems that it was felt unnecessary to incorporate it into the document. Whether the accounts of *terra regis* were originally similarly separate in Exon is as yet to be determined. Welldon Finn considered that they were largely the work of scribes G and A, but he is unclear as to what else they wrote; Flight concurs but his analysis suggests that they worked extensively on the other entries.[69] Duplication of material, however, does hint at discrete sources. Matters treated in the king's *breves* frequently make a second appearance in seigneurial contexts, usually in more expansive terms. In the account of the king's manor of Axminster in Devon, for example, dues from Charlton, Honiton, Smallridge, Membury, and Rawridge are noticed, but the lands themselves are more fully described in the *breves* of the bishop of Coutances, the count of Mortain, Ralph de la Pommeraye, William Chevre, and the church of St Mary of Rouen.[70]

In the compilation of his text, the GDB scribe sometimes suppressed anomalies of this kind,[71] one suspects where he spotted them, but not always. Similar duplication of material throughout GDB suggests that the special procedure for the king's demesne lands was widespread. It is more especially evident in the aberrant forms of the *terra regis*. Typically, the king's chapter in each county is untidy. There are numerous additions; common sequences of hundreds and vills, ubiquitous elsewhere, are ignored; there are different sequences for the demesne estates as opposed to the king's other lands; the order of entries is haphazard; common forms of expression are absent; and unusual formulas are employed. These anomalies also provide some indication of the scope of the survey. If the account of the land between Ribble and Mersey, again a geographically arranged section,[72] is at all typical, it was not confined to the issues of the estates in the narrowest sense. Accounts were drawn up of the more important tenants and the

---

[68] ICC, 6, 83; GDB, 189v: *DB Cambs*, 1,13. It can be seen that the main scribe was at times confused by his source. He duly entered an account of the king's manor of Soham from the *breve regis* at the beginning of the king's chapter, but when he started to use the ICC exemplar for the tenanted royal manors he entered the ICC note that Soham could be found in the king's record, misreading the assessment in the process: 'In Soham King William has 6 hides and 40 acres in his record (*in breve suo*).' The neutral 'record' is here preferred to Alecto's 'return'.

[69] R. Welldon Finn, 'The Exeter Domesday and its Construction', *Bulletin of the John Rylands Library*, 41 (1958–59), 368, 385; Flight, *The Survey of the Whole of England*, 55–9.

[70] Exon, 84b, 135, 216b, 343, 111, 195.

[71] Some twenty parcels of land belonging to the royal manor of Winnianton in Cornwall are described in the king's *breve* in Exon and more fully in the Count of Mortain's chapter. The GDB scribe suppressed the duplication (Exon, 99–100, 224–7; GDB, 120a: *DB Cornwall*, 1,1). For a comparison of the accounts, see *DB Cornwall*, 1,1n.

[72] GDB, 269v–270: *DB Cheshire*, R1–7. The account proceeds vill by vill and hundred by hundred.

services they rendered; in West Derby all the thegns paid two *orae* of sixteen pence for each carucate, and were obliged to repair the king's hall, fisheries, woodland enclosures, and stag beats, and cut the king's corn in August. The customs and sokes from which the king derived an income were recorded; failure to acquit services incurred a fine of 4s, absence from the hundred one of 5s, and rape, bloodshed, or absence from the shire moot 10s. Finally, an account was made of the value of individual holdings and the renders that the king received from each hundred.[73]

Much the same sorts of information were collected throughout the country.[74] Renders in kind are frequently noticed, and details of their management are recorded in the accounts of the farms of one night in the western and south-western shires.[75] Hundredal jurisdiction is also regularly noticed. In Oxfordshire, for example, the number of hundreds attached to Benson, Headington, Kirtlington, Wootton, Shipton-under-Wychwood, Bampton, Bloxham, and Adderbury are recorded.[76] In Worcestershire the shire presented that seven of the twelve hundreds were exempt, and the sheriff complained that he thereby lost much in farm.[77] In Norfolk the farms and soke of each hundred are noted at the end of each hundredal section.[78] In Gloucestershire a careful account is given of all land that had been taken out of the king's farm and brought into it since 1066, along with the circumstances of each change.[79] Here and there issues of courts are also recorded, along with the forfeitures that the king enjoyed. Thus, in Kent, Lincolnshire, Nottinghamshire, and Yorkshire the holders of sake and soke are noted as a measure of what the king might expect.[80]

There also seems to have been a survey of churches and ecclesiastical dues that in some way belonged to the king's demesne in many if not most counties.[81] Royal

---

[73] For a reconstruction of the 'articles' of inquiry, see C. P. Lewis, 'An Introduction to the Lancashire Domesday', *The Lancashire Domesday*, eds A. Williams and G. H. Martin (London, 1991), 10–12.

[74] Cf. Lewis, 'An Introduction to the Lancashire Domesday', 10, who compares Ribble and Mersey with Leominster.

[75] E. B. Demarest, 'The *Firma Unius Noctis*', *EHR*, 35 (1920), 78–89; P. A. Stafford, 'The "Farm of One Night" and the Organisation of King Edward's Estates in Domesday', *EcHR*, 2nd series, 33 (1980), 491–502. See below, pp. 127–32.

[76] GDB, 154c–d: *DB Oxon*, 1,1–7a.

[77] GDB, 172a: *DB Worcs*, C3.

[78] LDB, 109b–141b: *DB Norfolk*, 1.

[79] GDB, 162d–164b: *DB Gloucs*, 1.

[80] GDB, iv; 337, 280v, 298v: *DB Kent*, D25; *DB Lincs*, T5; *DB Notts*, S5; *DB Yorks*, C36. These lists are not intended as a record of liberties, although, of course, they act as such. Incidental notices of sake and soke in the body of the text indicate that the lists are not complete.

[81] This procedure has hitherto remained unsuspected, although C. Holdsworth, 'The Church at Domesday', *Domesday Essays*, ed. C. Holdsworth, Exeter Studies in History, 14 (1986), 56, has suggested that only churches from which the king expected to derive an

churches generally are widely distinguished from run-of-the-mill foundations by notice of their dedication, details of their endowment, or tenure, but they are often further marked out. In some counties they are separately described. Thus, in Rutland churches and tithes are recorded at the end of the *terra regis*,[82] as are priests and their churches in Wiltshire and Somerset.[83] In others, such as Berkshire, Hampshire, Herefordshire, and Suffolk, they are marked out by distinctive scribal conventions within the account of the manor. Typically, churches are entered at the end of the entry in a separate paragraph indicated by a rubricated capital letter, a gallows sign, or similar device. In all these cases the assets of each are described in great detail. It is recorded of Collingbourne in Wiltshire, for example, in what is probably a postscriptal passage, that 'To the church belongs half a hide. Gerald, the priest of Wilton [Church], holds the tithe of this church, and it is worth 10s. The church itself is waste and dismantled.'[84] All these characteristics contrast with the enrolment of seigneurial churches as simple manorial appurtenances[85] and suggest that the information for royal foundations was drawn from a schedule solely concerned with ecclesiastical matters. The detailed account of the lands of St Martin in Dover, which is entered with the borough of Dover, may well be drawn from an example.[86] In Norfolk a note on the value of churches is inserted at the end of each section of the *terra regis* and elsewhere.[87] The churches themselves are entered in the account of the appropriate manor, but the regular appearance of the comment indicates that there was some sort of article on the matter.

Boroughs, at least in part, were surveyed at the same time.[88] They were in their own way but a specialized variant of royal estates, and their descriptions, usually but by no means always, entered at the beginning of each county, exhibit a disregard for system and order similar to that in the account of the *terra regis*. Typically, they open with an account of customary land, that is the tenements that owed their dues to the king. Where GDB gives totals of the number of tenements, LDB names every individual who rendered dues. Inquiry was clearly detailed. Then, a value is given, usually a render indicating that the sum was some sort of farm, that is an agreed amount of money paid by the sheriff in return for the

income were entered in the Devon folios. In Cheshire information relating to churches was 'supplied or processed' by the hundred (A. T. Thacker, P. H. Sawyer, 'Domesday Survey', *VCH Cheshire*, i, ed. B. E. Harris (London, 1987), 296–7).

[82] GDB, 294: *DB Rutland*, R21.

[83] GDB, 65v, 91, 91v: *DB Wilts*, 1,23a–j; *DB Somerset*, 15.16.

[84] GDB, 65: *DB Wilts*, 1,19.

[85] There is nothing quite comparable to the treatment of royal churches in seigneurial fees, apart from the separate enrolment of Ely's churches in IE (136–7). If there was a separate survey of churches outside the royal demesne, it would seem that it was quickly abandoned.

[86] GDB, iv, 2a: *DB Kent*, M, P.

[87] LDB, 116, 159v, 172, 208, 219v, 234v, 265: *DB Norf*, 1,60.8,14;136.13,23.17,44.21,36.48,8.

[88] For a more detailed discussion, see chapter 4.

issues of the town. Non-customary tenements follow. These were urban lands that were held by tenants-in-chief or other privileged tenants and typically they were attached to rural manors. Often, however, this type of tenement was entered in the relevant chapter of the tenant-in-chief and, indeed, where it was not, there are indications that the information usually came from a source other than that of the account of the customary land. The material is sometimes postscriptal and often distinguished from the royal section by gallows signs. Moreover, it occasionally exhibits the forms of the body of the text. In the description of Buckingham, for example, the order of tenants-in-chief is the same as that of the body of the text.[89] The borough proper, like the royal demesne, was afforded a separate survey.[90]

The account of the king's demesne estates and their related dues is the most visible product of this process. It was not, however, the only or even main business of the survey. That was a geld inquest. Galbraith was the first to demonstrate that the *inquisitio geldi* was contemporary with the Domesday inquest, but assumed that it was an independent initiative.[91] In concurring, Harvey has argued the case.[92] For her the progress of the geld inquest can be traced in the folios of Domesday Book by the incidence of reassessment as indicated by TRW geld figures. The pattern of distribution is patchy and she concludes that the *inquisitio* was still in progress in the course of the Domesday inquiry and the commissioners made use of its findings where available, but that the whole process was a separate enterprise. This argument is not entirely satisfactory. As we have seen,[93] the record of TRE assessments does not preclude a reassessment but, more to the point, there is little evidence that reassessment was the primary purpose of the *inquisitio*: the surviving records of the process suggest more of a concern with collection and the enforcement of liability.[94] The account of Melsham Hundred in Wiltshire is typical:

> In the hundred of Melsham there are 86 hides and 13 carucates of Harold's land which never pay geld. These the king has in demesne. Of the aforesaid hides the barons have in demesne 32½ hides and ½ virgate. Of these the king has in demesne 9 hides of the land of Harold; Bristric has 8½ hides;

---

[89] GDB, 143: *DB Bucks*, B2–13.

[90] See below, pp. 113–19.

[91] V. H. Galbraith, *The Making of Domesday Book*, 87–101, especially at 92.

[92] S. P. J. Harvey, 'Domesday Book and its Predecessors', *EHR*, 86 (1971), 768–9.

[93] Above, pp. 55–6.

[94] Exon, 1–10, 13–24, 65–82. The process that produced them was ongoing. Of the three accounts of Wiltshire, C appears to be earlier than A and B, for it records sums which were outstanding that had been discharged in the other two. All, however, drew on earlier sources from which they were abstracted. Thus, much of the detail given is perceptibly earlier than the GDB state of affairs (*DIB*, 134). The debate as to whether the accounts relate to the 1084 geld or another in 1085 is irrelevant. See J. F. A. Mason, 'The Date of the Geld Rolls', *EHR*, 69 (1954), 283–9.

Alvric 2 hides; Lieman 2 hides; Ernulf de Hesdin 1 hide and 3 virgates; William Corniola 3 hides and 3 virgates; Ansger 4 hides and 1 virgate; Edilt the widow 1 hide and 1½ virgates. And for 15 hides and ½ virgate have been rendered to the king £4 11s. Odo Culus Lupi and Godwin retain the geld of ½ virgate. And the king's villains retain the geld from 38 hides of the land of Harold.[95]

The *inquisitio geldi* was a geld audit.

In fact, there is little beyond the internal logic of the Galbraithian schema to divorce the geld inquest from the Domesday survey. Robert of Hereford notes that 'the land was vexed with much violence arising from the collection of the king's taxes' in the wake of the inquest,[96] while the Anglo-Saxon Chronicle explicitly links the survey of 'what land and cattle the king himself had in the country, or what dues he ought to have in twelve months from the shire' with 'how many hundred hides there were in the shire'.[97] The account of Rutland opens with a statement of geld liability[98] and in the description of the City of Lincoln, in Harvey's judgement an area that was yet to be 'reassessed' in 1086, there even survives a geld account which, in its urban context, is identical in form to those preserved in Exon.

Those written below have not paid the king's geld as they ought:

The land of St Mary on which Theodbert dwells in the high street has not paid geld; nor has the bishop's land situated at St Laurence's paid geld in respect of 1 house.

The abbot of Peterborough has not paid geld in respect of 1 house and 3 tofts.

Earl Hugh has not paid geld in respect of all his land; nor Turold of Greetwell, nor Losuoard, nor Ketilbert.

Hugh fitzBaldric has not paid geld in respect of 2 tofts; nor Geoffrey Alselin likewise in respect of 2 tofts.

Nor has Gilbert paid geld in respect of 3 houses. Nor has Peter de Valognes in respect of his house. Nor has the Countess Judith in respect of her house.

---

[95] Exon, 15; R. R. Darlington, 'Wiltshire Geld Rolls', *VCH Wiltshire*, ii, eds R. B. Pugh and E. Crittall (Oxford, 1955), 193. The additional material from MSS B and C has been excluded.

[96] W. H. Stevenson, 'A Contemporary Description of the Domesday Survey', *EHR*, 22 (1907), 74. This passage is echoed in a copy of Marianus' History probably from Worcester (BL, Cotton MS, Nero C v). It reads: 'William, king of the English, ordered all of the possessions of the whole of England to be described, in fields, in men, in all animals, in all manors from the greatest to the smallest, and in all payments which could be rendered from the land of all. And the land was vexed with much violence proceeding therefrom.' See Stevenson, 'A Contemporary Description of the Domesday Survey', 77.

[97] *ASC*, 166.

[98] GDB, 293v: *DB Rutland*, R1–3.

Nor has Ralph Paynel in respect of 1 house. Nor has Ralph de Bapaume in respect of his house. Nor has Ertald in respect of his house.

The house in respect of which the abbot of Peterborough has not, as they say, paid geld, Norman Crassus claims as of the king's fee, for Guthrothr his predecessor had it in pledge for 3½ marks of silver.[99]

Sometimes there are explicit complaints about exemptions. In Shrewsbury, for example, the burgesses complain that they are still paying geld on the same number of houses as in 1066 although many had been destroyed in building the castle and others had passed to French burgesses (who presumably did not pay).[100] Even more emphatic is the evidence of LDB; so emphatic indeed that it has completely eluded historians. For every vill in Norfolk and Suffolk there is a record of the amount of money that it owed when the hundred paid one pound in geld. Despite the entirely regular notice of carucates (here subdivided into probably 120 fiscal acres) at the beginning of each entry, this formula has been seen as evidence of a mode of *assessment* that is unique to East Anglia.[101] In reality, it can be seen as a record of *payment*.[102] It may not be paralleled elsewhere in the Domesday corpus; there is precious little about geld collection, but a comparable method of payment is evidenced in the Lincolnshire Pipe Rolls.[103] There can be no doubt that the *inquisitio geldi* was an integral part of the Domesday inquest.

Much of the information about geld assessment in the Domesday corpus must have come from this stage in the inquiry. Throughout we find references to geld exemption and even occasionally, as at Lincoln, non-payment.[104] But the most substantial contribution to the extant documents is probably the assessments themselves. It seems hardly credible that the Domesday commissioners would allow the record of such a vital statistic without testing the information in some formal way or another. This, however, was not a matter of jurors dredging up figures from the depths of their memories. From time to time they got their heads together to recall an assessment, but the main source was clearly taxation records. Only one direct reference is found to their use: in Huntingdonshire it is stated that 'The villeins and sokemen pay geld according to the hides written in the records.'[105] But such

---

[99] GDB, 336b–c: *DB Lincs*, C20–1. Although this entry is slightly misaligned with the column above, it does not seem to be postscriptal.

[100] GDB, 252: *DB Salop*, C14. This entry is postscriptal, although rubricated.

[101] See C. R. Hart, *The Danelaw* (London, 1992), 93–7, for the latest statement of the case. Carucates are interpreted as the missing ploughlands of East Anglia. They can be no such thing, as the ploughland summaries of IE indicate. See below, pp. 94–5, 205.

[102] D. R. Roffe, 'Introduction', *Little Domesday Book, Norfolk* (London, 2000), 18.

[103] *The Great Roll of the Pipe for the Sixth Year of the Reign of King Richard the First, Michaelmas 1194*, ed. D. M. Stenton, Pipe Roll Society, 43 (1928), 118; D. R. Roffe, 'The Lincolnshire Hundred', *Landscape History*, 3 (1981), 35.

[104] J. D. Foy, *Domesday Book Index: Subjects* (Chichester, 1992), 229–32.

[105] GDB, 203: *DB Hunts*, B21.

records have left their mark on the texts in common sequences of vills and regular geographical circuits. In Yorkshire, for example, the pattern is so pronounced that the ubiquitous *Torps* of the area can be identified with a singular degree of confidence.[106] We see here less the footprints of Domesday commissioners than those of earlier tax collectors. the sheriff must have brought local records to the inquest so that the hundredmen could attest their accuracy.[107]

It is of the nature of financial administration that most of this information must have gone by on the nod. There were more controversial matters to discuss. The proceedings of the geld inquest are probably most accurately represented by the presentments of juries recorded in the various Domesday texts. This, of course, is not most immediately apparent. It has long been recognized that jurors appear to have pronounced on a very limited range of subjects. There are a handful of comments on geld assessment and slightly more on value, but there is a resounding silence on the human resources, livestock, and infrastructure of estates. Of the 3000 passages that are explicitly presentments or are arguably derived from them, over 95 per cent are directly concerned with title to land. Some report rival claims; others record the transfer of dues from one tenurial context to another. It is little wonder that historians have often seen these verdicts as proof positive that the Domesday inquest was concerned with the determination of title.[108]

Of course, the inquest was no glorified assize. Indeed, as we shall see,[109] from beginning to end it was less concerned with right than tenure. The jurors' presentments are symptomatic of wider concerns. At an early stage in the proceedings tenants-in-chief seem to have been invited to claim their lands.[110] As early as the reign of Cnut the right to land was predicated on the performance of the service due from it, and Hemming records in the earliest Worcester cartulary that estates were seized by the expedient of paying the geld due upon them.[111] Here and there in Domesday Book itself we encounter vestiges of such a relationship between taxation and tenure.[112] Questions about geld payment inevitably led to more unsettling questions about right. According to Domesday and Exon the bishop of

---

[106] H. C. Darby and I. S. Maxwell, *The Domesday Geography of Northern England* (Cambridge, 1962), 481–94.

[107] So Harvey, 'Domesday Book and its Predecessors', but, as we have seen (pp. 54–6), her suggested examples are as likely to emanate from the Domesday inquest.

[108] For the latest statements of this view, see P. Hyams, '"No Register of Title": The Domesday Inquest and Land Adjudication', *ANS,* 9 (1986), 127–41, and J. C. Holt, '1086', *Domesday Studies*, ed. J. C. Holt (Woodbridge, 1987), 41–64.

[109] Below, pp. 85, 275.

[110] *DIB*, 136–8.

[111] Robertson, II Cnut, 79; *Hemingi Chartularium*, i, 278.

[112] GDB, 141, 216v: *DB Herts*, 36,9; *DB Beds*, 46,1. It has been doubted that there was any continuity between the reign of Cnut and the Domesday inquest in this area on the ground that there was a discontinuity in the collection of geld between 1051 and 1066 (Hyams, '"No Register of Title": The Domesday Inquest and Land Adjudication', 128). However, while

Exeter produced charters to demonstrate title to his estates. I have suggested elsewhere that documents like Domesday Monachorum A, the Descriptio Terrarum
of Peterborough, and Worcester A represent schedules of land that lords presented
to make good their title.[113] The Domesday presentments are precisely the sort of
arguments that the process might be expected to have produced.

The gathering of the *inquisitio geldi* into the Domesday fold explains much
that has been ignored or glossed over in discussions of the Domesday inquest and
the making of Domesday Book. Sally Harvey could explain away geld assessments
generally by positing the use of pre-existing documentation and the record of
exemption, avoidance, and non-payment in particular as leakage of information
from a separate and on-going fiscal reassessment.[114] It has proved more difficult
to account for regular sequences of hundreds and vills. Galbraith was clearly right
to point out that much Domesday data was the stuff of estate management and
could only have been furnished by the lord of the manor, his bailiffs, or agents:
as much as local jurors may have taken an interest in Farmer Brown's prize bull
(or female slave), it is hardly credible that they were *au fait* with the minutiae of
his less interesting livestock, let alone the resources of demesne.[115] Yet how do we
account for the fact that the data, in early sources like Bath A as well as LDB and
GDB, follow a common villar and hundredal structure in each county? Notions
of a progress from hundred meeting place to hundred meeting place were long
ago discarded, and the assertion that the sequence emanates from local government documentation merely begs the question. Radical recensionism has seemed
to be the only possibility. Both Sawyer and Galbraith were forced by the logic of
their respective arguments to assert that the extant texts were produced through
a series of re-writes.[116] By rearranging his material the author of the Domesday
enterprise slowly edged from the chaos of raw data to the finely honed forms of
the GDB text.

This was a conclusion that was inherently implausible. Was it really credible that
there were so many 'editions' of Domesday Book? And, moreover, produced in the
limited time frame of Christmas 1085 to the death of William the Conqueror in
September 1087? The notion might have been accepted in the absence of any better
explanation, but it is no longer tenable in the light of the discovery that Domesday

---

the collection of *Danegeld* may have been suspended in the reign of Edward the Confessor,
other dues were, of course, still levied.

[113] D. R. Roffe, 'The Descriptio Terrarum of Peterborough Abbey', *Historical Research*, 65
(1992), 15–16.

[114] Harvey, 'Domesday Book and its Predecessors'.

[115] Galbraith, *The Making of Domesday Book*, 82.

[116] Galbraith, *The Making of Domesday Book*, 28–44; P. H. Sawyer, 'The "Original Returns"
and Domesday Book', *EHR*, 70 (1955), 177–97.

entries were formulated by reference to the geld.[117] The folios of Circuit VI, and especially those of Lincolnshire, have provided the decisive evidence. There the manor appears to be precisely articulated. The manorial demesne is distinguished from berewicks and sokeland by forms that seem precisely to lay bare the internal structure of the estate. In reality, however, the structure is a Domesday artefact. The content of entries was determined less by the economy of the manor than by its assessment to the geld. Where the manor was situated in its entirety in a single twelve-carucated hundred (the equivalent of the East Anglian leet and the vill of hidated England) it was described in one entry failing any elements that had a distinct tenurial identity. Inland and sokeland were only accorded their own entries when they were situated in a hundred other than that in which the *caput* lay. The point is illustrated by the Domesday representation of the estates in the wapentake of Elloe in the Holland division of Lincolnshire (Table 3.2). Here there were six twelve-carucate hundreds and it will be noticed that berewicks and soke-lands are always in a different hundred from the manorial centre unless a parcel of tributary land has a status (such as tenure by another tenant or the render of soke to a manor other than the *caput*) which marks it out as anomalous. Elsewhere we find that whole groups of manors could be entered together in 'multiple manor entries', even though they were demonstrably discrete entities in 1086, when they were situated in the same hundred.[118]

Similarly, the leet or vill determined the extent of entries in the Norfolk and Suffolk folios.[119] Elsewhere there is only limited evidence of this mechanism of entry

---

[117] For the following, see D. R. Roffe, 'Place-Naming in Domesday Book: Settlements, Estates, and Communities', *Nomina*, 14 (1990–91), 47–60, and Roffe, 'The Lincolnshire Hundred'.

[118] D. R. Roffe, 'An Introduction to the Lincolnshire Domesday', *The Lincolnshire Domesday*, eds A. Williams and G. H. Martin (London, 1991), 13. Manors were grouped together only when they shared a common tenurial nexus (see below, p. 160). The process is most clearly illustrated by an entry in Count Alan's Lincolnshire *breve*. Six manors were held in 1066 by six thegns, one of whom was a certain Holmchetel. The place was originally identified as 'Hagworthingham' in the wapentake of Hill, but the name was subsequently deleted and 'Mumby', in the wapentake of Calcewath, interlined. The entry ends with the comment that 'these *seven* manors were worth ten pounds TRE; now they are worth sixteen pounds' (GDB, 348v: *DB Lincs*, 12,96). Assessed at four bovates and held by Holmkell, the seventh manor was in fact in Hagworthingham and had already been described. The entry notes that 'its value [is assessed] in other manors' (GDB, 348v: *DB Lincs*, 12,85). It seems that all seven had formed an extended tenurial group, but Holmkell's estate had been enrolled in a separate entry because it was situated in a different hundred and wapentake. However, when the scribe came to the remaining manors, he inadvertently enrolled the whole group. He subsequently realized his mistake, however, and changed the place-name. But he omitted to delete the record of Holmkell and subtract the four bovates of his manor from the total. The assessment of Mumby Hundred is precisely twelve carucates once Holmchetel's four bovates are subtracted. See further GDB, 348v, 355, 360: *DB Lincs*, 12,93;96.24,55–6.29,32.

[119] Roffe, 'Introduction', *Little Domesday, Norfolk*, 15.

Table 3.2 *Hundreds and Domesday Book entries in Elloe Wapentake*

Hundred	Constituent vills	Holder	Status	Car.	bov.	Total	
PINCHBECK	Pinchbeck	Ivo Taillebois	S of Spalding	10	0	12	0
		Guy de Craon	S of Holbeach/Whaplode	2	0		
SPALDING	Spalding	Crowland Abbey	B of Crowland	2	0		
		Ivo Taillebois	M	9	0	12	0
		Guy de Craon	M	1	3		
WESTON, MOULTON	Weston/ Moulton	Ivo Taillebois	S of Spalding	10	1	12	0
		Guy de Craon	S of Holbeach/Whaplode	1	7		
HOLBEACH, FLEET	Holbeach	King	S of Gedney	8	6		
	Holbeach/Whaplode	King	S of Gedney	5	0		
		Count Alan	S of Gedney	13	6*		
WHAPLODE		Count Alan	B of Fleet	1	0	24	0
		Crowland Abbey	M	1	0		
		Guy de Craon	M	2	2		
	Fleet	King	?M	6	0		
GEDNEY, LUTTON	Gedney	King	M	8	0	12	0
	Lutton	King	M	4	0		
TYDD	Tydd	King	M	5	1		
		King	B of Lutton	2	1	12	0
		Ivo Taillebois	B of Spalding	3	2		
		Guy de Craon	S of Holbeach/Whaplode	1	4		

M = manor, B = berewick, S = sokeland

* duplicate entry. Crowland was uncarucated and therefore unsurveyed.

formation in Domesday Book; with manor and vill coterminous throughout much of England, the phenomenon is confined to areas where manors were extensive.[120] Nevertheless it is significant. Domesday entries of this kind are accounting devices that were clearly foreign to the tenant-in-chief. The lands of Peterborough Abbey are entered hundred by hundred in the Lincolnshire folios in this way,[121] but the Descriptio Terrarum, a document apparently furnished by the abbey itself at the

[120] There are, however, different mechanisms of entry formation elsewhere. In Derbyshire, for example, there is evidence that place-names relate to an ancient unit of assessment known in pre-Conquest charters as the *mansio*. See below, p. 295. Vill and estates names were variously used throughout the Domesday text (Roffe, 'Place-Naming').

[121] GDB, 345v–346: *DB Lincs*, 8.

beginning of the proceedings, provides an account of the same lands vill by vill. The detailed seigneurial return was made by the tenant-in-chief, but its form was dictated by the processes of the inquest. The conclusion is clear: the *inquisitio geldi* produced up-to-date lists of lands, their lords, and assessment to the geld, and those lords were invited to make more detailed presentments on the basis of schedules drawn up from them.[122]

There are several candidates among the surviving schedules that might be examples of such documents. Ely C, Evesham K, Evesham P, and the Kentish Assessment List may in one way or another have been derived from lists of lands to which the tenants-in-chief were expected to make a return,[123] although the strongest claims can perhaps be made for Bury A and B.[124] However, none can be positively identified as such. Rather it is Bath A that is the most eloquent testimony to the process. As we have seen,[125] the document is perceptibly earlier in the Domesday process than Exon, and, as its editor argued, if it is not a seigneurial presentment, it is the closest that we have to one. And yet it already has the hundredal order common to the other chapters of Exon.

We can begin to appreciate that the collection of seigneurial details was as directed as the parallel survey of royal lands and interests. The king needed sharply defined items of data and he needed them from the estates that he specified. In recent years Domesday scholarship has tended to emphasize the subjective element in the seigneurial presentments.[126] The occasional enrolment of disputed land in two or more *breves* apparently lends itself to the concept of a free-for-all. However, the significance of the phenomenon of parallel entries of this kind should not be exaggerated. They are relatively uncommon and usually betoken a division of rights over land; the representation of the intricacies of soke often appears contradictory within the tightly defined schema of Domesday Book. Thus it is that various lands appear in the king's *breve* as well as those of tenants-in-chief. Sokemen in Marsham in Norfolk, for example, were in some unspecified way 'in Cawston' and were thus entered, presumably in the survey of regalia, in the account of the king's demesne estates. They appear in more detail, however, in the *breves* of the bishop of Thetford and Walter Giffard, for their predecessors had held the land.[127] By and large tenure, sanctioned or otherwise, defined the extent of the land to which returns were made.

---

[122] *DIB*, 143–6.
[123] *DIB*, 146.
[124] *DIB*, 138–9.
[125] Above, p. 58.
[126] Galbraith, *The Making of Domesday Book*, 82, 119–20; A. Williams, 'Apparent Repetitions in Domesday Book', *Domesday Book Studies*, eds A. Williams and R. W. H. Erskine (London, 1987), 91–2; S. Baxter, 'The Representation of Lordship and Land Tenure in Domesday Book', *Domesday Book*, eds E. Hallam and D. Bates (Stroud, 2001), 73–102.
[127] LDB, 115, 196v, 241v: *DB Norfolk*, 1,57.10,40–1.25,10.

It has always seemed a truism that a survey of seigneurial estates was intended from the inception of the Domesday enterprise. In reality there is nothing that demands such a conclusion.[128] Throughout the Middle Ages articles of inquiry were frequently supplemented, and even radically changed, as early returns showed the dimensions of the problem to be addressed. In 1255 the initial commission seems to have been confined to the issues of the forest but was soon expanded to cover all regalia.[129] The Ragman inquest of 1274–5 saw a complete change of focus: it too was initially conceived of as a survey of regalia, but the need for a review of local and seigneurial administration was quickly realized and a new commission was issued.[130] Both of the primary witnesses to the Domesday inquest understood the enterprise to be a two-stage process. The Anglo-Saxon chronicler is non-committal as to the relationship between the two, while Robert of Hereford's emphasis on estates may have been conditioned by hindsight: there can be no doubt that it was this aspect of the inquest that excited the most comment.

What is certain is that the collection of seigneurial data marked a change in the procedure of the inquiry. As Robert of Hereford hints and the enrolment of the Rutland lands in Lincolnshire more directly indicates,[131] the forum moved from the shire to the circuit. Armed with the documentation from the *inquisitio geldi*, the commissioners appointed to supervise the business of this, the second stage of the inquest, must have issued articles of inquiry. The prologue to IE cannot represent them,[132] but nevertheless, the remarkable consistency of the main items of data from *breve* to *breve* and county to county suggests that something very like them, albeit considerably more detailed, must have been provided. The process began with what was essentially a private estate survey conducted by the tenant-in-chief and his agents. In Herefordshire we hear that the bishop of Hereford's men did not do the job comprehensively; elsewhere accounts were not rendered.[133] The bailiff of the manor or the sitting tenant was probably the main informant for each estate.[134] There has been some debate about the form of the presentments

---

[128] *DIB*, 229–30.

[129] Roffe, 'The Hundred Rolls of 1255', 201–10.

[130] Cam, *The Hundred and the Hundred Rolls*, 37.

[131] See above, pp. 71–2.

[132] *DIB*, 113–17.

[133] GDB, 182v: *DB Hereford*, 2,57. 'In all there are in the bishopric [of Hereford] 300 hides, although of 33 hides the bishop's men have given no account.' In Gloucestershire there are a number of instances in which accounts were not rendered (GDB, 164, 166v, 170: *DB Gloucs*, 1,63; 28,7; 75,2).

[134] The distinctive diplomatic of Roger de Lacy's fee in Shropshire extends to the manors he held from other tenants-in-chief, suggesting that he or his bailiff supplied the data directly (C. P. Lewis, 'Introduction to the Shropshire Domesday', *The Shropshire Domesday*, eds A. Williams and R. W. H. Erskine (London, 1990), 9). Bath A, the closest Domesday text to a seigneurial return, is confined to the demesne manors of the church of Bath, describing seven out of nine. Presumably the abbey's tenants made their own returns. See

that ensued.[135] That most were written seems likely, for it is hardly credible that complex statistics were presented from the memory of the reeve, much less the tenant-in-chief. What is clear is that a time and a place were then assigned to each tenant-in-chief to have his say. Thus, in the Norfolk *invasiones* Robert Malet speaks of 'the day when it [the account of his lands] was recorded in writing (*inbreviatus*)', that is, enrolled.[136] Regional *breves*, like those of Exon, would seem to have been the result of the subsequent inbreviation.[137]

Inbreviation may have marked the end of the process in some areas, but it did not everywhere. It would appear from ICC that in Cambridgeshire the evidence of the tenants-in-chief was formally presented by the hundred jurors in a further court session. The form of the jurors' presentments and how common was the procedure is the subject of the next section.

Circuit reports

The inquest was, by its nature, a reflexive process, that is, the government asked a question or series of questions and expected answers in due course. From the time of Round those answers have been called 'returns'. Here, however, we shall refer to them as the more neutral 'reports'. *Retornum* is a later medieval term. It refers to the process by which the crown oversaw the operation of local government by requiring shrieval or franchisal officials to endorse a writ with an account of the action taken which was then returned to the issuing department. The process was essentially a bureaucratic one and its application to the inquest has had a considerable impact on the interpretation of the Domesday process. The form of the returns has been seen as the key to the understanding of the government's intentions.[138] Within the investigative process that was the inquest, they of course do no such thing.

To start with, it is clear that not just one type of document found its way back to central government. It is often assumed that the account of the king's demesne manors was already incorporated into reports.[139] There is, however, little evidence to demonstrate the fact. On the contrary, the uncertainty of organization of many king's *breves* and the frequent addition of materials often suggests that the scribe

G. A. Loud, 'An Introduction to the Somerset Domesday', *The Somerset Domesday*, eds A. Williams and R. W. H. Erskine (London, 1989), 3.
[135] Galbraith, *The Making of Domesday Book*, 81–4.
[136] LDB, 276v: *DB Norfolk*, 66,61. See also LDB, 277v: *DB Norfolk*, 66,81, for a reference to Roger Bigod's return (*breve*). Here, as in other notices of *breve*, it is not clear whether the scribe is referring to a chapter in the work in hand, i.e. LDB, or a separate document.
[137] *DIB*, 172–3.
[138] *DIB*, 67–8, 169.
[139] F. R. and C. Thorn, 'Writing of Great Domesday Book', *Domesday*, eds E. Hallam and D. Bates (Stroud, 2001), 64–6.

was compiling his text (as opposed to abbreviating a fully formulated text before him) from a discrete source.[140] More explicit is the return of hundredally arranged schedules of land. Both Abingdon A and the Crowland Domesday assert that they were derived from 'hundred rolls' kept with Domesday Book in the Exchequer. There is no pressing reason to believe with Harvey that these were pre-existing taxation records.[141] Given their close association with Domesday, both chronological and formal, the best explanation of the documents is that their exemplars were produced in the *inquisitio geldi*. Bury A, Bury B, Domesday Monachorum B, and the Excerpta of St Augustine's, Canterbury, exhibit similar characteristics and may have been extracts or abstracts of similar sources.[142] If the enforcement of geld liability was an aim of the Domesday inquest, it would be strange if the king did not demand some report on the findings.

Documents of this type were but a small part of the material that found its way back to central government. For most historians today, Exon is the quintessential return. That perception is largely owed to the force of Galbraith's devastating demolition of Round's account of the making of Domesday Book.[143] His case has, to all appearances, been in no way weakened by the realization that it is the direct source of the GDB account of much of Circuit II.[144] There can be no doubt that Exon was the main documentation to come out of the Domesday inquest in the South West. It is another matter, however, to claim that it was typical. We have already seen that it was a series of working files and we have suggested that it is perhaps best interpreted as the product of what we have termed the process of 'inbreviation'.[145] These are characteristics that are in marked contrast with those of LDB, which Galbraith identified as a directly comparable source.[146] LDB is a fair copy and a compiled document to boot, that is, it was shaped from a complete archive into a pre-conceived form. Conceiving of a similar recension intermediate between Exon and GDB, for Galbraith this was of little moment. And indeed it would be of little moment if LDB was compiled from a series of inbreviations. It was not.

Despite the Galbraithian consensus, students of LDB have continued to voice reservations about the sources of the volume. As Sawyer pointed out in 1955, the accounts of all three counties of Circuit VII exhibit a highly regular hundredal sequence (albeit with repetitions and the like, although irregularities are usually

---

[140] The fact is most clearly apparent in the king's chapters in Yorkshire and Lincolnshire in which there is a number of additions, corrections, and changes of plan.

[141] See above, p. 55–6.

[142] *DIB*, 138–40.

[143] Galbraith, *The Making of Domesday Book*.

[144] F. and C. Thorn, 'Writing of Great Domesday Book', 67–9.

[145] Above, p. 59.

[146] Galbraith, *The Making of Domesday Book*, 30–2.

fully signposted).[147] In 1969 Barbara Dodwell drew attention to the equally regular sequence of vills in some parts of the Norfolk folios.[148] The text itself reinforces these observations. The most cursory examination of the manuscript gives the impression of a pronounced geographical structure: it is not the lord or manor that is visually dominant, but the hundred rubric. Both Sawyer and Dodwell suspected, but could not prove, that a geographically arranged source like ICC lay behind LDB. That their intimations were correct is suggested by diverse, but together compelling, evidence.[149]

First, there is diplomatic. The usage of the Essex folios may be *sui generis*, but that of Norfolk and Suffolk Domesdays is quite distinctive. Throughout LDB tenurial relations of all kinds are noticed. Berewicks are explicitly linked with the demesnes to which they belonged; sokemen and free men are regularly associated with the manors to which they rendered their dues; various sokerights are made explicit. Nevertheless, estate structures articulated in this way have little affect on the form of the text; hundredal structure is rigidly maintained throughout. This in itself does not necessarily indicate anything more than the use of a hundred-ally arranged schedule. However, the layout is accompanied by diplomatic that is elsewhere associated with hundredally arranged accounts. Five main entry forms are found in the text (Table 3.3). Forms 1 and 2 of Norfolk and Suffolk, '*X tenuit Y pro z carucatis*' and '*X tenet A quam Y tenuit pro z carucatis*', echo the '*X pro z hidis se defendit*' formula of the GDB account of Cambridgeshire which, as John Palmer has shown,[150] is taken from the opening formula '*X pro z hidis se defendit*' of the ICC account of each vill. A similar origin is suggested by the distribution of the forms. Where vills are divided between a number of holdings there is a tendency for only the main or principal holding to exhibit the forms. There were five holdings in Martley in Suffolk, for example; the account of Hervey de Bourges' manor commences with '*Martele tenuit Brihtmarus commendatus Haroldi TRE pro manerio lxxx acros ...*' but the remaining four holdings exhibit form 3, '*In Martele ...*'[151]

[147] Sawyer, 'Original Returns', 188.
[148] B. Dodwell, 'The Making of the Domesday Survey in Norfolk: The Hundred and a Half of Clackclose', *EHR*, 84 (1969), 79–84.
[149] For the following, see *DIB*, 177–9.
[150] J. J. N. Palmer, 'The Domesday Manor', *Domesday Studies*, ed. J. C. Holt (Woodbridge, 1987), 144.
[151] LDB, 293v, 294, 327v, 348, 443v: *DB Suffolk*, 3,35;52.6,293.8,28.67,27.

Table 3.3 *Entry forms in LDB*

VIIA	*X* [the place] held *Y* [TRE holder] for *z* carucates …
VIIB	*X* held *A* [TRW tenant] which *Y* held for *z* carucates …
VIIC	A berewick *X* of *z* carucates …
VIID	In *X* holds *A z* carucates which held *Y* a free man TRE …
VIIE	In *X* a free man *z* acres TRE …

Second, some Norfolk and Suffolk entries contain information that relates directly to the vill as opposed to the estate. The statement of the burden of taxation in terms of the number of pence due from each vill when the hundred paid one pound is linked with a statement of what is ostensibly an estimate of the dimensions, and that both items of information express a communal assessment is sometimes explicit. Count Alan's holding in Foulden in Norfolk is said to be measured with the land of William de Warenne where the data are duly found, while in Suffolk the formula is frequently accompanied by the statement that 'others hold here'.[152] It is also indicated by the fact that the sums add up to in some cases, or, more often, approximate to, the one pound total for each hundred and fall into the 20d or 30d units owed by the leets.[153] Like entry form 1, the distribution of the information is not haphazard. It is often associated with undivided vills and is thus appended to entries commencing with the formula '*X* tenuit *Y*'. Where there was more than one holding it is almost invariably tacked onto a subsidiary entry of the form 'In *X* …'[154] The implication must be that the dimensions of the vill and its liability to the geld were at the end of a geographical account and the information was attached to the last holding in the vill when it was transferred to LDB.

Third, certain expressions and items of information are mediated by hundred rather than fief.[155] Some such may have been derived from the geld survey or the schedules that were drawn up from it. In South Greenhoe Hundred in Norfolk, for example, values are given for *quando recepit* or *quando invenit*, when the land was acquired, where elsewhere the term *post*, later, is used, while in Docking, Smethdon, and South Greenhoe carucates to the geld are frequently omitted. Others, however, must have come from a full hundredal recension. In North Greenhoe, Eynesford, Earsham, Henstead, and Loddon, in part a distinct group of hundreds within the

---

[152] LDB, 144v, 167–167v, 328v–329: *DB Norfolk*, 4,3.8,90; *DB Suffolk*, 6,308.

[153] B. A. Lees, 'Introduction to the Suffolk Domesday', *VCH Suffolk*, i, ed. W. Page (London, 1911), 361; C. Johnson, 'Introduction to the Norfolk Domesday', *VCH Norfolk*, ii, ed. W. Page (London, 1906), 6; *The Kalendar of Abbot Samson of Bury St Edmunds and Related Documents*, ed. R. H. C. Davis, Camden Society, 3rd series, 84 (1954), xvi–xxv.

[154] *Pace* Dodwell, 'Domesday Survey in Norfolk', 80.

[155] R. Welldon Finn, *Domesday Studies: The Eastern Counties* (London, 1967), 54, 59.

common sequence,[156] the unusual formulation *inter omnes*, or *inter homines* is used of the total number of ploughs, and in the hundreds in central Norfolk *sochemannus* is preferred to *liber homo* where the opposite obtains in the south-east.

All these characteristics point to the existence of a geographically arranged recension of the data from which LDB, or at least the Norfolk and Suffolk sections, was compiled. It was presumably from this source that the textually earlier, and apparently hundredally arranged, East Anglian sections of IE were copied.[157] A key element of Galbraith's structure comes tumbling down. Similar characteristics indicate that the Domesday data of probably as many as a further nineteen counties were originally drawn up vill by vill and hundred by hundred.[158] The ICC-derived diplomatic of the Cambridgeshire folios is found throughout Circuit III, suggesting that the Bedfordshire, Buckinghamshire, Hertfordshire, and Middlesex data were also derived from an ICC-like source. Differences in diplomatic and content are indeed manifest from hundred to hundred in this area.[159] Similar forms are also found in Circuit I.

Equally compelling is the evidence from Circuit VI. In the Nottinghamshire and Yorkshire folios there survive two sections of the GDB text that are still geographically arranged. The account of Rutland proceeds by vill and twelve-carucate hundred with the assessment of each of the wapentakes recorded in the opening rubric (Table 3.4). That of the eighty-four carucates of York is arranged by vill alone, but again the assessment of each is given before the various elements are described.[160] Both, it is true, were royal estates, but a third geographically arranged passage in a seigneurial context indicates that the form was general. The account of the Isle of Axholme, which was held in its entirety by Geoffrey de la Guerche, exhibits a hundredal cadastre as neat as that of Rutland (Table 3.5).[161] Vestiges of a similar source are found in the Huntingdonshire section of IE. There,

[156] The adjacent hundreds of Earsham, Henstead, and Loddon with Diss were nos 21–4 in the common hundredal sequence. There is some evidence to suggest that hundreds were grouped together for some purposes. Two parts of the soke of three hundreds were attached to the farm of the borough of Yarmouth (LDB, 118–118v: *DB Norfolk*, 1,67). This may represent a purely *ad hoc* arrangement, for hundreds were often joined together for especially weighty legal occasions, but it is perhaps more likely to indicate a ship soke, that is, a group of three hundreds that provided a ship for the royal fleet. Hundredal sequences often coincide with propinquity to suggest other Norfolk groups, but no others coincide with diplomatically defined entities.

[157] See above, p. 58.

[158] *DIB*, 173–6.

[159] Cottesloe Hundred in Buckinghamshire, for example, records no woodland in an otherwise densely wooded shire, while seven hundreds in the Aylesbury 'circuit' do not use the *pro manerio* formula (J. Bradbury, 'Introduction to the Buckinghamshire Domesday', *The Buckinghamshire Domesday*, eds A. Williams and R. W. H. Erskine (London, 1988), 9, 17).

[160] GDB, 298–298v: *DB Yorks*, C23–35.

[161] GDB, 369–369v: *DB Lincs*, 63,5–23.

Table 3.4 *The Rutland Domesday*, GDB, 293v: *DB Rutland*, R

Hundred	Manor	Lord in 1086	Assessment		
			car.	bov.	
Alstoe I	Greetham	King	3	0	
	Cottesmore	King	3	0	
	Mk Overton				
	Stretton	Countess Judith	3	4	
	Thistleton	Countess Judith	0	4	
	Ibidem	Alvred of Lincoln	0	4	
	Same hundred (Teigh)	Robert Malet	1	4	12 car.
Alstoe II	Whissendine	Countess Judith	4	0	
	Exton	Countess Judith	2	0	
	Whitwell	Countess Judith	1	0	
	Awsthorp	Ogier fitzUngemar	1	0	
	Burley	Gilbert de Ghent	2	0	
	Ashwell	Earl Hugh	2	0	12 car.
Martinsley	Oakham (5 berewicks)	King	4	0	
	Ibidem	Fulcher Malsor	1	0	
	Hambleton (7 berewicks)	King	4	0	
	Ridlington (7 berewicks)	King	4	0	13 car.

Words in brackets are interlineations.

as in ICC-derived sources, undivided vills commence with the formula 'X [the place]. Abbot Thurstin had a manor …', while divided vills are of the form 'In X Thurstin has …'[162] Throughout the circuit certain items of data are mediated by hundredal structure. In Lincolnshire, for example, the record of churches is largely determined by wapentake rather than fee. In some there are no churches at all and in others a comprehensive record, some represented by a church, others by a church and priest, and yet others by a priest alone.[163]

In circuit V the record of churches and priests in the Cheshire folios is similarly mediated by hundredal structure.[164] In Hamestan Hundred no churches at all are noticed, but in the remaining hundreds a distinct pattern emerges. In Duddestan, Warmundestrou, Rushton, Willaston, and Tunendune a priest alone is recorded, while in Ruloe, Bucklow, Ati's Cross, and Exestan the formula is a church or a church and priest. In like wise woodland is differently described in Shropshire from hundred to hundred. In Culvestan, Leintwardine, Merset, and Wrockwardine

[162] Colne is an apparent exception, for only Ely held within the settlement. However, it would seem that, assessed at 6 hides, it was joined with some other settlement to form a vill.

[163] *DIB*, 176.

[164] Thacker and Sawyer, 'Domesday Survey', 296–7.

Table 3.5 *The Isle of Axholme*

Ref.	Vill	Assessment		Status	
		car.	bov.		
63,5	Epworth	8	0	manor	
63,6	Owston	4	0	manor	12 car.
63,7	Haxey	3	0	manor	
63,8	Eastlound Graizelound	1	6	two manors	
63,9	*Ibidem*	1	1	soke of Epworth	
63,10	*Ibidem*	0	1	berewick of Belton	
63,11	The Burnhams	6	0	soke of Belton	12 car.
63,12	Belton	5	0	two manor	
63,13	Beltoft	1	0	soke, unspecified	
63,14	Althorpe	1	0	soke, addition	
63,15	Crowle	5	7	manor	
		0	1	inland of Upperthorpe	13 car.
63,16	Amcotts	2	0	soke of Crowle	
63,17	*Ibidem*	0	3	inland of Westwood	
63,18	*Ibidem*	0	5	soke of Garthorpe	
63,19	Garthorpe Luddington	4	4	soke of Crowle	
63,20	*Ibidem*	1	0	manor	
63,21	*Ibidem*	0	4	soke of Belton	
63,22	Butterwick	3	0	soke and inland of Owston	12 car.

it is given in linear measurements, while in Alnodestou, Baschurch, Conditre, Condover, Hodnet, Overs, Patton, Reweset, and Rinlau by the number of swine it could support.[165] The GDB account of both counties may thus have also been derived from ICC-like precursors.

It is only in the remaining three shires of Circuit V and Circuit IV that there are no obvious traces of a geographical recension. In both areas estates from one shire were frequently enrolled, apparently erroneously, in GDB in the folios of other shires. This is also a characteristic of Circuit II and there it is possible to perceive that such errors were a function of the supra-comital arrangement of Exon. Had all three accounts gone through a geographically arranged stage such anomalies would no doubt have been spotted and eliminated. With the majority of circuit reports appearing in ICC-like format, the best interpretation of Exon

---

[165] C. P. Lewis, 'Introduction to the Shropshire Domesday', 10. Only the demesne of Earl Roger of Montgomery breaks the rule in using linear measurements regardless of where the woodland was situated. The land was probably extra-hundredal.

would seem to be that for some reason the Domesday commissioners did not proceed to a fully compiled report.[166] Why this should be so is, of course, now impossible to determine. It is, however, a phenomenon that is relatively common in the records of inquisitions in the later Middle Ages. To take but one example from the original returns that survive from the thirteenth century, the verdicts of the Ragman inquest of 1274–5 are generally neatly copied replies to the articles of inquiry painstakingly compiled from the presentments of knights of the shire, hundreds and vills. In Whittlesford Hundred in Cambridgeshire, though, the raw data were returned seemingly because there was no time to compile a conventional report.[167] The use of Exon, and similar sources in the West Midlands, may be indicative of a little local difficulty of the same kind.

It seems clear, then, that the intention of the commissioners was to present the survey of lands in a geographical format. This does indeed tell us something of their perception of what was required of them. They clearly understood that an account of the resources of the lord's Domesday demesne was to be rendered within the context of the vill and hundred. Galbraith would seem to have us believe that subsequently, in Cambridgeshire at least, the commissioners recast the reports into a seigneurial form. 'Would seem', for he is at his most obscure at this point in his argument.[168] He avers that the failure to include the *terra regis* indicates that they had already begun to compile in terms of the GDB form and we are left to conclude that ICC was some idle exercise. In fact, the *breve regis* indicates nothing more than a separate report from a discrete process (the survey of regalia). There is no necessity beyond the demands of the recensionist hypothesis itself to conceive of an intermediate recension between ICC-like sources and GDB.[169] Pre-existing schedules of the lands of tenants-in-chief would have been adequate enough to enable the GDB scribe to construct the present text from the geographically arranged sources like ICC.

[166] *DIB*, 173.
[167] London, National Archives, SC5/ Cambridge/Chapter House/4.
[168] Galbraith, *The Making of Domesday Book*, 123–35.
[169] The case for 'circuit volumes' similar to Exon (and LDB) has been most fully put by Frank and Caroline Thorn, 'Writing of Great Domesday Book', 64–6. Most of their evidence is drawn from Circuits II and IV and interpolated for the rest of the MS. They argue that it would be difficult to compile from ICC-like sources and the result would be more mistakes than are apparent. They do not discuss the geographically arranged sections of GDB and their import. It may be noted that seigneurially arranged 'breves' were drawn up from hundredally arranged sources in the great scutage of 1242–3 without any great loss of data or unacceptable inaccuracy (*The Book of Fees*, Public Record Office, 2 vols in 3 (1920–31)).

The extent of the commissioners' interest in the fee itself is probably indicated by a series of documents, compiled at this stage in the proceedings, that have been called 'summaries'.[170] That relating to Ely Abbey's lands in Essex is typical:

> The same abbot [of Ely] has in demesne in Essex 5 manors [assessed] at 49½ hides. There are 14 ploughs in demesne, and 102 villeins, 45 bordars, and 44 slaves who have 39 ploughs. The whole is worth £64 10s.
>
> His knights have 2 manors in the same county [assessed] at 5 hides. There are 3 ploughs in demesne, and 6 villeins, 7 bordars, and 7 slaves who have 6 ploughs. It is worth £8. This land suffices for 61 ploughs (*Hec terra sufficit lxi carucis*). It has increased in value (*emendata de*) by £9 in the hands of Abbot Symeon.

Twenty-four of these summaries survive (Table 3.6). Two are to be found in the folios of GDB itself,[171] the remainder in Exon (13) and IE (9).[172] Despite these various provenances, all are remarkably consistent in content and expression. They open with a statement of the number of manors held in demesne and indicate the total assessment to the geld, the number of ploughs of the lord and his men, the numbers of the dependent peasantry, and the total value. Similar statistics are then given for the enfeoffed estates. Finally, the number of ploughlands in the whole of the fee is given, usually as a single figure, along with a sum for the increase in

---

[170] It has been suggested that the summaries were written, in part at least, when the abbey of Ely was in the hands of the king in 1093, on the ground that the figure for the increase in value during the time of Abbot Symeon is unlikely to have been recorded in 1086 when Simeon was still alive (Galbraith, *The Making of Domesday Book*, 141–2). A similar increase in value is given for the lands of Glastonbury Abbey which was in the hands of the king in 1086 (Exon, 173, 527v–528), but the information is also found for Picot the sheriff's fee in Cambridgeshire (IE, 121–3) and (as a depreciation) in the count of Mortain's in the South West (Exon, 531). By definition, the texts must postdate the collection of evidence. Their transmission with Exon and IE, however, indicate that they precede the drafting of GDB. C. P. Lewis, 'An Introduction to the Lancashire Domesday', 12, suggests that the Ribble and Mersey summary emanates from a presentment of the shire on the ground that the discrepancies between summary and text preclude the one being compiled from the other. In fact the differences are within the range of accuracy of Domesday summary figures – arithmetic was not a strong point of medieval scribes. The other summaries must be derived from the Domesday returns since shires elsewhere were not competent to make such presentments.

[171] Vestiges of a third summary are probably to be found in Shropshire. There Earl Roger is said to have had 12 manors that had belonged to the king, with 57 berewicks attached, and 11 others. A total value is provided of £330 and 115s of farm (GDB, 254: *DB Salop*, 4,1,37).

[172] There are a further seven summary-like accounts of the Ely thegnlands and sokelands held by Hardwin de Scales, Picot the sheriff, and Guy de Raimbeaucourt in Cambridgeshire and Hertfordshire (IE, 121–4). These may be *ex parte* Ely documents. However, if they were produced by the commissioners, they presumably relate to the special circumstances of the abbey's claims.

Table 3.6 *The Domesday summaries*

Reference	Lord	Location	Circuit
GDB, 270: *DB Ches*, R7	The king	Ribble and Mersey	4
GDB, 381: *DB Yorks*, SN,CtA45	C. Alan of Brittany	Yorkshire: Richmondshire	6
Exon, 527b	Glastonbury Abbey	Wiltshire	2
	Glastonbury Abbey	Dorset	2
	Glastonbury Abbey	Devon	2
Exon, 528	Glastonbury Abbey	Somerset	2
Exon, 528b	St Petroc	Cornwall	2
Exon, 530b	Ralf de Mortimer	Wiltshire	2
	Miles Crispin	Wiltshire	2
	Robert son of Gerald	Wiltshire and Dorset	2
	Robert son of Gerald	Dorset	2
	Robert son of Gerald	Wiltshire, Dorset, Somerset	2
Exon, 531	Durand of Gloucester	Wiltshire	2
	Gilbert of Breteuil	Wiltshire	2
	Count of Mortain	Wiltshire, Dorset, Devon, Cornwall	2
IE, 121	Ely Abbey	Cambridgeshire	3
IE, 122	Ely Abbey	Hertfordshire	
	Ely Abbey	Essex	7
	Ely Abbey	Norfolk	7
	Ely Abbey	Suffolk	7
IE, 123	Ely Abbey	Huntingdonshire	6
	Picot the sheriff	Cambridgeshire	3
	Hardwin de Scales	Cambridgeshire	3
IE, 124	Hardwin de Scales	Hertfordshire	3

value since acquired. With two notable exceptions (the GDB instances), the phrase used for the latter is the unvarying 'This land is sufficient for so many ploughs. It has increased in value by so many pounds.'

A final class of document that was of interest to the king appears to have been schedules of disputes, one of which is noticed in IE.[173] The *terre occupate* of Exon and the *invasiones* of LDB are probably examples or are derived from examples. With details of stocking the *terre occupate* must, in their present form, postdate the geld survey; thereafter they could have been extracted from the inbreviations at any time up to the collecting of the Exon manuscript together. Further palaeographical research will, no doubt, clarify the matter. The *invasiones* of LDB, however, tend to suggest an early point in the Domesday process. Again, like the *terre occupate*, they contain details of stocking, but here it is unlikely that they were abstracted from

[173] IE, 127.

the survey of vills since they are arranged by tenant-in-chief. Inbreviations were evidently the immediate source, but already at that stage they may have been in the form of a separate schedule. In the Norfolk folios Bishop William's *invasiones* are anomalously entered after his *breve*.[174] If this reflects the form of his return, then it would seem that disputed estates were already distinguished at inbreviation.

Schedules of claims, then, albeit summary, could have been drawn up in the aftermath of the geld survey. That seems to be the best explanation of the fact that the *clamores* of Circuit VI are organized in the common wapentake sequence of the body of the text. Of course, the pleas themselves postdate inbreviation. It can be doubted, though, that such a procedure was followed throughout the country. In Circuit III, at least, claims are fully integrated into ICC, and it would therefore seem that they had not been pruned out of the inbreviations. That is not to say, however, that there might not also have been separate schedules, for Ely D may have been derived from one such.

The dénouement: the Oath of Salisbury

If the circumstances were exceptional, the inquest was a trusty well-oiled mechanism; once initiated it worked itself almost unprompted. But it was no automaton, and thus no description of the process is complete without an account of its dénouement. One might be forgiven for thinking that in the reign of Edward I information was sometimes collected for its own sake: the Dunstable chronicler famously opined that 'nothing came out of [the Ragman Inquest]' of 1275 and the Hundred Roll survey of 1279–80 may well have been pulled because it served no useful purpose.[175] However, medieval kings were of course generally not train spotters. Inquests presaged furious activity. Legal action was a universal sequel; it usually dragged on for years and years. More immediately, there was government action to tackle the problem that initiated the inquest. The Domesday inquest was no exception in this respect.

For many that business is still the compilation of Domesday Book. The concept of 'original returns' introduced by Round subliminally suggests that the documentation that the inquest produced was in some way preliminary. The diversity of its forms indicates that it was anything but. The survey of the royal demesne, geld inquest, the survey of vills, summaries, claims, even the inbreviations of Exon, evidently served their own purposes. One of the most important contributions to Domesday studies of the last fifty years has been Sir James Holt's placing of the Oath of Salisbury in early August 1086, back at the centre of the process.[176] The

---

[174] LDB, 197v–201v: *DB Norfolk*, 10,48–93.
[175] *Annales Monastici*, ed. H. R. Luard, Rolls Series, 36, 5 vols (1864–69), iii, 263; *DIB*, 225.
[176] J. C. Holt, '1086', *Domesday Studies*, ed. J. C. Holt (Woodbridge, 1987), 41–64,

event, as recorded in the Anglo-Saxon Chronicle,[177] is not explicitly associated
with the inquest, but the act of mass homage that took place there must have been
performed in return for land (the quid pro quo), and so an association with the
Domesday inquest seems certain. It was presumably at Salisbury that 'the writings'
were brought to William. There is indeed a possible reference to the process. In the
Exon account of the bishop of Winchester's lands in Somerset it is recorded that
at a meeting at Salisbury King William ordered the bishop of Durham to write
down in his records (*in brevibus*) a grant to the bishop of Winchester of additions
to his manor of Taunton which he, King William, had just acknowledged.[178] The
terms of the deal worked out at Salisbury are not stated. They will become clear
in the discussion of geld and service.[179]

The making of Domesday Book

Galbraith's equation of LDB with Exon was inspired. At once he could point to a
format apparently embodied in the so-called articles of inquiry that informed an
early stage of data enrolment and an immediately pre-GDB text. LDB was clearly
later than Exon but equally it represented a circuit return which, in the event, was
never entered into the final work. These are perceptions that have informed almost
all thinking about the making of Domesday Book in the last forty years. Galbraith
believed that it was the death of William the Conqueror that brought the enterprise
to a close before the end of the work.[180] More recently, Pierre Chaplais has argued
that it was the exile in 1088 of William de St Calais, his candidate for the 'man
behind the book', which aborted the project.[181] Less personal reasons have been
advanced by others. For Welldon Finn the social structure of East Anglia was of a
complexity that defied abbreviation in the normal way and the GDB scribe threw
up his hands in despair,[182] while for Loyn the sheer volume of material would have
made GDB unwieldy and it was decided to exclude it on these grounds.[183] All are
agreed, however, that Domesday Book is a mongrel source, cobbled together *faute
de mieux*. Rumble has rounded off the argument by demonstrating how scribe 7
rubricated LDB to disguise as much as possible its separate origin.[184]

---

[177] *ASC*, 162.
[178] Exon, 175.
[179] Below, pp. 176–209, 309–10.
[180] Galbraith, *The Making of Domesday Book*, 205.
[181] P. Chaplais, 'William of Saint-Calais and the Domesday Survey', *Domesday Studies*, ed.
J. C. Holt (Woodbridge, 1987), 77.
[182] R. Welldon Finn, *The Domesday Inquest* (London, 1961), 190.
[183] Loyn, 'A General Introduction to Domesday Book', 6–7.
[184] A. R. Rumble, 'The Domesday Manuscripts: Scribes and *Scriptoria*', *Domesday Studies*,
ed. J. C. Holt (Woodbridge, 1987), 80–1.

We can now see that this elaborate structure is fatally flawed. Whatever the origins of the IE prologue, it almost certainly relates to a very late stage in the whole Domesday process, while, as a working document, Exon is of a different order from the carefully crafted LDB. Above all, the compilation of the LDB text from an ICC-like source severs all formal links with Exon. LDB's affinities are with GDB. It is almost certainly earlier, for it includes demesne statistics which the compiler of GDB strove to omit, but it is of a piece with it. The production of LDB saw the realization of the GDB form – the juxtaposition of the king's land with the land of the tenants-in-chief and the ordering by fee and county – for the very first time. We might best conclude that LDB and GDB exist in contradistinction to the records of the inquest as the products of a common and discrete programme. It is precisely this that the horizontal diplomatic of the two texts, the forms that the compilers brought to their work, demonstrates. A developing schema underlies LDB and GDB.

In LDB horizontal diplomatic reveals itself in a number of idiosyncrasies. The most prominent is the inclusion of the *invasiones* section at the end of each county. Normally, this feature has been considered a vertical element (that is, content derived from the source documents).[185] However, it would seem that similar material was recorded throughout the country and it was the compiler's decision whether to include it or not. Thus, *clamores* appear in the Circuit VI folios of GDB but not in those of Circuit II even though recorded in Exon, its source.[186] The record of vill and manor dimensions would seem to be of the same order. They are universal in Norfolk and Suffolk (although absent from Essex) but only sporadic in GDB, although regularly found in earlier sources like ICC. Less prominent, but nonetheless significant, is the usage of the six LDB scribes who wrote the text.[187] The periodic change of scribe, however, makes it impossible to determine in detail the order in which the text was written and thus precludes an analysis of developing forms within the volume. There are no such constraints in the case of GDB and there the horizontal diplomatic reveals a neat development.

The present order of the text dating from the time when it was first bound, there are a number of textual links between quires that indicate a fragmentary sequence of writing. With the one county finishing half way through a quire and the other beginning straight after, it is clear that Devon was written before Cornwall,

---

[185] See, for example, Wormald, 'Domesday Lawsuits: A Provisional List and Preliminary Comments', 64–9.

[186] The *terre occupate* of Exon are not pleas like many, although not all, of the *clamores* (see below, p. 278). As collections of evidence in anticipation of pleas, however, they are directly comparable to the *invasiones*.

[187] See above, pp. 38–41.

Gloucestershire before Worcestershire, Shropshire before Cheshire,[188] Yorkshire before Lincolnshire, and probably Nottinghamshire before Derbyshire.[189] Otherwise, there are no explicit indications. Rulings, however, suggest that some quires go with others. In much of GDB the scribe carefully marked out the lines and columns of each quire, often with the aid of a template to prick the folios, before he started to write.[190] Variations are considerable, but, postulating a progressive compression of the text with the scribe's growing awareness of the urgency of the task before him, Galbraith suggested that the Circuit III folios, with 44 lines per column, were written first, followed by Circuits VI, I, and IV with 50 lines, and finally II, and V in which the rulings were ignored altogether.[191]

Unfortunately, the analysis was based on the maxima and minima given in the 1953 PRO publication *Domesday Rebound* which do not reflect the variations in ruling or indeed of lines of writing which do not always respect the layout. Subsequently, Michael Gullick has undertaken a more searching analysis (now revised by Frank and Caroline Thorn), identifying four distinct ruling patterns.[192] Number 1 consists of eight vertical and usually forty-four horizontal lines; 1b is distinguished from 1a by the use of ruling template B. Number 2 has seven vertical and fifty horizontal lines, template A being employed, and number 3 four and fifty to fifty-seven. Finally, 4 has only two vertical and two horizontal lines to define the writing space, but is otherwise unruled.[193] The distribution of the forms suggests four distinct sequences (Table 3.7).[194] But Gullick has shown that compression often reflects the scribe's desire to enrol a shire within the confines of a single quire or group of quires. The assumption of increasing haste is unwarranted.

Ruling patterns can only be used effectively to work out the order of writing in conjunction with diplomatic.[195] The initial problem here is where to start. I

---

[188] In Shropshire this seems to have been an oversight since the list at the beginning of the account of the county indicates that the scribe was unaware of the existence of the fees after number four: they are listed postscriptally. Had he known of their existence he would, presumably, have added extra leaves to the first quire (Lewis, 'Introduction to the Shropshire Domesday', 7–8).

[189] *Domesday Book Rebound*, end pull-outs, and M. Gullick, 'The Great and Little Domesday Manuscripts', *Domesday Studies*, eds A. Williams and R. W. H. Erskine (London, 987), 93–112 and appendix III.

[190] Gullick, 'The Great and Little Domesday Manuscripts', 94–6.

[191] Galbraith, *The Making of Domesday Book*, 203–4.

[192] Gullick, 'Great and Little Domesday Manuscripts', 96'; F. and C. Thorn, 'Writing of Great Domesday Book', 40–4.

[193] A type 4a (Somerset, Devon, and Cornwall) has been distinguished from 4b on the basis of the height of the frame and the distance between the prickings (F. and C. Thorn, 'Writing of Great Domesday Book', 43).

[194] Gullick failed to notice that Oxfordshire was ruled with pattern 3.

[195] *DIB*, 194.

Table 3.7 *Ruling patterns and diplomatic forms*

	Quire	Pattern	Formula
CIRCUIT VI	38 Yorks 1	1b	VIA–F
	39 Yorks 2	2	VIC,F–I
	40 Yorks 3	1b	VIJ,K
	41 Yorks 4	1b	VIK
	42 Yorks 5	1b	VIK
	Lincs 1		VIK/M–O
	43 Lincs 2	1b	VIK/M–O
	44 Lincs 3	1b	VIK/N–Q
	45 Lincs 4	1b	VIK/Q
	46 Lincs 5	1b	VIK/Q
	47 *Clamores*	2	
	36 Notts 1	1b	VIK/Q
	37 Notts 2 & Rutland	1b	VIK/Q
	35 Derby	1a	VIK/Q/S
	26 Hunts	1a	VIK/Q/S
CIRCUIT III	24 Cambs 1	1a	IIIA–D
	25 Cambs 2	1a	IIIA–D
	17 Middlesex	1a	IIIA–D
	27 Beds	1a	IIIA–D
	19 Bucks	1a	IIIA–D
	18 Herts	1b	IIIA–D
CIRCUIT I	1 Kent 1	2	IA=IIIC
	2 Kent 2	1b/2	IA–B
	3 Sussex 1	2	IB–C
	4 Sussex 2	2	IB, IIID
	5 Surrey	2	IB, IIID
	6 Hants 1	2	IB
	7 Hants 2	2	IB
	8 Hants 3	2	IB
	9 Berks	2	IB
CIRCUIT II	10 Wilts	3	IIA–B
	11 Dorset	3	IIA–C
	12 Soms 1	4	IIB–C
	13 Soms 2	4	IIC–D
	14 Devon 1	4	IID
	15 Devon 2	4	IID
	16 Devon 3	4	IID
	& Cornwall		IIC,E,F
CIRCUIT V	21 Gloucs 1	2	
	22 Gloucs 2	4	VA–D

	Quire	Pattern	Formula
	& Worcs		VC,E
23	Hereford	4	VC–E
32	Salop 1	4	VC–F
33	Salop 2	4	VF
	& Ches 1		VF
34	Ches 2 & Lancs	4	VF
CIRCUIT IV 31	Staffs	4	IVA=VF,B–E
30	Warks	4	IVB–E
28	Northants	4	IVD–E
20	Oxon	3	IVD–E
29	Leics	2 & 4	IVD–E

suggested a way forward in 1990.[196] Circuit VI exhibits ruling pattern 1 and here by and large the scribe was at his most disciplined. He adhered to his grid and the resulting text is well drafted. Curiously, however, Circuit VI has the widest spread of diplomatic. A score or so of different opening forms and other distinguishing features can be identified (Appendix) and, once postscriptal entries are flagged, it can be seen that they fall into a neat sequence. The scribe was clearly feeling his way into an acceptable format for the text. It was a format that he was to apply widely. In the course of compiling his account of the North he worked out conventions that were to become standard throughout the rest of the text. Thus, the representation of ploughlands went through a number of permutations before lighting upon the formula 'land for so many ploughs' which is otherwise the norm in GDB. Conversely, forms that appear elsewhere in GDB, such as 'x *tenuit*', are postscriptal in the account of the North. The conclusion is plain: the scribe began the writing of GDB with the Yorkshire folios of Circuit VI.

The evolving forms indicate that, after Lincolnshire, Nottinghamshire, and Derbyshire, Huntingdonshire was probably the last shire in that circuit to be entered. From there the scribe proceeded to Circuit III.[197] There ruling pattern 1 is again used and marginal M, a formula developed in Yorkshire to draw attention to manors, appears in the Cambridgeshire, Middlesex, Bedfordshire, and Buckinghamshire folios. Hertfordshire only exhibits the form in three places and was probably the last in the circuit to be enrolled. Four distinctive entry forms are found, but in all of them the TRE tenant is recorded at the end. It is this characteristic that indicates that Circuit I came next. Ruling pattern 2 is found throughout the circuit but, significantly, the second Kent quire is a re-ruling of a

[196] D. R. Roffe, 'Domesday Book and Northern Society: A Reassessment', *EHR*, 105 (1990), 310–36; *DIB*, 194–203.
[197] *DIB*, 203–11.

pattern 1 quire. Nevertheless, in the early Kent folios the TRE tenant continues to be recorded at the end of the entry, but from *breve* no. 9 onwards it appears at the beginning, a characteristic that the Domesday Monachorum B suggests was a vertical element derived from the GDB sources. Kent was undoubtedly written first, but only a tentative sequence can be suggested for the rest of the circuit, although it is likely that Berkshire was last.

There are no diplomatic links with the remaining three circuits beyond the common ploughland formula, but layout suggests Circuit II came next. Wiltshire and Dorset exhibit ruling pattern 3 but Somerset, Devon, and Cornwall number 4.[198] The change marked a significant decision to dispense with horizontal rulings which are subsequently found in GDB only in the first ten lines of the first quire of Gloucestershire, Oxfordshire, and Leicestershire folios (and there by sheet rather than membrane). The writing of the Circuit II folios, then, would appear to bridge a change of policy in the layout of GDB. Within the circuit six developing forms indicate that after Dorset, Somerset, Devon, and Cornwall were entered in that order. A neat sequence of twelve forms indicates that Gloucestershire, Worcestershire, Herefordshire, Shropshire, and Cheshire in Circuit V were followed by Staffordshire and Warwickshire, and then probably Northamptonshire, Oxfordshire, and Leicestershire in Circuit IV to finish the volume.[199]

All this seems ineffably arcane, but an important point emerges from it. The GDB scribe wrote in an ordered sequence starting in the North, going on to the East Midlands, South East, South and South West, West Midlands and North West, and finishing with the Central Midlands. What is significant about this textual itinerary is that East Anglia plays no part in it; had the GDB scribe intended abbreviating the East Anglian shires he would have done so after Circuit VI or

---

[198] The change also mirrors the twofold division of Exon (T. Webber, 'Salisbury and the Exon Domesday: Some Observations Concerning the Origins of Exeter Cathedral MS 3500', *English Manuscript Studies 1100–1700*, I, eds P. Beal and J. Griffiths (Oxford, 1989), 1–18).

[199] Frank and Caroline Thorn ('Writing of Great Domesday', 40–4) transpose Circuits II and IV on the ground that there is greater compression in the latter. Their analysis, however, is based solely on rulings and to what extent they were observed. Flight, *The Survey of the Whole of England*, 15–20, again transposes Circuits II and IV on the ground of vertical rulings. At what point the *clamores* and Yorkshire Summary were written cannot be determined from the formulas since the data are of a different order from those of the body of the text. F. and C. Thorn, 'Writing of Great Domesday Book', 46, postulate that the section was last to be written, for, although using ruling pattern 2, it was an update to the body of the text that, by definition, came in late. This conclusion, of course, begs the question as to when GDB was written. Moreover, the Summary content is demonstrably earlier than the text (D. R. Roffe, 'The Yorkshire Summary: A Domesday Satellite', *Northern History*, 27 (1991), 242–60). In fact, it seems more likely that the section was written early with the rest of the northern material. It is implausible to group it with Circuit 1 in which ruling pattern 2 is also used and it should be noted that the same pattern is used in the second Yorkshire quire.

Circuit III. That he did not do so because he considered it the first part of the programme is indicated by horizontal diplomatic links between the two volumes. The characteristic record of dimensions and *invasiones* in LDB is echoed in the record of similar data at the beginning of GDB. Both are found in the Yorkshire folios which, unlike the rest of the circuit, exhibit the same hundredal structure as the LDB folios and (at least initially) the same running heads indicating holders of land.[200] Claims, akin to *invasiones*, subsequently appear in Lincolnshire and Huntingdonshire but thereafter are quietly dropped. The implications are clear: LDB and GDB belong to a common programme. The former was no work of the compiler of the latter, but nevertheless he conceived of it as one work. What is now volume 2 of Domesday Book is rightly volume 1.

The date of Domesday Book has become one of the most contentious issues in Domesday studies in the last few years.[201] Hitherto, despite the absence of hard evidence, it had hardly been a problem. Although Roundians and Galbraithians differed on the form of the 'original returns', none of them had any doubt that the inquest was about decisions, and decisions had to be recorded for later use. Domesday Book was clearly intended to be a register of title and it was therefore logical to assume that it was drafted as soon as possible after the inquest from the unwieldy documentation that the process had spawned. Content seemingly confirms this assumption. There is, it is argued, no indication of data dating after 1086[202] and references to Rufus as the son of the king and the like firmly indicate that the bulk of the work belongs to the reign of the Conqueror.[203] Of late it has been fashionable even to conceive of an indecent haste: it is argued

---

[200] For this last observation, see F. and C. Thorn, 'Writing of Great Domesday Book', 44–5. In the Yorkshire folios the names, confined to the first two quires, were subsequently erased and 'Yorkshire' was added. County names appear as the only headings in the rest of GDB.

[201] The question was opened up in *DIB*, 242–8. For responses, see J. C. Holt, 'Domesday Studies 2000', *Domesday*, eds E. Hallam and D. Bates (Stroud, 2002), 23–4; F. and C. Thorn, 'Writing of Great Domesday Book', 69–72; S. Baxter, review of *DIB*, http://www.history. ac.uk/reviews/paper/baxterStephen.html, and D. R. Roffe's reply, http://www.history.ac.uk/ reviews/paper/roffeDavid.html.

[202] There is, of course, a nasty circularity here: anything that is in Domesday Book must date from 1086 since Domesday Book was compiled in 1086. The text has always been treated as a gold standard for dating. It should no longer be necessarily treated so. As an abbreviation of the inquest records it may well be expected that it largely confined itself to that material. Nevertheless, future work may well indicate that some items of information are of a later date. The cases recorded in the *clamores* may well be of this type; see below, p. 276.

[203] J. C. Holt, '1086', *Colonial England 1066–1215* (London, 1997), 57, asserts that an interlineation in the Hampshire folios indicating that Geoffrey the chamberlain was the chamberlain 'of the king's daughter' (GDB, 49: *DB Hants*, 67,1) is proof positive that the passage was written before the death of William the Conqueror. This 'demonstrably later addition' is a current gloss.

that the complex stratigraphy of additions, corrections, and emendations indicate that the production of Domesday Book was begun before all the returns were in. With the satisfying picture of a scribe sending off messengers to find out more information by ordering the recall of juries, there has seemed no trouble in seeing the completion of the GDB by the end of September 1087 when William died or, at the latest, in the early months of 1088 before the revolt against Rufus, his successor.[204]

These are all certainties that dissolve once the inquest is recognized as the investigative process it was. While it is formally possible that Domesday Book embodied the decisions made at Salisbury in August 1086, it cannot have been the aim of the inquest itself, for there are no formal or logical connections between Domesday Book and the inquest texts, apart from the fact that it was compiled from them. Furthermore, at whatever date it was compiled one would not expect the data to be updated.[205] Numerous twelfth- and thirteenth-century inquests were to be abbreviated in the Red Book of the Exchequer, the Black Book, and the Book of Fees as late as the early fourteenth century, but of course no attempt was made to revise them. Abbreviations were drawn up to preserve useful information and to change that information would be to subvert its purpose.[206]

Chronologically, Domesday Book is therefore cast adrift. Any date between 1086 and 1099–1101, when 'the king's book' is first referred to, is possible. For myself, I have suggested that the most likely date for the compilation of Domesday Book is 1088–90.[207] With a firm indication of the order in which GDB was written, a period in the reign of Rufus seems certain, for the first reference to Earl William de Warenne in the Huntingdonshire folios occurs only some hundred folios into the work. What other evidence there is points in the same direction. Orderic Vitalis reports that Rannulf Flambard 'revised' the survey of England in 1089:

> This man unsettled the young king with his fraudulent suggestions, inciting
> him to revise the survey of all England (*incitans ut totius Angliae reuiseret*
> *descriptionem*), and convincing him that he should make a new division of

---

[204] For a restatement of the case, see F. R. and C. Thorn, 'Writing of Great Domesday Book', 37–72.

[205] The references to 'Earl' William de Warenne were an anachronism that the GDB scribe would surely have eradicated if he had noticed it (http://www.history.ac.uk/reviews/paper/roffeDavid.html).

[206] On these grounds it is perhaps unwarranted to assume that, like scripture, every jot and tittle is significant; so R. W. Eyton, *Domesday Studies: Somerset*, 11: 'the Commissioners and scribes did not crowd nearly every sentence ... with a vain tautology, nor yet indite which, well and literally translated, would fail to be significant in its every word'. The sentiment is echoed by Thorn and Thorn, 'Writing of Great Domesday Book', 55: '... nothing is there by accident, is merely descriptive.' Later practice would suggest that a scribe was often anxious to write down what was there, even if he was unaware of its import or utility, simply because it was there. Source, authority, was paramount.

[207] *DIB*, 242–8.

the land of England and confiscate from his subjects, invaders and natives alike, whatever was found above a certain quantity. With the king's consent he measured all the ploughlands, which in English are called hides, with a rope, and made a record of them; setting aside the measures which the open-handed English freely apportioned by command of King Edward, he reduced their size and cut back the fields of the peasants to increase the royal taxes. So by reducing the land which had long been held in peace and increasing the burden of the new taxation he brutally oppressed the king's helpless and faithful subjects, impoverished them by confiscations, and reduced them from comfortable prosperity to the verge of starvation.[208]

Surely this is a reference to the compilation of Domesday Book.[209]

It seems to me that the aftermath of the revolt of 1088 provides a likely context in the light of the tenurial uncertainty that the rebellion had occasioned.[210] The need for information on the tenure of land, both the king's and that of his tenants-in-chief, before the revolt is patent. Royal demesne was plundered throughout the kingdom and the supporters of both parties seized estates of their opponents where they could.[211] The relevance of the Domesday data after this is, arguably, less convincing. Nevertheless, this dating of Domesday Book is speculative – it could indeed be later and Rannulf's interest in the exploitation of regalia to its fullest extent would have been a sufficient motive at any time[212] – and moreover it does not satisfactorily date LDB. As I have argued, LDB was indubitably the model for GDB, but one cannot assume that it was written with something like GDB in mind. It is certainly the same type of creature as the GDB that it inspired, but it is not inconceivable that it was originally compiled for other purposes. Was it an enterprise that was recognized as a good idea and taken over by the scribe of GDB? There will be no answers until LDB has received the detailed study that it deserves and has so far been denied.

Rannulf Flambard has figured before as the likely man behind the Domesday project. Speculation on the author of the whole enterprise has been one of the minor but diverting themes of Domesday studies. Galbraith fingered Samson the priest, later bishop of Worcester, on the somewhat flimsy ground that the

---

[208] *The Ecclesiastical History of Orderic Vitalis*, ed. M. Chibnall, 6 vols (Oxford, 1969–80), iv, 172.

[209] Orderic is vilified by those who strive to maintain Galbraithian orthodoxy, but it must be remembered that his account, the first of the purpose of the Domesday inquest, is well informed as to the centrality of the ploughland and service.

[210] Sir James Holt ('Domesday Studies 2000', 24) asserts that the tenurial chaos of 1088 has been exaggerated. The Anglo-Saxon Chronicler stresses that *terra regis* was widely seized by the rebels (*ASC*, 166–8). For the forfeitures and grants of land in the aftermath of the rebellion, see J. A. Green, *The Aristocracy of Norman England* (Cambridge, 1997), 274–7.

[211] F. Barlow, *William Rufus* (London, 1983), 53–98.

[212] J. O. Prestwich, 'The Career of Ranulf Flambard', *Anglo-Norman Durham, 1093–1193*, eds D. Rollason, M. Harvey, and M. Prestwich (Woodbridge, 1994), 299–310.

account of his manor of Templecombe is entered in Exon by the scribe of GDB.[213] Chaplais has made a somewhat more substantial case for William de St Calais, the bishop of Durham, based on the Durham affinities of the same hand.[214] Sally Harvey has identified Rannulf who, she claims, as master of St Martin's Dover was responsible for the anomalous survey of the foundation, preserved in Domesday Book but compiled before 1085, that was to be the model for the survey of the England of the following year.[215] However, it should be noted that the argument here is that he was only the man behind Domesday *Book*. Although it seems extremely likely that the brains behind the work had been closely involved in the inquest, there is no evidence that Rannulf was the main instigator. Indeed, once we dispose of the concept of a fully integrated executive Domesday process, there is no necessity to believe that a single individual was the driving force behind it. William consulted with his council, and, as we know, the survey was undertaken through the normal channels of local government with only the guiding hand of commissioners. Whatever decisions came out of it were again thrashed out within a consultative context. The inquest was first and foremost a communal activity invoked to tackle communal problems.[216]

Abbreviations were another matter. By their nature they were compiled to preserve what was considered to be of more than ephemeral value in the data collected in the inquest. It is hardly surprising, then, that names of jurors, the record of livestock, and claims were jettisoned: they were of little intrinsic interest outside the specific context in which the data had been demanded. By the same token, the resulting abstracts had no legal force, at least at the time when they were first compiled. In the eleventh and twelfth centuries writing was authoritative because it was writing, but clearly the fact of writing down cannot have immediately changed the nature of the verdicts presented by the jurors in 1086. It was time that conferred authority.

Domesday Book was almost certainly compiled for administrative purposes within the king's government. As we have seen, the earliest references to it do not suggest great familiarity with its contents and indicate that it was not widely

[213] Exon, 153v; GDB, 87d: *DB Somerset*, 4,1; V. H. Galbraith, 'Notes on the Career of Samson, Bishop of Worcester (1096–1112)', *EHR*, 82 (1967), 86–101.
[214] P. Chaplais, 'William of Saint-Calais and the Domesday Survey', *Domesday Studies*, ed. J. C. Holt (Woodbridge, 1987), 65–77.
[215] S. P. J. Harvey, 'Domesday Book and Anglo-Norman Governance', *TRHS*, 5th series, 25 (1975), 190–3. The peculiarities she cites are the placing of the account in the 'shire' section of the Kent Domesday, anomalous diplomatic, a summary account of the lands lost to Odo of Bayeux, the absence of ploughlands, and the appearance of TRE geld assessments where the rest of the Kent text has TRW. In reality, none of these is particularly odd in the context of Domesday accounts of county towns and customs. The best explanation would be that St Martin's was surveyed in the initial survey of the royal demesne and customs as a royal foundation. See below, p. 131 and note 109, for a discussion.
[216] D. R. Roffe, 'Talking to Others: The Domesday Inquest' (forthcoming).

disseminated.[217] Significantly, the work is first referred to as 'the king's book', and thereafter it is known variously as 'the book of the treasury', 'the book of the Exchequer', and 'the register'.[218] It was evidently compiled for the king's use alone. It is perhaps appropriate that someone like Rannulf, one of the greatest administrators in medieval England, was its begetter.

[217] See above, p. 2.
[218] V. H. Galbraith, *Domesday Book: its Place in Administrative History* (Oxford, 1974), 100–4.

4

The Domesday Boroughs

THERE WERE 120 or so settlements in Domesday Book that can be categorized as in some sense urban. Fifteen are called cities (*civitas*), the remainder, either directly or by implication, boroughs (*burgus*).[1] *Civitas* translates OE *cæster*, 'city, walled town, fortification', and refers to former Roman settlements. *Burgus*, representing OE *burh*, 'stronghold', had less specific connotations.[2] There was many a borough, even major ones like Derby, that had never been defended.[3] By the eleventh century *burgus* had come to mean something like the modern 'town', and as such embraced all settlements of the kind, including cities.[4] A vibrant urban economy had long characterized English society. York, Lincoln, Norwich, London, Winchester had been major urban centres of an international stature from at least the early tenth century. Many smaller county boroughs had flourished as local and regional markets from the same period.[5] Archaeological excavations in the last forty years have demonstrated just how diversified was their industrial base and how wide were their trading contacts. The boroughs that the Normans found in 1066 were rich, complex settlements with a long history of urban life.[6]

---

[1] H. C. Darby, *Domesday England* (Cambridge, 1977), 289–320. Forty-eight are expressly termed 'borough', the rest are characterized by the presence of burgesses (*burgenses*).

[2] D. N. Parsons and T. Styles, *The Vocabulary of English Place-Names (Brace-Cæster)*, Centre for English Names Studies (Nottingham, 2000), 74–85, 158–62.

[3] In 917 four of Æthelfæda's thegns were killed within the gates of 'Derby' (*ASC*, 64–5), but the defences were those of the Roman fort at Little Chester (R. Birss and H. Wheeler, 'Roman Derby: Excavations 1968–83', *Derbyshire Archaeological Journal*, 105 (1985), 11).

[4] S. Reynolds, 'Towns in Domesday', *Domesday Studies*, ed. J. C. Holt (Woodbridge, 1987), 295. Chester, Exeter, Chelmsford, Gloucester, and Worcester are each referred to as both cities and boroughs.

[5] H. Swanson, *Medieval British Towns* (New York, 1999). The view that there were no truly urban settlements until after the Conquest (C. Stephenson, *Borough and Town: A Study of Urban Origins in England* (Cambridge, Mass., 1933)) is no longer tenable.

[6] J. Schofield and A. Vince, *Medieval Towns* (London, 1994).

It is now realized that their origins and patterns of development were various. In the past most thinking about towns had been reductionist.[7] From the nineteenth century attempts were made to define urban status as if it was a legalistic quantity founded in charters of liberties or the like. The work of Ballard, himself a town clerk, epitomizes the approach of historians who were steeped in Victorian notions of rational town government.[8] But not all accounts were so simplistic. Maitland was not immune to the intellectual climate of the time, but his account of boroughs, in *Domesday Book and Beyond* and his study of Cambridge in *Township and Borough*, was by far the most nuanced.[9] He recognized that boroughs were settlements that retained rural characteristics; most had fields[10] and agriculture was still a significant activity for townsmen in the eleventh century. Nevertheless, he accepted that they had a special status that distinguished them, both legally and functionally, from the surrounding countryside. For him the defining feature was tenurial heterogeneity – despite the pre-eminence of the king, no lord had a monopoly of land or rights – and this was a direct function of their origin as garrisons. In the late ninth and early tenth centuries a network of boroughs was set up to counter the Danish settlement of England and then contain it. The lords of the shire assigned to each borough were burdened with the duty of repairing its defences and attending its court and so in the discharge of their obligations they acquired houses in town to accommodate their men. In 1066 their successors, their men now merchants and tradesmen, still owed the same types of service and so it was that the borough was afforded special treatment in the Domesday inquest as the centre of shire administration.

Tait effectively demolished this, the garrison theory, in his review of *Domesday Book and Beyond*.[11] Repair of the borough defences was indeed incumbent on the thegns of the shire in a system set out in minute detail in the tenth-century document known as the Burghal Hidage.[12] But estates had been burdened with borough defence long before the Danish settlements and, furthermore, many rural

---

[7] For a review of the historiography and an important contribution to the debate, see G. H. Martin, 'Domesday Book and the Boroughs', *Domesday Book: A Reassessment*, ed. P. H. Sawyer (London, 1985), 143–63.

[8] A. Ballard, *The Domesday Borough* (Oxford, 1904).

[9] F. W. Maitland, *Domesday Book and Beyond* (Cambridge, 1897); *Township and Borough* (Cambridge, 1898).

[10] In the Domesday account of Grantham in Lincolnshire it is stated that 'There is no arable land outside the vill' (GDB, 337v: *DB Lincs*, 1,9). The town has never had fields, the territory of surrounding vills coming right up to the Mowbeck, the boundary ditch of the town. Lack of fields is characteristic of some post-Conquest plantations in which borough and manor remain distinct. Grantham, however, is not obviously of this type.

[11] J. Tait, Review of F. W. Maitland, *Domesday Book and Beyond*, *EHR*, 12 (1897), 768–77.

[12] A. R. Rumble, 'An Edition and Translation of the Burghal Hidage', *The Defence of Wessex: The Burghal Hidage and Anglo-Saxon Fortification*, eds D. Hill and A. R. Rumble (Manchester, 1996), 14–35.

estates had from an early period maintained houses in boroughs for access to their courts and markets.[13] Clearly some towns were initially created as fortresses and garrisons, but not all. It is now recognized that tenurial heterogeneity can be a function of a number of processes. Major east-coast and south-coast ports such as Boston, King's Lynn, and Hastings were established around, probably originally seasonal, markets in marginal locations.[14] They do not feature in Domesday Book or only vestigially so, and yet by the mid twelfth century they exhibited every bit as much tenurial heterogeneity as any Domesday borough. The characteristic is not even particularly urban. All and sundry had salt pits and houses in the salterns around Droitwich, and the great and good of Lindsey had estates in the immediate vicinity of the remote Lissingleys where the court of Lindsey seems to have met.[15]

All sorts of urban origins and functions are now recognized. In addition to fortress foundations, towns developed around castles, markets, churches or shrines, major estate centres, even convenient locations, or, indeed, any combination of these. In 1086 there was no common denominator that defined a borough. Susan Reynolds has even argued that we should abandon the term 'borough', because of the legal connotations of the word, in favour of the vaguer 'town'.[16] For her, just as townies today see themselves as different from countrymen, so did burgesses in 1086. Although they were aware of all sorts of continuities between the urban and rural, continuities eloquently described by Robin Fleming,[17] they knew that they were other in the variety of their occupations and the diversity of their urban society and economy. This was a consciousness, the argument goes on, that was recognized by the Domesday commissioners in accepting a special procedure for these especially complex settlements. Towns did not fit into the seigneurial schema of the Domesday process, and burgesses thus presented their evidence as a community. So it was that the compilers of Domesday Book chose to enter them, regardless of lordship, 'above the line' in Maitland's phrase, at the head of each

[13] N. P. Brooks, 'The Development of Military Obligations in Eighth- and Ninth-Century England', *England before the Conquest*, eds P. Clemoes and K. Hughes (Cambridge, 1971), 69–84; J. Tait, *The Medieval English Borough* (Manchester, 1936), 26.
[14] D. M. Owen, 'The Beginnings of the Port of Boston', *A Prospect of Lincolnshire*, eds N. Field and A. White (Lincoln, 1984), 42–5; D. M. Owen, *The Making of King's Lynn*, British Academy, Records of Social and Economic History, new series, 9 (1984); M. Gardiner, 'Shipping and Trade between England and the Continent during the Eleventh Century', *ANS*, 22 (1999), 71–94.
[15] There were manors with appurtenances in Droitwich, itself apparently some sort of town, in Buckinghamshire, Gloucestershire, Herefordshire, Oxfordshire, Shropshire, Warwickshire, and Worcestershire. For Lissingleys, see D. R. Roffe, 'Lissingleys and the Meeting Place of Lindsey', online at http://www.roffe.co.uk/lindsey.htm.
[16] Reynolds, 'Towns in Domesday', 295.
[17] R. Fleming, 'Rural Elites and Urban Communities in Late Anglo-Saxon England', *Past and Present*, 141 (1993), 3–37.

county. The result, messy and incomplete as it has seemed to generations of urban historians, is a reasonably comprehensive account of a phenomenon that was as difficult for the Domesday scribe to categorize as for us.

Reynolds' final admonition to stop the moaning and be thankful for what we have is well deserved. Her analysis succinctly summarizes the present consensus on the distinctiveness of the Domesday borough. But how far is it consistent with what can be perceived of the Domesday scribe's perception of 'towns'? We shall have to start with the sources of the Domesday accounts, the various juries that made presentments. We shall also have to consider the various forms that the accounts take. Why should there have been such diversity? Above all we shall have to examine why descriptions of boroughs are not the only items of information to be entered above the line. Borough customs might be considered imperceptively to merge into county customs to account for their inclusion,[18] but why were the Welsh commotes of Archenfield and what was later known as Monmouthshire treated in the same way? The scribe of GDB did indeed have an idea of what he should insert into the spaces he left at the head of each county, and that idea comprehended much more than accounts of towns.

In the present discussion the term 'borough' is retained. The reader will understand that it is not intended to carry overtones of charters, borough farms, or municipal reform acts. Borough was, though, a term that was used by the scribe to describe something meaningful for him. We shall pay little attention to many settlements, which may or may not be called boroughs, in which burgesses are found. In some cases it might be suspected that such burgesses paid their dues to the lord of the manor and were otherwise resident elsewhere.[19] Others must indicate nascent urban development. But we shall consider them only where there is evidence of a degree of tenurial heterogeneity.[20] In looking at this sample of boroughs, whether they be entered above the line or in the body of the text, we shall better be able to see how the Domesday scribes dealt with their sources and what perceptions they brought to the job of representing them.

[18] See, for example, Chester (GDB, 262v: *DB Cheshire*, C).

[19] There were three burgesses rendering 30d in the bishop of Winchester's manor of Houghton in Hampshire, for example, but there was no borough (GDB, 40v: *DB Hants*, 2,20 and note). The burgesses were resident in either Winchester or Stockbridge.

[20] Domesday evidence alone is considered. The dividing line is not always clear cut. In Grantham there were 77 tofts 'of the sokemen of the thegns', but no tenant-in-chief owned up to having land in the town apart from the bishop of Durham, who claimed tofts in succession to Earnwine the priest, and the abbot of Peterborough and/or Kolgrimr (GDB, 337v: *DB Lincs*, 1,9).

The borough and the Domesday inquest

At the outset, it is clear that there was no special inquest procedure and no single burghal presentment. It is an apparent truism to state that boroughs are described as settlements rather than as a series of estates, but the reality is somewhat different. Of the sixty-two boroughs studied here, only twelve conform to this supposed norm (Table 4.1). Most of the remaining fifty have some sort of account at the head of the county, but references to various parcels of land occur throughout the body of the text in the account of rural manors. This disparity has been explained as a failure by the Domesday scribes to assimilate the comments of rural juries into the main presentment by the burgess community.[21] That, however, begs the question; the information from the rural juries is additional as opposed to supplementary. Furthermore, an examination of the manuscripts shows that even in the twelve compound borough entries the unity of the account is illusory. It has already been noted that the dues of the king are entered first, often followed by a value for the whole, and then various devices like the *paragraphos* distinguish the rights of other holders of land as in some way different.[22]

These peculiarities of the accounts of boroughs are perfectly explicable in terms of the two-stage Domesday inquest process we have already described.[23] It is clear from a relatively large number of presentments that the lands and dues of the king were surveyed in the first stage by the officers of the shire.[24] In line with an inquest into the resources of the crown, jurors from the burgess community appear to have presented verdicts on what dues were rendered TRE, what in 1086, what the town was worth, and the reason for any shortfalls.[25] Additionally, they made an account of geld payment.[26] Judging from the description of Colchester, detailed evidence might be provided: here the text provides a long list of named burgesses with an account of the tenements that each held.[27] There is a similar, although shorter, list of burgesses who held wall houses in Oxford and were therefore quit of custom.[28]

---

[21] Reynolds, 'Towns in Domesday', 302–3.

[22] See above, pp. 77–8.

[23] Above, pp. 74–87.

[24] GDB, 13, 32, 56, 163, 252, 298, 336: *DB Kent*, 9,9; *DB Surrey*, 5,28; *DB Berks*, B1; *DB Gloucs*, 1,21; *DB Salop*, C14; *DB Yorks*, C2; 10; *DB Lincs*, C4; 16.

[25] GDB, 56, 13, 336, 298: *DB Berks*, B1; *DB Kent*, 9,9; *DB Lincs*, C4; 16; *DB Yorks*, C2; 10.

[26] See the account of Lincoln for the geld inquest (GDB, 336: *DB Lincs*, C20). The burgesses of Shrewsbury complained about the increased burden of geld that they had to bear because of the number of tenements that had become exempt in one way or another. Note that this entry is apparently postscriptal. Robert of Stafford appears to have given evidence in Stafford on the borough farm, probably in his capacity as sheriff (GDB, 246: *DB Staffs*, B12).

[27] LDB, 104–6: *DB Essex*, B3a.

[28] GDB, 154: *DB Oxon*, B10.

Table 4.1 *Domesday borough entry forms*

County	Borough	Separate chapter	King's chapter	Lords' chapters
Essex	Colchester	k?t		t
	Maldon		k	t
Norfolk	Norwich		c	
	Thetford		c	
	Yarmouth		c	
Suffolk	Sudbury		k	
	Ipswich		k	t
	Dunwich			t
Yorkshire	York	c		
Lincolnshire	Lincoln	c		
	Stamford	c		
	Torksey	c		
Nottinghamshire	Nottingham	c		
	Derby	c		
Derbyshire				
Huntingdonshire	Huntingdon	c		
Cambridgeshire	Cambridge	k		t
Middlesex				
Bedfordshire	Bedford	d		
Buckinghamshire	Buckingham	c		
Hertfordshire	Hertford	c		
Kent	Dover	k		
	Canterbury	k		t
	Rochester			t
Sussex	Chichester			t
	Arundel			c
	Pevensey			c
	Lewes			c
	Hastings			t
Surrey	Guildford		kt	t
	Southwark		k	t
Berkshire	Wallingford	k		t
Hampshire	Southampton	kt		t
	Winchester			t
Wiltshire	Malmesbury	k?t		t
	Wilton	d		t
	Cricklade	d		t
	Salisbury	d		

County	Borough	Separate chapter	King's chapter	Lords' chapters
Dorset	Dorchester	k		t
	Bridport	k		t
	Wareham	kt		t
	Shaftesbury	kt		
	Wimbourne			
Somerset	Bath		k	t
	Langport		k	t
	Ilchester		d	t
	Bruton		d	t
	Frome		d	
Devon	Exeter	k		t
	Barnstaple	d	k	t
	Lydford	d	k	t
	Totnes	d		t
Cornwall				
Gloucestershire	Gloucester	k		t
	Winchcombe	d		t
	Bristol			
Worcestershire	Worcester	d		t
Herefordshire	Hereford	d		t
Shropshire	Shrewsbury	k		t
Cheshire	Chester	k		t
Staffordshire	Stafford	kt		t
Warwickshire	Warwick	kt	d	t
Northamptonshire	Northampton	c		
Oxfordshire	Oxford	kt		t (1)
Leicestershire	Leicester	kt		t

c = composite account, k = king's lands, d = king's dues only, t = tenants-in-chief's lands

In Chester and Shrewsbury fines that accrued to the king and earl from all manner of misdeeds are described in full.[29] All of this information, however, looks as if it was derived from written sources.[30] Verbal presentments were probably more

[29] GDB, 262v, 252: *DB Cheshire*, C3–14; *DB Salop*, 2–12.
[30] Martin, 'Domesday Book and the Boroughs', 157. None of the information is obviously postscriptal, but various calligraphic devices suggest discrete sources. The list of Colchester burgesses (LDB, 104–6: *DB Essex*, B2a) is headed by a title ('These are the burgesses of the king who render customary dues'), and, unusually for LDB, entries are not pointed up by the *paragraphos* (gallows sign). For the most recent discussion of the section, see P. Taylor,

concise; at the very least, the data were summarized at an early stage. Thus, the summary form of the GDB accounts of the West Country boroughs is already evident in Exon. By and large, the result is remarkably consistent. There are, of course, lacunae. Bedford might as well not appear at all for all the information that the Domesday account affords. However, the town had never been assessed in hides and so it is likely that it simply fell outside Domesday's remit.[31] Just the bare details are provided for Wilton, Cricklade, Salisbury, Winchcombe, and Hereford.[32] Otherwise, the number of tenements owing services to the king and the value of the town as a whole are generally fully recorded.

As in the survey of the king's lands in Winchester of *c.*1110, the inquiry process must have uncovered much information about the tenements held by tenants-in-chief.[33] Since 1066 many lords had encroached onto the king's dues, burdening the remaining burgesses with increased rents and taxes. Many a reference to messuages that 'ought to render all customs' must have been supplied by the local jurors. The geld inquest may have uncovered others. The tenements proper of the tenants-in-chief, however, were probably surveyed in the second stage of the Domesday inquest before the commissioners. Only one explicit presentment has been identified, delivered, significantly, by the shire rather than the burgesses, and it concerns the right of the bishop of Bayeux to properties in Guildford in Surrey as lord of the manor of Bramley.[34] It is typical of the verdicts relating to rural estates, and there therefore seems no reason to doubt that urban possessions of tenants-in-chief

'Introduction', *Little Domesday Book, Essex*, eds A. Williams and G. H. Martin (London, 2000), 13–14. The so-called 'Laws of Chester' (GDB, 262v: *DB Cheshire*, C3–14) are clearly distinguished from the rest of the Chester text. The account begins with an enlarged square rubricated capital P for the first entry (*Pax data manu regis* ...), and the end is indicated by a smaller but again rubricated O for *Omnium harum forisfacturarum* ... The following section, 'county customs' is signalled by an enlarged square and rubricated S. Similar devices are used in the account of Shrewsbury. Susan Reynolds has doubted that schedules were widely used because they were so soon out of date in the rapidly changing society of the borough ('Towns in Domesday', 302). There was certainly much change between 1066 and 1086, but there was continuity of tenurial units. In Winchester, for example, boundaries remained constant from the tenth century into the modern period. The messuage had a legal identity that paralleled this physical continuity and that is what the commissioners were interested in. Schedules of holders could and did remain of relevance to administrators long after the demise of the tenants. The Winchester survey of *c.*1110 was based on a schedule of *c.*1057 (*Winchester in the Early Middle Ages: An Edition and Discussion of the Winton Domesday*, ed. M. Biddle, Winchester Studies, 1 (Oxford, 1976), 9–10, 407).

[31] GDB, 209: *DB Beds*, B. For the relationship between the Domesday inquest and the geld, see below, pp. 183–209, 312–3.
[32] GDB, 64v, 162v, 179: *DB Wilts*, B1;3–4.*DB Gloucs*, B1.*DB Hereford*, C1.
[33] *Winchester in the Early Middle Ages*, 9–18.
[34] GDB, 30: *DB Surrey*, 1,1. The hundred of Brixton testified in relation to a dispute between Odo of Bayeux and the sheriff of Surrey in Southwark. By contrast, 'the men of Southwark' bore witness about toll (GDB, 32: *DB Surrey*, 5,28).

were surveyed at the same time and in the same way. This is certainly the best explanation for how urban properties came to be enrolled with the manors to which they belonged throughout much of Domesday Book (Table 4.1). How thorough the account was is difficult to gauge. Boroughs like Oxford, Wallingford, Northampton, and Leicester seem to have been host to just about every major lord, and many more minor ones, in their respective shires and beyond.[35] It is, then, suspicious that only six lords are named in the Cambridgeshire account.[36] Later documentation can sometimes suggest that Domesday lords did not always record all their urban properties. Some properties, of course, may well be silently included in the list of 'king's' burgesses if customs were rendered to the king.[37] However, many, as appurtenances of rural manors, may have simply been omitted, like many another appurtenance. In other words, the account of seigneurial lands in boroughs is probably no worse than that of the corresponding rural estates.

The process of data collection must have produced documentation that was similar in form to that which more generally emanated from each stage of the inquiry.[38] As Galbraith divined,[39] the decision to enter boroughs as a whole above the line was taken by the compilers of Domesday Book. In Exon urban lands are entered in the chapter of the appropriate lord (the king or otherwise) where a context can be determined.[40] In LDB Ipswich and Sudbury exhibit the same form as the boroughs of Exon,[41] and Colchester is similar, although the customary

---

[35] GDB, 154, 56, 230, 219: *DB Oxon*, B; *DB Berks*, B; *DB Leics*, C; *DB Northants*, B.

[36] GDB, 189: *DB Cambs*, B.

[37] In the Exon account of Devon, however, such customary houses are noticed at the end of each lord's chapter.

[38] The first stage of the inquest is probably represented by three documents. An account of Canterbury is enrolled in the Excerpta of St Augustine's, Canterbury (*Excerpta*, 6–10). It is more expansive than the GDB account and, significantly, is part of a document that almost certainly emanates from the first stage of the Domesday inquest (*DIB*, 130–40, 174n). The lands of Ely Abbey in Cambridge are described ward by ward in IE (121), but apart from naming the second ward and omitting the lands of other tenants-in-chief, the account does not differ from the GDB counterpart. The customary lands of Gloucester and Winchcombe are entered in Evesham K in far more detail than GDB (*DB Gloucs*, EvK1). Although numerous tenants-in-chief are named, none are so in respect of non-customary lands. The second stage of the inquest before the commissioners may be represented by a York document known as 'The Rights and Laws of the Archbishop of York' (D. M. Palliser, *Domesday York* (York, 1990), 25). It is witnessed by the sheriff, along with five other Norman lords, but also twelve men of York and all the city bore witness. The document is not securely dated and it cannot be firmly associated with the Domesday inquest.

[39] V. H. Galbraith, *Domesday Book: its Place in Administrative History* (Oxford, 1974), 152–3.

[40] Wareham and Shaftesbury contain accounts of some seigneurial lands, but they were probably customary.

[41] The two boroughs were otherwise anomalous, for the dues of Ipswich belonged to the queen and earl (LDB, 290: *DB Suffolk*, 1,122a) and Earl Morcar's mother held Sudbury (LDB, 286v: *DB Suffolk*, 1,97).

lands are entered in a separate section after the *invasiones* at the end of the county folios.[42] Norwich, Thetford, and Yarmouth, by contrast, are described in compound accounts – royal and seigneurial lands together – after the main section of the *terra regis*.[43] The further decision to enter boroughs at the head of each county was taken by the compiler of GDB. Accordingly, a space was left for a borough (although it was not always filled) in every county except Surrey, Somerset, and Cornwall.[44] Compound accounts, however, were not always inserted (Table 4.1). The boroughs of Circuits VI and III caused no problems. Burgesses of Lincoln, Stamford and Cambridge are described in the manors of Scotton, Uffington and Linton, but they duplicate information entered in the respective borough.[45] Thereafter, however, only Northampton is unambiguously entered as a compound account. Sometimes the king's dues alone are listed at the head of the county. More often, a few tenements of the tenants-in-chief are also included while others are found in the appropriate *breves*.

There is little or no overlap of this material; if a lord's own land appears in the account of the borough at the head of the county it will generally not appear in his *breve* and vice versa.[46] It is possible, then, that the GDB scribe attempted to rearrange his materials better to realize his programme for the boroughs.[47] How successful he was seems to have been dependent on the form of his sources. The compound accounts predominantly occur in those circuits (VII, VI and III) in which the verdicts were geographically arranged. There the scribe presumably had before him an account of the lands of the tenants-in-chief in each borough, as he had for the vills in the rest of the county.[48] He simply had to join it with the account of the king's lands. Where his sources were like Exon, it was too difficult to rearrange the materials, and he merely copied what he had before him.

From this perspective the lamentations about the deficiencies of the Domesday record of boroughs can often be shown to be misplaced. The absence of Winchester,

---

[42] LDB, 104–7v: *DB Essex*, B. There are echoes here of the treatment of the *taini regis*.

[43] LDB, 116–19: *DB Norfolk*, 1,61–70.

[44] Guildford is entered as the first estate in the *terra regis* in Surrey. In Berkshire Wallingford is anomalously entered after the list of landholders, but still before the king's lands (GDB, 209: *DB Berks*, B).

[45] GDB, 336, 336v, 345v, 358, 189, 194: *DB Lincs*, C20.S11.8,15.27,35; *DB Cambs*, B,12.14,12. Duplication here suggests that the GDB scribe was following his sources.

[46] In Colchester there may be some duplication; the figures given in the *breves* are, however, different from those in the main account.

[47] He is known to have rearranged Exon material in Devon. There the account of the customary tenements held by the tenants-in-chief had been postscriptally appended to the end of each section. But in the process of compilation, the GDB scribe moved the entries to the head of each chapter rather than to the account of the borough at the head of the county.

[48] The account of Ely's lands in Cambridge in IE may be taken from such a document (IE, 121).

for example, is frequently remarked. But in reality, much of the account is there in the Hampshire *breves*. It is unlikely that the scribe ever seriously considered putting together all the notices of city tenements in the account of rural manors (he did not do so for all boroughs, either in the area or at that stage in his work). Had he done so, though, it is unlikely that the account of the non-customary lands in Winchester would have said much more than:

> *The following have the customary dues from their houses in Winchester by grant of King William: the King 13, the Bishop of Winchester 8, Archbishop Thomas 1, St Peter of Westminster 1, Romsey Abbey 14, the Church of Wherwell 31 and a mill worth 48s, Earl Roger 1, Hugh de Port 1, Ralf de Mortimer 8 Bernard Pauncevolt 1, Hugh fitzBaldric 1, Miles the porter 1, Odo of Winchester 8, the sons of Godric Malf 1.*[49]

What is missing is any information about customary tenements and the render of the city. No doubt some comment would have been made about the land 'on which is the king's house in the city', which was acquired from St Peter's in exchange for land in Kingsclere, and such like.[50] Otherwise, a summary total of tenements would have been given: the Winchester Survey of *c.*1110 suggests that the figure would have been in the region of 250, of which as many as 33 may have ceased to render customs in 1086.[51] There were, of course, many other tenements – the later twelfth-century survey suggests at least 750 – but many, probably most, of these were probably beyond the remit of the Domesday inquest.[52] Finally, there may have been a statement of the value of the city (although this is absent in the account of Southampton) which, twelfth-century evidence would suggest,[53] was no more than £80. Winchester is not absent from Domesday Book. The account may be incomplete – and it may not satisfy what we would like – but it is only deficient if a composite description is considered the norm. It was not.

[49] GDB, 38v, 39, 40v, 42, 43v, 43v, 44, 44v, 45, 46v, 47v, 48, 49v, 51v: *DB Hants*, 1,19;25;42.2, 11.4,1.8,1.15,1.16,7.21,2.23,19.29,3.39,3.44,3.68,7.69,2;7.NF9,37. The form adopted is based on the account of Southampton. The various manorial accounts give values but these would probably not have been reproduced. For possible omissions, see *Winchester in the Early Middle Ages*, ed. Biddle, 382–4.

[50] GDB, 43: *DB Hants*, 6,9; *Winchester in the Early Middle Ages*, ed. Biddle, Survey I, 57.

[51] *Winchester in the Early Middle Ages*, ed. Biddle, 11. A further 22 tenements may have been 'taken away' by tenants-in-chief.

[52] In Survey II of *c.*1148 131 of the bishop's 402 tenements are marked as *de terra baronum*, *de t' b'* or *de B*. Were these entries the only ones that were *warland*, i.e. liable to the geld, and therefore the proper concern of the king? The formulas confused the editors, but they do at least indicate that the status of holdings was not uniform (*Winchester in the Early Middle Ages*, ed. Biddle, 18–25).

[53] Tait, *The Medieval English Borough*, 171.

Society and economy

The diverse sources of the Domesday account of boroughs reflect a basic dichotomy in tenurial structure. Townsmen, sheriffs, and commissioners seem to have believed that burgesses or properties (the terms are apparently interchangeable) either paid customs to the king or they paid them to another lord. The distinction informs every entry in the texts. What we shall call the 'customary tenements', the ones that paid the customs to the king, were royal demesne and they constituted the borough proper.[54] In contrast to the practice in LDB, they are generally treated in a cursory manner in GDB; only totals are given, with justification for any shortfall from the TRE figure, along with a note of appurtenant churches, mills, and land. The dues they owed are rarely explicit, but can be reconstructed from the many exemptions that are noted in the text. A tenement might render geld, heriot, tolls, landgable, mint tax, baking dues, and soke to the king and earl.[55] These were the sorts of dues that were owed from the land of free men and sokemen in the countryside.[56] In Stamford seventy-seven townsmen are explicitly called sokemen and indeed in later medieval legal treatises a broad similarity between tenure in burgage and tenure in socage is apparent.[57] Occasionally burgesses were obliged to render light labour dues like cartage,[58] but the burden of service was not great, and they seem to have had full freedom of person, property, and trade.[59]

It was these burgesses who paid the borough farm, the annual sum owed to the king from each borough, which is typically recorded immediately after the account of their tenements. They also owed renders in kind, such as honey and iron, like royal manors.[60] Non-customary lands were of a different order. Some were of recent origin and were not always licit. We repeatedly hear of tenements

[54] For an explicit notice of tenements 'of the borough', see GDB, 280: *DB Notts*, B4: 'In Nottingham there is 1 church in the king's demesne, to which belong 3 messuages of the borough and 5 bovates of land of the above-mentioned 6 carucates with sake and soke, and to the same church belong 5½ acres of land of which the king has sake and soke.'

[55] Tait, *Medieval English Borough*, 96–108.

[56] W. Stubbs, *Constitutional History of England*, i, 409; F. Pollock and F. W. Maitland, *The History of English Law*, 2nd edn, 2 vols (Cambridge, 1923), i, 293–6.

[57] GDB, 336v: *DB Lincs*, S4. W. H. Stevenson, 'Land Tenures in Nottinghamshire', *Old Nottinghamshire*, 1st series, ed. S. P. Briscoe (Nottingham, 1881), 66–71. Pollock and Maitland, *History of English Law*, i, 647; ii, 279. Borough English, inheritance by the youngest son, is the most apparent common custom.

[58] GDB, 179: *DB Hereford*, C3. In Nottingham the 'works' of the burgesses may have been labour dues (GDB, 280: *DB Notts*, B11).

[59] A certain Edstan in Norwich could not withdraw his land without the king's permission (LDB, 116: *DB Norfolk*, 1,61). In Hereford townsmen had to ask permission to sell their land and the reeve was entitled to a third of the proceeds (GDB, 179: *DB Hereford*, C2). Their heriot was somewhat less than that of a lesser thegn. However, these two instances would seem to be very much the exception.

[60] See, for example, Colchester, Gloucester, Leicester, Oxford, and Warwick.

that had formerly rendered custom and no longer did so. The Norman settlement
had seen the grant of some dues and the wholesale appropriation of many others;
a principal aim of the Domesday inquests in the towns was to determine what
dues the king had lost since 1066. Others had been exempt from custom in 1066
and, no doubt, long before. The circumstances were various. Some were held by
especially privileged townsmen. In both Lincoln and Stamford there were twelve
lawmen who, holding with sake and soke, rendered no customs.[61] They were
probably expert doomsmen who declared the law in the borough court and formed
an urban patriciate.[62] The lawmen of Cambridge may have been of similar status:
with a heriot of £8 and 'the arms of 1 knight' they were directly comparable to a
king's thegn.[63] Especially privileged burgesses, like the nineteen in Warwick who
held with sake and soke, the eight in Bedford with land outside the borough,
and the 'better citizens' in Shrewsbury,[64] may represent urban movers and shakers
elsewhere. Moneyers were also quit. In Wallingford one rendered no custom as
long as he did the coining; seven in Hereford held with sake and soke as did six
in Lincoln who seem also to have been lawmen.[65] Others made a separate render
as moneyers, suggesting a similar status and accounting for the designation of
some of their class as thegns on some eleventh-century coin issues.[66] Holders of

[61] GDB, 336, 336v: *DB Lincs*, C2–3.S5.

[62] In Stamford they survived until the late thirteenth century. They then had their own
courts for the assize of bread and ale. It has been doubted that they had any formal function in 1086 (F. M. Stenton, 'Introduction', *The Lincolnshire Domesday and Lindsey Survey*,
Lincoln Record Society, 19 (1924), xxix–xxx). It seems to me, however, that there is more
than an outside chance that the twelve coroners who kept the king's pleas and made attach-
ments in the town in the early thirteenth century were their successors in office (*Stamford
in the Thirteenth Century: Two Inquisitions from the Reign of Edward I*, ed. D. R. Roffe
(Stamford, 1994), 30). The Lincoln lawmen are uniquely named and some of their successors can be traced through the descent of their lands in Lindsey. Siward the priest's lands
descended to Rumfar who founded a cell of St Mary of York in Lincoln. Aghmund son
of Wælhræfn is represented by the de Paris family which provided numerous bailiffs and
mayors of Lincoln between 1163 and 1245 (J. W. F. Hill, *Medieval Lincoln* (Cambridge, 1948),
339–40, 379–81).

[63] GDB, 189: *DB Cambs*, B13; Robertson, II Cnut 71. Four judges in York had been granted
the customs by the king for as long as they lived (GDB, 298: *DB Yorks*, C1). The judges of
Chester are frequently compared with the lawmen, but they were apparently men of the
king, bishop, and earl: 'There were then 12 judges in the city and these were [chosen] from
the men of the king and of the bishop and of the earl' (GDB, 262v: *DB Cheshire*, C20.
They were presumably of lesser status.

[64] GDB, 238: *DB Warks*, B2; GDB, 218: *DB Beds*, 56; GDB, 252: *DB Salop*, C3. The land
of the Bedford burgesses was enrolled in a separate *breve* before the *taini regis*. Some of
the lawmen of Lincoln held manors in Lindsey TRE, but had lost them by 1086 (Roffe,
'Lissingleys and the Meeting Place of Lindsey', http://www.roffe.co.uk/lindsey.htm).

[65] Hill, *Medieval Lincoln*, 40.

[66] In many towns the land of the moneyer remained as a separate fee held in chief of the
crown throughout much of the Middle Ages. See, for example, Nottingham, where the

major churches and even town mills might also escape customs, as did some who had special duties. The holders of wall houses in Oxford were quit in return for repairing the town wall when it was required.[67]

These urban liberties, for such they became in the later Middle Ages, often under the name of sokes,[68] are probably under-represented in Domesday Book. Within the perceivable procedure of the Domesday inquest in the boroughs they were neither fish nor fowl and may therefore have often escaped notice. Indeed, there is many a town fee with its own court that looks as if it ought to be ancient and yet is not obviously represented in Domesday.[69] This is less true of those fees that belonged to honours. Most non-customary lands in 1086 were held by tenants-in-chief with sake and soke, toll and team, and the dues which normally accrued to the king were rendered to the lord. As always, geld was generally reserved, but otherwise these lands were free of royal service. In Warwick it is said of such tenements that they 'belong to the lands which the barons themselves hold outside the borough and are valued there'.[70] This was the reality of most of them. In

moneyers' land appears year after year in the Pipe Rolls (*PR 1194*, 84; *1195*, 17; *1196*, 267; *1197*, 144). For the operation of the mints in the Domesday boroughs, see D. M. Metcalf, 'The Taxation of Moneyers under Edward the Confessor', *Domesday Studies*, ed. J. C. Holt (London, 1987), 279–93.

[67] GDB, 154: *DB Oxon*, B.

[68] So in Huntingdon (D. R. Roffe, 'An Introduction to the Huntingdonshire Domesday', *The Huntingdonshire Domesday*, eds A. Williams and R. W. H. Erskine (London, 1989), 20–1). The sokes of London are directly comparable: C. N. L. Brooke, *London 800–1216: The Shaping of a City* (London, 1975), 155–7.

[69] Nottingham provides an example. In 1219, Gilbert le Gluton held land and an oven in Nottingham by sergeancy as a royal bailiff errant (*Book of Fees*, 288). The fee was held in chief, and was probably quite extensive. A case brought against Gilbert in the *curia regis* in 1225 by William son of Simon, sought the seisin of seven crofts and half an oven in Nottingham (*Curia Regis Rolls*, xii, 124). Subsequently, it was described as tenements, and later a messuage, with an oven (*Calendar of Patent Rolls 1258–1266*, 29; *List of the Inquisitions Ad Quod Damnum Preserved in the Public Record Office* (New York, 1963), 94). Part of the fee may have been situated in the Saturday Market, for John son of Geoffrey le Gaoler, who was granted the estate in 1306, held at least one toft there within the English Borough (*Rufford Charters*, ed. C. J. Holdsworth, Thoroton Society Record Series, 29, no. 33; *Calendar of Patent Rolls 1301–1307*, 487). But the oven was probably located off Wheeler Gate, possibly in the present Eldon Chambers, for in 1395/6 a tenement on that street was said to abut on a common lane (*venella*) leading to Gilbert le Gluton's oven (Nottinghamshire Record Office, CA 1295, Nottingham Borough Court Enrolments, fol. 2v). The fee can be traced into the late fourteenth century, and throughout the possession of an oven or bake house is carefully noted (*Calendar of Patent Rolls 1334–1338*, 437; *1339–1340*, 258; *1343–1345*, 250–1; *Placita de Quo Warranto*, ed. W. Illingworth, Record Commission (London, 1818), 617; *Inquisitions Ad Quod Damnum*, 365; *Calendar of Close Rolls 1377–1381*, 287). Since the property was a capital tenement, this might imply that Gilbert and his successors had the assize of bread.

[70] GDB, 238: *DB Warks*, B2.

Circuits I, II, IV, and V the manor is identified if the tenements are not entered in the description of the same. In Circuits III, VI, and VII, where compound accounts are found, Domesday is silent, but later evidence shows that the same sorts of relationship obtained.

Non-customary lands, then, stood outside the borough as the compilers of Domesday Book chose to view it. Here and there a contrast is drawn between tenements 'of the borough' and non-customary lands.[71] Some of these non-customary tenements were held in demesne and functioned as a house in town for their lord. Toki son of Auti had a hall in Lincoln, and Thorbiorn a hall and court in Colchester.[72] Most were held by tenants and they were still known as burgesses. Bizarrely, there was one in Ipswich who was a slave.[73] But, although they belonged to rural manors, they generally seem to have been of a similar status to the king's burgesses in 1086. They apparently held their lands by burgage tenure, typically rendering a few pence to their lord, and were as free as their royal counterparts; there is nothing to suggest that their tenements were the real estate of their lords.[74] Some were undoubtedly commended to them and therefore represented their interests in the borough as a sort of affinity, but this was probably the exception.[75] Earl Harold's twenty-seven burgesses in Hereford had 'the same customs as the other burgesses'.[76] In the later Middle Ages their successors are indistinguishable from the body of the urban community lest it be by paying suit to their lord's court in respect of the assizes of bread and ale, that is the regulation of baking and brewing,

[71] See GDB, 280: *DB Notts*, B4. In Chester we hear of 'the bishop's borough', presumably, as opposed to the king's (GDB, 262v: *DB Cheshire*, C1). The bishop of Lincoln's 'little' manor outside Lincoln was known as the borough of Willingthorpe in 1127 (Hill, *Medieval Lincoln*, 61–2).

[72] GDB, 336: *DB Lincs*, C4; LDB, 106: *DB Essex*, B3b.

[73] LDB, 393: *DB Suffolk*, 25,52. Richard son of Count Gilbert, and presumably Fin his predecessor, had sake and soke and commendation over him and several other burgesses.

[74] *Pace* Fleming, 'Rural Elites and Urban Communities', 13–16. The right to soke did not confer rights to land. See below, pp. 153–5. The difference between the hall and tenanted properties is explicit in the account of Toki son of Auti's fee in Lincoln (GDB, 336: *DB Lincs*, C4): 'Toki son of Auti had in the city 30 messuages besides his hall and 2½ churches, and he had his hall quit of every custom, and with respect to another 30 messuages he had rent; and besides this [he had] from each [messuage] 1d, that is landgafol. In respect of these 30 messuages the king had toll and forfeiture, as the burgesses testified.'

[75] Thirty-three men in Thetford were commended to Roger Bigod, forty-one in Ipswich to Robert fitzWimarc, and thirty-two in Norwich to Harold and fifty to Stigand, while the king's burgesses in Thetford are said to be able to be men of whom they chose (LDB, 116, 173, 402: *DB Norfolk*, 1,61.9,1; *DB Suffolk*, 27,8). Otherwise commendation is not noticed even though LDB took a particular interest in the relationship. In GDB burgesses in Buckingham are said to have been 'men' of certain lords (GDB, 143: *DB Bucks*, B), but again the relationship is not prominent. Of course, the issue may not have been raised in urban contexts. Most townsmen, though, were probably in frankpledges of one kind or another.

[76] GDB, 179: *DB Hereford*, C11.

and paying landgable.[77] It is, perhaps, unlikely that there were such courts in 1086; the dues that accrued from the right to sake and soke were probably enjoyed in the communal court.

In 1086 this, the borough court, seems to have been the hundred.[78] In LDB the larger towns appear under hundredal headings of their own – Norwich, Thetford, Ipswich, Colchester, Maldon.[79] In GDB Cambridge and Winchcombe are explicitly said to be hundreds and Bedford a half hundred.[80] The assessment of Huntingdon and Chester at 50 hides each might point to two further half hundreds and there was presumably a hundred of Shrewsbury, for the borough was assessed at 100 hides.[81] Elsewhere there is no comparable evidence, but it seems likely this pattern was typical, at least of the major boroughs.[82] Such a status puts in context the numerous references to the military service due from townsmen.[83] The precise duties varied from area to area. In Hereford and Shrewsbury townsmen had to fight in Wales when the sheriff went with an army;[84] in Maldon a ship had to be provided, in Warwick boatmen;[85] horses had to be found at Leicester and Maldon;[86] more widely townsmen had to 'go on expedition' by land or sea. A money payment could be made in lieu in Oxford and Warwick.[87] However, all these were of the same type that free men owed in the hundred.[88]

---

[77] The existence of such courts occasionally surfaces in routine administrative documents, like inquisitions *post mortem*, but are most fully described in the Ragman Rolls of 1275 (*Rotuli Hundredorum*, ed. W. Illingworth, Record Commission, 2 vols (1812–18)) and the Quo Warranto Rolls (*Placita de Quo Warranto*). For an appreciation of the importance of these two sources for the study of Domesday boroughs, see *Stamford in the Thirteenth Century*, ed. Roffe, 1–43.

[78] Tait, *English Medieval Borough*, 43–63.

[79] LDB, 116, 118v, 290, 104, 5v: *DB Norfolk*, 1,61;69; *DB Suffolk*, 1,122a; *DB Essex*, B1;1,25. For Sudbury, see *the Kalendar of Abbot Samson*, ed. R. H. C. Davis, Camden 3rd series, 84 (1954), xvii, xxv. It was constituted as three leets.

[80] GDB, 189, 162v, 209: *DB Cambs*, B; *DB Gloucs*, B1; *DB Beds*, B.

[81] GDB, 203, 262v, 252: *DB Hunts*, B15; *DB Cheshire*, C1; *DB Salop*, B13. Huntingdon was a quarter of the double hundred of Hurstingstone.

[82] Stamford was assessed at 12½ hundreds (GDB, 336v: *DB Lincs*, S1), that is 150 carucates, representing precisely one twelfth of the assessment of Kesteven and a quarter of the assessment of a Lindsey riding (D. R. Roffe, 'Hundreds and Wapentakes', *The Lincolnshire Domesday*, eds A. Williams and G. H. Martin (London, 1992), 32–42).

[83] This was, apparently, a communal impost as opposed to a specifically royal one imposed on the king's tenants. In Maldon, Swein of Essex performed military service with the burgesses but otherwise had all customs (LDB, 48: *DB Essex*, 24,63); in Stamford the borough as a whole was assessed at 12½ hundreds for army service, boat service, and Danegeld (GDB, 336v: *DB Lincs*, S1).

[84] GDB, 179, 252: *DB Hereford*, C10; *DB Salop*, C4.

[85] LDB, 48: *DB Essex*, 24,63; GDB, 238: *DB Warks*, B6.

[86] GDB, 230: *DB Leics*, C2; LDB 48: *DB Essex*, 24,63.

[87] GDB, 154, 238: *DB Oxon*, B2; *DB Warks*, B6.

[88] See below, pp. 264–71.

In neither tenure nor services, then, was there any substantial difference between townsmen and rural free men. In the terms of the Domesday inquest the only peculiarity of urban dwellers was that they lived in or close to a defended settlement or town and might in consequence (although not necessarily) be referred to as burgesses (*burgenses*). The activities of townsmen did, of course, distinguish towns, but they are largely invisible in Domesday Book because they were not central to the concerns of the Domesday inquest. Boroughs were still agricultural settlements in 1086. Many encompassed within their bounds more or less rural settlements and references to villeins and bordars, as at, for example, Nottingham,[89] probably relate to those who worked the land. All had fields of greater or lesser extent which the burgesses might till. But agriculture was peripheral to the urban economy. Most townsmen made their living from trade and industry. In Bury St Edmunds (not explicitly called a borough) alone is there anything to indicate the diversity of occupation: there bakers, brewers, tailors, washerwomen, shoemakers, robe makers, cooks, porters, and bursars are said to have served St Edmund.[90] In reality the range, both there and generally, was considerably greater. We are dependent on other types of evidence, notably archaeology, for what we know of it. Towns were the hub of a burgeoning mercantile economy which is only hinted at by the odd reference to toll in Domesday Book.[91]

Even here, however, there was merely a difference in degree rather than kind between town and country. Neither trade nor industry was confined to boroughs. There are far more references to rural markets in Domesday Book than urban ones (48 to 5 by my reckoning) and, likewise, numerous crafts are noticed. If anything the inquisitors took more interest in non-agricultural matters in the countryside than in the town. In the inquest records they treated the boroughs like other settlements that were divided between a number of lords. Why, then, did the GDB scribe choose to distinguish the borough above other settlements? It was clearly not because of its economy. The answer points to the wider context of the boroughs. They were of interest to the scribe not because of any special characteristic of their own but because they were adjuncts of royal and comital estates with extensive administrative functions throughout the shire.

The Domesday borough (that is, the customary lands alone) was royal demesne, but it was usually but one element in a complex of royal lands in the vicinity.

---

[89] GDB, 280: *DB Notts*, B1.

[90] LDB, 372: *DB Suffolk*, 14,167.

[91] For the distinction between *toll*, 'toll', and *tolnea*, 'through toll', see D. R. Roffe, 'The Origins of Derbyshire', *Derbyshire Archaeological Journal*, 106 (1986), 102–22. The one went with sake and soke and was confined to a single estate; the other was collected from a district regardless of tenure. In Derbyshire and Nottinghamshire through toll boundaries have been associated with the establishment of legal markets by King Athelstan.

Gloucester extended to Kingsholm,[92] Northampton to Kingsthorpe and its appurtenances,[93] Derby to Little Chester, Quarndon, Little Eaton, and Litchurch,[94] York to eighty-four carucates of land in thirteen vills,[95] to name but a few. Burgesses might be obliged to work within the wider estate from time to time; those of Hereford reaped at Marden for the king[96] and similar obligations are known from later documentation in other boroughs. However, as in Hereford and Maldon,[97] the king's hall was more usually situated in the borough itself and dues were usually rendered there. This was, though, but one of its functions. In county towns the shire met there and it was the headquarters of the sheriff as the representative of the king in the shire. From there the sheriff managed the king's estates, levied the geld, and, most importantly of all, coordinated the services due from the tenants-in-chief and the community of the shire. In the lesser towns the king's hall could not have had such elevated functions, but it still served as an estate centre and tributary nexus. In parallel the earl had a similar establishment, often, it would seem, adjacent to the borough. In York the 'Earlsburgh' was situated outside Bootham Bar to the west of the City; after the Conquest the abbey of St Mary of York was founded on the site.[98] Earl Tosti's estate in Nottingham was to the west of the English borough and became the nucleus of the French Borough after the Conquest.[99] At Warwick, Earl Edwin's hall was in the adjoining settlement of Coten to which the issues of the Borough and the earl's third penny belonged in 1086.[100] By contrast, *Irlesbiri*, 'the earl's residence', was within the City of Exeter

[92] A. Williams, 'An Introduction to the Gloucestershire Domesday', *The Gloucester Domesday*, eds A. Williams and R. W. H. Erskine (London, 1989), 8. The king's hall was probably situated in Kingsholm (GDB, 162, 172v: *DB Gloucs*, G1; *DB Worcs*, 1,7).

[93] G. Foard, 'The Early Topography of Northampton and its Suburbs', *Northamptonshire Archaeology*, 26 (1995), 109–22, at 112. Kingsthorpe was a chapelry of St Peter's, Northampton, but was itself the caput of a manor that extended into several surrounding vills (GDB, 219v: *DB Northants*, 1,18).

[94] GDB, 280: *DB Derby*, B1,3. There were extensive ecclesiastical links between churches in Derby and this complex of vills along with several others (D. R. Roffe, 'An Introduction to the Derbyshire Domesday', *The Derbyshire Domesday*, eds A. Williams and R. W. H. Erskine (London, 1990), 19–24).

[95] GDB, 298, 298v: *DB Yorks*, C22–35; P. R. Newman, 'The Domesday Inquest and the Norman Land Settlement in the Yorkshire Wapentake of Ainsty', *Nottingham Mediaeval Studies*, 46 (2002), 1–24.

[96] GDB, 179: *DB Hereford*, C3.

[97] GDB, 179: *DB Hereford*, C4; LDB, 6: *DB Essex*, 1,25.

[98] D. W. Rollason, *Sources for York History to AD 1100*, The Archaeology of York, 1 (York, 1998), 171, 175. The name Earlsburgh survives from no earlier than the eighteenth century.

[99] D. R. Roffe, 'Anglo-Saxon Nottingham and the Norman Conquest', *A Centenary History of Nottingham*, ed. J. V. Beckett (Manchester, 1997), 35–7.

[100] GDB, 238, 243: *DB* Warks, 1,6.26,1; D. Desborough, 'An Introduction to the Warwickshire Domesday', *The Warwickshire Domesday*, eds A. Williams and G. H. Martin (London, 1991), 15–16. Budbrooke was also part of the estates.

to the north-west of the cathedral in the vicinity of the modern Fiernhay Street.[101] Less is known about the functions of the earl's estate. There is some evidence that the earl's thegns rendered their services at the earl's hall in Nottingham,[102] and it seems likely that this was the norm.

By 1086 the crown had resumed most comital lands.[103] Some remained in the king's hands, others had been granted piecemeal to Norman tenants-in-chief. However, the king's hall, or its functional successor, the king's castle, remained the centre of shire administration. It figured little in the Domesday inquest, for the focus of the inquiry was the vill and the lord. But with the compilation of Domesday Book shire administration moved to centre stage. The writing of LDB saw the organization of the inquest material by fee within counties for the first time.[104] In moving boroughs above the line the GDB scribe was probably attempting to provide some sort of account of the income of the king from the customary dues of the shire. It was presumably for that reason that in some Domesday counties he coupled the data with what are usually called 'county customs'.

County customs and tributes

In ten counties there is a record of diverse matters relating to the sheriff's administration of the shire. There is no one item of information that is common to all, but in broad terms each and every one relates to the dues of the king (Table 4.2). Some sections, it is true, do look like a record of liberties of tenants-in-chief and their predecessors. Stori is said to have had the right to make a church on his own lands and in his soke and to dispose of his tithe as he saw fit.[105] The passage is unparalleled and it is therefore difficult to know what to make of it. Another liberty, though, is more comprehensible. Dozens of pre-Conquest holders of land had sake and soke over their estates, and here the point would seem to be that the king was entitled to their forfeitures should they default in whatever obligations they owed to the king in return. The other items are more explicitly forfeitures, the issues of courts, and the yield of the county farm.

[101] J. Allen, C. Henderson, and R. Higham, 'Saxon Exeter', *Anglo-Saxon Towns in Southern England*, ed. J. Haslam (Chichester, 1984), 402.
[102] The honour of Peverel, which met within the earl's estate in Nottingham, in large measure perpetuated the pre-Conquest organization (Roffe, 'The Anglo-Saxon Town and the Norman Conquest', *A Centenary History of Nottingham*, 36; D. R. Roffe, 'Nottinghamshire and the North: A Domesday Study', unpublished PhD thesis, Nottingham, 1987, 143–77, online at http://www.roffe.co.uk/phd/phd070.htm).
[103] C. P. Lewis, 'The Early Earls of Norman England', *ANS*, 13 (1990), 207–23.
[104] See above, pp. 99–104.
[105] GDB, 280: *DB Derby*, B16. This right was not confined to the borough of Derby (Fleming, 'Rural Elites and Urban Communities', 16); it is enrolled after the account of the customs of Appletree Wapentake.

Table 4.2 *The county customs*

	Sake and soke	King's peace/forfeit	Communications	Reliefs	Dues of king & earl	Military obligations	Laws/customs	Geld	Hundreds	Pleas of shire	County renders/royal manors	Miscellaneous
Essex												
Norfolk												
Suffolk												
Yorkshire	✓	✓	✓	✓	✓		✓					
Lincolnshire	✓	✓			✓							
Nottinghamshire	✓	✓	✓[1]	✓	✓		✓					
Derbyshire					✓							✓
Huntingdonshire								✓				
Cambridgeshire												
Middlesex												
Bedfordshire												
Buckinghamshire												
Hertfordshire												
Kent	✓		✓ ✓[2]	✓			✓					
Sussex												
Surrey												
Hampshire												
Berkshire		✓		✓		✓	✓	✓				
Wiltshire												
Dorset												
Somerset												
Devon												
Cornwall												
Gloucestershire												
Worcestershire		✓			✓	✓		✓	✓	✓	✓	
Herefordshire							✓[3]				✓[4]	
Shropshire												
Cheshire												
Staffordshire												

	Sake and soke	King's peace/forfeit	Communications	Reliefs	Dues of king & earl	Military obligations	Laws/customs	Geld	Hundreds	Pleas of shire	County renders/royal manors	Miscellaneous
Warwickshire						√5				√	√	
Northamptonshire											√	
Oxfordshire		√6				√6					√6	
Leicestershire												√

[1] In the account of Nottingham, but probably postscriptal. It might refer only to the borough.

[2] In the account of Canterbury and related to the city. The information is entered in a different section signalled by an enlarged P.

[3] Customs of the Welsh of Archenfield.

[4] In the *terra regis*.

[5] Warwick only.

[6] Entered at the end of the king's *breve*.

Where this type of information has been discussed at all, it has been tacitly assumed that it was in some way related to the borough's presentment. It is clear, however, that it was drawn from a different source or series of sources. In Kent county customs were not provided by burgesses but by 'the men of the four lathes', while in Derbyshire the dues were acknowledged by 'the two shires' (Derbyshire was twinned with Nottinghamshire) and in Worcestershire by the shire.[106] That this was the norm is indicated by the forms of the text. In Oxfordshire the information is recorded at the end of the account of the *terra regis* rather than with the borough of Oxford; likewise there is a note on the dues of the county in the Herefordshire *terra regis*. A different source is indicated. In the other eight examples various calligraphic devices – enlarged capital letters, spacing in the text etc. – are employed which suggest that the section was considered other than what went before.

The fact is important, for it puts the account of the borough in context as one of a series of renders that accrued to the king. The account of Worcester makes the point very well:

In the City of Worcester, King Edward had this customary due: when the coinage was changed, each moneyer gave 20s at London for receiving the dies for the coinage. When the shire paid geld, the city was reckoned at 15 hides.

[106] GDB, 1, 280, 172: *DB Kent*, Dii; *DB Derby*, B15; *DB Worcs* C4.

From the same city the king himself had £10 and Earl Edwin £8. The king took no other customary due there except the rent on the houses according to the liability of each.

Now King William has in demesne both the king's part and the earl's part. Thence the sheriff pays £23 5s by weight, for the city; and for the demesne manors of the king he pays £123 4s by weight. For the shire he pays £17 by weight; and he further pays £10 of pennies, at 20 to the ora, or a Norway hawk; [...] and to the queen also 100s by tale; and 20s, at 20[d] to the ora, for a sumpter horse. These £17 by weight and £16 by tale are for the pleas of the shire and for the hundreds, and if he does not receive [so much] thence, he pays it out of his own [means].

In this shire are 12 hundreds; 7 of these are so quit, the shire says, that the sheriff has no [rights] in them, and therefore, as he says, he loses much on the farm.

Here the farm of the borough and the renders of the moneyers are just two items in the list of sums that are owed by the sheriff. The account of Warwickshire is directly comparable:

in the time of King Edward the shire of Warwick with the borough and with the royal manors rendered £65 and 36 sesters of honey, or £24 8s. in place of all [dues] pertaining to honey.

Now, including the farm of the royal manors and the pleas of the shire, it renders £145 a year by weight, and £23 for the customary payment for dogs, and 20s. for a sumpter horse, and £10l for a hawk, and 100s. to the queen for a benevolence.

Besides these it renders 24 sesters of honey by the greater measure and from the borough 6 sesters of honey, that is, a sester for 15d. From these the Count of Meulan has 6 sesters and 5s.

And Oxfordshire is very similar:

The shire of Oxford renders a farm of 3 nights, that is £150. As increment £25 by weight. From the borough £20 by weight.

From the mint £20l [...] in pennies at 20 to the ora. For weapons 4s.

From the queen's exactions 100s by tale. For a hawk £10.

For a sumpter-horse 20s. For hounds £23 in pennies at 20 to the ora; and 6 sesters of honey and 15d as a customary due.

From the land of Earl Edwin in Oxford [shire] and in Warwickshire the king has £100 and 100s.

The similarity of dues presumably reflects the close relationship between these three counties that met from time to time, with Gloucester, at *Gildberg*.

Northamptonshire has a brief account of county dues in comparable terms, and a truncated list was postscriptally appended to the description of Malmesbury in Wiltshire (here after the list of holders of land). Substantial gaps left between the accounts of the boroughs and the lists of tenants-in-chief in Nottinghamshire, Derbyshire, Berkshire, Somerset, Devon, and Staffordshire may have been left in anticipation of supplying similar information. In three counties other types of information relating to the king's dues were also entered above the line. In the Herefordshire folios there is an account of the customs of Archenfield and the sum rendered by Rhys of Wales.[107] Between the Wye and the Monnow, Archenfield was a part of Wales that had been conquered by the English in the reign of Edward the Confessor but, still under Welsh law, was not yet integrated into the kingdom of England. Its administration was entrusted to the sheriff. The account of the rights of the king, in what would later be called Monmouthshire, in Wales, which follows the city of Gloucester is more specific. It outlines the king's dues (including some of the earl's) and then, like the description of boroughs, lists the lands held by tenants along with the rights that they enjoyed over them. Again, the land was not incorporated into the kingdom and was directly administered by the sheriff. There is also a short note on the castlery of Chepstow which was similarly administered. Finally, there is the land of St Martin of Dover in the Kent folios.[108] It is by far the most difficult to understand but it seems that it too was in some way related to royal dues, here in the borough of Dover, for the church was royal demesne and apparently considered customary land.[109]

[107] GDB, 179: *DB Hereford*, A. There is an abbreviated account of the same customs in the king's chapter (GDB, 181: *DB Hereford*, 1,49).

[108] The account comes in two sections. The first follows Dover and consists of a general statement of the 24 sulungs held by St Martin's and is followed by a detailed description of 17 sulungs, 4½ yokes, 3 virgates, and 235 acres in the hundreds of Bewsbury and Cornilo in Eastry Lathe (GDB, IV: *DB Kent*, M1–24). The second section is separated from the first by the account of Canterbury (somewhat compressed at the end to allow enough space for all the material that had to be entered), and consists of an account of 3 sulungs in Street, Bircholt, and Blackbourne in Limen Lathe, and a few odd notes on dues from Dover and pleas in which St Martin's was involved (GDB, 2: *DB Kent*, P1–20).

[109] 'The Priory of Dover', *A History of the County of Kent*, ii, ed. W. Page (London, 1926), 133. The enrolment of the lands of an institution that did not hold in chief with the boroughs has been seen as evidence that the scribe was unsure of his programme at this point or was unwilling to impose it on the material with which he was presented (R. Eales, 'An Introduction to the Kent Domesday', *The Kent Domesday*, eds A. Williams and G. H. Martin (London, 1992), 4). The former possibility is implausible. At this stage in the writing of GDB the scribe was well into his work and would have been well aware of what he was doing. The latter is clearly indicated since the land is associated with Dover in the Excerpta which probably precedes the compilation of Domesday Book. Noting the TRE assessments of the account and the absence of ploughlands, Harvey has suggested that the account was a pilot survey of 1085 undertaken by Rannulf Flambard, the master of St Martin's (S. Harvey, 'Domesday Book and Anglo-Norman Governance', *TRHS*, 5th series, 25 (1975), 191–2). In fact TRE assessments and the absence of ploughlands are typical of the accounts of boroughs (only Buckingham and Derby have a record of ploughlands). The decision to keep the land above the line was clearly intentional. St Martin's had some of the dues of Dover and so the most likely explanation for the special treatment of its lands is

The account of county customs and revenues is as unrealized as that of the boroughs. It cannot be doubted, however, that it was as much a part of the scribe's programme. He clearly felt that each Domesday county should be prefaced with something of a summary of the king's dues. Why he failed to complete the project is a fascinating question, but one that is probably unanswerable. The information must have been potentially available to him. There was no special procedure for either the customs or the boroughs, and, after all, royal income was the subject of the first stage of the Domesday inquest. Nevertheless, judging from the spaces left in the text, more information was anticipated than present. Is it possible that all the information simply did not find its way back to central government? It was not all of equal value. Where the commissioners had a pressing use for the geld survey to inform their own inquest, they had less need of documentation that did not. Geld lists were more vital than surveys of boroughs; these latter may on occasion have remained with the sheriff who supervised the survey. The cursory statement of dues may have been his usual reply.

The Domesday inquisitors, then, did not recognize any especial status in towns or townsmen and did not accord them any extraordinary procedure. Customary lands were surveyed with the larger royal estates of which they were an element; non-customary lands as separate estates or as part of the rural manors to which they belonged. Further, the scribes of Domesday Book took no interest in boroughs *per se*; they noticed them as only one item in a series of county renders. Boroughs as urban communities, 'towns' in Reynolds' sense, are not described in Domesday Book. Where the dues alone are recorded the social and economic historian, the topographer and historical geographer must turn to other sources to reconstruct eleventh-century towns.[110] We can, however, usually go further when the accounts are fuller. Here the tenurial complexity of urban settlements is a godsend.

that it was merely an especially detailed account of customary land, here, in all likelihood, derived from the survey of royal churches in the initial stages of the Domesday inquest. It should be noted that the burgesses of Dover are associated with the Canons of St Martin's in a presentment relating to Atherton in the body of the text (GDB, 13: *DB Kent*, 9,9).

[110] The usual approach is to rush into topographical analysis of town plans, often with little regard for the documentation. Elements – castles, markets, planned blocks etc. – are identified and a stratigraphy is developed by observing the relationship between them. Road 'diversions', for example, may suggest that one element is later than another. Plan elements are also used comparatively. It would now seem that any triangular market place is by definition an early one, external to a defended settlement. The literature is vast, but for an introduction, see D. M. Palliser, T. R. Slater, and E. P. Dennison, 'The Topography of Towns 600–1300', in D. M. Palliser (ed.), *The Cambridge Urban History of Britain, vol. 1: 600–1540* (Cambridge, 2000), 153–86; T. R. Slater, 'English Medieval New Towns with Composite Plans: Evidence from the Midlands', in T. R. Slater (ed.), *The Built Form of Western Cities: Essays for M. R. G. Conzen on the Occasion of his 80th Birthday* (Leicester, 1990), 60–82; T. R. Slater, 'English Medieval Town Planning', in D. Denecke, Dietrich and G. Shaw, *Urban Historical Geography: Recent Progress in Britain and Germany* (Cambridge, 1988), 93–105. All of this is often claimed to be scientific, but of course it can be as assumption-

Topography and demographics

In 1066 most boroughs had a long history behind them. The Norman Conquest came as a period of radical change. The construction of urban castles saw the wholesale destruction of properties.[111] In times of war and conquest the niceties of property rights could be ignored. The bald statements indicating that so many messuages were destroyed may conceal the workings of other factors. More than one castle was sited with an eye for the pre-Conquest foci of authority, suggesting that the king or lord had more rights in the tenements that were swept way than is immediately apparent from Domesday Book.[112] Nevertheless, it cannot be doubted that the construction of most castles was a radical intrusion into urban topography. The new boroughs associated with them could be similarly disruptive. At Nottingham the French Borough was founded to the west of the English Borough within the earl's estate, but its streets were probably laid out anew to communicate with the east gate of the castle.[113] The creation of a French borough in Norwich, significantly within the earl's demesne yet again, seems to have also seen replanning.[114] By contrast, the new borough in Northampton was laid out in the open fields to the east of the pre-Conquest borough.[115] In Lincoln, it would seem, there was the added disruption of the development of a cathedral complex with the movement of the bishopric of Dorchester on Thames to the city.[116]

bound as any von Daeniken analysis. Chronologies have all-too-often assumed unifocal development where a polyfocal development is equally possible. Common sense assumptions can just be plain wrong. Everyone knows that planned boroughs have axial roads and so, for example, it has been assumed that Nottingham's had been blocked at some point. A wider perspective using archaeological and historical data, however, indicates that a central axial road had never existed; it was an intramural road (a functionally secondary element in plan-analysis theory) that had always been the main street of the borough (Roffe, 'Anglo-Saxon Nottingham and the Norman Conquest', *A Centenary History of Nottingham*, 24–42). This is not by way of saying that plan analysis is never to be used. It can be useful as an analytical tool. However, it is no model for synthesis. The study of the origins and development of towns (as indeed of other settlements) must usually be founded in the simultaneous use of different categories of evidence since no one is complete.

[111] See C. Drage, 'Urban Castles', in J. Schofield and R. Leech (eds), *Urban Archaeology in Britain*, CBA Research Report, 61 (1987), 117–32; B. English, 'Towns, Mottes and Ringworks of the Conquest', *The Medieval Military Revolution*, eds A. Ayton and J. L. Price (London, 1995), 45–61.
[112] C. Coulson, 'Peaceable Power in English Castles', *ANS*, 23 (2000), 69–95.
[113] Roffe, 'Anglo-Saxon Nottingham and the Norman Conquest' *A Centenary History of Nottingham*, 36–7.
[114] *Current Archaeology*, October 2000, Norwich Special Edition, 'The French Borough', 64–8.
[115] Foard, 'The Early Topography of Northampton and its Suburbs', 113–15.
[116] In some quarters there is scepticism as to whether St Mary in Lincoln was the site of the cathedral church of the diocese of Lindsey. See D. M. Owen, 'The Norman Cathedral at Lincoln', *ANS*, 6 (1983), 189–99; S. Bassett, 'Lincoln and the Anglo-Saxon See of Lindsey',

The Conquest did indeed see unprecedented urban change and development. However, it by no means obliterated the Anglo-Saxon borough. Inherent in all boroughs was a degree of tenurial heterogeneity that discouraged subsequent change in tenurial structure. A settlement that is characterized by a web of interlocking and equal rights is more difficult to change than one in which there is a single authority. Villages typically underwent several restructuring episodes between the tenth and the nineteenth centuries, usually through the initiative of lords, whereas ancient boroughs had to wait until the various parliamentary reform acts of the nineteenth century before they were fundamentally changed. Continuity of interests is pronounced in boroughs; archaeological excavation has repeatedly demonstrated that urban property boundaries persist for centuries.[117] Indeed, much of the pre-Conquest borough survived, for lords succeeded to the lands of pre-Conquest individuals and they held them in 1086 under similar terms.[118] The later history of these fees can reveal much about the eleventh-century borough.

Churches are undoubtedly the best markers. Most are not named in Domesday Book, but it is usually possible to identify them by tracing the history of the land with which they were associated. My introduction to Domesday studies began with wondering about the identity of the two churches in the borough of Stamford in Lincolnshire which were held before the Conquest by Earnwine the priest and by Eudo the steward at the time of the Domesday inquest.[119] With no references to named churches before the late twelfth century, the problem seemed insoluble until I began to examine the wider interests of Eudo and his family. In 1086 Eudo also held the manor of Wakerley in Northamptonshire and William de Lanvalie, his successor there, granted the church of St Clement in Stamford to the nuns of St Michael in the same town in about 1200. That church, then, was almost certainly one of the ones held by Earnwine and its site, well attested in the later Middle Ages, indicates a suburban focus of settlement before the Conquest. Stray archaeological finds in the area have confirmed the antiquity of the site.[120]

Eudo's second church has remained unidentified. But using the same technique it proved possible to locate several other churches and the fees associated with them

Anglo-Saxon England, 18 (1989), 1–32. For Norwich, see B. Dodwell, 'The Honour of the Bishop of Thetford/Norwich in the Late Eleventh and Early Twelfth Centuries', *Norfolk Archaeology*, 33 (1965), 185–99.

[117] Schofield and Vince, *Medieval Towns*, 63–9, 76–8. Plot division was, of course, common. Amalgamation was also possible, but was mostly confined to areas that were not intensely used.

[118] Urban properties were usually attached to rural manors. For the process, see below, pp. 163–75.

[119] GDB, 336v: *DB Lincs*, S6.

[120] D. R. Roffe, 'Rural Manors and Stamford', *South Lincolnshire Archaeology*, 1 (Stamford, 1977), 12–13.

to build up a fairly detailed picture of Stamford in the eleventh century.[121] St Peter's church is of especial significance in the history of the town. It belonged to a fee of seventy *mansiones* held by Queen Edith in 1066 with all customs. Abutting on the market place of Stamford, this estate was nevertheless a manor belonging to Rutland that stood outside the borough.[122] Excavation has shown that its nucleus was defended in the late ninth century, and the church would therefore seem to point to an ancient centre of authority, probably the king's hall. Here was clearly an origin (if not necessarily the only one) of the town of Stamford.

The account of Stamford is one of the more detailed in Domesday Book, but this is still a considerable haul for such a terse and seemingly intractable source. The technique is the more successful where the later sources are fulsome. Urry was able to expound the Canterbury Domesday in minute detail with the aid of comprehensive twelfth-century surveys of the City.[123] Hill had nothing similar for Lincoln. Nevertheless, with the survival of a great number of twelfth- and thirteenth-century charters in the archives of the Dean and Chapter of Lincoln, he was still able to reconstruct the topography of Lincoln in 1086 in consider-able detail.[124] Much work of this kind has been undertaken, especially in the North where the Domesday accounts are full,[125] but the evidence has not yet been exhausted in many boroughs. Detailed analysis of sources still throws up connections that have not been made before to elucidate an otherwise dark age.

Whether such work can uncover the internal organization of boroughs has yet to be seen. Wards are noted in Cambridge and Stamford, quarters in Huntingdon, and shires in York.[126] Nothing is known of the function of these divisions. Given

---

[121] C. M. Mahany and D. R. Roffe, 'Stamford: The Development of an Anglo-Scandina-vian Borough', *ANS* [*Proceedings of Battle Conference*], 5 (1983), 199–219, reprinted with updated references in *Anglo-Saxon History: Basic Readings*, ed. D. A. E. Pelteret, Garland Reference Library of the Humanities, 2108 (New York and London, 2000), 387–417.

[122] GDB, 336v, 294, 219v: *DB Lincs*, S13; *DB Rutland*, R21; *DB Northants*, 1,5; D. R. Roffe and C. M. Mahany, 'Stamford and the Norman Conquest', *Lincolnshire History and Archae-ology*, 21 (1986), 5–9.

[123] W. Urry, *Canterbury under the Angevin Kings* (London, 1967).

[124] Hill, *Medieval Lincoln*, 42–63.

[125] Chester: A. T. Thacker, 'The Early Medieval City and its Buildings', *Medieval Archae-ology, Art and Architecture at Chester*, ed. A. T. Thacker, British Archaeological Association, Conference Transactions, 22 (Leeds, 2000), 16–30; Derby: D. R. Roffe, 'An Introduction to the Derbyshire Domesday', *The Derbyshire Domesday*, eds A. Williams and R. W. H. Erskine (London, 1989), 19–24; Huntingdon: D. R. Roffe, 'An Introduction to the Huntingdon Domesday', *The Huntingdonshire Domesday*, eds A. Williams and R. W. H. Erskine (London, 1989), 19–22; Leicester: P. Courtney, 'Saxon and Medieval Leicester: The Making of an Urban Landscape', *Transactions of the Leicestershire Archaeological and Historical Society*, 72 (1998), 110–45; Nottingham: D. R. Roffe, 'An Introduction to the Nottinghamshire Domesday', *The Nottinghamshire Domesday*, eds A. Williams and R. W. H. Erskine (London, 1990), 24–7; York: Palliser, *Domesday York*.

[126] GDB, 189, 336v, 203: *DB Cambs*, B; *DB Lincs*, S; *DB Hunts*, B.

that the borough court was a hundred, it seems likely that each was a tithing
of some kind and was responsible for the policing of the area, like the wards of
London which are evidenced from the twelfth century.[127] Little is known from
later records, however. Ten wards are noted in Cambridge. One was occupied by
the castle and a second was known as Bridge Ward according to IE.[128] It may be
possible to localize the others from the record of the holders of land preserved
in Domesday Book. There were six in Stamford. One was situated south of the
Welland and can be identified with the suburb of St Martin's, the site of the English
borough built by Edward the Elder in 918. The remaining five cannot be located;
it is possible, however, that they are associated with the five principal roads, and
the gates that controlled them, that come into the town.[129] A similar explanation has been given for the ferdings of Huntingdon.[130] A little more is known
about the shires of York.[131] Of the seven, one, belonging to the archbishop and
encompassing the Close, has been plausibly identified with the north-east part of
the City. A second, of which the archbishop had the third penny, is described in a
possibly contemporary inquest as consisting of Monkgate, Layerthorpe, Walmgate,
Fishergate, Clementhorpe, and Bishopshill. A third was wasted in the construction
of the castle(s). If the plural is intended, then this shire spanned the Ouse, for there
was a second motte across the river from Clifford's Tower and Castle Yard.[132]

Domesday provides the evidence for assessing something of the physical extent
of boroughs. There is less data for determining size and population. Many boroughs
had defences that encompassed large areas but only a portion was fully developed.
Much of the western side of the Lower City in Lincoln was given over to gardens and
orchards in the Middle Ages, and the low number of churches in the area suggests
that it had been underdeveloped in the eleventh century. In part this was a function
of the siting of the two urban fees of the manor of Hungate (later Beaumont Fee)
and Bolingbroke after the Conquest. Excavation, however, has demonstrated that

[127] C. N. L. Brooke and G. Keir, 'Streets and Wards', *London 800–1216* (London, 1972),
149–82.
[128] IE, 121.
[129] D. R. Roffe, 'Walter Dragun's Town? Lord and Burghal Community in Thirteenth-
Century Stamford', *Lincolnshire History and Archaeology*, 22 (1987), 43–6.
[130] Roffe, 'An Introduction to the Huntingdonshire Domesday', 19; P. Spoerry, 'The
Topography of Anglo-Saxon Huntingdon: A Survey of the Archaeological and Historical
Evidence', *Proceedings of the Cambridge Antiquarian Society*, 89 (2001), 35–47.
[131] For a summary of the evidence, see Palliser, *Domesday York*, 11–12. The main studies of
Domesday York are A. G. Dickens, 'The Shire and Privileges of the Archbishop in Eleventh-
Century York', *Yorkshire Archaeological Journal*, 38 (1953), 131–47; S. R. Rees Jones, 'Property,
Tenure and Rents: Some Aspects of the Topography and Economy of Medieval York',
unpublished DPhil. thesis, University of York, 1987; R. Hall, 'The Making of Domesday
York', *Anglo-Saxon Settlements*, ed. D. Hooke (Oxford, 1988), 233–47.
[132] Palliser, *Domesday York*, 25.

sparse development characterized the area before the Conquest.[133] Much of intramural Leicester was similarly deserted.[134] The accounts of most boroughs provide
statistics, but the units are of indeterminate significance. The number of burgesses
is the most common measure, but *mansiones, mansure, domus,* or *hage* are preferred
elsewhere. The first three are common throughout the country, the last is confined
to Circuit I, although it is not used exclusively in Kent or Hampshire. All the terms
might be considered more or less equivalent. In Shrewsbury we hear of 252 houses
with as many burgesses in them[135] and elsewhere the various terms appear apparently interchangeably from entry to entry in the same borough. But the equation is
less informative than it seems. In Nottingham there were three *mansiones* in which
there were eleven houses and in Hereford there were men who did not have 'whole
tenements (*integras mansuras*)'.[136] Here *mansio* and *mansura* relate to entities from
which dues were owed: indeed in the Domesday inquest both were used of rural
manors.[137] Neither, then, primarily signifies a house in the everyday sense. *Haga*,
with the root meaning of hedge and by extension enclosure, is used in the same
way.[138] We cannot assume that the equivalent burgess is any more than the person
responsible for the dues assessed upon the standard unit.

It is thus clear that Domesday is at best telling us about a class of townsmen
who were charged with paying the customs in person. The statistics do not tell
us about the number of houses, much less population. There is some sense in
which the data can be used to rank boroughs, but the categories must always be
broad.[139] There is nothing to prove that the *mansio* in one place is the equivalent
of a *mansio* in another. One in Lincoln that belonged to Stori, for example, can be
identified with a large group of tenements bounded by the Strait, Danes Terrace,
and Flaxengate, while many in York were apparently small.[140] Moreover, since
it is inherently likely that customary tenements are more consistently recorded

---

[133] B. J. J. Gilmour and D. R. Roffe, 'Medieval and Later Occupation of the South-Western
Part of the Lower City: Archaeological and Historical Evidence', *The Defences of the Lower
City: Excavations at The Park and West Parade 1970–1972 and a Discussion of the Other Sites
Excavated up to 1994*, ed. M. J. Jones, The Archaeology of Lincoln VII–2, Council for British
Archaeology, 1999, 262–7.

[134] Courtney, 'Saxon and Medieval Leicester'. The focus of the city subsequently shifted
to the eastern edge.

[135] GDB, 252: *DB Salop*, C1.

[136] GDB, 280, 179: *DB Notts*, B8; GDB, 179: *DB Hereford*, C3–4.

[137] See below, pp. 176–82.

[138] A. H. Smith, *English Place-Name Elements*, English Place-Name Society, 25 and 26
(1956), i, 221.

[139] Darby, *Domesday England*, 302–9, 364–8.

[140] GDB, 336: *DB Lincs*, C10. Part of the insula bounded by Danes Terrace, Flaxengate,
Grantham Street, and The Strait rendered soke dues to Bolingbroke in the sixteenth century
(Lincoln Archives Office, FL MSS, 3/1). I shall be publishing a detailed analysis of the area
in due course. For York, see Palliser, *Domesday York*, 16.

than non-customary, boroughs like Nottingham in which the rights of the crown were pronounced may not be directly comparable with other boroughs with a greater degree of tenurial heterogeneity.[141] The figures that are bandied about of the population of the Domesday boroughs are nothing more than guesses based upon uninformed notions of the nature of the data.

The odd incidental detail may, however, be illuminating. Six pence were paid in Colchester from each house 'that can render [them]' for the victuals of the king's soldiers TRE. In total £15 5s 3d was collected, suggesting a minimum of 610½ houses.[142] In York there are two references that suggest intense street frontage development.[143] William de Percy had seven small messuages that were 50 feet wide, indicating a frontage of seven feet each.[144] Excavation in Coppergate has shown that sixteen feet was the norm. Again, a Gamal had a messuage with four *dingis*, a word that can probably be translated as 'shop' or 'cellar'.[145] In Nottingham there is a reference to twenty-three houses built in the town ditch.[146] Here the English borough was not intensely developed throughout its area, but structures of the period have been excavated in the town ditch on Drury Hill which, adjacent to the main thoroughfare of the borough, was one of the more desirable areas of Nottingham. Likewise, there were eleven houses in the City ditch in Canterbury.[147] The construction of a suburb, that of Butwerk to the east of the Lower City, is recorded in the Lincoln account, perhaps indicating pressure on space within the eastern half of the Lower City itself.[148] Conversely, there were crofts in Chichester, perhaps indicating less intense development.[149] In Malmesbury, as in many other boroughs, there were waste tenements, although the meaning of the term is not transparent, while in Dorchester, Bridport, Wareham, and Shaftesbury there were 100 that had been 'completely destroyed'.[150]

[141] Roffe, 'Anglo-Saxon Nottingham', 37–9.

[142] LDB, 107: *DB Essex*, B6. The moneyers paid £4 of the total. However, Rumble (*DB Essex*, B6 note) suggests an emendation to the text, arguing that *propter* is a mistake for *preter*, to read 'And apart from these 6d., the whole city rendered TRE £15. 5s. 3d. a year, in addition to all dues. Of these, the moneyers rendered 4 TRE. Now it [the city] renders £80 and 4 sesters of honey or 40s. 4[d.]. And in addition to this, [they render] 100s. to the sheriff for exactions. And [they render] 10s. 8d. for feeding the prebendaries'.

[143] Palliser, *Domesday York*, 16.

[144] GDB, 298: *DB Yorks*, C10.

[145] GDB, 298: *DB Yorks*, C3. Alecto has 'drengs' for *dingis*. For 'shop', see Palliser, *Domesday York*, 16, citing J. R. Boyle, 'The Dings in York', *Notes and Queries*, 9th series, 4 (1899), 181–2.

[146] GDB, 280: *DB Notts*, B17.

[147] GDB, 2: *DB Kent*, C1.

[148] GDB, 336v: *DB Lincs*, C22; Hill, *Medieval Lincoln*, 133–4. It should be noted, however, that Kolsveinn was granted the land by the king and he may therefore have speculatively developed an area that was available to him.

[149] GDB, 23: *DB Sussex*, 11,1.

[150] GDB, 64v, 75: *DB Wilts*, M; *DB Dorset*, B. For waste, see below, pp. 250–6.

None of this helps with ranking boroughs. If one must, the best measure is probably the renders of the boroughs, their farms. All farms are in some sense conventional. Occasionally, there is the record of what looks like a real render, that is the sum of the a large number of discrete payments. Most sums, however, are round numbers suggesting that they are agreed amounts paid by a reeve or the community to acquit the borough of its obligations (Table 4.3). There is some indication of system: units of £15, £30, and multiples recur. Norwich, Thetford, Ipswich, Lincoln, Stamford, Huntingdon, Chichester, Wallingford, Shrewsbury, Oxford, and Leicester rendered one or the other TRE, Norwich, Torksey, Nottingham, Derby, Huntingdon, Guildford, Bath, Gloucester, Hereford, Chester, Oxford TRW; Hertford was valued at £7 10s TRE, £15 afterwards, and £30 at the time of the survey. In Northamptonshire £30 was the value of three nights' farm (here the farm of the shire),[151] and it is possible that it was a food render that originally lay at the heart of the system. How such figures relate to cash payments is impossible to say. In many boroughs various sources of income – landgable, tolls, customs, etc. – are itemized and some appurtenances are separately valued, but there seems little correlation between the sums. Only in Huntingdon, it seems, is landgable explicitly additional to the borough farm.[152] In whatever they consist, however, the borough farms are probably related to prosperity in one way or another. Indeed, the value of Dover when it was acquired was unknown because the town had been burnt.[153]

By and large, the figures tell the same story as tenements totals. There was a premier league of boroughs in the North and East – York, Lincoln, Norwich – which rendered about £100. Some way behind is a first division of about £60: Colchester, Thetford, Stamford, Canterbury, Wallingford, Wilton, Bath, Langport,[154] Gloucester, Hereford, Chester, and Oxford. The remainder paid in the region of £30, although some, like Stafford (£7) and Cambridge (£14 2s 10d), paid somewhat less.

---

[151] GDB, 219: *DB Northants*, B36. There was, though, no standard cash equivalent for the farm of one night in the countryside. See below, p. 248.
[152] GDB, 203: *DB Hunts*, B16–17.
[153] GDB, 1: *DB Kent*, D7.
[154] It must be suspected that the totals for Wilton, Bath, and Langport incorporate profits from other sources, like the associated hundreds.

Table 4.3 *Borough farms and renders*

County	Borough	TRE value (£ s d)	Later value (£ s d)	TRW value (£ s d)	Render (£ s d)	Sesters of honey	Blooms of iron	Skins/hides	Mint (£ s d)
Essex	Colchester	15 5 3		80					20
	Maldon	13 2 0	24	16w					
Norfolk	Norwich	30		70w+20b	6	6			
	Thetford	30t		50w+20b	6t	4		14	40
	Yarmouth	27		27 16 4					
Suffolk	Sudbury	18		28t					
	Ipswich	15	40	37		6/			4/20
Yorkshire	York	53		100w					
Lincolnshire	Lincoln	30		100t					75
	Stamford	15		50	28				
	Torksey	18		30					
Nottinghamshire	Nottingham	18		30					
	Derby	24		30					10
Derbyshire									
Huntingdonshire	Huntingdon	30		30					2
Cambridgeshire	Cambridge			14 2 10					
Middlesex									
Bedfordshire	Bedford								
Buckinghamshire	Buckingham	10t		16b					
Hertfordshire	Hertford	7 10 0t	15t	20w	10t				
Kent	Dover	18	?	40	54				
	Canterbury	51	51	50	54				
	Rochester		5	5	20	40			
Sussex	Chichester	15		25	35				
	Pevensey	3 16 9		5 19 0					1
	Lewes	26		34					5 12 0
Hastings									
Surrey	Guildford	18 0 3		30	32				
	Southwark		16						
Hampshire	Southampton								
Winchester									
Berkshire	Wallingford	30	40	60	80t				
Wiltshire	Malmesbury	12		12					5
	Wilton			50					
	Cricklade								
	Salisbury								

County	Borough	TRE value (£ s d)	Later value (£ s d)	TRW value (£ s d)	Render (£ s d)	Sesters of honey	Blooms of iron	Skins/hides	Mint (£ s d)
Dorset	Dorchester								
	Bridport								
	Wareham								
	Shaftesbury								
	Wimbourne								
Somerset	Bath			60 13 4					5
	Langport			79 10 7					
	Ilchester								
	Bruton								
	Frome								
Devon	Exeter			12t+6b					
	Barnstaple								
	Lydford								
	Totnes								
Cornwall									
Gloucestershire	Gloucester	36t		60xx		12	36		20
	Winchcombe	6	20	28xx					
	Bristol								
Worcestershire	Worcester	18		23 5 0w					
Herefordshire	Hereford	18		60t					
Shropshire	Shrewsbury	30		40					
Cheshire	Chester	14 or 45	30	70+1m				3	
Staffordshire	Stafford	9		7					
Warwickshire	Warwick	With manors							
Northamptonshire	Northampton			30 10 0					
Oxfordshire	Oxford	30		60t	20	6/			20
Leicestershire	Leicester	30t				15			

Notes: Total values, farms, only are noted here; they apparently encompassed individual renders.

In Dorset and Warks value of boroughs in county renders.

w = weight; t = tale; b = blanched; xx 20d to the *ora*.

Boroughs in relation

Size matters for the economic historian. There is little else to use to reconstruct the market hierarchies and marketing networks of Domesday England. Thiessen polygrams may look pretty, but there is little in Domesday on which to found them. Archaeological data afford a much sounder basis for such analyses. The texts do, however, hint at wider relationships of a different kind. We have already seen that locally many boroughs fit into a network of royal and comital estates. They might also be grouped with other boroughs. In the Midland shires there was generally only one 'county borough'. Elsewhere there were several. Sometimes the fact merely points at the amalgamation of diverse political entities. In 1086 Winchcombe was indubitably a part of Gloucestershire, but it was described as a 'ferding' (quarter) and rendered £28 with the three hundreds associated with it.[155] In the early eleventh century it had had its own shire.[156] Likewise, Stamford was part of Lincolnshire, but the £28 which it too paid is probably identical with the £28 in customs that 'Sudlincolia' rendered in 1086, recalling a time when it had been the county borough of Kesteven and Holland.[157]

To all appearances the enrolment of the account of Derby with Nottingham betokens a recent association of a similar kind. In 1086 Derbyshire and Nottinghamshire were administered by a single sheriff, but were otherwise seemingly separate administrative entities. The relationship, however, was probably early and of a more structural nature. Thirteenth-century evidence indicates that before the twelfth century the toll banlieu of Nottingham not only embraced much of Nottinghamshire, as would be expected of a county town, but also southern Derbyshire, indicating that the whole area had formed a proto-shire.[158] Pre-Conquest Nottingham was a major administrative centre, but, with an essentially command economy, there are few signs that it had ever been truly urban. Derby, by contrast, was economically buoyant judging by the impressive output of its mint in the tenth century, but was never fortified. In consequence it has been suggested that it was Nottingham's *port*, that is its market.[159]

A relationship of a similar type is believed to have obtained between Southampton and Winchester before the Conquest.[160] With the account of Winchester incomplete, there is, however, no indication of the relationship in Domesday Book. The only explicit link between two boroughs in the text is of a different order. Torksey is said to have been a suburb (*suburbium*) and it enjoyed the same

---

[155] GDB, 162v, 166: *DB Gloucs*, B1;12,10.
[156] *Hemingi Chartularium*, i, 280–1.
[157] GDB, 336v: *DB Lincs*, C28.
[158] D. R. Roffe, 'The Origins of Derbyshire', *The Derbyshire Archaeological Journal*, 106 (1986), 102–22.
[159] Roffe 'Anglo-Saxon Nottingham and the Norman Conquest', 38.
[160] *Winchester in the Early Middle Ages*, ed. Biddle, 461–2.

customs as Lincoln, accounting for one fifth of the geld thereof.[161] Situated on the Trent at the western end of the Foss Dyke it seems to have complemented Lincoln's role in defending a key line of communication between the South and the North. Borough and city may have operated as a single mercantile community.[162] Despite the reticence of the texts, other Domesday boroughs may have had similar relationships. Thus, in Devon Barnstaple, Lydford, and Totnes rendered the same service as Exeter, perhaps suggesting some degree of military cooperation.[163] Further connections are indicated by the coin record, but here we stray into numismatics.[164]

---

[161] GDB, 337: *DB Lincs*, T2. Both the Alecto and Phillimore translations render *suburbium* as 'small town', but there seems no reason not to take the term literally. Cf. the use of *suburbani* at GDB, 39: *DB Hants*, 1,42.

[162] Hill, *Medieval Lincoln*, 186, 307–10.

[163] GDB, 100: *DB Devon*, C6.

[164] A. Freeman, *The Moneyer and the Mint in the Reign of Edward the Confessor 1042–1066* (Oxford, 1985).

5

Lordship, Land, and Service

L ORDSHIP was central to Domesday Book and clearly important in the
Domesday inquest. Its nature both before and after the Conquest has been a
major concern of politicians and historians alike from at least the mid thirteenth
century when Matthew Paris opined 'here the manifest oppression of England
began'.[1] Various notions have collided in the debate: the free Saxons and the
Norman yoke, anarchy and reason, native and foreign, innocence and experience.[2]
Steering a course through the minefield is one of the greatest challenges in Anglo-
Norman history. All agree that King William replaced the Old English aristocracy
with his followers, but otherwise there has been little common ground.

As in much else, Round has set the terms of the debate. He argued forcibly that
knight service was a post-Conquest phenomenon and further that it was introduced by William the Conqueror.[3] No one now would accept that the system was
introduced at one fell swoop (Round seems to have believed it was more or less in
place by 1086 in its entirety). Research in the last fifty years or so has demonstrated
that the Norman settlement was far more protracted than previously thought,
extending well into the reign of Rufus and even Henry I in the North.[4] The
formation of the honours of the twelfth and thirteenth centuries was incomplete
in 1086 and feudal customs were not established. The Domesday inquest was, in
part, responsible for definition of much that was inchoate, but feudal lordship was
a twelfth-century construct. All of this, though, was merely a refining of Round's
essential thesis. The concept of knight service, personal attendance on a lord in
return for land, was generally seen as a Norman importation.[5]

---

[1] *Matthei Parisiensis, Monachi Sancti Albani, Historia Anglorum*, ed. F. Madden, 3 vols, Rolls
Series, 44 (1866–68), iii, 172.
[2] For the most recent review, see M. Chibnall, *The Debate on the Norman Conquest*
(Manchester, 1999).
[3] J. H. Round, 'The Introduction of Knight Service into England', *Feudal England* (London,
1895), 225–314.
[4] J. A. Green, *The Aristocracy of Norman England* (Cambridge, 1997), chapters 1–4.
[5] There are, of course, some notable exceptions. See, for example, J. Gillingham, 'The
Introduction of Knight Service into England', *ANS*, 4 (1981), 53–64, 181–7 (notes).

For the most dyed-in-the-wool Normanists this was self-evident.[6] Normans fought on horseback and to do so needed a warhorse and chain mail birnie. Such equipment was beyond the means of the ordinary free man and so lordship over men and land was a necessary corollary for the accumulation of enough capital to purchase them. The castle, where donjon originally meant lord and keep, became at once the symbol of that lordship and the home of the lord. Feudalism was defined by the mounted knight and the castle and neither was known in pre-Conquest England. Domesday appears to put flesh on this skeleton. There is found a picture of a Norman settlement in which a handful of Norman tenants-in-chief holding of the king succeeded, *de facto* or *de jure*, to the land of a mass of free men to whom the bonds of lordship had been of little moment. Domesday, of course, attests the existence of some pre-Conquest castles – Richards Castle and possibly Ewyas Harold, for example[7] – but they belonged to Normans and Frenchmen who settled in England in the reign of Edward the Confessor, and other sources, notably the Anglo-Saxon Chronicle,[8] show just how foreign they were to English culture.[9]

Arguments in this vein largely eclipsed earlier discussions on the relation-ship between the pre-Conquest units of assessment and post-Conquest tenure which informed much of the debate in the nineteenth century and sometimes subsequently.[10] The Berkshire folios of Domesday Book certainly suggest a link between geld assessment and military service before the Conquest. Nevertheless, it is unlikely that twelfth-century formulas like twelve carucates to the knight fee which are widely found in Yorkshire and Lincolnshire are related to the system. They were probably no more than useful rules of thumb for measuring service from sokeland in areas where grants of land for military service had made few inroads on more traditional modes of tenure.[11] Neither is the measurement of knight fees in hides here or there, not the least because a five-hide unit is not apparent.[12]

[6] R. A. Brown, *The Normans* (London, 1984), 49–78.

[7] *Contra* Round, C. P. Lewis identifies Osbern Pentecost's castle as most likely Hereford rather than Ewyas Harold (Lewis, 'An Introduction to the Herefordshire Domesday', *The Herefordshire Domesday*, eds A. Williams and R. W. H. Erskine (London, 1988), 11).

[8] *ASC*, 119 (E 1051): 'The Foreigners then had built a castle in Herefordshire in Earl Swein's province, and had inflicted every possible injury and insult upon the king's men in those parts.'

[9] C. G. Harfield, 'A Handlist of Castles Recorded in the Domesday Book', *EHR*, 106 (1991), 371–92. For the French in England before the Conquest, see C. P. Lewis, 'The French in England before the Norman Conquest', *ANS*, 17 (1994), 123–44.

[10] E. John, *Land Tenure in Early England* (Leicester, 1964), 147–9.

[11] Reading successive thirteenth-century inquest records from Yorkshire it is difficult to escape the impression that scribes had to improvise in translating services into familiar terms in an area where the carucate had always been the only measure.

[12] M. Hollings, 'The Survival of the Five Hide Unit in the Western Midlands', *EHR*, 68 (1948), 453–87.

However, pre-Conquest analogues of post-Conquest services have been identified. It is now recognized that bookland was a precarious tenure dependent on, *inter alia*, military service.[13] Other correlates between Anglo-Saxon and Norman forms have also been noted. The distribution of religious houses from which William the Conqueror demanded a quota of knights conforms to a decidedly pre-Conquest pattern and in the post-Conquest period legal notions of what later became known as tenure in barony and enfeoffment were couched in Old English terms. Where a vavassour was equated with a thegn,[14] his pre-Conquest counterpart qualified by the ownership of five hides and a bell tower, what in other contexts is called a *burh* or defence. Excavation has shown that his *burh* was a castle in everything but name.[15] Above all, recent studies have shown that pre-Conquest England was not immune to the great changes around the year 1000 that saw a concentration of resources and a greater degree of social differentiation. In the early eleventh century the king's thegn became richer and he increasingly distinguished himself from his men by displays of conspicuous consumption.[16]

Where was then the gentleman? There is now a tendency to play down the differences between pre- and post-Conquest societies.[17] Susan Reynolds, in particular, has been at pains to show that the language of lordship, notably *feudum*, does not seem to have any specific content. She argues therefrom that the Norman Conquest saw no radical changes in the modes of lordship: lordship was as territorialized before the Conquest as after and heredity was a constant throughout.[18] Vagueness of vocabulary, however, does not mean that there are no differences there to be described. What was lordship? What the heritable 'land' over which it was exercised? In concentrating on words, historians have tended to ignore processes. So, much of the debate on the Norman Conquest has largely been formulated in terms of an equation of lordship with land and the antithesis of

---

[13] R. P. Abels, 'Bookland and Fyrd Service', *ANS*, 7 (1984), 1–25.

[14] GDB, 56v: *DB Berks*, B10: 'When a thegn or a knight of the king's demesne was dying he left all his weapons to the king as heriot, and 1 horse with a saddle and 1 without a saddle. But if he possessed hounds or hawks these were presented to the king, to have if he wished.' Part of the manor of Potterne in Wiltshire was held by an Englishman who was 'a knight by the command of the king'; later in the entry he is described as a thegn (GDB, 66: *DB Wilts*, 3,1). See *Die Gesetze der Angelsachsen*, ed. F. Liebermann, 3 vols (Halle, 1903–26), i, 507, 647; F. M. Stenton, *The First Century of English Feudalism* (Oxford, 1932), 141.

[15] C. Coulson, 'Peaceable Power in English Castles', *ANS*, 23 (2000), 69–95, esp. at 89–95. See also A. Williams, 'A Bell-House and a Burh-geat: Lordly Residence before the Norman Conquest', *The Ideals and Practice of Medieval Knighthood*, 4 (Woodbridge, 1992), 221–40.

[16] R. Fleming, 'The New Wealth, the New Rich and the New Political Style in Late Anglo-Saxon England', *ANS*, 23 (2000), 1–22.

[17] For a review of the present orthodoxy, see D. R. Bates, 'England and the "Feudal Revolution"', *Il Feudalesimo Nell'Alto Medioevo*, Settimane de Studio Del Centro Italiano di Studi Sull'Alto Medioevo (Spoleto, 2000), 611–49.

[18] S. Reynolds, *Fiefs and Vassals: The Medieval Evidence Reinterpreted* (Oxford, 1994), 342–52.

geld and service. It is argued here that both were anachronisms. Twelfth-century concepts of the knight fee have been projected into the previous century where they are unwarranted.

Pre-Conquest lordship

There are some 20,000 names of people in the Domesday texts who held land in 1066 or before. The basic study of this corpus was undertaken by Olaf von Feilitzen.[19] He has been responsible for producing a list of forms that approximate to English phonology and orthography. This is a not inconsiderable achievement. The transmission of the names by scribes who were not always *au fait* with English pronunciation and usage has produced forms that even now at times defy definitive explanation. Onomasticians, notably Cecily Clarke and Gilliam Fellows-Jensen, have more recently revisited the material and have added nuances to von Feilitzen's taxonomy.[20] With the greater awareness of the genesis of the Domesday texts, further refinements may be possible. Nevertheless, von Feilitzen's analysis remains the standard reference in determining to what name any particular form points.

His analysis is of less use in determining ethnicity. Von Feilitzen's approach is strictly linguistic, attributing names to groups that are sometimes grossly unhistorical. This has led him wrongly to multiply the number of names present and sometimes to misidentify their country of origin. Moreover, he took no account of social patterns in naming. Fashions in nomenclature are related to all sorts of political and social mechanisms that are not simply signalled by their etymology. The origins of names are in themselves of little use for telling us about the origins of those who bore them. Thus, in attempting to identify the French element in the corpus, Christopher Lewis could not simply list all the continental forms since many were also native English: some Norman names come from a common Germanic stock. Rather he has had to assume that post-Conquest naming patterns in continental families are a reasonable clue to origins before the Conquest. This approach leaves many uncertainties, but there remains a significant group that can be identified as 'French' with considerable confidence.[21] Whether other groups can be identified using similar techniques remains to be seen.

The problem is less a philological one than an historical one. It is a preliminary to the identification of individuals and their families, and this is a task that presents a formidable challenge to the historian. Whatever the Domesday

---

[19] O. von Feilitzen, *Pre-Conquest Personal Names of Domesday Book* (Uppsala, 1937).

[20] C. Clark, *Words, Names, and History: Selected Papers of Cecily Clark*, ed. P. Jackson (Woodbridge, 1995); C. Clark, 'English Personal Names *ca* 650–1300: Some Prosopographical Bearings', *Medieval Prosopography*, 8 (1987), 31–60; G. Fellows-Jensen, *Scandinavian Personal Names in Lincolnshire and Yorkshire* (Copenhagen, 1968).

[21] Lewis, 'The French in England before the Norman Conquest', 123–44.

inquest was about, it clearly did not aim to compile a *Who's Who* of pre-Conquest England.[22] To compound the problem, the scribes who compiled Domesday Book from the circuit reports edited out much of the detail that was recorded. By and large, no systematic attempt was made to distinguish individuals. The scribe of GDB attempted to identify the more important personages. As a rule churches are personified by their patron saint and are thus easily spotted, and churchmen are usually accorded their titles from first drafting. The identification of secular lords was probably an afterthought.[23] The same scribe interlined titles such as earl, dapifer, and the like on a wide scale, but not consistently or, one suspects, always accurately. The references to such individuals provide, at best, minima. Regional and local worthies are also at times distinguished by a cognomen, patronymic, toponymic, or other distinguishing epithet, but these are the exceptions. For most the name stands alone. Where it is rare, one can often be confident in identifying two occurrences with a single person. But any such confidence would be misplaced with the commonality of names. Regional patterns of naming vary, but locally Sweins, Godwins, Azors, Leofrics, Ediths, and the like are as ubiquitous as modern-day Shauns, Darrens, Sharons, and Traceys.

The surest means of positive identification is, of course, evidence from other contemporary sources. By far the majority of names, however, are only known from Domesday. Other techniques must be employed. In many cases the only indication is the tenure of the land in 1086. Where a Leodwine is found as a predecessor of Geoffrey de la Guerche in Gainsborough in Lincolnshire there is a *prima facie* case for identifying him with the person of the same name who preceded him in Epworth in the same county.[24] There is, furthermore, also a good chance that he is identical with the individual of the same name noticed in Geoffrey's Leicestershire and Warwickshire *breves*.[25] The assumption here is that land of the same individual tended to be granted to the same lord after the Conquest. It does not follow from this that all his land was disposed of in this way. Where it passed to a number of new lords a longer view is often the only way of arriving at an identity. In Lincolnshire and Yorkshire a series of references is found to a Kolgrimr holding both before the Conquest and after as a tenant-in-chief in his own right and as a tenant of other tenants-in-chief. The Domesday evidence is intractable, but the subsequent history of the various fees shows that many passed into the

[22] The Prosopography of Anglo-Saxon England (PACE a joint Cambridge University and King's College, London, research project), promises to remedy the omission by identifying as many individuals as possible (http://www.pase.ac.uk/).
[23] Whether the interlineations are current or more strictly postscriptal is not always immediately apparent from the facsimile. F. R. and C. Thorn, 'Writing of Great Domesday Book', *Domesday*, eds E. Hallam and D. Bates (Stroud, 2002), 53, are of the opinion that most are current.
[24] GDB, 369: *DB Lincs*, 63,2;5.
[25] GDB, 235v, 243v: *DB Leics*, 29,3;18; *DB Warks*, 31,12.

same family.[26] The presumption must be that a single Kolgrimr provided title to the lands they held.

More tenuous, but nonetheless useful at times, is geographical proximity. Where the same name occurs as the predecessor of two or more fees in the same vill or adjacent vills there is a distinct possibility of identity. Clearly, the more uncommon the name, the more confident the identification. Ann Williams has been able to suggest many plausible identifications on these grounds in Gloucestershire and Worcestershire.[27] But sometimes the coincidences are so pronounced as to countenance the identity of a common name. Osfram is a case in point. The name occurs widely in Lincolnshire in a number of tenurial contexts, but there is a large concentration of references in adjacent vills in southern Kesteven. It occurs twice each in Keisby, Dowsby, and Kirkby Underwood, and once in Southorpe, Elsthorpe, Bulby, Avethorpe, and Little Lavington.[28] There is no common tenurial denominator to this series of estates either in 1086 or subsequently. The repeated occurrence of the name must, however, point to either a local Lothario who owned to his offspring or a single person.

In the reconstruction of families we are largely at the mercy of the texts. Relationships are sometimes explicit, but most details come from claims and other *obiter dicta*. Only one textual form has direct bearing on families. Here and there not one, but two or more pre-Conquest holders are given for a single tenement. On their own such entries are open to a number of interpretations; post-Conquest amalgamation of fees or the concatenation of estates that were too small to be separately described are explanations that are commonly advanced. But a significant relationship looks more likely where the same two names are linked in a series of entries or one name appears repeatedly with other names in similar entries. The phenomenon is presumably a representation of tenure in parage consequent to partible inheritance[29] or tenure from a common lord.[30] Ann Williams has made

---

[26] GDB, 337v, 341, 346v, 347v, 348, 348v, 368v: *DB Lincs*, 1,9.3,35.11,5;7.12,48;52;55;91–2.67,1;7;13;14;17;20–1;24–5. *Early Yorkshire Charters*, v, *The Honour of Richmond*, ed. C. Clay (Wakefield, 1937), 255–7; C. Clay and D. E. Greenway, *Early Yorkshire Families* (Wakefield, 1973), 46–7; F. M. Stenton, 'English Families and the Norman Conquest', *TRHS*, 4th series, 26 (1944), 332–3.

[27] A. Williams, 'An Introduction to the Worcestershire Domesday', *The Worcestershire Domesday*, eds A. Williams and R. W. H. Erskine (London, 1988), 1–39; A. Williams, 'An Introduction to the Gloucestershire Domesday', *The Gloucestershire Domesday*, eds A. Williams and R. W. H. Erskine (London, 1989), 1–39.

[28] GDB, 354v, 358v, 367, 368, 370v, 371, 377: *DB Lincs*, 24,26.27,55–6;57,12;41;45;57.67,23;68,21–2;CK47.

[29] So, presumably, GDB, 35v: *DB Surrey*, 19,37. 'Robert holds of Richard Shalford. 2 brothers held it TRE. Each one had his own house, and yet they resided in 1 court, and could go where they would.'

[30] See, for example, GDB, 27: *DB Sussex*, 12,35. 'William de Vatteville holds Perching. Azur held it of King Edward, and 2 men [held] of Azur. It was assessed at 5½ hides then,

good use of it to reconstruct the families and estates of a number of worthies like Earl Ralph of Hereford and Beorhtric son of Ælgar.[31] It is a technique, nevertheless, that must be used with care. Hopscotching from one multiple-lord entry to another may provide a chain, but it cannot claim validity without a common thread or independent corroboration.[32]

Consideration of family and kin leads on naturally to matters of lordship. A generation ago it was axiomatic that pre- and post-Conquest lordship and tenure were as chalk and cheese. Knight service and the fee were seen as the basis of *Normanitas* and, by contrast, Old English society was viewed as inherently less hierarchical. These are certainties that have dissolved in recent years as this reductionist approach has been abandoned in the wake of a more critical analysis of the pre-Conquest sources and Domesday Book. Although many historians still aver that the Norman settlement saw the introduction of fundamental forms and organizations that were to stamp their character on England and mould its society in the later Middle Ages, it is probably true to say that there is now a universal appreciation of a significant role for forms approximating to 'feudal' lordship in pre-Conquest society. Attention has been drawn to the distinction that the Old English law codes make between the king's thegn and the median thegn and how it informed relationships with the king.[33] Bookland here is of the essence and it has been redefined as a tenure dependent on service.[34] More emphatically, pre-Conquest hierarchies of tenure have been identified in Domesday Book.[35] It is becoming increasingly clear that the older generation of historians were projecting

as now. Then there were 2 halls. Now [it is] in 1 manor.'

[31] A. Williams, 'The King's Nephew: The Family, Career, and Connections of Ralph, Earl of Hereford', *Studies in Medieval History Presented to R. Allen Brown*, eds C. Harper-Bill and J. L. Nelson (Woodbridge, 1989), 327–43; A. Williams, 'A West-Country Magnate of the Eleventh Century: The Family, Estates and Patronage of Beorhtric son of Ælgar', *Family Trees and the Roots of Politics*, ed. K. S. B. Keats-Rohan (Woodbridge, 1997), 41–68.

[32] Not all individuals in grouped entries are related. It can sometimes be shown that the first is the lord of the second; the relationship is probably signalled by the notice of two or more halls or manors. For a discussion of the multiple manor entry, see D. R. Roffe, 'An Introduction to the Lincolnshire Domesday', *The Lincolnshire Domesday*, eds A. Williams and G. H. Martin (London, 1991), 13.

[33] Robertson, II Cnut, 71.

[34] R. Abels, 'Bookland and Fyrd Service in Late Saxon England', *ANS*, 7 (1985), 1–25.

[35] The existence, and something of the structure, of these lordships was first identified in the Domesday account of the northern shires (D. R. Roffe, 'Norman Tenants-in-Chief and their Pre-Conquest Predecessors in Nottinghamshire', *History in the Making*, ed. S. N. Mastoris (Nottingham, 1985), 3–7; D. R. Roffe, 'Nottinghamshire and the North: A Domesday Study', PhD thesis, Leicester 1987 (now posted at http://www.roffe.co.uk/phdframe.htm). The concept was developed by P. H. Sawyer, '1066–1086: A Tenurial Revolution?' *Domesday Book: A Reassessment*, ed. P. H. Sawyer (London, 1985), 71–85. It now informs many analyses of pre-Conquest tenure. See, for example, A. Williams, *The English and the Norman Conquest* (Woodbridge, 1995).

an earlier medieval, and it has to said continental, pattern of lordship onto Old English society. They have used the freedom that the myriad of Domesday free men and sokemen enjoyed to characterize lordship as *königsfreiheit*, that is freedom given by the king in return for service, or bookright, that is, complete freedom from constraint.[36] This, however, is a unitary concept of lordship that is not consonant with the realities of eleventh-century English society. Generally speaking there was no simple equation of superiority with land.

It is true that it is possible to point to a large number of estates in the Domesday corpus which display what might be considered 'classic' features of lordship. The type is found throughout the country but is best exemplified, since minutely described, by the monastic estates of the East Midlands and East Anglia. The demesne manors of the abbeys of Bury St Edmunds, Ely, and Ramsey were in part directly exploited and in part worked by tenants of varying degrees of freedom but the respective abbots owned the soil and enjoyed all the services, rents, and dues that accrued from it. Bury's manor of Nowton in Suffolk stands for the type.[37] Assessed at 4 carucates, the manor had the usual complement of villeins and bordars and a fair range of demesne ploughs and livestock. In addition, there were ten sokemen on ½ carucate over whom St Edmund 'had then, and now has, sake and soke and commendation with all the customary dues. And they could not give or sell the land without the abbot's permission.' This is a litany of 'feudal' rights that any Marxist of the old school would recognize at a thousand paces. Jurisdiction, homage, service, and rights to land lie at the heart of what is popularly understood as medieval lordship. And so they did in pre-Conquest England. What is peculiar about Nowton is not the expectations of superiority but their investment in a single lord. Sake and soke, commendation, and land were entities informing degrees of lordship that usually did not coincide. GDB accords a special place to sake and soke or simple soke and so we shall start with that.

The nature of soke is most clearly seen in the folios of Circuit VI where it informed the processes recorded in the *clamores*. Its characteristics, however, are manifest throughout the country. *Soca*, soke, can, and often does, refer to simple jurisdiction, frequently called 'the king's two pennies' (the third went to the earl), which was essentially personal.[38] It might command suit of court, forfeitures, and sundry minor dues, but otherwise did not confer substantial rights over land. Without the grant or assumption of leet jurisdiction or the return of writs, soke in

---

[36] A. K. G. Kristensen, 'Danelaw Institutions and Danish Society in the Viking Age', *Medieval Scandinavia*, 8 (1975), 27–85; R. Welldon Finn, 'Some Reflections on the Cambridgeshire Domesday', *Proceedings of the Cambridge Antiquarian Society*, 53 (1960), 29–38; R. P. Abels, *Lordship and Military Obligation in Anglo-Saxon England* (London, 1988), 143.

[37] LDB, 357: *DB Suffolk*, 14,4.

[38] D. R. Roffe, 'From Thegnage to Baronage: Sake and Soke, Title, and Tenants-in-Chief', *ANS*, 12 (1990), 164–5.

this sense never subsequently sanctioned a private court.[39] In the eleventh century the earl's penny was always reserved and the kin of injured parties had rights to compensation. It would therefore seem that the soke lord enjoyed his *soc* within the courts of hundred (which he may also have held) and shire. More usually, though, the term *soca* embraced more extensive bonds; IE and other Ely sources show that it could also comprise labour dues, sundry customs, services, and farm.[40] These are the *consuetudines*, 'customs', that are occasionally noticed in the Domesday texts.[41] It is rare to find the Domesday corpus so expansive, but nevertheless it is clear that the scribes used the portmanteau word *terra*, 'land', to convey the rights to this assortment of dues and renders.[42] *Saca et soca*, 'sake and soke', expressed the right to *soca* in both these senses, jurisdiction and land, and it brought the holder into a special relationship with the crown. He held his lands with full rights, although again apparently without a court,[43] only making his forfeitures and rendering an exceptional heriot to the king and earl. Known as a *landhlaford* or *landrica* in the law codes, he was a king's thegn and the estates over which his soke extended was bookland.[44]

Bookland was a dependent tenure.[45] As is clear from the Berkshire and Worcestershire folios of GDB,[46] the lord who enjoyed it was obliged to perform military service for the king in person and, if he failed, might suffer the loss of his estate. Otherwise, however, it was at the full disposal of the lord, not the least of its attractions being that it was, apparently exceptionally, heritable. It was, then, a

---

[39] It is usually invisible after the eleventh century.

[40] *Inquisitio Comitatus Cantabrigiensis … Subjicitur Inquisitio Eliensis*, ed. N. E. S. A. Hamilton (London, 1876), 193–4; Roffe, 'From Thegnage to Barony', 164.

[41] For a gloss of the *soc* of the Laws of Cnut with *consuetudines*, see 'Instituta Cnuti' in *Die Gesetze der Angelsachsen*, i, 359.

[42] Roffe, 'From Thegnage to Barony', 165.

[43] See, for example, GDB, 32: *DB Surrey*, 5,28: 'The men of Southwark testify that TRE no one took toll on the strand or on the water front except the king, and if anyone committing a trespass there had been charged, he paid a fine to the king. If, however, he had escaped uncharged to [the jurisdiction of] him who had sake and soke, that man was to have the fine from the accused.' There was a court (*placitum*) at Acton in Cheshire in 1086 (GDB, 266v: *DB Cheshire*, 8,16), but Acton had been a comital manor before the Conquest.

[44] Attenborough, VI Athelstan 1.1; Robertson, I Edgar 2.1, III Edgar 7.1, II Edgar 3.1, I Æthelred 1.7, III Æthelred 4.1, II Cnut 71.1–3. Susan Reynolds has denied that the term bookland had any specific content in the eleventh century ('Bookland, Folkland and Fief', *ANS*, 14 (1991), 211–27). She has not, however, examined the intricacies of soke and its relationship to land as it is articulated in Domesday Book. Likewise, Baxter and Blair examine the law code and charter evidence in isolation (S. Baxter and J. Blair, 'Land Tenure and Royal Patronage in the Early English Kingdom: A Model and a Case Study', *ANS*, 28 (2005), 19–46). The Domesday evidence affords perspective to the various references to soke and forfeiture of bookland in the laws of Cnut and the Leges Henrici Primi.

[45] Abels, 'Bookland and Fyrd Service', 1–18; Abels, *Lordship and Military Obligation*, 116–31.

[46] GDB, 56v, 172: *DB Berks*, B10; *DB Worcs*, C5.

lordship of the highest order.[47] Consisting in essentially regalian rights, it was, in theory at least, created by the king who had used it to endow religious houses and reward his men. It was a precious commodity and recipients were careful in its use. Monasteries frequently leased bookland out for a term of lives in return for a hefty rent and/or the performance of the service due.[48] The bishop of Worcester's lands in Oswaldlow Hundred in Worcestershire were let under such terms.[49] Equally, churches might grant such *laenland* or 'loanland' on advantageous terms to local or national power-brokers in return for protection.[50] King's thegns, often reserving their soke *qua* jurisdiction, used their bookland in a similar way to support a band of retainers. As median thegns, these latter held the bookland from their lord and were dependent upon him.[51]

To the modern ear, *terra*, *landhlaford*, bookland all speak of real estate, but in the eleventh century the tenure of 'land' did not always extend to the soil. That the king's thegn usually had a demesne is clear, but most of his bookland was in reality confined to the right to the customs listed in IE and other sources from otherwise freely held land. Stenton made much of the freedom of the sokeman of the Northern Danelaw to alienate his land at will; numerous twelfth-century charters show him acting without consultation with his lord.[52] Neither grantor nor grantee, however, could withdraw the soke dues that accrued from their lands.

[47] For a full discussion, see D. R. Roffe, 'Brought to Book: Lordship and Land in Anglo-Saxon England', http://www.roffe.co.uk/bookland.htm.

[48] Services could be entirely of a soke variety, that is farm (as in *Anglo-Saxon Charters*, ed. A. J. Robertson, 2nd edn (Cambridge, 1956), nos 56, 58) or exclusively military, that is the common burdens (as *Anglo-Saxon Charters*, nos 42, 46, 55). The former appears to be called *earnignclande* in a note appended to S1367 (*Anglo-Saxon Wills*, ed. D. Whitelock (Cambridge, 1930), 178), and the *boclonde* of the same charter and S1347, which both refer to grants for a term of lives, probably refers to the latter. Beorhtric son of Ælgar who held Bushley in Worcestershire 'rendered to the soke of the bishop whatever he owed to the king's service' (GDB, 173: *DB Worcs*, 2,30).

[49] For the leases, see *Hemingi Chartularium*.

[50] Beorhtric son of Ælgar held Barley and Bushley in Worcestershire thus of the bishop of Worcester (GDB, 173: *DB Worcs*, 2,30;37; Williams, 'Introduction to the Worcestershire Domesday', 23), and Hereward ('the Wake') Rippingale in Lincolnshire of Crowland Abbey (GDB, 377: *DB Lincs*, CK48; D. R. Roffe, 'Hereward "the Wake" and the Barony of Bourne: A Reassessment of a Fenland Legend', *Lincolnshire History and Archaeology*, 29 (1994), 7–10).

[51] Housecarls are now seen as men, probably of Danish descent, of this kind, albeit at a high social level, rather than a standing army with its own organization. See N. Hooper, 'The Housecarls in England in the Eleventh Century', *ANS*, 7 (1984), 161–76.

[52] F. M. Stenton, *The Free Peasantry of the Northern Danelaw* (Oxford, 1969); *idem*, 'The Danes in England', *Preparatory to Anglo-Saxon England*, ed. D. M. Stenton (Oxford, 1970), 136–65; *Documents Illustrative of the Social and Economic History of the Danelaw from Various Collections*, ed. F. M. Stenton, British Academy Records of Social and Economic History, 5 (1920).

Thus it is that, despite a vigorous land market, Domesday sokes survived well into the thirteenth century and beyond.[53]

Freedom of alienation in this way was no peculiarity of an area of Danish colonization. Throughout the Domesday corpus free men and sokemen are repeatedly said to be free to go with their lands or to have held *in alodio* (that is as an alod, in 'freehold')[54] and yet they were in the soke of a lord or belonged to a manor.[55] Lydeard and Leigh in Somerset, for example, had always rendered customs and services to the bishop of Winchester's manor of Taunton, but they were held TRE by a thegn who was free to go with his land to whatever lord he wished, and the bishop's tenure of the estate was only warranted by a specific grant of the king after the Conquest.[56] In East Anglia the attachment of free men to the manor was often a post-Conquest development, but the *invasiones* reveal that such encroachments were usually at the expense of another manor.[57] Here and there the rights of the king's thegn in 1066 is even made explicit. Thus, Eskil, for example, who gave title to Earl Hugh of Chester, had sake and soke over nine parcels of land which were freely held by other thegns in Northamptonshire.[58]

Many of these free men themselves held manors that incorporated the land of other free men. Soke was reserved to the king's thegn, and the 'land' with which they were free to go was presumably the dues that the free men under them rendered. It was in these latter free men that the soil was vested. It can perhaps best be characterized as family land. In the Danelaw sokemen clearly acted

[53] D. R. Roffe, 'An Introduction to the Lincolnshire Domesday', *The Lincolnshire Domesday*, eds A. Williams and G. H. Martin (London, 1992), 27–9.

[54] The term *alodium* is confined to Circuit I where it stands for the more usual 'could go with his land' etc. A. Williams, 'How Land was Held Before and After the Conquest', *Domesday Book Studies*, eds A. Williams and R. W. H. Erskine (London, 1987), 37–8).

[55] *Contra* S. Oosthuizen, 'Sokemen and Freemen: Tenure, Status, and Landscape Conservatism in Eleventh-Century Cambridgeshire', *Anglo-Saxons: Studies Presented to Cyril Roy Hart*, eds S. Keynes and A. P. Smyth (Dublin, 2005), 186–207, they did not have sake and soke. GDB, 170: *DB Worcs*, C5, of course, explicitly refers to a king's thegn.

[56] GDB, 87v: *DB Somerset*, 2,9; *Regesta Regum Anglo-Normannorum*, i, ed. H. W. C. Davis (Oxford, 1913), no. 386.

[57] D. R. Roffe, 'Introduction', *Little Domesday, Norfolk*, eds A. Williams and G. H. Martin (London, 2000), 26–31.

[58] GDB, 224v: *DB Northants*, 22,9. More obliquely, many urban tenements which were held with sake and soke, and were consequently non-customary, can be shown to have been appurtenant to rural manors held by king's thegns. In the Leicestershire folios land is said to have been held freely but to have belonged to the fees (*feudum*) of Earl Waltheof and the queen before the Conquest (GDB, 232, 232v, 233: *DB Leics*, 13,3;11;45;67;73). *Honor*, although strictly anachronistic, is widely used in the same way to express bookright. For the most recent discussion of the term *feudum*, see P. Taylor, 'The Endowment and Military Obligations of the See of London: A Reassessment of Three Sources', *ANS*, 14 (1991), 307–8, and H. Tsurushima, 'Feodum in Kent c.1066–1215', *Journal of Medieval History*, 21 (1995), 97–115.

independently of their lords, but they could not so easily ignore the interests of the kin. A grantee was wise to solicit and record the assent of a wife and heirs, for many a twelfth-century grant was subsequently challenged, often successfully, by such interested parties.[59] Sokeland was frequently subject to the custom of partible inheritance, and the closely related practice of Borough English, that is ultimogeniture, and it would thus seem that it was entailed within the family.[60] This was perhaps the reality of all freely held land in the eleventh century. Partible inheritance was subsequently only widely prevalent in Kent,[61] although it was still inherent in socage tenure, but GDB frequently asserts that land in the South and South West was held *in paragio* or *pariter*, that is in parage or equally, where Exon records that it was freely held.[62]

Commendation is only explicitly noticed in LDB, but a similar relationship is expressed in Circuit III where sokemen are said to have been the men of certain lords. Here again was a form of superiority that was independent of land holding. Time and again a lord is said to have had the commendation of a man, but 'he was free to go with his land'. The disputes recorded in the *invasiones* of LDB repeatedly underline the point: numerous tenants-in-chief in 1086 had taken land on the ground that their predecessor had the commendation, but successive juries ruled the seisin unjust because the lord in 1086 had had no more than that. Commendation was, moreover, independent. As at Nowton, where a lord held the soil he was also likely to command the commendation of his men; this was a relationship that informed the dependent thegnages of Ely Abbey in Cambridgeshire.[63] But these were very much the exception. Throughout the area free men and sokemen tended to be commended to a man other than their soke lord. In Bedfordshire, Hertfordshire, and Suffolk a concerted plan seems to be at work to avoid local power brokers: a sokeman's commendation more often than not belonged to a lord with no interests in the hundred in which the sokeman resided.[64]

---

[59] *Danelaw Charters, passim.* The same was, of course, true throughout the country.
[60] F. Pollock and F. W. Maitland, *History of English Law* (Cambridge, 1895), i, 647; ii, 279.
[61] It was called 'gravelkind'. It, too, was coming under increasing pressure in the thirteenth century (F. R. H. Du Boulay, *The Lordship of Canterbury: An Essay on Medieval Society* (London, 1966), 145).
[62] R. Welldon Finn, *Domesday Studies: The Liber Exoniensis* (London, 1964), 71–2, 86–93; *DB Devon*, 1,15 note.
[63] *Inquisitio Comitatus Cantabrigiensis*, 193–4.
[64] R. Abels, 'An Introduction to the Bedfordshire Domesday', *The Bedfordshire Domesday*, eds A. Williams and R. W. H. Erskine (London, 1991), 38–40; R. Abels, 'An Introduction to the Hertfordshire Domesday', *The Hertfordshire Domesday*, eds A. Williams and R. W. H. Erskine (London, 1991), 30–2; A. Williams, 'Little Domesday and the English: The Hundred of Colneis in Suffolk', *Domesday Book*, eds E. Hallam and D. Bates (Stroud, 2001), 103–20.

These are characteristics that go to the very heart of the relationship. Despite the soke exercised over them, free men were not subject to the court of the king's thegn. They rendered their own geld and, judging from the obligation of their descendants to make suit of court in the twelfth and thirteenth centuries, performed all the duties of the law-worthy man in the hundred and shire; sokeright was exercised in these communal courts.[65] In the later Middle Ages the lord was to mediate this direct relationship with the machinery of local government through the grant or assumption of leet jurisdiction or the more weighty liberties of return and estreat of writs: he was effectively to guarantee the law-worthiness of his men. Commendation performed a similar function but in a non-seigneurial context. In Domesday Book it is explicitly associated with protection in several passages. Authgi, who held land in Easton in Bedfordshire, was commended by King William to Ralph Taillebois that he should protect him as long as he lived;[66] a free man in Tiscott in Hertfordshire turned to Vigot of Wallingford for protection.[67] Such protection seems to have included surety in court. Robert fitzWymarc, for example, was brought into the hundred when Brungar his man was accused of stealing horses.[68] It is thus clear that lordship of this type can be equated with that embodied in the *hlaford* of the late tenth- and eleventh-century English law codes. Up to *c*. 950 surety for the maintenance of the peace largely devolved upon the kin, but thereafter it was invested in lordship.[69] Unruly kin had long posed a challenge to order

[65] The most comprehensive account of thirteenth-century liberties is to be found in the Hundred Rolls and *Quo Warranto* Rolls (*Rotuli Hundredorum*, ed. W. Illingworth, Record Commission, 2 vols (1812–18); *Placita de Quo Warranto*, ed. W. Illingworth, Record Commission (1818)). Domesday sake and soke is never paralleled by hundredal jurisdiction at the later date unless there was a specific grant of return of writs. The only correlation is with the assize of bread and ale which was often exercised in private (as opposed to public) courts.

[66] GDB, 211v: *DB Beds*, 17,5.

[67] GDB, 137v: *DB Herts*, 19,1.

[68] LDB, 401v–402: *DB Suffolk*, 27,7. This reference helps to explain a correlate of the relationship in the Norfolk and Suffolk folios. Foldsoke was a due that was rendered for use of the lord's fold and it has usually been interpreted as a manorial incident; the lord required his tenants to put their sheep in his pasture to fertilise his land (*VCH Norfolk*, ii, ed. W. Page (London, 1906), 31). There are, indeed, a few references that contrast the right with free tenure (LDB, 203v, 204, 204v, 208v, 230, 249v, 250). But more generally foldsoke is associated with commendation, and here it must be related to the warranting of title. From the early tenth century purchase of livestock had to take place before witnesses and a warrantor and surety had to be invoked to make good title where cattle had strayed or other claims were made upon them (Attenborough, I Athelstan 3; Robertson, II Cnut 24, Laws of William I, 5.1, 5.2, 6.1, 21, 45). The render of foldsoke presumably guaranteed right to livestock kept within the fold. It was, then, a natural corollary of a relationship that ensured the law-worthiness of a free man.

[69] Robertson, III Edmund 7, I Æthelred 1.5, I Æthelred 1.7, II Cnut 30.3b. Lords stood surety for their men in the reign of Athelstan (III Athelstan 7), but the context is probably the household. Abels (*Lordship and Military Obligation*, 257) has argued that the *landhlaford* also provided surety, but the two texts he cites do not support his case. Attenborough, III

that peace gilds had failed to check. The new provisions effectively neutralized recalcitrant families, for henceforward every free man was required to have a lord (*hlaford*) who would vouch for his good behaviour. In return the lord was vested with the warrantee's wergeld, but otherwise typically received only small monetary payments in recognition of his superiority.[70] Lordship of this kind was a public matter; it was declared in the hundred or shire court and could not be repudiated without raising suspicion of criminality.[71] It was, however, terminated by the gross misconduct, outlawry, or death of either party.[72]

There must, of course, have been many considerations that impinged on the choice of lord, but in its essence commendation was a recognition of superiority that was freely entered into. That free men often sought protection from someone other than their soke lord must in large part account for the failure of the king's thegn, either in his capacity as soke lord or surety, to aggregate and territorialize his rights in the pre-Conquest period.[73] The corollary was strong and effective local government underpinned by the king's peace. Royal power and the free community of the shire both maintained and sustained each other throughout the tenth and eleventh centuries. It was a reality that was quickly appreciated. From the late tenth century onwards, the target of lords on the make turned from real estate to the machinery of local government. In the 970s and 980s the crown granted groups of hundreds to the abbeys of Bury St Edmunds, Ely, Peterborough, and Ramsey, and at the same time much of the church of Worcester's local power was founded in its rights (albeit somewhat less than the immunity claimed in Domesday) in Oswaldslow Hundred, while in 1015 Ealdorman Eadric Streona orchestrated opposition to the king in the West through the system of local government.[74]

Athelstan 7 does not mention land, but simply asserts that every man should hold his men in pledge. Robertson, III Edmund 7 reads 'Et omnis homo creditabilis faciat homines suos et omnes qui in pace et terra sua sunt' and it seems unlikely that the relative clause qualifies the *homines suos* (so, Robertson, p. 15, but see also p. 299 where she recognizes the possibility). Rather it refers to another group, that is those who were on his demesne; they can be identified with those who could not recede and did not have freedom of commendation. Cf. those in the household (Robertson, 1 Æthelred 1.10, II Cnut 31). In reality, however, a lord must usually have been a booklord as well as a liege lord.

[70] Typically, where explicit, monetary renders were the regular services owed (GDB, 141v; LDB, 149: *DB Herts*, 37,10;12; *DB Norfolk*, 4,41), but the fact is usually only apparent from the sharing of *commendatio* by a number of lords (LDB, 182v, 188: *DB Norfolk*, 9,111; 196). The close association of commendation with foldsoke in East Anglia emphasizes the judicial element, and one case in Suffolk illustrates the role of lords in legal proceedings which ensued (LDB, 402: *DB Suffolk*, 27,7).

[71] Robertson, II Edward 7, II Athelstan 22, 22.1, 22.2, III Athelstan 4, III Edgar 7.3, II Cnut 57, 77. But cf. Attenborough, Alfred 37.

[72] See, for example, GDB, 211v: *DB Beds*, 17,5; LDB, 311: *DB Suffolk*, 6,79.

[73] Roffe, 'Brought to Book'.

[74] N. D. Hurnard, 'The Anglo-Norman Franchises', *EHR*, 64 (1949), 316–27; W. E. Kapelle, *The Norman Conquest of the North: The Region and its Transformation 1000–1135* (London,

For Maitland and Round, as for some historians today, the high incidence of freedom in some areas was proof positive of the weakness of Old English lordship. This, however, is to equate lordship only with land. If lordship was trammelled by an alliance between the free man and the crown, soke and commendation were nevertheless the mediums of patronage and aristocratic power. Through them lords could command the loyalty of large groups of men who could be relied upon to support their interests in the courts of the shire as in the wider world. Any geography of power that only plotted the hundreds of 1066 would be woefully incomplete. The king's thegn was a nexus of real power and influence, and identifying his interests is a fundamental challenge for the historian. It is a challenge not least because Domesday was no survey of pre-Conquest lordship. Outside Circuits III and VII there are few indications of status and none of them is systematic. Commendation was universal and it seems clear that the repeated insistence that a thegn held freely was a reminder that the commendation lord's successor had no rights in the land.[75] There is, however, no means of determining who those lords were, give or take the extremely rare reference. Sokeright is another matter. There are characteristics of the texts that facilitate the identification of its loci.

A priori, it seems likely that ecclesiastics and the greater secular lords held bookland and, despite the difficulties we have already noted, they are relatively easily identifiable. The title *tainus regis* seems to promise the identification of less exalted holders of bookland. Here and there it may well do precisely that,[76] but that is not usually its significance. Typically, it describes a class of thegn who held directly of the king in return for sundry more or less minor services. The land they held, although entered in a separate chapter at the end of the account of each county, was *terra regis* and was as often as not in close proximity to royal estate centres.[77] Their successors were royal sergeants and they can best be characterized as median

---

1979), 95–8; *ASC*, 94–6. For Oswaldslow and the other ecclesiastical hundreds of Worcestershire, see A. Williams, 'The Spoliation of Worcester', *ANS*, 19 (1996), 384–408, and P. Wormald, 'Oswaldslow: an "Immunity"?', *St Oswald of Worcester: Life and Influence*, eds N. P. Brooks and C. Cubitt (Leicester and New York, 1996), 117–28.

[75] *DIB*, 34.

[76] In Essex there are a number of entries in the body of the text in which the TRE tenant is called a king's thegn. Diplomatically, these have the form of a holder of sake and soke, but the number and distribution must introduce an element of doubt. This is one of many peculiarities of the Essex folios.

[77] The GDB scribe was initially ambivalent about their status. In the Yorkshire Summary their manors are said to be the king's, but subsequently he decided to enter them in their own chapter at the end of the Yorkshire *breves*. At some point, however, he had another change of mind. Three hundred and thirty-two manors of *taini regis*, either waste in 1086 or without tenants (i.e. without a thegn or dreng), were entered on two separate sheets and appended to the end of the king's *breve*. For a full discussion, see D. R. Roffe, 'The Yorkshire Summary: A Domesday Satellite', *Northern History* (1991), 242–60. Throughout the text, land of this kind continued to be enrolled in the king's chapter.

thegns who served the king.[78] King's thegns, in the sense of the law codes, are more reliably identified by the record of sake and soke. Holders of the liberty are listed in the Derbyshire, Kent, Lincolnshire, Nottinghamshire, and Yorkshire folios in the 'shire customs'.[79] Many are only known from these lists but, not surprisingly, those who are found in other sources can be seen to have occupied leading roles in their communities before and immediately after the Conquest. Unfortunately, none of the lists is complete; incidental references to sake and soke in the body of the text reveal that there were more king's thegns, perhaps of more modest means, who escaped notice.[80] The circumstance in which their liberty is recorded is normally disputed tenure and we must suppose that there were many others who have gone unrecorded in this way.[81]

This is generally typical of the rest of Domesday. LDB is more expansive than GDB, but by and large sake and soke is only mentioned in exceptional circumstances.[82] Locally, certain features of the text supplement this scant record. In Derbyshire and Nottinghamshire sake and soke is explicitly associated with a place: Henry de Ferrers in Ednaston, Doveridge, and Brailsford, Alsige son of Karski in Worksop, Walter d'Aincourt in Granby, Morton, and Pilsey. This usage draws attention to some sixteen references to a 'chief manor (*capitale manerium*)', suggesting that it too was a centre of tribute and its lord a king's thegn.[83] It has been suggested, perhaps somewhat more tenuously, that the right to a church was a similar marker in Cheshire.[84] More clearly, the same may be indicated when the value of one manor is said to be included in another.[85] More subtle, and tricky, are

---

[78] For the most recent discussion, see R. Lavelle, 'All the King's Men? Land and Royal Service in Eleventh-Century England', *Southern History*, 26 (2005 for 2004), 1–37.

[79] GDB, iv, 337, 280v, 298v: *DB Kent*, D25; *DB Lincs*, T5; *DB Notts*, S5; *DB Yorks*, C36.

[80] There are ten names in the Yorkshire list (Earl Harold, Mærle-Sveinn, Ulf Fenman, Thorgot Lag, Toki son of Auti, Edwin and Morcar, Gamal son of Osbeorht, Kofse, Knut), for example, while the text supplies a further ten (Archbishop Ealdræd, St Peter's of York, Karli, Thorfinnr, Thor, Haldor?, Ligulf, Beornwulf, William Malet, Thorulf).

[81] Nevertheless, Domesday provides a reasonably comprehensive sample in these areas. Its structure sometimes reflects the underlying sokeright. In Lincolnshire, for example, there are a number of *breves* with successive repetitions of wapentake sequence, pointed up by the use of blank lines in the text, in each of which there is a single holder of sake and soke.

[82] Fleming lists 103 named individuals in all who held sake and soke (R. Fleming, *Domesday Book and the Law* (Cambridge, 1998), 527–8).

[83] GDB, 11, 18, 26, 41v, 58, 104, 163, 164, 166, 173, 173v, 181, 223, 367v, 377: *DB Kent*, 5,192; *DB Sussex*, 9,4;12,6; *DB Hants*, 3,9; *DB Berks*, 1,46; *DB Devon*, 6,13; *DB Gloucs*, 1,24;52.19,1; *DB Worcs*, 2,41;55; *DB Hereford*, 1,61; *DB Northants*, 18,8; *DB Lincs*, 57,14.CK27.

[84] N. J. Higham, 'Patterns of Patronage and Power: The Governance of Late Anglo-Saxon Cheshire', *Government, Religion and Society in Northern England, 1000–1700*, eds J. C. Appleby and P. Dalton (Stroud, 1997), 1–13.

[85] Multiple-manor entries have one value, often a conventional sum that indicates that it is not the total of a number of discrete renders. Otherwise, in fifty or so entries one holding is said to be valued in another. It is not always possible to demonstrate that both

calligraphic devices. Square initial I's are the norm for principal entries in the text, with the rustic variety reserved for subordinate tenements. On occasion, though, the account of a manor begins with the latter, and the supposition must be that there is a relationship to a superior lord in an adjacent manor.[86] Nevertheless, the conclusion is not invariable. As we have seen,[87] in the later folios of GDB rustic I may mark nothing more than the use of a schedule in the compilation of the text. However, all of these are characteristics that are exceptional.

The diplomatic of the text goes some way to filling the gaps. Throughout the Domesday corpus there are found entries in which two or more manors are described together with a record of the corresponding number of holders in 1066.[88] This form has frequently been explained as merely a function of the amalgamation of small estates after the Conquest by rationalizing Norman lords. Sometimes this is an appropriate interpretation. There were three manors in Gravesend TRE held by Leofric, Wulfwine, and Godwine, but in 1086 there was only one held by Herbert fitzIvo.[89] More often, however, it does not tell the full story. One assessment to the geld and a single TRE value hint at a pre-Conquest identity of the complex, while sometimes the disparate elements still functioned as discrete tenurial units in 1086, that is, the number of TRE holders is matched by an equal number of TRW tenants. Rather the form seems to point to interdependent manors (both within and without the family) which were situated in the same vill. Sometimes the TRE holders were dependent on a common lord outside the complex.[90] At others, the first-named TRE holder can be identified with an individual of regional standing who held sake and soke in at least some of his estates, while the second and subsequently named individuals are otherwise relatively obscure.

Multiple-manor entries of this type were not intended to represent lordship; they are a prosaic function of entry formation in GDB.[91] It is, nevertheless, significant that there is usually no qualification of the tenure where a lord is one of the TRE holders. The usual form (outside Circuit VI which displays its own unique diplomatic) was the bald statement 'X and Y held (*X et Y tenuit*)'. This is a form that is otherwise almost invariably associated with earls and the like and

were manors (one is often called simply 'land'), but the occurrence of named TRE holders indicates dependence of some sort.

[86] See, for example, the two manors in Oakham (GDB, 293v: *DB Rutland*, R17–18).

[87] See above p. 43.

[88] For a detailed discussion of the form, see D. R. Roffe, 'Nottinghamshire and the North: A Domesday Study', http://www.roffe.co.uk/phd/phd040.htm.

[89] GDB, 7v: *DB Kent*, 5,54.

[90] See, for example, GDB, 27: *DB Sussex*, 12,35. 'William de Vatteville holds Perching. Azur held it of King Edward, and 2 men [held] of Azur. It was assessed at 5½ hides then, as now. Then there were 2 halls. Now [it is] in 1 manor.'

[91] See above, p. 83.

those who held with sake and soke.[92] It is possible to point to the odd entry in which a man is said to have held freely or could go with his land who also enjoyed sake and soke elsewhere,[93] but generally the contrast is pointed. The implications seem clear. As we know from the *invasiones*, the function of the *libere* clause was to draw attention to the fact that the successor to the commendation lord had no right in the land and, by implication, in the soke.[94] King's thegns, of course, had no such lord, for they made their forfeitures directly to the king. It would seem that to state that they held 'freely' was redundant. The *tenuit* formula is clearly not always a variation on *tenuit libere* and the like. It is, then, probably a fair indication that the lords it distinguishes were king's thegns.[95]

Initial analysis of these patterns goes a long way to confirm this observation.[96] There are limitations. Exon shows that the GDB scribe did not always assidu-ously copy his sources, for where the one has *tenuit libere*, the other sometimes has *tenuit* alone, and vice versa. In some counties like Essex the *tenuit libere* formula is comparatively rare and a distinction may not have been made at all.[97]

---

[92] *DIB*, 34–8. Indeed, in the Northamptonshire and Leicestershire folios the formula is expanded to '*tenuit cum soca et saca*' in 20 per cent and 40 per cent of cases respectively.

[93] The implication here would seem to be that the estate was family land, often held of another soke lord. See below, p. 162, for a discussion of the phenomenon.

[94] *DIB*, 34.

[95] The point is nicely made in the Berkshire folios where the variant '*X tenuit de rege*' is found. *Pace* N. Hooper, 'An Introduction to the Berkshire Domesday', *The Berkshire Domesday*, eds A. Williams and R. W. H. Erskine (London, 1988), 18, the usage is contrasted with the *in alodio* formula.

[96] Lists are posted at http://www.roffe.co.uk/thegns.htm. For the Leicestershire thegns, see D. R. Roffe, 'Great Bowden and its Soke', *Anglo-Saxon Landscapes in the East Midlands*, ed. J. Bourne (Leicester, 1996), 107–20; for Norfolk, D. R. Roffe, 'Introduction', *The Norfolk Domesday*, eds A. Williams and G. H. Martin (London, 2000), 26–34. The charter evidence is largely consonant with this conclusion. See, for example, Baxter and Blair ('Land Tenure and Royal Patronage in the Early English Kingdom: A Model and a Case Study', 19–46). They did not consider the *tenuit* and *tenuit libere* formulas in detail in their analysis of pre-Conquest tenure in Bampton Hundred (Oxon). However, it should be noted that Witney, the one bookland estate that is explicitly identified in GDB, exhibits the simple *tenuit* formula (S701, S1001; GDB, 155: *DB Oxon*, 3,1). They identify Yelford as possibly book-land, but the *tenuit libere* formula is found (GDB, 160: *DB Oxon*, 45,1). Conversely, what they term 'ministerial' tenures almost all exhibit the *tenuit libere* formula – Bromscott and Pemscott, Black Bourton, Westwell, Brize Norton, Weald, and Averscot (GDB, 158, 160, 160v: *DB Oxon*, 27,3.40,1.45,2.58,17–8;21). Lew, which they identify as ministerial, has the *tenuit* formula but was nevertheless probably bookland – it was granted in 984 to Ælfwine the *scriptor* (S853; GDB, 160v: *DB Oxon*, 58,20). Of the comital estate, Langford held by Earl Harold exhibits the *tenuit* formula, while Broughton Poggs was explicitly held by 3 freemen and therefore, quite appropriately, the *tenuit libere* formula is found (GDB, 154v, 160: *DB Oxon*, 1,8–9.50,1). Finally, Broadwell is identified as possibly comital, although the *tenuit libere* formula is again found (GDB, 160: *DB Oxon*, 54,1).

[97] In this, as in many other features, Essex is distinctive and it is simply possible that king's thegns were thicker on the ground. See below, pp. 303–4.

Furthermore, three further classes of tenure are also distinguished by the *tenuit* form. Land held in alms is almost never said to be freely held; since it was quit of all custom and service the formula is perhaps inappropriate. Bookland held in laenage also exhibits the form. *Beneficia* of this type are generally only identifiable when explicitly noticed, although irregularities in other forms may hint at their existence.[98] Finally, royal and comital estates almost invariably exhibit the form. Although they were clearly primary nexus of soke, they were not bookland in the sense that they were not heritable.[99]

By and large, these are the exceptions. They are, however, exceptions that underline an important aspect of status and tenure in 1066. Where lordship is identified with land, tenure tends to define status. In pre-Conquest England matters were by necessity otherwise. The tenant of *laenland* had sokeright but he was not a king's thegn, although he might discharge part of his lord's obligation to the king. Conversely, a man might be a king's thegn by virtue of bookland, but he did not necessarily have equal right in all of his lands. In addition to laenages, he might also hold family land which owed soke to another king's thegn: time and again, an individual who is otherwise known to have had sake and soke is said to have held freely.[100] While some of these references are probably mistakes on the part of the Domesday scribe, not all can be so. The disjunction of lordship and land before the Conquest means that there was not always a single relationship between a man and every parcel of land that he had rights in. It is a characteristic of tenure that is of importance to an understanding of the Norman settlement.

[98] Some thegns, for example, are said to have held 'under (*sub*)' or 'from (*de*)' a lord, perhaps indicating that the estate was leased. Typical of the form is a reference to land in Codicote and 'Oxwyce' in Hertfordshire held by Ælfwine of Gotton under the abbot of St Albans; Ælfwine could not alienate it from the church (GDB, 135v: *DB Herts*, 10,6). Stephen Baxter, 'The Leofwinesons: Power, Property and Patronage in the Early English Kingdom', unpublished DPhil. thesis, University of Oxford (2002), has undertaken a detailed study of these forms and their referents.

[99] Baxter and Blair, 'Land Tenure and Royal Patronage in the Early English Kingdom', 19–46, have forcibly made the point, but, of course, it does not follow that the form cannot be a marker of bookland or, *a fortiori*, that the concept of bookland had no content in 1066.

[100] Roffe, 'Introduction', *The Norfolk Domesday*, 26–34. Robertson, II Cnut 77 presupposes that a thegn might have different types of land: 'Concerning the man who deserts his lord. And the man who, through cowardice, deserts his lord or his comrades on a military expedition, either by sea or by land, shall lose all that he possesses and his life, and the lord shall take back the property and the land which he has given him. And if he has bookland it shall pass into the king's hands.'

Post-Conquest lordship

Identifying lords in 1086 is a great deal easier than identifying those of 1066. Tenants-in-chief, who held their lands directly from the king, occupy a central position within the county divisions of Domesday Book. It is important to realize, however, that they did not exclusively do so. The *taini regis* were also accorded separate chapters, albeit usually as a group, like tenants-in-chief. As we have seen, they were subordinate tenants who held directly from the king but were in every other respect the equivalent of lowly median thegns.[101] Others like sergeants and almsmen were also often given their own chapters. Once these classes are excluded, however, some 200 tenants-in-chief can be readily identified by collating the lists given at the beginning of each county section and the *breves* themselves.[102] Here and there are uncertainties,[103] but by and large it is clear that this is an exhaustive list.

Tenants, holders of manors under the tenants-in-chief, are more erratically recorded. Numerous earlier or contemporary documents notice tenancies where Domesday is silent[104] and little attempt was made to distinguish those that do appear: Richards, Rogers, and Williams follow each other without any indication of identity.[105] There is evidence that a more concise record was made of them in the inquest itself. In ICC and Exon distinguishing cognomina are usually provided, albeit only on the first occasion that they appear in each hundred.[106] The Domesday scribes either did not understand the convention or they were not too fussed by tenants.

The deficiencies of the record can be rectified in a number of ways where contemporary evidence is absent. Individuals can normally be identified by tracing the subsequent history of the fees in question. There must be a presumption that where two manors are held by one family in the twelfth and thirteenth centuries the Domesday tenants will be an individual if they share a name. Such evidence suggests that Domesday tenants tend to be early representatives of what was later

---

[101] Above, pp. 158–9.
[102] K. S. B. Keats-Rohan, *Domesday People: A Prosopography of Persons Occurring in English Documents, 1066–1166: 1. Domesday Book* (Woodbridge, 1998), 23.
[103] For the status of the lists, see V. H. Galbraith, *The Making of Domesday Book* (Oxford, 1961), 190–8.
[104] They can be identified in the COEL database.
[105] The exception is in the accounts of the great territorial lordships like Chester.
[106] Count Alan's tenants in Cambridgeshire, for example, are undifferentiated in the folios of GDB. In ICC, however, almost all are positively identified the first time they appear in each hundred unless they have a very rare name, such as the Gollan who appears only once. Thus, in Longstowe Hundred Almær of Bourn's toponym is given in the entry for Bourn itself but not in those of Caldecote, Longstowe, and Hatley St George that follow (ICC, 89). The pattern in Exon has not been systematically explored; it would repay more attention.

known as the honorial barony, the major tenants of a lord.[107] This realization in
its turn has prompted an examination of enfeoffment patterns in Northern France.
Lords brought their men with them, and so it is often possible to suggest the
continental origins of various tenants.

Using these techniques Katharine Keats-Rohan has identified almost all the
holders of land in 1086.[108] Less than a handful of English nobles remained to
represent the pre-Conquest order at its highest level.[109] The holders of land who
had fought at Hastings had immediately forfeited their lands where they survived
the battle; the remaining earls and king's thegns succumbed in the following ten
years in the aftermath of the successive rebellions that punctuated the Norman
settlement. By the time of Domesday the tenants-in-chief of native descent, or at
least with pre-Conquest antecedents, were confined to Kolgrimr, Edward of Salisbury, Thorkil of Warwick, Kolsveinn, Gospatric son of Arnketil, and Iudichael of
Totnes. At a lower level in the social hierarchy, however, there were more survivors.
Median thegns holding of the king, the *taini regis* of the Domesday texts, are the
most visible: in every county there are scores of English men who continued to
enjoy an estate under King William where they or their father had done so under
Edward the Confessor. They were, however, not immune from forfeiture, for some
of their manors were held by the king or had passed to Norman lords by 1086.
Many, probably all, were subject to a process of delivery of their lands after 1066.[110]
Median thegns are less conspicuous in the honours of the tenants-in-chief. In the
North they are relatively common, especially in the West Riding of Yorkshire and
parts of Nottinghamshire, where they appear as Domesday tenants.[111] Likewise,

---

[107] Keats-Rohan, *Domesday People*, 24–6. There was nothing of the lower classes about these
men. For a debate on the status of the more lowly knight, see S. P. J. Harvey, 'The Knight
and the Knight's Fee in England', *Past and Present*, 49 (1970), 3–43; D. F. Fleming, 'Landholding by *Milites* in Domesday Book: A Revision', *ANS*, 13 (1991), 83–98; J. Gillingham,
'1066 and the Introduction of Chivalry into England', in *Law and Government in England
and Normandy: Essays in Honour of J. C. Holt*, eds G. Garnett and J. Hudson (Cambridge,
1994), 31–55; J. Gillingham 'Thegns and Knights in Eleventh-Century England: Who was
then the Gentleman?', *TRHS*, 6th series, 5 (1995), 129–53. The low status of those classified
as *milites* cannot be used to categorize the holders of manors. See below, pp. 219–20.

[108] COEL database; Keats-Rohan, *Domesday People*, 23–4.

[109] For the following, see Williams, *The English and the Norman Conquest*; H. M. Thomas,
'The Significance and Fate of the Native English Landholders of 1086', *EHR*, 118 (2003),
303–33.

[110] See, for example, GDB, 211: *DB Beds*, 14,1: Earnwine the priest held land in Harrowden
and 'the father of this aforesaid man held this land. He was a man of King Edward. He
has no livery officer nor writ for this, but he took possession of it to the king's loss, as
the hundred attests.' Not all *taini regis* succeeded to their own land, but equally might be
granted the lands of others.

[111] Where a pre-Conquest holder of land survived as a tenant in 1086, it is usually assumed
that, in being subject to a Norman lord, he had suffered a depression in status. This is,
of course, possible. However, it is as likely that he merely 'stayed in place' just like the

there were large numbers in the Count of Mortain's fee in Cornwall.[112] Elsewhere, English tenants are an apparent rarity.[113]

One of the great achievements in Domesday studies in the last ten years has been to demonstrate that this is a Domesday artefact. Christopher Lewis has formulated the criteria for identifying Englishmen in Domesday Book and has succeeded in recognizing many that have previously gone unsuspected.[114] More crucially, however, he has demonstrated that beyond the great castleries, subtenants, that is tenants of Domesday tenants, are largely absent from the record.[115] It is precisely at this level that English survivors were probably ubiquitous. Ann Williams has chronicled the fate of many of them into the twelfth century.[116] Domesday misrepresents the extent of English tenure in 1086 because it was a survey of the lands of the tenants-in-chief and their honorial barons, that is, their most influential tenants.

There remained a substantial substratum of English tenure in 1086 and it is becoming increasingly clear that the Norman Conquest was in large part a seizure of the levers of power.[117] The Conquest has always been perceived, and rightly so, as a point of departure in English history; it is therein that most medieval families and institutions find their origins and from the very beginning they were anxious to record their descent and to preserve records that demonstrated it. In consequence, much more is known about the tenants-in-chief and their tenants in 1086 than of their pre-Conquest predecessors. That, combined with the focus of Domesday Book, has fostered the notion that England was thoroughly Norman-ized in every sense in 1086. And yet there was no attempt to quantify the extent of Norman settlement since the resources were not available. That is only now possible with the publication of the COEL database. Through her tireless prosopographical

---

taini regis who held in both 1066 and 1086. For an analysis of such thegns in Dorset, Kent, Cambridgeshire, and Shropshire, see Williams, *The English and the Norman Conquest*, 78–97. Edward held Hambledon in Hampshire from Earl Godwine before the Conquest and from Earl Roger, Godwine's successor, in 1086 (GDB, 44v: *DB Hants*, 21,19). An initial examination of 371 incidences in GDB suggests that this situation, or something like it, was common. A thorough survey of the phenomenon would be desirable.

[112] I. N. Soulsby, 'An Introduction to the Cornwall Domesday', *The Cornwall Domesday*, eds A. Williams and R. W. H. Erskine (London, 1988), 11–12.

[113] For a list, see Thomas, 'The Significance and Fate of the Native English Landholders of 1086', 331–3.

[114] C. P Lewis, 'Joining the Dots: A Methodology for Identifying the English in Domesday Book', *Family Trees and the Roots of Politics: The Prosopography of Britain and France from the Tenth to the Twelfth Century*, ed. K. S. B. Keats-Rohan (Woodbridge, 1997), 69–87.

[115] C. P Lewis, 'Domesday Jurors', *The Haskins Society Journal*, 5 (1993), 17–44; Lewis, 'Joining the Dots: A Methodology for Identifying the English in Domesday Book', 69–87.

[116] Williams, *The English and the Norman Conquest*.

[117] For a contrary view, see Thomas, 'The Significance and Fate of the Native English Landholders of 1086'.

researches, Katherine Keats-Rohan has been able to demonstrate that there are probably no more than 2500 newcomers named in the Domesday corpus.[118] There must have been, of course, additional settlers who do not appear in the texts, but the fact remains that the Norman Conquest largely saw the replacement of one elite by another.

How that transfer took place has been the subject of one of the more lively debates of the last few years. Six mechanisms have been recognized. First, there was a process which has been dubbed 'antecession',[119] whereby a tenant-in-chief was granted the lands of a single pre-Conquest holder of land, his predecessor (*antecessor*), and thereby succeeded to all the latter's interests and obligations. Geoffrey de Mandeville, for example, succeeded to the lands of Esger the Staller in nine or so counties. Second, estates were granted individually. Here and there throughout Domesday Book there are references to writs and charters whereby the king conveyed the title to a manor to a tenant-in-chief. Third, land was apparently granted to individuals on a geographical basis regardless of pre-Conquest tenure.[120] In Sussex the Rapes of Arundel, Hastings, Lewes, and Pevensey were granted in 1067 to Roger of Montgomery, Humphrey de Tilleul, William de Warenne, and Robert of Mortain as castleries on the continental model to guard the south coast. The fifth Rape of Bramber was in existence by 1084. Similarly, Herefordshire was granted to William fitzOsbern in 1069 along with the Isle of Wight and possibly the New Forest area,[121] Cheshire to Gerbod the Fleming and then to Earl Hugh d'Avranches in 1069–70, and Shropshire to Roger of Montgomery at about the same date to create a strong Norman presence in the Welsh Marches. Cornwall was likewise given to Robert of Mortain to hold the West Country. There may have been a comparable plan to grant Kent to Odo of Bayeux, and elsewhere strategic areas seem to have been conferred on a single tenant-in-chief. Drogo de la Beuvriere held Holderness and Count Alan of Brittany what became known as Richmondshire in the North Riding of Yorkshire, and land was granted to Richard fitzGilbert in Kent to form the lowy of Tonbridge.[122] In all cases, the tenant-in-

[118] Keats-Rohan, *Domesday People*, 23, puts the total at 2468. There are additionally 992 names of people of native descent who were holding land in 1086. The number of individuals, while clearly smaller than this total, has not been determined. Palmer suggests about 8000 newcomers in 'The Wealth of the Secular Aristocracy', *ANS*, 22 (1999), 286–7.

[119] Fleming, *Kings and Lords in Conquest England*, 180.

[120] Fleming, *Kings and Lords in Conquest England*, 145–8.

[121] K. Mew, 'The Dynamics of Lordship and Landscape as Revealed in a Domesday Study of the *Nova Foresta*', *ANS*, 23 (2000), 155–66.

[122] P. Grierson, in 'Weights and Measures', *Domesday Studies*, eds A. Williams and R. W. H. Erskine (London, 1987), 82, suggests that the *leuga* was a square league. But surely the referent is less a measure than a jurisdiction in the same way that *banleuca* is. This is evidently the meaning of the *leuga* that belonged to Ripon in Yorkshire (GDB, 303v: *DB Yorks*, 2W7). The fact that Tonbridge itself is not described in Domesday Book suggests that it was indeed privileged inland. See below, pp. 202, 313.

chief had title to the estates of all pre-Conquest holders of land except those of the church. Fourth, newcomers married English heiresses and widows. The Breton Geoffrey de la Guerche, for example, had title to much of the lands of Leodwine and his son Leofric Cild in Leicestershire, Lincolnshire, Northamptonshire, and Nottinghamshire through marriage to Leodwine's daughter and heir Ælfgifu;[123] the Fleming Walter de Douai came into possession of Uffculme in Devon by marriage to an English woman, Eadgytha widow of Hemming;[124] and Richard Iuvenis married the widow of Alfwine, sheriff of Gloucestershire, and succeeded to his estates in Gloucestershire.[125] Fifth, land was acquired by officials through the exercise of their office. Sheriffs were undoubtedly in the best position to profit in this way. Eustace, sheriff of Huntingdon, is an egregious and well-documented example.[126] Sixth, and finally, land was simply taken by powerful local lords as the opportunity arose. Throughout Domesday there are references to land illegally taken by tenants-in-chief.

Of these six mechanisms of land transfer it is generally agreed that three were of peripheral importance. Individual grants, it is true, could sometimes convey a group of estates,[127] but the use of writs and charters to distribute a significant proportion of the land of England would presuppose a land register even more detailed than Domesday Book itself. Intermarriage was also rare. There can be no doubt that it was more common than is apparent from the extant sources, but it was a device that was not favoured by the Norman aristocracy: the tenants-in-chief who are known to have sought English heiresses were either drawn from the lesser Norman nobility or were non-Norman.[128] Finally, sheriffs and the like accumulated many parcels of land in the exercise of their office, but most of the tenements were small and in total do not amount to much.

The importance of illegal seizures has probably also been exaggerated. Robin Fleming has argued that the *clamores*, *invasiones*, and *terre occupate* attest a free-for-all in the Norman settlement of England. But this is to be dazzled, not to

---

[123] *Charters of the Honour of Mowbray 1107–1191*, ed. D. E. Greenway, Records of Social and Economic History, New Series, 1, British Academy (1972), xx–xxi.

[124] *The Great Chartulary of Glastonbury*, ed. A. Watkin, 3 vols, Somerset Record Society, 59, 63, 64 (1947–56), i, 126–8.

[125] GDB, 167: *DB Gloucs*, 34,8; Williams, 'Introduction to the Gloucestershire Domesday', 35.

[126] R. Abels, 'Sheriffs, Lord-Seeking and the Norman Settlement of the South-East Midlands', *ANS*, 19 (1997), 19–50.

[127] The grant of Sleaford to the bishop of Lincoln (*Registrum Antiquissimum of Lincoln*, ed. C. W. Foster, Lincoln Record Society, 27 (1931), i, 2–3) certainly included extensive sokeland in seven vills in the wapentake of Aswardhurn in Lincolnshire. It may also have included an extensive group of estates in Lincolnshire, Leicestershire, and Rutland which the bishop of Lincoln held in 1086 in succession to Barthi, the pre-Conquest lord of Sleaford (GDB, 230, 344, 344v, 221: *DB Leics*, 3,11; *DB Lincs*, 7,38–43;45–50; *DB Northants*, 5,1–4.

[128] Keats-Rohan, *Domesday People*, 28.

say misled,[129] by the historical goodies. Disputes do indeed command attention in the Domesday texts, not least because they are often the only relief in
a turgid litany of statistics. They reveal much about Domesday procedures and
the workings of eleventh-century society,[130] but their historiographical importance
has exaggerated their relevance as an index of the settlement. The seizure of land
and the long-drawn-out legal actions that ensued had a long and, no doubt to
the perpetrators, honourable history in pre-Conquest England. The conquerors
and settlers of William's reign had no monopoly in that respect. In reading any
monastic chronicle one might be forgiven for concluding that a sizeable proportion
of church lands was always illicitly in the hands of aggressors. In reality there is
no way of determining what was 'normal'. But it seems clear that disputes affected
only a small proportion of the lands of England in 1086. A few statistics. By my
estimation there are 1199 claims in the Domesday corpus (that is, in Exon as well
as LDB and GDB) out of a total of some 29,000 separate entries in Domesday
Book. This figure, of course, relates to causes and there has never been an analysis
of the extent of the lands involved: many include small parcels of land, although a
small minority concerned a number of manors. Lincolnshire, however, will serve to
illustrate the magnitude of the problem.[131] More claims are recorded in the county
than anywhere else and yet they relate only to 148 parcels of land, assessed at 266
carucates, out of the 1655 described with a total assessment of 4316 carucates.[132]
Title to only 6 per cent of holdings in the county was in question in 1086, and

[129] Since presentments have been seen as judgements, the claimant has usually been seen as
the injured party. In reality, they can often be shown to be 'shooting a line' as much as the
aggressors. Ely Abbey, for example, frequently laid claim to land where it was only entitled
to soke or commendation (*DIB*, 23). In such cases the tenurial arrangements of DB may
represent a fairer picture of right. A *locus classicus* is the various accounts of land in Shelford
in Cambridgeshire. Ely had the soke in 1066, Eadgifu 'the Fair', the commendation, and
6 or 7 sokemen the land. By 1086 Ely still had the soke, Count Alan the commendation,
and Hardwin de Scales the land (GDB, 191, 194, 198: *DB Cambs*, 5,27.14,22.26,18; IE
107). Despite its protestations to the contrary, there are no grounds for assuming that Ely
was hard-done-by in this distribution of the spoils, although it might have amounted to
a defeat for its aspirations. The 'spoliation of Worcester' was also not quite as the church
of Worcester chose to represent it. Ann Williams, 'The Spoliation of Worcester', *ANS*, 19
(1996), 399, has argued that, in a contest between a powerful and wealthy corporation and
officers of local government with limited resources, it was probably the church that was
the villain of the piece. St Paul's, London, even seems to have preyed on another church:
it claimed Caddington in Hertfordshire by right of its predecessor Leofwine Cild who had
held it in laenage from St Albans Abbey (GDB, 136: *DB Herts*, 13,2; S1235). The canons
were equally predatory in Essex (P. Taylor, 'Introduction', *Little Domesday Book, Essex*, eds
A. Williams and G. H. Martin (London, 2000), 25).
[130] Fleming, *Domesday Book and the Law: Society and Legal Custom in Early Medieval
England*.
[131] For the following, see *DIB*, 23–4.
[132] Roffe, 'Hundreds and Wapentakes', 35. Claims to soke *qua* jurisdiction alone have been
excluded.

moreover most of this concerned soke dues, that is jurisdiction, rather than land. If Lincolnshire is anywhere near typical – and there is nothing to suggest that it was unusually lightly affected by illegal seizures – then the Domesday claims hardly attest a land at the mercy of a predatory aristocracy.

Further debate has centred on the relative importance of the remaining two mechanisms, that is antecession and distribution by district. The creation of the great castleries has usually been seen as a species of pragmatic strategic thinking, but in the past antecession was seen as the means by which most land was transferred. For Stenton it was axiomatic that almost every TRE holder of land was a 'lord' and he therefore assumed that there must have been an explicit grant (if not necessarily in writing) for every one.[133] Research on the Northern Danelaw modified this perception by suggesting a role for overlordship.[134] In Circuit VI there is a handful of references that demonstrate that title to some manors in 1086 was not derived from the sitting tenant, but from his lord. An entry in the Lincolnshire *clamores* relating to 1 carucate of land in Billingborough exemplifies the type.[135] The men of Aveland Wapentake asserted that Robert of Stafford claimed the manor unjustly because Karli, who is ascribed the land in the text, held it from Ralph the staller. Robert held the rest of Karli's estates in the area, but here Count Alan had title since he had succeeded to the lands of Ralph. Likewise, Ely claimed manors held by various tenants-in-chief in Cambridgeshire, Hertfordshire, Norfolk, and Suffolk on the ground that the manors concerned were sokeland of the abbey.[136] In some cases, it would seem the grant of one manor could convey title to all the manors that were held from it.

Peter Sawyer identified this type of relationship with the various forms of lordship found elsewhere in the text, notably with commendation of Circuits III and VII and, adducing various references throughout the Domesday corpus, argued that the Norman Conquest saw a change of personnel but heralded no tenurial revolution.[137] This conclusion has in its turn been roundly dismissed by Robin Fleming.[138] She accepts that antecession was a mechanism of land transmission, but avers that the number of references to pre-Conquest overlordship in Domesday Book is small and insufficient to argue for continuity. Further, a computer-aided analysis of lordship in the eastern counties, as indicated by explicit notice of commendation in GDB and LDB, reveals that bonds of lordship were usually not respected in the post-Conquest period. There she sees free enterprise as a significant factor. Antecession, she argues, was generally of limited importance.

[133] F. M. Stenton, *Anglo-Saxon England*, 3rd edn (Oxford, 1971), 626.
[134] Roffe, 'Norman Tenants-in-Chief and their Pre-Conquest Predecessors in Nottinghamshire', 3–7; Roffe, 'Nottinghamshire and the North: A Domesday Study'.
[135] GDB, 377v: *DB Lincs*, CK51.
[136] IE, 123–4.
[137] Sawyer, '1066–1086: A Tenurial Revolution?', 71–85.
[138] Fleming, *Kings and Lords in Conquest England*, 107–231.

It appears to have been employed in the earliest stages of the Norman settlement and was confined to the demesne estates of English lords. Geographical distribution was a far more significant mechanism. In Nottinghamshire, Derbyshire, parts of Lincolnshire, Kent, Sussex, and Yorkshire land distribution echoed the divisions of shire, hundred, and wapentake more closely than pre-Conquest lordship. Fleming concludes that by any standard the Norman settlement saw a massive reorganization of land of unprecedented proportions.

Fleming is clearly right in reasserting what Domesday tells us time and again: commendation conveyed no land. She is also right in pointing out that some Norman lords might opine differently when it suited them. Both she and Sawyer, however, fail to recognize the role of soke. That it was a significant characteristic of post-Conquest tenure might be suspected from its continuing citation in charters.[139] Right up to the late twelfth century sake and soke is a liberty that is regularly granted. Nor was it any empty form; it is only an attribute of land that was granted in hereditary fee. The echoes of bookland are resounding. And they are echoes that are articulated in contemporary legal thinking. In cc. 9 and 20 of the Leges Henrici Primi it is asserted that sake and soke was inherent in the tenant-in-chief's honour.[140] As Reid showed in 1920,[141] the liberty, and the 'nighness' to the king to which it gave rise, defined what later became known as tenure by barony.

The equation of barony with thegnage is remarkably precise. The tenant-in-chief, like the king's thegn, rendered a relief that was higher than that of a lord holding by knight service; he was free of local juries and made his forfeitures directly to the king; he was personally responsible for the services due from his honour and, in consequence, his honorial *caput* was deemed to be indivisible.[142] Moreover, his tenants apparently stood in a similar relationship to him as did median thegns to the king's thegn, for, possibly apart from the honorial barony, they did not generally have hereditary right to their lands. They were thus subject to their lord's court rather than the courts of hundred and shire.

The equivalence of baron and thegn in the Leges Henrici Primi is explicit in five passages;[143] it was apparently no slip of the pen. The identification of king's thegns in the Domesday texts allows us to chart how the one succeeded to the soke of the other. Where soke was confined to simple jurisdiction it conferred no right over land. Otherwise, however, it invariably conveyed *terra* (that is the soke dues from land) unless there was an explicit royal writ disposing it elsewhere. A

---

[139] Roffe, 'From Thegnage to Barony', 174–6.

[140] *Leges Henrici Primi*, ed. L. J. Downer (Oxford, 1972).

[141] R. R. Reid, 'Barony and Thanage', *EHR*, 35 (1920), 161–99.

[142] *Tractatus de Legibus et Consuetudinibus Anglie qui Glanvilla Vocatur*, ed. G. D. G. Hall (London, 1965), 108; *Bracton on the Laws and Custom of England*, ed. G. E. Woodbine, trans. Samuel E. Thorne, 2 vols (Cambridge, MA, 1968), i, 8; ii, 39.

[143] *Leges Henrici Primi*, cc. 35.1a, 37.1, 41.1b, 80.9b, 87.5.

predecessor's right to sake and soke was above all the surest guarantee of title in 1086. In those counties in which lists are given – Derbyshire, Kent, Lincolnshire, Nottinghamshire, Yorkshire[144] – the lands of earls are widely dispersed.[145] Each king's thegn, by contrast, tended to give title to only one tenant-in-chief. It is a pattern that is repeated in other counties. Oxfordshire provides an example. There king's thegns have to be identified by the *tenuit* formula (Table 5.1). In thirty-four *breves* there is no indication of bookland, and in the remaining, it is clear that the lands of earls were likewise dispersed but, remarkably, each king's thegn had only one successor.[146] Oxfordshire, like Leicestershire and several other counties, provides a near perfect example. Exceptions there are aplenty elsewhere. Some are explained by extraordinary circumstances like grants, mortgages, marriage, exchanges, and illegal seisin. In Norfolk, for example, almost all irregularities can be assigned to such causes.[147] Others attest the dismemberment of large fees, often on a county basis,[148] while many remain unexplained. Nevertheless, a tendency is clear: the right to sake and soke was transferred in an orderly way between 1066 and 1086.

With sake and soke went the lands over which it was exercised. In a number of Lincolnshire *breves* groups of manors are defined in the text by spacing and the repetition of wapentake sequence and in each there is one holder of sake and soke and indications that the remaining tenants were of dependent status (Table 5.2).[149] Here the form of the GDB text apparently betrays the structure of extended pre-Conquest bookland estates which were transferred *en bloc*. Elsewhere it is not so easy to identify the lands. And yet repeated references to 'the honour'

---

[144] There is a also list of holders of sake and soke in the lathes of Sutton and Aylesford in the Kent folios, but all of the land went to Odo of Bayeux.

[145] This is especially true of King Harold's lands. C. P. Lewis, 'The Formation of the Honor of Chester, 1066–1100', in *The Earldom of Chester and its Charters: A Tribute to Geoffrey Barraclough*, ed. A. T. Thacker, *Journal of the Chester Archaeological Society*, 71 (1991), 45–6, plausibly suggests that King William's wide distribution of Harold's lands in southern England was a symbolic act designed to reward his followers at the expense of the usurper and ensure that as many of his barons as possible had a stake in the new order.

[146] The division of Vigot's lands dates from Easter 1084 when Miles Crispin married the daughter and heiress of Robert d'Oilly and his English wife, the daughter of Vigod of Wallingford (K. S. B. Keats-Rohan, 'The Devolution of the Honour of Wallingford', *Oxoniensia*, 54 (1989), 311–18).

[147] Roffe, 'Introduction', *Little Domesday, Norfolk*, 26–34. The lands in the North went predominantly to Earl Hugh and William de Warenne sometime after 1071.

[148] Beorhtric son of Ælfgar's demesnes in Cornwall, Devon, Dorset, Gloucestershire, Wiltshire, and Worcestershire, for example, passed to some eighteen different tenants-in-chief by various routes (A. Williams, 'A West Country Magnate of the Eleventh Century: The Family, Estates and Patronage of Beorhtric son of Ælgar', *Family Trees and the Roots of Politics*, ed. K. S. B. Keats-Rohan (Woodbridge, 1997), 41–68, esp. at 63–5).

[149] There has been no systematic examination of these patterns. For the techniques employed, see below, pp. 287–91.

Table 5.1 *The* tenuit *formula in the Oxfordshire folios*

Ref.	Pre-Conquest holder	Post-Conquest holder
9,9	Abingdon, St Mary of	Abingdon, St Mary of
7,4	Æthelnoth of Kent	Bayeux, bishop of
39,3	Esger	Geoffrey de Mandeville
35,17	Azur	Miles Crispin
35,12	Beorhtric	Miles Crispin
14,4	Brun the priest	Oxford, canons of, and others
2,1	Canterbury, archbishop	Canterbury, archbishop
24,6	Cynewig	Henry de Ferrers
20,4	Edith, Queen	Walter Giffard
34,2	Edith, Queen	Berengar de Tosny
35,2	Edith, Queen	Miles Crispin
1,7a	Edwin, Earl	King
13,1	Edward, King	Paris, St Denis
35,10	Edwin	Miles Crispin
35,11	Engelric	Miles Crispin
29,4	Fourteen thegns	Roger d'Ivry
32,1	Hakun	Richard de Courcy
1,9	Harold, Earl	King
10,1	Harold, Earl	Battle Abbey
15,4	Harold, Earl	Hugh, Earl
15,3	Hugh the chamberlain	Hugh, Earl
35,34	Ketil	Miles Crispin
51,1	Ledric	Osbern Giffard
35,20	Leofnoth	Miles Crispin
5,1	Leofric, bishop of Exeter	Exeter, bishop of
8,4	Leofwine	Lisieux, bishop of
6,5	Lincoln, St Mary of	Lincoln, bishop of
14,2	Oxford, canons of	Oxford, canons of, and others
4,1	Salisbury, bishop of	Salisbury, bishop of
3,1	Stigand, Archbishop	Winchester, bishop of
15,2	Stigand, Archbishop	Hugh, Earl
34,2	Thorgot	Berengar de Tosny
38,1	Tonni	Gilbert de Ghent
20,5	Tosti, Earl	Walter Giffard
38,2	Ulf	Gilbert de Ghent
28,2	Vigot	Robert d'Oilly
35,1	Vigot	Miles Crispin
3,2	Winchester, bishop of	Winchester, bishop of
40,3	Wulfweard White, Ælfric Whelp	Ernulf de Hesdin

Table 5.2 *Goups of manors in the Lincs breves of Walter d'Aincourt and Peterborough Abbey (source Roffe, 'Hundreds and Wapentakes', 37)*

Lord 1086	Lord and tenant 1066	Division and wapentake
Walter d'Aincourt	1. Thorir,* Siward, Alwig	K30,24,21/
	2. Arnketil, Hemming,* Godric	K21,26,23/
	3. Healfdene,* his two brothers	K23
Peterborough Abbey	1. Peterborough Abbey*	LWR14/,K20/,21/,28,H31,K24
	2. Alnoth, Rolf, Hereweard, Alnoth, Eskil	LWR14,17,19,K20,21,20 (?add)

* = holder of sake and soke, LWR = Lindsey West Riding, K = Kesteven, H = Holland.
Obliques indicate spaces in the text and the numbers refer to wapentakes by their position in the common Lincolnshire sequence.

of predecessors, albeit pointing out that land did not belong to it, indicate that transfer *en bloc* was a common occurrence.[150] Claims of one sort or another are persistently made on the basis of the sake and soke of a predecessor rather than the rights of a tenant.[151] This characteristic accounts for many apparent anomalies of distribution. Although a tenant-in-chief succeeded to the lands and interests of his predecessor, there was no simple transfer of all of his lands. The newcomer had no right in his predecessor's *laenland*, although he might negotiate a continuation of the lease with the new soke lord; he did not necessarily succeed to his family land, although again he might seek to become the man of the lord who succeeded to its soke.[152] The combined interests of a single individual might legitimately

[150] See, for example, LDB, 393: *DB Suffolk*, 25,52: 'In the same borough Richard has 13 burgesses whom Fin held TRE. Over 4 of these he had soke and sake and commendation. One of them is a slave. And over 12 [he had] commendation only but they dwelt on land of their own and they paid the whole of the customary due in the borough. And this is part of Fin's honour.' *Feudum*, 'fee' or 'fief', was probably used in the same way in some contexts. See, for example, GDB, 233, 239, LDB, 26: *DB Leics*, 13,67; *DB Warks*, 7,1; *DB Essex*, 19,1. However, the term is more used of post-Conquest fees. In the Essex and Hertfordshire *breves* of the bishop of London it distinguishes the lands bought after the Conquest from those of the pre-Conquest bishopric, while a similar usage is found in the bishop of Thetford's Norfolk *breve* (Taylor, 'The Endowment and Military Obligations of the See of London: A Reassessment of Three Sources', 307–8).

[151] See, for example, GDB, 377v: *DB Lincs*, CK66: 'Guy de Craon holds 4 bovates of land in Drayton and 10 bovates in Bicker Hundred of the land of Æthelstan son of Godram. Count Alan claims these, and Algar his man has given to the king's barons a pledge to prove by ordeal or by combat that Æthelstan himself was not seized of these 14 bovates TRE. On the other hand, Ælfstan of Frampton, Guy's man, has given his pledge to prove that he was seized of them with sake and soke, and Guy was seized of them from the time of Ralph the staller until now, and holds them now.'

[152] This, of course, did not stop him claiming full rights. Hardwin de Scales had taken much land from Ely Abbey in this way, although pleas in the 1070s adjudged them to the

pass to a number of lords in 1086, but his own sokeright would be vested in one alone.[153] Sake and soke was as near as most lords got to land in 1066 and so it was in 1086.

In such a context it is not surprising that centres of pre-Conquest authority continued to exercise a powerful hold on the mental landscape of post-Conquest England. It is a sobering thought for the military historian to ponder that many, probably most, castles built before 1135, and many after, are situated within manors held by a king's thegn with sake and soke in 1066.[154] In some cases it is even possible to demonstrate that the site itself was determined by the location of the lordly residence in 1066. Stamford Castle, for example, was situated on a small knoll to the west of the late pre-Conquest town in a position that was remote from the main road and river crossing. It was not the most defensible of positions, but the authority that a major pre-Conquest manorial centre on the site commanded seems to have overridden purely strategic considerations in the building of the castle there in 1068.[155] Castellogists are increasingly becoming aware that the symbolism of the castle was as important as, and sometimes more important than, its military function. Castle Rising was conceived as the focus of what can almost

abbey. Monasteries were an easier touch than lay lords. Many a fee is held by one tenant-in-chief from another without comment. Some such instances must attest patronage – either to buy protection or to give it – but most probably reflect pre-Conquest relationships between predecessors.

[153] Ann Williams, in 'Meet the *Antecessores*: Lords and Land in Eleventh-Century Suffolk', *Anglo-Saxons: Studies Presented to Cyril Roy Hart*, eds S. Keynes and A. P. Smyth (Dublin, 2005), 275–87, has doubted that *antecessor* has much meaning in this context. The examples she gives, however, nicely illustrate the point. She cites the cases of Acwulf and Rada who are called *antecessores* but whose respective lands passed to two tenants-in-chief. In both cases it seems that they only had sake and soke in one of their manors (Rada explicitly so, and Acwulf by implication) and title to the other did not therefore pass with it. The term *antecessor* might, then, have clear legal connotations without it necessarily meaning that the land of the individual so named all went to the same person.

[154] Coulson, 'Peaceable Power in English Castles'; C. Coulson, 'Cultural Realities and Reappraisals in English Castle Study', *Journal of Medieval History*, 22 (1996), 171–208. For local studies, see D. R. Roffe, 'Castles', *An Historical Atlas of Lincolnshire*, eds S. Bennett and N. Bennett (Hull, 1992), 34–43; R. Liddiard, 'Castle Rising, Norfolk: A "Landscape of Lordship"?' *ANS*, 22 (2000 for 1999), 169–86; O. H. Creighton, 'Early Castles in the Medieval Landscape of Wiltshire', *Wiltshire Archaeological and Natural History Magazine*, 93 (2000), 105–19; O. H. Creighton, 'Early Castles and Rural Settlement Patterns: Insights from Yorkshire and the East Midlands', *Medieval Settlement Research Group Annual Report*, 14 (1999), 29–33; O. H. Creighton, 'Early Castles in the Medieval Landscape of Rutland', *Transactions of the Leicestershire Archaeological and Historical Society*, 73 (1999), 19–33; O. H. Creighton, 'Early Leicestershire Castles: Archaeology and Landscape History', *Transactions of the Leicestershire Archaeological and Historical Society*, 71 (1997), 21–36. There has been no systematic study of castle sites and patterns of pre-Conquest tenure.

[155] C. M. Mahany and D. R. Roffe, 'Stamford: The Development of an Anglo-Scandinavian Borough', *ANS* [*Proceedings of Battle Conference*], 5 (1983), 199–219.

be described as a ritual landscape that dramatized its lord's power.[156] Legitimacy, and demonstrating it, was a vital issue in the fifty years after the Conquest.

Soke and its nexus were of fundamental importance in the Norman settlement. In these terms, then, even the most obvious geographical grants must be questioned. Fleming has made much of the distribution of land by hundred and wapentake in the North and there are indeed some neat patterns.[157] What she does not explain is why these structures are necessarily post-Conquest. Some, at least, have decidedly pre-Conquest characteristics that suggest a soke nexus. The honour of Peverel in Nottinghamshire is a case in point.[158] There William Peverel appears to have been granted almost all of the lands surrounding the borough of Nottingham in the wapentakes of Rushcliffe and Broxtow, and it seems clear that his fee was a castlery of a classic kind. However, the complex incorporated the comital manor of Clifton and that fact, combined with a high proportion of English tenants in 1086 and the meeting of the honour in the fee of Earl Tosti in Nottingham itself, suggests that William was granted the lands and services of the earl's thegns. It may be true that he was not granted all of those lands, but nevertheless it is misleading to characterize the complex as an innovation.

The case for a pre-Conquest identity for the honours of Roger de Bully and Henry de Ferrers, equally fixed points in Fleming's argument, is likewise strong.[159] Those for the honour of Chester and the Sussex Rapes are perhaps less robust.[160] Nevertheless, the point is well made that the Normans could adhere to traditional legal forms while adapting them to the needs of the Conquest and settlement. It is a tired cliché, but it was continuity and change that characterized the Norman Conquest and settlement at all levels. There was, indeed, a tenurial revolution after 1066, but it was a revolution predicated on the continuity of legal forms. William the Conqueror had no option but to think in terms of predecessors endowed with sake and soke, for this was what constituted land. But in those terms he could distribute it to best suit his purposes and those of his tenants-in-chief. To one he might grant the lands of two or more king's thegns, to another the lands of the earl in a hundred. For both he negotiated terms of service that reflected the size of the new agglomeration of land and the circumstances in which it was granted. It is the nature of those services that we shall consider next.

---

[156] Liddiard, 'Castle Rising, Norfolk: A "Landscape of Lordship"?'

[157] Fleming, *Kings and Lords in Conquest England*, 145–82.

[158] D. R. Roffe, 'Anglo-Saxon Nottingham and the Norman Conquest', *A Centenary History of Nottingham*, ed. J. V. Beckett (Manchester, 1997), 24–42.

[159] *DIB*, 37–8.

[160] For Cheshire, see Higham, 'Patterns of Patronage and Power: The Governance of Late Anglo-Saxon Cheshire', 1–13; for Sussex, see F. R. Thorn, 'Hundreds and Wapentakes', *The Sussex Domesday*, eds A. Williams and R. W. H. Erskine (London, 1990), 29–33, for the most recent discussion, along with a bibliography of the various arguments.

The manor and service

The manor appears to have figured large in the minds of those who collected the Domesday data. In the folios of Circuit VI it is an institution that organizes the text, in Circuit III it is carefully distinguished from land, and in the remainder of the Domesday corpus it is a constant, if mysterious, presence. Two words were employed to describe the creature. *Mansio* is the norm in Exon and the prologue to IE, but it is found in GDB and LDB only in the description of boroughs where it is the usual word for an urban tenement. *Manerium* is the preferred word in these sources and the remainder of the Domesday corpus. The first, then, may be indicative of usage in the earliest stages of the Domesday inquest, but otherwise there is little difference between the two terms: of their root meaning there can be no doubt; they both signify a house.

In the Circuit VI and I folios this connotation is not infrequently underlined by references to the hall: the apparently exceptional lack of a hall is noted in several entries and land and commodities are occasionally said to belong to it. The referents, however, are not just to physical structures;[161] the manor was also an abstract entity. Its nature has been the subject of much debate. Maitland was the first to describe the variety of estates and relationships that it encompassed and he concluded that the common denominator was taxation: a manor was a house at which geld was charged.[162] Welldon Finn concurred and John Palmer has recently restated the case by demonstrating that there was only one manor per vill in Cambridgeshire and Bedfordshire.[163] But generally the notion has been rejected.[164] The manor and the vill, the unit of geld assessment and collection,[165]

---

[161] In Irish Hill in Berkshire 'the hall and other buildings and the livestock' were transported to another manor by Hugolin the steersman (GDB, 63: *DB Berks*, 58,2).

[162] F. W. Maitland, *Domesday Book and Beyond* (Cambridge, 1897), 140–63.

[163] R. Welldon Finn, *The Domesday Inquest* (London, 1961), 60–73; J. J. N. Palmer, 'The Domesday Manor', *Domesday Studies*, ed. J. C. Holt (Woodbridge, 1987), 139–54. Unfortunately, the equation breaks down elsewhere: in some areas as many as ten manors were situated in a single vill. The hypothesis would also demand that no manor could at one and the same time be part of another manor. In reality, there are many subordinate manors of this kind. Roger de Lacy, for example, held three manors in the king's manor of Kingsland in Herefordshire (GDB, 179v: *DB Hereford*, 1,5). Welldon Finn's explanation that 'occasionally the member of a manor, perhaps by reason of its distance from the head of a manor, might pay its geld direct, and so in this respect be thought of by the bewildered and not always English clerks as being what the term "manor" implied' is as ingenious as unconvincing. His further attempts to explain away numerous references in Exon which were 'corrected' by the suddenly expert GDB scribe is merely special pleading.

[164] J. H. Round, 'The Domesday Manor', *EHR*, 15 (1900), 294; J. Tait, Review of *Domesday Book and Beyond*, *EHR*, 12 (1897), 768–77; F. H. Baring, *Domesday Tables for the Counties of Surrey, Berkshire, Middlesex, Hertford, Buckingham and Bedford and the New Forest* (London, 1909), 79, 82, 94, 139–42, 177.

[165] See below, pp. 190–7, 258–64.

are essentially non-commensurate, and the tendency has been to maintain that 'manor' was no technical term.

At the outset, it would seem that the balance of the evidence is against this proposition. Numerous passages in Domesday demonstrate that the scribe had a precise understanding when he applied the term *manerium*. To take but one example, in Startforth in Yorkshire one tenant had two carucates and another four but 'the former had a manor; the other not'.[166] Throughout LDB and GDB people are said to have held tenements 'for a manor' and simple 'land' is often consistently distinguished from the unit.[167] Maitland was clearly right in pointing to such entries as evidence of a clear concept of the manor. He seems to have erred only in confining his understanding of geld to Danegeld.[168] It seems to me that the Domesday manor articulated soke and was thus a measure of service.[169]

This is most apparent in the North. Circuit VI is distinguished by its concern with the structure of the manor.[170] In Yorkshire each parcel of land is explicitly assigned to one, while in Lincolnshire, Nottinghamshire, Derbyshire, and Huntingdonshire the manor provides the organizing principle of each chapter. The *caput*, that is the place where the hall was located, is identified by a marginal M, and its subordinate berewicks and sokelands, signalled by marginal B and S respectively, are described below it, often with a rubric 'sokeland of this manor'. Difference in the status of the various elements is emphasized by the rubrication of 'manorial' place-names and the use of a square initial I as opposed to a rustic I in inland and sokeland entries. The essence of these manors was neither geld payment nor jurisdiction; both can be frequently shown not to coincide with it.[171] Rather it consisted in the rents and dues that constituted what Domesday simply calls *terra*, 'land'. The TRE recipient of these dues is recorded in the account of the *caput* (names are not regularly recorded in inland and sokeland entries).

---

[166] GDB, 309v: *DB Yorks*, 6N18.

[167] In Cambridgeshire, for example, the usage is quite deliberate; the scribe changed the *terra* of his source to *manerium* on twelve occasions, but *manerium* to *terra* only once (Palmer, 'Domesday Manor', 141–2).

[168] See below, 193–4, 310–11.

[169] *DIB*, 239–41.

[170] D. R. Roffe, 'Domesday Book and Northern Society: A Reassessment', *EHR*, 105 (1990), 310–36; *DIB*, 211–16.

[171] Geld was articulated in the twelve-carucate hundred, which was independent of tenure (D. R. Roffe, 'The Lincolnshire Hundred', *Landscape History*, 3 (1981), 27–36). Thus, the bishop of Lincoln had tenements in Lincoln which belonged to a small manor outside the City and which were quit except that they paid geld with the citizens (GDB, 336: *DB Lincs*, C11). There are numerous 'forinsec' soke entries that indicate that the soke of part of one manor belonged to another. Occasionally it is noted that the whole of a manor was in the soke of another. See, for example, Denton in Lincolnshire (GDB, 368v: *DB Lincs*, 59,1): 'M. In Denton, Uhtbrand had 1 carucate of land and 6 bovates to the geld. [There is] land for as many ploughs and oxen. [It is] sokeland belonging to Grantham.'

This was a relatively simple principle: the manor was a tributary centre. In practice, though, the GDB scribe had problems with his taxonomy.[172] In Yorkshire he was promiscuous with his identifications: he applied the term manor to thegnages and drengages (that is, ministerial tenements of one sort or another) as well as bookland demesnes, the holdings of free men, and leaseholds. By the time he came to compile the Lincolnshire folios, however, he thought better of the classification and confined his definition solely to these latter three tenures. Halfway through the county he developed the series of conventions that was to inform his work throughout the remainder of the circuit.

Nowhere else in Domesday is the manor so precisely articulated as a matter of course. Nevertheless, similar structures can be identified throughout the country.[173] LDB exhibits almost exactly the same forms as the Yorkshire Domesday account: it retains a rigid hundredal structure but more or less consistently identifies manors and their immediately dependent elements.[174] In the rest of GDB large tributary estates are enrolled in much the same terms as in the North wherever they occur; examples can be found in every county. There are sufficient references to indicate that smaller ones existed, and that soke was of their essence, but their structure is rarely made explicit. The scribe, it would seem, lost interest in the manor as such after he compiled the Circuit VI folios. In Circuit III, the second to be enrolled, he at first gamely tried to apply the forms that he had developed in the North to the material that constituted his sources. He retained the marginal M and the use of rustic initial I's for subordinate entries. But he abandoned any attempt to reconstruct manors, or his sources prevented him from doing so, reverting to a more strictly hundredal arrangement of the text. From Hertfordshire onwards he even gave up that remnant of his taxonomy and thereafter studiously ignored the manor. Thus, an examination of Exon shows that he disregarded much of the detail that his source afforded him.[175] By the time he came to the Leicestershire folios the institution plays only a bit part in a rewritten script. The manor of Domesday became the victim of an editorial decision.

The manor was clearly no great part of the evolving programme that produced GDB. It was, however, central to the Domesday inquest. The commissioners returned summaries of fees in every county and one of the statistics that they furnished was the number of manors held by each tenant-in-chief. Two examples are preserved in GDB itself, several others are found in Exon and IE (Table 3.5). By and large, perhaps not surprisingly in the light of the purpose of the surviving documentation, the figures they provide cannot be reconciled with manors recorded

---

[172] Roffe, 'Domesday Book and Northern Society: A Reassessment', 310–36.

[173] DIB, 216–20.

[174] For identifying the manor in East Anglia, see Roffe, 'Introduction', *Little Domesday, Norfolk*, 11–15. The lands of free men are rarely given a tenurial context but were as much manorial appurtenances as sokeland. See below, pp. 220–1, 300.

[175] DB Devon, 3,8n.

in the Domesday corpus. Rather they usually seem to have been derived from a count of the number of TRE tenants recorded.[176] This, nevertheless, accords well with the northern evidence where only the recipients of soke dues are named in the text. It is, moreover, a characteristic of the manor which points to service as its essential point of interest for the commissioners.

As has been seen,[177] the TRE holders of the Domesday corpus were not constituted as a homogeneous class. However, they had one thing in common: in one way or another they all held rights in land that were derived from bookright. Bookright carried with it the corollary of personal service and, as a point of interception of the tributes and dues that made it up, the manor was evidently an indicator of the obligation. Holders of manors owed services to their lords and they in their turn owed services to the king. The connection is indeed explicit in the folios of Circuit VI. There it is stated that those with more than six manors paid their reliefs (a payment on succession in recognition of service due) to the king, while those with six or less paid to the sheriff.[178]

This much is clear. It does not require any belief in tenurial continuity between 1066 and 1086 to appreciate that it was in these terms that the manor was of interest to the Domesday commissioners. The honour was founded in bookright and it was therefore not surprising that its nodes, the points at which service was rendered, should figure largely in the Domesday inquest. Count Eustace had originally been granted a hundred manors[179] and a careful record was evidently kept of the number held by other tenants-in-chief: several references are found to the estates in 'the number' of a lord's manors or the like.[180] There was, moreover, a clear concept of what was an appropriate size; there are references to a small manor, a half manor, and lands added to an estate to make up manors.[181] Regularly in Exon and LDB, and intermittently in GDB, land is said to be held 'for a manor (*pro*

---

[176] *DIB*, 182; R. Welldon Finn, 'The *Inquisitio Eliensis* Re-considered', *EHR*, 75 (1960), 385–409 at 394–7; *idem*, *Domesday Studies: The Liber Exoniensis*, 124; *idem*, *The Domesday Inquest and the Making of Domesday Book* (London, 1961), 67. The 188 manors between the Ribble and Mersey, for example, are probably represented by the 182 thegns and drengs who held in 1066.

[177] Above, pp. 147–62.

[178] GDB, 280v: *DB Notts*, S3: 'A thegn having more than 6 manors does not give relief for his land except £8 to the king alone. If he has only 6 or less he gives 3 marks of silver to the sheriff as relief wherever he dwells, in the borough or without.' See also GDB, 298v: *DB Yorks*, C40.

[179] Two hides in Orsett and 'Gravesend' in Essex 'did not belong to his 100 manors' (LDB, 9v,26v: *DB Essex*, 3,2. 20,4–5). For this reading of the passage, see Welldon Finn, *Domesday Inquest*, 10n. His renewed doubts, in *Domesday Studies: The Eastern Counties* (London, 1967), 15n, seem unwarranted.

[180] LDB, 100, 121, 170v, 246: *DB Essex*; 90.17; *DB Norfolk*, 1,78; 8,117; 29,7.

[181] GDB, 45v, 336: *DB Hants*, 23,41; *DB Lincs*, C11; LDB, 170b, 206b, 242b, 257b, 258, 336, 435b: *DB Norfolk*, 8,120–1; 13,10; 25,24; 34,13; 34,18–19; *DB Suffolk* 7,55; 55,1.

manerio)' or for a number of manors even where there is only one lord or tenant.[182] Less widely, a concern is evident to identify land that had been added or taken away.[183] All these references clearly point to the manor as a measure of service in 1086. Conversely, placing land or men outside a manor constituted exemption.[184]

Domesday does not tell us what that service was, nor would we expect it to as a collection of evidence. Fees held by engineers, arblasters, foresters, and the like almost invariably emerge as sergeancies in the thirteenth century, and it would therefore seem likely that the specific personal service enjoined upon the tenant then represents the terms of tenure in 1086.[185] Most fees, however, were probably held for military service of one kind or another. The various duties that made up the service only play a walk-on part in the Domesday corpus. In Kent and Surrey there are a handful of references to the service as a render to the lord,[186] while Drayton Parslow in Buckinghamshire was said to be held of the king by the service of providing two mail-clad men for castle guard at Windsor.[187] There are indications, however, that military service figured large in the discussions at Salisbury in early August 1086. According to the Anglo-Saxon Chronicle, William demanded an oath of loyalty and homage from all those who held land in England. An echo of what lay behind the oath may been found in clause two of the text known as 'The Laws of William the Conqueror':

> We decree also that every free man shall affirm by oath and compact that he will be loyal to King William both within and without England, that he will preserve with him his lands and honour with all fidelity and defend him against all his enemies.[188]

---

[182] See, for example, Chilfrome in Dorset which William de Moyon claimed for two manors (Exon, 48b). The information was omitted from GDB, 81v: *DB Dorset*, 36,6.

[183] The matter is explicitly noticed in the so-called articles in the Prologue to IE (IE, 97).

[184] See, for example, GDB, 180v: *DB Hereford*, 1,44: 'Earl William put outside his manors 2 foresters, one from Hanley Castle [Worcs.] and the other from Bushley [Worcs.], in order to guard the woods.'

[185] It has been suggested that in Bedfordshire sergeancy is indicated by the *x tenet de rege* (Abels, 'An Introduction to the Bedfordshire Domesday', 48). In fact, the formula is not confined to this type of entry, but is generally found in the opening entry of chapters or sub-chapters throughout Domesday Book. It perhaps emphasizes the rights that the king claimed in all land.

[186] Sunridge in Kent provided one knight in the service of the archbishop, and Coombe and Thames Ditton in Surrey another each. GDB, 3, 10v, 32: *DB Kent*, 2,5.5,165; *DB Surrey*, 5,27.

[187] GDB, 151v: *DB Bucks*, 40,1.

[188] *Die Gesetze*, i, 486; *EHD*, ii, 399.

This text is not without its difficulties,[189] but, since it refers to the recognition of liege lordship, it would seem to embody a memory of events in 1086. What is striking, then, is the insistence on the free men's duty to defend the realm. The implication seems to be that there was at the same time a redefinition of the *servitium debitum*, the duty to fight in defence of the king and his realm.

This is indeed a theme that was central to Orderic Vitalis' understanding of the Domesday process.[190] There can be no doubt that he viewed the Domesday inquest as a decisive point in the definition of military service in England. Wherein the changes lay is far from clear, but it was evidently not in the fact of service. Round was the first to formulate the idea that the *servitium debitum* was introduced by the Conqueror, and he believed that the quotas of the *carte baronum* of 1166 were by and large established by the time of the Domesday inquest.[191] If a writ addressed to Æthelwig of Evesham is substantially authentic, then it is clear that the abbey's quota of five knights was fixed (or at least not subsequently changed) before Æthelwig's death in 1077.[192] Domesday itself records large numbers of tenants whose successors in 1166 understood them to have held by knight service. Nevertheless, it cannot be assumed that the duties of those knights were identical with those of their twelfth-century counterparts. What is decidedly odd about William's response to threatened invasion in 1085 was his apparent reliance on mercenaries alone to defend the realm.[193] Tenants-in-chief were, however, responsible for billeting the troops, a service that does not appear to have been demanded subsequently. As I have suggested in *Domesday: the Inquest and the Book*, the meeting at Salisbury may well have seen the imposition of more onerous service in return for a confirmation of lands.[194]

Was, then, twelfth-century feudalism (and I use the term advisedly) knocked out at Salisbury in 1086? It may well have been.[195] The meeting had far-reaching

[189] J. C. Holt, '1086', *Domesday Studies*, ed. J. C. Holt (Woodbridge, 1987), 63–4.
[190] *The Ecclesiastical History of Orderic Vitalis*, ed. M. Chibnall, 6 vols (Oxford, 1969–80), ii, 267.
[191] Round, 'The Introduction of Knight Service into England', 225–314.
[192] *Regesta Regum Anglo-Normannorum: The Acta of William I 1066–1087*, ed. D. Bates (Oxford, 1998), no. 131.
[193] Later kings made extensive use of mercenaries, but they believed enough in the fiction of the feudal army to demand scutage from their tenants-in-chief.
[194] *DIB*, 234–42.
[195] This is not a new view, although the reasons for saying so may be. The idea was first expressed by Martin Wright in *Introduction to the Laws of Tenure* (London, 1730), 56: 'as this general homage and fealty was done about the time that Domesday Book was finished, and not before, we may suppose that the Survey was taken upon or soon after our ancestors' consent to tenures in order to discover the quantity and to fix his homage'. The idea was taken up by W. Blackstone, *Commentaries on the Laws of England*, 4 vols (Oxford, 1770), ii, 49–50. It was subsequently abandoned since knight service is not mentioned in Domesday Book. The only recent exponent has been D. C. Douglas in *The Domesday of Christchurch*

effects. If tenants-in-chief were confirmed in their lands in return for their homage, so in their turn were their men, the honorial barony. In 1989 I suggested that one of the results of the Domesday inquest was the realization that many tenants held their land hereditarily with sake and soke and that the oath at Salisbury was intended to bring them into direct relationship with the king.[196] It is equally possible that the fact of the oath conferred hereditary right. It is certainly true that in the three charters from the reign of William the Conqueror that record enfeoffment for knight service the grant was only for a life and was more of the character of a *beneficium*, a specifically pre-Conquest form of tenure.[197] Thereafter, however, grants in hereditary fee became the norm. By creating a direct bond with the king William in effect recognized the tenant's land as bookland. Where at times the Domesday commissioners seem to have been vague as to what constituted a manor, one of the results of the inquest and the negotiations that followed it was probably a closer definition of the concept of the manor.

These were remarkable changes with long-term consequences. But it is another matter to say that they were revolutionary. There was nothing particularly Norman about the fact of personal service. As we have seen, it lies at the root of sokeright. The nighness to the king that the possession of soke implied had always entailed attendance on him in person. In the nature of these things, the terms must have ever been a matter of negotiation. What may distinguish the business at Salisbury was its scale. 'Contracts' with subjects were probably not unknown before the Conquest. Edward the Confessor's remittance of Danegeld at the London witan in 1051 was presumably part of a general agreement of one kind or another associated with the exile of Earl Godwine and his sons.[198] It may well have been primarily directed at their thegns or it may have had a wider constituency. There is no doubt about the scope of the Salisbury meeting. Attended by 'all those who held land in England', it evidently marked a new dispensation in the relations between the king and his subjects.

Canterbury, ed. D. C. Douglas (London, 1944), 26–7, on the basis of John of Worcester's assertion that '*quot feudatos milites?*' was one of the questions asked in the inquest.
[196] 'From Thegnage to Barony', 175–6.
[197] T. S. Purser, 'The Origins of English Feudalism? An Episcopal Land-Grant Revisited', *Historical Research*, 73 (2000), 80–92.
[198] *ASC*, 116–22; J. Campbell, *The Anglo-Saxons* (London, 1982), 244.

6

The Vill and Taxation

W<small>HILE</small> personal service as an attribute of land tenure is no longer perceived as an exclusively Norman phenomenon, it is generally still seen as the antithesis of taxation. Gentlemen fought for their lords, while peasants paid their taxes. This dichotomy is again artificial. Tax and service were closely inter-linked exactions. At first sight this may surprise. It is clear from the records of the geld inquest in the South West that the demesne of GDB held by tenants-in-chief (but not their tenants) did not pay geld. In hundred after hundred the non-gelding land can be equated with the land *in dominio* in Exon and GDB.[1] That this was the norm in the reign of William the Conqueror is illustrated by the pre-Domesday Northamptonshire Geld Roll in which substantial amounts of land in the lord's hands did not pay.[2] There is no doubt that the demesne was exempt before the Domesday inquest.

However, this is to say less than it seems. Exemption was not inherent in the idea of (Domesday) demesne. Both Exon and the Northamptonshire Geld Roll indicate that the exempt demesne was hidated. Unlike, say, royal lands that rendered the farm of one night, it had been assessed to the geld. It was, in the language of English estate surveys and lawcodes, *warland*, that is land that was liable to all the king's taxes.[3] Land liable to service was assessed even if geld was not paid on it. We can take the argument little further from the Domesday texts, but the relation of service to geld is explicit in clause eleven of Henry I's coronation charter.

> I grant by my own gift that the demesne ploughs of those knights who hold by knight service should be free from all gelds, so that, being relieved of such a great burden, they may furnish themselves so well with horses and arms

---

[1] R. R. Darlington, 'Wiltshire Geld Rolls', *VCH Wiltshire*, ii, eds R. B. Pugh and E. Crittall (Oxford, 1955), 169–221. For comment, see p. 178.

[2] *EHD*, ii, 483–6; R. S. Hoyt, *The Royal Demesne in English Constitutional History, 1066–1272* (Cornell, 1950), 52–8; J. H. Round, *Feudal England* (London, 1895), 147–56.

[3] From OE *wara*, 'defence', and land, hence the Domesday formula *x* defends itself for *y* hides of land.

that they may be properly equipped and prepared to discharge my service and to defend my kingdom.[4]

Service was a condition of exemption: it complemented taxation. Any change in the one affected the other. The way in which they interacted in the Domesday inquest is explored in this chapter.

Taxation was generally assessed upon the community as opposed to the estate. It was the focus of the first stage of the Domesday inquest, while the manor was a primary concern of the second. Our first task, then, is to examine the place-names of Domesday Book to determine to what they refer.

Names and places

There are some 29,000 place-names in the Domesday corpus. Thumbing through a modern translation of Domesday Book it is not difficult to conclude that the identification of most is obvious. In reality, however, a great deal of hidden scholarship lies behind the confident ascription of a modern name to an eleventh-century place-name form. The basic problem is philological. For the vast majority of places Domesday provides the earliest reference and on this account each should command especial authority; modern place-name studies insist on argument from the earliest forms. But the authority of the Domesday names is compromised by the people and processes that recorded them. Exon and LDB were written by francophone scribes and their orthography was shaped by an ear that could not always comprehend English phonology. The influence that they exerted on forms is described by Sawyer.[5] The bilingual scribes of GDB and the schedules were more au fait with the vernacular, and their forms are often closer to contemporary English usage.[6] But they were no less immune to misunderstandings and absurdities. By and large, however, each Domesday place-name can be identified with a small group of modern forms or names that survived in later medieval and early modern documents.

Onomastics is an exacting science; here be dragons, and the layman ventures into the area at his own peril. Place-name scholars are best left to their disputes over the meaning and origins of names unless historical sources and methods suggest alternative explanations. Identification is another matter. The process requires further

---

[4] W. Stubbs, *Select Charters*, 9th edn (Oxford, 1913), 119. Translation from J. A. Green, 'The Last Century of Danegeld', *EHR*, 96 (1981), 246. Hoyt saw this as an extension of the privilege to all knights (Hoyt, *Royal Demesne*, 53).

[5] P. H. Sawyer, 'The Place-Names of the Domesday Manuscripts', *Bulletin of the John Rylands Library*, 38 (1955–56), 483–506.

[6] See C. Clark, 'Domesday Book – a Great Red-herring: Thoughts on some Eleventh-Century Orthographies', *England in the Eleventh Century*, ed. C. Hicks, Harlaxton Medieval Studies, 2 (1992), 317–31, who argues that the aim of the GDB scribe was to Latinize. It is inevitable, then, that forms only approximate to English orthography and pronunciation.

analysis which calls on expertise in less arcane disciplines.[7] Undoubtedly the first among these is textual criticism. The scribe of GDB took no great pains positively to identify places; he was not engaged on the compilation of a post office gazetteer. Those of LDB and Exon were only marginally more careful. Nevertheless, their sources were often more explicit. Where circuit drafts were arranged geographically the vill and hundred in which a place-name was recorded were precise indicators of locality. Identifying rubrics were usually lost when these texts were rearranged to compile Domesday Book, but vestiges survive in the hundredal and villar sequences of GDB and LDB. Position in a chapter is the most important clue to the identity of a place-name and in some cases provides the only clue. Yorkshire is character-ized by a proliferation of Anglo-Scandinavian names in -*thorpe*, that is 'hamlet'. Nowadays the names are prefixed by a distinguishing element, but in GDB many are identified only by the simplex *torp*. However, the Yorkshire Summary preserves a record of an earlier geographical arrangement of the materials, and one *torp* can be reliably distinguished from another. Even where an number of *torp*s occur in the same wapentake, a regular geographical sequence of vills permits accurate differentiation.[8]

The textual context of a name, then, is a primary clue. It must be remembered, however, that it is not infallible. A regular sequence of hundreds or wapentakes is the norm in many counties; Cambridgeshire and Norfolk are prime examples.[9] But elsewhere more complex patterns are found attesting other processes and procedures. Here the historian is in danger of employing bootstrapping: the area of hundreds is largely determined by place-names and so place-names cannot be identified wholesale by reference to hundreds where the pattern is irregular. In such circumstances other sources of evidence must be adduced. Twelfth- and early thirteenth-century records are usually as elliptical as Domesday but, increasingly from 1250, public and private documents strove to define locality with a legal precision. Where a continuous chain of tenure from 1086 to a later period can be established later medieval localizations can be used to identify names at the time of Domesday.

For a secure identification, philology, textual criticism, and manorial history must all be brought to bear on a Domesday name. In practice only the first two have been regularly employed and new identifications are regularly reported as the

---

[7] J. S. Moore, 'The Gloucestershire Section of Domesday Book: Geographical Problems of the Text, Part I', *Transactions of the Bristol and Gloucestershire Archaeological Society*, 105 (1987), 110–11; F. R. Thorn, 'The Identification of Domesday Places in the South-Western Counties of England', *Nomina*, 10 (1986), 41–59.

[8] H. C. Darby and I. S. Maxwell, *The Domesday Geography of Northern England* (Cambridge, 1962), 481–94.

[9] See above, pp. 47–50.

descent of individual fees is studied.[10] Nevertheless, the vast majority of names
have now been assigned to a locality if not a place. There are only 698 names
that have defied identification completely.[11] Where a tenurial chain is not documented and a Domesday name is not evidenced in later sources, the historian must
resort to interpretation, guesswork, or acceptance of an insoluble problem. By and
large the spade work has been done and the conclusions silently presented to the
reader by the various editors of Domesday Book. Early volumes of the *VCH* and
Domesday Geography of England might give the impression that there are no further
interpretative problems. Place-names are regularly represented in older maps as
dots with the clear implication that each represents a nucleated village, that is a
group of houses and farms huddled around the communal lifelines of church and
pub, on the site of its modern counterpart. These are certainties that have dissolved
in the last thirty years.

In origin most Domesday place-names are toponyms, that is, they refer to a
feature precisely located in space.[12] District names, it is true, are known; names
in *-feld* like Hatfield in Yorkshire and the river names Piddle, Westbourne, and
Tarrant in Dorset are of this type, while tribal areas are indicated by names in
-ing and the like. But the generic of names is more usually a topographical feature
or a habitative location such as an enclosure, homestead, or cottage. *Tun*, for
example, the most common element in English place-names, has the root meaning
of 'fence' or 'hedge', *ham* 'a safe dwelling'. All sorts of other names refer to farms,
crofts, clearings, and the like. However, from a very early period such names were
transferred to social and economic units – *tun* became 'village', *ham* 'estate' – and
they themselves were then transferred to communal organizations such as the vill
and the hundred.

The problem with Domesday place-names is determining their referents in these
terms. Nowadays no one would contend that they are all settlement names.[13]
It is more usual to assume that they are estate names or names of subdivisions
thereof.[14] The IE prologue is couched in terms of the *mansio*, that is 'manor', and

---

[10] In researching the Domesday place-names of Lincolnshire for *The Lincolnshire Domesday*
(London, 1992) I was able to suggest over fifty new identifications.

[11] This total is of names rather than places, i.e. some names occur more than once, as
they appear in the Phillimore edition of Domesday Book. H. C. Darby, *Domesday England*
(Cambridge, 1977), 15, gives a total of 561, but this seems to be of places rather than entries.
Several of these names have subsequently been identified with a greater or lesser degree of
confidence.

[12] M. Gelling and A. Cole, *The Landscape of Place-Names* (Stamford, 2000), xii.

[13] Darby, *Domesday England*, 14–26, is ambivalent. He cites many names which are clearly
those of estates, but nevertheless maintains that the Domesday record is 'incomplete',
apparently because it does not name all vills or settlements.

[14] F. R. Thorn, '"Another Seaborough", "The Other Dinnaton": Some Manorial Affixes in
Domesday Book', *Names, Places, and People: An Onomastic Miscellany for John McNeal
Dodgson*, eds A. R. Rumble and A. D. Mills (Stamford, 1997), 345, prefers the term 'holding',

it might be logical to assume that this organization was the point of reference in Domesday place-names. The reality is more complex.[15] There is no consistency in Domesday Book, for its sources were communal as well as seigneurial, and even names in the same entry may have different referents. The diversity in usage is eloquently illustrated in Circuit VI. In the Lincolnshire folios the name of a twelve-carucate hundred, a peculiarly northern unit of local government, is used on thirty-nine occasions to identify parcels of land in preference to an estate name. It must be suspected that many others were silently used, for in a significant number of instances a name is employed that is never subsequently used to identify the manor.[16]

Sometimes the choice of name is transparently purposeful. In Count Alan's Lincolnshire chapter three consecutive parcels of land are described as 'in Drayton Hundred', 'in the same Drayton', and 'in Drayton itself'.[17] Here a hundred name is opposed to what is probably an estate name, and a settlement name ('Drayton itself' surely points to a nucleus) to the end of clarifying an otherwise confusing series of entries. More often hundred, estate and settlement names are used seemingly without rationale. The lost name *Bredestorp* in south Lincolnshire is a Scarlet Pimpernell of a name. In GDB the name primarily identifies a manor held by Drogo de la Beuvriere which was subsequently known as Holywell and included the settlement of Aunby.[18] But it is also found in the Descriptio Terrarum of Peterborough Abbey (a Domesday schedule) where it refers to the estate known as *Adewelle* in GDB and as Careby in thirteenth-century and later sources, and it is consequently clear that the *Bergestorp* to which a berewick in Little Bytham is said to belong in GDB refers to the same manor.[19] *Bredestorp*, then, is the name of a settlement, probably an early name for Holywell, which is also the name of a hundred and as such, in the deviant form *Bergestorp*, identifies a manor with its hall in a place called *Adewelle*. Why the one type of name should be preferred in any one context to the others in this onomastic and historical nightmare is entirely unclear.

Domesday place-name analysis is rarely that complex, but similar considerations apply elsewhere. In Nottinghamshire and its satellite Rutland the twelve-carucate

a unit that could either be separately valued or was responsible for the geld; it might consist of a number of 'manors'.

[15] D. R. Roffe, 'Place-Naming in Domesday Book: Settlements, Estates, and Communities', *Nomina*, 14 (1990–91), 47–60.

[16] D. R. Roffe, 'An Introduction to the Lincolnshire Domesday', *The Lincolnshire Domesday*, eds A. Williams and G. H. Martin (London, 1992), 8–12.

[17] GDB, 348: *DB Lincs*, 12,58–60.

[18] GDB, 360v: *DB Lincs*, 30,28; *Book of Fees*, Public Record Office, 3 vols (London, 1920–31), 182, 1050.

[19] GDB, 345v: *DB Lincs*, 8,5; *Book of Fees*, 182.

hundred is also found, but in only one instance did it directly affect nomenclature.[20] Outside Lincolnshire the unit was more extensive in area and more specific names had to be employed to distinguish places. Generally, estate names were used. Southwell, for example, embraced the manorial centre and twelve further unnamed berewicks.[21] On occasion, however, settlement names may have been employed. The sokelands of the manor of Mansfield are minutely described and may be of this type.[22] In Derbyshire a different system can be observed.[23] The place-names of High Peak Wapentake are derived from an antique system of royal estate manage-ment dating from the early tenth century (if not earlier) and in 1086 they probably bore little relation to contemporary social, political, or economic reality. Similar structures can be identified in Yorkshire but the majority of names are derived from the Yorkshire Summary and are evidently those of vills, that is communities with defined responsibilities.[24] In Norfolk there are indications that the area of the East Anglian leet had some affect on naming, but the vill seems to have been the predominant determinant.[25]

Beyond the Northern Danelaw the problem has been little addressed. In Huntingdonshire vill names were employed where a manor did not extend beyond its area. Conversely, estate names occur when it did.[26] A similar usage has been observed in Gloucestershire and Worcestershire.[27] Contemporary charters and leases indicate that large demesne estates, like the church of Worcester's manors of Fladbury and Bibury, consisted of numerous townships and vills, but either the estate name itself is used in GDB or the various elements are noticed only incidentally in the same entry. Smaller fees, by contrast, such as the monks of Worcester's demesne and tenanted lands which encompassed whole vills or parts of vills are identified by vill names or probably, in some cases where they are different, by township names. A similar pattern has been observed in Kent.[28] In the east and north, an area of primary settlement and large estates, manor names

---

[20] GDB, 293v: *DB Rutland*, R10. A manor held by Robert Malet was initially identified as 'in the same hundred', that is the second twelve-carucate hundred of Alstoe Wapentake, and subsequently 'in Tie', Teigh, was interlined above it.

[21] GDB, 283: *DB Notts*, 5,1. The twelve berewicks of the estate are identified in a charter of 956 (S659).

[22] GDB, 281: *DB Notts*, 1.23–30.

[23] Roffe, 'Place-Naming in Domesday Book', 52–3. See below, p. 295.

[24] D. R. Roffe, 'The Yorkshire Summary: A Domesday Satellite', *Northern History*, 27 (1991), 242–60.

[25] D. R. Roffe, 'Introduction', *Little Domesday, Norfolk*, eds A. Williams and G. H. Martin (London, 2000), 15.

[26] Roffe, 'Place-Naming in Domesday Book', 53.

[27] J. D. Hamshere, 'The Structure and Exploitation of the Domesday Book Estate of the Church of Worcester', *Landscape History*, 7 (1985), 44–5.

[28] R. Eales, 'An Introduction to the Kent Domesday', *The Kent Domesday*, eds A. Williams and G. H. Martin (London, 1992), 18.

predominate. The smaller fees on the Downland, by contrast, are identified by settlement names. Finally, in Shropshire estate names are the norm except where a separate presentment was made for subordinate elements, and there settlement names were probably employed.[29]

Elsewhere the referents of Domesday place-names have not been studied in detail. But enough evidence has been cited to demonstrate that it would be naive to assume that all Domesday names are equal. It is now self-evident (although not so much so fifty years ago) that Domesday Book is not a simple settlement gazetteer. Independent documentation frequently indicates that an estate or vill name stands for a number of hamlets and villages and archaeology has further demonstrated that hidden habitations are legion.[30] What, then, can Domesday Book tell us about settlement structure? The bottom line is a minimum of *settlement nuclei*. Where neighbouring estates or vills shared a name the Domesday sources distinguished one from another apparently to avoid confusion and such differentiating elements were often, if not always, transferred to the extant texts. Great, little, north, south, east, west, upper, lower were all used as distinguishing epithets. More rarely, in Exon the name of a lord, either TRE or TRW, was sometimes appended. But such instances are the exception. Domesday Book alone can tell us little more.

It is in consequence that editors of Domesday Book have resorted to later documentation. The VCH, Alecto, and Phillimore editions all recognize the existence of settlements undifferentiated in the Domesday text where the history of the fees thereby identified indicates two or more nuclei.[31] In most cases I am sure that the assumption is warranted; where a Domesday estate in A is consistently placed in B in later documentation, it would be perverse always to insist that B was a post-Domesday settlement. However, Frank Thorn, following Darby, has recently reminded us that the method has its dangers.[32] Hitherto the use of 'the other' or 'another' with a place-name has been seen as a cast-iron indication of two settlement nuclei. But he has adduced evidence to show that sometimes the word is used to connote 'another one like this', that is, another estate in the same place. Curiously, in most cases later documentation indicates two settlements. Whether the usage necessarily precludes the existence of two settlements in 1086 is another matter. Nevertheless, it is as well to acknowledge that the retrospective method is an interpretative one and the historian must be aware of the prevailing trends in settlement morphology.

---

[29] C. P. Lewis, 'Introduction to the Shropshire Domesday', *The Shropshire Domesday*, eds A. Williams and R. W. H. Erskine (London, 1990), 13.

[30] Darby, *Domesday England*, 23–6.

[31] The Phillimore editors are generally more cautious in their interpretation, confining differentiations to notes or index.

[32] Thorn, '"Another Seaborough", "The Other Dinnaton": Some Manorial Affixes in Domesday Book', 345–77; Darby, *Domesday England*, 20.

A generation ago it was axiomatic that all Anglo-Saxon settlement was nucle-ated. In the last thirty years intensive archaeological field work has shown that the predominant form in the middle Saxon period was dispersion.[33] Many parts of the country still exhibit this pattern of settlement today and Domesday Book some-times hints that it was a locally significant form in 1086: the references to Drayton in Lincolnshire already cited seem to contrast a scatter of settlement in the hundred of Drayton with a central nucleus. Elsewhere in the same county a number of estates identified by a single name seemingly match an equal number of discrete earthworks within the parish, sometimes even adjacent to each other.[34] Dispersed settlement has always been a characteristic of the fenland and Wold. Holdings with one or two inhabitants must often generally represent a farm or hamlet.[35] But for many areas, notably the Midland counties, the change from dispersion to nucleation has eluded researchers. Various mechanisms, from population growth to the development of lordship, have been proposed, but the chronology remains vague.[36] The interpreter of Domesday must make a choice. For an adherent of early nucleation, the splitting of a settlement might be indicative of late population growth, while a believer in later nucleation might see it as a vestige of dispersed settlement.

Domesday evidence cannot resolve these issues. It merely provides a framework, be it ever so incomplete, in which the discussion can take place. Domesday is more eloquent in what it has to say about its central concerns, that is, vills and estates.

The hide, the geld, and local government

Almost every entry in Domesday has an assessment to the geld. The unit employed varies from area to area. In the Danelaw counties of Yorkshire, Lincolnshire, Nottinghamshire, Derbyshire, Leicestershire, Norfolk, and Suffolk, the carucate is found. The name *carucata* is derived from Latin *caruca*, 'plough', and is a trans-lation of the Anglo-Scandinavian term *plogsland*, that is, 'ploughland'. In Kent a similar unit is found called the sulung, from OE *sulh*, 'plough'. In the rest of England covered by the survey the hide is all but universal. The term has the root meaning of 'family', and, unlike the carucate and sulung, it is notionally a measure

[33] For a recent review of settlement studies, see C. Lewis, P. Mitchell-Fox, and C. Dyer, *Village, Hamlet, and Field: Changing Medieval Settlements in Central England*, 2nd edn (Macclesfield, 2000).
[34] P. Everson, C. C. Taylor, and C. J. Dunn, *Change and Continuity: Rural Settlement in North-West Lincolnshire* (London, 1991), 13–28.
[35] See, for example, Church Stoke near Montgomery and Brockton in Shropshire (GDB, 257v, 259v: *DB Salop*, 4,12,1;4,27,25; Lewis, 'Introduction to the Shropshire Domesday', 13).
[36] H. S. A. Fox (ed.), *The Origins of the Midland Village*, Department of English Local History, University of Leicester (Leicester, 1992).

of the total resources of a holding (as opposed to its arable component), but by the eleventh century the term was probably closer to yardland. The three units had emerged in different contexts, but by the time of the Domesday inquest there was probably felt to be a high degree of equivalence between them as a measure of the taxable capacity of an estate or tenement, although notionally the sulung was twice the area of the hide.[37]

By and large historical accounts of the hide have been reductionist.[38] It is most often likened to a rate assessment; more recently, though, statistical analysis has been employed to argue that it is an actual measure of resources, even an income tax coding.[39] It is a debate that continues: the fiscal and the real are often seen as irreconcilable opposites. Nevertheless, both camps tend to agree that by 1086 the assessment was primarily used to levy the Danegeld. This was an impost that was first demanded in the late tenth century by Æthelræd the Unready to buy off Danish invaders. With Cnut's Danish conquest it became a regular tax upon land which survived, with a caesura in the reign of Edward the Confessor, into the Norman period. The Anglo-Saxon Chronicle makes much of the burden that the tax imposed upon the people[40] and this has encouraged the notion that the geld was an exploitative device first imposed by necessity and then sustained by predatory kingship. These are notions that misrepresent both the hide and the geld.[41]

The idea of Domesday Book as a terrier appealed to the Victorians. Throughout the nineteenth century countless parish priests pored over their tithe maps to determine the area of the hide. Round put an end to all that in a magisterial analysis that introduced that other Victorian notion, the rate. Thereafter, elucidating the pattern of hidation became the primary task of all Domesday historians; the subject is the first item in every VCH Domesday introduction. Not even Galbraith's dismissal of the geld as a primary concern of the Domesday inquiry has entirely dispelled interest in the matter.[42] The drift of the work was in one direction: the geld was a function of a top-down assessment rather than measured survey.

[37] H. R. Loyn, *The Governance of Anglo-Saxon England, 500–1087* (London, 1984), 119–20.
[38] For exceptions, see R. P. Abels, *Lordship and Military Obligation in Anglo-Saxon England* (London, 1988), 113–14, and, more recently, R. Faith, *The English Peasantry and the Growth of Lordship* (London and Washington, 1997), 89–125.
[39] J. McDonald and G. D. Snooks, 'Were the Tax Assessments of Domesday England Artificial? The Case of Essex', *EcHR*, 2nd series, 38 (1985), 353–73; A. R. Bridbury, 'Domesday Book: A Re-interpretation', *EHR*, 105 (1990), 284–309.
[40] *ASC*, 82, 83, 86, 88, 89, 91, 93, 97, 106.
[41] *DIB*, 58–64.
[42] For references and reviews of the literature for each county, see Frank Thorn's discussion of the 'Hundreds and Wapentakes' in each volume of *Great Domesday Book: County Edition*, eds Ann Williams and R. W. H. Erskine, 30 vols (London, 1986–92). See also K. Bailey, 'The Hidation of Buckinghamshire: Part 1, Domesday', *Records of Buckinghamshire, 32* (1990),

It seems to me that much of this primary research into the mechanics of the geld remains sound. The evidence for geld quotas, that is the assignment of a burden of taxation to a district, is overwhelming. Two quotas are recorded in Domesday Book itself; Rutland was assessed at three units of twelve carucates and the vills that gelded with York at seven similar units.[43] Many Domesday assessments can be shown to be identical with quotas recorded elsewhere. The 1189 hides at which the twelve hundreds of Worcestershire were assessed in 1086 seem to be represented by the 1200 hides assigned to the shire in a pre-Conquest document known as the County Hidage.[44] A similar equation obtains with a further six quotas recorded in the same document. Finally, the ridings of Lindsey were assessed to within a few bovates of the fifty twelve-carucate hundreds assigned to them in the Lindsey Survey of 1115.[45]

The list is impressive. It is nevertheless true that the majority of assessments of Domesday hundreds and counties exhibit no such neat totals. The widespread incidence of conventional units of assessment at a more local level, however, attests an original pro rata distribution of quotas throughout the country. R. A. Leaver has shown that in a sample of ten shires 40 to 62 per cent of estates in nine were assessed at five hides or a multiple of five hides (only Essex was significantly lower at 4.5 per cent).[46] In the Northern Danelaw a twelve-carucate unit is ubiquitous, often forming a regular cadastration that can be reconstructed from consecutive entries in the Domesday text.[47] The burden of assessment was clearly higher in some counties than others. Taking into consideration differences in resources and landscape, Kent, for example, is comparatively lightly assessed compared with neighbouring Sussex and Surrey.[48] Even within a shire rates could vary. In Lincolnshire, Kesteven and Holland had to pay three or four times the geld of Lindsey and in the twelfth century the men of the two divisions complained to the Exchequer on more than one occasion of the inequality.[49] Nevertheless, area by area (as opposed

1–34; *idem*, 'The Hidation of Buckinghamshire: Part 2, Before Domesday', *Records of Buckinghamshire*, 34 (1992), 87–96; C. R. Hart, *The Danelaw* (London, 1992), 231–430.

[43] GDB, 293v, 298: *DB Rutland*, R1–4; *DB Yorks*, C22.

[44] F. W. Maitland, *Domesday Book and Beyond* (Cambridge, 1897), 524–9.

[45] D. R. Roffe, 'Hundreds and Wapentakes', *The Lincolnshire Domesday*, eds A. Williams and G. H. Martin (London, 1992), 35.

[46] R. A. Leaver, 'Five Hides in Ten Counties: A Contribution to the Domesday Regression Debate', *EcHR*, 2nd ser., 41 (1988), 525–42. The shires are Bedfordshire, Berkshire, Buckinghamshire, Essex, Hertfordshire, Huntingdonshire, Middlesex, Oxfordshire, Surrey, and Wiltshire.

[47] Roffe, 'Hundreds and Wapentakes', 33–9. See above, pp. 91–3.

[48] Darby, *Domesday England*, 336. Assessing rates of hidation can only be approximate. Dividing assessment to the geld by recorded population gives a figure of 0.1 sulungs/person in Kent, which equals 0.2 hides/person, 0.33 hides/person in Sussex, and 0.5 hides/person in Surrey.

[49] D. R. Roffe, 'The Lincolnshire Hundred', *Landscape History*, 3 (1981), 34–5.

to nationally)[50] statistical analysis displays a high degree of positive correlation between these assessments and other Domesday data, that is, hidation is regularly proportional to the value and resources of an estate.[51] It would seem that while the geld was assigned through quotas the burden of distribution was locally equitable. At the level of the shire and hundred it seems likely that there was some degree of survey, probably confined to a count of ploughs or ploughlands, to ensure that no free man was disadvantaged.[52]

All this looks as bureaucratic as any Victorian administrator might wish. In reality, the system was far from a simple administrative instrument subservient to executive fiat. How the burden of geld was determined from area to area is unknown, but it seems clear that it was a function of negotiation. In some shires, like Worcestershire, the original hidation survived until 1086 (although the burden was by then no longer equally distributed).[53] Elsewhere it was subject to reduction. At the time of the County Hidage, Northamptonshire was assessed at 3200 hides and so there were 32 hundreds in the county at Domesday but their assessment had been reduced by 60 per cent.[54] Hundreds throughout the country enjoyed reassessments at varying rates if not always pro rata. Individual lords might also negotiate special terms for their estates, as numerous references to exemption in part or whole testify. These were modifications to the system that were common-place enough before the Conquest, but thereafter they gathered pace. By 1086 it was a matter of course that the demesne of all tenants-in-chief was exempt.[55]

The geld, then, was flexible and accommodating. It mediated the relationship between the king and his subjects in the matter of Danegeld. But this was not its only function. Domesday Book tells us that Stamford was assessed at twelve and a half hundreds, that is 150 carucates, 'for military service by land and sea and for danegeld'.[56] Hides were used to determine military service in Berkshire,

---

[50] I am not aware of a statistical study that takes *all* the shires of Domesday England as its basis. If correlation is to prove that assessment is related to resources, then it has to be more than local.

[51] McDonald and Snooks, 'Were the Tax Assessments of Domesday England Artificial?', 353–73.

[52] J. McDonald, 'Tax Fairness in Eleventh-Century England', *The Accounting Historians Journal*, 29 (2002), 173–94, suggests that lesser free men fared better than the larger land-holders. The analysis, however, is based on post-Conquest tenurial units and pre-Conquest assessments and assumes that values are a measure of net annual income.

[53] GDB, 172: *DB Worcs*, C3.

[54] There were twenty-two hundreds, two double hundreds, and four hundreds and a half, that is thirty-two hundreds (22+4+6). For a speculative reconstruction of the process, see C. R. Hart, *The Hidation of Northamptonshire*, Department of English Local History, University of Leicester, Occasional Papers, 2nd series, 3 (1970).

[55] *DIB*, 63. In counties like Surrey, where TRE and TRW assessments are given, the exemption of demesne estates can be directly observed (S. P. J. Harvey, 'Taxation and the Economy', *Domesday Studies*, ed. J. C. Holt (Woodbridge, 1987), 257–9).

[56] GDB, 336v: *DB Lincs*, S1.

and one man was sent from each in Cheshire to repair the bridge and walls of Chester, while in the South West hides determined contributions to the king's farm (a food render).[57] More significantly still, the geld also mediated the duties of policing incumbent on the community of the vill. In the North the twelve-carucate hundred paid eight pounds for breach of the peace, and by implication was responsible for the maintenance of tithings (a frankpledge system in which groups of free men were held responsible for the good behaviour of their fellows).[58] This was a penalty that was apparently instituted, or perpetuated, by the Wantage Code of c.997.[59] No similar provision is explicit in the parallel laws for hidated England, although the Hundred Ordinance suggests that something like the five-hide vill must have had similar duties.[60] Here we begin to see that the hide was not only some sort of measure of the obligations of a free man. It also constituted the essential cohesion of local societies.

It is thus no surprise to find that the hide was an integral part of the structure of local government. The hundred of a hundred hides is a relatively rare occurrence; so-called 'beneficial hidation', the exemption of land, may often account for shortfalls. Excesses, however, are also common. Sometimes the hundred concerned was a hundred and half or a double hundred: both are phenomena which were common in the East Midlands and East Anglia, although the fact is not always explicit in Domesday Book. The special status of royal estates may also have played a part. Most, although by no means all, were hidated, but since they rendered a farm they did not always participate in the local government structure. This may well be the explanation for the small hundreds coterminous with royal estates in the South and West.[61] The phenomenon has, however, been little studied beyond the Danelaw,[62] but there the pattern is decided. *Terra regis* stood outside geld

[57] GDB, 565v, 262v: *DB Berks*, B10; *DB Cheshire*, C21. For the king's farm, see, for example, GDB, 50v: *DB Hants*, 69,41: 'Edwin the huntsman holds 2 hides of the king's farm. King Edward gave them to him. They were then, as now, assessed at 1 virgate.'
[58] Roffe, 'Lincolnshire Hundred'.
[59] Robertson, III Æthelræd, 3.1; *EHD*, i, 403. In East Anglia the leet performed much the same functions as the twelve-carucate hundred.
[60] Robertson, The Hundred Ordinance.
[61] For the exemption of royal estates in the South West, see Darlington, 'The Wiltshire Geld Rolls', 75–7. H. M. Cam, '*Manerium cum Hundredo*: The Hundred and the Hundredal Manor', *EHR*, 47 (1932), 353–76, assumed that the phenomenon lay at the heart of the hundred as an institution. For a critique of this analysis, see below, pp. 283–4.
[62] But see R. P. Abels, 'An Introduction to the Bedfordshire Domesday', *The Bedfordshire Domesday*, eds A. Williams and R. W. H. Erskine (London, 1991), 6, *contra* F. R. Thorn, 'Hundreds and Wapentakes', in *eodem*, 58–9, citing GDB, 209v: *DB Beds*, 1,5: 'Ralph Taillebois [...] added [Biscot] to Luton, the king's manor, for the additional payment which it gave him, and alienated it from the hundred in which it was assessed TRE. On the other hand he took another 5 hides from another hundred and placed them in Flitton Hundred.'

quotas and often the twelve-carucate hundred, emerging in the twelfth century as separately constituted vills and quasi extra-hundredal sokes.[63]

Hundreds in their turn were often grouped in twelves, twenty-fours, and thirty-twos to form the shire, as witnessed by the County Hidage, but again there was no great regularity. The integration of the system is most fully seen in the North where in 1086 it had been more recently introduced. In Nottinghamshire and Derbyshire there were consistently seven twelve-carucate hundreds to the wapentake and six wapentakes to the shire. Elsewhere other systems were employed but the figures 84 (7x12) and 504 (7x12x6) recur. In Lincolnshire wapentakes were often assessed at seven or fourteen hundreds, but overall there was a fifty-hundred unit: each of the three ridings of Lindsey weighed in at precisely that figure, Kesteven at 150 hundreds (incorporating the 12½ hundreds of Stamford), and Holland at 25. In Yorkshire and its dependent territories no overall system has been identified but again assessments of 84 and 504 carucates are common.[64]

The hide and carucate became the cornerstone of local government in the tenth century. As a unit of assessment the hide had had a longer history. From the seventh century it had been used as an indicator of extent in the grant of estates to monasteries. Here and there the same assessment might persist into the eleventh century, but by then its connotations had changed. In a late seventh-century document known as the Tribal Hidage the hide seems to be a measure of tribute: the various 'tribes' that owed allegiance to Mercia (or Northumbria) were measured, often in duodecimal groups, in hundreds of hides.[65] The cadastre, however, cannot be related to later assessments. Undoubtedly, the Domesday system finds its origins in the network of boroughs set up by Alfred in the late ninth century to counter Danish raids. Its principles are set out in the probably early tenth-century document known as the Burghal Hidage.[66] There for the first time is stated the obligation of the hide to the defence of the borough. It is from this time that continuity of assessment into the eleventh century can generally be traced. A proto-shrieval system was born. Not all of the early boroughs and their territories were to survive, but the network was adapted and extended as Mercia and the Midlands were conquered in the early tenth century.

Despite its supposed Danish associations, the carucate seems to have been an English innovation consequent on the incorporation of the North into the

---

[63] D. R. Roffe, 'The Origins of Derbyshire', *The Derbyshire Archaeological Journal*, 106 (1986), 102–22; Roffe, 'Hundreds and Wapentakes', 33–9.

[64] Roffe, 'Hundreds and Wapentakes', 33–9.

[65] W. Davies, and H. Vierck, 'The Contexts of the Tribal Hidage: Social Aggregates and Settlement Patterns', *Frühmittelalterlichestudien*, 8 (1974), 223–93; Loyn, *Governance of Anglo-Saxon England*, 34–8.

[66] A. R. Rumble, 'An Edition and Translation of the Burghal Hidage', *The Defence of Wessex: The Burghal Hidage and Anglo-Saxon Fortification*, eds D. Hill and A. R. Rumble (Manchester, 1996), 14–35.

kingdom of England in the later tenth century.[67] Domesday here provides the decisive evidence. The twelve-carucate hundred was independent of tenure; it took no cognizance of the structure of manors and, in the eleventh century at least, was not attached to any partial interest. It was a communal organization and, as a tithing, it cannot therefore have been any earlier than the late tenth century when surety ceased to be vouched by the kin and was vested in the community. In hidated England the functions of the hide and the hundred were adapted to the developing demands of local government. In the North the term wapentake may have been borrowed from earlier popular assemblies, but the integrated Domesday system seems to have been instituted in its entirety at this point in time.

By 1066 the courts of hundred, wapentake, and shire were the forums in which the law-worthy men of the shire assumed their responsibilities as members of a free community. It was the duties that the hide ordained that defined and maintained their status. Failure to render geld held up the prospect of losing land. In the Laws of Cnut (II Cnut 79) it is stated that he who serves by land or sea by the witness of the shire shall have his land unmolested by lawsuits. Hemming, the compiler of the earliest surviving Worcester cartulary, recorded that laymen often appropriated land before the Conquest by paying the geld due on it, and Domesday Book itself notes a handful of instances in which land was lost since the geld was paid by someone else.[68] The geld entailed a series of obligations to the king – the Danegeld in particular was a tax that was paid into the royal treasury for the king's use – but those obligations were also public. Ultimately, the geld defined the freedom of the free man.

It was this that conferred legitimacy on eleventh-century government and administration, and it underlines the reciprocal nature of the geld. There can be no society in the world in which taxation, if grudgingly tolerated, is not resented. That the demands of a polity should be perceived as an imposition go back to the very roots of the word and in modern English to tax still carries with it not a little of the notion of *unfair* demands. But governments and prime ministers have ignored at their peril the truth that they ultimately only tax with consent. In liberal circles it is a commonplace to aver that taxation is our subscription to a civilized society. And so it is only if it is perceived to be so. If this is a political reality now, so it was the more so in eleventh-century England. The geld was no arbitrary imposition. In its essentials it mediated relationships between the crown and the various communities over which it exercised sovereignty.

---

[67] Roffe, 'Hundreds and Wapentakes', 33–9.

[68] *Hemingi Chartularium*, I, 278; GDB, 141, 216v: *DB Herts*, 36,9; *DB Beds*, 46,1. It has been doubted that there was any continuity between the reign of Cnut and the Domesday inquest in this area on the ground that there was a discontinuity in the collection of geld between 1051 and 1066 (P. Hyams, '"No Register of Title": The Domesday inquest and Land Adjudication', *ANS*, 9 (1986), 128). However, while the collection of *Danegeld* may have been suspended in the reign of Edward the Confessor, other dues were, of course, still levied.

Within this context it becomes clear that the record of an assessment to the geld in the Domesday inquiry was always going to mean something more than the note of a tax liability. In calling the inquest the king clearly had in mind, among other things, an audit of his revenues and this was a matter in which the community of the shire had an interest as tax-payers. But their interest went deeper. The acknowledgement of an obligation to pay the geld was tantamount to a confirmation of freedom and the right to land and, conversely, their absence would put their land in jeopardy. The concealment of land or liability would clearly have been a dangerous strategy, and hence it is likely that great pains were taken to discover land and note sanctioned immunities. The Domesday inquiry could not fail to be about geld at the level of the community of the shire.

For the tenant-in-chief it was probably of less interest. In most entries he is to all appearances represented as assuming responsibility for the burden of geld assessed on his land. However, beyond the demesne his rights in his estate were confined to dues and it was the tenants who paid the geld. Time and again the Exon geld rolls show that free men and villeins not named in GDB were personally in arrears for their Danegeld or were exempt. In Huntingdonshire we are told that 'the villeins and sokemen paid geld according to the hides written in the records'.[69] Throughout the Domesday corpus a separate assessment is often given for their lands. In Middlesex the text details the amount paid by almost everyone. With the lord's demesne exempt, the burden of taxation largely fell upon the peasantry. It was probably only where he held non-gelding land that the tenant-in-chief's interest was engaged. Normally, the grant of exemption is seen as relieving the lord of taxation but, since he was not responsible for it in the normal course of events, it looks more likely that exemption was in fact a grant of the geld to himself.[70]

---

[69] GDB, 203: *DB Hunts*, B21. 'Records' rather than Alecto's 'return' for *breve*, since it is not clear that a Domesday return is referred to.

[70] In cases of total exemption the lord seems to have levied the geld himself. Thus, Exon records (202) that Padstow in Cornwall never gelded 'except for the use of the church [of St Petroc]'. LDB records that the geld of Bury St Edmunds was diverted to the monks of the church and this arrangement seems to have been a function of the exemption of the vill by King Cnut in 1021 (LDB, 372: *DB Suffolk*, 14,167; S980). For a more ambiguous reference, see GDB, 174: *DB Worcs*, 2,74. 'Under-assessment' was probably no different in kind. Urban tenements that belonged to rural manors certainly paid their geld to the lord, for *geldum* was apparently one of 'the customs' that he enjoyed. In Huntingdon, for example, the abbot of Ramsey, the abbot of Ely, and Ulf Fenman had had all customs except geld, but the bishop of Lincoln (*recte* Dorchester), Earl Siward, and Gos and Hunæf had held all customs and sake and soke without reservation (GDB, 203: *DB Hunts*, B1–5,14). An explicit reference to payment to a lord is found in the Sussex folios; a Leofwin held ½ a hide of the 59 at Washington and gave geld to his lord, but the latter 'gave nothing' (GDB, 28: *DB Sussex*, 13,9).

The forest and inland

The hide was a fundamental reality of Old English society that still informed its Anglo-Norman successor. One might be forgiven for believing that it represented all land in England in 1086, but this is not so. It is true that almost all land described in Domesday was geldable, that is *warland*. Historians have not always grasped the fact. *Warland* is frequently identified with the land of the peasantry and is therefore contrasted with the lord's demesne. It is clear from the Domesday corpus, however, that demesne was equally *warland*. The fact is often explicit. In Spaldwick in Huntingdonshire, for example, it is stated that 'the abbot of Ely had 15 hides to the geld. [There is] land for 9 ploughs. There is now in demesne 4 ploughs, on 5 hides of this land.'[71] Similar references are widely found in the Wiltshire and Dorset folios. In Exon the hidage of the demesne and tenanted land is separately recorded as a matter of course and the two figures regularly add up to the total for which the estate defended itself. Elsewhere the information is only sporadic. The implication is nevertheless clear. Where GDB states that a tenant-in-chief holds x and it defends itself for y hides, land for z ploughs, in demesne x ploughs, that demesne is to be understood to be part of the geldable land. Here and there we find accounts of tenements that had never been hidated, but these are the exceptions, being predominantly royal lands subject to the special procedure of the first stage of the Domesday inquest. Otherwise, it follows, all land in Domesday either paid geld or had been exempt.

The Domesday inquest was clearly about geldable land. However, the hide was not an exclusive measure. Many of the royal manors assessed to the farm of one night in Wessex were unassessed to the geld. On the fringes of the kingdom there were lands that had not been hidated. Along the Welsh marches newly conquered territory was yet to be incorporated into the shrieval system in 1086 and is measured in terms of carucates that represent ploughlands or simply ploughs.[72] Entered above the line or in a separate section of the king's chapter, it too owes its enrolment to the special procedure of the first stage of the Domesday inquest. In the survey of the non-royal estates, land outside the cadastre of this kind was simply omitted. The forest is a prime example. Woodland, of course, is ubiquitous in the Domesday texts. What characterized forest was not trees but legal status: as the royal hunting domain it was land that was *foris*, 'outside', the normal law. In consequence its existence is generally apparent only from incidental references in the text. In the lost *Haswic* in Staffordshire and Ellington in Huntingdonshire land was said to be waste because it had been placed in the forest;[73] Robert Gernon had taken a swineherd from the manor of Writtle in Essex and made him a forester

---

[71] GDB, 204: *DB Hunts*, 4,4.
[72] GDB, 162, 181, 269: *DB Gloucs*, W; *DB Hereford*, 1,49–60; *DB Cheshire*, FT.
[73] GDB, 247v, 204v: *DB Staffs*, 7,6; *DB Hunts*, 6,26.

of the king's wood, and in Worcestershire two foresters had been placed outside
the manors of Hanley Castle and Bushley for the keeping of the woods;[74] the
bishop of Worcester lost dues from his wood at Malvern because it was placed in
the forest, and, conversely, at Walton on Thames a forester paid 10s to Edward of
Salisbury.[75] Only the New Forest in Hampshire is explicitly mentioned, but even
there the intention was less a description of assets than a justification of what had
been taken away from various manors that would have otherwise enjoyed them.[76]
Welldon Finn rightly asserted 'that the men and their teams (in some settlements at
any rate) had disappeared only from the record and not from the land' as afforest-
ation put them 'beyond the scope of the inquest'.[77] Land put in the forest no
longer paid the geld,[78] and so it is that only TRE details of the estate are recorded
unless part remained outside the forest.

[74] LDB, 5v: *DB Essex*, 1,24. GDB, 180v: *DB Hereford*, 1,44.

[75] GDB, 173, 36: *DB Worcs*, 2,31; *DB Surrey*, 27,1.

[76] There has been considerable debate about the New Forest entries. Royal manors in the
forest are described in the *terra regis* and further references occur throughout the *breves*.
There is, however, a separate section towards the end of the Hampshire folios, before
the account of Southampton and the Isle of Wight, entitled *In Nova Foresta et circum
eam*. Some seventy-one parcels of land are described, some wholly in the forest, others in
part. Round believed that the section was postscriptal ('Introduction to the Hampshire
Domesday', *VCH Hampshire*, i, ed. H. A. Doubleday (London, 1900), 445–6). It is indeed
cramped, with the final entries added to the end of the previous quire after the account of
the lands of the king's thegns. But Julian Munby has argued convincingly from the existence
of a list of landholders at the beginning of the Hampshire folios and from compression in
the writing before the New Forest section that it was anticipated (*DB Hants*, Appendix). It
has, nevertheless, still been interpreted as a failed attempt to describe the forest as a whole
even though some of the land was remote from it. It should be noted, however, that the
information evidently came from a different source from the other references to forest, for
many of the entries start with the (in Circuit I) anomalous formula *X habuit*... That source
must be a schedule of the rights of the king, as ever probably issuing from the first stage
of the Domesday inquest. Dr Karin Mew ('The Dynamics of Lordship and Landscape as
Revealed in a Domesday Study of the *Nova Foresta*', *ANS*, 23 (2000), 155–66) has argued
that the identity of the area was not derived from the New Forest at all – *Nova Foresta* is
merely a topographical marker – but from its earlier tenure by Earl William fitzOsbern as
a military lordship or quasi rape along with Southampton and the Isle of Wight.

[77] R. Welldon Finn, 'Hampshire', *The Domesday Geography of South-East England*, eds
H. C. Darby and E. M. J. Campbell (Cambridge, 1971), 331. This is not to deny that
some settlements may have been destroyed in the interests of hunting, as William of
Malmesbury graphically relates (*William, of Malmesbury, ca.1090–ca.1143 – Gesta Regum
Anglorum: The History of the English Kings*, eds and trans. R. A. B. Mynors, R. M. Thomson,
M. Winterbottom, 2 vols (Oxford, 1998), i, 504).

[78] See, for example, GDB, 61v: *DB Berks*, 3–4: 'Walter [fitzOther] holds Bucklebury, 1 hide;
and a certain man of his [holds] of him. It lies in the forest and has never paid geld, so the
shire says', and again 'In Kintbury the same Walter holds half a hide, which King Edward
gave to his predecessor out of his farm, and freed from all customary dues in consideration
of wardenship of the forest – except such forfeiture to the king as is [due from] theft, and

These are clearly exceptional circumstances, but the omission of land was not confined to the forest. There is evidence that beside the geldable there was non-geldable land, both seigneurial and royal, throughout the country which also fell outside the terms of reference of the Domesday commissioners. In the Exon geld accounts there are numerous reference to 'carucates of land', usually royal, that do not obviously appear in GDB.[79] Except in the North (where the term is the usual word for a berewick), this type of land is normally called *inland* where it is noticed in Domesday Book.[80] It is most frequently recorded in Oxfordshire where it is consistently contrasted with the hidated demesne.[81] The account of Stanton Harcourt exemplifies the type: 'The same bishop [of Bayeux] holds Stanton Harcourt. There are 26 hides which paid geld TRE. There is land for 23 ploughs. Now in demesne [is] 1 hide and 1 virgate of this land in addition to the inland.'[82] Similar formulas are found in Northamptonshire and Warwickshire, and in Huntingdonshire a non-hidated demesne is consistently recorded in the hundred of Hurstingstone.

Elsewhere Domesday Book is silent on this subject apart from sporadic notices of unassessed lands.[83] Nevertheless, inland was clearly not the local phenomenon that this handful of references might suggest. The early twelfth-century surveys of the abbey of Burton's estates in Staffordshire and Derbyshire continually make reference to inland, there defined as land that does not pay the king's geld, which is contrasted with the hidated and carucated demesne.[84] Similarly, the monks of

---

manslaughter, and housebreaking, and breach of the peace. It is worth 5s.' Here the special status of 'forest' has pre-Conquest antecedents.

[79] Darlington, 'Wiltshire Geld Rolls', 175–7.

[80] The Domesday inland in Banbury is almost certainly represented by *karruatas* in a memorandum of *c*.1072 relating to the same land (*contra* J. Blair, 'Estate Memoranda of c.1070 from the See of Dorchester-on-Thames', *EHR*, 116 (2001), 114–23). For a discussion of inland of fundamental importance, see R. Faith, *The English Peasantry and the Growth of Lordship* (London and Washington, 1997), chapter 2.

[81] Faith supposes a continuum between inland and Domesday demesne in a process whereby ancient inland, cultivated by demesne tenants, metamorphosed into the directly exploited demesne or 'home farm' (*The English Peasantry and the Growth of Lordship*, 49–50). That there was a change in management of inland and Domesday demesne in the eleventh and twelfth centuries is not denied, but here attention is drawn to the distinction between non-assessment and exemption. Occasionally, inland might be measured in hides, but Domesday Book makes it clear that it had never been assessed to the geld. It is, then, to be contrasted with Domesday demesne that had been assessed but was exempt in 1086 which was *warland*.

[82] GDB, 155v: *DB Oxon*, 7,3. All was unhidated except that in Wykham, Garsington, Watlington, and Water Eaton, which, nevertheless, seem never to have paid geld.

[83] In Taunton in Somerset, for example, there were 54 hides and 'besides this the bishop [of Winchester] has in demesne land for 20 ploughs that have never paid geld' (GDB, 87v: *DB Somerset*, 22,1).

[84] 'The Burton Abbey Twelfth Century Surveys', ed. C. G. O. Bridgeman, *Collections of the History of Staffordshire*, William Salt Archaeological Society (1916), 236, 244.

Ramsey in Huntingdonshire recognized demesne of this type throughout their East Anglian estates, as did the canons of St Paul's, London, in their Middlesex, Hertfordshire, and Essex manors.[85] Apart from that of Ramsey in Hurstingstone Hundred in Huntingdonshire, none of this land is noticed in GDB or LDB. We must conclude that there was land outside the cadastre which was not noticed by the Domesday commissioners.

How common it was remains to be determined. Unhidated and non-geld paying areas of land, usually at estate centres, have been identified in Essex, Northampton- shire, and Worcestershire in the later Middle Ages, and more widely distributed references to inland, especially when contrasted with *outland, sulingland,* and the like, may point to others.[86] We may suspect that inland was rare in the highly taxed counties. In Lincolnshire there is no unambiguous sign of uncarucated demesne in the early twelfth-century survey of the lands of Peterborough Abbey, although the same survey appears to notice it in the lowly assessed Nottinghamshire: the abbey's demesne in Collingham seems to stand outside the 4 carucates of the villeins and sokemen which equate with the 4 carucates of GDB.[87] Conversely, unhidated land is more likely in areas in which the burden of geld was lower. Nottingham- shire generally was pre-eminently such a county. There vills were typically assessed at one or two carucates and there are relatively few manors compared with the neighbouring more highly rated shires of Lincolnshire and Leicestershire. Twelfth- century charters, however, indicate intricate subinfeudation which is every bit as complex.[88]

Neither is it clear that all this 'inland' was necessarily the lord's demesne. In Huntingdonshire it is frequently found that there is precisely one villein per fiscal virgate, implying that the liability to the geld was attached to a certain tenement in much the same way as duties such as suit of court were in the later Middle Ages.[89] It is thus conceivable that other tenements could coexist with the hidated land but were not noticed in GDB. However, in the light of the close relation- ship of geld and freedom, it seems unlikely that unhidated peasant land could remain independent for very long in areas of strong lordship. Indeed, we find that the fiscal tenements formed the basis of service throughout the Middle Ages but were subdivided between a number of families. By and large, it seems likely that

[85] See, for example, Elsworth in Cambridgeshire where there were said to be 'three caru- cates of land in demesne (*tres carucatae terrae*)' (*Cartularium Monasterii de Rameseia*, eds W. H. Hart and P. A. Lyons, Rolls Series, 79, 3 vols (1884–89), iii, 248). For St Paul's, London, see *The Early Charters of the Cathedral Church of St Paul's, London*, ed. M. Gibbs, Camden, 3rd series, 53 (1939), 118–21.

[86] Faith, *The English Peasantry and the Growth of Lordship*, 15–55.

[87] *Chronicon Petroburgense*, ed. T. Stapleton, Camden Society, Old Series, 47 (1849), 159.

[88] See, for example, the d'Aincourt fee (*The Thurgarton Cartulary*, ed. T. Foulds (Stamford, 1994), xxix–cxc).

[89] D. R. Roffe, 'An Introduction to the Huntingdonshire Domesday', *The Huntingdonshire Domesday*, eds A. Williams and R. W. H. Erskine (London, 1989), 11.

peasants maintained their freedom by contributing pro rata for the geld assessed upon the whole tenement. This is clearly the reality of the hide of eight virgates in the banlieu of Battle Abbey in Sussex.[90] More clearly, the widespread occurrence of free men in both earlier and later surveys where Domesday records none may well indicate non-seigneurial interests that were beyond the remit of the Domesday inquest.[91]

Until some idea is formed of the extent of inland no complete account can be made of its origins and functions. Nevertheless, some possibilities come to mind. As a seigneurial phenomenon, it might best be interpreted as the landed element of bookright. Inland is the usual term for the lord's demesne in pre-Conquest sources and in some contexts at least it is associated with king's thegns.[92] In Domesday Book the inland that is recorded is almost exclusively found on the tenant-in-chief's demesne manors. This interpretation is consonant with notable 'omissions' from Domesday Book. The settlements of Crowland, Thorney, and Ramsey in the fenland of eastern England, and Glastonbury, Athelney, and Muchelney in the South West were all within highly privileged ecclesiastical sanctuaries and none is described in the text. Inland, or something like it, might also be created by the simple expedient of remitting assessment. Battle Abbey's *leuga*, which is not described in Domesday Book, was created in this way by William the Conqueror as an act of expiation after the Battle of Hastings. If a significant non-seigneurial phenomenon, inland may be related to areas of weak lordship consequent on reclamation, assarting, or isolation. This may well be the import of a reference to 'men who dwell in the woodland' in the account of Newport Pagnell in Buckinghamshire.[93]

The problem has remained largely unexplored. Later medieval surveys need to be looked at anew to determine whether discrepancies in estate structure attest later developments or limitations to the Domesday data. Patterns of hidation and carucation still remain to be elucidated, but the greater challenge is to identify inland. Its occurrence in GDB and near contemporary sources stands to remind us that the hide is no absolute measure of the total landed resources available to a lord. Inland made an important contribution to the economy of estates in

---

[90] *The Chronicle of Battle Abbey*, ed. E. Searle (Oxford, 1980), 48. In the light of the evidence here presented, it seems unlikely that the phenomenon indicates a sliding scale of fiscal assessment for newly assarted land as previously suggested (E. Searle, 'Hides, Virgates and Settlement at Battle Abbey', *EcHR*, 2nd series, 16 (1963–64), 297).

[91] For the omission of free men in Circuit II see, for example, A. Williams, 'The Abbey Tenants and Servants in the 12th Century', *Studies in the Early History of Shaftesbury Abbey*, ed. L. Keen (Dorchester, 1999), 134–5; Circuit VII: P. Taylor, 'Introduction', *Little Domesday, Essex*, eds A. Williams and G. H. Martin (London, 2000), 19–20; Faith, 'The Topography and Social Structure of a Small Soke in the Middle Ages: The Sokens, Essex', 202–13; Circuit IV: Faith, *The English Peasantry and the Growth of Lordship*, 121–5.

[92] Faith, *The English Peasantry and the Growth of Lordship*, chapter 2.

[93] GDB, 148v: *DB Bucks*, 17,17.

the eleventh and early twelfth centuries and yet it is a resource that Domesday ignores. No account of Domesday society and its origins can be complete without an examination of the problem. The initial task is one of identification and this is one on which the ploughland data of Domesday cast some light.

The ploughland

The statement 'land for so many ploughs' is at once the most simple of formulations and the most complex of Domesday problems. The formula is found in most entries but not all (it is absent in LDB in its entirety and is rare in the Gloucestershire, Herefordshire, Worcestershire, half of the Shropshire, and the Lancashire folios of GDB), and yet it answers to none of the so-called articles of inquiry preserved in IE. It is ostensibly an estate statistic, and yet in the North it is assessed upon the vill and the twelve-carucate hundred. It normally exceeds the number of available ploughs, but in a large minority of estates there were more ploughs than ploughlands (a phenomenon known as 'overstocking'). In some areas it resembles a real measure of land, while in others it is closely related to the assessment to the geld. Finally, despite its prominence in Domesday the ploughland has not been unambiguously identified in either earlier or later records.

The ploughland is a nightmare for the tidy-minded. Hitherto all attempts to square these circles have been less than satisfactory. A. R. Bridbury has tried to cut the Gordian knot by arguing that the statistic refers to service capacity, the number of ploughs assessed to day work.[94] This is a possible reading of some entries in Exon, but hardly comes to grips with the usual formula of GDB. The ploughland is about land as well as ploughs[95] and so it has been widely interpreted. Two broad schools of thought have emerged. Realists have taken the ploughland phrase at face value, it is a measure of land. For Maitland it represented the extent of arable in 1066 and for Cyril Hart an ancient assessment, but for most proponents of the realist school, the datum was 1086 and the referent the yardland in contradistinction to the fiscal hide.[96] Nominalists, by contrast, see the ploughland as a further fiscal assessment. For Hart it represents a Danish carucation or an earlier hidation. But again the preferred referent is 1086; Stenton and more emphatically

---

[94] Bridbury, 'Domesday Book: A Re-interpretation', 304–5.
[95] So, for example, in Buckinghamshire it is recorded 'In the same vill [Horsenden] Robert holds of the bishop half a hide. There is land for half a plough, but the plough is not there' (GDB, 144: *DB Bucks*, 4,9). There are many similar entries in Circuit III.
[96] Maitland, *Domesday Book and Beyond*, 482–513; Hart, *Hidation of Northamptonshire*, 28; J. S. Moore, 'The Domesday Teamland: A Reconsideration', *TRHS*, 5th series, 14 (1964), 109–30; N. Higham, 'Settlement, Land Use and Domesday Ploughlands', *Landscape History*, 12 (1990), 33–44. P. Vinogradoff, *English Society in the Eleventh Century* (Oxford, 1908), 153–74, believed that the ploughland was a measure of the potential for assarting.

Sally Harvey are of the opinion that it is the assessment for a new tax to replace the geld.[97]

By and large it is the nominalists who have made the running. Their case is based upon the improbability of overstocking and the patent artificiality of many ploughland figures. The plough team was a capital intensive asset which required extensive maintenance, that is it had to be fed through the winter, and it is thus inconceivable that more teams were kept than were needed. The ploughland cannot be an actual measure of arable land. As an assessment no overall system can be found in the various figures that GDB presents – ploughlands are variously based upon hidation, working ploughs, or simple estimation – but this is in the nature of assessments: principle gives way to expediency where homogeneous taxes are assessed upon heterogeneous economies. Harvey cites the Roman *iugum* as a parallel. The Domesday commissioners used the economic indicator that most closely represented the wealth of the society they were assessing.

Elegant as this critique is, it does not explain why East Anglia and the West Midlands were apparently not reassessed and, more critically, why there is no trace of the supposed new assessment after the Domesday survey. Realists have further countered that the objections to the ploughland as a measure of agricultural potential are misconceived. Nicholas Higham has argued that overstocking can be adequately explained by the inefficiencies of land exploitation in a landscape of dispersed settlements, while in areas like Northamptonshire seemingly artificial patterns of assessment have been shown to be firmly grounded in agricultural reality.[98] However, the realists have in their turn failed to explain convincingly why the data were collected. It has been suggested that the aim was to improve agricultural yields by identifying areas of inefficiency, but the notion of the Conqueror as Farmer William is somewhat anachronistic.

Neither side has been able fully to convince a wider audience. It seems to me that that is because the terms of the debate are misconceived. If the realists and nominalists are agreed on anything it is that the Domesday inquest was an executive process, it was about decision making. In these terms, the dichotomy

---

[97] F. M. Stenton, 'Domesday Survey', *VCH Nottingham*, i, ed. W. Page (London, 1906), 211–13; F. M. Stenton, 'Introduction', *The Lincolnshire Domesday and Lindsey Survey*, eds C. W. Foster and T. Longley, Lincoln Record Society, 19 (1921), xv–xix; S. P. J. Harvey, 'Taxation and the Ploughland in Domesday Book', *Domesday Book: A Reassessment*, ed. P. H. Sawyer (London, 1985), 86–103; S. P. J. Harvey, 'Taxation and the Economy', *Domesday Studies*, ed. J. C. Holt (Woodbridge, 1987), 249–64.

[98] D. Hall, 'An Introduction to the Northamptonshire Domesday', *The Northamptonshire and Rutland Domesday*, eds A. Williams and R. W. H. Erskine (London, 1987), 15–17. To take but one example, Great Billing was assessed at 4 hides in 1086 and there were 8 ploughlands there with two ploughs in demesne, and these were represented in the seventeenth century by 48 yardlands of which 12 were in demesne (GDB, 229: *DB Northants*, 57,1; P. Whalley, *The History and Antiquities of Northamptonshire, Compiled from the Manuscript Collection of John Bridges* (Oxford, 1791), 405).

of the real and the fiscal is absolute. The result is the impasse that I have just
described. But of course the Domesday inquest was less about decision making
than collecting information to inform decisions yet to be made, and in this context
we don't have to think in terms of either/or. The ploughland begins to make sense
if the real and the fiscal are not seen as mutually exclusive but different stages in
a *process* of assessment.

In elucidating to what the unit refers, we must first clear the ground by determining the importance of the ploughland in the surviving manuscripts. This is
instructive. The ploughland was central to the purpose of neither of the two
volumes of Domesday Book. In LDB the data are not recorded at all,[99] but the
item was clearly omitted as opposed to being unavailable.[100] The IE summaries of
Ely Abbey's lands in Norfolk, Suffolk, and Essex all afford totals, indicating that
the matter of ploughlands was considered in East Anglia as elsewhere.[101] The GDB
scribe clearly accorded the information more importance, but he also does not seem
to have viewed the statistics as absolutely essential. In some areas he failed to enter
the figures or could not find a record of them. In the Kent folios he left gaps which
were never filled, and in the West Midlands he appears to have simply thought
the matter otiose. In the bishop of Worcester's chapter it is stated that there were
as many ploughlands as ploughs and this was probably the reality throughout the
area.[102] Only halfway through Shropshire does he seem to have thought better of
this omission and decided once more to make the ploughland explicit, thereafter
generally succeeding in recording a figure of some kind or another.[103]

The ploughland loomed large only in the Domesday inquest, and it would seem
from the summaries that it was a central item of inquiry. Ploughland figures are
recorded in all the complete summaries and are expressed in a common language
(*Hec terra sufficit* x *carucis*) that indicates that they are the reply to an article of
inquiry. Moreover, they stand out from the rest of the figures. In most instances,
the statistics are the only ones given for the whole fee: where assessment to the
geld, value, and the like are presented in two sequences relating to the demesne

---

[99] J. E. A. Jolliffe, 'A Survey of Fiscal Tenements', *EcHR*, 1st ser., 6 (1935–36), 136, argued
that the carucates of Norfolk and Suffolk were the ploughlands, given that geld was assessed
on the leet, but this is untenable. Elsewhere in Domesday *carucate terre* are always assessments to the geld. If they are not read as such in East Anglia, it is difficult to see how
the sums levied on each vill were distributed between the men who were liable to pay.
Moreover, if the same argument is applied to Essex (where geld was rendered in much the
same fashion as in the rest of England) and the hides are read as ploughlands, then there is
no statement of assessment to the geld at all. The East Anglian carucate is an assessment to
the geld. There are, however, sporadic references to 'ploughs that could be restored' where
there were fewer ploughs in 1086 than earlier.
[100] *DIB*, 163–5.
[101] IE, 122.
[102] GDB, 174: *DB Worcs*, 2,80.
[103] GDB, 257: *DB Salop*, 4,11,17.

and enfeoffed lands respectively, there is only one summary ploughland figure. Nevertheless, the information from which the totals were derived was apparently presented late in the proceedings. No verdict of vill, hundred, or shire recorded in the text mentions the matter. Furthermore, the ploughland is signally absent from the schedules that appear to have emanated from the earliest stages of the inquiry, the geld inquest and the survey of the *terra regis*.[104] The data first make an unambiguous appearance in Bath A which, if not a seigneurial return, is very close to that stage in the inquiry. Significantly, in the south-east and Leicestershire the pattern of omission is seigneurial rather than geographical.[105] The ploughland was an item of information that could evidently be provided by the lord or his agent.

This in itself does not preclude the ploughland as an existing fiscal unit. But such thorough-going self-assessment is unlikely, and it must be remembered that the information is given in the present tense: there *is* land for so many ploughs. What the tenant-in-chief understood by the ploughland seems to have been more concrete. It is simply untrue to say that the ploughland does not appear in later sources. It does, and significantly it is not an assessment. In the early twelfth-century surveys of the lands of the abbeys of Burton and Ely 'land for so many ploughs' was the regular way of indicating the quantity of land in unassessed demesne; the ploughland was a non-fiscal measure of land.[106] That is, it is as real as it gets without getting out a tape measure. The phrase is used in a similar context in GDB. We have already noted that unhidated land in the Welsh marches was measured in carucates. The connection is sometimes explicit. The measurement of the lands of Clifford Castle in ploughlands, for example, seems to be a function of the fact that it 'is part of the kingdom of England; it is not subject to any hundred nor any customary due'.[107] Even more exactly, demesne is sometimes measured in ploughlands. In Bluntisham in Huntingdonshire, for example, there was unassessed demesne for two ploughs.[108] Similar references can be found in Buckinghamshire, Northamptonshire, Oxfordshire, Dorset, and possibly Rutland.

Here, surely, we perceive a non-fiscal understanding of the ploughland. However, we cannot agree with the realist that it is always a measure of arable or that it has

---

[104] Burton B has been claimed as a Domesday satellite (J. F. R. Walmsley, 'Another Domesday Text', *Medieval Studies*, 39 (1977), 109–20), but is more likely to be a post-Domesday schedule (*DIB*, 151). The document styles itself *Scriptura sicut continetur in libro regis*. However, ploughlands are recorded in the form 'terra *n* carucis' which, in the North at least, was developed in the course of composition of GDB itself. Burton B would therefore seem to be an abstract from GDB; it can probably be associated with the survey of 1114 with which it is enrolled. Ely D is a schedule of claims that is later in the proceedings (*DIB*, 106, 167 and n).

[105] Darby, *Domesday England*, 348–9.

[106] 'Burton Surveys', 209–47.

[107] GDB, 183: *DB Hereford*, 8,1.

[108] GDB, 204: *DB Hunts*, 5,2.

no fiscal referents. That the Domesday ploughland in many parts of the North is conventional is irrefutable. In Rutland, for example, it is stated that Alstoe Wapentake was divided into two hundreds in each of which were 24 ploughlands.[109] In some parts of Lincolnshire the same ratio of carucate to ploughland is found in estate after estate.[110] Land *per se* was not the focus of the ploughland figures. Rather it seems to have been the fiscal hide. In the early Yorkshire folios of GDB there are entries of the form 'In Pickering there are 37 carucates of land to the geld which 20 ploughs can plough'.[111] The referent of the ploughland is the assessment to the geld. That this is to be understood throughout is indicated by GDB's sources. In ICC many entries are of a form that anticipates GDB usage; others are more expansive. Thus, it is recorded that 'In this village of Triplow Hardwin [de Scales] holds under the king 1 hide of the supplies of the monks [of Ely] ... In this hide is land for one plough.'[112] In Exon the linking of assessment and ploughlands is the norm. Entries are of the form 'The Count [of Mortain] has a manor called Buckland, which Eadmær Ator held TRE and it rendered geld for 3 hides less ½ virgate; 20 ploughs can plough these.'[113]

The ploughland is clearly a non-fiscal measure of fiscal land. What it is telling us is that, although this land is paying tax at so many hides there is in fact that much land there. We can begin to perceive, then, that the ploughland was a measure of the capacity of the hidated land to pay the geld assessed upon it. Where ploughland matches hide there was a balance between field and fiscal units, while an excess indicated a surplus of land for the geld assessed upon it. Conversely, a deficit indicated over-taxation. In these terms, it is clear that the ploughland figures could most easily be assessed by the tenant-in-chief by simply counting the number of ploughs that could work the hidated area of his manor. But where this was not possible an estimate could be made to the same end. Why such an expedient should have been employed in the North is not entirely clear. It may have been a function of the complexity of tenure, the relative weakness of lordship, the predominately pastoral nature of the economy, or simply the prominence of the twelve-carucate hundred in the communal life of the Danelaw. Elsewhere a different expedient was employed: in Leicestershire and Norfolk a sporadic record of TRE ploughs served the same purpose.[114] However, from the point of view of

---

[109] GDB, 292b: *DB Rutland*, R1–4.

[110] Stenton, 'Introduction', xv–xix.

[111] GDB, 299v: *DB Yorks*, 1Y4. Alecto has erroneously 'could plough' for *possunt*.

[112] ICC, 43–4.

[113] Exon, 210v.

[114] For Leicestershire, see Darby, *Domesday England*, 348–9. In Norfolk the *restaurari* formula, the number of ploughs that could be restored compared with those in use in 1066, directly links the statistic with tax capacity (D. R. Roffe, 'Introduction', *Little Domesday, Norfolk*, eds A. Williams and G. H. Martin (London, 2000), 22–3.

the commissioners, the effect was the same: the ploughland figures afforded some measure of the efficiency with which the wealth of hidated England was taxed.

In this formulation it becomes clear why the ploughland never became an assessment in itself. It was a measure of reality which took no account of the circumstances that mediated all assessments to taxation. In uncovering the physical extent of geldable land the king clearly seems to have had in mind an increase in the yield of the geld. In the event geld was only re-imposed upon the lord's demesne (certainly by 1096, and almost certainly in 1086).[115] Beneficial hidation and exemption of demesne had indeed made considerable inroads into tax returns but it had done so by diverting geld into the lord's pocket.[116] This, at least after the Conquest, was seen as the corollary of personal service, a legitimate perk if you like. Sensibilities, then, had to be observed. Even in his most avaricious dreams William cannot have believed that the ploughland figures could ever constitute a new assessment. A compromise was struck. The king assumed the right to geld over the hidated demesne while the tenant-in-chief retained the spare capacity that existed in the lands of his tenants. The ploughland figures would seem to have informed a process of negotiation.

It is a process which probably underlies the reality of assessment in general. Hide, carucate, and sulung are all terms with areal referents that speak of agricultural practice. To be credible all taxation must be founded in fact. Equally, taxation is about people and relationships: whatever assessment is imposed upon a community must reflect agreement. The real and the fiscal are not an irreconcilable dualism but complementary quantities. The Domesday corpus preserves a record of one aspect of a single activity, that of data collection. One might expect the second stage to have been the business, or part of the business, of the meeting at Salisbury in August 1086, but no record of the agreements there made is preserved. We have the evidence but not the judgement that was drawn from it. The ploughland figures are, then, the more precious because they uniquely attest a stage in a process of assessment that is otherwise unrecorded in English medieval sources. The nearest approach is the assessment of the carucage of 1198, but there only a handful of returns survive.[117]

---

[115] B. R. O'Brien, *God's Peace and King's Peace: the Laws of Edward the Confessor* (Philadelphia, 1999), 168–9; DIB, 235–8.

[116] For an attempt to formulate a method to identify beneficial hidation and quantify it, see McDonald, 'Tax Fairness in Eleventh-Century England'. The Beneficial Hidation Index (BHI) there developed highlights smaller, often enfeoffed, estates where the documentary sources, notably the Exon geld lists, suggest that it was the larger demesne estates held in chief that were exempt.

[117] *Chronica Rogeri de Houedene*, ed. W. Stubbs, 4 vols, Rolls Series, 51 (1868–71), iv, 46–7. For an account of the procedure of the inquest, see J. H. Round, 'The Great Carucage of 1198', *EHR*, 3 (1888), 501–10.

What light, then, does the ploughland cast on late eleventh-century England? Clearly, it is of only limited and local use in determining the extent of arable in 1086. Were all land in England assessed to the geld, then it would presumably provide a fairly accurate measure. Here and there, indeed, it can be shown that ploughlands are directly related to the yardlands of the later medieval period. But the equation is far from the rule. A real measure of fiscal land is as uninformative as the fiscal assessment itself when its extent is unknown. At most the ploughland provides an index of minima. The figures are, however, a measure of the rate of hidation. Patterns of distribution vary within and between areas. Regionally, these patterns may merely echo the rate of hidation, but the figures do provide a firm datum established by the commissioners themselves and therefore afford an index which is more valid than those normally employed. Locally, variations in distribution remain to be studied.

More obliquely, in conjunction with the record of ploughs the ploughland may cast light upon the extent of inland. It seems to me that overstocking, the excess of ploughs over ploughlands, is best explained by the inclusion of the ploughs of unassessed land in the account of the Domesday manor. On the overstocked Burton estates in Staffordshire the extra ploughs in 1086 correspond with the ploughs on the inland in 1114 (Table 6.1). Tenants of the *warland* also held inland and it would seem that the Domesday commissioners counted all of their ploughs, probably because they owed service with all of them at their lord's hall. This is a pattern that is repeated wherever inland is noticed in later sources. Overstocking is characteristic of under-assessed shires where unassesed land is likely to be the most prevalent. The phenomenon is the best guide we have to a phantom Domesday resource.

Table 6.1 *Burton Abbey's overstocked manors and inland in 1114*

Manor	GDB			1114	
	P/l	P/d	P/v	P/l	P/i
Burton	2	2	2	2	2
Stretton	2	1	5	3	2
Bromley	1	1	1	2	1
Leigh	3	1	5		2
Winshill	3	2	1½	2	2

P/l = ploughlands, P/d = demesne ploughs, P/v = villagers' ploughs, P/i = inland ploughs. Burton is mistakenly identified as Stafford in GDB, 247v: *DB Staffs*, 4,1 and n.

7

————

The Economy and Society

I N THE TRANSITION from lordship and tax assessment to stocking and value, the Domesday entry appears to move from the ineffable to the real. And as such, with a collective sigh of relief, have economic and social historians tended to treat the details of the lord's demesne, his ploughs, the population of the manor, and its resources in ploughs, meadow, woodland, pasture, churches, mills and the like, and finally value. None would now espouse the nineteenth-century view that Domesday is an exhaustive survey of communities, but it is widely assumed that it provides a comprehensive picture of the economic underpinning of lordship in 1086. In any assessment of Domesday data, it would seem that it is *de rigueur* to protest that commodities in land and services were recorded because they contributed to the income of the lord's demesne.[1]

This much has been common ground. Where there has been disagreement, it has been over the degree to which Domesday Book provides a measure of real incomes and how those incomes represent the wealth of England. While accepting that the inquest was an inventory survey, many have followed Lennard's lead in interpreting Domesday values as actual or potential lease values.[2] Most of the figures are multiples of standard units of account, whether they be shillings, pounds or *orae* of sixteen pence, and as such can hardly represent the sum totals of discrete renders. Moreover, many estates produced more than what they were assessed at. Domesday provides what is essentially a rental value. The actual productivity of estates, it is argued, must have been higher to allow for the subsistence and profit of the lessee, suggesting that the dependent peasantry produced a surplus that is not represented in Domesday Book.[3] Against this, Graeme Snooks has argued that the statistical 'fit' between value and resources is so exact that it will not allow any

---

[1] A. R. Bridbury, 'Domesday Book: A Re-interpretation', *EHR*, 105 (1990), 284–309.

[2] R. Lennard, *Rural England 1086–1135: A Study of Social and Agrarian Conditions* (Oxford, 1959), 123–8; S. Harvey, 'Domesday England', *The Agrarian History of England and Wales*, ii, ed. H. E. Hallam (Cambridge, 1988), 45–136.

[3] N. Mayhew, 'Appendix 2: The Calculation of GDP from Domesday Book', *The Commercialisation of English Society, 1000–1300*, eds R. H. Britnell and B. M. S. Campbell (Manchester, 1993), 195–6.

possibility of a surplus of this kind. Domesday values must be a measure of the net income of the lord, that is the productivity of the estate less the subsistence of the dependent peasantry. Only the lands of free men and sokemen, usually separately valued, stand outside the lord's demesne.[4]

All of this is much of a muchness when it comes down to the lord's take-home pay, as it were, given that many demesnes were indeed leased out. However, the two views embody contrasting interpretations of the status and economic standing of the dependent peasantry. On the one hand villeins, bordars, and the like are seen as producers with resources of their own; on the other as merely stock. The difference in approach is highlighted by attempts to estimate gross domestic product (GDP) in 1086. Nicholas Mayhew, on the assumption that the £77,000 of Domesday values represent rents, has suggested a figure in the region of £300,000 to £400,000.[5] Conversely, Snooks comes up with a much lower figure of £137,000 as his interpretation must demand.[6]

Both Mayhew and Snooks recognize the speculative element in calculating such figures: neither would claim that either was anything other than an order of magnitude. However, they do not own to inherent contradictions in their respective analyses. If the value of estates is rent, why did the commissioners go to so much trouble to uncover the minutiae of stocking? Later medieval rentals were confined to a simple record of issues. If values represent incomes, the inventory becomes comprehensible. But why, in that case, does Domesday Book not provide an account of all the estate's resources? Inland, for example, is unappraised and communal assets like common grazing, without doubt an equally valuable seigneurial resource, are omitted. And yet the underlying contradictions have not been addressed, for the economic models that have informed the analyses have appeared unassailable. Statistical analyses have demonstrated highly significant relationships between all the Domesday variables. Assessment to the geld, resources, and value are interdependent quantities just as the notion of Domesday as a survey of estates would suppose. Disagreement has centred on statistical method.[7] The assumption that Domesday is about real economies has not been questioned.

[4] G. D. Snooks, 'The Dynamic Role of the Market in the Anglo-Norman Economy and Beyond, 1086–1300', *The Commercialisation of English Society, 1000–1300*, eds Britnell and Campbell, 27–54.

[5] N. Mayhew, 'Modelling Medieval Monetisation', *The Commercialisation of English Society, 1000–1300*, eds Britnell and Campbell, 60–2.

[6] Snooks, 'The Dynamic Role of the Market in the Anglo-Norman Economy and Beyond, 1086–1300', 29–35.

[7] J. McDonald and G. D. Snooks, *The Domesday Economy: A New Approach to Anglo-Norman History* (Oxford, 1986) and their 'Were the Tax Assessments of Domesday England Artificial? The Case of Essex', *EcHR*, 2nd series, 38 (1985), 353–73, and 'The Suitability of Domesday Book for Cliometric Analysis', *EcHR*, 2nd ser., 40 (1987), 252–61; and J. D. Hamshere, 'Regressing Domesday Book: Tax Assessments in Norman England', *EcHR*, 2nd ser., 40

It can be. Domesday variables can correlate for any number of reasons. That they do so because they relate to estates is the least likely explanation. At the outset it is clear that this, the accepted view, has always been more than a little ambiguous. Few, it seems, have been willing to allow that the *manerium*, the manor, of Domesday has any meaningful content as a term. And yet at the same time no one has demurred in the assumption that the *mansio*, manor, of Robert of Hereford's account of the Domesday inquest or of the so-called articles of inquiry in IE refers to a well-defined estate of an immediately comprehensible type. That estate has remained remarkably elusive. Manorial structure seems to have been of little interest to the commissioners. There was a concern to identify what had been added or taken away. But, as the identifying place-names of entries indicate, all too often no attempt was made precisely to fix the location of manors; vill names are probably more common than estate names in the Domesday texts. Furthermore, it was the extent of these vills (or twelve-carucate hundreds or leets) that mediated the representation of manors rather than the internal organization of the manor itself.[8] In Circuit VI a concerted effort was made to identify (Yorkshire) or put together (Lincolnshire, Nottinghamshire and Rutland, Derbyshire, and Hunting-donshire) these artificial blocks as territorial units. But this probably reflects more of the GDB scribe's programme than the commissioners'.[9]

Elsewhere, it is only in the royal demesne that estate structure is regularly indi-cated, presumably reflecting the concerns of the initial stage of the Domesday inquest. Berewicks are more or less consistently identified in LDB. Otherwise, the realities of the estate office rarely obtrude. The account of the bishop of Worcester's hundred of Oswaldlow in Worcestershire seems to have issued directly from his reeve.[10] It commences with a unique, and *ad partem*, account of the bishop's liber-ties and then continues, in language that is entirely its own, to describe its estates manor by manor with a rehearsal of the appurtenances of each, as identified by distinctive diplomatic, in a form that is not dissimilar to that found in Circuit VI. Here, presumably, is an account of the estates of Worcester as the church itself perceived them. Such insights into estates are, however, conspicuous by their rarity.[11]

(1987), 247–51; J. McDonald, *Production Efficiency in Domesday England, 1086* (London and New York, 1998).

[8] See above, pp. 82–5.

[9] See above, p. 178.

[10] GDB, 172v–174: *DB Worcs*, 2; *DIB*, 143; S. Baxter, 'The Representation of Lordship and Land Tenure in Domesday Book', *Domesday Book*, eds E. Hallam and D. Bates (Stroud, 2001), 82–9.

[11] The lands of Glastonbury are described in an order that departs from that of the rest of the text (G. A. Loud, 'An Introduction to the Somerset Domesday', *The Somerset Domesday*, eds A. Williams and R. W. H. Erskine (London, 1989), 5); the various groups of manors may define discrete bailiwicks. In the account of the bishop of Lincoln's estates in Lincolnshire, Stow St Mary, its most important manor, is entered first where Welton by Lincoln might

What, then, is being described in the accounts of Domesday manors? Land *per se* was not the focus of the Domesday inquest. Its concerns were the interrelated matters of the geld and service and so its subject matter was hidated land, which mediated both. We might therefore expect that commodities were only recorded in so far as they were liable to taxation and rendered soke dues. We might also expect a significant statistical correlation between commodities chosen in this way. It is precisely this that the details of population, manorial stock, and value indicate.

The demesne

The term 'demesne', *dominium*, lordship, is used in three distinct senses in medieval documents. At its most specific it refers to that part of an estate that was held in the lord's hands, often for the supply of his household, and is usually referred to as his home farm. Secondly, it is additionally used of the land of the villeins who owed labour dues to it. Thirdly, it might refer by extension to those estates in which a lord had such land, that is the ones which had not been granted out to a tenant for service. Which usage is found in the Domesday corpus, and in what contexts, is central to the debate on the economy. The last is common enough, appearing most regularly in the summaries.[12] It presents few problems of interpretation. Whether Domesday Book describes the first or second has been more problematic. For Lennard and those who have followed him, the Domesday demesne of the ordinary entry is primarily the home farm and its stock alone. For Snooks, by contrast, it embraces the land and stock of the dependent peasantry. Both and neither are right.

Throughout the Domesday corpus the demesne is contrasted with the land of the men. Sometimes it is given a separate assessment, although it might be exempt from geld payment, and is often distinguished by distinctive diplomatic and calligraphic forms and content. Thus, in Exon its extent is regularly measured

---

have been expected, perhaps reflecting its management. Peterborough Abbey's lands are divided between demesne and enfeoffed lands wherever they occur, a form that cannot have been entirely unrelated to the accounting methods that they employed. By contrast, the demesne/enfeoffed dichotomy of Circuit IV may reflect the commissioners' practice. The head of the fee was commonly described first in the Herefordshire *breves* (C. P. Lewis, 'An Introduction to the Herefordshire Domesday', *The Herefordshire Domesday*, eds A. Williams and R. W. H. Erskine (London, 1988), 3–4). In Somerset, however, the GDB scribe seems to have been responsible for such rearrangements (Loud, 'An Introduction to the Somerset Domesday', 5). For a discussion of seigneurial returns, see Baxter, 'The Representation of Lordship and Land Tenure in Domesday Book', 73–102.

[12] Bridbury, 'Domesday Book: A Re-interpretation', 302–3, seems to think that the demesne in the summaries is in the sense of home farm. This is a possible reading of the Count of Mortain's summary that he examines, but in the light of the whole corpus, it can be shown to be a misreading. The other summaries are explicit in indicating that the land in demesne is those manors not held by tenants.

in hides, while in the Descriptio Terrarum of Peterborough Abbey land *in dominio* is contrasted with land *in socagio* and in Exon, ICC, and LDB its livestock alone is recorded. Furthermore, the occasional equation of *dominium* with 'land belonging to the hall' reminds us that we are dealing with seigneurial households.[13] That the demesne was effectively a farm (in the everyday modern sense) is often apparent from the record of ploughs. Typically, large numbers of ploughs are found on the demesne manors close to lordly residences and it is difficult to escape the conclusion that food was being produced for the lord's table.[14] Direct exploitation may also be indicated by the record of livestock. High concentrations of sheep, especially in certain areas of East Anglia, suggest that the resources of the demesne were fully realized where conditions were right. But conditions had to be right. Otherwise, a different management regime was employed. The fact is most clearly illustrated by the *terra regis*.

In the south and west royal manors, or groups of manors, rendered in kind a farm of one or more nights before the Conquest, that is enough food to supply the king's household for a certain number of days. Produce was either eaten on the spot when the court visited the estate or was transported to a suitable venue for consumption. After the Conquest the farm was commuted to monetary payments at varying rates and the use of the word *reddit*, 'it renders', suggests that the estates were leased out.[15] Other manors were let from before 1066 at agreed sums. The reign of William the Conqueror saw a great increase in the sums demanded. According to the Anglo-Saxon Chronicle:

> The king sold his land on very hard terms – as hard as he could. Then came somebody else, and offered more than the other had given, and the king let it go to the man who had offered more. Then came the third, and offered still more, and the king gave it into the hands of the man who offered him most of all, and did not care how sinfully the reeves had got it from poor men, nor how many unlawful things they did. But the more just laws were talked about, the more unlawful things were done. They imposed unjust tolls and did many other injustices which are hard to reckon up.[16]

Here and there Domesday Book does indeed notice the oppression of lessees.[17] Equally, it is evident that land could be granted at an advantageous rate to reward.[18]

---

[13] GDB, 203v, 293v, 299, 299v, 337v, 338v, 368v; LDB, 350v: *DB Hunts*, 1,6; *DB Rutland*, R17; *DB Yorks*, 1Y1;10; *DB Lincs*, 1,11;66.59,14; *DB Suffolk*, 8,52. In all but two instances this formula is found on the royal demesne.

[14] Harvey, 'Domesday England', 115–17.

[15] P. A. Stafford, 'The "Farm of One Night" and the Organisation of King Edward's Estates in Domesday', *EcHR*, 2nd series, 33 (1980), 491–502; Harvey, 'Domesday England', 85–95.

[16] *ASC*, 162–3.

[17] LDB, 284v: *DB Suffolk*, 1,60.

[18] R. P. Abels, *Lordship and Military Obligation in Anglo-Saxon England* (London, 1988), 151–5.

Both Beorhtric son of Ælgar and Hereweard made advantageous deals with religious houses before the Conquest.[19] The practice was no less common after the Conquest. Numerous tenants-in-chief held land from other lords, often churches, at low rents. Some of these arrangements perpetuate pre-Conquest agreements; others were apparently new.[20] Nevertheless, by and large the renders are probably broadly related to the output of estates.

Manorial renders, as indicated by the use of *reddit* and *reddidit*, are found outside the royal demesne but are rarer, occurring most commonly in ecclesiastical estates. The archbishop of Canterbury, for example, leased out many of his manors for mostly cash payments.[21] In thirty or so cases demesne appears to have been rented out to *censores*.[22] The number of references is small but it is likely that Domesday conceals other instances. A methodology for elucidating different strategies of estate management was pioneered by Lennard[23] and is now well established. It distinguishes between demesne and enfeoffed estates of various sizes in the hands of royal, ecclesiastical, and lay lords, and represents the characteristics of each by calculating percentage increases in value between 1066 and 1086 and the ratios between demesne ploughs, the peasants' ploughs, ploughlands, and a variety of other resources.[24]

Using these techniques, J. D. Hamshere has argued that demesne leasing was a management expedient that was widely employed in large fees.[25] In an analysis of estates in Gloucestershire, Worcestershire, and Warwickshire, he expressed assessment to the geld, ploughteams, the various classes of population, and value as a percentage of the total for large (>10 hides), medium (5–10 hides) and small (<5 hides) manors. In the large manors he found that there were significantly fewer demesne ploughs and higher values than the average and concluded that their demesnes were largely let at rent. It would seem that the return for lords of

---

[19] GDB, 173, 377–377v: *DB Worcs*, 2,30; *DB Lincs*, CK48. For both, see D. R. Roffe, 'Hereward "the Wake" and the Barony of Bourne: A Reassessment of a Fenland Legend', *Lincolnshire History and Archaeology*, 29, (1994), 7–10.

[20] There has been no general study of the type of tenure. At times, however, it seems to have been related to family arrangements. See D. R. Roffe, 'Welbourn Castle, Lincolnshire', *Nottingham Medieval Studies*, 41 (1997), 54–6.

[21] Harvey, 'Domesday England', 95–115.

[22] They are found in Dorset and Essex, but only otherwise in the Northern Danelaw. The rent they paid is usually, but by no means always, given. See also GDB, 368v: *DB Lincs*, 60,1: 'In Burton, Godric had 2 carucates of land to the geld. [There is] land for 2 ploughs. [It is] sokeland of Scampton, but nevertheless there was a hall there. Now Peter de Valognes has there 1 villein and 4 bordars with half a plough, and 5 acres of meadow. The demesne is tilled and leased. TRE worth 15s; now 11s.'

[23] Lennard, *Rural England 1086–1135*.

[24] For a succinct account of the methodology, and some of its results, see A. Wareham, 'The "Feudal Revolution" in Eleventh-Century East Anglia', *ANS*, 22 (2000), 294.

[25] J. D. Hamshere, 'The Structure and Exploitation of the Domesday Book Estate of the Church of Worcester', *Landscape History*, 7 (1985), 41–52.

extensive estates like the king was somewhat greater than that from direct cultivation and sale of the produce. By contrast, the statistical profile of the smaller estates
suggested more direct exploitation. A higher proportion of ploughs and lower value
seems an appropriate pattern for the lords with modest resources who lived on the
estates that they exploited.

Using the ratio of demesne to men's ploughs, Sally Harvey has argued along
similar lines for the country as a whole.[26] Arable land was not always the most
valuable asset – the bulk of the income was sometimes to be found in dues from
suit of court, soke, and the like – and it therefore often made better sense to
rent it out where it was not required for the lord's subsistence.[27] Both arguments
are founded in the assumptions that the plough figures are comprehensive and
Domesday values are transparent. These are big assumptions. Nevertheless, Harvey
is surely right in suggesting that the Conquest saw a decrease in direct demesne
exploitation. It is, of course, possible to point to the creation of new demesnes.
This, however, was a local phenomenon of limited importance.[28] Even after taking
account of hierarchies of lordship in 1066, the Norman settlement had generally
seen a concentration of power in fewer hands.[29] In consequence, there was less
need for home farms. The same was probably true of the lord's inland, where
he had any. Burton Abbey's was let to *censarii* in the early twelfth century and
probably the bishop of Lincoln's in Banbury *c.*1072.[30]

The Domesday demesne was, then, often a farm distinct from the other farms
that made up the manor, although it might not always be exploited directly by its
lord. But all of this was of little moment to the Domesday commissioners: the texts
are largely silent as to modes of demesne exploitation. The focus of the Domesday
inquest was other. That it was nexus of geld and service is indicated by the record

[26] S. P. J. Harvey, 'The Extent and Profitability of Demesne Agriculture in England in the
Later Eleventh Century', *Social Relations and Ideas: Essays in Honour of R. H. Hilton*, eds
T. H. Aston, P. R. Coss, C. Dyer and J. Thirsk (Cambridge 1983), 45–72.

[27] The profits could, nevertheless, be considerable. In Leominster, for example, 'The villeins
ploughed 140 acres of the lord's land and sowed them with their own wheat-seed and gave
as a customary due £11 and 52d' (GDB, 180: *DB Hereford*, 1,10a).

[28] *Contra* M. Chibnall, *Anglo-Norman England* (London, 1986), 141, and R. Faith, *The
English Peasantry and the Growth of Lordship* (Leicester, 1997), 198. For the fate of free men
and sokemen, see below, p. 220–1.

[29] But see C. P. Lewis, 'Introduction to the Shropshire Domesday', *The Shropshire Domesday*,
eds A. Williams and R. W. H. Erskine (London, 1990), 21–3, who argues that there was little
change in the number of sitting tenants between 1066 and 1086 in Shropshire. A. Williams,
'An Introduction to the Gloucestershire Domesday', *Domesday Book: Gloucestershire*, eds
A. Williams and R. W. H. Erskine (London 1989), 16–19, makes the same point for Gloucestershire, although there the figures are less convincing.

[30] 'The Burton Abbey Twelfth-Century Surveys', ed. C. G. O. Bridgeman, *Collections for the
History of Staffordshire*, William Salt Archaeological Society (1916), 20–47; J. Blair, 'Estate
Memoranda of *c.*1070 from the See of Dorchester-on-Thames', *EHR*, 116 (2001), 114–23. The
laici homines of the Banbury survey are probably equivalent to the Burton *censarii*.

of the assets of the manor. These assets were neither exclusively the lord's property
nor his exclusive right.

Ploughs

Like assessment to the geld, a record of ploughs occurs in just about every entry
in Domesday Book. The ploughs on the demesne are distinguished from those
of the men, both villeins and free men, but the position of both in Domesday
Book indicates that they were the most important asset of the estate. They head
the list of demesne appurtenances and are the only item of peasant stock that
is noticed. Their prominence is even more marked in earlier documentation.
Where Domesday Book records demesne ploughs, population, and then the men's
ploughs, Bath A, Exon, and ICC group plough statistics as a single item after the
ploughland figures. So, for example, it is said of Buckland Brewer in Devon that it
paid geld for 3 hides, less half a virgate of land, 'and 20 ploughs can plough these.
Now Ansger the Breton holds it from the Count [of Mortain]. Ansger has ½ hide
and 3 ploughs in demesne and the villeins have 2 hides and 1½ virgates and 8½
ploughs.'[31] Ploughs were a major concern of the Domesday inquest. Indeed, they
are duly entered in the summaries.

Here and there *obiter dicta* provide background information. Ploughs are said
not to be there[32] or land was tilled by ploughs 'from another manor'.[33] The
informants are nowhere identified, although there seems little doubt that they
were the lord, his agents, or his men. This is not to say, however, that the record is
unmediated by the preconceptions of the Domesday process. On occasion ploughteams of three, four, five, and six oxen are recorded, but numerous parallel entries
indicate that the eight-ox team was the norm. It was clearly conventional. Later
records reveal that the reality was sometimes more, sometimes less, depending on
conditions.[34] How 'real' teams were transformed into the teams of the text is
unexplained, but there are some indications that the GDB scribe rounded up the
figures of his sources.

In all, over 81,000 ploughs are recorded throughout England. It is, nevertheless, unlikely that this figure represents anything close to the total for the country
in 1086. We have already suggested that some ploughs on unassessed land are
recorded in the text,[35] but they are only so because they also worked the assessed

[31] Exon, 210b.
[32] The fact is most widely recorded in Circuit VII with a significant number occurring in
Circuit III. The referent is usually the ploughland.
[33] GDB, 139, 376v: *DB Herts*, 31,3; *DB Lincs*, CK2.
[34] H. C. Darby, *Domesday England* (Cambridge, 1977), 121–6. Variation has been noted
in Circuit II (R. Lennard, 'The Composition of the Domesday Caruca', *EHR*, 81 (1966),
770–5).
[35] Above, p. 209.

demesne. The juxtaposition of the men's ploughs with those of the lord in the surviving inquest records strongly suggests that they were largely the ones that owed ploughing service. Villagers who did not plough were certainly an exception worthy of note.[36] As A. R. Bridbury has argued,[37] there is no pressing reason to suppose that villeins did not plough elsewhere on their own account with their own teams. Overstocking, the excess of ploughs over ploughlands, is direct evidence of surplus capacity above the needs of the fiscal demesne.

The uncertainty makes the statistics more difficult to use. Clearly, plough figures are not by necessity directly related to actual arable. The supposition must often be that its area is greater. However, what do we make of the manor in which there are more ploughlands than ploughs? In Circuit III the number of additional ploughs that might be employed is widely recorded. The supposition here may be that there was a surplus of potential arable as yet to be exploited, but not necessarily so. If the ploughland was a measure of the tax capacity of the *warland*, and as such was as likely to be estimated as counted where it served the same end, then the low level of ploughs may merely reflect the relative importance of arable farming in a mixed or pastoral economy.

All this would be the more comprehensible if we had a better idea of how agriculture was organized. Unfortunately, Domesday Book affords few clues as to the nature of field systems and the like. Inland in Garsington in Oxfordshire is said to have been 'dispersed among the king's land',[38] perhaps suggesting strip cultivation, but the entry is all-but unique. There is more indirect evidence. If the geld assessments of Northamptonshire are truly related to field units, then it might be argued that the Domesday account of the county hides few assets within more or less fully developed field systems. David Hall has identified strips that are organized in furlongs and furlongs in fields in patterns determined by hidation.[39] Even here, however, the fact does not necessarily preclude other assets beyond a common system. Certainly, there are areas in which non-Domesday sources indicate that demesne was consolidated in blocks where villagers' lands were dispersed and there is evidence that land of this type might be unassessed.[40] Elsewhere attempts to extrapolate the organization of agriculture from Domesday sources have been more tenuous.[41] Here and there field systems like those of Northamptonshire can be

---

[36] GDB, 167, 315v, 323v, 330, 346v, 350, 370v: *DB* Gloucs, 38,4; *DB Yorks*, 9W25.9W33.14E1.28W35; *DB Lincs*, 11,6.14,11.68,10–11.

[37] Bridbury. 'Domesday Book: A Re-interpretation, 304–5.

[38] GDB, 156v: *DB Oxon*, 9,7.

[39] D. Hall, 'An Introduction to the Northamptonshire Domesday', *The Northamptonshire and Rutland Domesday*, eds A. Williams and R. W. H. Erskine, (London, 1987), 15–17; D. Hall, *The Open Fields of Northamptonshire*, Northamptonshire Record Society, 38 (1995).

[40] Faith, *The English Peasantry and the Growth of Lordship*, 15–55.

[41] See, for example, J. A. Sheppard, 'Pre-Conquest Yorkshire: Fiscal Carucates as an Index of Land Exploitation', *Institute of British Geographers Transactions*, 65 (1975), 67–78.

identified from other fragmentary sources,[42] but equally it is clear that common open fields were not universal in the eleventh century. In some areas they developed only in the twelfth or thirteenth century; in others they never emerged at all. Generally, the matter remains problematic precisely because Domesday is largely silent on the subject.[43]

Population

The enumeration of the population of the manor normally follows the account of the lord's demesne and his ploughs. The various classes are apparently sharply defined both vis-à-vis the holders of land TRE and TRW and themselves. It is clear, however, that they did not form entirely discrete categories. As we have seen,[44] in the Circuit VI folios the GDB scribe only slowly developed a workable taxonomy. Initially, he brought thegns and dregns of one kind or another above the salt and, where they were not too numerous, named them. Subsequently, however, he seems to have thought better of his classification and recategorized them as sokemen, being content to just number them. This did not stop him, however, from committing an apparent solecism in referring to '5 sokemen upon 5 manors' in Deeping in Lincolnshire.[45] In LDB unnamed free men held manors, but elsewhere in GDB holders of a manor were explicitly free but as named individuals were distinguished from other free men. There was probably a steeper status gradient between both types and other classes of rural population, but the edges were again perhaps fuzzy. Free men and sokemen are known to have had villeins 'under' them, whatever that should mean, but not vice versa. Bordars always seem to have been dependants of one kind or another and slaves were chattels.

At the top end of the scale were what Domesday Book calls *milites*, 'knights'. Typically, these were subtenants (although in other contexts the word *miles* might be used of any soldier, aristocratic or otherwise). In Berkshire there are a number who held from (*de*) the tenant.[46] Most are attributed a number of hides within the manor, although a significant number are recorded as demesne appurtenances.[47] Many are unnamed and must clearly be distinguished from the holders of manors;

---

[42] For the Domesday evidence, see H. Clarke, 'Agriculture in Late Anglo-Saxon England', *Domesday Studies*, eds A. Williams and R. W. H. Erskine (London, 1987), 43–7.

[43] The literature on the origins of field systems is enormous. For an introduction, see C. Taylor, *Fields in the English Landscape* (Stroud, 2000).

[44] Above, p.178.

[45] GDB, 366: *DB Lincs*, 51,3. The translation is from *The Lincolnshire Domesday and Lindsey Survey*, eds C. W. Foster and T. Longley, Lincoln Record Society, 19 (1921), 51/3. Phillimore and Alecto read *v. soc super v. maneria*, as '5 sokes over 5 manors', which is otherwise unparalleled.

[46] GDB, 61, 61v, 62v: *DB Berks*, 22,5.29,1.31,6.46,4.

[47] Earl Hugh, for example, had 2 hides in Hartham in Wiltshire of which '1 hide is in demesne, and there are 2 ploughs, and 2 slaves. There is 1 knight, and 3 cotsets, and 5 acres

it is a mistake to categorize all knights in their terms. The value of their holdings is usually small, and it has been suggested that they were household knights, hired soldiers, or sergeants of low status within the military hierarchy.[48] This analysis begs the question of the nature of values, but in general it probably represents the reality. Where they can be traced in later records, subtenants of this kind were usually of modest standing, little different form the richer free men. Nevertheless, some were clearly a cut above the ordinary in 1086. In Potterne in Wiltshire an English man was 'a knight by order of the king'; he was the nephew of Bishop Herman of Ramsbury and Sherborne.[49] Most, by virtue of their calling, must have been closer to their lords than the ordinary run of the rural peasantry.[50]

The status of the free man, the *liber homo*, is clearer, being more or less consistently defined throughout the Domesday texts in various formulas. In the areas in which he is found he is normally said to be 'free to go with his land', able 'to recede to another lord', or he simply held 'freely'. As with the holders of manors, it has usually been assumed that he held allodial land, that is land that was unencumbered with anything other than services to the king.[51] That the free man had title to his land seems clear. There were free men in East Anglia who were held in demesne by lords,[52] but generally, it would seem, no lord had an unconditional right to his land. However, this does not imply that the free man had full rights of alienation. The odd reference indicates that land was frequently held in parage, that is, it was shared within the family, and the substitution of *in paragio* in GDB for the *libere* of Exon suggests that this was its normal condition.[53] It was held in what would later be called socage and was land that was entailed within the

---

of meadow, and 3 acres of woodland and 12 acres of pasture. It is worth 40s.' (GDB, 68v: *DB Wilts*, 22,3). The type is most common in Circuit IV.

[48] S. P. J. Harvey, 'The Knight and the Knight's Fee in England', *Past and Present*, 49 (1970), 3–43; D. F. Fleming, 'Landholding by *Milites* in Domesday Book: A Revision', *ANS*, 13 (1991), 83–98.

[49] GDB, 66: *DB Wilts*, 3,2.

[50] J. Gillingham, 'Thegns and Knights in Eleventh-Century England: Who Was Then the Gentleman?', *TRHS*, 6th series, 5 (1995), 135–6.

[51] See, for example, C. R. Hart, 'Land Tenure in Cambridgeshire on the Eve of the Norman Conquest', *Proceedings of the Cambridge Antiquarian Society*, 84 (1996 for 1995), 59–90; S. Oosthuizen, 'Sokemen and Freemen: Tenure, Status, and Landscape Conservatism in Eleventh-Century Cambridgeshire', *Anglo-Saxons: Studies Presented to Cyril Roy Hart*, eds S. Keynes and A. P. Smyth (Dublin, 2005), 186–207. Since free men and sokemen rendered customs, albeit at times to the king, they did *not* hold with sake and soke: there can be found throughout Circuits III, VI, and VII sokemen and free men who belonged to manors over which a named lord had sake and soke.

[52] In Finningham and Westhorpe in Suffolk, for example, two free men held 10 acres and could not sell their land (LDB, 309v: *DB Suffolk*, 6,59–60).

[53] The formula *in paragio* is as often used of the holding of one person as of a number in Domesday Book, thereby indicating something more and less than parage.

family. Soke dues – light labour services, rents and the like[54] – were, moreover, rendered by the free man, and, it would seem, his land was in some sense part of a manor.[55] Although he may often have had more demands made upon him, his status was little different from what it was before the Conquest: the supposed wholesale 'manorialization' of the free man between 1066 and 1086 is a myth.[56]

Rights of alienation and freedom from lordship, then, hardly characterize the free man. Rather it would seem to be his right of receding to a lord of his choosing that distinguished him. Here the context was commendation, the choice of a lord to provide surety and warrant him in courts of law.[57] Again, his freedom was not unqualified. He had to declare his lord in the hundred and only death or outlawry could terminate the relationship; to do otherwise was to invite the suspicion of wrong-doing.[58] But, nevertheless, it was a considerable liberty for all that. Where his lord is noticed in Domesday Book he seems to have taken pains to ensure that he was sponsored by a powerful local lord other than the lord of the manor to which his land belonged. With soke and surety vested in different individuals, it would seem that he was best able to maintain his own freedom and control over his family land.[59] This was a balancing act which Norman lords were often keen to upset by claiming land on the basis of commendation alone. It was a tactic that was to lead to increased 'manorialization' in the following century.

In GDB the free man is largely confined to Circuits I, II, V, and part of IV. Otherwise he is represented by the *sochemannus*, 'sokeman'. In Circuit III his tenure is characterized by freedom to 'go with his land' and the right to commend himself to a lord of his choosing. Circuits IV and VI afford no comparable information on commendation, but the sokeman seems similarly to have held his land freely. Broadly speaking, he is clearly the local equivalent of the free man. In the past it has often been assumed that the sokeman was a peculiarity of the Danelaw. He is, however, also to be found in Middlesex and Kent and it must therefore be suspected that, in part at least, the distribution of free men and sokemen, echoing as it does the order of writing, is a function of the processes of compilation (Table 7.1). Nevertheless, it should be noted that in LDB free men and sokemen

---

[54] See above, p. 152.

[55] The East Anglian evidence is collected in D. R. Roffe, 'Introduction', *Little Domesday, Norfolk*, eds A. Williams and G. H. Martin (London, 2000), 34–7. Almost all free men were valued, often TRE, and this must mean that they belonged to someone. See below, pp. 245–6. For patterns of tenure and manorial structure, see below, p. 300.

[56] Freedoms might survive even where Domesday apparently records unfree tenures. See P. Taylor, 'Introduction', *Little Domesday Book, Essex*, eds A. Williams and G. H. Martin (London, 2000), 19–20; R. Faith, 'The Topography and Social Structure of a Small Soke in the Middle Ages: The Sokens, Essex', *Essex Archaeology and History*, 27 (1997), 202–13.

[57] See above, pp. 155–7.

[58] See, for example, GDB, 211v: *DB Beds*, 17,5; LDB, 311: *DB Suffolk*, 6,79.

[59] A. Williams, 'Little Domesday and the English: The Hundred of Colneis in Suffolk', *Domesday Book*, eds E. M. Hallam and D. Bates (Stroud, 2001), 103–20.

Table 7.1 *The distribution of free men, sokemen, and radmen/knights*

	Free man	Sokeman	Radman/knight
Essex	✓	✓	
Norfolk	✓	✓	
Suffolk	✓	✓	
Yorkshire		✓	
Lincolnshire		✓	
Nottinghamshire		✓	
Derbyshire		✓	
Huntingdonshire		✓	
Cambridgeshire		✓	
Middlesex		✓	
Bedfordshire		✓	
Buckinghamshire		✓	
Hertfordshire		✓	
Kent	✓	✓	
Sussex	✓		
Surrey	✓		
Hampshire	✓		✓
Berkshire	✓		✓
Wiltshire	✓		
Dorset	✓		
Somerset	✓		
Devon	✓		
Cornwall			
Gloucestershire			✓
Worcestershire	✓		✓
Herefordshire	✓		✓
Shropshire	✓		✓
Cheshire	✓		✓
Staffordshire	✓		
Warwickshire	✓		
Northamptonshire		✓	
Oxfordshire	✓		
Leicestershire		✓	

are distinguished one from the other.[60] Wherein lay the difference between them as here defined has never been satisfactorily explained. The most likely explanation is that the sokeman was not free to commend himself and, like the villein, was in frankpledge.[61] It is probable that some sokemen in the North likewise belonged to tithings: many a twelve-carucate hundred in Lincolnshire is seemingly composed of sokeland alone. The fact serves to remind us that neither free men nor sokemen were necessarily constituted as a homogeneous class. As we have seen, some held manors and might have been considered thegns in their own right. Others, like the drengs of the North, were a cut above the communality by virtue of ministerial tenure. Finally, some sokemen, like those in Feltwell in Norfolk, were not free to go with their land but held by the tenure known as thegnage.[62] Many sokemen with their one or two virgates or bovates can have been little distinguished from the lower orders of the rural population. Like the free man, each had always belonged to a manor, albeit at times a hundredal manor.[63]

The Norman settlement undoubtedly saw the disappearance of some sokemen. Where new manors were created, usually to accommodate newly enfeoffed knights, there might be depression in status. But this was a local phenomenon of limited extent – post-Conquest tenants usually held the estates of pre-Conquest counterparts – and even then manorialization was not inevitable.[64] In Hertfordshire, it is true, a count of *sochemanni* reveals a reduction in numbers from 224 in 1066 to some forty-five in 1086, a pattern repeated generally in the southern

[60] In some instances differentiation may be merely editorial. The free men in Lynn and Upwell of LDB are styled sokemen in IE, and in the Ely schedules individuals are variously styled sokemen and free men. Again, sokemen are more commonly recorded in some Norfolk hundreds than others. Nevertheless, the scribe often seems to have used the terms with deliberation. In Roudham, for example, there were two free men with one carucate of land and three sokemen and five bordars (fol. 164v).

[61] Roffe, 'Introduction', *Little Domesday, Norfolk*, 35–7. In the Suffolk folios, in contrast to those of Essex and Norfolk, the lords of free men are consistently identified, whereas almost no sokeman is said to have a lord. Sokemen, while no less free, may well have been warranted by tithings.

[62] LDB, 213–213v: *DB Norfolk*, 15,7. Typically the sokeman of this kind owed relatively heavy services. In Feltwell, he ploughed, sowed, reaped, and carried for the Abbot of Ely at will (*Inquisitio Comitatus Cantabrigiensis ... Subjicitur Inquistitio Eliensis*, ed. N. E. S. A. Hamilton (London, 1876), 193–4).

[63] In Circuit VI many a sokeman is entered in the account of the manorial *caput*. F. M. Stenton, *Types of Manorial Structure in the Northern Danelaw*, Oxford Studies in Social and Legal History, 2 (Oxford, 1910), 46–9, drew a distinction between these 'intra-manorial sokemen' and those who are described in their own entries. In reality, there is no distinction, the difference being merely a function of entry formation (Roffe, 'Introduction to the Lincolnshire Domesday', 19). For sokemen of hundredal manors, see below, pp. 266–7.

[64] See, for example, LDB, 134: *DB Norfolk*, 1,201: 'Caister was held by 80 free men TRE and likewise now [as] 4 carucates of land. Then [there were] 22 ploughs, and of the whole of this Earl R[alph] made a manor.'

portion of Circuit III.[65] But the statistic does not compare like with like. The sokemen of 1066 held manors, and, although unnamed, they are the equivalent of any other free men or thegns who held manors TRE. They shared the same status in 1066 and the same fate subsequently. The forty-five 'manorial' sokeman of 1086 may represent some of the disseized, but it is as likely that they were different individuals who had always been part of the manor. Nor is there any guarantee that these represent the full extent of the class. What appear as fully manorialized holdings in Domesday Book often supported a substantial free population in the later Middle Ages by a socage tenure that is unlikely to have had post-Conquest origins.[66]

Radmen and radknights, 'riding men' recorded only in Circuit V, appear to have been roughly comparable with free men and sokemen.[67] Here and there they are said to be free men – although how they were distinguished from the *liberi homines* who occur in more limited numbers in the same circuit is unexplained – and they too typically held land within the manor with villeins and bordars under them. Again, their recorded services are directly comparable: in addition to the escort duty implied by their name, they owed labour dues. At Deerhurst in Gloucestershire radknights 'all ploughed and harrowed, mowed, and reaped for the lord's use', and at Tewkesbury they 'ploughed and harrowed for their lord's court'.[68] As a class they are probably identical with the geneats of the Tidenham survey of *c.*1050 (although none is recorded there in 1086) who 'must labour either on the estate or off the estate, whichever he is bidden, and ride and furnish carrying-service and supply transport and drive herds and do many other things'.[69]

Free men, sokemen, radmen, and radknights account for some 14 per cent of the recorded Domesday population in 1086. Their contribution to the manorial economy is often invisible, but, where they are separately valued, it would seem that they could be a sizeable asset derived from the money rents and light labour services of sokeright. More valuable was the villein, and it is perhaps not coincidental that it is this class that is most commonly represented in Domesday Book, being found in every county and accounting for almost half of the Domesday

[65] Abels 'An Introduction to the Hertfordshire Domesday', 16.
[66] D. R. Roffe, 'Domesday Book and Northern Society: A Reassessment', *EHR*, 105 (1990), 332; A. Williams, 'The Abbey Tenants and Servants in the 12th Century', *Studies in the Early History of Shaftesbury Abbey*, ed. L. Keen (Dorchester, 1999), 134–5; Taylor, 'Introduction', *Little Domesday, Essex*, 19–20; Faith, 'The Topography and Social Structure of a Small Soke in the Middle Ages: The Sokens, Essex', 202–13; Faith, *The English Peasantry and the Growth of Lordship*, 121–5.
[67] Williams, 'An Introduction to the Gloucestershire Domesday', 5; Lewis, 'An Introduction to the Herefordshire Domesday', 5.
[68] GDB, 163, 166: *DB Gloucs*, 1, 24;14,1. This may merely imply that their men, like those of the Ribble and Mersey thegns (GDB, 269v: *DB Cheshire*, R1,40a), owed the service on their behalf.
[69] *Anglo-Saxon Charters*, ed. A. J. Robertson, 2nd edn (Cambridge, 1956), no. 109.

population. In the later Middle Ages his lineal descendent was usually unfree, and in 1086 there were probably some villeins who were close to serfdom. It seems likely, however, that most were still personally free. They certainly seem to have been responsible for the geld assessed upon their land. In the Huntingdonshire folios it is recorded that 'The villeins and sokemen pay geld according to the hides written in the records'[70] and there are explicit references to them gelding elsewhere: in Alton in Hampshire it is stated that there were 10 hides and the villeins there gelded for 5, while in Cornwall a formerly exempt estate gelded 'as villeins' land'.[71] In Exon the *terra villanorum* is regularly assessed separately from the demesne and in the North Midlands villeins appear to have gelded within the twelve-carucate hundred.

Nevertheless, the villein is sharply distinguished from the free man and sokeman in the Domesday texts. Precisely wherein the distinction lies is not explicit. Contemporary and later evidence, though, indicates that his services were more onerous, and this points to a closer seigneurial interest in his lands. Whereas the free man and sokeman 'could go with their land to another lord', the villein's freedom was more circumscribed. He certainly seems to have had no right to seek a lord. The villein was in a tithing, what later became known as a frankpledge, which assumed the responsibility for his surety and the like: the villein, *tunesman* in English, was after all the inhabitant of a *vill*, the basic unit of policing. The tithing was still a communal organization in 1086; seigneurial encroachment, which was to result in leet jurisdictions of the later Middle Ages, was only just beginning to be felt.[72] Nevertheless, the villein's lack of strong patronage other than his immediate lord must have left him vulnerable to seigneurial encroachment on his land. As a geld payer he was free and had title to his land, but he may well have needed his lord's consent to alienate it. It should not be concluded from this, however, that he belonged to the *Untermenschen* of the medieval countryside. His holding was often large, typically amounting to a virgate or more. In Fulham in Middlesex, for example, there were 5 villeins with 1 hide each, 13 with one virgate each, and 34 with ½ a virgate each, as well as sundry other tenants with smaller amounts of land.[73] Three or four day-works per week may have been demanded from each

---

[70] GDB, 203: *DB Hunts*, B21.

[71] GDB, 43, 121: *DB Hants*, 6,1; *DB Cornwall*, 4,29.

[72] See, for example, GDB, 363: *DB Lincs*, 37,2. The three [twelve-carucate] hundreds of Normanton, Frieston, and West Willoughby belonged to Robert de Vessey's manor of Caythorpe. Elsewhere this type of hundred was communal and was to remain so for the next hundred years or so (D. R. Roffe, 'The Lincolnshire Hundred', *Landscape History*, 3 (1981), 27–36). For the tithing as a communal organization equivalent to the vill, see W. L. Warren, *The Governance of Norman and Angevin England, 1066–1272* (London, 1987), 40.

[73] These quantities are, of course, fiscal measures, but we cannot doubt that they represent at least equal quantities of real land.

tenement,[74] but it must be remembered that the service was generally acquitted by one person (only at harvest time might more labour have been demanded). In return the villein and his family had a full share in the resources of the village in arable, meadow, and pasture and their interests were protected by the customs of the manor.

In moving from the free man and villein to the bordars and cottars the Domesday entry crosses a greater social divide. The bordar (*bordarius*) is ubiquitous, appearing in various proportions in every Domesday county. The cottar (*cotarius, cotsetus*) is confined to southern counties. Despite the fact that the distribution of the two classes overlaps, it would appear that they were of a similar status.[75] Both were smallholders who might have a plough in common but did not have a regular share in the fields of the village: in Sawbridgeworth in Hertfordshire forty-six bordars each had eight acres of land.[76] Some were settled on the demesne and would appear to have worked for the lord as wage-earners; in some counties such as Cambridgeshire and Bedfordshire they are numbered in the manorial stock rather than with the villagers. They may have also been tradesmen of one kind or another. Others were seemingly undertenants of villeins and free men. It has been suggested that still others were dwellers on newly cleared land.[77] *Cotarius* clearly points to a cottage dweller, but bordar comes from French *borde*, equally wooden cottage, but also cognate with *borde* meaning plank or edge, suggesting that the derivative *bordarius* might be a dweller on the fringe of settlement.[78] However, it seems unlikely that bordar was widely used in this sense. There are five references in Domesday Book to *hospites*, that is settlers, who might well have held assarts, and they seem to have rendered a monetary rent.[79] New land is unlikely regularly to have been incorporated into the structure of the vill; were bordars of a similar

---

[74] Domesday perhaps indicates something less; 238 villeins in Leominster ploughed and sowed with their own seed 140 acres of the demesne (GDB, 180: *DB Hereford*, 1,10b). Others of unspecified station worked two days a week on the same manor (GDB, 180v: *DB Hereford*, 1,38). In West Derby (Lancs) villeins 'made the king's houses and whatever belonged to them … and the fisheries and the enclosures in the woodland, and the deer hays' (GDB, 269v: *DB Cheshire*, R1,40a), although here the thegns performed the same services.

[75] Harvey, 'Domesday England', 58–64. The two terms are used apparently interchangeably in Domesday and IE. For example, the bordars in Soham in the one are represented by cottars in the other (GDB, 189: *DB Cambs*, 1,1; IE, 101). Only in Middlesex is a consistent distinction drawn between the two.

[76] GDB, 139v: *DB Herts*, 33,17.

[77] S. P. J. Harvey, 'Evidence for Settlement: Domesday Book', *Medieval Settlement*, ed. P. H. Sawyer (London, 1976), 197–9.

[78] Harvey, 'Domesday England', 58. For an examination of the local distribution of such bordars in these terms, see D. Postles, 'The Bordars of Domesday Derbyshire', *Derbyshire Archaeological Journal*, 106 (1986), 123–6. The conclusion is equivocal.

[79] GDB, 184v, 259, 259v, 264: *DB Hereford*, 10,47; *DB Salop*, 4,23,17. 4,25,3.4,27,27; *DB Cheshire*, 2,9. All references are in Circuit V.

status it might therefore be expected that their renders would also be valued. They are not.

The last major class of inhabitant is the slave (*servus, ancilla*).[80] Male slaves are widely found throughout the country except in the counties of Circuit VI (barring the odd reference in Nottinghamshire and Derbyshire), where, it would seem from Ely A,[81] they were all-but-completely edited out at some stage before GDB was compiled. Female slaves are largely confined to the West Midland and South Western shires. The GDB scribe unequivocally identified them with the lord's demesne (Table 7.2). Thus, in Circuits II, IV, and Cheshire and Shropshire in V they are entered with the demesne ploughs, while in Circuits III and I they appear as the first or second item in the manorial stock (as indicated by *ibi* in the normal way). His sources, however, often allude to a more complex reality. ICC, Exon, LDB, and the earliest folios of GDB group slaves with the other classes of peasant, albeit sandwiched between the free and the stock, thereby suggesting a less intimate relationship with the lord. Females (*ancillae*) were undoubtedly employed in his household and may well have lived in his hall. Males, by contrast, were usually married (therefore representing a family in Domesday) and can often be shown to have had their own land. In many respects they can have been very little different from the bordars who are likewise enrolled in the manorial stock. Socially, they may have enhanced the status of their lord,[82] but their economic role was specific. Like the ploughman (*bovarius*) of the Welsh Marches with whom they have sometimes been identified,[83] the slave's main task was probably to work the lord's demesne ploughs: throughout the country there is a consistent pattern of two slaves to every plough.[84]

Boors and *coliberti*, 'freedmen', glossed as equivalents in the Hampshire and Worcestershire folios,[85] were manumitted slaves, but apparently still remained of low status, for they are usually recorded with the unfree despite often holding

---

[80] J. S. Moore, 'Domesday Slavery', *ANS*, 11 (1989), 191–220; D. A. E. Pelteret, *Slavery in Early Medieval England* (Woodbridge, 1995), 185–240.

[81] Ely A, 169. In total 23 slaves are recorded for Somersham, Bluntisham, and Spaldwick. The information is absent from IE, suggesting that it was omitted at some stage prior to the production of the county report.

[82] Slavery also seems to have been a social construct. See D. Wyatt, 'The Significance of Slavery: Alternative Approaches to Anglo-Saxon Slavery', *ANS*, 23 (2000), 327–47.

[83] Harvey, 'Domesday England', 64–9. A difference in status between oxman and slave is, however, implied by an emendation in the Shropshire folios. In the account of Huntington the scribe originally wrote 'In demesne are 2 ploughs and 4 slaves', but subsequently underlined *servi* for deletion and interlined *bovarii* (GDB, 256v: *DB Salop*, 4,11,2).

[84] For a local study underlining this conclusion, see K. A. Bailey, 'Buckinghamshire Slavery in 1086', *Records of Buckinghamshire*, 33–7 (1995), 67–78. Bailey discounts any correlation between Domesday slaves and areas of British survivals.

[85] GDB, 38, 38v, 174v: *DB Hants*, 1,10;23; *DB Worcs*, 8,10a.

Table 7.2 *The position of slaves in the Domesday entry*

	With demesne	With stock	With villeins
Essex			✓
Norfolk			✓
Suffolk			✓
Yorkshire			
Lincolnshire			
Nottinghamshire			✓
Derbyshire			✓
Huntingdonshire			
Cambridgeshire		✓	
Middlesex		✓	
Bedfordshire		✓	
Buckinghamshire		✓	
Hertfordshire		✓	
Kent		✓	
Sussex		✓	
Surrey		✓	
Hampshire		✓	
Berkshire		✓	
Wiltshire	✓		
Dorset	✓		
Somerset	✓		
Devon	✓		
Cornwall	✓		
Gloucestershire		✓	
Worcestershire		✓	
Herefordshire		✓	
Shropshire	✓		
Cheshire	✓		
Staffordshire	✓		
Warwickshire	✓		
Oxfordshire	✓		
Northamptonshire	✓		
Leicestershire	✓		

considerable amounts of land.[86] They were much of a muchness with various other miscellaneous classes of people that are noted in the text. Smiths, iron-workers, shepherds, millers, rent payers, and above all priests,[87] are usually recorded as an adjunct of a commodity owned or enjoyed by the lord. Most members of these heterogeneous classes were probably unfree, but some were clearly not. The priest, for example, was not of servile status. Nevertheless, it was predominantly his lord's church that he served and his horizons must accordingly have been limited.

Some 269,000 inhabitants are noted in the two volumes of Domesday Book. Statistics on this scale are unique in medieval records and it is therefore not surprising that attempts have been made to exploit them to the full. Attitudes to the figures have on the whole been bullish. Postan, it is true, doubted that they could be meaningfully used since Domesday is first and foremost a survey of demesnes, but in his chosen calling he has largely stood alone.[88] Historical geographers and social and economic historians have generally been loath to accept that population figures are anything other than a gift horse. However, they have not failed to notice the odd dodgy tooth here and there and they have therefore expended a considerable amount of effort to demonstrate that the dataset is basically coherent once 'correction' factors are applied. The case has been most cogently put by John Moore.[89] He starts out by rejecting as 'muddle-headed' the claims of a fundamentalist tendency in Domesday studies that sees the figures as more accurate than sixteenth-century hearth tax returns. It is patent that the GDB scribe often mis-transcribed, was confused, or lacked information. These are givens of any source, be it medieval or modern. The Domesday commissioners laboured under additional problems, not the least being the use of roman numerals in a process that required numerous recensions. Moore accepts that the data will never amount to a census. But he believes that it is possible to determine a 'standard error' and proceeds to calibrate the data. Here the decisive yardstick is early twelfth-century

---

[86] King's Worthy, a berewick of the manor of Barton Stacey in Hampshire, was unassessed apart from 6 hides held by an unspecified number of coliberts (GDB, 38v: *DB Hants*, 1,17).

[87] For the equation of priest and church, see, for example, LDB, 4: *DB Essex*, 1,13: 'To this manor [of Wethersfield] belonged 30 acres of land TRE which 1 priest held in alms and he rendered soke, and 8½ acres belonging to another church.' This is not to say, however, that a priest may not at times be recorded simply as a holder of land. See, for example, C. P. Lewis, 'Introduction to the Shropshire Domesday', *The Shropshire Domesday*, eds A. Williams and R. W. H. Erskine (London, 1990), 24–5. There were priests in Broughton, Astley, and Yorton but subsequently no churches (GDB, 252v, 253: *DB Salop*, 3d,1–2;3f,4). The estates belonged to the minsters of St Mary and St Chad in Shrewsbury, and it seems likely that the priests were canons who held the endowments.

[88] M. M. Postan, *The Medieval Economy and Society: An Economic History of Britain in the Middle Ages* (London, 1972), 30–1.

[89] J. S. Moore, '"Quot homines?": The Population of Domesday England', *ANS*, 19 (1997), 307–34.

estate surveys from the abbeys of Holy Trinity, Caen, Evesham, Peterborough, and Shaftesbury. Unlike Domesday schedules and circuit reports, these sources are independent of the Domesday process and authoritative since the estate managers who drew them up were in a position to know the facts and had every incentive to record them in full. The comparison indicates a margin of error of ±2–3% in the Domesday statistics (a figure close to the error in modern censuses) with a further error of perhaps 10% in under-recording. Estimates have to be made for those classes of population that are not adequately represented in Domesday: burgesses are under-recorded, garrisons, religious communities and the like are largely omitted. The individuals in each category all represent heads of households and, with the size of each set at about five, a population of 2 million for Domesday England is reached.

Some economic historians might quibble with various assumptions made in this analysis. In particular the size of households has been questioned, A. Nash, for example, suggesting that a higher multiplier is appropriate for richer villeins than for the relatively poorer bordars.[90] But it is generally agreed that whatever the deficiencies of the data they are quantifiable; what errors exist are errors in a survey of people. It is this underlying assumption that must be questioned. That the bordars and slaves on the demesne represent individuals (and their families) seems likely. They are little different from churches or mills and no one would suggest that they are notional;[91] Moore has persuasively argued that, outside the Northern Danelaw, slaves and bordars are consistently and accurately recorded in Domesday Book.[92] This, however, is far from manifest with villeins and sokemen. The problem is illustrated by the entry for Newport Pagnell in Buckinghamshire:

> William [fitzAnsculf] himself holds Newport Pagnell. It is assessed at 5 hides. There is land for 9 ploughs. In demesne [are] 4 carucates of land, and there are 4 ploughs; and 5 villeins have 5 ploughs. The burgesses have 6 ½ ploughs, and [the ploughs] of other men working outside the 5 hides. There are 9 slaves, and 2 mills rendering 40s, meadow for all the ploughs and 10s [besides], woodland for 300 pigs and 2s [besides], and, in addition, 4s from men who dwell in the woodland; and in all other rents it renders yearly 100s and 16s 4d.[93]

---

[90] A. Nash, 'The Population of Southern England in 1086: A New Look at the Evidence of Domesday Book', *Southern History*, 10 (1988), 1–28.

[91] Mills may, however, refer to millstones rather than separate buildings. It seems clear that the Domesday mill was a watermill, but whether it was the more simple horizontal mill or the technically more advanced vertical mill is unclear (J. Landon, 'Watermills and Windmills in the West Midlands, 1086–1500', *EcHR*, 44 (1991), 433).

[92] J. S Moore, 'Domesday Slavery', *ANS*, 11 (1989), 191–220.

[93] GDB, 148v: *DB Bucks*, 17,17.

Hitherto, 'the men working outside the 5 hides' and the 'men who dwell in the woodland' have been adduced as fine evidence of the difficulties under which the GDB scribe laboured. We can now perceive that they are indicative rather of his focus. The land in question was non-geldable and, as in other references to inland, we are given no population figures. The Domesday inquest was about geldable land and population figures are directly related to its extent.

The problem of inland as regards population figures has been broached before, if its significance has not been recognized. In 1896 Baring drew attention to the *censarii* in the Burton surveys who are not explicitly represented in GDB, and Walmsley subsequently argued that their land was included in the ploughland figures.[94] The conclusion cannot be sustained – Walmsley's figures cannot be reconciled with the surveys – but in the light of other references to inland in GDB their analysis stands: there were substantial numbers of tenants who are not recorded in Domesday Book (Moore maintains that the Burton *censarii* attest post-Domesday recolonization).[95] Walmsley's reaction was to increase the multiplier for the Domesday population, suggesting a factor somewhere in the region of fifteen. This figure may well be locally appropriate, but there is a wider point. Neither Walmsley nor Baring noticed, or at least attached significance to, the fact that the *censarii* held inland as well as *warland* and that it was there that the under-recording of Domesday population occurred. Population figures are not only confined to the geldable land but are also directly related to it. We have already noted that on many Huntingdonshire estates there was one villein per fiscal virgate.[96] This is a pattern that is evident elsewhere, although by no means general.[97] In Middlesex a half virgate seems to have been the holding of most villeins, elsewhere no trend has been identified.[98] Nevertheless, there are other indications that population figures were notional; half, quarter, and even one sixth free men, villeins, and sokemen, for example, make no sense except in fiscal terms.[99] Indeed, inhabitants may have been

[94] F. H. Baring, 'Domesday Book and the Burton Cartulary', *EHR*, 11 (1896), 98–102; J. F. R. Walmsley, 'The Censarii of Burton Abbey and the Domesday Population', *North Staffordshire Journal of Field Studies*, 8 (1968), 73–80.

[95] Moore, 'Quot Homines?', 328.

[96] See above, pp. 201–2.

[97] See, for example, Buckinghamshire where the number of villeins is closely related to the hidage (J. Bradbury, 'Introduction to the Buckinghamshire Domesday', *The Buckinghamshire Domesday*, eds A. Williams and R. W. H. Erskine (London, 1988), 27).

[98] *DIB*, 157. Only Exon regularly provides the data to determine the extent of the land of the men, thus allowing such analyses. There has been no comprehensive study of the figures, but initial analysis suggests correspondence in about 20 per cent of cases at a rate of one virgate/villein. This compares with 40 per cent in Huntingdonshire where data allow an analysis (*DIB*, 156).

[99] There are references to 24 half villeins, 35 half sokemen, 1 quarter sokeman, 238 half free men, 3 quarter free men, and 1 one sixth free man. Most occur in LDB. Some historians have argued that the half villeins are half-virgaters, that is they had half the usual amount

a matter of official record rather than seigneurial presentment in 1086. In LDB population figures are juxtaposed with the geld assessments and the two items of information are the subject of Bury A and B which probably emanated from the geld inquest. As the Huntingdonshire folios tell us, the villeins paid the geld and it is geld-payers who are recorded in the text.

We are left, then, with fiscal inhabitants who are difficult to relate to the warm-blooded variety. The twelfth-century surveys are here of little use as controls since they too are often concerned with the fiscal peasant. In Peterborough's Lincolnshire lands the geld was the datum of service in the early twelfth century,[100] while day work was levied on Ramsey's fiscal virgates into the fourteenth century and probably beyond.[101] A reality is only occasionally glimpsed. Virgates were held in parage or were locally redefined as five, six, seven, or eight virgates.[102] Otherwise, we are in the dark. That fiscal villeins and people often coincided cannot be doubted, but it cannot be assumed that this was always the case. With due provision made for omissions and the like, the Domesday statistics represent a bare minimum of inhabitants in 1086.

Domesday hardly provides a solid base for demographic analysis. Numerous studies have employed the data to demonstrate a population explosion in the twelfth and thirteenth centuries. Now it must be suspected that this so-called growth, in part at least, represents a stratum of eleventh-century society that was hidden by the form of the Domesday data. To take but one example, Hallam employed numerous sources to demonstrate rapid growth in the fenland wapentake of Elloe in Lincolnshire in the 150 years after the Domesday inquest.[103] Reclamation of the fen and salt marsh in this period clearly suggests some upward demographic trends, but the dominance of sokemen in the later records must give pause for thought. The class is poorly represented in the GDB account of Elloe and yet it seems unlikely that so many were created by predominantly ecclesiastical lords in

of land of a villein. But comparison with twelfth-century surveys suggests that service is the datum. The two half villeins in Ivedon in Devon were one person whose services were divided between two tenants-in-chief (GDB, 110v, 114v: *DB Devon*, 19,43.34,45). Cf. the account of Onibury in Shropshire (GDB, 252: *DB Salop*, 2,2) where there were '4 whole villeins and 6 half (*iiii villani integri et vi dimidii*)'.

[100] In 1125 Fiskerton, for example, was assessed at 11 carucates and 6 bovates 'to the king's geld and the service of Peterborough Abbey' (*Chronicon Petroburgensis*, ed. T. Stapleton, Camden Society, old series, 47 (1849), 164).

[101] D. R. Roffe, 'An Introduction to the Huntingdonshire Domesday', *The Huntingdonshire Domesday*, eds A. Williams and R. W. H. Erskine (London, 1989), 11. In Holywell in Huntingdonshire, for example, *c.*1135 the 26 villagers of the GDB account are seemingly matched by 25 or 26 tenants of virgates.

[102] *DIB*, 159.

[103] H. E. Hallam, *The New Lands of Elloe* (Leicester, 1954); H. E. Hallam, 'Some Thirteenth-Century Censuses', *EcHR*, 2nd series, 10 (1958), 340–61.

the century after the Domesday inquest.[104] It must be suspected that they were already represented in the wapentake in the late eleventh century, but did not pay geld and therefore escaped the notice of the Domesday commissioners.

Livestock

In demographic terms only the record of bordars, slaves, and other ancillary workers approaches anything like a straightforward census, and that because the servants of the demesne were most closely akin to stock. Livestock itself, though, was not of central interest to the compiler of GDB. The record of ploughs, of course, presupposes oxen,[105] but its purpose was fiscal: the actual size of the ploughteam was irrelevant as was the stock management that underlay it. Pigs have a similarly notional existence. In Circuit III woodland is measured in terms of the number of swine that it could support, but the round totals that are usually given indicate that the figures are estimates.[106] Whether those pigs were actually there or not is indeterminate. In Circuit I we may come closer to the beasts. In the South East 19,361½ pigs were rendered for pannage, and the formula 'woodland for so many swine' must often indicate the numbers that passed from the peasants to their lord's table. Again, though, what this represents in reality is difficult to determine. In Leominster 1 in 10 pigs were rendered in pannage,[107] but that was in Circuit V and the record of incidental swine renders for pasture in the South East of between 1 in 3 and 1 in 7 suggests that other figures may have applied there.[108] None of this helps with determining how many pigs the lord had in demesne.

Otherwise, there is the occasional reference to stock, but, one suspects, only in very exceptional circumstances or where the GDB scribe nodded.[109] The systematic record is to be found in earlier documentation. LDB, IE, ICC, Exon, Bath A all variously record sheep, wethers, swine, goats, cows, calves, oxen, bulls, horses, rounceys, mares, foals, mules, and donkeys in substantial numbers for Norfolk, Suffolk, and Essex in Circuit VII, for Cambridgeshire, Hertfordshire, and Huntingdonshire in Circuit III, and for Cornwall, Devon, Dorset and Somerset in Circuit II. Here the record is explicitly related to the Domesday demesne. In East Anglia as in the East Midlands details of stock are entered after the description of

---

[104] Roffe, 'Introduction to the Lincolnshire Domesday', 19.

[105] *Pace* L. Keen, 'An Introduction to the Dorset Domesday', *The Dorset Domesday*, eds A. Williams and G. H. Martin (London, 1991), 9, who argues that the Domesday *caruca* refers to the plough itself, the implement, rather than the draught animals that go with it. While this formulation might be one solution to the problem of overstocking, it hardly comes to terms with such formulations as '1 plough and 5 oxen' and the like.

[106] See, for example, Bradbury, 'Introduction to the Buckinghamshire Domesday', 9–10.

[107] GDB, 180: *DB Hereford*, 1,10a.

[108] Darby, *Domesday England*, 177.

[109] See Darby, *Domesday England*, 167–70, for references to stock elsewhere in GDB.

the manorial appurtenances, but in Exon they precede it with the enumeration of
the population. First and foremost, however, stock is only recorded where there
was a demesne. The animals of the men were of no interest to the Domesday
commissioners unless, of course, they were rendered to the lord.[110]

The data have been conveniently tabulated by H. C. Darby in *Domesday
England*.[111] Unlike the pig estimates of GDB, the figures usually have every
appearance of being a count of heads. This is not to say, however, that they are
comprehensive. Cows and bulls, for example, are under-represented. Nevertheless,
there is little to suggest that the figures are not a measure of the resources of the
lord in the main categories. Inevitably, correlations are found between some of the
statistics and value. It is asserted that 'horses were not an economic resource in
Norman England', putting them in the same category as beehives, but otherwise
livestock figures are a fair indicator of wealth.[112] The main focus of study has been
on geographical distributions, especially of sheep, which form the largest group of
recorded animals. Not surprisingly, concentrations are found on the silt fens and
coastal marshes of East Anglia as well as on the Brecklands of Norfolk and the
chalky heath of eastern Cambridgeshire. Generally smaller flocks are found in the
West Country, but again the distribution favours Downland and marsh.[113]

Sally Harvey has essayed more nuanced distributions.[114] Distinguishing between
demesnes and 'small producers', she has observed that sheep were of importance to
both. In Essex, for example, there are 141 manors in which the demesne livestock
can be compared with total pasture measured in terms of the number of sheep
it could support. Overall the figures suggest that two-thirds of sheep were run
by demesnes and in one-third of cases they took up the whole of the available
pasture. Harvey suggests that the smaller farmers must have made supplementary
use of long-term fallow for grazing.[115] Pigs, by contrast, seem to have figured more
largely in the peasant economy. In the West Country there are relatively few on
demesnes, and, although more are found in East Anglia, there woodland measured
in swine suggests that lords supplied only 22 per cent of the total that the woods
could sustain.

East Anglia certainly suffered a pasture crisis in the later Middle Ages, but
Harvey's assumption that manors were fully stocked in the eleventh century is

---

[110] See, for example, LDB, 249: *DB Norfolk*, 31,6. At *Schieteshaga* [in Hempnall] there
were 'always 5 horses. Then [there were] 9 head of cattle; now 12. Then [there were] 100
pigs; now 60. Then [there were] 5 sheep; now 186.' However, 'apart from this the whole
of this manor renders 6 cows and 20 pigs and 20 rams'. Presumably the render came from
the peasantry.
[111] Darby, *Domesday England*, 164.
[112] McDonald and Snooks, *Domesday Economy*, 88–9.
[113] Darby, *Domesday England*, 165–70.
[114] Harvey, 'Domesday England', 121–31.
[115] Harvey, 'Domesday England', 125.

another matter. The shortfall in pasture in Essex is equally likely to be a function of under-recording. Laurence Keen has described a somewhat more complex picture in his study of animal husbandry in Domesday Dorset.[116] He starts out with the rule of thumb that 'one ox, cow, or horse needs about one acre of grazing a year, together with one acre of hay for supplementary winter feeding. Sheep and goats would also need approximately an acre each for summer grazing.' He then proceeds to compare how well the needs of the recorded stock tally with the pasture and meadow said to be available. The results are interesting. There are some instances in which manors are apparently grossly overstocked. Cerne Abbey's manor of Little Puddle, for example, suggests a ratio of 9.4 beasts to each acre. The record of pasture is clearly deficient. More usually there is a better fit, with a trend towards understocking. In Abbotsbury Abbey's manors, for example, Abbotsbury itself has a ratio of 1:6.7, but otherwise it is round about 1:1.

This analysis also assumes that pasture is accurately recorded, but here it inspires confidence in the conclusion, for under-recording would suppose an even higher degree of understocking. Patterns of this kind, and their interpretation, remain to be explored elsewhere. The record of livestock has been little exploited as an historical resource. The data would repay more attention.

Manorial appurtenances

Whereas the record of livestock seems to be sharply focused as specifically demesne stock, the account of the manorial infrastructure is less so. In Domesday as a whole a great variety of assets are recorded. That the data are intrinsically uneven is undeniable. The scribes of LDB and GDB were dependent on their sources, and they were various: from circuit to circuit commissioners interpreted their brief as they would and juries and tenants-in-chief made their returns as they could. Some items of information are peculiar to a particular area. Hawk eyries, parks, and heys are only found in Circuit V, for example, but must have been equally common in other forested areas of the country.[117] Even in Circuit V, though, there is no guarantee that they are consistently recorded. Appurtenances were often erratically enrolled. There is a record of churches throughout the Domesday texts, but it is remarkably uneven at both the local and the national level. In some counties there appears to be a comprehensive survey. The Derbyshire folios illustrate the type.[118] Foundations that can be shown to have been dependent chapels find no place in the text, even though independent evidence demonstrates that they were in existence in 1086, but the well-established parish churches with burial rights are consistently noted. Here the Domesday church is a seigneurial institution that is

---

[116] Keen, 'An Introduction to the Dorset Domesday', 11–13.
[117] R. Liddiard, 'The Deer Parks of Domesday Book', *Landscapes*, 4:1 (2003), 4–23.
[118] D. R. Roffe, *The Derbyshire Domesday* (Darley Dale, 1986), 16–17, 20.

recorded with some degree of accuracy at the level at which it rendered dues to its lord. In Circuit VI this might act as a reasonable characterization of many of the churches that are noted in the text. Major churches, like the royal free chapel of Blyth in Nottinghamshire, first noticed in 1088,[119] simply do not appear, and most that do can be shown to be or have become private churches. But the account is nowhere as comprehensive as in Derbyshire. Elsewhere there is even more variation. In Circuit II the ordinary church is conspicuous by its total absence with only a few minsters appearing in the text in their own entries as holders of land, here emanating from the first stage of the Domesday inquest. Circuit I falls between the two extremes: in Surrey there was probably a comprehensive record of parish churches,[120] while in Kent as many as half were omitted.[121]

The sources were not uniform. Thereafter, the scribes of Domesday Book brought their own editorial priorities to bear on the data which imposed other changes. Much of the detail collected was transferred to LDB, but subsequently it seems to have been realized that the essentially ephemeral had no place in a more permanent record. From the start, the GDB scribe omitted livestock, confining himself to what was of long-term value, the essentials of the manorial infrastructure; the absence of slaves from the Circuit VI folios may be evidence of an even narrower initial view of the relevant. In good accounting style he often imposed a structure on his data. He usually began with what he seems to have perceived as the most tangible entities. Where they occur in this position, slaves and bordars are recorded first and are followed in approximate order by churches, mills, fisheries, meadow, pasture, and woodland. Separate values are often given for churches, mills and fisheries and the considerable renders that they yielded suggests that the order of enrolment approximates to the size of the return that they made, beginning with the most valuable.

Variation in the data is a fact; it can be readily appreciated in the detailed distribution maps of Darby's *Domesday Geography* series and in summary form in his *Domesday England*. In consequence, studies of individual items of data have generally been pragmatic. John Blair, for example, has not made any assumption about the distribution of churches, his area of study, but has attempted to use the differing diplomatic of the text to map both local and regional variations in the status of foundations.[122] The criteria that he has developed for classifying churches

[119] *The Blyth Cartulary*, ed. R. T. Timson, Thoroton Society Record Series, 27–8 (1973), no. 293.

[120] J. Blair, 'Local Churches in Domesday Book and Before', *Domesday Studies*, ed. J. C. Holt (Woodbridge, 1987), 276–8; J. Blair, 'An Introduction to the Surrey Domesday', *The Surrey Domesday*, eds A. Williams and R. W. H. Erskine (London, 1989), 5–6.

[121] Darby, *Domesday England*, 24–6.

[122] Blair, 'Local Churches in Domesday Book and Before', 265–78; J. Blair, 'Secular Minster Churches in Domesday Book', *Domesday Book: A Reassessment*, ed. P. H. Sawyer (London, 1985), 164–74.

have undoubtedly cast light on ecclesiastical organization in the pre-Conquest period, albeit in terms of a model that has recently been challenged.[123] Likewise, Oliver Rackham has greatly increased our understanding of the organization of woodland.[124] There have been a number of studies of the salt industry. In particular, Della Hooke has examined the inland production at Droitwich and Lawrence Keen coastal production throughout the country.[125] Domesday mills have also been studied extensively.[126] All studies of this kind have accepted that the limitations of the data are essentially unquantifiable.

To a greater or lesser degree, scribal ignorance or plain carelessness must always be an underlying factor. Nevertheless, the random element in the data can be over-stressed. The commonly occurring commodities – meadow, pasture, fisheries, woodland – are almost certainly as thoroughly recorded as demanded by the commissioners' brief. Something of that brief can be reconstructed from the characteristics of those commodities. At the outset, there is nothing to suggest that the assets recorded in Domesday are anything other than those of *warland*, the land assessed to the geld. There are no details of assets given in the few references to inland. In the Burton surveys there was 'surplus' pasture and meadow that does not seem to be represented in Domesday Book.[127] There can be no doubt, however, that the commissioners' focus was that part of the *warland* held by the lord, that is, the Domesday demesne. Despite the Anglo-Saxon Chronicler's propaganda, it was no business of the Domesday inquest to inquire into the cattle, sheep, horses, goats, and the like of the peasantry. By and large, all the commodities recorded in the Domesday text were those that were in some way appurtenant to the lord's demesne.

This, however, it not to say that the sole criterion for inclusion was what contributed to seigneurial income. Far from it. Throughout the country there

---

[123] D. Rollason, 'The Ecclesiastical Context', *The Origins of the Midland Village*, ed. H. S. A. Fox (Leicester, 1992), 73–90; D. Rollason, 'Monasteries and Society in Early Northumbria', *Monasteries and Society in Medieval Britain*, ed. B. Thompson, Harlaxton Medieval Studies, 6 (Stamford, 1999), 59–74; E. Cambridge and D. W. Rollason, 'Debate: The Pastoral Organization of the Anglo-Saxon Church: A Review of the "Minster Hypothesis"', *Early Medieval Europe*, 4 (1995), 87–104; J. Blair, 'Debate: Ecclesiastical Organization and Pastoral Care in Anglo-Saxon England', *Early Medieval Europe*, 4 (1995), 193–212.

[124] O. Rackham, *The History of the Countryside* (London, 1986).

[125] D. Hooke, 'The Droitwich Salt Industry: An Examination of the West Midland Charter Evidence', *Anglo-Saxon Studies in Archaeology and History*, 2 (1981), 123–70; L. Keen, 'Coastal Salt Production in Norman England', *ANS*, 11 (1988), 133–80.

[126] R. A. Holt, *The Mills of Medieval England* (Oxford, 1988); Landon, 'Watermills and Windmills in the West Midlands, 1086–1500', 424–44; P. A. Rahtz and D. A. Bullough, 'The Parts of an Anglo-Saxon Mill', *Anglo-Saxon England*, 6 (1977), 15–37; K. A. Bailey, 'Mills in Domesday Buckinghamshire', *Records of Buckinghamshire*, 39 (1997), 67–72; Keen, 'An Introduction to the Dorset Domesday', 13–17.

[127] 'The Burton Abbey Twelfth-Century Surveys', 209–47.

were vast areas of upland moor and heathland, sea marsh and fen, which provided extensive grazing for the communities that abutted on them. There is nothing to suggest that the lord did not share in these amenities. Indeed, later evidence would suggest that his rights were such that he could subsequently claim them as exclusively his own. And yet there are only a few incidental references – notably eel renders in Cambridgeshire – to such assets.[128] Rather it would seem that it was only the stock of the fiscal demesne and what rendered service to it that was included. The distinction is hinted at in the record of mills in an entry in the Cambridgeshire folios. In Badlingham there were '2 mills, one rendering 6s. and the other milling for the demesne'.[129] The circumstance is all but unique,[130] but the distinction is common. Numerous references to mills that 'serve the hall', or court, that were 'without rent' or that were 'grinding corn for his court' are also unvalued. The implication seems to be that mills that were valued served the community and rendered soke to the lord for the privilege.[131] They correspond to the mills attached to free and customary tenures in the twelfth-century surveys.[132]

---

[128] Darby, *Domesday England*, 159–62. In eastern England there are twenty-nine or so references to marsh, but only in Huntingdon is it measured in leagues. In probably all cases the marsh was peat fen which was subject to appropriation from at least the early tenth century. Thus, for example, in the 950s the bounds of estates in Yaxley, Farcet, and Conington in Huntingdonshire encompassed fenland (S595, S649). According to the Ramsey Cartulary, the fen around Sawtry, again in Huntingdonshire, was divided by Thurkil of Harringworth by order of the king in the reign of Cnut (*Cartularium Monasterii de Rameseia*, eds W. H. Hart and P. A. Lyons, Rolls Series, 79, 3 vols (1884–9), i, 164). The pasture lands of the silt fens of eastern England, probably the most valuable grazing in England, are not recorded in Domesday; only the large flocks of sheep in north-west Norfolk hint at their presence (P. H. Sawyer, 'The Wealth of England in the Eleventh Century', *TRHS*, 5th series, 15 (1965), 145–64). Substantial amounts of moor are recorded in the Somerset Levels, reflecting early division (M. Costen, *The Origins of Somerset* (Manchester, 1992), 15), but a minuscule amount in Devon, and none in Cornwall. In Cheshire at Edge it is simply stated 'There are moors' (GDB, 264: *DB Cheshire*, 2,8). In the North there are only sporadic notices of sometimes substantial areas of waste. Some areas of marsh and moor were subsequently afforested, but there is no indication that they were in the forest in 1086 (F. Barlow, 'An Introduction to the Devon Domesday', *The Devon Domesday*, eds A. Williams and R. W. H. Erskine (London, 1991), 10).

[129] GDB, 195v: *DB Cambs*, 14,67.

[130] It is paralleled by a reference to mills in Boarhunt, Hampshire, and in Abingdon, Berkshires and another to fisheries in Swanscombe in Kent where there were '5 fisheries rendering 30d, and a sixth which serves the hall' (GDB, 44v, 58v, 6: *DB Hants*, 21,1; *DB Berks*, 7,38; *DB Kent*, 5,2).

[131] Cf. B. J. Golding, 'An Introduction to the Hampshire Domesday', *The Hampshire Domesday*, eds A. Williams and R. W. H. Erskine (London, 1989), 13. Keen, 'An Introduction to the Dorset Domesday', 13–17, argues that the value of mills is dependent on the amount of water available, showing that value increases the further a mill is from the source of the river on which it is situated.

[132] R. A. Holt, 'Whose were the Profits of Milling? An Aspect of the Changing Relationship between the Abbots of Glastonbury and their Tenants, 1066–1350', *Past and Present*, 116

Many other commodities are less a physical structure than a right. There are, for example, references to the construction of fisheries and the site of fisheries which point to a weir or the like.[133] More usually, however, the lord did not get his hands wet. In Yorkshire and East Anglia and along the Thames a *piscaria* was usually the right to an eel render, while in Devon it was salmon.[134]

We must conclude that assets were recorded not just because they were stock in the widest sense. Clearly, a need was felt to set down the physical assets of the fiscal demesne. Slaves and livestock were infrastructure of the hall, a measure of its size and worth. Much of the recorded pasture, meadow, and woodland must also have been what was later called 'several', that is private, and therefore conveyed a similar message.[135] That which was valued, by contrast, was that which merely rendered dues. On the one hand, then, we do not have a comprehensive stocktaking of the lord's demesne, nor, on the other, do we have a survey of the resources of an estate or community. The focus seems to have been the resources of a nexus of soke. Assets find their way into Domesday Book because they were 'geldable' in the broadest sense, not because they contributed to the income of the lord's demesne, still less simply because they were there. Domesday represents the resources of neither the lord nor his dependent tenants.

This reformulation may begin to make sense of some distributions. The churches that are noticed in the Kent folios were clearly appurtenant to estates of one kind or another. As is clear from three late eleventh-century lists of Kent churches, some of those that were omitted were daughter churches, and an independent record of their existence might not be expected in Domesday Book. Others, by contrast, apparently had full parochial rights.[136] Their omission may well be due to the fact that there was no soke nexus. Those on the Weald in particular look as if they

---

(1987), 6–8, 11–12, assumed that all mills were attached to demesnes in 1086, but argued that many were converted to free or customary tenure in the early twelfth century because of the unprofitability of demesne agriculture and the general leasing out of manors. Rather it would seem that there had been no fundamental change: not all Domesday mills belonged to the demesne.

[133] GDB, 31, 269v, 288, 310, 340, 354v: *DB Surrey*, 2,3; *DB Cheshire*, R1,40a; *DB Notts*, 10,55; *DB Yorks*, 6N31; *DB Lincs*, 2,40.24,12. It is significant that none of these fisheries is valued: that in Surrey is specifically said to be 'without rent (*sine censu*)'.

[134] H. S. A. Fox, *The Evolution of the Fishing Village: Landscape and Society along the South Devon Coast, 1086–1550*, Leicester Explorations in Local History, 1 (Oxford, 2001), 54.

[135] Only in Middlesex, Hertfordshire, and Cambridgeshire, all in Circuit III, is (unmeasured and unvalued) 'pasture for the livestock of the vill' regularly recorded. Elsewhere there are only intermittent references (Darby, *Domesday England*, 153–4). In some instances, where the calculation can be made, the recorded pasture is hardly sufficient for the recorded livestock (Keen, 'An Introduction to the Dorset Domesday', 11–13).

[136] R. Eales, 'An Introduction to the Kent Domesday', *The Kent Domesday*, eds A. Williams and G. H. Martin (London, 1992), 34–9.

were unburdened by soke dues to lowland manors.[137] Again, the great number of churches recorded in Lincolnshire, Norfolk, and Suffolk may well simply attest the scarcity of unassessed land in the three counties rather than circuit procedure. Whether the distribution of other commodities can be explained in similar terms has as yet to be determined. A wider point, however, remains. The record of appurtenances is not necessarily the measure of seigneurial dominance in the economy that a straightforward account of his income would imply. Some assets clearly did 'serve the hall'; others merely rendered dues. All, though, were part of the service equation.

In mapping appurtenances, then, it cannot be assumed that assets were in close proximity to the lord's hall. Coastal salt production is a case in point. In Norfolk there are many seemingly discrete upland manors that had salterns in 1086. Castle Rising, for example, had thirteen and yet there is no sign in the Domesday text that the manor had land on the coast some five miles away.[138] In Kent, Sussex, and Surrey pasture noticed in lowland manors might be as many as twenty miles away in the Weald.[139] In Warwickshire numerous Felden villages had woodland in the Forest of Arden.[140] Even in the supposedly classic champion country of Northamptonshire, replete with its nucleated villages and open-field systems, woodland can sometimes be shown to have been remote from the manor in which it is described.[141] Locating such appurtenances is not possible from Domesday evidence alone – the maps of the *Domesday Geographies* series here are misleading. Later sources must be collated. Using twelfth- and thirteenth-century charters, extents, and surveys, Du Boulay has shown that the archbishop of Canterbury's manor of Wingham in Kent extended over an area of twenty square miles.[142] Many studies of a similar kind have already been undertaken, but much work still remains to be done.

Value

Manorial renders, as indicated by the use of *reddit* and *reddidit*, are the norm on the royal demesne, and are often recorded for ecclesiastical estates. Otherwise, the

---

[137] Golding, 'An Introduction to the Hampshire Domesday', 9–11, has suggested that such an exclusion criterion may have been at work in the Hampshire folios, especially on the estates of New Minster.

[138] LDB, 142v: *DB Norfolk*, 2,4.

[139] Eales, 'Introduction to the Kent Domesday', 1; K. P. Witney, *The Jutist Forest: A Study of the Weald of Kent from 450 to 1380 AD* (London, 1976), 207–75.

[140] W. J. Ford, 'Some Settlement Patterns in the Central Region of the Warwickshire Avon', *Medieval Settlement*, ed. P. H. Sawyer (London, 1976), 279–81.

[141] D. Hall. 'An Introduction to the Northamptonshire Domesday', *The Northamptonshire and Rutland Domesday*, eds A. Williams and R. W. H. Erskine (London, 1987), 5. The woodland belonging to Titchmarsh, for example, was located in the parish of Sudborough.

[142] F. R. H. Du Boulay, *The Lordship of Canterbury: An Essay on Medieval Society* (London, 1966), 52–113.

issues of estates are almost always represented by a value, expressed in the term *valuit* or *valebat*, 'it was worth', and *valet*, 'it is worth'. These statistics are a leit-motif of almost all the Domesday texts. Three figures, TRE, when acquired, and TRW, are commonly given in documents that emanated from the inquest and in the IE prologue, LDB, and intermittently in GDB, and it would therefore seem that change in value between 1066 and 1086 was of primary interest at the earliest stage of the Domesday survey. The surviving summaries provide the figures.[143] It was, moreover, changes in value of holdings as opposed to manors. In circuit VI, it is true, a value is only regularly appended to 'manorial' entries – dependent bere-wicks and sokelands are separately appraised only when the soke was forinsec, the land was enfeoffed, or there was some other peculiarity of tenure – but this is very much the exception. Values are appended to the vast majority of Domesday entries regardless of status in the rest of the country, the exceptions being mostly confined to waste estates where the information was not appropriate or was unavailable. It was fluctuations in value within the vill that exercised the commissioners.

It has been widely assumed that these values are equivalent to renders, repre-senting the actual or potential sums that the estates would garner if let to farm,[144] or, alternatively, the net income of the lord.[145] The close relationship between the figures and other Domesday statistics has long been recognized. Maitland was the first to notice the equation of one pound to the hide[146] and subsequently economic historians have adduced a series of close correlations between value and other resources.[147] It is now generally held that, like renders, Domesday values are a more or less accurate index of the productive capacity of estates.

This analysis is difficult to sustain, a whole barrage of sophisticated statistical tools notwithstanding. In a small number of entries both renders and values are given and invariably the sum which the lord received is greater than the supposed worth of the land; farms are always bigger than values.[148] The fact, of course, has

---

[143] For a discussion of intermediate values in LDB, see L. Marten, 'The Impact of Rebellion on Little Domesday', *ANS*, 27 (2005), 132–50. Lucy Marten is currently (2006) extending her analysis to the whole country in a research project entitled 'The Value of Rebellion: A New Interpretation of the Domesday Survey'.

[144] For dissent, see *DIB*, 40–2, and now J. J. N. Palmer, 'Values', http://www.domesday-book.net/hs2370.htm.

[145] Bridbury, 'Domesday: A Re-interpretation', 284–309; Snooks, 'The Dynamic Role of the Market in the Anglo-Norman Economy and Beyond, 1086–1300', 27–54.

[146] F. W. Maitland, *Domesday Book and Beyond* (Cambridge, 1897), 532–45.

[147] McDonald and Snooks, *Domesday Economy: A New Approach to Anglo-Norman History*; J. McDonald and G. D. Snooks, 'The Determinants of Manorial Income in Domesday England: Evidence from Essex', *Journal of Economic History*, 45 (1985), 541–56; McDonald and Snooks, 'Were the Tax Assessments of Domesday England Artificial? The Case of Essex', 353–73.

[148] The account of Marsh Gibbon in Buckinghamshire makes the point nicely: Æthelric held the manor TRE, 'but he now holds it at farm of William [fitzAnsculf] in heaviness

not gone unnoticed and has been variously explained away. Farmers, it is argued, always demanded more to make up for their own expenses and to turn a profit. There are indeed many references to exploitative farmers and lords.[149] Again, it is averred that values relate to agricultural output alone, while renders include additional sources of income like the pleas of hundreds.[150] All very neat, but the fact remains that estates regularly produced more than the supposed agricultural or wider value. Renders in kind are explicitly additional,[151] as presumably were the payments from appurtenances like the church and mill,[152] while separate payments were also made for regular incidents like *taillia*[153] and *gersuma*.[154] The *valuit* and *valet* figures can hardly be an index of productive capacity.

and misery'. Nevertheless, the value of the manor remained 70s throughout (GDB, 148v: *DB Bucks*, 17,16).

[149] See, for example, West Meon in Hampshire (GDB, 40v: *DB Hants*, 2,11): 'TRE it was worth £20; and afterwards £16; now £30; yet it renders £40 at farm, but it cannot support it for long.'

[150] Harvey, 'Domesday England', 93.

[151] Typically, they appear alongside the monetary value. Darley in Derbyshire, for example, was 'TRE worth 40s and 2 sesters of honey; now £4' (GDB, 272: *DB Derby*, 1,11).

[152] The value of the mills and the like of Leominster were included in a render of £23 2s, but the manor was not valued. The shire stated 'that if it were freed this manor could be valued at six-score pounds, that is 120' (GDB, 180: *DB Gloucs*, 1,10b). For an explicit indication that sums were other than the value, see GDB, 155: *DB Oxon*, 6,1–2. McDonald and Snooks (*Domesday Economy*, 88) found no correlation between the mill renders and Domesday values, pointing to the same conclusion. Elsewhere appurtenances are sometimes worth more than the total value. In West Drayton in Nottinghamshire, for example, there were three mills rendering 50s, where the value was 30s TRE and 17s 4d in 1086 (GDB, 285: *DB Notts*, 9,31). There was a mill in Bromham in Bedfordshire that rendered 40s and 100 eels where the value of the manor was only 20s (GDB, 217: *DB Beds*, 53,9). The value of appurtenances was also independent of renders: see Houghton Regis in Bedfordshire (GDB, 209v: *DB Beds*, 1,3). It is frequently stated that 'The whole is worth ...' This formula, though, begs the question as to what 'the whole' is.

[153] The word is cognate with *tallagium* and the like of the later Middle Ages which connoted a more or less arbitrary levy raised by a lord from his (unfree) tenants. Its significance in 1086 is unclear. It is not found in the *terra regis*, but otherwise appears sporadically in almost every Lincolnshire *breve*. It was always a considerable sum, sometimes almost equalling the recorded value of a manor, and was enjoyed by the most exalted to the smallest thegn. It is possible that the due is silently included in the value in other counties. Thistleton is valued at 60s in the Rutland folios, but a parallel entry in Lincolnshire indicates that it was soke of the manor of South Witham which was valued at 50s with 10s *taillia* (GDB, 293v, 358v: *DB Rutland*, R8; Elc7). C. R. Hart, *The Danelaw* (London, 1992), 188–93, suggests that it was a due paid to the crown, but this interpretation is difficult to square with the fact that *taillia* was paid from Blankney to Branston which was in no sense royal (GDB, 361: *DB Lincs*, 32,16). *Taillia* remains a mystery.

[154] A customary payment made by the peasantry to the lord of the manor. See P. Vinogradoff, *English Society in the Eleventh Century: Essays in English Medieval History* (Oxford, 1908), 143.

It can be agreed, though, that values are sums of money that are rendered in one direction or another. The value of many manors is attached to others, usually demesne estates, and there is a significant number of instances in which it can be shown to be the sum that a tenant paid to an overlord (TRE and TRW). Thus, for example, Thaxted in Essex is said to have been valued at £50 but Richard son of Count Gilbert granted it to an Englishman for £60.[155] Domesday values are often identical to the renders specified in contemporary charters for the lease of an estate. The value of Onibury in Shropshire in 1086 was the render that Roger de Lacy agreed to pay the bishop of Hereford for the estate in the previous year, and the 10 shillings at which Ticknall and Stanton by Newball in Derbyshire were valued was the rent that two tenants paid to Burton Abbey in the early twelfth century.[156] The monetary farms of the Canterbury manors of Croydon, Mortlake, and Hayes in Surrey, and Harrow in Middlesex of 1086 were likewise approximately the same as the Domesday values.[157] The income that the king derived from his estates in Worcestershire (which is noted in the account of the City of Worcester) is within a few shillings of the sum total of the renders and values (the *reddit* and *valet* figures) recorded in his *breve*.[158]

What, then, were Domesday values? From the evidence of twelfth-century surveys, A. R. Bridbury has suggested that many are simply money rents.[159] I concur. I shall further argue that they are no more and no less than soke dues rendered in coin, and, as such they supplement other cash renders and food rents. They are a measure of petty cash rather than of productive capacity. We can best begin by determining the source of the data. Explicit evidence is limited. There are three references to the presentment of values by the shire and hundred.[160] A further eight by Englishmen, Frenchmen, or English and Frenchmen could refer to presentments by the vill, hundred or shire,[161] while one to 'the men' is presumably a reference to a seigneurial source. This last is instructive.

---

[155] LDB, 38v: *DB Essex*, 23,2.

[156] V. H. Galbraith, 'An Episcopal Land-Grant of 1085', *EHR*, 44 (1929), 357; 'Burton Surveys', 240; GDB, 252, 273, 274: *DB Salop*, 2,2; *DB Derby*, 3,7.6,21.

[157] *The Domesday Monachorum of Canterbury*, ed. D. C. Douglas, Royal Historical Society (1944), 10, 99

[158] GDB, 172, 172v: *DB Worcs*, C2.1,1–4. The sheriff of Worcester is said to have rendered £123 4s from the king's estates, while the total of the *reddit* and *valet* figures in the king's *breve* is £124 6s. Kinver (Staffs) appears to have rendered in Worcestershire, but Trodebrigge and Clent (Worcs) in Staffordshire.

[159] A. R. Bridbury, *The English Economy from Bede to the Reformation* (Woodbridge, 1992), 111–32.

[160] GDB, 166v; LDB, 15v, 343: *DB Gloucs*, 28,7; *DB Essex*, 7,1; *DB Suffolk*, 7121.

[161] GDB, 2v, 65, 70; LDB, 18, 38v: *DB Kent*, 1,1; *DB Wilts*, 1,10–12.26,5; *DB Essex*, 9,7.23,2. Another communal presentment is probably recorded in the entry for Sherrington in Sussex where it is recorded that 'For the half-hide which is not there they deduct 20s' (GDB, 20v: *DB Sussex*, 10,18).

The whole manor [of Damerham in Wiltshire] TRE was worth £36. It now renders £61, but by the men [the lands] are not valued at more than £45, on account of the confusion of the land, and on account of the farm, which is too high.[162]

The evidence of the men is opposed to the recorded value and it would therefore suggest that there was an input from both shrieval and seigneurial sources. What evidence Domesday affords indicates that values were not entirely the privileged data of estate management. That they were in some sense public is inherently likely. Values are consistently given for 1066 and when the estate was acquired, and yet these were statistics that tenants-in-chief cannot regularly have been in a position to know. They can only have been a matter of official record or communal presentment or both. The Domesday Monachorum B of Canterbury and the Excerpta of St Augustine's, Canterbury, would appear to be examples. Both documents lack details of population and stock and would therefore appear to precede the seigneurial returns, and yet values are consistently recorded. If these documents have been correctly identified as the product of the geld inquest, then it would appear that the information was regularly presented by the juries of vill, hundred, and shire.

Values were apparently public knowledge. As sums that went out of manors, they were therefore probably grounded in wider tributary relationships. The valuation clause of the entry for Osmaston by Derby in GDB is unique; it is, nevertheless, thought-provoking in this context. It records that Osmaston was worth 40s in 1066 and 20s at the time of the inquest and continues 'of this money 2 parts are the king's, the third Henry's'.[163] Henry was Henry de Ferrers who succeeded to the estates of the local earl in Derbyshire and thus it is inevitable that the division of the value in the ratio of two to one should remind us of sake and soke and the rights that that liberty conferred upon a king's thegn or a tenant-in-chief.[164] The receipt of the king's two pennies was of the essence of soke, and so it is clear that the value is a record of its render in this entry.

We have no further statement of value in these terms, but the figures that are recorded in the Domesday texts must often represent similar soke renders. The ancient royal estate and soke of Rutland rendered £150 to the king in 1086.[165] The statement is attached to the account of Alstoe and Martinsley Wapentakes in the Nottinghamshire folios, but a handful of references in the Northamptonshire text indicates that the soke also encompassed Witchley Hundred in Northamptonshire.[166] Much of the land was in the hands of the king, but by no means all

[162] GDB, 66v: *DB Wilts*, 7,1.
[163] GDB, 275v: *DB Derby*, 6,88.
[164] See above, pp. 151–5.
[165] GDB, 293v: *DB Rutland*, R4.
[166] GDB, 219, 219v, 228v: *DB Northants*, 1,3;4.56,36.

of it. Six of these latter estates are pointedly said to have been held with sake and soke (an unusual feature of the Northamptonshire folios) and if their valets are excluded the total value of the whole soke in 1086 as set out in GDB is £153 8s.[167] Here surely is the farm of £150 that Rutland rendered.

More precise evidence comes from Bury St Edmunds' sources. In the Suffolk folios of LDB the lands of the abbey's free men are occasionally separately valued and in most cases the same tenements can be identified in Bury C. In this document each free man is named and the amount of land that he held is recorded along with a sum of money. Totals are given for these sums and, although neither they nor the aggregates of the individual figures equate exactly with the LDB values, they are all of the same magnitude and some are very close (Table 7.3). They can be further traced in the Kalendar of Abbot Samson, a late twelfth-century inventory of the dues of Bury St Edmunds in the hundreds of its Suffolk liberty,[168] and there they are identified. The renders were additional to a series of light labour services and a food rent called foddercorn and were known as hidage, sheriff's aid, carriage, and wardpenny. LDB makes it clear that the abbey had the soke of these men and it seems clear that Bury C and the Kalendar preserve a record of the sorts of due that made up their Domesday value.

Table 7.3 *The value and renders of Bury free men*

| | LDB | | Bury C | Kalendar | |
	TRE	TRW		Summa	Total
Timworth	30s	20s	26s 0½d	26s 3d	26s 3d
Thurston		40s	10s 5d	10s 8d+20s	30s 10d
Tostock	10s	10s 8d	3s 9½d	8s 6½d	8s 8½d
Hessett		40s	48s 1d	40s+14s 4d	49s 1d
Woolpit		10s 8d	10s 11d		10s 8d
Bradfield		6s	4s 4d	5s 8d	5s 7d
Rushbrooke	16s	21s 11d	19s 2d	21s 4d	22s 11½d

Summa refers to the total given in the text, *Total* to the sum of the individual items recorded in each entry.

The nature and origins of the dues have been discussed by the editor of the Kalendar, R. H. C. Davis.[169] Sheriff's aid, carriage, and wardpenny can be

---

[167] T. Cain ('Introduction to the Rutland Domesday', *The Northamptonshire and Rutland Domesday*, eds A. Williams and R. W. H. Erskine (London, 1987), 27) equates the farm with the TRE value of the Martinsley and Witchley estates alone of £156 12s.

[168] *The Kalendar of Abbot Samson of Bury St Edmunds and Related Documents*, ed. R. H. C. Davis, Camden Society, 3rd series, 84 (1954), 6–22. Selection of entries has been dictated by a separate assessment and value in LDB and a comparable assessment in the Kalendar.

[169] *Kalendar of Abbot Samson*, xxxii–xlvii.

characterized as public duties which were incumbent on all land. In financial terms they were of minor value and were probably not included in the Domesday *valet* figures. Hidage, by contrast, was a more substantial source of income which was confined to sokeland. Here it was a hundredal due, having its origins in the renders that free men and sokemen made to the king, but it seems to represent the soke dues that were conferred by the right of sake and soke. Some sokemen may have paid in addition a manorial rent, but by and large hidage seems to have represented their full value. And it was a value that was essentially fiscal. Hidage was generally assessed on the fiscal carucate at the rate of 1d per *ware* acre or at 16d for every 15 acres, yielding 10s 8d each.

This is an equation that can be widely observed in East Anglia; time and again the value of subholdings works out at exactly 1d per *ware* acre.[170] In Lancashire a custom directly comparable to hidage is called 'geld of the carucates of land', customs, or simply 'geld'. In the account of West Derby it is stated that each thegn 'had by custom to render 2 *orae* of pennies for each carucate of land'.[171] Two Danish *orae* work out at 32d, and an examination of the value of the manors they held reveals that two-thirds of the figures are based on this sum (Table 7.4). The fifteen or so instances in which there is no correspondence can be attributed to exemption from the payment where a lord had compounded for a different, usually higher, figure, or simple scribal error.[172]

Burton Abbey sources indicate that manorial values were also related to soke dues in Staffordshire and Derbyshire.[173] The Burton Survey A of *c*.1125, like the earlier Survey B, distinguishes between inland and *warland*. As we have seen, the former is not represented in Domesday Book which concerns itself solely with the latter. Survey A further distinguishes this, the *warland*. First it describes that part that was held *ad opus*, that is, by day work, which is not valued, and then goes on to described the remainder held *ad malam* with a note of the sums that were rendered therefor. *Mala* signifies 'rent' but, levied at between 1s and 2s per bovate, with a mode of 1s 6d, the impost appears to be more akin to the hidages of Suffolk. Table 7.5 shows that in one case the total is the same as the Domesday value for the whole manor, while in the remaining six the figures are close to or in the same order as their Domesday counterparts.

A similar relationship between some Domesday manorial values and soke dues can be observed in twelfth-century Ely, Glastonbury, Peterborough, Ramsey, St Paul's, London, Shaftesbury, and Winchester sources.[174] The equation is not

---

[170] R. Welldon Finn, *Domesday Studies: The Eastern Counties* (London, 1967), 172–3.

[171] GDB, 269v: *DB Cheshire*, R1,40a.

[172] C. Stephenson, 'The Firma Unius Noctis and the Customs of the Hundred', *EHR*, 39 (1924), 169–72.

[173] 'Burton Surveys'.

[174] Bridbury (*The English Economy from Bede to the Reformation*, 126–32) tabulates the information.

Table 7.4 *Assessments and values in West Derby Hundred in Lancashire*

Vill	Assessment car.	bov.	Value	Vill	Assessment car.	bov.	Value
Toxteth	2		4s	Aughton	1		32d*
Toxteth	2		4s	Formby	4		10s
Septon	6		16s*	Ainsdale	2		64d*
Kirkdale	3		10s	Upholland	2		64d*
Walton	2	3	8s	Dalton	1		32d*
Litherland	3		8s*	Skelmersdale	1		32d*
Ince	3		8s*	Litherland	1		32d*
Thornton	3		8s*	Argarmeles	2		8s
Meols	3		8s*	Meols	3		10s
Woolton	2		64d*	Lathom	3		10s 8d
Smithdown	1		32d*	Hurlston/Marton	3		10s 8d
Allerton	3		8s*	Melling	2		10s
Speke	2		64d*	Lydiate		6	64d
Childwall	3		8s*	Downholland		6	2s*
Wibaldslei	2		64d*	Altcar	3		waste
Woolton	1		30d	Barton	1		32d*
Wavertree	2		64d*	Halsall	2		8s
Bootle	2		64d*				

Assessments in hides have been translated into carucates at the rate of 6 carucates to the hide as at GDB, 267v: *DB Ches*, R1,44.

* indicates values at the rate of 32d/carucate.

Table 7.5 *Lands* ad malam *in the Burton Survey*

	GDB values		Burton Survey A	
	TRE	TRW	Total	Summa
Winshill	20s	60s	54s 8d	
Branston	60s	40s	21s 4d† + 20s?	23s 5d
Bromley	10s	20s	50s†	64s
Leigh	40s	40s	40s	44s
Mickleover	£25	£10	£6 13s 8d*	
Stapenhill	60s	60s	29s 6d*	29s 6d
Appleby	20s	60s	23s*	

* estate smaller than that in 1086

† inland not distinguished from *warland*

always precise: of the 118 manors for which comparative figures survive, the twelfth-century values of only twenty-four come within 10 per cent of their TRW values. However, the Burton survey of 1125 shows that tenements that were converted to day work between 1086 and the time of that survey ceased to render monetary

dues. Elsewhere the same processes were probably at work after 1086 to account
for discrepancies in value. This see-saw relationship between value and service is
consonant with a widely occurring characteristic of Domesday values: *valet* figures
complement renders in kind. Thus, figures often subsist side by side with services,
but where the render was totally in kind, as in the farm of one night, no valuation
is given. We can conclude, then, that Domesday values are soke dues rendered in
cash. They do not represent any sort of overall return from the manor as whole.
Thus it is that they appear in Domesday Book alongside the renders of churches,
mills, and the like as any other render in kind or cash.

This formulation might occasion disappointment, but it should cause little
surprise. It was beyond the capacity, or the inclination, of the compilers of the
twelfth-century terriers and customals to value their own lands in the modern
sense: what was recorded was what was tangible, namely renders, services, rents.
There is no reason to believe that the situation was otherwise in 1086. A notional
monetary value was as meaningless then as it was throughout much of the Middle
Ages. A more meaningful description of an estate was to describe what the lord
got out of it. In the eleventh century this was broadly services and renders in kind
and cash and that is precisely what Robert of Hereford understood as one of the
articles of inquiry: where the Anglo-Saxon Chronicle merely refers to 'how much
money it was worth', he reports that 'the services and payments (*servitio et censu*)
due from all the men in the whole land' were recorded.[175] We must suspect that
Domesday Book affords us precisely that, statistical analyses notwithstanding.

At once we can perceive that the Domesday commissioners were demanding
something that was concrete. They did not require the application of abstruse
equations to arrive at the data they requested. They simply asked for the sum
of the rents and dues that the lord enjoyed in each vill. On occasion there were
simply none and so no value is recorded. It is said of Blackburn in Lancashire,
for example, that:

> Roger de Poitou gave the whole of this land to Roger de Bully and Albert
> Greslet, and there are as many men who have 11½ ploughs, [to] whom they
> themselves have granted quittance [from rent] for 3 years, and therefore it
> is not now valued.[176]

---

[175] John of Worcester gives a similar account (*The Chronicle of John of Worcester, 3: The
Annals from 1067 to 1140 with the Gloucester Interpolations and the Continuation to 1141*,
ed. and trans. P. McGurk (Oxford, 1998), 44–5). The anonymous Worcester chronicler,
writing *c.*1140, apparently understood the same even though he was following the Anglo-
Saxon Chronicle: his formula reads 'He inquired what these were worth, and how much
they then rendered, and how much they were able to render in the time of King Edward'
(*EHD*, ii, 853).
[176] GDB, 270: *DB Cheshire*, R4,2.

More usually there were renders. Bury C may well be an example of the type of record returned. It was a task that was clearly within the competence of seigneurial officials and local jurors alike and so it is that we encounter no management consultants or quantity surveyors in Domesday Book. Values were but one more resource that underlay the lord's share of the wealth of the vill. In the seigneurial summaries its significance is even more pointed. It is clearly recorded as a complement to the number of hides and ploughs rather than as a summary of what went before. All of these data are in apposition to ploughlands and increase in value. The record of values is subservient to the wider concern with taxation capacity.

If Domesday values are a record of monetary renders, they clearly cannot be used as an index of the fee's annual return on capital. Like the Domesday commissioners, we have no way of putting a value on the resources of the manor in demesne ploughs, livestock, appurtenances, and services; we only have a measure of them in their own terms. Nor, *a fortiori*, it is possible to use the information as a measure of productive capacity. Economic historians must look again at their evidence where they have used Domesday values as a datum for economic growth in the twelfth century and later.[177] The figures can only be used as what they are, a measure of the extent of rents and renders. It is, however, a characteristic that opens up an insight into estate management in the reign of the Conqueror. In East Anglia the comprehensive record of changing levels of stock between 1066 and 1086 shows that rising values are often accompanied by falling resources in ploughs and population. This was a correlation that frankly flummoxed Welldon Finn; he could only conclude that Norman tenants-in-chief were demanding more from an increasingly economically depressed peasantry.[178] Likewise, Desborough has observed an inverse correlation between ploughs and value in Staffordshire, although the fact confused him.[179] But as an index of monetary dues, the rising values clearly indicate a decline in demesne agriculture.

This is a relationship that Hamshere has noted in passing in the West Midlands.[180] He argued for a decrease in demesne farming on the *terra regis* from the relatively low proportion of demesne ploughs on royal estates and attributed the increase in value to the contribution of rents to the annual return in the more efficient management regime. Conversely, he associated stable or falling values with demesnes with a high proportion of ploughs that were directly exploited by religious foundations and lords with a small local power base. A similar pattern can be observed in the demesne and enfeoffed estates of the Count of Mortain in

---

[177] Bridbury, *The English Economy from Bede to the Reformation*, 121–5.
[178] Welldon Finn, *Domesday Studies: The Eastern Counties*, 169–76.
[179] D. Desborough, 'An Introduction to the Staffordshire Domesday', *The Staffordshire Domesday*, eds A. Williams and G. H. Martin (London, 1991), 14.
[180] Hamshere, 'The Structure and Exploitation of the Domesday Book Estate of the Church of Worcester', 41–52.

Cornwall, and it too must surely indicate different management strategies rather than the varying efficiency of local husbandry suggested by I. N. Soulsby.[181] These are patterns that could well repay further local study.

More widely, Domesday values remain an index of baronial wealth. Corbett was the first to rank tenants-in-chief by Domesday value and John Palmer has more recently reviewed the evidence.[182] Both assumed that the figures represented global incomes in some way. This we must modify. The figures represent only income in cash. In demesne estates, of course, cash was only part of the total value to the lord. Additionally there were renders in kind and the issues of inland, both of which were unappraised. How indicative the *valet* and *valuit* figures are of wealth in that context will therefore depend on all sorts of largely unquantifiable variables such as the rate of hidation and the extent of demesne exploitation. In enfeoffed estates, by contrast, they are more likely to approximate to the sum total of the lord's tangible income, for if the soke dues went out of manors, presumably the other issues went to the sitting tenant. Nevertheless, as a measure of the readies at the lord's disposal, the figures are probably as good an index of status as overall wealth.

Waste

Lack of values, and dramatic falls, present further problems of interpretation. They are usually discussed in relation to waste. There are over 2000 places in Domesday Book which are said to have been waste (*wasta*) in whole or in part or laid waste (*wastata*). Typically, entries of the kind record assessment to the geld and ploughlands, but otherwise no other details of waste in 1086. Wastage at an earlier date, either when the estate was acquired or in 1066, is specifically linked to value. So, for example, it is said of Bexhill that 'the whole manor TRE was worth £20; and afterwards it was waste; now [it is worth] £18 10s.'[183] The expectation that waste was worthless is further emphasized by the exceptions. Where a value is recorded, the anomaly is expressly signalled. Foxley in Northamptonshire was waste, but 'nevertheless (*tamen*) it is worth 5s'.[184] The same qualification occurs in almost all similar entries. Wastage raised the expectation that a holding was without value. That much is clear, but what it actually meant on the ground has been the subject of yet another debate in Domesday studies.

[181] I. N. Soulsby, 'An Introduction to the Cornwall Domesday', *The Cornwall Domesday*, eds A. Williams and R. W. H. Erskine (London, 1988), 11–12.
[182] W. J. Corbett, 'The Development of the Duchy of Normandy and the Norman Conquest of England', *The Cambridge Medieval History*, ed. J. R. Tanner, vol. 5 (Cambridge, 1926), 481–520, 885–94; J.J.N. Palmer, 'The Wealth of the Secular Aristocracy in 1086', *ANS*, 22 (2000), 279–91.
[183] GDB, 18: *DB Sussex*, 9,11.
[184] GDB, 223v: *DB Northants*, 18,39.

The uncertainty has stemmed from the reticence of the Domesday texts as to why land was waste. Wrangle in Lincolnshire was devastated on account of the flooding of the sea, and it is reported that King Gruffydd and Bleddyn laid waste Archenfield TRE 'and so it is not known what it was like at that time'.[185] Such glosses, however, are rare. Nevertheless, that waste often involved physical destruction cannot be doubted. In Oxford 'within the wall as without, there are 243 houses paying geld, and besides these there are 500 houses, less 22, so waste and destroyed that they cannot pay geld'.[186] Even more emphatic is the entry for Netheravon in Wiltshire: 'Nigel the physician holds the church of this manor with 1 hide. This with all its appendages is worth £32. [The church] itself, however, is waste, and the roof so damaged, that it is almost tumbling down.'[187]

Military action has most often been assumed to be the cause. The wasting of land by burning crops and killing stock was a common tactic in early medieval warfare.[188] It at once provided an army with supplies and denied them to their opponents and might equally well be used offensively to punish an area as defensively to discourage invasion. It was employed by the Welsh kings in the marches in 1065, the Normans in Sussex in 1066 and, most brutally, in the North in 1069. As recently as 1085 William had ordered coastal areas to be wasted in anticipation of the Danish invasion (although there is little sign of it unless it was confined to the North Yorkshire coast).[189] The twenty years before the Domesday inquest had seen more than usual devastation and it cannot be entirely coincidental that its main centres are precisely those areas in which Domesday waste is concentrated.

However, not all have agreed that *wastum* always signifies physical devastation. A reassessment of the nature of waste emerged in a revisionary debate on the extent of the damage inflicted by William the Conqueror on the North in 1069. There are more waste holdings in Yorkshire than any other county, accounting for no less than two-thirds of the total, and this fact has been linked with a large number of other tenements in which no details of stock are provided in Domesday Book to argue that the area was still suffering from the after-effects of the Harrying of the North seventeen years later in 1086. This simple picture, however, is seemingly belied by the distribution of the waste. In 1948 Bishop observed that waste was predominantly found in upland areas whereas it might be expected that devastation would be concentrated on the richer lowland soils. He concluded that tenants-in-

[185] GDB, 367v, 181: *DB Lincs*, 57,36; *DB Hereford*, 1,49.
[186] GDB, 154: *DB Oxon*, B4.
[187] GDB, 65: *DB Wilts*, 1,18.
[188] N. Hooper, 'The Anglo-Saxons at War', *Weapons and Warfare in Anglo-Saxon England*, ed. S. C. Hawkes (Oxford, 1989), 191–201; M. Strickland, *Anglo-Norman Warfare* (Woodbridge, 1992), 150–5, 199–201, 214–17, 232–4.
[189] *ASC*, 161. Welldon Finn, *Domesday Studies: The Eastern Counties*, 167, suggests that the wasting may be evidenced by the failure of manors in coastal hundreds to appreciate, and indeed for some to decline, in value between 1066 and 1086.

chief must have restocked these their core estates at the expense of more peripheral assets.[190] The pattern of waste in 1086 reflects the response to the Harrying rather than its immediate effects. Wightman subsequently developed the argument.[191] He conceded that the waste on the Pennine uplands and the coastal plain was a direct testimony to the events of 1069. The pattern of distribution elsewhere, however, pointed less to destruction than unrelated changes in estate management. Some waste holdings still had resources in stock, manpower, and value, indicating that waste did not necessarily indicate complete destruction. Moreover, the wastage of one is often offset by an increase in resources of another close by. In such cases, *wastum* seems to indicate that where formally there had been two or more holdings there were now fewer. Wightman concluded that the classification of a holding as waste was an accounting device to signal that a holding no longer existed as a separate entity when its resources had been assigned to another demesne.

The wider conclusion that the extent and severity of the Harrying of the North has been exaggerated is echoed by David Palliser.[192] He accepts Wightman's reinterpretation of waste and further argues that most of the summary accounts of land in the Yorkshire Domesday are less a function of wastage than lack of information in a survey that was incomplete in the satellite regions attached to the county. For hundreds of manors nothing more than a TRE holder, assessment to the geld, and often ploughlands is given. Parallel entries indicate that some of these were waste, but others were not. For the majority, information is simply inadequate. It would seem that the Domesday inquest got little further than the first stage, the geld audit.

Both propositions have recently been revisited by John Palmer.[193] Drawing for the first time on a comprehensive data set generated by the *Domesday Explorer* database, he has criticized this reassessment of waste in an endorsement of the realist analysis in the area covered by GDB (there are only nine references to waste in LDB and they in no way contradict his argument). Wightman's distributions do not stand up to systematic examination: in the majority of entries there is nothing to suggest that the resources of waste land are entered in adjoining holdings. His conclusions are, moreover, contradictory. The amalgamation of estates is indicated in Domesday Book by the statement of the number of manors that were there TRE. The record of waste is clearly not another method since estates that were so

[190] T. A. M. Bishop, 'The Norman Settlement of Yorkshire', *Studies in Medieval History Presented to Frederick Maurice Powicke*, eds R. W. Hunt, W. A. Pantin, and R. W. Southern (Oxford, 1948), 1–14.
[191] W. E. Wightman, 'The Significance of "Waste" in the Yorkshire Domesday', *Northern History*, 10 (1975), 55–71.
[192] D. M. Palliser, 'Domesday Book and the Harrying of the North', *Northern History*, 29 (1993), 1–23.
[193] J. J. N. Palmer, 'War and Domesday Waste', in *Armies, Chivalry and Warfare in Medieval Britain and France*, ed. M. Strickland (Stamford, 1998), 256–75.

in 1066 or later are still identifiable entities in 1086. As for the summary entries in Domesday Book, the frequent record of ploughlands and sometimes value indicate that a survey had taken place and that there was nothing to report.

The debate goes on. And it proceeds in the usual reductionist fashion of either/or. In reality, an administrative definition of *wastum* does not necessarily exclude physical waste when the phenomenon is examined within the terms of the Domesday inquest. The anecdotal evidence in Domesday Book does indeed suggest that waste usually implied dilapidation. The use of the alternative *wastata*, the norm in Circuit I, is difficult to translate as anything other than 'laid waste'. But it is another matter to claim that the Domesday commissioners recorded the fact for its own sake. Regional aid for reconstruction was not part of their remit. The yield of the geld was. In Herefordshire the matter is consistently linked with waste. The account of Huntington, near Hereford, is typical of a number of entries in the bishop of Hereford's *breve*: 'In Huntington are 10 hides. Of these, 4 are waste, and the others pay geld.'[194] Payment of the geld is also linked with waste in the king's *breve*.[195] It seems to have been a common association. Of Malmesbury in Wiltshire we read that there were '25 messuages in which are houses which pay no more geld than waste land'; of Oxford that there were '243 houses paying geld, and besides these there are 500 houses, less 22, so waste and destroyed that they cannot pay geld'; of Embley in Hampshire that 'it then paid geld for half a hide; now for nothing. There is land for half a plough. It was worth 10s. It is now waste.'[196] Land taken into the 'king's wood' in Ellington in Huntingdonshire was presumably waste because it too no longer paid geld, although whether it was also physically waste is not clear.[197]

The linking of waste and geld payment is not peculiar to the Domesday process. It was apparently a commonplace of administration, being attested, *inter alia*, in both the pre-Domesday Northamptonshire geld roll and the 1156 Pipe Roll.[198] It would be a mistake, however, to conclude that Domesday waste was just land that did not pay geld. There were, of course, estates that were unassessed that were said to be waste. Bistre in Cheshire (now in Wales) was unhidated in 1086 and had never paid geld; and yet it had been waste in 1066 and when Earl Hugh had received it.[199] Service must also have been part of the equation. It is only once explicitly linked with waste. Again in Malmesbury there was 'half a waste messuage, [part] of

---

[194] GDB, 182: *DB Hereford*, 2,40.
[195] GDB, 181: *DB Hereford*, 1,69.
[196] GDB, 64v, 154, 47v: *DB Wilts*, M1; *DB Oxon*, B4; *DB Hants*, 39,5.
[197] GDB, 204v: *DB Hunts*, 6,26. Wightman considered this type of entry as indicative of 'administrative' waste. There is little, however, to indicate that the land was still stocked. Undeveloped land undoubtedly was incorporated into the forest. In Cheshire there was much land that 'was waste' and 'is now in the forest'.
[198] J. H. Round, *Feudal England* (London, 1895), 148–9.
[199] GDB, 269: *DB Cheshire*, FT3,1.

the fief of the Bishop of Bayeux, which renders no service'.[200] But more obliquely it may be hinted at in references to waste manors. In Herefordshire a postscriptal note asserts that three manors were waste; more pointedly, the summary of Count Alan's fee in Yorkshire carefully notes that 108 of his manors were waste.[201]

The important point here is that for the commissioners, and probably the compilers of Domesday Book too, waste was defined in relation to the main concerns of the Domesday inquest. Land in itself was of little interest to them; whether it was cultivated or not was of even less moment. What was important was its capacity to pay tax and render service. This perspective makes sense of the supposed anomaly of waste land with stock and value. Where land was completely destroyed there was no question of capacity to pay. Destruction was reason enough for removal of land from considerations of tax and service. But this did not preclude the making of similar allowances for other estates with limited resources. This is precisely how waste seems to have been used in the early Pipe Rolls. Emily Amt has demonstrated that *wastum* is not a portmanteau word for any loss of income. Assets which were granted out and the like are explicitly said to be so; waste refers to physical devastation. And yet sheriffs seem to have negotiated for allowances where resources were not adequate for the burdens assessed upon the tenement.[202] It is a reality recognized by administrators the world over. Even today the local tax known as the Community Charge in England is not levied on houses undergoing major structural repairs or are unoccupied. Such properties remain upstanding and valuable, but yield no tax for the local authority. The Domesday commissioners would, no doubt, have written them down as waste.

Where does that leave us in using the data? Well, clearly waste in 1086 is precisely that. The fact tells us about expectations of geld and service at the time of the inquest. What it does not tell us directly is what happened fifteen or twenty years before. As Palmer has eloquently argued,[203] Yorkshire may well have still been reeling from the effects of the Harrying of the North when the Domesday commissioners visited the county, but it is another matter to claim that Domesday Book affords an accurate inventory of the damage. The intervening years saw all sorts of changes that conditioned the choices made in 1086. Some of those changes must have included the restructuring of estates, by internal colonization as well as amalgamation. Waste in itself, however, does not seem to point to them. There is indeed little to show that resources had been transferred elsewhere. If LDB is anything to go by, the commissioners were expressly instructed to identify changes in manorial structure and waste was no part of their vocabulary in reporting it.

---

[200] GDB, 64v: *DB Wilts*, M2.
[201] GDB, 181, 381: *DB Hereford*, 1,69; *DB Yorks*, SN,CtA45.
[202] E. M. Amt, 'The Meaning of Waste in the Early Pipe Rolls of Henry II', *EcHR*, 2nd ser., 44 (1991), 240–8.
[203] Palmer, 'War and Domesday Waste', 256–75.

Waste in 1066 and later provides better evidence for assessing the effects of wasting and the responses to it. The fact was presumably a matter of record or memory and therefore it might not be expected that it had such a narrow focus as a textual form as waste in 1086. Indeed, most land that was 'laid' waste (*wastata*) had been so in 1066 or 'later'. Waste at earlier periods is more likely, then, to refer to events than geld payment or service. The waste in Cheshire, Shropshire, and Staffordshire can reasonably be attributed to the Harrying of the North. Likewise, the waste around Hastings looks like the collateral damage from the campaign of conquest in 1066. Hitherto, the evidence has been used almost exclusively to reconstruct the movements of the armies. The principle first surfaces in the work of William Hayley, a Sussex antiquary of the late eighteenth century, who argued that King Harold's progress to his defeat at Hastings can be mapped in the record of waste manors in 1066.[204] Ellis, Freeman, Round, and Maitland all accepted the analysis (although Freeman was aghast at the suggestion that King Harold was to blame). But it was Baring who developed the method to the full. In an influential paper published in 1898 he argued that military action could also be detected in falls in value between 1066 and the 'later' of the texts. The observation informed an analysis of William the Conqueror's campaign of 1066 which put flesh on the scanty chronicle accounts of the Normans' march on London. He claimed not only to be able to map the route of the main army, but also the sorties of detachments and the landing places of reinforcements.[205]

Baring's techniques have now been used in all areas in which Domesday affords a valuation at an intermediate period (predominantly Circuits I and III), and indeed beyond,[206] to recover 'the Conqueror's footprints' in Domesday Book. However, generally the conclusions are unconvincing. The distribution of waste looks authentic enough, but there are no coherent patterns in loss of value. In a recent review of the data John Palmer noted a group of manors with low intermediate values in the vicinity of Dover, which was burnt in 1066, but no similar pattern around Wallingford through which the Conqueror's army is known to have passed on its way to London.[207] Most of the routes suggested by Baring and those who have re-worked his evidence do not stand out from a background 'noise' of depression in values. Declining values do not seem to point to the footprints of passing armies. They may betoken general disruption – even as rents, falling values

[204] Quoted in H. Ellis, *A General Introduction to Domesday Book*, 2 vols (London, 1833), i, 314–20.

[205] F. H. Baring, 'The Conqueror's Footprints in Domesday', *EHR*, 13 (1898), 17–25.

[206] G. H. Fowler, 'The Devastation of Bedfordshire and the Neighbouring Counties in 1065 and 1066', *Archaeologia*, 72 (1922), 41–50, advocated an 'inductive' method in areas in which there were only two dates, that is he plotted percentage rises.

[207] J. J. N. Palmer, 'The Conqueror's Footprints in Domesday Book', in A. C. Ayton and J. L. Price (eds), *The Medieval Military Revolution: State, Society and Military Change in Medieval and Early Modern Europe* (London and New York, 1995), 23–44.

may indicate non-collection. But further conclusions must await a comparative survey of intermediate values throughout the country.[208] Dips are evident in Essex and East Anglia, where wasting is probably less likely. This material may provide clues to what was happening when estates were taken over by their new lords.

The record of pre-Domesday waste does not satisfy the demands made upon it by military historians. But in areas like Cheshire, where the data are extensive, it may resolve many of the issues raised by Bishop and Wightman in Yorkshire. With data for 1066, when estates were acquired, and 1086, it should be possible to assess the strategies employed for dealing with wastage. Such a study would have to characterize the location and tenure of each waste and cultivated estate and track the fortunes of each type. It is a study that has yet to be undertaken.[209]

[208] For East Anglia, see Marten, 'The Impact of Rebellion on Little Domesday', 132–50.
[209] For preliminary accounts, see R. Welldon Finn, *The Norman Conquest and its Effects on the Economy 1066–1086* (London, 1971), 168–78, and, more recently, J. S. Matthews, 'William the Conqueror's Campaign in Cheshire in 1069–70: Resistance in the North-West', *Northern History*, 40 (2003), 53–70.

8

The Communities of the Shire

I T IS, of course, a truism to assert that Domesday Book is about lords and manors. The GDB scribe made a half-hearted attempt to enter boroughs as settlements, but otherwise communities hardly get a look-in. However, the same cannot be claimed for the earliest stage of the Domesday inquest. Tenants-in-chief as holders of land were, of course, major participants in the process throughout, but it was local communities – the vill, the hundred, the riding, the shire – that presented and validated the evidence that they provided. In the initial sessions local communities were even its subject. The geld inquest was *par excellence* about communal affairs. We know from the surviving sources that the matter of who owed what was bound up with the obligations of communities, what was customary and what was not. Much of the data was already written. Routine administrative documents seem to lie behind the earliest Domesday texts. Presentments confirmed and expanded on their data.[1]

The result must have been a comprehensive overview of the obligations of the free communities of the shire. In its turn, the documentation set in train a review. The question of who paid geld was inextricably linked to title in the mind of the free man. It is surely not fanciful to assume that there had been something like a stampede to register liability. Rival claims were inevitable and so the process demanded resolution of claims. Pleas were probably no part of the Domesday inquest. The business of 1086 was too urgent to be held up by messy and protracted private litigation (royal claims may have been another matter). However, such sessions must have been scheduled at an early stage.

The second stage of the Domesday inquest was peripheral to all this furious activity. Schedules of the lands held by each tenant-in-chief were drawn up from the records of the geld inquest and detailed survey was requested in what can only have been a private matter. It was primarily this subset of data that engaged the interest of the compilers of Domesday Book. The communal was largely superfluous to their purpose, and therefore what does survive in the text is largely incidental. It is a fact that often makes the evidence difficult to interpret. Communal concerns

----

[1] Above, pp. 64–86.

intrude in exceptional circumstances, and there is no way of knowing whether they too are exceptional. Nevertheless, the evidence is the more valuable because there is often nothing else to elucidate the workings of local communities in the late eleventh century.

Much of the data is difficult to classify. Hundred penny, escort, and cartage were rendered in the hundred or shire and were, then, 'public'. In other respects they were tenurial, for they were rendered at a hundred manor. The distinction is, however, largely artificial. The vill and the hundred, in their different forms, as they presented themselves in 1086, were a function of the shrieval system: their activities and responsibilities were those which were accorded and coordinated in a system of local government founded in the community. In many areas, probably all, they inherited duties that were personal and tenurial from a time when there was nothing else. But these were shaped and fashioned to meet the needs of local administration. Thus, in Wessex the ancient food rents that made up the farm of one night had been reorganized, probably in the early eleventh century, to provide resources more efficiently for the crown in parallel with the system of local government.[2]

The vill

The community of the vill was the focus of the Domesday inquest and of most of the reports that the commissioners compiled from the presentments thereof. It is not surprising, then, that communal dues relating to it were widely recorded. We know from ICC that the assessment of each vill was enrolled and it might be suspected from those quotas that are found in GDB that hundred assessments were also determined in the *inquisitio geldi*.[3] Such information, however, was of less relevance to the evolving schema of Domesday Book and much of the data was omitted at the beginning of the enterprise; the villar assessments of ICC did not make it into GDB and elsewhere they are only found, exceptionally, in the account of Rutland and of the land attached to York.[4] Nevertheless, the scribes of LDB and GDB developed their programme slowly, and thus it is that communal obligations were not rigorously excluded at the beginning of their work. Some obligations of the community survive in LDB and the earliest folios of GDB, allowing some insight into communal organizations.

[2] P. A. Stafford, 'The "Farm of One Night" and the Organisation of King Edward's Estates in Domesday', *EcHR*, 2nd series, 33 (1980), 491–502; R. Lavelle, 'The "Farm of One Night" and the Organization of Estates in Late Anglo-Saxon Wessex', *Haskins Society Journal*, 14 (2005 for 2003), 54–82.
[3] According to the Anglo-Saxon Chronicle, William 'sent his men over all England into every shire and had them find out how many hundred hides there were in the shire …' (*ASC*, 161).
[4] GDB, 292v, 298–298v: *DB Rutland*, R1–3; *DB Yorks*, C22–35.

Such obligations have long been recognized in the Norfolk and Suffolk folios. As is normal throughout Domesday Book, each holding is given a rating to the geld in carucates or acres. In some there is recorded after the valuation clause a further statement of the burden of taxation in terms of the number of pence due when the hundred paid one pound. As we have seen,[5] the distribution of this type of entry indicates that the information came from the geographically arranged predecessor of LDB and was a statement of the liability of the whole vill as opposed to the holding to which it is attached in the surviving text. It has been widely supposed that the system was unique to East Anglia, and indeed there is nothing comparable in Domesday Book.[6] But there is a parallel if it is seen as the method of *payment* that it was rather than an assessment. Norfolk and Suffolk vills owing a combined total of one pound to the geld were organized into leets, and these units were similar in function to the twelve-carucate hundreds of the Northern Danelaw. They too consisted of a number of vills and were known in the later Middle Ages as *ville integre*. There survives nothing comparable to Abbot Samson's Kalendar to demonstrate how the geld was collected in the North, but it is perhaps significant that an attempt to reduce the assessment of Kesteven in 1194 was couched in terms of the sum levied on each carucate or hundred. The twelve-carucate hundred may well have functioned in the same way as the leet.[7] If so, all reference to its functioning was edited out of GDB.

The same was not true of the item of information that follows the LDB record of contribution to the geld. A measurement of land is consistently noted in the Norfolk and Suffolk folios in the same clause. The association has led some writers to assume that the data have something to do with the geld.[8] In reality, it seems to be yet another item of communal data that was tacked onto the end of the geographically arranged predecessor of LDB. There are numerous statements that 'other fees are here', and 'it is measured in another fee', and the like and it seems clear that the dimensions are those of the vill. The function of the data is far from clear. Welldon Finn has suggested that the measurements refer to pasture land or common, but such commodities are often recorded alongside the data and it does seem as if the figures are intended to be inclusive.[9] C. R. Hart has argued that the

[5] Above, p.90.
[6] For the basic discussion of the institution, see D. C. Douglas, *The Social Structure of Medieval East Anglia* (Oxford, 1927), 55–8, 191–2, 213–14; R. Welldon Finn, *Domesday Studies: The Eastern Counties* (London, 1967), 105–21.
[7] *The Great Roll of the Pipe for the Sixth Year of the Reign of King Richard the First, Michaelmas 1194*, ed. D. M. Stenton, Pipe Roll Society, 43 (1928), 118; D. R. Roffe, 'The Lincolnshire Hundred', *Landscape History*, 3 (1981), 35.
[8] B. A. Lees, 'Introduction to the Suffolk Domesday', *VCH Suffolk*, ed. W. Page (London, 1911), i, 363–8. Ial in Wales has dimensions of 5 by 1½ leagues instead of an assessment to the geld, but, of course, the manor had never been hidated (GDB, 254: *DB Salop*, 4,2,1).
[9] Welldon Finn (*Domesday Studies: Eastern Counties*, 58–9). He ultimately believed that the problem was insoluble.

data are a measure of arable and as such they are the East Anglian equivalent of ploughlands.[10] This conclusion, however, is not easily reconciled with the independent record of East Anglian ploughlands in the Ely summaries.

It is, moreover, at odds with the northern evidence, where carucates to the geld, ploughlands, and dimensions are juxtaposed. In GDB measurements of the kind are regularly found only in the Yorkshire folios. There they are first encountered in the account of the 84 carucates of York where they are explicitly the dimensions of vills. Osbaldwick and Murton were assessed at 6 and 4 carucates respectively, with land for 3 and 2 ploughs, and 'these two vills are 1 league broad and 1 long'.[11] Thereafter the measurements are often said to refer to the manor. In some cases this, the referent is unambiguous, but the figures are associated with those manors that were enrolled as a whole in the Yorkshire Summary. The distribution of the remainder is difficult to assess since, due to the summary form of some Yorkshire entries, many figures are seemingly omitted. Nevertheless, there are indications that the remainder are associated with groups of estates within vills. Further investigation is called for. After Yorkshire the information is recorded sporadically. It is found in Lincolnshire, Nottinghamshire, Derbyshire, Shropshire, and Cheshire, and in the IE account of Huntingdonshire (although not in the corresponding passages in GDB). It would therefore appear that the data had been more widely collected but that a conscious choice was made to omit them from the GDB text.

Throughout the units used are furlongs and leagues. These units are also used to measure woodland and, in a few instances in Circuit VI, arable, and there is therefore little reason not to take them at face value: they are measures of area. There seems little prospect of taking the matter of dimensions further. With a greater body of evidence surviving, the leet may be another matter. What communal functions its constituent vills had is not immediately clear. They must have assumed many of the responsibilities of the vill elsewhere in the country as a forum for its inhabitants. The leet itself, however, formed the unit of local government charged with wider communal affairs.[12] Besides the geld, it was responsible for policing and relationships with other communities. It was the leet that managed communal assets like pasture and fen and represented the interests of its constituent vills when they were challenged or compromised. It is, then, of considerable interest as a unit of communal organization (as opposed to territorial: it was not always constituted as a discrete territory), and two attempts have been made to reconstruct

[10] C. R. Hart, *The Danelaw* (London, 1992), 97–103. For a restatement of the case, see M. Hesse, 'Domesday Land Measures in Suffolk', *Landscape History*, 22 (2002), 21–36.
[11] GDB, 298: *DB Yorks*, C23.
[12] Douglas, *Social Structure of Medieval East Anglia*, 191–201. It will be noted that the leet was independent of the manor. Thus, in Marshland, for example, a sharp distinction was drawn between the courts of the leet and the manor (*ibid.*, 199).

the network.[13] Neither, however, would claim to be definitive. In some hundreds villar contributions to the geld can be arranged in neat fractions of a pound. In Walsham Hundred in Norfolk, for example, there were five groups of vills which each paid four shillings when the hundred owed one pound in geld (Table 8.1). But in most hundreds such patterns are not apparent. The data are incomplete and/or incorrect and it is usually not apparent which vills should go with which. Domesday only mentions leets in passing: there are said to be fourteen leets in the hundred of South Greenhoe (fol. 119v) and ten in the hundred and a half of Clackclose (fol. 212v) in Norfolk.[14] Even later evidence does not help. The structure of the leets of Thedwestrey, Thingoe, and Blackbourn Hundreds in Suffolk is evidenced in the Abbot Samson's Kalendar, but by and large the Domesday evidence has not been reconciled with it.[15]

It is possible that leets were formed and reformed as circumstances demanded. The twelfth-century discontinuity in Suffolk is paralleled by a pre-Conquest discontinuity in Norfolk. The earliest reference to leets is probably to be found in a Bury St Edmunds estate memorandum of 1045×1065 in which seven 'hundreds' are named; they were all in the north-west of Norfolk, but again are unrecognisable in Domesday.[16] However, it is more likely that by 1086 exemption and partial exemption from the geld had dislocated a consistent relationship between the leet and hundred on the one hand and assessment and geld payments on the other. The functionally similar twelve-carucate hundred of the Northern Danelaw was, at least in some areas, stable over a period of at least two hundred years, and its characteristics suggest a way forward.

Reconstructing this network encounters problems not unlike those experienced in East Anglia. As we have seen, Rutland is explicitly said to have been divided into three hundreds in two wapentakes; the three groups of twelve carucates can be reconstructed by adding up the assessments of consecutive entries. The four

[13] Lees, 'Introduction to the Suffolk Domesday', 412–16; C. Johnson, 'Introduction to the Norfolk Domesday', *VCH Norfolk*, ii, ed. W. Page (London, 1906), 5–9.

[14] LDB, 119v, 212v: *DB Norfolk*, 1,71.15,1.

[15] *The Kalendar of Abbot Samson of Bury St Edmunds and Related Documents*, ed. R. H. C. Davis, Camden Society, 3rd series, 84 (1954), esp. at xv–xxx. P. Warner, *The Origins of Suffolk* (Manchester, 1996), 159–65, has suggested that the structure of leets in Suffolk is represented by the *ville integre* of the fourteenth century. It is, however, too easy to assume basic continuity. Elsewhere the twelfth and thirteenth centuries saw considerable change in these types of structure. The Domesday hundreds of the East Riding of Yorkshire, for example, were tidied up to form the later medieval wapentakes, while in Leicestershire the *ville integre* are not easily reconciled with early twelfth-century hundreds. See D. R. Roffe, 'The Yorkshire Summary: A Domesday Satellite', *Northern History*, 27 (1991), 242–60; C. F. Slade, *The Leicestershire Survey c.A.D. 1130*, Department of English Local History, University of Leicester, Occasional Papers, 7 (Leicester, 1956).

[16] D. C. Douglas, 'Fragments of an Anglo-Saxon Survey from Bury St Edmunds', *EHR*, 43 (1928), 376–83.

Table 8.1 *Geld payments and leets in Walsham Hundred, Norfolk*

Folio	Vill	Payments			
		s	d	s	d
216	Woodbastwick	1	4		
129	Panxworth and Ranworth	1	4	4	0
129	Hemblington	1	4		
128	South Walsham	4	0	4	0
129	Upton	2	0		
128v	Acle	2	0	4	0
129	Fishley		10		
194v	Beighton	1	0		
129v	Moulton St Mary	1	3½	4	0
129v	Wickhampton		10½		
239v	Tunstall		8		
128v	Halvergate	2	0	4	0
224	Reedham	1	4		

hundreds of Axholme in Lincolnshire, held in their entirety by Geoffrey de la Guerche, can be identified in the same way.[17] Elsewhere it is a matter of manipulating assessments. Many hundreds are named, with some idea given of their extent, and so guesswork is minimized. Others suggest themselves by peculiarities in entries. Two hundreds in Nottinghamshire can be identified by the unique equation of the ploughlands of their constituent vills with the carucates assessed upon them (Table 8.2). In some wapentakes, like Elloe (Table 3.2), the whole system can be reconstructed, but elsewhere ragged edges remain. Two carucates of land in Pickworth are said not to be enumerated in any hundred, 'nor have they [their] like in Lincolnshire',[18] but, again, our evidence is not complete enough to reconstruct the system completely. Much more is known about it, however, than about the network of leets, and one significant characteristic is clear: royal lands stood outside the network of twelve-carucate hundreds.[19]

If this is a characteristic of East Anglia, then the leet might begin to make more sense when royal land is placed on one side. No explicit evidence is likely to be found in corroboration, but the structure of vills in the later Middle Ages may

---

[17] Above, pp. 91–2.

[18] GDB, 357v: *DB Lincs*, 26,53.

[19] D. R. Roffe, 'Hundreds and Wapentakes', *The Lincolnshire Domesday*, eds A. Williams and G. H. Martin (London, 1992), 32–42. The geld quotas of the Lindsey Survey weigh in at 50 hundreds per riding, but *terra regis* is not included in the system; the assessment of Kesteven is another 150 hundreds, including the 12½ of Stamford, again excluding the lands of the king.

Table 8.2 *Twelve-carucate hundreds in Nottinghamshire*

Ref.	Vill	c	b	p	o	Ref.	Vill	c	b	p	o
10,63	Newthorpe	0	2	0	2	10,66	Bulwell	2	0	2	0
10,43	Watnall	1	0	1	0	*1,45*	*Arnold*	*3*	*0*	*3*	*0*
10,47	Kimberley	1	0	1	0	10,51	Basford	2	3	2	3
10,40	Nuthall	0	4½	0	4½	10,52	Basford	0	1		
30,32	Nuthall	0	3½	0	3½	30,34	Basford	0	4	0	4
10,36	Cossall	0	6	0	6	10,15	Radford	3	0	3	0
13,12	Cossall	0	6	0	6	*1,48*	*Lenton*	*0*	*4*		
10,27	Strelley	0	6	0	6	10,19	Lenton	2	0	2	0
10,28	Strelley	0	3			10,24	Lenton	0	4	0	4
30,31	Strelley	0	3	0	3	10,17	Morton	1	4	1	4
1,50	*Bilborough*	*0*	*1*	*0*	*1*	B1	*Nottingham*	6	0		
10,39	Bilborough	0	7	0	7						
1,49	*Broxtow*	*0*	*1*								
28,3	Broxtow	0	3	0	3						
29,2	Trowell	1	4	1	4						
30,30	Trowell	0	4	0	4						
30,50	Trowell	0	4	0	4						
30,51	Trowell	0	4	0	4						
1,47	*Wollaton*	*1*	*0*	*1*	*0*						
10,35	Wollaton	1	4	1	4						
Total		**12**	**0**	**11**	**3**			**12**	**0**	**11**	**5**

c = carucate, b = bovate, p = plough, o = oxen. The king's lands (italicized) were non-geldable.

be suggestive. In Derbyshire royal estates in divided settlements were constituted as separate vills in the fourteenth century.[20] The constitution of the vills in the Norfolk and Suffolk Nomina Villarum returns of 1316 may well repay closer study for such clues to earlier structures.

In Cambridgeshire, of course, the vills of the county are identified in ICC.[21] Elsewhere we are left juggling geld assessments. As we have seen,[22] there is a considerable body of evidence to demonstrate a five-hide unit (perhaps grouped in twos) throughout much of the country, but where vills are assessed at more or less there are few indications as to how they should be combined. Unlike in

[20] D. R. Roffe, 'The Origins of Derbyshire', *Derbyshire Archaeological Journal*, 106 (1986), 106. Kilburn, Chellaston, Normanton, Swarkestone, Osmaston, Over Haddon, and Hope and Shatton were each divided between the king and Henry de Ferrers and were each constituted as two vills by the time of the Lay Subsidy of 1334 (*The Lay Subsidy of 1334*, ed. R. E. Glasscock, British Academy (London, 1975), 43, 44, 47).
[21] For an analysis, see C. R. Hart, 'The Hidation of Huntingdonshire', *Proceedings of the Cambridge Antiquarian Society*, 61 (1968), 55–66.
[22] Above, p. 192.

Lincolnshire, the evidence of the vill is not explicitly noticed in the text. For many counties something of the pattern has been plausibly reconstructed,[23] for others it has remained elusive. In Essex, for example, no system at all has been identified, and it might be doubted that the five-hide unit ever existed there.[24] Whether exemption of royal demesne would make sense of the pattern remains to be determined. In the South West 'ancient demesne' of the crown, like the *terra regis* of the North, certainly did not pay geld,[25] but here again there has been no recent detailed study of the patterns of hidation.

On the fringes other systems of communal organization can be dimly perceived. In Wales, not surprisingly, a Welsh organization of communities in groups of vills held by reeves is apparent.[26] Similar structures obtained in Ribble and Mersey and Lancashire, and can be dimly perceived in the High Peak of Derbyshire.[27] They all speak of more ancient arrangements than the geld-related vills of lowland England. They are discussed in detail in the next chapter.

The hundred

Leet, twelve-carucate hundred, and five-hide vill all organized free men in communal activities at the lowest level of local government. There were other duties to discharge in the hundred or wapentake and shire. These are rarely explicit in Domesday Book. An exception is the account of the hundred manor of Taunton:

> These customs belong to Taunton: borough-right; thieves; breach of the peace; house-breaking; hundred pence and St Peter's pence; church-scot; thrice in the year the bishop's pleas to be held without summons; setting out on service with the bishop's men.
>
> These lands render the said customs at Taunton: Tolland, Oake, Holford, and Upper Cheddon and Cheddon Fitzpaine, Maidenbrook, Ford, Hillfarrance and Hele, Nynehead, Norton Fitzwarren, Bradford-on-Tone,

---

[23] Some account will be found in the relevant *VCH* volume for each county, and likewise in F. R. Thorn's 'Hundreds and Wapentakes' sections of the Alecto County Edition of the Domesday Book. See also, for Buckinghamshire: K. Bailey, 'The Hidation of Buckinghamshire: Part 1, Domesday', *Records of Buckinghamshire*, 32 (1990), 1–34; K. A. Bailey, 'The Hidation of Buckinghamshire: Part 2, Before Domesday', *Records of Buckinghamshire*, 34 (1992), 87–96. Middlesex: K. A. Bailey, 'The Hidation of Middlesex', *Transactions of the London and Middlesex Archaeological Society*, 39 (1988), 165–86; S. Doree, *Domesday Book and the Origins of Edmonton Hundred* (Enfield, 1986).
[24] J. H. Round, 'Introduction to the Essex Domesday', *VCH Essex*, i, ed. H. A. Doubleday (London, 1903), 333–4.
[25] R. R. Darlington, 'Wiltshire Geld Rolls', *VCH Wiltshire*, ii, eds R. B. Pugh and E. Crittall (Oxford, 1955), 176–7.
[26] GDB, 162: *DB Gloucs*, W and notes.
[27] D. R. Roffe, 'Place-Naming in Domesday Book: Settlements, Estates, and Communities', *Nomina*, 14 (1990–91), 47–60.

Halse and Heathfield, Shopnoller, and Stoke St Mary. These 2 estates do not owe military service. Those of West Bagborough owe the same customs except military service and burial.[28]

Here the dues are explicit because laymen held manors within the ecclesiastical hundred. Apart from burial, church-scot, and St Peter's pence (specifically ecclesiastical dues), they are, however, probably more or less typical of the sorts of obligation that obtained throughout England.

The jurisdiction of Taunton Hundred, outlined in more detail in an English document from early in the reign of King William,[29] may in part reflect the liberties of the church of Winchester that held the hundred. But they are not out of line with what were considered to be the king's pleas in the Laws of Cnut.[30] Here and there Domesday notes one or other of them as appurtenant to various hundreds (albeit in private hands), and it therefore seems clear that the Taunton list is fairly representative. Although relatively minor, these pleas could be lucrative to the king or lord of the hundred. Much of the not inconsiderable value of the king's manors in Oxfordshire, for example, seems to have been derived from the hundredal jurisdictions attached to them.[31]

Hundred pennies were much discussed in the 1920s. Demarest believed they were identical with all sorts of customs mentioned in Domesday Book and were vestiges of the obligation of all free men to contribute to the king's farm.[32] Stephenson countered that they were merely a hundredal impost.[33] He was clearly right. Later evidence shows that in Taunton the hundred penny was a poll tax of one penny on every male over the age of twelve. The incident is widely found in the thirteenth-century hundred rolls, but elsewhere it was commuted for a lump sum. There seems no doubt that it was the fine paid in the view of frankpledge for the maintenance of tithings. Demarest identified three instances of rents or customs that were paid to the hundred as hundred pennies, but none is specific and one she misread.[34]

Hundred courts were notionally royal and the profits of many still accrued to the king in 1086. However, from at least the late tenth century hundredal jurisdiction had been granted out, notably to religious houses, just like any other due. The bishop of Winchester's hundred of Taunton is paralleled in just about every

[28] GDB, 87v: *DB Somerset*, 2,2–3.
[29] H. P. R. Finberg, *The Early Charters of Wessex* (Leicester, 1964), no. 544.
[30] Robertson, II Cnut.
[31] GDB, 154v: *DB Oxon*, 1,1–12.
[32] E. B. Demarest, 'The Hundred-Pennies', *EHR*, 33 (1918), 62–72; E. B. Demarest, 'Consuetudo Regis in Essex, Norfolk, and Suffolk', *EHR*, 42 (1927), 161–79.
[33] C. Stephenson, 'The Firma Unius Noctis and the Customs of the Hundred', *EHR*, 39 (1924), 161–74.
[34] LDB, 277v: *DB Norfolk*, 66,81. It was Roger Bigod who rendered the rent in the hundred since he held the free man in question on behalf of the king.

county south of the Welland. In Worcestershire seven of the twelve hundreds had been alienated in this way and the sheriff complained that in consequence he could not meet his farm.[35] In East Anglia lands in the hundred are sometimes said to be in the soke of the hundred manor or of the lord of the hundred. Archbishop Stigand had soke over land and men in Mintlyn, Islington, Middleton, Lynn, West Winch, Wiggenhall, East Winch, West Walton, Gayton Thorpe, Gayton, and Lynn.[36] Nevertheless, he did not hold the land itself – it was in the hands of other holders and did not pass to Bishop Odo of Bayeux, Stigand's successor – and it therefore seems likely that the soke was hundredal jurisdiction pertaining to his hundred manor of Snettisham.[37]

The due, of course, usually entailed a more substantial bond than that of mere jurisdiction: soke embodied exclusive title to 'land', that is dues over land.[38] In the Northern Danelaw, though, 'forinsec soke' of the Snettisham kind (soke over land which is held by another lord) may commonly refer to a similar relationship. As far as can be seen, wapentakes were generally in the king's hands in 1086. Well Wapentake in Lincolnshire and the adjacent Newark Wapentake in Nottingham-shire belonged to the church of Lincoln,[39] but otherwise no other interests are apparent. The fact probably reflects the absence of major ecclesiastical founda-tions in the area. But persistent rights to soke, but not land, held by both clerics and laymen, may often indicate *ad hoc* grants of wapentake jurisdiction. Forinsec soke is usually absent from later records, but significantly that which belonged to Kimbolton in Huntingdonshire in 1086 was represented by a view of frankpledge in the late thirteenth century.[40] In some instances, by contrast, a tenurial nexus may be a more appropriate explanation of the relationship. A concerted study of the type is needed.

A related problem is that of king's sokemen who rendered 'soke in the hundred'. A few are scattered about in the East Midlands,[41] but the highest concentrations are found in East Anglia where, as free men, they are glossed as those who did not

---

[35] GDB, 172: *DB Worcs*, C3.

[36] LDB, 197v, 207, 222, 238, 251v, 274v, 276, 277, 278v: *DB Norfolk*, 8,48.9,6–7.10,50.13,1 3.19,6.23,10.31,32.34,1.

[37] LDB, 142v: *DB Norfolk*, 2,4.

[38] Above, pp. 151–5.

[39] GDB, 283v, 376: *DB Lincs*, Cw9–11; *DB Notts*, 6,1.

[40] GDB, 205v: *DB Hunts*, 13,1–5; D. R. Roffe, 'An Introduction to the Huntingdonshire Domesday', *The Huntingdonshire Domesday*, eds A. Williams and R. W. H. Erskine (London, 1989), 13.

[41] It is widely assumed that all sokemen were the king's before the Conquest. See, for example, R. P. Abels, 'An Introduction to the Hertfordshire Domesday', *The Hertfordshire Domesday*, eds A. Williams and R. W. H. Erskine (London, 1991), 16–17. However, this assumes a unitary concept of pre-Conquest lordship that cannot be sustained. All free men and sokemen were in some sense 'manorialized' in that soke dues were rendered to a hall, be it the king's or another lord's. See above, p. 220–1.

belong to any farm.[42] This terminology, however, is probably misleading. Most had been snapped up by various lords by 1086 – hence the reference to farms – but before the Conquest their dues accrued to the king. The hundred manor was almost certainly the nexus. We read in the Cambridgeshire folios '5 hides of this land [in Chippenham] were in King Edward's farm, and 2 sokemen had 2 hides from the king and could give their land to whom they would, and yet each one provided 18s 8d or 1 horse in the king's service, and paid their forfeitures in Fordham'.[43] Elsewhere cartage, watch and ward, and escort duties were also demanded by the sheriff, or sums of money taken in lieu. These were dues that differed little from those of free men, sokemen, and probably radmen who belonged to manors. King's sokemen and the like indubitably owed suit to the hundred court, but their soke has something of a tenurial aspect to it. Nevertheless, it would be a mistake to see their lands as vestiges of ancient estates. Unless there is evidence to the contrary, we must assume that the association with both the hundred and the hundred manor is no earlier than the origins of the hundredal system.

Finally, military service. As we have already seen, king's thegns were personally summoned to the host. Other free men acquitted their obligations in the hundred. Thus, in the Huntingdonshire folios we read: 'The men of the shire bear witness that King Edward gave Swineshead [Beds] to Earl Siward [with] sake and soke, and so Earl Harold had it, except that [the men] paid geld in the hundred, and went against the enemy with them.'[44] Not all of the men fought. In Berkshire one man was sent from every five hides and 'for his sustenance or pay 4s for 2 months was given him from each hide'.[45] As in Chippenham in Cambridgeshire, various items of equipment might be supplied.[46] The burden varied from area to area. Not surprisingly, it was heavier in the Welsh Marches than in central England. Throughout, however, the burden was apparently distributed by the geld.

Some animal renders may also be hundredal. Manors in North Bradon, Ashill, Donyatt, South Bradon, and Hatch Beauchamp each rendered a sheep and a lamb to Curry Rivel in Somerset, and Bickenhall rendered five sheep and five lambs along with a bloom of iron from each free man.[47] Similar renders were made to South Petherton, Williton and Cannington, Dulverton, Crewkerne, and Carhampton, also in Somerset,[48] while oxen were rendered to South Tawton in

---

[42] LDB, 272, 446: *DB Norfolk*, 64,1; *DB Suffolk*, 74,4.

[43] GDB, 197: *DB Cambs*, 22,6.

[44] GDB, 208: *DB Hunts*, D14.

[45] GDB, 56v: *DB Berks*, B10.

[46] GDB, 197: *DB Cambs*, 22,6: '2 sokemen had 2 hides from the king and could give their land to whom they would, and yet each one provided 18s 8d or 1 horse in the king's service, and paid their forfeitures in Fordham'.

[47] GDB, 92: *DB Somerset*, 19,17;18;23–25;27; 29.

[48] GDB, 86, 96v, 87v, 96v: *DB Somerset*, 1,4.3,1.

Devon.[49] Demarest considered these renders were made in respect of the farm of one night. All, however, were paid by non-royal manors, and at least one was apparently a post-Conquest custom: 'From Alvred's manor of Monksilver has been added to this manor a customary due, that is, 18 sheep a year. TRE this did not belong to Williton.'[50] Stephenson suggested that the renders are better understood as pasture dues paid in the hundred.[51] Other renders in cash are impossible to categorize. For example, thirty-four free men in various places rendered customs to Witham in Essex.[52] The obligation would appear to devolve upon soke of some kind, but the value of their lands belonged to various tenants-in-chief

Of the workings of the hundred, the most remarkable survivals are the geld accounts preserved in Exon. Three, A, B, and C, survive for Wiltshire, and one each for the counties of Cornwall, Devon, Dorset, and Somerset. They are arranged by hundred, but vary in formula, form, and the detail of content. Nevertheless, each generally notes the total number of hides in every hundred, those held in demesne by the king and his barons, which were apparently exempt, the amounts for which geld was owing or had not been paid at the time of the inquest, and the sums received and for how many hides.[53] Galbraith and Harvey associate them with a re-assessment to the geld,[54] but the accounts clearly relate to the payment and collection of the geld. Thus, the thegns of Walter de Douai gave evidence that a holding belonged to the hundred of Bempstone; Lambert of Wheathill was adjudged to be quit for a hide by the testimony of the collectors; lands of the Count of Mortain in Cornwall had always been exempt from the geld according to the testimony of the hundredmen.[55] There are numerous other references of a similar kind, but little to suggest a reassessment.

Eyton, who first studied the geld accounts in detail, believed that they referred to the geld of 6s per hide which was levied in 1084.[56] This remains possible (although an unrecorded geld in 1085 is equally likely).[57] There seems no doubt, however, that the existing records relate to an audit of 1086. The process that produced them was clearly ongoing. Of the three accounts of Wiltshire, C appears to be earlier than A and B, for it records sums which were outstanding that had been discharged

[49] GDB, 116v, 117v: *DB Devon*, 43,1.51,2.
[50] GDB, 86v: *DB Somerset*, 1,6.
[51] Stephenson, 'The Firma Unius Noctis and the Customs of the Hundred', 168.
[52] LDB, 2: *DB Essex*, 1,2.
[53] R. Welldon Finn, *Domesday Studies: The Liber Exoniensis* (London, 1964), 98.
[54] V. H. Galbraith, *The Making of Domesday Book* (Oxford, 1961), 87–101, especially at 92; S. P. J. Harvey, 'Domesday Book and its Predecessors', *EHR*, 86 (1971), 768–9.
[55] Exon, 77v, 81v, 72, 72v, 68v.
[56] R. W. Eyton, *Domesday Studies: An Analysis and Digest of the Somerset Survey and of the Somerset Gheld Inquest of AD 1084*, 2 vols (London, 1880), 87–93; R. W. Eyton, *A Key to Domesday: The Dorset Survey* (Dorchester, 1878), 4–5, 109.
[57] For which, see Galbraith, *The Making of Domesday Book*, 87–101.

in the other two.[58] All drew on earlier sources from which they were abstracted, but there is material that is perceptibly later than 1084. Although produced in and for the Domesday inquest, the geld accounts are probably typical of the routine documentation produced in the hundred. Indeed, they bear a remarkable similarity to the so-called Northampton Geld Roll which dates from the 1070s.

Not much of these summary records found its way into Domesday Book. But, as we have seen,[59] the individual geld assessments of the sources from which they were compiled inform every entry. Perhaps the closest document in the Domesday corpus to these sources is the Yorkshire Summary.[60] Demonstrably earlier than the Yorkshire folios of GDB, it reproduces the geographical form of the 84 carucates attached to York at the very beginning, and in the same section notes TRE tenants, as in the comparable summary lists of lands in Amounderness and Craven.[61] Thereafter, it is more limited in scope. Nevertheless, it seems likely that it was the source of the assessments of the Yorkshire text. Thus, for example, the order of entries in the GDB account of the inland of North Allerton is derived from an interlineation (probably carried over from its exemplar) in the Yorkshire Summary.[62] As the formal archetype of the GDB text, the Summary may have been abstracted from its exemplar to guide the compiler in the composition of the Yorkshire folios. But in its essentials it probably represents the business of the geld inquest in Yorkshire.

Ultimately, the hundredal rubrics of Domesday Book must come from similar sources.[63] In LDB they are assiduously recorded, with few gaps. The GDB scribe, by contrast, was more cavalier. He transcribed many in the Yorkshire folios, although by no means all of them. In Lincolnshire the record is much more haphazard. Only in chapters 3, 12, 30, and 31 are wapentakes consistently noted, and then merely from the point at which lands in Kesteven are described. All these rubrics are probably postscriptal; indeed, in chapter 12 it can be seen that they have been squeezed into whatever spaces (end of line, blank line, in between lines, or, if all else failed, the margin) were available.[64] Thereafter in Circuit VI, wapentakes are indicated only erratically. Circuit III, I, and V hundreds are more regularly noticed, while they are absent in Circuit II, and much of Circuit IV. The distribution more

[58] Darlington, 'Wiltshire Geld Rolls', 171–2.

[59] Above, p. 85.

[60] GDB, 379–82: *DB Yorks*, SW–SE; Roffe, 'The Yorkshire Summary', 242–60.

[61] GDB, 301v–302, 332: *DB Yorks*, 1L.30W.

[62] GDB, 299, 381: *DB Yorks*, 1Y2;SN,A1.

[63] Name forms of hundreds in Domesday Book are sometimes different from those of the places from which they derive their name. In the Lincolnshire folios, for example, the hundred rubric *Hag* (Hough on the Hill) is followed by the description of a manor in *Hache* (Hough on the Hill) (GDB, 347v: *DB Lincs*, 12,43). A different source for the two forms seems likely. There has been no systematic comparison of such pairs of names.

[64] D. R. Roffe, 'Hundreds and Wapentakes', *The Lincolnshire Domesday*, eds A. Williams and G. H. Martin (London, 1992), 34.

or less reflects the sources that the scribe drew upon. Only in Circuit VI, where those sources were geographically arranged as in ICC, did he experience uncertainty as to what was appropriate. Thus it is that there the vill (in the guise of the twelve-carucate hundred) is named in rubrics. The fact is further evidence of the experimental nature of the Circuit VI folios.

The hundred rubrics are the starting point for any reconstruction of the hundredal system. However, it must be borne in mind that not all are correctly placed in the text. This can be a boon: an error in the Lincolnshire folios that is perpetuated in the Crowland Domesday provides the decisive evidence that elements of both are derived from a geographically arranged precursor.[65] It is usually not, but even then, hundreds, and subdivisions thereof, sometimes identify themselves by the grouping of vills in the text. Freebridge Hundred and a Half in Norfolk is undifferentiated in the text, but the constituent vills occur in two distinct sequences (Table 2.5). The first starts with Lynn and proceeds clockwise from east to west through Marshland (Walsoken, and Walpole cannot be placed since they occur only once). The second begins with Middleton and, by contrast, proceeds anticlockwise north and east. The two sequences seem to correspond to the half hundred and the hundred respectively. In Amounderness a similar change in direction in the sequence of entries defines two divisions of the district north and south of the River Calder, while likewise the order of places in West Derby Hundred describes two discrete areas.[66] But such patterns are fortuitous and, as we have seen,[67] where they are absent, the Domesday rubrics have to be supplemented by later sources.

Here and there hundreds acted together for certain purposes. Groups of three are found in Oxfordshire (Dorchester, Thame and Banbury) and Norfolk (East Flegg, West Flegg, and Happing),[68] while Pershore and Oswaldslow in Worcestershire were triple hundreds.[69] The last is called a 'ship soke' in a near contemporary source,[70] that is an area or estate liable to provide a ship for the king's fleet.[71] Larger groupings are also found. Yorkshire was divided into ridings, that is thirds, as was Lindsey. In both counties riding juries provided evidence, but otherwise

---

[65] D. R. Roffe, 'The Historia Croylandensis: A Plea for Reassessment', *EHR*, 110 (1995), 100.

[66] C. P. Lewis, 'An Introduction to the Lancashire Domesday', *The Lancashire Domesday*, eds A. Williams and R. W. H. Erskine (London, 1991), 25–7.

[67] Above, p.185.

[68] GDB, 155; LDB, 118: *DB Oxon*, 6,1–4; *DB Norfolk*, 1,67.

[69] GDB, 172v, 175v: *DB Worcs*, 2,1.9,7.

[70] *Hemingi Chartularium*, i, 77–8.

[71] For the suggestion that the ship soke was assessed on the holding, see P. Taylor, 'The Endowment and Military Obligations of the See of London: A Reassessment of Three Sources', *ANS*, 14 (1991), 300.

their function is unknown.[72] Lathes are found in Kent, four of which provided evidence on the customs of eastern Kent.[73] The Rapes of Sussex were castleries, but it is possible that they had pre-Conquest antecedents.[74] They remain largely mysterious. Riding-like divisions of north Nottinghamshire called Hatfield and the Clay are only noticed in the later Middle Ages, but the grouping of their vills together in the Nottinghamshire folios betrays their existence in 1086.[75] Likewise, two divisions of Buckinghamshire of nine hundreds and three ship sokes each are defined by hundredal sequences, the southern one being centred on Aylesbury to which numerous sokemen owed suit,[76] and there were probably four ferdings in Gloucestershire.[77] Elsewhere, hundreds might meet together for certain purposes on an *ad hoc* basis, but there was generally no regular forum of communal activity between the hundred and the shire.[78]

The shire

Entered 'above the line' with the account of the boroughs, the shire customs are only sporadically recorded (Table 4.2). Nevertheless, it is clear from them just how central the shire was to English society both before and after the Conquest. The shire, of course, was a node in local government, a link between the king and court and local communities. Here the free men of the shire paid suit and, no doubt, executed much of the king's business, just as the knights of the shire were to do in the later Middle Ages, under the supervision of the king's representative, the sheriff. Here also presided the earl through whom regional defence was coordinated. But the shire was more than that. It was, no less, the forum in which the personal duties inherent in bookright and then barony were discharged towards the king.

Of the duties of bookright, bridge repair and fortification were in this respect the most obviously local. In Cheshire one man was called up from each hide for

---

[72] There were riding courts in the later Middle Ages, but little is known of them except the fact that they met and where they did so.

[73] GDB, 1–1v: *DB Kent*, D11–25. For a balanced discussion of the origins of the lathes, see R. Eales, 'An Introduction to the Kent Domesday', *The Kent Domesday*, eds A. Williams and G. H. Martin (London, 1992), 11–14.

[74] See F. R. Thorn, 'Hundreds and Wapentakes', *The Sussex Domesday*, eds A. Williams and R. W. H. Erskine (London, 1990), 29–33, for the most recent discussion, along with a bibliography of the various arguments.

[75] M. S. Parker, 'The Province of Hatfield', *Northern History*, 28 (1992), 42–69.

[76] J. Bradbury, 'Introduction to the Buckinghamshire Domesday', *The Buckinghamshire Domesday*, eds A. Williams and R. W. H. Erskine (London, 1988), 14.

[77] A. Williams, 'An Introduction to the Gloucestershire Domesday', *Domesday Book: Gloucestershire*, eds A. Williams and R. W. H. Erskine (London 1989), 13.

[78] The ferding of Winchcombe and the Parts of Kesteven and Holland in Lincolnshire were formerly separate 'proto-shires' which had been incorporated into the larger unit.

the work, but it was the lord who was fined by the sheriff for default.[79] Service in the host, however, also appears to have been a county matter, at least if the penalties for default are anything to go by. Sake and soke is recorded as a shire custom and the fact suggests that the forfeitures implied by the liberty were also local. Indeed, in Nottinghamshire the earl had a share as he did in many other shires.[80] More emphatically local were heriots and reliefs. Again in Nottinghamshire and in Yorkshire they were paid to the sheriff if the thegn had six manors or less but to the king if he had more.[81] The king's thegn was no bodyguard: the nighness to the king that bookland entailed appears to have usually been no closer than the county town and the personal summons that he received was evidently to accompany the earl.

Likewise, the tenant-in-chief also seems to have rendered his service in the shire. A writ directed to Abbot Æthelwig of Evesham (d.1077) ordered him 'to summon all who are under his authority (*ballia*) and jurisdiction to have as many warriors as they owe to the king ready in the king's presence at Clarendon at the Octave of Whitsun'. Æthelwig was also ordered to bring along the five knights that he himself owed.[82] The Evesham Chronicle identifies his *ballia* as Worcestershire, Gloucestershire, Oxfordshire, Shropshire, Staffordshire, Herefordshire, and Warwickshire, substantially the area of Mercian law.[83] If the writ is authentic, then it would appear that the feudal host was mustered through the apparatus of local government in the reign of William the Conqueror.[84] Certainly in the twelfth and thirteenth centuries writs of muster were always addressed to the sheriff.[85]

What later evidence there is for royal castle guard points in the same direction: the tenant-in-chief tended to render his service in the county in which the *caput* of his honour was situated.[86] All of this adds dimension to the most compelling evidence of all, namely the form of Domesday Book. In modern historiography it is a truism that it is a seigneurial survey. The reality, of course, is that the primary organizing principle of the work is the *shire*. Whether Domesday was a register of land, service, or geld, the implication is plain: whatever obligations the tenant-in-chief had towards the king were acquitted in the shire. Again, the principle is reflected in later records. In 1166, for example, tenants-in-chief made their returns,

---

[79] GDB, 262v: *DB Cheshire*, C21.

[80] GDB, 280v: *DB Notts*, S4: 'If a thegn having sake and soke forfeits his land, the king and earl between them have half his land and resources, and his lawful wife with his legitimate heirs, if there are any, have the other half.' Presumably, the king and earl divided the issues in the ratio of 2:1 as they did with other dues.

[81] GDB, 280v, 298v: *DB Notts*, S3; *DB Yorks*, C40.

[82] *Regesta*, ed. Bates, no. 131.

[83] *Chronicon Abbatiae de Evesham, ad Annum 1418*, ed. W. D. Macray, Rolls Series, 29 (1863), 89.

[84] R. R. Darlington, 'Aethelwig, Abbot of Evesham', *EHR*, 48 (1933), 10–14.

[85] *Regesta*, ed. Bates, no. 131.

[86] S. Painter, 'Castle Guard', *The American Historical Review*, 40 (1935), 450–9.

the *carte baronum*, of the number of knights they owed to the county in which their *caput* was situated. The honour certainly had an identity as a community, but it rendered its service through the apparatus of local government.

The king's thegns undoubtedly made suit to the shire court in 1066, and so, it would appear, did the tenants-in-chief or their representatives after the Conquest. Their appearance there in the first stage of the Domesday inquest, as attested by their numerous presentments, was evidently not exceptional. Collectively, their's, in part, must be the voice that Domesday Book laconically attributes to 'the men of the shire'.[87] The *barones* of the shire, to whom writs were addressed in the early twelfth century, included all tenants-in-chief no matter how great or small their fee.[88] The business of the court in normal session is only fleetingly evidenced in Domesday Book. A handful of shire verdicts hinge on whether the jurors had seen a royal writ for a certain transaction; whether these jurors were one and the same as the deliverers who conveyed the land is unclear.[89] The Domesday sessions were clearly exceptional and do not therefore necessarily attest normal procedure. Nevertheless, they are witness to the actions of all the communities of shire, of which the tenants-in-chief were one, most conspicuously in the processes of dispute resolution.

Disputes

For most historians it has been axiomatic that legal action to restore rightful tenure began with the Domesday inquest. In folio after folio juries pronounce on the rights and wrongs of rival claims and it seems clear that they were recognizing the right of the causes brought before them. It is an axiom, however, as has become increasingly clear in the last few years, that introduces impossible contradictions. Patrick Wormald has pointed out that the jurors sometimes availed themselves of the language of judgement – 'justly', 'ought to', 'attest to the use of', and the like – and found it impossible not to believe that they were involved in legal actions.[90] He was, then, frankly confused to find just how ramshackle the process was. Using his own criteria to distinguish 'judgements', he noticed that the distribution was far from even. By far the most are found in Circuit VI, while in Circuit IV there are none at all. Was the process demand-led? Or were some

---

[87] There were probably also suitors of lower status, for in Wiltshire reference is made to 'the thegns of the shire' (GDB, 69, 70v, 71: *DB Wilts*, 23,7.26,19.28,10). As in the Domesday inquest, half of the jurors may have been English and half French.

[88] R. Sharpe, 'The Emergence of the English County Town, c.950–1300', forthcoming.

[89] It should be noted that sight of writs is more often linked with verdicts of the hundred.

[90] P. Wormald, 'Domesday Lawsuits: A Provisional List and Preliminary Comments', *England in the Eleventh Century*, ed. C. Hicks, Harlaxton Medieval Studies, 2 (Stamford, 1992), 61–102.

commissioners more sympathetic than others? Was there more time in some areas than in others? Variations within circuits suggest that none of these explanations is entirely satisfactory. But the problem of uneven distribution pales into a mere oddity compared with the tangible effect of such judgements. Some were indeed implemented: the land was entered in the *breve* of the rightful tenant in Domesday Book. The majority, however, were still enjoyed by the aggressor and the later history of the fees shows that 'judgements' were usually never effected.

These are contradictions that are easily resolved. As we have seen,[91] the inquest was not concerned with judgements; it collected evidence for later action. The presentments of Domesday jurors may sometimes have been viewed as incontrovertible, since uncontested, and have led to the immediate transfer of land; but this was more a case of 'fair cop, guv' than a formal legal procedure. A prima facie case of gross infringement of the king's rights might likewise have led to the immediate seizure of an estate into the king's hands.[92] But these were exceptional circumstances. In their essence the jurors' presentments regarding the disputes of subjects are merely evidentiary. There seems little doubt that neither the king nor the commissioners were primarily concerned with title to land, and it was an issue that occupied the compilers of Domesday Book less and less as the work progressed.[93] In LDB the problem of disputes is met head-on by the assignment of a section of the text in each county, the *invasiones*, to lands that were the subject of rival claims (although not to the complete exclusion of such material from the body of the text). This was a format that was retained in the early folios of GDB: *clamores* sections are found in the Yorkshire, Lincolnshire, and Huntingdonshire folios.[94] Thereafter, disputes progressively commanded less of the GDB scribe's

---

[91] Above, pp. 64–7.

[92] Several passages indicate that the king took lands into his hands. In Exon, for example, it is recorded that the predecessor of the abbot of Tavistock had held the manor of Werrington in Devon 'and the abbot had been seized of it when King William sent his barons (*barones*) to inquire into the lands of England; his predecessor before him had been in possession of it. He was disseized by them because the English testified that it did not belong to the abbey on the day King Edward was alive and dead.' (Exon, 178v). In Herefordshire land in Yatton was said to have been thegnland TRE but that afterwards it was turned into reeveland, 'therefore the king's commissioners (*legati*) say that this land and the revenue issuing from it is being stealthily taken away from the king' (GDB, 181: *DB Hereford*, 1,75). In Essex Geoffrey de Mandeville had annexed land in Mashbury, but the king had recovered the estate and granted it to a certain Wulfric (LDB, 100: *DB Essex*, 90,20). Elsewhere reference is found to estates 'adjudged for the use of the king' without any indication of the agency responsible (GDB, 348c, 367b–c: *DB Lincs*, 12,84.57,14; LDB, 133a: *DB Norfolk*, 1,195; GDB, 158d: *DB Oxon*, 29,13). In all cases the land concerned appears in the king's *breve* in Domesday Book, and it is therefore clear that action had been ordered; when – before, during the inquest, or indeed after – is not always clear.

[93] *DIB*, 165–8.

[94] The absence of *clamores* for Nottinghamshire and Derbyshire is mysterious. The VIS formula (see appendix) suggests that both were written before the Huntingdonshire folios.

attention.[95] In Circuit II he made no attempt to incorporate the material from the *terre occupate* sections of Exon and by the time he reached the end of his task with the Leicestershire folios he omitted almost all reference to disputed title (Table 8.3).

Table 8.3 *The number of claims by county and circuit*
(after Wormald, 'Domesday Lawsuits')

Circuit VI: 185	Yorkshire	41	Circuit II: 7	Wiltshire	6
	Lincolnshire	126		Dorset	
	Nottinghamshire	1		Somerset	
	Derbyshire	1		Devon	1
	Huntingdonshire	16		Cornwall	
Circuit III: 46	Cambridgeshire	16	Circuit V: 10	Gloucestershire	1
	Middlesex	2		Worcestershire	3
	Bedfordshire	17		Herefordshire	1
	Buckinghamshire	2		Shropshire	1
	Hertfordshire	9		Cheshire	4
Circuit I: 19	Kent	2	Circuit IV: 0	Staffordshire	
	Sussex	1		Warwickshire	
	Surrey	4		Northamptonshire	
	Hampshire	10		Oxfordshire	
	Berkshire	2		Leicestershire	

It might seem that the real issue is why title is as prominent as it in the Domesday corpus. This, however, is to misunderstand the matter of the geld. As the glue of local societies, it defined the freedom of the free man and his right to the tenure of his land.[96] Thus, it was that any inquiry into the geld inevitably brought to light questions of title. For the king the Domesday inquiry might only be about taxation; for his subjects it could not help but also be about right to land. The commissioners had created a demand that had to be satisfied. The Domesday references are vestiges of a process that was not central to its purpose. Nevertheless, the main outlines of the procedures employed are clear. Commissioners might

However, the differences in formulation in the three counties are not great and it is there-fore possible that Huntingdonshire came after Lincolnshire. The suggestion that there were simply fewer claims in Nottinghamshire and Derbyshire – there are only two in the text – remains a possibility (D. R. Roffe, 'Domesday Book and Northern Society: A Reassessment', *EHR*, 105 (1990), 325–6), but, of course, begs the question in the present context.
[95] The annotation of the GDB text with 'k' for *kalumpnia*, 'claim', in Lincolnshire, Huntingdonshire, and Derbyshire alone is further indicative of uncertainty at this stage in the writing of the text (C. Thorn, 'Marginal Notes and Signs in Domesday Book', *Domesday Studies*, eds A. Williams and R. W. H. Erskine (London, 1987), 124–6).
[96] Above, pp. 193–7.

clear the ground for actions. There was a dispute over Ashfield in Suffolk 'when the king's barons came into the county', but they merely brokered a peace 'until there is a judgement (*donec sit derationatus*)'.[97] It would seem that proceedings might be initiated fairly quickly afterwards. The *clamores* are records of sessions in the Northern circuit. The accounts are subsequent to the inquest: they determine cases that are raised for the first time in the body of the text.[98] They are, moreover, ostensibly judgements: the *clamores* of the South Riding of Lindsey are headed 'The disputes which are in the South Riding of Lincoln, and their settlement [...] by the jurors'.[99] They are largely organized by wapentakes in an order that is found in the body of the text and it must be assumed that a list of cases had been drawn up from inbreviations or the circuit reports and systematically heard sometime before the compilation of GDB.

How common was this procedure is unclear. IE refers to a schedule of disputes[100] and the *terre occupate, invasiones*, and Ely D may be extant examples. There is even a judgement, albeit postscriptal, in the Hampshire folios.[101] Nevertheless, the *clamores* are probably not typical (unless, of course, GDB was compiled later than 1090). Speedy recognition of right was not always possible. Despite the explicit assertion that they are judgements, not even all the *clamores* represent completed business: on more than one occasion a decision is postponed to the king's court or another determination had yet to be made.[102] This was apparently the norm elsewhere. The law was an arthritic behemoth in its operations; there was generally

---

[97] LDB, 377: *DB Suffolk*, 16,34.

[98] The cases themselves overlap with presentments preserved in the body of the text, but there is no exact correlation; disputes are found in the one that are not noticed in the other and vice versa. While there is no doubt that these *clamores* belong firmly within the Domesday process (i.e. they took place before GDB was compiled), in the Lincoln-shire instances at least, they were heard independently of the presentments in the text and probably on a later occasion, for the twelve-carucate hundred, ubiquitous in the text, is absent.

[99] GDB, 375: *DB Lincs*, CS1.

[100] IE, 127. Ely claimed land in Essex *secundum breves regis*. Welldon Finn thought that the reference is to Domesday Book (*Domesday Studies: Eastern Counties*, 87). The entries that follow, however, are drawn from material predating LDB. It is conceivable that LDB's immediate precursor is the referent – the entries are undoubtedly derived from that source – but the scribe may have had a schedule of claims like Ely D in mind.

[101] GDB, 48: *DB Hants*, 44,1. The nuns of St Mary, Winchester, claimed the manor of Itchen Abbas in Hampshire which was held by Hugh fitzBaldric. In the margin there is a postscriptal 'r', for *require*, 'enquire', and subsequently the main scribe added 'King William has restored it to the same church'. The fact that the king delivered judgement, or at least endorsed a decision reached by his agents, suggests that this was no part of the Domesday process. With a later date for Domesday Book, the judgement may well have been made after the inquest.

[102] The claims that Drogo de la Beuvriere made on the lands of Morcar in the wapentake of Aveland in Lincolnshire were remitted to the king's decision, while in Kirton Wapentake in the same county pledges were given by the opposing sides to prove by ordeal or battle

no speedy resolution of disputes unless, perhaps, in the king's respite.[103] It is preliminary legal proceedings that above all characterize the *invasiones* of LDB. Judgements are conspicuous by their apparent absence; nor are pleadings anywhere in evidence. Rather there is a litany of preliminaries: lands had been seized and offenders were in mercy awaiting further developments;[104] warrantors had been pledged but had not supported claims,[105] while others had yet to be produced;[106] pledges were made to prove right and sureties secured;[107] some cases had proceeded no further than the fact of the claim itself.[108]

By necessity legal action continued after the Domesday commissioners had come and gone. David Bates has recently shown that a Ramsey case that was resolved in 1087 had been brought to light by the Domesday inquest.[109] At the time of the survey Eustace, the sheriff of Huntingdonshire, held land at Isham in Northamptonshire which he had appropriated by force from the abbey.[110] In 1087 William II issued a writ to William of Cahagnes to convene a shire court at Northampton to determine whether the land had paid a farm to Ramsey; if it had, it was to be placed in the abbey's demesne, but if, on the other hand, it had been thegnland, the tenant was to hold of the abbey.[111] Abbot Æthelsige proved his right at the county court by the oath of witnesses and a second writ of the same year ordered the sheriff to put him in possession of the estate.[112] Here can

rival claims made by Count Alan and Guy de Craon to lands in Drayton, Bicker, and Gosberton (GDB, 377–377v: *DB Lincs*, CK50;66;69).

[103] It has been claimed that the king's right to jurisdiction over the highways of Kent was confirmed in a judgement in Kent in the course of the Domesday inquest (A. Cooper, 'Extraordinary Privilege: The Trial of Penenden Heath and the Domesday Inquest', *EHR*, 116 (2001), 1167–92). The matters appear in two passages (GDB, 1, 2: *DB Kent*, D11–16.C6–7), and the verb *concordare*, 'to agree', is used in both, the first in the present tense and the second the perfect. Dr Cooper argues that the agreements were current because the decisions are couched in the future tense ('It is agreed that they shall …'). In fact, the present subjunctive, a normal way of expressing an obligation or consequence, is almost as often used. Other 'customs' sections alternate between present and future, active and subjunctive. I think we can draw few conclusions as to the date of 'pleas' from this sort of evidence.

[104] LDB, 99, 99v, 276v, 278, 278v, 279, 279v, 446v, 447, 449, 450: *DB Essex*, 90,4;6;8;9; *DB Norfolk*, 66,60;84;86;98;99; *DB Suffolk*, 76,13–16;19.77,4.

[105] LDB, 101v, 103: *DB Essex*, 90,48;77;78.

[106] LDB, 448v, 449: *DB Suffolk*, 76,13–15.

[107] LDB, 99, 100v, 101, 103, 174, 278v, 287, 448v, 449: *DB Essex*, 90,1;2;29;41;74;76;78; *DB Norfolk*, 66,5;88;106; *DB Suffolk*, 76,13;15;17.

[108] LDB, 101, 102v: *DB Essex*, 90,35;64;66.

[109] D. Bates, 'Two Ramsey Writs and the Domesday Survey', *Historical Research*, 63 (1990), 337–9.

[110] GDB, 228: *DB Northants*, 55,1.

[111] *Regesta Regum Anglo-Normannorum 1066–1154*, eds H. W. C. Davis, C. Johnson, H. A. Cronne, and R. H. C. Davis, 4 vols (Oxford, 1913–69), i, no. 383.

[112] *Regesta Regum*, i, no. 288b. Davis assigned this writ to William I, but Bates has demonstrated that it must have been issued by William II between his accession and the death of

be perceived the routine workings of the shire court to resolve disputes outside the extraordinary processes of the Domesday survey. This must have been the reality of most of the claims that came to light in the course of the Domesday inquest. That so many were unsuccessful, despite an apparently strong case, underlines the difficulty that any eleventh-century plaintiff had in making good his claim against a sitting tenant.

The inquest was a fact-finding exercise and could never supersede the due processes of law. Why, then, did the commissioners' reports, and, even more so, Domesday Book, accord as much space to claims as they did? The answer to this puzzle seems to be that claims, *clamores, invasiones*, and *terre occupate*, were in fact intended as no such record. Here the peculiarities of the Exon claims come to the fore. The entries therein are ostensibly 'occupied lands', and yet as often as not the aggressor is not identified. What use is such a record if drawn up to inform ongoing legal proceedings? The focus of each entry is on the land itself. The TRE tenant is named, its assessment is given, and its value is carefully recorded. The *invasiones* of LDB exhibit an even greater concern with the resources and issues of the estate: there a complete description is given. Significantly, in Essex and Suffolk they are said to be *super regem*, 'upon the king'.[113] Surely the intention is to make clear the assets of the land in question to the end of informing the king of the dues that he might expect from custody, potential or actual.[114] The first step in many actions was the taking of an estate into the king's hands. The *terre occupate* and *invasiones* sections are a handy guide to what profits the king might make from them. That such a document should find a place in Exon is understandable; the geld accounts that are also found there illustrate that the king was concerned about the issues of his regalia. But routine administrative records of this kind were less appropriate for the land register that was Domesday Book. The scribe of GDB soon realized just how irrelevant the material was and took early steps to eliminate it.

An inquest into the geld inevitably brought to the notice of the world illegal seizures of land. But there was a penalty to pay for both the defendant and plaintiff. As likely as not the matter was brought into a royal court and invited the intervention of the king into a private matter. Forfeiture and 'deraignment to the king's use' were probably a pain for both sides. Just how typical is this of the law of the period? Domesday has been studied and used as a source of legal procedure in the late eleventh century[115] and clearly it shines a light on many corners of Anglo-Norman law that would otherwise remain in the dark. But our analysis would suggest that many of the procedures that are extracted were extraordinary.

Abbot Æthelsige late in 1087.
[113] LDB, 90, 447v: *DB Essex*, 90; *DB Suffolk*, 76.
[114] *DIB*, 184–5.
[115] R. Fleming, *Domesday Book and the Law: Society and Legal Custom in Early Medieval England* (Cambridge, 1998).

By its nature the inquest must always have been a meddle-fest for the crown, but equally by its nature the inquest was an exceptional process. The normal processes of law were probably very different.[116] Above all the evidence is partial: it presents but one part of a larger picture. In the past Domesday Book has repeatedly been used to demonstrate that the jury superseded the Old English processes of compurgation through oath-helpers. Yet this is to view the matter solely from a Domesday perspective. The wider view reveals that the jury was by no means a Norman innovation.[117] It was inherent in the concept of the geld and was probably widely used in legal proceedings. It was, moreover, not the antithesis of the so-called traditional procedures; presentment by jurors sat easily beside determination through compurgation. The Isham case nicely illustrates the relationship after the Conquest: the Domesday jury presented the illegal tenure and the matter was subsequently determined by oath of witnesses in the shire court. That was normal procedure and continued to be so. Compurgation was a given in the Leges Henrici Primi and continued to be a valid means of proof in procedure by appeal into the thirteenth century.[118] To view the Domesday evidence in isolation is to misunderstand the procedure of the inquest and misrepresent the development of English law.

The Domesday claims are no treatise on everyday law. Much less are they an insight into the chaos occasioned by the Norman Conquest. As we have seen,[119] only a tiny proportion of the land of England was in dispute in 1086. And yet mechanisms were invoked to right those wrongs that had not been remedied. Paradoxically, the claims of Domesday Book stand to emphasize just how orderly the Conquest had been. There were problems at the edges but, in making them public, Domesday demonstrates just how clear-cut the principles of land tenure were. The explicit writ of the king could never be gainsaid in court (although the basis on which it was issued might be questioned), but here were plaintiffs who again and again asserted the rights of inheritance from a pre-Conquest predecessor. These are demands based on principles that command authority because the causes in which they were invoked were the exception.

[116] See J. Hudson, 'Court Cases and Legal Arguments in England, c. 1066–1166', *TRHS*, 6th series, 10 (2000), 91–115, for the process of teasing legal norms out of Domesday evidence.
[117] See above, pp. 64–7.
[118] *Leges Henrici Primi*, ed. L. J. Downer (Oxford, 1972), 120, 208; F. Pollock and F. W. Maitland, *The History of English Law*, 2nd edn, 2 vols (Cambridge, 1898), ii, 600–1, 633–7.
[119] Above, pp. 167–9.

9

_____

The Beyond of Domesday

D OMESDAY BOOK incorporates history into its very fabric. It may not have
been compiled to document the Norman Conquest and settlement, but it
does so because 'the day on which King Edward was alive and dead' was set as the
term of the assize for the changes which the Domesday inquest wished to document.
This perspective has, perhaps, been one of the most important characteristics that
have ensured a continuing fascination with the record. From early on in its history
Domesday has been used to reconstruct Old English society, becoming, as we have
seen,[1] first a pawn in successive political debates, and then latterly the stuff of
academic discourse. As much as to recreate the present of 1086, Domesday Book
is today used to reconstruct the past, the 'beyond of Domesday'.

That evocative phrase has been coined in reference to Frederick Maitland's great
book *Domesday Book and Beyond*.[2] Maitland was by no means the first to attempt
a systematic reconstruction of Anglo-Saxon England from the folios of Domesday
Book, but in his masterpiece he formulated a manifesto that has resonated down
to the present day. In the final paragraph of the work he wrote:

> There is every reason why the explorers of ancient English history should
> be hopeful. We are beginning to learn that there are intricate problems to
> be solved and yet that they are not insoluble. A century hence the student's
> materials will not be in the shape that he find them now. In the first place, the
> substance of Domesday Book will have been rearranged. Those villages and
> hundreds that the Norman clerks tore into shreds will have been reconstituted
> and pictured in maps, for many men from over all England will have come
> within King William's spell, will have bowed themselves to him and become
> that man's men. Then there will be a critical edition of the Anglo-Saxon
> charters in which the philologist and the palaeographer, the annalist and the

[1] See above, pp. 1–21.
[2] F. W. Maitland, *Domesday Book and Beyond* (Cambridge, 1897). The phrase 'the beyond of
Domesday' can be attributed to H. R. Loyn, 'The Beyond of Domesday', *Domesday Studies*,
ed. J. C. Holt (Woodbridge, 1987), 1–13. Loyn does not treat of the hidden agendas in the
methodology.

formulist will have winnowed the grains of truth from the chaff of imposture. Instead of a few photographed village maps, there will be many; the history of land-measures and field-systems will have been elaborated. Above all by slow degrees the thoughts of our forefathers, their common thoughts about common things, will have become thinkable once more. There are discoveries to be made; but also there are habits to be formed.[3]

A hundred years later Maitland would probably have thought his prediction over-cautious. His legacy has been no less than a new discipline, that of landscape history, and an unprecedented interest in the 'origins of estates'. The last twenty-five years have seen an explosion in the number of publications on the subject.

Without Domesday much of this work would not have been possible. It is the more surprising, then, that landscape history has founded its analyses not in the Domesday text but in Welsh law codes of the twelfth and thirteenth centuries and Northumbrian customals of even later dates. In the hands of first Jolliffe and then Davis and Glanville Jones,[4] these sources yielded a picture of primitive societies which were highly structured. *Regiones*, or subkingdoms, were divided into 'multiple estates' which each consisted of a balanced mix of land and resources from which a tributary population could provide the royal household with all the commodities that it required. The large estates of Domesday Book were interpreted as vestiges of similar organizations and so began a hunt for the building blocks of the English landscape.

In some schools of history the approach has now become institutionalized. As in the sequencing of genes, undergraduates and postgraduates are each given their own part of the code to crack; soon there will not be a single area of England that has not been populated with multiple estates.[5] Enthusiasm for the model has, however, sometimes done violence to the evidence. Whether Welsh legal tracts can

---

[3] Maitland, *Domesday Book and Beyond*, 596.

[4] J. E. A. Jolliffe: 'Northumbrian Institutions', *EHR*, 41 (1926), 1–42; 'A Survey of Fiscal Tenements', *EcHR*, 1st series, 6 (1935–36), 157–71; *Pre-Feudal England: The Jutes* (Oxford, 1933). G. R. J. Jones: 'The Portrayal of Land Settlement in Domesday Book', *Domesday Studies*, ed. J. C. Holt (Woodbridge, 1987), 183–200; 'Multiple Estate and Early Settlement', *Medieval Settlement*, ed. P. H. Sawyer (London, 1976), 15–40. R. H. C. Davis: *The Kalendar of Abbot Samson and Related Documents*, Camden Society, 3rd series, 84 (1954), ix–l.

[5] For local views of the evidence, see D. Kenyon, *The Origins of Lancashire* (Manchester, 1991); M. Costen, *The Origins of Somerset* (Manchester, 1992); T. Williamson, *The Origins of Norfolk* (Manchester, 1993); N. J. Higham, *The Origins of Cheshire* (Manchester, 1993); J. Blair, *Anglo-Saxon Oxfordshire* (Stroud, 1994); P. Dalton, *Conquest, Anarchy and Lordship: Yorkshire, 1066–1154* (Cambridge, 1994); P. Warner, *The Origins of Suffolk* (Manchester, 1996); P. H. Sawyer, *Anglo-Saxon Lincolnshire* (Lincoln, 1998). For critiques of the multiple estate model, see N. Gregson, 'The Multiple Estate Model: Some Critical Questions', *Journal of Historical Geography*, 11 (1985), 339–51, and D. Hadley, 'Multiple Estates and the Origins of the Manorial Structure in the Northern Danelaw', *Journal of Historical Geography*, 22 (1996), 3–15.

be treated as history is a debatable point and it is equally doubtful that late medieval customals are relevant to the organization of seventh-century Northumbria. More to the present point, the model is not entirely consistent with Domesday. That large estates survived into the eleventh century from an early period is undisputed. Manors like Fladbury in Worcestershire, for which early charters are known, seem to have changed little in extent between the seventh century and Domesday.[6] Equally, it can be demonstrated that some Domesday manors and sokes came into being through the fission of larger units sometime before 1086. A memorandum of *c.*972, for example, indicates that the soke of Helperby in the East Riding of Yorkshire had been created out of the soke of Ripon at some point prior to that date.[7] Numerous pre-Conquest charters indicate that small parts of larger estates were frequently hived off, increasingly so from the tenth century.

Fission of this kind, however, was demonstrably not the only mechanism of estate formation. Throughout the Domesday corpus there are repeated references to lands that have been added to manors or taken away from them. Some of these changes were undoubtedly irregular; a degree of chaos had accompanied the Norman Conquest and settlement. But the seizure of land was no preserve of invaders. It had as long a history in pre-Conquest England as in Normandy.[8] The point here is that perceptions of right did vary and the fact demonstrates that there was no recognized order of estates carved in stone. More to the point, many of the changes in estate structure recorded in Domesday were licit; exchanges, mortgages, pledges, forfeitures, and grants all altered the structure of manors. This was of the nature of sokeright.[9] It seems to have been the main medium of patronage in Anglo-Saxon England and when granted as bookland its basic attraction was that it was alienable. Booklords could grant the dues that they enjoyed in sokeland to whomsoever they wished.

Many of the manors that we find in Domesday clearly owe their existence to these sorts of process. Changes to the structure of Tewkesbury in Gloucestershire are recorded in GDB: a number of thegns had 'TRE submitted themselves and their lands under the power of Beorhtric [son of Ælfgar]'.[10] Others can be deduced from other sources: by 1086 Conisbrough in Yorkshire had gained sokelands that had formerly owed their dues elsewhere.[11] Fusions of this kind must have been commonplace. Equally there may have been repeated reallocations of lands. The most cursory of glances at the distribution of Domesday manors reveals

[6] S76, 185.

[7] *EHD*, i, no. 114.

[8] Cf. the seizure of lands in the anti-monastic reaction after the death of Edgar in 975.

[9] See above, p.158.

[10] GDB, 163–163v: *DB Gloucs*, 1,24–46.

[11] M. S. Parker, 'Some Notes on the Pre-Norman History of Doncaster', *Yorkshire Archaeological Journal*, 59 (1987), 29–43.

that there are many estates that can be assigned to neat schemas only with the eye of faith.[12]

The introduction of extraneous evidence only obfuscates the issue. Parish and hundred boundaries, along with patterns of intercommoning and place-names, are often introduced to 'prove' ancient associations. They may indeed be old. But such analyses usually depend on an *a priori* assumption of fission in estate formation. In reality, supra-manorial structures can often be shown to be late adaptations. Hundred boundaries are the least useful for landscape historians. The concept of the *manerium cum hundredo*, that is, the close relationship between early royal manors and the bounds of hundreds, is a hare that was first set up by Helen Cam.[13] The institution certainly has some being in some parts of southern and western England as it is represented in the late thirteenth-century hundred rolls, and hundred dues can be shown to have been appurtenant to many hundreds in Domesday. That some such hundred manors were *ville regales* in the pre-Conquest period and even at the time of the Domesday inquest is also indisputable. But none of this is evidence of continuity. The association of manor and hundred was demonstrably recent in some cases. Wootton in Oxfordshire, for example, had the dues of three hundreds attached to it despite the fact that it had only recently come into the hands of the king.[14] This is hardly surprising. The hundredal system of the tenth century that superseded the system of royal administration based upon the *ville regales* performed completely different functions and over much of England north of the Thames it was set up anew without regard for tenurial patterns.[15] As we have seen, along with its infrastructure of vills, it was essentially a product of geld quotas.[16] Hundred boundaries are the physical representation of an institution that was largely unrelated to tenure. They

---

[12] See, for example, M. W. Bishop, 'Multiple Estates in Late Anglo-Saxon Nottinghamshire', *Transactions of the Thoroton Society*, 85 (1981), 37–47.

[13] H. M. Cam, '*Manerium cum Hundredo*: The Hundred and the Hundred Manor', *EHR*, 47 (1932), 355–76.

[14] So in Oxfordshire: see J. Blair, 'An Introduction to the Oxfordshire Domesday', *The Oxfordshire Domesday*, eds A. Williams and R. W. H. Erskine (London, 1990), 13.

[15] It is common to find appurtenances of a manor in one county in another, even across major boundaries like the Thames (N. Hooper, 'An Introduction to the Berkshire Domesday', *The Berkshire Domesday*, eds A. Williams and R. W. H. Erskine (London, 1988), 3–4, 8). It is often difficult to assess how ancient such links are, but the evidence can be compelling. For example, there are indications from Waltham Holy Cross sources to suggest that the definition of the boundaries of Hertfordshire, Essex, and Middlesex along the River Lea disrupted earlier groupings of estates (S. Doree, *Domesday Book and the Origins of Edmonton Hundred*, Edmonton Hundred Historical Society Occasional Paper No. 48 (Enfield, 1986), 13–15). See also P. Taylor, 'Boundaries and Margins: Barnet, Finchley, and Totteridge', *Medieval Ecclesiastical Studies in Honour of Dorothy M. Owen*, eds M. J. Franklin and C. Harper-Bill (Woodbridge, 1995), 259–79; P. Taylor, 'The Endowment and Military Obligations of the See of London: A Reassessment of Three Sources', *ANS*, 14 (1991), 302–3.

[16] See above, pp. 192–3.

may incidentally perpetuate pre-tenth-century systems of land management, but it cannot be assumed that they do so unless there is independent evidence.[17] Where the manor and hundred equation does apply it effectively relates to an intrinsic hundred (hundredal jurisdiction confined to a demesne estate),[18] and must be seen as an adaptation to administrative concerns of the tenth century or later.[19] Many royal estates were never fully incorporated into the hundredal system since, assessed to a food farm rather than the geld, they were administered directly by the king's reeve,[20] while many churches were soon granted immunities in their own lands. Nevertheless, Pauline Stafford has shown how dangerous it is to assume that even here their Domesday forms are necessarily ancient. The very neatness of the system of royal farm management in much of Wessex suggests that it was a recent innovation.[21]

The parish is equally problematic. Until recently, the origins of parishes have been viewed almost exclusively as a mirror image of estate formation. The ur-church in England was characterized by a network of minsters founded in *regiones* and multiple estates, and the *parochia* was conterminous with their areas; the evolution of the parochial system of the Middle Ages was a function of a fragmentation of these units that paralleled the formation of manors.[22] David Rollason has shown

---

[17] Frank Thorn has provided a sober evaluation of the evidence for the whole of England, except for Lincolnshire, Norfolk, Suffolk, and Essex, in his notes on hundreds and wapentakes in the Alecto County Edition of Domesday (London, 1987–92). For Lincolnshire, see D. R. Roffe, 'Hundreds and Wapentakes', *The Lincolnshire Domesday*, eds A. Williams and G. H. Martin (London, 1992); Norfolk, D. R. Roffe, 'Introduction', *Little Domesday, Norfolk*, eds A. Williams and G. H. Martin (London, 2000), 37–9; Suffolk, M. Bailey, 'Introduction', *Little Domesday, Suffolk*, eds A. Williams and G. H. Martin (London, 2000), 9–13. The name of the hundred – OE of an early form, folk names, Danish elements etc. – is the least satisfactory evidence of antiquity. A traditional meeting place may well be old, suggesting an unbroken chain of memory of function, but that is hardly evidence of continuity of boundaries. Other evidence is required. That is precisely what, for example, Williamson (*The Origins of Norfolk*, 126–33) does for Norfolk.

[18] Maldon in Essex, for example, was divided between the king's hundred of Maldon and Wibertsherne (LDB, 4v: *DB Essex*, 1,17a).

[19] For the general point, see B. J. Golding, 'An Introduction to the Hampshire Domesday', *The Hampshire Domesday*, eds A. Williams and R. W. H. Erskine (London, 1989), 20–1.

[20] Roffe, 'Hundreds and Wapentakes', 32–42; C. P. Lewis, 'Introduction to the Shropshire Domesday', *The Shropshire Domesday*, eds A. Williams and R. W. H. Erskine (London, 1990), 10. In Shropshire distinctive diplomatic differing from the norm of the local hundred suggests that all but one of Earl Roger de Montgomery's manors were extra-hundredal; twelve had been held TRE by Edward the Confessor.

[21] P. A. Stafford, 'The "Farm of One Night" and the Organisation of King Edward's Estates in Domesday', *EcHR*, 2nd series, 33 (1980), 491–502. See also R. Lavelle, 'The "Farm of One Night" and the Organization of Estates in Late Anglo-Saxon Wessex', *Haskins Society Journal*, 14 (2005 for 2003), 54–82, where the earlier organization of the system is explored.

[22] The model is now known as the 'minster hypothesis'. See *Minsters and Parish Churches: The Local Church in Transition 950–1200*, ed. J. Blair (Oxford, 1988), and *Pastoral Care before*

how misconceived an assumption this can be. There is abundant evidence of a reorganization of the church in various areas in the tenth century and later.[23] Wharram Percy in the East Riding of Yorkshire provides a salutary example of this process. Its parish is, relatively speaking, extensive, encompassing in addition to Wharram itself, the adjacent townships of Burdale, Thixendale, Raisthorpe, and Towthorpe. The fact has inevitably suggested to some that the area was an early estate of some local importance; the discovery of a fragment of a Middle Saxon cross shaft in the vicinity of the church has raised the possibility that it was a major ecclesiastical centre.[24] My own analysis has shown that the parish is more likely to be a skeuomorph.[25] In common with other large parishes in the area like Kirby Underdale, the Wharram complex is characterized by the presence of a large number of thegnages and drengages. Pre-Conquest booklands, by contrast, are almost invariably associated with small parishes conterminous with the manor. If these latter parishes represent the extent of the ecclesiastical dues that were conferred by the grant of a book or similar, then the former may be simply those lands that were never booked. The extent of the parish of Wharram probably represents nothing more than a residue of dues that were formerly owed to a minster church in the vicinity; it probably only dates from the time when tithes were territorialized in the eleventh and twelfth centuries, Wharram may well have a large parish because its church was the nearest convenient one to which to attach the dues. It is clearly as unwarranted to assume that a large parish necessarily represents an early estate as does a hundred.

Intercommoning is an even less reliable indicator of ancient associations. It is, after all, as likely to represent compromise between two separate communities as the sharing of resources by one. This is a fact that is evident to anyone who has tried to follow the often tortuous negotiations between the fenland abbeys in the twelfth and thirteenth centuries in the allocation of pasture in the waste between Lincolnshire and Norfolk, Huntingdonshire and Cambridgeshire.[26] And it is a phenomenon which is demonstrably early. Della Hooke has shown that there was

---

the Parish, eds J. Blair and R. Sharpe (Leicester, 1992).

[23] D. Rollason, 'Monasteries and Society in Early Northumbria', Monasteries and Society in Medieval Britain, ed. B. Thompson, Harlaxton Medieval Studies, vi (Stamford, 1999), 59–74, esp. at 68–74. For the debate and a response, see E. Cambridge and D. Rollason, 'Debate: The Pastoral Organisation of the Anglo-Saxon Church: A Review of the "Minster Hypothesis"', and J. Blair, 'Debate: Ecclesiastical Organisation and Pastoral Care in Anglo-Saxon England', Early Medieval Europe, 4 (1995), 87–104, 193–212.

[24] M. Beresford and J. Hurst, Wharram Percy: Deserted Medieval Village (London, 1990), 83–4.

[25] D. R. Roffe, 'The Early History of Wharram Percy', The South Manor Area, Wharram: A Study of Settlement on the Yorkshire Wolds 8, eds P. A. Stamper and R. A. Croft, York University Archaeological Publications, 10 (York, 2000), 1–16, esp. at 14–15.

[26] N. Neilson, A Terrier of Fleet, Lincolnshire, from a Manuscript in the British Museum (London), v–lxxxv; D. R. Roffe, 'The Historical Context', Anglo-Saxon Settlement on the

common between the territories of the *Tomsaetan* and *Pencersaetan* in Worcestershire in the Middle Saxon period.[27] Throughout the country hundred meeting places are commonly characterized by a marginal site on common land.[28]

Finally, place-names present too many imponderables. It is no longer believed that name forms necessarily date settlements, but it is widely held that they provide a hierarchy. District names, like Hatfield, and so-called tribal names in *-ingaham* and *-ingas*, like Folkingham and Hastings, are said to point to early central places.[29] Subordinate elements of their estates then identify themselves in functional or directional names, such as Barton, 'the barley farm', and Norton, Sutton, Easton, and Weston, while personal names combined with the element *-tun*, indicate settlements that have been hived off. In reality, however, such names do not unambiguously provide independent corroboration of the multiple estate model. Other referents can be observed. Many 'tribal' names could as easily be names of more local kins or merely topographical descriptions. The *Clencwara* of Clenchwarton in Norfolk were probably less a people with a defined territory than simply 'the dwellers on the hill' (the hill being a silt bank in the fens).[30] Again, the directional names often only relate to a higher level mental map. *Northworthig*, the pre-Danish name of Derby, was 'the northern enclosure' because it was north of the Trent as opposed to Repton to the south.[31] It was in no way 'subordinate' to it, however, as a dependent estate.[32] Likewise, Astbury in Cheshire was the 'eastern fortification', but was no less important than its western neighbour Sandbach.[33] Above all, it is not possible to demonstrate when the names applied. Functional names may often indicate subordination (although they could as simply be merely

Siltland of Eastern England, eds A. Crowson, T. Lane, K. Penn, and D. Trimble, Lincolnshire Archaeology and Heritage Reports Series, 7 (2005), 264–88.

[27] D. Hooke, *The Anglo-Saxon Landscape: The Kingdom of the Hwicce* (Manchester, 1985), 85–6.

[28] See, for example, A. L. Meaney, 'Gazetteer of Hundred and Wapentake Meeting-Places of the Cambridge Region', *Proceedings of the Cambridge Antiquarian Society*, 82 (1994), 67–92; C. J. Balkwill, 'Old English Wic and the Origin of the Hundred', *Landscape History*, 15 (1993), 5–12; V. G. Swan, B. E. A. Jones, D. Grady, 'Bolesford, North Riding of Yorkshire: A Lost Wapentake Centre and its Landscape', *Landscape History*, 15 (1993), 13–28; D. R. Roffe, 'Linwood and the Meeting Place of Lindsey', http://www.roffe.co.uk/lindsey.htm.

[29] M. Gelling, *Signposts to the Past: Place-Names and the History of England*, 3rd edn (Chichester, 1997).

[30] A. D. Mills, *A Dictionary of English Place-Names* (Oxford, 1995), 82.

[31] T. L. Tudor, 'Repton, Northworthy (Derby), and Wirksworth', *Journal of the Derbyshire Archaeological and Natural History Society*, 44 (1922), 44–57.

[32] K. Cameron, *The Place-Names of Derbyshire*, English Place-Name Society, 27–9 (1959), ii, 446, suggests that the River Trent was the referent of the place-name. Nevertheless, the same point remains.

[33] Higham, *Origins of Cheshire*, 169–71.

descriptive), but they do not tell us at what date: they are as likely to be late as early.

The multiple estates hypothesis has its merits as a model (that is, in synthesis), but it is woefully lacking as a methodology for reconstructing the beyond of Domesday. Nowadays, no one accepts Round's view of the Domesday process. Much of the data may have been organized by vill at one time or another in the course of the Domesday inquest, but few would doubt that the process was about lordship. And yet the perspective of the multiple estate hypothesis is unremittingly geographical and local: its starting point is the vill. Like Round, its proponents still begin their analysis by reordering the text. In this respect, the model ignores the insights that have been gained into the Domesday process in the last hundred years. Its agenda is Maitland's.

It is the texts and lordship that should be placed at the centre of any analysis. Domesday Book is a record of a living society; it is at its most eloquent on the here and now of the late eleventh century. It must, then, be axiomatic that the text as it stands is no guide to the tenurial roots of England, although it does, of course, hint at the antiquity of some estates and estate centres. Neither is it an ancient customal, although it informs us of practices that are old. We must, however, resist the temptation to deconstruct it and interpret its data in terms of extraneous sources. In respecting the integrity of the texts and their concerns, we can begin to perceive what is ancient and what is modern in the interstices of Domesday forms, the patterns of data. The manor or estate cannot be studied in isolation. It has to be examined in the context of a landscape of lordship. The basic unit of analysis must be the holding, both TRE and TRW, and it, in its turn, must be examined in relation to surrounding holdings.

Structures of lordship

First the holding. In our discussion of the manor we have seen that all manors are equal, but some manors are more equal than others.[34] The manor was a point at which soke dues were intercepted in return for some kind of service (whether it be geld or a personal duty). Some, however, were higher up the tenurial pyramid than others. An 'ordinary' manor creamed off the dues of the peasant population of a certain area and rendered a service to another lord for the privilege. A 'chief' manor, by contrast, might receive dues from a number of these smaller estates and in return its lord performed military service for the king in person. The initial task in the study of any individual fee is not to examine the land but rather the person who holds it. The primary distinction that must be made, then, will be between what was held by the tenant-in-chief in demesne in 1086 and what was granted out to his tenants. It has often been argued that major Norman estate

---

[34] See above pp. 176–82.

centres and patterns of enfeoffment were a function of post-Conquest strategic considerations,[35] but of late it has been realized that status was at least of equal importance. Castles dominated the landscape as a Norman symbol of power, but their effect was the more potent when they were founded in existing centres of power.[36] People and their status mattered and it is therefore likely that important people lived in important places. Major demesne centres in 1086 are inherently likely to perpetuate pre-Conquest centres of power.

The equation, however, will not be invariable. In some counties and large fees we have to look further down the social scale for such markers. Where large areas of land were granted en masse to a single lord, such subtle distinctions have to be sought at the level of the honorial barony. In Cheshire each major tenant is conveniently identified in the text; in Shropshire and Cornwall the fee of each can be easily reconstructed.[37] More leg work has to be done in Kent and Sussex. Here, however, the vital distinction is between the land of the honorial baron and that held by the subtenant. Likewise, national figures like Robert of Mortain did not have remote demesnes and important estate centres were granted to their principal tenants. Their identity may often only be apparent from later documentation like the *carte baronum* of 1166.

Needless to say, though, continuity of tenure and site is not invariable. An all-but unremarked onomastic characteristic of the Domesday texts is the comparatively large number of holdings called Newbold.[38] Most of the estates so identified were held in demesne, but with the meaning of 'new hall'[39] most were apparently

---

[35] This went, of course, with the notion that William the Conqueror designed the whole process to ensure that none of his vassals received dangerous concentrations of power. See above, pp. 163–75.

[36] C. Coulson, 'Peaceable Power in English Castles', *ANS*, 23 (2000), 69–96; R. Liddiard, 'Castle Rising, Norfolk: A "Landscape of Lordship"?' *ANS*, 22 (1999), 169–86; O. Creighton, 'Early Castles in the Medieval Landscape of Rutland', *Transactions of the Leicestershire Archaeological and Historical Society*, 73 (1999), 19–33. Major royal castles regularly perpetuated sites of authority. There has been little published work on other castles; for a local study, see D. R. Roffe, 'Castles', *An Historical Atlas of Lincolnshire*, eds S. Bennett and N. Bennett (Hull, 1992), 40–1. On the choice and siting of demesne estates still less has been published. A good starting point might be to compare what can be perceived of liberties in 1086 (sake and soke etc.) with immunities and privileges in the later Middle Ages. There are remarkable correlations with the record of view of frankpledge, the right to courts, and the like in sources like the Hundred Rolls.

[37] For a speculative but interesting review of status in Cheshire, see N. J. Higham, 'Patterns of Patronage and Power: The Governance of Late Anglo-Saxon Cheshire', *Government, Religion and Society in Northern England 1000–1700*, eds J. C. Appleby and P. Dalton (Gloucester, 1997), 1–13.

[38] GDB, 232, 233, 233v, 236v, 239, 240v, 243v, 244, 267, 272, 281v, 302v, 381v. *DB Leics*, 13,11;74.14,33; *DB Warks*, 31,3.39,3; *DB Cheshire*, 18,1; *DB Derby*, 1,1.

[39] E. Ekwall, *The Concise Oxford Dictionary of English Place-Names*, 4th edn (Oxford, 1959), sv Newbold; *The Vocabulary of English Place-Names (Á-Box)*, eds D. Parsons, T. Styles, and

not primary sites and in some cases may have been of post-Conquest origin.[40] In East Anglia new manors were created after 1066 and were sometimes held in demesne. Widely throughout England small manors had been aggregated by 1086 to form units which were more appropriate to the needs of the new ruling classes and their men.[41]

Patterns of post-Conquest tenure, then, have to be tested against the corresponding pre-Conquest patterns. Sooner or later the landscape historian must hunt the king's thegn. As we have already seen, if a man is explicitly said to be a *tainus regis*, the chances are that he is not of the highest status.[42] The pre-Conquest equivalent of the tenant-in-chief is a rarer creature, but he is nevertheless quite distinct. The very top ranks of the class identify themselves easily enough by the recurrence of their names. Mærle-Sveinn had lands in Devon, Somerset, Gloucestershire, and Lincolnshire; he was clearly a figure with whom to reckon. Most king's thegns, however, were not national figures. Their holdings were more modest. Various differentiating criteria have been suggested to distinguish the more locally based king's thegn from his lowly namesakes: explicit notice of status (*tainus Regis Edwardi*), the right to sake and soke, possibly the tenure of a church (as in Cheshire), calligraphic and diplomatic forms (square initial letters and the *tenuit* formula), and the like.[43]

Identifying the men who owed service to these king's thegns and the land from which they owed it, is generally a somewhat more difficult business. Here and there a man is said to have held land from or under another or to have been in one way or another indebted to him. The record of the value of one manor in another is a sure sign of dependence. Likewise, a 1086 tenant who also held in 1066 may well have been a subordinate at both dates.[44] Many of the earl's thegns in Nottinghamshire apparently survived until 1086 to hold from William Peverel

---

C. Hough, Centre for English Names Studies (Nottingham, 1997), 135–7, suggests that the element *boðl* has some hint of importance in some contexts; the editors, however, do not look at the status of the Domesday entries.

[40] This is apparently true of Newbold Astbury in Cheshire (D. R. Roffe, 'Astbury in Domesday', http://www.roffe.co.uk/astbury.htm), and may be true of the Newbold in Derbyshire which is named in Domesday as the *caput* of the ancient manor and soke of Chesterfield (P. Riden, 'The Origin of the New Market of Chesterfield', *Derbyshire Archaeological Journal*, 97 (1978 for 1977), 5–15).

[41] Many multiple manor entries, however, may be merely a function of entry formation even when held by a single person. See above, p. 83.

[42] See above, pp. 158–9.

[43] See above, pp. 159–62.

[44] Depression of status is always assumed in these contexts, but no one suggests the same of the *taini Regis*; most historians have been happy to see them as ministers both before and after the Conquest. My impression is that the phenomenon of survival is greater in the North than elsewhere, probably reflecting the greater survival of the English undertenant there. A general survey of the type would be useful.

seemingly under little different terms of tenure.[45] Many are entered in multiple
manor entries, yet another indication of interdependence.[46] In the Oxfordshire,
Northamptonshire, and Leicestershire folios subordinates are often not recorded
at all: only predecessors are named in the normal course of events. But here we
are at least given some idea of the land they held. In Leicestershire Hearding was
presumably a king's thegn, for he is distinguished by the *tenuit* formula. A helpful
note at the end of the account informs us that 'Hearding with his men held all
these lands', some seventeen parcels in all.[47]

However, the more or less explicit notice of dependence is the exception. Is it
possible, then, to go any further? Well yes, a little. Sometimes anomalies in procedure may indicate groups of thegns and estates. Hundredal sequences are ubiquitous
in Domesday Book, but they are rarely simple. One of the most common of the
anomalies is that they are repeated in the same chapter: land is listed in the order
of hundreds 1, 2, 3, 4 ... 1, 2, 3, 4 ... etc. Formerly, the characteristic was explained
as an indication that a jury had been recalled to give further evidence. But this
supposes a simplistic understanding of Domesday procedure, and it is now realized
that it is related to the form in which the tenant-in-chief presented the information about his lands. This is most apparent when a lord listed his demesne lands
separately from the enfeoffed.[48] Many religious houses did this and each section
has its own hundredal sequence. As we have already noted,[49] others were related
to title. Ralph Baynard's Norfolk *breve* provides an example. It is divided into two
sequences, 247v–250v and 250v–253v. In each there are a few parcels of land that
were acquired by exchange or invasion, but only one king's thegn (as identified
by the *tenuit* formula). The first was Thorn who held Hempnall, Boyland, and
Raveningham in demesne. A further two manors in Kerdiston and Wheatacre
(fols 247v, 250) had been held by Thorth, described in one entry as a free man
and in another as a thegn. No claim is made to either estate. The second holder of
bookland was Æthelgyth who held six manors in demesne in Shouldham All Saints
and St Margaret, Wiggenhall, Boughton, Merton, and Wilby. A further manor that
she held as a free woman was claimed by Ely, but there were no claims to possible
manors in Tittleshall and Wicklewood held by Northmann and Ulf, both free men,
respectively in 1066 (fols 252v, 253). In both sections the inclusion of additional

[45] For the significance of this pattern, see D. R. Roffe, 'Anglo-Saxon Nottingham and the
Norman Conquest', *A Centenary History of Nottingham*, ed. J. V. Beckett (Manchester,
1997), 35–42.
[46] See above, pp. 83, 160. Note, however, that the first named holder is sometimes the lord.
[47] GDB, 231v; *DB Leics*, 10,1–17.
[48] The practice is common in Warwickshire and Leicestershire, but is otherwise sporadic.
It is, however, frequent in the king's *breves*. It would seem that only the king's demesne
estates were surveyed in the initial stages of the Domesday inquest; the adding of lands
held of him often resulted in a second sequence, and occasionally a third or more when
there were additional sections to add. See, for example, Norfolk.
[49] Above, pp. 172–3.

subordinate land (appurtenances of other manors etc.) indicates that content was primarily dictated by management in 1086. Nevertheless, it can be concluded that title to manors held by free men was derived from the two predecessors.

Many patterns like this remain to be identified, not to say interpreted. Counties like Hampshire are said to exhibit no coherent hundredal order, and yet under-lying groupings of estates may be concealing regular sequences. Such sequences, however, are comparatively rare. Moreover, like the holdings of the greater lords of pre-Conquest England, they can be difficult to relate to the actual organization of estates on the ground. The proximity of dependent manors to each other may suggest a coherent unit, but how can limits be determined? To do this the holding must be examined in relation to other holdings.

Metastructures of lordship

Various notions have collided to discourage such analyses hitherto. Where pre-Conquest England was seen as a land of free men behoven to none and the Norman settlement as the grant of their estates individually or by regions to the newcomers, it followed that patterns of manors were inevitably random. The widespread record of the delivery of men in Domesday Book merely reinforced the notion that there was little rhyme or reason in the organization of land beyond the personal. However, underlying patterns in both pre- and post-Conquest estate structures are there to be readily observed if a wider focus is adopted. The wapentake of Asward-hurn on the Kesteven fen edge provides an example (Table 9.1). The principal estate in the area was the manor of Sleaford. In 1086 it enjoyed the soke of tenements in the settlements of Ewerby, Howell, Heckington, Quarrington, Laythorpe, and Evedon.[50] Set out thus, the soke looks decidedly *ad hoc*. But its form takes on significance when it is perceived that the structure is substantially reproduced in the king's manor of Kirkby La Thorpe,[51] Kolsveinn's manors of Ewerby Thorpe, Heckington, and Laythorpe,[52] and Kolgrimr's extended group of manors and soke-lands in Aswardhurn,[53] and vestigially in two other estates.[54]

These are patterns that are ubiquitous in the North and the East Midlands.[55] They are also common in East Anglia.[56] There seems no doubt that in these

[50] GDB, 344v: *DB Lincs*, 7,43–50.
[51] GDB, 337v: *DB Lincs*, 1,1–3.
[52] GDB, 357, 357v: *DB Lincs*, 26,27–30. Burg was the northern part of the settlement of Kirkby (http://www.roffe.co.uk/burg.htm).
[53] GDB, 370: *DB Lincs*, 67,1–6.
[54] GDB, 341, 355: *DB Lincs*, 3,35–8.24,39–40.
[55] *Pace* Hadley, *The Northern Danelaw: its Social Structure, c.800–1100*, 144–6, who implies that the phenomenon is of limited distribution.
[56] Roffe, 'Pre-Conquest Fenland'; D. R. Roffe, 'Introduction', *Little Domesday, Norfolk*, eds A. Williams and G. H. Martin (London, 2000), 39–41.

Table 9.1 *The soke of Sleaford and related estates*

	1	*7*	*26*	*67*
Sleaford		1*		
Kirkby La Thorpe	1*			
Burg				3
				5
Ewerby		2		1
Ewerby Thorpe	3a		1	
Howell	3b	3	3	2
Heckington	3c	4	2	6
Quarrington	3d	5		
Laythorpe		6	4	
Evedon	2	7	5	4

Numbers in *italics* at the head of columns refer to chapters in the Lincs section of GDB. The remaining numbers refer to the order of entries within each chapter.

* indicates a manor held with sake and soke.

contexts manors had been created by the ordered division of large estates element by element sometime before the Conquest.[57] Indeed, the mechanism is occasionally documented. The archbishop of York's Nottinghamshire manor of Laneham possessed appurtenances in the same vills as the king's soke of Oswaldbeck in 1086 and, according to a thirteenth-century source, had formerly belonged to the larger estate.[58] The rights of the crown were probably finally relinquished by a writ of 1065 whereby Edward the Confessor granted all the soke to the archbishop.[59] Again, the abbot of Crowland's holdings in Elloe Wapentake in Lincolnshire interlock with Earl Ælfgar's holdings, and, according to a charter preserved in the Historia Croylandensis, they had been granted to the abbey in one transaction by the same earl sometime in the 1050s or early 1060s.[60] Although the document is clearly a forgery in the form in which it survives, it evidently records an authentic tradition, for the transaction is noted in the twelfth-century patronage list known as the Guthlac Roll.[61] In the twelfth century the baronies of Bywell and Bolebeck in Northumberland were created by a similar division of the various elements of Bywellshire.[62]

[57] D. R. Roffe, 'An Introduction to the Lincolnshire Domesday', *The Lincolnshire Domesday*, eds A. Williams and G. H. Martin (London, 1992), 11.

[58] GDB, 281–281v, 283: *DB Notts*, 5,4; *Rotuli Hundredorum*, ed. W. Illingworth, Record Commission (London, 1812–18), ii, 25.

[59] *Anglo-Saxon Writs*, ed. F. E. Harmer (Manchester, 1952), no. 119.

[60] *Ingulph's Chronicle of the Abbey of Crowland and the Continuations by Peter de Blois and Anonymous Writers*, trans. H. T. Riley (London, 1854), 196.

[61] BL, Harleian MS Y 6.

[62] J. C. Hodgson, *History of Northumberland*, vi (Newcastle, 1902), 14–15.

By 1066 the interlocking elements were generally held with full rights: each manor or group of manors rendered dues to a single king's thegn. In origin, however, it seems likely that, as in Oswaldbeck, rights were limited to certain renders and they were collected in a central court. Thus it is that ecclesiastical dues are rarely appurtenant to the subsidiary elements in the later Middle Ages. Churches, as evidenced by Domesday Book or subsequent records of rights of presentation, were usually vested in the fee of the main soke lord, suggesting that tithes had been reserved.[63] The fact is occasionally explicit. In 1086 jurors declared that 'the tithes and customary church dues of Winnibriggs Wapentake and Threo Wapentake, in respect of all the sokes and inlands which the king has there, belong to the church of Grantham'.[64] In the later Middle Ages the right to tithe both within and without the soke was vested in the church. The area thus indicated may define something of the *parochia* (that is, parish) of such major minster churches.[65] This characteristic is in marked contrast to estates that were booked. There the lord seems to have been granted (or assumed) unequivocal right, and typically he had his own church within a smaller, discrete territory.

There are signs that such patterns were not just a characteristic of the Danelaw. The granting of elements out of royal estates to various lords on a more or less temporary basis is attested throughout Domesday Book. To take but one example, 16½ of the 50 hides of Keynsham in Somerset were in one way or another leased out of the manor before the Conquest. By 1086 they had come into the hands of five different lords.[66] Vestiges of a unity are sometimes apparent. Eleven of the 15 hides of Winnianton in Cornwall, situated in 21 vills, were held TRE by 17 thegns who 'could not be separated from the manor' (GDB) and 'rendered customary dues to the manor' (Exon).[67] By 1086 they had passed to the Count of Mortain: in Exon they are entered in his *breve* as well as the king's, while in GDB they appear only in the latter's. The lands were still attached to the original manor at the time of Domesday, although they were soon to realize their independence. In Pershore there are even signs of interlocking, here a division apparently effected in the reign of Edward the Confessor between the abbeys of Westminster and

---

[63] D. R. Roffe, 'Great Bowden and its Soke', *Anglo-Saxon Landscapes in the East Midlands*, ed. J. Bourne (Leicester, 1996), 107–20.

[64] GDB, 377: *DB Lincs*, CK24.

[65] For a detailed exposition of the method, see http://www.roffe.co.uk/rand.htm. Here a major church in Wragby, only previously suspected from a pre-Conquest sculptural fragment, was identified. The method has also been applied to Waltham in Lindsey with similar results (G. F. Bryant, *Domesday Book: How to Read it and What its Text Means*, Workers Education Association (Waltham, 1985)). The evidence of advowsons is an unexploited source which would repay further investigation. None of this, of course, prejudices the origins of these rights.

[66] GDB, 87: *DB Somerset*, 1,28.

[67] GDB, 120: *DB Cornwall*, 1,1; Exon 99a.

Pershore (Table 9.2).[68] This, however, is generally difficult to spot since vills were more rarely divided than in the east and north. Nevertheless, there is evidence that some groups of vills were related to each other.

Table 9.2 *Interlocking patterns of tenure in Pershore Hundred, Worcestershire*

Vill	8	9
Pershore	1	1a
Wick	2	1g
Chivington		1b
Abberton		1c, 1f
Wadborough		1d
Pensham	3	
Birlingham	4	
Bricklehampton	5	
Defford	6	
Eckington	7	
Besford	8	
Longdon	9	
Powick	10	
Snodsbury	11	
Hussingtree	12	
Droitwick	13	
Dormston	14	
Piddle	15, 18	
Naunton	16	
Grafton	17, 20	
Pirton	19	
Peopleton	21	
Comberton	23, 27	1h
Broughton Hackett	24	
Broughton, Drakes		1e
Nafford	25	
Stoke, Severn	26	
Beoley		2
Alderminster		3
Broadway		4
Leigh, Bransford		5

Numbers in *italics* at the head of columns refer to chapters in the Worcestershire section of GDB. The remaining numbers refer to the order of entries within each chapter.

[68] GDB, 174v–175v: *DB Worcs*, chapters 8 and 9.

It has long been recognized that there is something contrived about the vills of *Hamestan* Wapentake in the High Peak of Derbyshire. There, as in much of England, they are generally undivided. And yet a system appears to underlie the number assigned to each manor. Precisely twelve each belonged to Longendale and Ashford. Darley, Bakewell, and Hope had three, eight, and seven respectively,[69] but interlocking patterns and parochial structure point to the existence of three further groups of twelve vills (Table 9.3).[70] In pre-Conquest charters many of the elements can be identified in assessments in *mansiones* or *manentes*. Both of these terms are usually translated as 'hide', but they here clearly refer to groupings of vills which precede the Domesday estate structure.[71] The whole complex of sixty vills in *Hamestan* Wapentake can be identified with the sixty *manentes* 'in Hope and Ashford' confirmed to Earl Uhtred in 926.[72]

Table 9.3 *Groups of vills in north Derbyshire*

Manor	Appurtenances	Total
Darley	3 berewicks + Middleton, Youlgreave, Gratton, Elton, Harthill, Stanton, Winster, Cowley, Birchover	12
Bakewell	8 berewicks + Pilsley, Edensor, Chatsworth, Beeley	12
Ashford	12 berewicks	12
Hope	7 berewicks + Hathersage, Bamford, Hurst, Stoney Middleton, Eyam	12
Longendale	12 manors	12

Vestiges of a duodecimal grouping of vills is widespread, but the evidence can be difficult to interpret. Numerology can quickly degenerate into pyramidiocy. Clearly, arguments for a grouping are the most compelling when the fact is more or less explicit. On these grounds we might be confident that something like the Derbyshire system is to be found in southern Lancashire. Precisely forty-eight vills are said to belong to the manor/hundred of West Derby and there were twelve manors in Leyland.[73] But how do we interpret the 37 appurtenances of Warrington? Can we really say that it really represents 36? Likewise, to what extent is it really convincing to assert that the 21 vills of Blackburn conform to the system?[74] In

---

[69] GDB, 272–272v: *DB Derby*, 1,11;27;27–30.

[70] D. R. Roffe, 'The Origins of Derbyshire', *Derbyshire Archaeological Journal*, 106 (1986), 120–1.

[71] How widespread the meaning of vill is in pre-Conquest documents has not been determined. *Mansio*, of course, is used of manors in the Domesday texts. It is, however, deemed to be a post-Conquest usage.

[72] S397.

[73] GDB, 169v–170: *DB Cheshire*, R1. R6.

[74] GDB, 169v–170: *DB Cheshire*, R3. R4. In societies in which mixed base arithmetic is the norm, all sorts of patterns can be perceived that may be insignificant; after all, reckoning in tens, twelves, sixteens, and twenties is designed to make calculation easier where the

tackling these problems I have tried to formulate some principles for counting based upon the Derbyshire evidence.[75] First, the vill in which the *caput* of the manor is situated is not counted, for it apparently did not participate in the system unless a subgroup has been formed by the fission of a larger unit. Second, all vills associated with the *caput*, whether inland, soke, or forinsec soke (land where the soke belonged to one lord in 1086 and the soke to another), are included.[76] Land is more easily alienated than the soke over it. Third, linked settlements with only one assessment which formed a single vill in the later Middle Ages are counted as single vills. Finally, no distinction is made between inland (in the northern sense) and soke in the same vill: they are counted as one.

Of thirty-eight manors with more than nine appurtenances in Yorkshire seven display a perfect duodecimal pattern and a further ten come within one.[77] Other groups can be suggested where interlocking indicates that existing manors and their appurtenances are the function of fission of larger units as in Derbyshire.[78] Leicestershire, Lincolnshire, Nottinghamshire, and Rutland[79] yield similar results. These patterns are clearly not specifically Danish and therefore local as the duodecimal base might suggest to some. Monastic endowments of six or twelve vills were common in Northumbria before the mid ninth century.[80] But how common they are elsewhere has been little investigated. Nevertheless, there may be good grounds for suspecting that they are widespread. Perhaps the most plausible reason for the pattern is that it is simply related to the organization of food farms throughout the twelve months of the year. And with the eye of faith something like such a system can be hypothesized in some areas. In Staffordshire, for example, twelve vills belonged to Eccleshall and eighteen to Lichfield.[81] Likewise, in Worcestershire there were twenty-four vills associated with Pershore of which six were berewicks of the abbey of Pershore's manor of Pershore.[82] Similarly the king's manor of Bromsgrove had eighteen berewicks and, with Droitwich, a further six parcels of

---

concept of nought is absent. So, virtually any old number can be interpreted as duodecimal or, come to that, decimal.

[75] Roffe, 'Wharram Percy', 12.

[76] W. E. Kapelle, *The Norman Conquest of the North* (Croome Helm, 1979), 80, for example, in counting the appurtenances of manors in Yorkshire, included only those in the main entry for each manor.

[77] Roffe, 'Wharram Percy', 12.

[78] See, for example, the sokes of Weaverthorpe, Buckton Holms, and Langton which interlock and have precisely eighteen vills between them (Roffe, 'Wharram Percy', 13–14).

[79] There are six vills in each of the two twelve-carucate hundreds of Alstoe Wapentake. Martinsley is divided into three manors with five, seven, and seven berewicks.

[80] C. R. Hart, *Early Charters of Northern England and the North Midlands* (Leicester, 1975), nos 139, 141, 151, 156.

[81] GDB, 247: *DB Staffs*, 2,10–11;16;22.

[82] GDB, 174v–175v: *DB Worcs*, chapters 8 and 9. Abberton is listed twice, apparently in error (Evesham A, *DB Worcs* 9,1a note) and has thus been counted as one berewick.

land associated with it.[83] Kidderminster, by contrast, had sixteen appurtenances, but whether other vills interlock with it remains to be determined.[84] Finally, six vills are associated with the bishop of Worcester's manor of Fladbury.[85]

This type of evidence is suggestive, but more work needs to be done to recognize the forms of other areas of England. Some may relate to other processes. Decimal groups of vills may merely be a function of hidation in areas like the double hundred of Normancross in Huntingdonshire where the five-hide unit of an original geld quota survived into the late eleventh century. Other types of structure more closely related to estate organization may be awaiting discovery. In many counties the forms of Domesday may militate against this type of analysis, or at least make it more difficult. It is (presumably) chance references in Gilbert de Ghent's *breve* in Cambridgeshire that make it clear that his manor of Fen Stanton in Huntingdonshire had six appurtenances.[86] There is little that is comparable in the Cambridgeshire folios where there is nothing to associate entries. But we shall not know until we look.

The recognition of metastructures can be a powerful tool for an understanding of both Domesday Book and earlier organizations of the lands depicted therein. The hundred and a half of Freebridge in Norfolk will serve as an example.[87] To Douglas,[88] as to most who have studied the area, Freebridge was the archetype of a free East Anglian society and of a prelapsarian England. Small manors held mostly by local thegns swam in a sea of unrestrained freedom. There is little of an explicit nature in LDB to discourage such a notion. And yet a detailed examination of the patterns of tenure reveals anything but a free-for-all. Single manors are found here and there, and there is a significant concentration in the Half Hundred in an area known as Marshland. Earlier documentation (as indeed the diplomatic forms of Domesday) shows that West Winch, Wiggenhall, West Walton, Terrington, Walsoken, and Walpole were discrete bookland estates before the Conquest.[89] Interlocking patterns are otherwise everywhere (Table 9.4). Islington, Clenchwarton, Middleton, North Runcton, and West Bilney to the east of Marshland are associated in four groups of estates, Pentney, East Walton, Castle Acre, Gayton Thorpe, and East Winch in three, and so on (groups are placed in the

---

[83] GDB, 172: *DB Worcs*, 1,1.

[84] GDB, 172: *DB Worcs*, 1,2.

[85] GDB, 172v–173: *DB Worcs*, 2,15–21.

[86] GDB, 197–197v, 207: *DB Cambs*, 23,1–6; *DB Hunts*, 21,1.

[87] For the following, see Roffe, 'The Historical Context', *Anglo-Saxon Settlement on the Siltlands of Eastern England*, 274–6. For the sake of simplicity, the evidence of Domesday churches and later advowsons has been omitted, as have indications of the extent of fees.

[88] D. C. Douglas, *The Social Structure of Medieval East Anglia* (Oxford, 1927).

[89] West Walton was divided into three fees (LDB, 160–160v, 213, 226), Terrington into two (LDB, 206v–207, 251v), but Wiggenhall, Walpole, West Winch, and Walsoken were undivided (LDB, 251, 266, 231v, 215v). For the earlier documentation, see C. R. Hart, *The Early Charters of Eastern England* (Leicester, 1966), 79–96, 215–30.

Table 9.4 *Patterns of tenure in the hundred and a half of Freebridge, Norfolk*

	1	2	4	5	7	8	9	10	13	14	15	16	18	19	20	21	22	23	29	31	34	35	49	51	66	66
Freebridge Half Hundred																										
Lynn												4					19			32					17	55
Winch, West																9									18	
Wiggenhall																				24					19	
Walton, West						21					4															
Terrington									12											31						
Walsoken												3														
Walpole																							9			
Islington			44						13	4	6		1					10								
Clenchwarton													2													56
Freebridge Hundred																										
Middleton			45							5								11								
Runcton, North									14				4	5												
Bilney, West																		12								
Pentney							2																			
Walton, East			45				2										15								21	
Acre, Castle						22					5						16									
Gayton Thorpe					1		3										17								22	
Winch, East		131					3										20								20	
Gayton						23								7				13							23	
Ashwicken				45												10										
Glosthorpe					1																					

	1	2	4	5	7	8	9	10	13	14	15	16	18	19	20	21	22	23	29	31	34	35	49	51	66	66
Bawsey		45		2																						
Well													1													
Leziate																								58		
Gaywood								**1**																		
Mintlyn								*50*																		
Wootton	132																									
Grimston		2				25	116																1			
Congham						26																		2		
Hillington						28												1						3		
Massingham	1		*1*			29	5							8		11			2							
Babingley																			3		1					
Dersingham																			4		2					
Sandringham																		1								
Harpley		3				**30**																				
Anmer				2		*31*																				
Snettisham		4																								
Flitcham		4				32	*4, 6*																			
Appleton							7														3					
Newton, West		4																								
Rising, Castle		4																								
Roydon		4																								

Numbers in *italics* at the head of columns refer to chapters in the Norfolk section of LDB. The remaining numbers refer to the order of entries within each chapter; those in **bold** indicate demesne holdings of king's thegns, those in *italics*, lands acquired by invasion, exchange, purchase etc. after 1066. Horizontal lines define probable pre-Domesday groupings of land.

same box defined by horizontal lines in the table). One king's thegn (as identified by the *tenuit* formula), but only one, can usually be identified in each group of fees, and a single soke nexus would therefore seem to underlie the various elements associated with him. At once we can see that seemingly independent free men must in reality have shared common obligations in both 1086 and 1066, that is they were in the same soke. Thus, for example, the eight free men that Hermer de Ferrers had illicitly annexed in Lynn, East Winch, East Walton,[90] and Gayton Thorpe (no 66, 20–22) were clearly not an *ad hoc* group (their distribution reflects that of the other groups of fees). There is insufficient evidence to assign each parcel of land to a specific manorial centre. The free men may have rendered their dues directly to the king's thegn; equally their immediate soke lord may have been any of his many thegns.[91] However, the important fact is that patterns of tenure indicate a common identity.

Above all the identification of the earlier structures that emerge from the analysis allows a much more nuanced interpretation of other types of evidence. Dersingham and Sandringham ('sand Dersingham') share a name, but hitherto there has been little to show that they also had a common tenurial context. More surprisingly, we can see that groups of settlements hailed as obvious communities in the join-the-dots schools of landscape history are no such thing. All the vills of Freebridge Half Hundred intercommoned in Marshland and the whole lot has been repeatedly interpreted as an early fenland community and estate.[92] Our analysis, however, shows that the vills to the east had decided links with the upland to the south and east (a fact reinforced by the record of salterns in the manors there), leaving only the western vills as purely fenland. Throughout the recorded history of the area, the two groups of vills remained distinct and were usually in conflict with each other,[93] and it would seem likely that for a long time before 1066, if not always,

---

[90] So F. Blomefield, *An Essay towards a Topographical History of the County of Norfolk*, 2nd edn, 11 vols, 1805–10 (London, 1808), ix, 145. *DB Norfolk*, 66,21, has West Walton, but there is no sign of the fee there in the later history of the vill. There is no reason to believe that the fee was absorbed into Ely's West Walton manor after the Domesday inquest (R. J. Silvester 'West Walton: The Development of a Siltland Parish', *Norfolk Archaeology*, 39 (1987), 109). Interlocking structures, can, then, also help in the identification of place-names.

[91] It is possible to cite instances of both in the Danelaw.

[92] N. Neilson, *A Terrier of Fleet, Lincolnshire, from a Manuscript in the British Museum* (London, 1920), xliii–xlvi.

[93] The links between Lynn, Islington and Clenchwarton on the one hand, and the fen edge on the other, look as ancient as the contrasting structures to the west, and there are indications that in the twelfth and thirteenth centuries they functioned as a separate community. The vills were outside the 'leta integra' of Marshland, consisting of West Walton, Walsoken, Terrington, and Walpole (Wiggenhall was also outside the leet although it is not explicitly grouped with the vills to the east), and from time to time as a group they came into conflict over rights in the fen with these their neighbours. In the early thirteenth century, for example, the abbot of Bury and his partners of Tilney and Islington on the one hand

they had been constituted as separate communities. At least two other groups of commoners to the south and east were similarly discrete. Marshland was clearly a frontier resource which was exploited by a number of peoples.

A similar analysis of the Domesday account of the whole of the fenland of Lincolnshire, Cambridgeshire, Huntingdonshire, and Norfolk reveals more general patterns.[94] In outline the reconstruction might not seem much different from that which a traditional approach to landscape history would produce. No one would doubt that Wisbech Hundred, and Elloe, Kirton, and Skirbeck Wapentakes were distinct entities. The detail, however, is highly significant. Crowland, for example, does not fit into the Elloe pattern and there is much earlier and subsequent evidence to show that it was attached to the highland. It was an island in the peat fen and, bordering the upland, was fully exploited from the fen edge.[95] By contrast, the silts towards the sea were, with the sole exception of the Marshland boundary, self-contained and socially distinct. The metastructures recovered from Domesday Book hint at societies somewhat older. The evidence provides a much firmer basis for interpreting earlier sources like the Tribal Hidage.

Landscape historians are at root romantics, for much of their approach to Domesday, as to other sources, tends to assume antiquity and continuity. There is, after all, great comfort to be had in, say, discovering that the layout of a modern housing estate perpetuates field boundaries that go back for over a thousand years. In reality Domesday Book records much that is new as well as old, and a study of the structures and metastructures of the text can easily reveal it. To all appearances the soke of Great Bowden in Leicestershire (Table 9.5, fee no. 1, entries 4a–k, 5, 11) is little different from that of Sleaford or any of the extensive estates in the fenland. It looks very like the archetype of an early organization of land, and accordingly it has been argued that it is a vestige of tributary bonds that bound a series of twelve multiple estates into a pagan Saxon *regio*, or subkingdom, which substantially occupied the area of and was, by implication, perpetuated by the wapentake of Gartree.[96] The whole area is perceived as a social and, to a lesser extent, as an economic entity which retained its integrity throughout many centuries.

Eloquent as this analysis is, there are, however, problems with it.[97] When examined in relation to others fees, it is apparent that the northern element of

reached an agreement with the bishop of Ely and his partners of the leet of Marshland on the other (Douglas, *Social Structure of Medieval East Anglia*, 195–8, 250–2).

[94] Roffe, 'The Historical Context', *Anglo-Saxon Settlement on the Siltlands of Eastern England*, 276–80.

[95] D. R. Roffe, '*On Myddan Gyrwan Fenne*: Intercommoning around the Island of Crowland', *Fenland Research*, 8 (1994), 80–6.

[96] C. Phythian-Adams, 'Lordship and the Patterns of Estate Fragmentation', *The Norman Conquest of Leicestershire and Rutland: A Regional Introduction to Domesday Book*, ed. C. Phythian-Adams (Leicester, 1986), 16–18.

[97] For what follows, see D. R. Roffe, 'Great Bowden and its Soke', *Anglo-Saxon Landscapes in the East Midlands*, ed. J. Bourne (Leicester, 1996), 107–20.

Table 9.5 *Interlocking patterns of tenure in Gartree Wapentake, Leicestershire*

	1	2	5	13	14	15	16	17	19	28	40
Bowden, Gt	4a										18
Medbourne	4b					2					
Blaston	4l					2					20
Prestgrave	5										
Easton, Gt			2								
Stockerston				15							21
Horninghold							1				
Hallaton										1	
Goadby										2	
Billesdon										4	
Rolleston										5	
Keythorpe		6								3	
Langton, Tur		1									
Langton, W		1	1								
Langton, E				57							
Thorpe Langton				14			6	18			
Welham		5						19			30
Othorpe											19
Slawston								17,20			
Stonton Wyville				56							28
Glooston											22
Cranoe	4c										29
Shangton	4d			55			5				
Carlton Curl	4e			17							
Illston	4f			13				16			
Galby	4g			53							
Norton, King's	4h										
Stretton	4i										
Noseley				18							
Burton Overy				16							
Evington				50				6			
Ingarsby				51							
Stoughton				52							
Frisby				54							
Glen, Gt				58							
Newton Harcourt							9				
Fleckney									10,12		
Wistow									13		
Kibworth Harcourt						8					

	1	2	5	13	14	15	16	17	19	28	40
Kibworth Beauchamp									14		
Smeeton West	*4j*			29					11		
Lubenham		3,4				9					15
Gumley							4				17
Foxton	*4k*										16
Theddingworth	*27,2*										31
Saddington	6										
Laughton						8					
Houghton					16						
Bosworth, Husbands								7	15		
Knossington	*11*										
Owston										**26**	

The numbers in *italics* at the head of columns refer to chapters and the remaining figures to entries in *DB Leics*.

Italics (other than at the head of columns) indicate sokeland and **bold** the notice of a king's thegn; their bookright extended over a usually indeterminate number of estates. Horizontal lines define probable pre-Domesday groupings of land.

Bowden's sokeland in Shangton, Carlton Curlieu, Illston, and Glaby interlocks with the estates of Hugh de Grandmesnil in the same vills, and it is clear that, along with King's Norton and Stretton, the complex had formerly constituted a single estate. The reservation of all of the ecclesiastical dues to the Grandmesnil fee in the later Middle Ages suggests that it was the primary element. By contrast, Bowden and the soke in its immediate vicinity are closer to a complex of royal and comital lands and estates that extended over the county boundary into Northamptonshire. It looks very much as if the creation of the two shires in the tenth century had seen the division of the Bowden estate and the two new shire reeves had restructured its administration to suit the new circumstances. The soke of Bowden as described in Domesday Book was apparently a skeuomorph of relatively recent creation in 1086.

In many areas metastructures are not manifest in the Domesday text at all. In counties like Middlesex and Wiltshire this may be a Domesday artefact. Estates such as Stepney and Corsham explicitly had dependencies but they are simply not named.[98] Later, or indeed earlier, evidence must be used to supplement the Domesday data in these circumstances. Elsewhere, by contrast, vestiges of earlier types of organization may not have survived or, alternatively, there may always have been a landscape of small and discrete entities. Essex is probably an example:

[98] GDB, 127–127v, 65: *DB Middlesex*, 3,1–11; *DB Wilts*, 1,11.

the county was characterized by a large number of king's thegns in 1066.[99] Such a tenurial profile is perhaps a function of an area of dense woodland and marsh in which many settlements owed their existence to assarting. Humberside has a similar profile but for different reasons. On both banks of the River Humber all the local and regional powers of pre-Conquest England had footholds, reflecting the vulnerability of a major boundary and line of communication in the north.[100]

A new manifesto

The identification of metastructures is not for the faint-hearted. The analysis can be complex as the tables used to illustrate the argument above amply demonstrate. Furthermore, there are numerous imponderables. No claims are made that the methods outlined here are definitive; they do not supersede other methods or devalue their data. What can be said, however, is that the analysis is not just a useful tool for landscape studies; it is an essential one to reveal the significance of the Domesday data. The habits that Maitland wished to be formed have been taken too much to heart. There is still no geographical rearrangement of Domesday Book, but almost every reconstruction of the beyond of the text has begun with its deconstruction. Discussion of the origins of estates and the like has been based in a primary analysis of the vill.

That Maitland should have found this the only starting place is not surprising. He accepted fully Round's analysis of the Domesday inquest. It was self-evident that it was originally about vills, and so the key to understanding Domesday Book and its data was to rewrite it as it was 'originally intended'. Maitland's perception of the manor as a house against which geld was charged was a direct result: lordship was defined in relation to the vill. It was, of course, a view that was quickly rejected and yet Stenton and Douglas,[101] who took up the baton in their respective studies of the Northern Danelaw and East Anglia, retained Maitland's local geographical perspective. Both were at pains to elucidate the nature of lordship in their areas of study, but manor and vill remained their points of reference. From this perspective it was clear that tenurial structures were largely the function of *ad hoc* and essentially contingent personal relationships. These views too are no longer accepted. They have been replaced by an orthodoxy that seeks meaning outside the Domesday folios. Nevertheless that orthodoxy has been shaped by the

---

[99] D. R. Roffe, 'The King's Thegns of Essex', http://www.roffe.co.uk/tes.htm. This is not to say, however, that there were no extensive estates in the county. See, for example, R. Faith, 'The Topography and Social Structure of a Small Soke in the Middle Ages: The Sokens, Essex', *Essex Archaeology and History*, 27 (1997), 202–13.

[100] D. R. Roffe, 'Barton upon Humber'.

[101] F. M. Stenton, *Types of Manorial Structure in the Northern Danelaw* (Oxford, 1910); Douglas, *Social Structure of East Anglia*.

analytical paradigm outlined by Maitland. The multiple estate model still depends on a primary analysis of Domesday data in terms of the vill.

Maitland's landscape history manifesto has had far-reaching consequences for our understanding of the Old English past. It has directed us along a road not completely lacking in vistas; insights into the nature and management of the geld would not have been realized without it. But the prospects are relatively few and the blind spots and pitfalls many. Nowadays we do not accept Round's thesis on the Domesday process. Many of the findings of the Domesday inquest may have been presented by hundred and vill, but no one doubts that it was also about lordship and the service that it entailed. We have to learn the consequences of that realization. We can only begin to appreciate the nature of eleventh-century societies once we take the forms and subject matter of their documentation seriously. The seigneurial focus of the Domesday texts was intentional: they are about lords and men. By recasting the texts into an ersatz ICC form we avert our eyes from vital evidence. The beyond of Domesday is more likely to be found in its own terms than in grand theories of the origins of estates derived from later sources and evidence.

10

Domesday Now

IN THE PRECEDING PAGES I have been at pains to argue that the abandon-
ment of the concept of a single purpose for the Domesday enterprise provides a
better basis for understanding Domesday data. Once released from the necessity of
thinking in black and white terms, it is possible to perceive *processes* (as opposed to
quantities) that make better sense of the often apparently contradictory evidence.
The result has been glimpses of a very different Anglo-Norman society and
economy. In this chapter these perceptions are summarized and put into the wider
context of the evolution of England from a tributary society to a feudal one. It
was a transformation in which Domesday Book itself was instrumental. The fact,
though, makes it all the more necessary to differentiate between what Domesday
became from what it was when it was first written.

Purpose and content

The inventory school of Domesday studies draws on a long history. Contemporary
sources are eloquent on the what and how of the Domesday inquest, but remarkably mute as to why. In this respect it is no different from most other medieval
inquests. It is, then, not surprising that subsequent commentators fixed on its
most visible product.[1] From at least the late twelfth century the production
of Domesday Book was understood as the purpose of the Domesday inquest.
It was a bureaucratic process, drawn up by executive fiat. As reformulated by
Round and then Galbraith, this view gave birth to an important corollary: the
forms and content of Domesday are a clue to its intent. The resulting hypotheses
– Domesday Book as geld survey (Round), feodary (Galbraith), social contract
(Holt), tax assessment (Harvey), quartermaster's manual (Higham), even tax return
(Bridbury) – have all been posited on its exhaustive scope. Content has defined
purpose and purpose validated content.

The premise of all of these analyses does violence to the Domesday sources.
Galbraith and his followers have produced a complex taxonomy of the Domesday

---

[1] Above, pp. 1–21.

texts which purports to prove that the production of the book was the aim of the Domesday inquest. But, as we have seen,[2] this is nothing more than wishful thinking. The so-called articles of inquiry preserved in IE can be no such thing, and no single activity can be identified in the inquest records. One thing, however, it clear. Whether one considers the seigneurially arranged Exon or the geographically arranged ICC the normal product of the Domesday inquest, its 'returns', the writing of LDB and GDB – both *compiled* accounts organized by county and tenant-in-chief – represents the most radical change in form in the whole Domesday corpus. Domesday Book is as different as it can be from what went before.

It was, furthermore, if dimly perceived, then set apart from the inquest records in the first forty or so years of its life. Domesday Book was known, but not widely disseminated. Extracts are not found in the handful of cartularies – St Augustine's, Canterbury, Peterborough, Rochester, Shaftesbury, Worcester – that survive from the period 1086–1135. Moreover, all of the charters that cite 'the king's book' or the like actually refer to other sources. It was, rather, the inquest records that were current and used. It would appear that the Book was used as an administrative aid within the treasury and little more. In this respect Domesday Book was typical of abbreviations as a class of document. Such records were always later, and usually *post hoc*, often as much as a hundred years after the event. The reasons for compilation were various, but the aim was to preserve data that were considered of permanent value for administrative purposes. Here what was chosen gives some indication of that reason. Content and intent are closely related. The same is not true of the records of the inquiry. The principal objective of an investigation is to gather evidence and establish fact, or at least what is agreed. It does not decide, for in itself it is not an executive process. The documents that it produces are therefore often contingent to the decisions that are subsequently made. Even today any particular record of, say, a Royal Commission will not necessarily anticipate the conclusions that the commissioners ultimately reach. Their concerns may not even be apparent. Paradoxically, the subject matter of an inquiry is often what its documents are not about. The contents of Domesday Book tell us at best what the *book* was compiled for. They do not necessarily reveal why the data were collected in the first place.

My understanding of the Domesday process begins with that simple proposition. I have argued, here and more fully in *Domesday: the Inquest and the Book*, that the inquest and the production of Domesday Book were two entirely different enterprises. The one was concerned with the collection of evidence to inform the forging of a new 'social contract' between William the Conqueror and 'all those who held land in England' in the aftermath of the crisis of 1085, a threat of invasion, that had thrown into relief deficiencies in national finances and defence.

[2] Above, pp. 54–61.

The other was an administrative initiative that used the records of the inquest, probably to effect a settlement sometime after the revolt against William Rufus in 1088. In re-dating the text my intention was not to question the chronological integrity of its data. Whatever its date, Domesday Book was compiled from the returns of the inquest of 1086. Abbreviations were precisely that: throughout the Middle Ages their compilers did not tamper with their sources. Give or take the odd slip or two, Domesday Book was not updated. By and large, it remains sound evidence for the reign of William the Conqueror.

My interest here lies in the nature of that evidence. We now know that much of it was provided by the tenant-in-chief. One of Galbraith's great contributions to Domesday studies was to point out that much of the Domesday data is privileged and could therefore only have been presented by the lord. But the tenant-in-chief was not alone in providing evidence. Representatives of the community of the shire also furnished key items of information – assessment to the geld, title, and values were their main contribution – and it has been their involvement that has characterized the whole process. It has been held as axiomatic that local juries were making recognitions, that is that the Domesday evidence represents tried and tested judgements. And yet where is it is possible to test them, they are remarkably insubstantial. The fact has confused, but, of course, it makes perfect sense if we see the inquest as an investigative process, a collecting of evidence. There are undoubtedly recognitions in Domesday Book. The *clamores* of the South Riding of Lindsey are explicitly said to be so. These pleas, however, are ostensibly later than the main Domesday inquest sessions. The presentments of the text are simply evidence, matters that the local community wished to air. There is indeed evidence that complaints, particularly against sheriffs, were specifically invited.[3] The acceptance of *querele* of this kind was a characteristic of inquests throughout the Middle Ages.[4] But it is one thing to invite juries to dish the dirt and another thing to accept what they say as gospel. Domesday presentments might pre-figure future action. As has been seen,[5] a claim in Northamptonshire was followed up in the county court after the Domesday inquest. But they were not recognitions in themselves.

This was the reality of all the Domesday data. All respondents to the inquest were of course expected to tell the truth. That was the nature of a verdict, a *veredictum*. But one man's truth is another man's livelihood. It was the role of the regular processes of the law to weigh the evidence. The inquest was there to collect it. So, our data are not self-validating, as we have been led to believe. Their nature and scope can only be determined in the light of the purpose of the Domesday

[3] Above, p. 69.
[4] A. Harding, 'Plaints and Bills in the History of English Law, mainly in the period 1250–1350', *Legal History Studies 1972*, ed. D. Jenkins (Cardiff, 1975), 65–86. Incorporating them into hundredal presentments in the general inquest was a commonplace. See L. E. Scales, 'The Cambridgeshire Ragman Rolls', *EHR*, 113 (1998), 553–79.
[5] Above, pp. 277–8.

inquest. The production of Domesday Book was not it. Furthermore, one would not expect Domesday Book to embody it. The inquest collected evidence for subsequent consideration. It did not prejudice the outcome. It is a sad fact that we have no reports of what was said and done when it was planned at Gloucester in December 1085. Neither do we have an account of the proceedings at Salisbury in August 1086 when the decisions were made in the light of the evidence that had been collected. All we know was that it was done and dusted with 'all those who held land in England' doing homage to William and swearing an oath of loyalty. However, context and procedure suggest a background. The inquest follows a threat of invasion which had seen the hiring of an unprecedented number of mercenaries. I have argued at length that the initial stage of the Domesday inquest was a survey of the royal demesne and a geld audit.[6] Faced with calls on his purse from all directions, the king would seem to be looking at ways of maximizing his income.

The survey of the lands of the tenants-in-chief followed. For me the key to how it all fits together is the summaries. There are twenty-four in all of these little-remarked documents, two in GDB, thirteen in Exon, and nine in IE, supplying statistical totals for the lands of various tenants-in-chief. They first list the number of manors held in demesne, their total assessment to the geld, the number of ploughs of the lord and his men, the numbers of the dependent peasantry, and the total value. Similar statistics are then given for the enfeoffed estates. Finally, the number of ploughlands in the whole of the fee is recorded, usually as a single figure, along with the increase in value since the land was acquired. This last item of information stands out. With the exception of the two GDB summaries, the information is given in unvarying words: this land suffices for so many ploughs, it has increased in value by so many pounds. With a formula drawn from no fewer than thirteen different shires in five circuits, here are surely statistics which were demanded by central government. They are the nearest we have to articles of inquiry. The ploughland and increase in value were central items of interest in the Domesday inquest.

Hitherto, the ploughland has been thought of in purely reductionist terms. Debate has centred on whether the unit is a real measure of land or a fiscal unit. The one hypothesis has foundered on the fact that working ploughs often exceed the land said to be available for them, the other on any sign of a new assessment after Domesday. Well, within our concept of the inquest as investigation we don't have to think in terms of either/or. It seems to me that all taxation must ultimately be based in a commonly agreed reality. Otherwise you get poll tax riots and defenestration. But whatever base you use for assessment it is only that, a common ground from which negotiation can proceed. The real and the fiscal are

---

[6] Above, pp. 74–82.

not mutually exclusive but different stages in a *process* of assessment. This is the context in which the ploughland begins to make sense.[7]

First, it is untrue to say that it does not appear after Domesday. It does, but significantly not as a new assessment. In the Burton, Ramsey, and Ely surveys of the early twelfth century the ploughland is regularly used as a measure of non-fiscal, that is unhidated, land. Here and there it is used in the same way in Domesday Book, and it is as close as we will get to real land without getting out a tape measure. However, the main referent of the ploughland in Domesday Book is the land assessed to the geld. Thus, the uninformative 'there are *x* hides there, land for *y* ploughs' of GDB is derived from the more expansive '*x* hides which *y* ploughs can plough', or the like, of its sources. What it is telling us is that although this land is paying tax at so many hides there is in fact that much land there. Sometimes working ploughs, TRW or TRE, were counted; at other times ploughlands were estimated. It mattered not. The result was the same. The ploughland is a measure of tax capacity.

With beneficial hidation before the Conquest and selective exemption of demesne after, the tax system was not producing to full capacity. The tenant-in-chief was profiting from the shortfall; the increase in value recorded in the summaries was some measure of the surplus cash that he enjoyed. These were potent data. We can reconstruct something of what was done with the new information from what we can perceive of the geld in the reign of William Rufus. No new tax was introduced, but by 1096 lay estates were paying for their demesnes. A hard bargain seems to have been struck. The tenant-in-chief retained the spare capacity in the land of his peasants in return for foregoing the exemption of his own demesne. It seems to me that this was almost certainly one of the decisions that was made at Salisbury.

Fiddling about with taxation inevitably had repercussions for service. In that reductionist way that characterizes so much of Domesday studies, the two quantities have often been viewed as mutually exclusive opposites. Gentlemen fight while peasants pay their taxes. It was not like that. Almost invariably geld has been understood as Danegeld: it has been reduced to an occasional, although increasingly annual, land tax. It was, of course, much more than that. Domesday Book tells us that Stamford was assessed at twelve and a half hundreds, that is 150 carucates, 'for military service by land and sea and for danegeld'. The geld was used to determine military service in Berkshire, and borough and bridge work in Cheshire, while in the South West it determined contributions to the king's farm. Most significantly of all, it mediated the duties of policing incumbent on the communities of the hundred and the vill, and as such it was the vital mechanism of the king's peace in the localities.[8]

---

[7] Above, pp. 203–9.
[8] Above, pp. 193–7.

Geld, then, was much more than a tax. It constituted the essential cohesion of local societies by articulating all the duties that a free man owed in respect of his station. Domesday demesne fitted seamlessly into it. If it did not render geld in 1086, it was clearly exempt rather than unassessed. All Domesday demesne is hidated: it was *warland*, that is it defended itself against the geld. We can take the argument little further from the Domesday texts, but the relation of service to geld is explicit in clause eleven of Henry I's coronation charter. There the freedom of demesne ploughs from geld is explicitly linked to defence of the realm. Service was a condition of exemption. It complemented taxation. Any change in the one affected the other.

So it is that the figures for manors in the summaries complement the data specifically relating to geld. At first these statistics surprise. There is nothing concrete in Domesday Book to correspond with them: the figures seem to relate more to entries or named holders than manors. However, the fact does not indicate that the manor was of no concern in the *inquest*. In LDB manorial structure is comprehensively recorded. And so it was when the GDB scribe began his work abbreviating the account of the North, but thereafter he progressively lost interest in the subject. By the time he reached the Leicestershire folios the manor hardly figures at all. There are, nevertheless, clues to its central role in the process of data collection. Throughout the Domesday texts there are innumerable references to land 'held for a manor'. Less widely, but still significantly, a concern is evident to identify land that had been added or taken away – an item, it will be remembered, that is specifically noted in the so-called articles of inquiry in IE.[9]

LDB hints at the reason for all these comments. From time to time we hear that a holding 'was of the number of his manors', or 'of his hundred manors' or whatever. More commonly land is said to have been granted 'to make up a manor'. Size mattered, so did number. Here surely is a proxy for service. The totals in the summaries indicate that the information was important. What was done with it is invisible. However, the homage made at Salisbury must have been made for land and surely service was a quid pro quo. Some forty years later Orderic Vitalis asserted, in what is the first account of the purpose of the Domesday inquest, that it was from this time that land was allocated to knight fees. You do not have to be convinced of Orderic's reliability, though, to understand that service was a fundamental part of the Domesday equation.

Content and soke

I would be guilty of reductionism myself were I to claim that the Domesday inquest was concerned only with the geld and service. The participants were manifold and, in so far as they all seem to have cooperated, they must have all expected

[9] IE, 97.

something out of the process, even if it was only avoiding an amercement. In reality all had much more to gain. As we know from the OE laws, payment of the geld and service in the fyrd were irreducible corollaries of freedom and right to land. Stating an assessment to the geld, then, and demonstrating that it had been acquitted, was tantamount to a confirmation of title. Non-participation in the inquest was not an option. Far from hiding land, there was probably a stampede to register tax liability. All sorts of information may have been presented in the same way just to be on the safe side. However, the fact merely emphasizes just how central taxation and service were to English society in the late eleventh century. They were the focus of the inquest for a king who had found national resources in both tax and service inadequate in the crisis of 1085. It is in these terms that we have examined the significance and referents of Domesday data.

First of all, it is clear that the Domesday inquest concerned itself only with land assessed to the geld. The claim seems like a truism, but its significance becomes apparent when it is appreciated that not all land was.[10] Some unhidated land, of course, is described. In the south and west many royal manors had never been assessed because they rendered a food rent, the farm of one or more nights. All, however, belonged to the crown and were surveyed in the initial stage of the Domesday inquest. The Welsh lands described in the Gloucestershire and Herefordshire folios are likewise unassessed but they too owe their inclusion to a special procedure: they are entered, 'above the line' in Maitland's phrase, with the borough before the body of the county texts. Otherwise, just about all other lands are hidated or carucated. 'Just about', for there are a few incidental references to 'inland' that indicate a reserve of land that was ignored. Outside the North where the term is used interchangeably with berewick, inland is most frequently recorded in Oxfordshire and there it is seemingly contrasted with the demesne. But a similar usage is widely found in Northamptonshire and Warwickshire, while in Huntingdonshire a non-hidated demesne is consistently recorded in the hundred of Hurstingstone.

Elsewhere Domesday Book is largely silent on land not assessed to the geld. But inland was clearly not the local phenomenon that this handful of references might suggest. The early twelfth-century surveys of the abbey of Burton's estates in Staffordshire and Derbyshire continually make reference to inland, there defined as land that does not pay the king's geld, which is contrasted with the hidated and carucated demesne. Similarly, the monks of Ramsey and Ely recognized demesne of this type throughout their East Anglian estates. Apart from that of Ramsey in Hurstingstone Hundred in Huntingdonshire, none of this land is noticed in GDB or LDB. We must conclude that there was land outside the cadastre which was not noticed by the Domesday commissioners.

---

[10] Above, pp. 198–203.

Much of this was clearly land that was so demesnal that it was entirely quit. The phenomenon helps to explain why some interests simply do not appear at all in Domesday Book. The estates of Crowland Abbey, for example, are described in detail, but Crowland itself is absent. The island was a sanctuary in which the writ of the king did not run. But not all inland was demesne. Some, probably most, was in service of one kind or another. Many counties were lowly rated and some tenements had no liability assessed upon them. In Nottinghamshire, for example, there were typically one or two carucates per vill and there are relatively few Domesday manors compared with the neighbouring more highly rated Lincolnshire. Twelfth-century charters, however, indicate intricate subinfeudation which is every bit as complex. Much land in Nottinghamshire, as elsewhere, does not find its way into Domesday Book. Some of this type of geld-free land may be a function of freehold assarting. Most of it looks like seigneurial assets. Thus, the Burton inlands were let to *censarii*. Geld liability was attached to certain tenements and the remaining lands went unnoticed.

The extent of inland is essentially unquantifiable. It is probable that its existence is sometimes hinted at by the statistics for ploughs.[11] In a large minority of entries there are more ploughs recorded than ploughlands. The unlikihood of overstocking of this kind has been a central plank in the fiscal interpretation of the ploughland. I agree on its implausibility but would maintain that the extra ploughs are real enough, being those of unassessed lands. The Burton figures nicely illustrate the point: the surplus ploughs of 1086 are balanced by the inland ploughs in 1115 (Table 6.1). Otherwise, inland does not appear to figure in the Domesday manor. Demesne ploughs and, where it is recorded, livestock ostensibly relate to the hidated demesne. Likewise, the dependent peasantry are those of the *warland*. Sometimes the connection is quite precise. Throughout the Ramsey Abbey estates there is a pronounced equation of one villein per fiscal virgate. Up into the fourteenth century service was demanded and rendered on the basis of these Domesday fiscal tenements. A similar equation is found on the Battle Abbey estates. As in East Anglia, the reality of field units is represented by redefining the hide as six, seven, or eight virgates, the tenants of which are unrepresented in Domesday. More widely, the assessment to the geld was the datum of service for free men and sokemen.

What, then, is this manor that does not include a sometimes sizeable asset in land, and that fails to notice a significant proportion of the peasantry? The answer would seem to be land that was assessed to service. For most of the manorial appurtenances the fact is invisible, but not so for values.[12] For most economic historians it would seem that the *valet* and *valuit* figures are a real measure that is related to output. For some they are net or even gross receipts, for others rents

---

[11] Above, p. 209.
[12] Above, pp. 240–50.

or farms. Both formulations present difficulties, not least because farms are often recorded and they are invariably different and larger than the values. It can be agreed, though, that values are sums of money that are rendered in one direction or another. The value of many manors is attached to others, usually demesne estates, and there is a significant number of instances in which it can be shown to be the sum that a tenant paid to an overlord (TRE and TRW).

The presentments recorded in Domesday Book and documents like the Domesday Monachorum B indicate that values were not just the preserve of estate managers. They were in some sense public knowledge: local juries were expected to furnish the information and even correct the figures given by the lord or reeve. As sums that went out of manors, they were therefore probably grounded in wider tributary relationships. This is precisely the import of the valuation clause of the Domesday entry for Osmaston in Derbyshire, in which the value was divided between the king and Henry de Ferrers in the ratio of two to one: the receipt of the king's two pennies was of the essence of soke. The various sources of the estates of Bury St Edmunds substantiate the fact. In some LDB entries the abbey's free men are separately valued and the individual renders that they made are identified in a Domesday schedule known as Bury C. Those sums can themselves be identified in the twelfth-century Kalendar of Abbot Samson where they are called hidage (Table 7.3). Here hidage was a hundredal due, having its origins in the renders that free men and sokemen made to the king, but it seems to represent the soke dues that were conferred by the right of sake and soke. Some free men may have paid in addition a manorial rent, but by and large hidage seems to have represented their full value. And it was a value that was essentially fiscal. Hidage was generally assessed on the fiscal carucate at the rate of 1d per *ware* acre or at 16d for every 15 acres, yielding 10s 8d each. This is an equation that can be widely observed in East Anglia; time and again the value of subholdings works out at exactly 1d per *ware* acre.

In West Derby Hundred in Lancashire hidage went under the guise of 'geld of carucates of land', and there manors were valued according to the amount due at the rate of 32d per carucate (Table 7.4). A similar relationship can be observed between Domesday manorial values and soke dues in Burton, Ely, Glastonbury, Peterborough, Ramsey, St Paul's, London, Shaftesbury, and Winchester sources. The equation is not always precise. The Burton survey of 1125 shows that tenements that were converted to day work between 1086 and the time of that survey ceased to render monetary dues. This is consonant with a widely occurring characteristic of Domesday values. *Valet* figures complement renders in kind. Thus, figures often subsist side by side with services, but where the render was totally in kind, as in the farm of one night, no valuation is given. Again, an inverse relationship between demesne ploughs and Domesday values has confused many a historian. Yet in these terms one would clearly expect monetary renders to go up when labour services go down. Domesday values seem to be soke dues rendered in cash. They do not represent any sort of overall return from the manor as whole. Thus it is that they appear in Domesday Book alongside the renders of churches, mills, and the like as any other render in cash.

The conclusion is entirely consistent with Robert of Hereford's account of the Domesday inquest. Where the Anglo-Saxon Chronicle merely refers to values, Robert reports that 'the services and payments due from all the men in the whole land' were recorded. The Domesday manor clearly articulates soke dues. As such it can be seen to fit into a wider context of fees and service.[13] In both 1066 and 1086 there was no simple equation of lordship with land. Real estate, to use a modern term, was predominantly in the hands of free men who are not named in the Domesday texts. What Domesday calls 'land' (*terra*) was in fact dues owed by these free holders, whether they be thegns or villeins. Lordship subsisted in those dues, what is generically called soke, which would otherwise belong to the king. A manor, or more precisely its hall, was a point at which they were intercepted. Its holder enjoyed the renders of his tenants in return for rendering dues and services to his lord's hall. Significantly, it was those names, it will be remembered, that were counted to determine the number of manors in the summaries.

The Domesday inquest was about taxation and service and so it confined itself to soke dues, for these were the tangible rights that the king had over his tenants-in-chief and over their land. The king had no rights over inland, and therefore his interest in land *per se* did not extend much beyond his own estates. The Domesday inquest generally did not deal with the matter. The results of the various statistical analyses are of a piece with the conclusion. Where recorded resources are related to a system of soke mediated by the geld, correlation of values with assessment and the like naturally follows. Figures that are calculated from each other are by definition related. Rather than asserting that Domesday Book is about estates because its data correlate, we conclude that its data correlate because it is about soke.

How, then, can we use its data? Only with difficulty, it would seem, if we wish to reconstruct anything other than the tributary economy. It is of course true that the issues of soke were part of the lord's resources and so the Domesday figures will by definition provide minima. At best, statistics like ploughlands indicate a potential for arable, numbers of peasants indicate a measure of population, values indicate a basic income. The problem is, of course, determining how representative these quantities are. Although a real measure of fiscal land, ploughlands are as uninformative as hides if we have no idea of the extent of inland. Where population figures are related to geld, they are little more than an index of the rate of assessment. As a record of renders in coin, values only tell us about the lord's petty cash tin. Domesday statistics are finite data cast adrift in an uncharted sea.

But if we accept the Domesday data for what they are we have to ask different questions of them. As I have tried to outline, there is a whole new range of

[13] Above, pp. 147–62.

interpretative possibilities out there. We can summarize as follows. First of all, the concept of Domesday as soke must shift our focus in a major way. I, as much as anyone, have been guilty of mouthing the mantra that resources found their way into Domesday because they contributed to the income of the lord. We have to reformulate that. Resources appear because soke dues are rendered in respect of them. A mere technicality? Well, no. It is a definition that indicates a difference in status. The record of churches illustrates the point. It is certainly eccentric. Churches appear in profusion in some counties and not at all in others. It has been rightly divined that procedural differences underlie distributions on a national scale. Locally, by contrast, we have tended to believe that the churches of Domesday are those that belonged to lords, they were *eigenkirken*. However, we know that not all private churches are recorded, even in circuits where they were well-represented. And if only those that owed soke dues are recorded we now have a reason. We also have an insight into the status of both types of church. How useful this will be has yet to be determined. It does seem to make sense, though, of the high number of churches recorded in areas where there was apparently little inland, such as Lincolnshire and Norfolk.

Reassessment of all items of manorial stock can be undertaken in similar terms. That is all bread and butter. It is possible to draw wider conclusions within the terms of the Domesday inquest. I have already suggested that overstocking is almost certainly a marker for inland. The phenomenon is the best guide we have to a phantom Domesday resource. Given the near invisibility of inland in the Domesday corpus, this was probably not an outcome that the commissioners appreciated, let alone anticipated. By contrast, it is certain that, in demanding the ploughland statistics, they had an even more lucrative phantom resource within their sights. Geld exemption did not relieve the lord of a tax burden, it diverted it from his tenants into his pocket. In the summaries the ploughlands are collected by fee and juxtaposed with geld assessment, ploughs, population, and value of the demesne and enfeoffed lands. Assessment, resources, and income are indexed against the land available, providing a measure of how much the tenant-in-chief raked off from the geld. The excess of ploughlands over hides is an index of a resource that is not otherwise quantified in Domesday Book. King William used the information to divert some of the income into the treasury. What use the historian can made of the figures remains to be seen.

Finally, values. The *valuit* and *valet* figures are only contingently related to output, but the figures are a measure of the importance of cash in the management of estates. Here change is of more importance than magnitude. Our analysis would suggest that increases may often indicate commutation of labour dues and food rents. Domesday values may well be the best measure we have of the extent of demesne exploitation in 1086. Moreover, if they were sums that regularly went out of manors, they may also be an excellent index of the income in cash of the great lords of Norman England.

Domesday Book in perspective

The Domesday inquest was, most emphatically, not an inventory survey. What it tells us about estates, as opposed to Domesday manors, is incidental. The conclusion goes a long way to explaining why the preferred form of the inquest records was geographical arrangement. The king certainly demanded service from his tenants-in-chief in person. They must often have been required to attend on him at time of crisis. At other times, the shire was probably the forum in which they discharged their duties. By contrast, the king's interests in their lands, the geld and soke, were predominantly those that were rendered in the hundred and vill. The inquest was about communal dues that accrued to lords. It was who held them in the vill that was of relevance.

Even lordship, then, was peripheral to the king's dues and their nexus. It only became central with the production of Domesday Book. But the limitations of the source precluded any reconstruction of estates, had it been felt desirable. LDB remains as geographical as the new schema allowed: the hundred rather than the manor is the basic unit of the text. The GDB scribe was probably responsible for the tenurial arrangement of much of the folios of Lincolnshire, Nottinghamshire, Derbyshire, and Huntingdonshire, but the effort was not worth the candle. Thereafter, the manor itself ceased to be of interest. In highlighting the county boroughs and the shire customs, the GDB scribe reveals that his focus was still the dues of the king. The lands of his subjects were only of interest in so far as they rendered him dues. Indeed, there was no alternative. Had the Domesday scribes wanted to make a silk purse, they would have been unable to do so out of the pig's ear that they had before them.

That was the reality of writing and almost certainly of early use. The perception of the process was somewhat different in the longer term. Domesday society was still tributary. The twelfth century was a different world. In 1166 Henry II ordered an inquest into the service owed by his tenants-in-chief. Each lord was required to declare his *servitium debitum*, the number of knights that he was obliged to provide for the host, and how many had actually been enfeoffed on his lands, both before 1135 and after. The declarations, the *carte baronum*, share nothing with the Domesday texts.[14] Geld assessment, stock, value, manors, estates were all of no account. A statement of service and a list of those who would discharge it for the lord was all that was relevant. Lordship was now firmly identified with land. Enfeoffment conferred a more or less absolute right which was heritable and the king therefore had no further interest in it. Charters continued to use the language of English law, but grants of sake and soke and the like, resounding rights of great moment in 1086, were now formulas of little content. Gone were all of the nuances of soke, and geld had become a mere land tax. The knight fee and knight service

---

[14] *The Red Book of the Exchequer*, ed. H. Hall, 3 vols, Rolls Series, 99 (1896).

represented a new order. Except in the North, the tributary society of 1086 was largely a thing of the past.

It was a development that was widely paralleled in Europe. If there is anything peculiar about the English experience it is that it was so late in coming. No one factor, then, can be said to have initiated the transformation. At any particular point continuities are as apparent as discontinuities. Thus, on the one hand, late Anglo-Saxon society had already witnessed the increased differentiation in wealth between the thegn and the common free man, at once the cause and effect of a society which was becoming increasingly militarized, and its localization in space. On the other, the early twelfth century saw the rise of 'new men', developments in the law, and the Anarchy which were all to fashion the character of English feudalism. The territorialization of lordship was a trend that had no one precipitating cause.[15]

Nevertheless, there seems no doubt that the aftermath of the Domesday inquest was seen in retrospect as a decisive moment. For the old-fashioned constitutional historian the Oath of Salisbury in August 1086 marked a departure that was to define a particularly English experience in the later Middle Ages. Liege lordship, the expectation that a free man's first allegiance was due to the king, was held to have prevented the fragmentation of authority that characterized European feudalism. We can now see that the geld meditated much the same sort of relationship before 1086. The oath was, however, a new dispensation. Homage brought all free men to the nighness to the king that had hitherto been the right of the king's thegn and baron. Performance of the quid pro quo of service warranted heritable title.

The equation of lordship and land thereby implied cannot have been immediate: the expectation of bequest and inheritance could only be realized in the second generation. But it is not difficult to see that thereafter right might be defended by reference to the oath rather than the geld. That was certainly the understanding of Richard fitzNigel: the Domesday inquest was undertaken so that 'every man may be content with his own rights, and not encroach unpunished on those of others'. It was self-evident, then, that its 'decisions' could not be contradicted. We have argued at length that the inquest had not and could not recognize title, and the mere fact of writing down did not change the fact. Domesday Book was no register of title, not even a survey of estates. But the long view changes perspective. It must have been seen as the embodiment of the new order from early in the twelfth century when the identification of lordship with land was becoming a reality. In the 1120s Henry I ordered that services be restored to the lands of Ely 'which my Winchester charter shows to have been sworn to its fee'.[16] That, in its

---

[15] For a nuanced discussion of these issues, see M. Chibnall, *Anglo-Norman England 1066–1166* (Oxford, 1986), and, more recently, M. Chibnall, *The Debate on the Norman Conquest* (Manchester, 1999).

[16] *Regesta Regum Anglo-Normannorum 1066–1154*, eds H. W. C. Davis, C. Johnson, H. A. Cronne, and R. H. C. Davis, 4 vols (Oxford, 1913–69), ii, no. 1500. For others, see

turn, changed perceptions of the nature of Domesday data: the manor became an estate and its recorded appurtenances its stock. It is probably no coincidence that it was the expatriate Orderic alone who could clearly perceive the true nature of the Domesday process in the 1120s.

Domesday Book was reinvented in the image of twelfth-century society (unless, of course, it was written much later than here suggested, in which case the inquest was reinvented). Its authority was thrust upon it in the service of an ideology. Richard fitzNigel links the production of the book with the imposition of written law. Domesday Book was the embodiment of the will of William the Conqueror. In accepting that reductionist perspective, historians have been forced to make stark choices, with all the contradictions that have ensued. With the recognition of the inquest as the information gathering activity that it was, we are freed from that tyranny of either/or. It is an understanding that also dispenses with the need to perceive the Domesday inquest as an exhaustive process. Its focus was wide, but it was not overarching. In suggesting that tax and service were its interlinked subjects, I have argued that Domesday data were selected to illuminate these concerns. The Domesday inquest was less about estates than soke dues. All of what we want Domesday Book to be – a register of title, a terrier, an index of wealth, a topography of power – it is not. In return, we have a truer understanding of the nature and workings of late eleventh-century society.

Regesta Regum, ii, nos 236, 373, 386a, 468, 976, 1000, 1488, 1515.

Appendix

———

The main entry forms of GDB

Here are listed the main entry forms that are found in GDB. Minor variations, especially where postscriptal, are not generally noted. Nor is the diplomatic of the king's chapters outside Yorkshire. Throughout the text the *terra regis* exhibits its own formulas without any discernible overall sequence within the series or continuity with the body of the text. The characteristic is a function of the collection of the data within the shire in the initial stage of the Domesday inquest. For a full discussion of the various forms and how they relate to each other, see *DIB*, chapter 8.

Circuit VI

VIA	Survey by vills: In x there y^t carucates which z ploughs can plough; of these a^1 had y^1 with a hall; now b^1 has them. And a^2 had y^2 ...
VIB	In x there are y carucates to the geld which z ploughs can plough; a held it for a manor, now b and c from him.
VIC	In x are y carucates; z ploughs possible; a had a manor, now b and c from him.
VID	In x are y carucates; land for z ploughs. The manor was and is a's.
VIE	In x are y carucates; z ploughs are possible; a had and has it.
VIF	In x a had a manor of y carucates; z ploughs possible. Now c has it from b.
VIG	In x a had a manor of y carucates; [there is land for z ploughs]. Now c has it from b.
VIH	MNR In x a had y carucates, [land for z ploughs]. Now b has it.
VII	MNR In x a had y carucates, z ploughs are possible. Now b has it.
VIJ	M In x a had y carucates, z ploughs are possible. Now b has it.
VIK	M In x a had y carucates, land for z ploughs. Now b has it.
VIL	In x a^2 held y carucates from a^1, land for z ploughs.
VIM	b has t^1 teams in demesne, and n^1 villagers, and n^2 bordars with t^2 teams, and n^3 sokemen with t^3 teams.
VIN	b has t^1 teams in demesne, and n^1 villagers, and n^2 bordars with t^2 teams, and n^3 sokemen on y^2 carucates with t^3 teams.

VIO   *b* has t^1 teams in demesne, and n^1 villagers, n^3 sokemen, and n^2 bordars with t^2 teams.

VIP   *b* has t^1 teams in demesne, and n^1 villagers, n^3 sokemen, and n^2 bordars with t^2 teams ... y^2 carucates are in soke.

VIQ   *b* has t^1 teams in demesne and n^3 sokemen on y^2 carucates, and n^1 villagers, and n^2 bordars with t^2 teams.

VIR   *b* has t^1 teams in demesne and n^3 sokemen, n^1 villagers, and n^2 bordars with t^2 teams.

VIS b^2 holds from b^1.

Circuit III

IIIA   M *x* is a demesne vill and defends itself for *y* hides ... Value now, when acquired, TRE. This manor *a* held.

IIIB   M *x b* holds, *y* hides are there ... Value now, when acquired, TRE. This M *a* held.

IIIC   M *b* holds *x*/in *x*, *y* hides are there/it defends itself for *y* hides ... Value now, when acquired, TRE. This manor *a* held.

IIID   In *x* b^2 holds *y* hides ... Value now, when acquired, TRE. a^2 held this land under a^1. He could sell etc.

Circuit I

IA   M *b* holds *x*/in *x*, *y* sulungs are there/it defends itself for *y* sulungs ... Value now, when acquired, TRE. This manor *a* held.

IB   *b* holds *x*; *a* held it and it defended itself for y^1 sulungs, now for y^2 ... It used to be worth ... when acquired ... now.

IC   In *x a* held *y* hides and now it defends itself for/it never gelded ... Valuit/valebat, valet

Circuit II

IIA B^1 holds *x* (and b^2 from him). *A* held it TRE; he/it used to geld for y^1 hides. Land for *z* ploughs. Of these y^2 hides in demesne ... *Valuit, modo.*

IIB B^2 holds from b^1 *x*. *A* held it TRE; he/it used to geld for y^1 hides. Land for *z* ploughs ... *Valuit, modo.*

IIC B^1 holds *x*. *A* held it TRE; he/it used to geld for y^1 hides. Land for *z* ploughs ... *Valuit, modo.*

IID B^1 holds *x*. *A* used to hold it TRE; he/it used to geld for y^1 hides. Land for *z* ploughs ... *Olim, modo.*

IIE   *B* holds *x*. There were y^1 hides TRE. Land for *y* teams. In demesne y^2 hides ... *Olim, modo.*

IIF   *B* holds *x*; *a* used to hold it TRE and he/it used to geld for y^1 hides. There are y^2 hides there, however ... *Olim, modo.*

Circuit V

VA   *B* held *x*, there were *y* hides. In demesne ... *Valebat, modo.*

VB   In *x* held *b* *y* hides. In demesne ... Render.

VC B^1 holds (and b^2 from him) *x, a* held and could go. There *y* hides gelding. In demesne ... *Valuit, modo.*

VD   *B* holds *y* hides in *x/b* holds in *x y* hides, *a* held ... In demesne ... *Valuit, modo.*

VE   In *x* are *y* hides ...

VF   *B* (b^2 from b^1) holds *x*. *A* held. There *y* hides gelding. Land for *z* ploughs ... *Valuit, modo.*

Circuit IV

IVA   *B* (b^2 from b^1) holds *x*. *A* held. There are *y* hides. Land for *z* ploughs ... *Valebat, modo.*

IVB   *B* (b^2 from b^1) holds *x*. *A* held. There are *y* hides. Land for *z* ploughs ... *Valuit, modo.*

IVC B^1 *y* hides in *x/*in *x y* hides (and b^2 from him). *A* held. Land for *z* ploughs ... *Valuit, modo.*

IVD   *B* (b^2 from b^1) holds *x*. There are *y* hides. Land for *z* ploughs ... *Valuit, modo. A* held ...

IVE   *B* (b^2 from b^1) holds *y* hides in *x/*in *x y* hides. Land for *z* ploughs ... *Valuit, modo. A* held ...

IVF   In *x* are *y* hides/In *x* holds *b* *y* hides.

Bibliography

Primary sources

Anglo-Saxon Charters, ed. A. J. Robertson, 2nd edn (Cambridge, 1956).

The Anglo-Saxon Chronicle: A Revised Translation, eds D. Whitelock, D. C. Douglas, and S. I. Tucker, 2nd edn (London, 1963).

Anglo-Saxon Wills, ed. D. Whitelock (Cambridge, 1930).

Anglo-Saxon Writs, ed. F. E. Harmer (Manchester, 1952).

Annales Monastici, ed. H. R. Luard, Rolls Series, 36, 5 vols (1864–69).

The Blyth Cartulary, ed. R. T. Timson, Thoroton Society Record Series, 27–8 (1973).

The Book of Fees, Public Record Office, 2 vols in 3 (1920–31).

Bracton on the Laws and Custom of England, ed. G. E. Woodbine, trans. Samuel E. Thorne, 2 vols (Cambridge MA, 1968).

'The Burton Abbey Twelfth Century Surveys', ed. C. G. O. Bridgeman, *Collections of the History of Staffordshire*, William Salt Archaeological Society (1916), 209–47.

Calendar of Documents Preserved in France, 918–1206, ed. J. H. Round, Public Record Office (1899).

Calendar of Inquisitions Post Mortem and Other Analogous Documents Preserved in the Public Record Office, Public Record Office, 1904 and in progress.

Calendar of Inquisitions Miscellaneous (Chancery) Preserved in the Public Record Office, Public Record Office, 7 vols (1916–1968).

Cambridge, University Library, MS 3021, the Red Book of Thorney.

Canterbury, Dean and Chapter, MS Lit. E28.

Cartularium Monasterii de Rameseia, eds W. H. Hart and P. A. Lyons, Rolls Series, 79, 3 vols (1884–89).

Cartularium Saxonicum, ed. W. de Gray Birch, 3 vols (London, 1885–93).

The Cartulary of Worcester Cathedral Priory (Register 1), ed. R. R. Darlington, Pipe Roll Society, new series, 38 (1968).

The Charters of Burton Abbey, ed. P. H. Sawyer (Oxford, 1979).

Charters of the Honour of Mowbray 1107–1191, ed. D. E. Greenway, Records of Social and Economic History, new series, 1, British Academy (1972).

Chronica Rogeri de Houedene, ed. W. Stubbs, 4 vols, Rolls Series, 51 (1868–71).

The Chronicle of Battle Abbey, ed. E. Searle (Oxford, 1980).

The Chronicle of John of Worcester, 3: The Annals from 1067 to 1140 with the Gloucester Interpolations and the Continuation to 1141, ed. and trans. P. McGurk (Oxford, 1998).

Chronicon Abbatiae de Evesham, ad Annum 1418, ed. W. D. Macray, Rolls Series, 29 (1863).

Chronicon Angliae Petroburgense, ed. J. A. Giles, Caxton Society (1845).

Chronicon Monasterii de Abingdon, ed. J. Stevenson, Rolls Series, 2, 2 vols (1858).

Chronicon Petroburgense, ed. T. Stapleton, Camden Society, old series, 47 (1849).

The Continental Origins of English Landholders 1066–1166 database and the COEL Database System on CD-ROM, K. S. B. Keats-Rohan, Coel Enterprises Ltd, 2002.

'De Injusta Vexatione Willelmi Episcopi Primi per Willelmum Regem Filium Willelmi Magni Regis', ed. H. S. Offler, *Chronology, Conquest and Conflict in Medieval England*, Camden Miscellany 34, Camden Society, 5th series, 10 (1997), 49–104.

Dialogus de Scaccario, the Course of the Exchequer, and Constitutio Domus Regis, the King's Household, ed. C. Johnson (London, 1950).

Die Gesetze der Angelsachsen, ed. F. Liebermann, 3 vols (Halle, 1903–26).

The Digital Domesday, CD-ROM, Alecto Historical Editions (London, 2002).

Documents Illustrative of the Social and Economic History of the Danelaw from Various Collections, ed. F. M. Stenton, British Academy Records of Social and Economic History, 5 (1920).

Documents Relating to the Manor and Soke of Newark-on-Trent, ed. M. W. Barley, Thoroton Society, Record Series, 16 (1956).

Domesday Book, eds R. W. H. Erskine, A. Williams, and G. H. Martin (London: Alecto Historical Editions, 1986–2000).

Domesday Book: A Complete Translation, eds A. Williams and G. H. Martin (London: Penguin Books, 2002).

Domesday Book; seu Liber Censualis Willelmi Primi Regis Angliae inter Archivos Regni in Domo Capitulari Westmonasterii Asservatus, ed. A. Farley, 2 vols (London, 1783).

Domesday Book; seu Liber Censualis Vocati Domesday Book, Indices, ed. H. Ellis (London, 1816).

Domesday Book: Bedfordshire, ed. J. Morris (Chichester, 1977).

Domesday Book: Berkshire, ed. P. Morgan (Chichester, 1979).

Domesday Book: Buckinghamshire, ed. J. Morris (Chichester, 1978).

Domesday Book: Cambridgeshire, ed. A. Rumble (Chichester, 1981).

Domesday Book: Cheshire, ed. P. Morgan (Chichester, 1978).

Domesday Book: Cornwall, eds C. Thorn and F. Thorn (Chichester, 1979).

Domesday Book: Derbyshire, ed. P. Morgan (Chichester, 1978).

Domesday Book: Devon, eds C. Thorn and F. Thorn (Chichester, 1985).

Domesday Book: Dorset, eds C. Thorn and F. Thorn (Chichester, 1983).

Domesday Book: Essex, ed. A. Rumble (Chichester, 1983).

Domesday Book: Gloucestershire, ed. J. S. Moore (Chichester, 1982).

Domesday Book: Hampshire, ed. J. Mumby (Chichester, 1982).

Domesday Book: Herefordshire, eds F. Thorn and C. Thorn (Chichester, 1983).

Domesday Book: Hertfordshire, ed. J. Morris (Chichester, 1976).

Domesday Book: Huntingdonshire, ed. S. Harvey (Chichester, 1975).

Domesday Book: Kent, ed. P. Morgan (Chichester, 1983).

Domesday Book: Leicestershire, ed. P. Morgan (Chichester, 1979).

Domesday Book: Lincolnshire, eds P. Morgan and C. Thorn (Chichester, 1986).

Domesday Book: Middlesex, ed. J. Morris (Chichester, 1975).

Domesday Book: Norfolk, ed. P. Brown (Chichester, 1984).

Domesday Book: Northamptonshire, eds F. Thorn and C. Thorn (Chichester, 1979).

Domesday Book: Nottinghamshire, ed. J. Morris (Chichester, 1977).

Domesday Book: Oxfordshire, ed. J. Morris (Chichester, 1978).

Domesday Book: Rutland, ed. F. Thorn (Chichester, 1980).

Domesday Book: Shropshire, eds F. Thorn and C. Thorn (Chichester, 1986).

Domesday Book: Somerset, eds C. Thorn and F. Thorn (Chichester, 1980).

Domesday Book: Staffordshire, ed. J. Morris (Chichester, 1976).

Domesday Book: Suffolk, ed. A. Rumble (Chichester, 1986).

Domesday Book: Surrey, ed. J. Morris (Chichester, 1975).

Domesday Book: Sussex, ed. J. Morris (Chichester, 1976).

Domesday Book: Warwickshire, ed. J. Morris (Chichester, 1976).

Domesday Book: Wiltshire, eds C. Thorn and F. Thorn (Chichester, 1979).

Domesday Book: Worcestershire, eds F. Thorn and C. Thorn (Chichester, 1982).

Domesday Book: Yorkshire, eds M. L. Faull and M. Stinson (Chichester, 1986).

Domesday Explorer, CD-ROM, J. J. N. Palmer, M. Palmer, and G. Slater, Phillimore (Chichester, 2000).

The Domesday Monachorum of Christ Church, Canterbury, ed. D. C. Douglas, Royal Historical Society (1944).

The Earliest Lincolnshire Assize Rolls A.D. 1202–1209, ed. D. M. Stenton, Lincoln Record Society, 22 (1926).

The Early Charters of the Cathedral Church of St Paul's, London, ed. M. Gibbs, Camden, 3rd series, 53 (1939).

Early Yorkshire Charters, ed. C. T. Clay, Yorkshire Archaeological Society, Record Series, extra series, vols 4–10 (1935–55).

Early Yorkshire Charters, ed. W. Farrer, 3 vols (Edinburgh, 1914–16).

The Ecclesiastical History of Orderic Vitalis, ed. M. Chibnall, 6 vols (Oxford, 1969–80).

An Eleventh Century Inquisition of St Augustine's, Canterbury, ed. A. Ballard, Records of the Social and Economic History of England, 4 (London, 1920).

The English Register of Oseney Abbey, ed. A. Clark, Early English Text Society (1907).

Facsimiles of English Royal Writs to A.D. 1100 Presented to Vivian Hunter Galbraith, eds T. A. M. Bishop and P. Chaplais (Oxford, 1957).

Feudal Documents from the Abbey of Bury St Edmund's, ed. D. C. Douglas, Records of the Social and Economic History of England and Wales, 8, British Academy (1932).

The Great Chartulary of Glastonbury, ed. A. Watkin, Somerset Record Society, 59, 63, 64 (1947–56).

Great Domesday Book: County Edition, eds A. Williams and R. W. H. Erskine, 30 vols (London, 1986–92).

Hemingi Chartularium Ecclesiae Wigorniensis, ed. T. Hearne, 2 vols (Oxford, 1723).

Henrici Archdiaconi Huntendunensis Historia Anglorum, ed. T. Arnold, Rolls Series, 74 (1879).

Henry de Bracton: On the Laws and Customs of England, 4 vols (Cambridge, Mass., 1968–77).

Herefordshire Domesday, circa 1160–1170, eds V. H. Galbraith and J. Tait, Pipe Roll Society 63, new series, 25 (1950).

Historia Ecclesie Abbendonensis: The History of the Church of Abingdon, vol. 2, ed. and trans. John Hudson, Oxford Medieval Texts (Oxford, 2002).

Ingulph's Chronicle of the Abbey of Crowland and the Continuations by Peter de Blois and Anonymous Writers, trans. H. T. Riley (London, 1854).

Inquisitio Comitatus Cantabrigiensis … Subjicitur Inquisitio Eliensis, ed. N. E. S. A. Hamilton (London, 1876).

Inquisitions and Assessments Relating to Feudal Aids; with Other Analogous Documents Preserved in the Public Record Office AD 1284–1431, Public Record Office, 6 vols (1899–1920).

The Kalendar of Abbot Samson of Bury St Edmunds and Related Documents, ed. R. H. C. Davis, Camden Society, 3rd series, 84 (1954).

The Laws of the Earliest English Kings, ed. F. L. Attenborough (Cambridge, 1922).

The Laws of the Kings of England from Edmund to Henry I, ed. A. J. Robertson (Cambridge, 1925).

The Lay Subsidy of 1334, ed. R. E. Glasscock, British Academy (London, 1975).

Leges Henrici Primi, ed. L. J. Downer (Oxford, 1972).

The Letters of Lanfranc Archbishop of Canterbury, eds and trans. H. Glover and M. Gibson (Oxford, 1979).

Liber Eliensis, ed. E. O. Blake, Camden Society, 3rd series, 92 (1962).

Libri Censualis, vocati Domesday Book, Additamenta ex Codic. Antiquiss. Exon Domesday; Inquisitio Eliensis; Liber Winton; Boldon Book, ed. H. Ellis (London, 1816).

Lincoln, Lincoln Archives Office, Longley 7.

The Lincolnshire Domesday and Lindsey Survey, eds C. W. Foster and T. Longley, Lincoln Record Society, 19 (1921).

The Lincolnshire Survey Temp. Henry I, ed. J. Greenstreet (London, 1884).

London, British Library, Arundel 178.

London, British Library, Cotton MS Vespasian E.

London, British Library, Cotton, Claudius C.5.

London, British Library, Harleian MS Y 6, the Guthlac Roll.

London, British Library, Harleian MS 61, the Shaftesbury Register.

London, National Archives, SC5 Extract Rolls.

London, National Archives, SC5/Cambs/Chapter House/4.

London, National Archives, SC5/Devon/Chapter House/1.

London, National Archives, SC5/Essex/Chapter House/1–3.

London, National Archives, SC5/Kent/Chapter House/1.

London, National Archives, SC5/Wilts/Chapter House/1a.

London, National Archives, SC5.

London, Society of Antiquaries, MS 60, the Black Book of Peterborough.

London, London University Library, Fuller MSS.

Matthei Parisiensis, Monachi Sancti Albani, Historia Anglorum, ed. F. Madden, 3 vols, Rolls Series, 44 (1866–8).

Memorials of St Guthlac of Crowland, ed. W. de Gray Birch (Wisbech, 1881).

Monasticon Anglicanum, eds J. Caley, H. Ellis, and B. Bandinel, 6 vols in 8 (London, 1817–30).

Northampton, Northampton Record Office, ZB 347.

Papsturkunden in England, ed. W. Holtzmann, 3 vols (Berlin and Göttingen, 1930–52).

Peterborough, Peterborough Dean and Chapter MS 1, The Book of Robert of Swaffham.

The Peterborough Chronicle 1070–1154, ed. C. Clark, 2nd edn (Oxford, 1970).

Placita de Quo Warranto, ed. W. Illingworth, Record Commission (London, 1818).

Radulphi de Coggeshall Chronicon Anglicanum, ed. J. Stevenson, Rolls Series, 66 (1875).

The Red Book of the Exchequer, ed. H. Hall, 3 vols, Rolls Series, 99 (1896).

The Red Book of Worcester, ed. M. Hollings, 4 vols, Worcester Historical Society (1934–50).

Regesta Regum Anglo-Normannorum 1066–1154, eds H. W. C. Davis, C. Johnson, H. A. Cronne, and R. H. C. Davis, 4 vols (Oxford, 1913–69).

Regesta Regum Anglo-Normannorum: The Acta of William I 1066–1087, ed. D. Bates (Oxford, 1998).

The Registrum Antiquissimum, eds C. W. Foster and K. Major, Lincoln Record Society, 27–29, 32, 34, 41, 42, 46, 51, 62, 67, 68 (1931–73).

Rerum Anglicarum Scriptores Post Bedam, ed. H. Savile (Frankfurt, 1601).

Rerum Anglicarum Scriptores Veteres, i, ed. W. Fulman (Oxford, 1684).

Rotuli de Dominabus et Pueris et Puellis de xii Comitatibus, ed. J. H. Round, Pipe Roll Society, 35 (1913).

Rotuli Hundredorum, ed. W. Illingworth, 2 vols, Record Commission (1812, 1818).

Rufford Charters, ed. C. J. Holdsworth, Thoroton Society Record Series, 29.

Scriptores Post Bedam, ed. H. Savile (London, 1596).

Select Charters, ed. W. Stubbs, 9th edn, revised by H. W. C. Davis (Oxford, 1913).

Some Sessions of the Peace in Lincolnshire 1360–1374, ed. R. Sillem, Lincoln Record Society, 30 (1937).

Southwell, Minster Library, MS 1, The White Book of Southwell.

The Statutes of the Realm, eds A. Luders *et al.*, 11 vols in 12, Record Commission (1810–28).

Symeonis Monachi Opera Omnia, ed. T. Arnold, Rolls Series, 75, 2 vols (1882–85).

A Terrier of Fleet, Lincolnshire, from a Manuscript in the British Museum, ed. N. Neilson (London).

Textus Roffensis: Rochester Cathedral Library Manuscript A.3.5. Pt 1, ed. P. Sawyer, Early English MSS in Facsimile 7 (Copenhagen, 1957).

The Thurgarton Cartulary, ed. T. Foulds (Stamford, 1994).

Tractatus de Legibus et Consuetudinibus Anglie qui Glanvilla Vocatur, ed. G. D. G. Hall (London, 1965).

Visitations and Memorials of Southwell Minster, ed. A. F. Leach (London, 1891).

Westminster Abbey Charters 1066–c.1214, ed. E. Mason, London Record Society, 25 (1988).

Willelmi Monachi Malmesbiriensis de Gestis Regum Anglorum Libri Quinque; Historiae Novellae Libri Tres, ed. W. Stubbs, Rolls Series, 90, 2 vols (1887–9).

William of Malmesbury, ca.1090–ca.1143 – Gesta Regum Anglorum: The History of the English Kings, eds and trans. R. A. B. Mynors, R. M. Thomson, and M. Winterbottom, 2 vols (Oxford, 1998).

Yorkshire Hundred and Quo Warranto Rolls, ed. B. English, Yorkshire Archaeological Society, Record Series, 151 (1996).

Secondary sources

Abels, R. P., 'Bookland and Fyrd Service', *ANS*, 7 (1984), 1–25.

——, *Lordship and Military Obligation in Anglo-Saxon England* (London, 1988).

——, 'An Introduction to the Bedfordshire Domesday', *The Bedfordshire Domesday*, eds A. Williams and R. W. H. Erskine (London, 1991), 1–53.

——, 'An Introduction to the Hertfordshire Domesday', *The Hertfordshire Domesday*, eds A. Williams and R. W. H. Erskine (London, 1991), 1–36.

——, 'Sheriffs, Lord Seeking, and the Norman Settlement of the South-East Midlands', *ANS*, 19 (1996), 19–50.

Aird, W. M., *St Cuthbert and the Normans: The Church of Durham, 1071–1153* (Woodbridge, 1998).

Allen, J., Henderson, C., and Higham, R., 'Saxon Exeter', *Anglo-Saxon Towns in Southern England*, ed. J. Haslam (Chichester, 1984), 385–414.

Altman, D. G., *Practical Statistics for Medical Research* (London, 1991).

Amt, E. M., 'The Meaning of Waste in the Early Pipe Rolls of Henry II', *EcHR*, 2nd ser., 44 (1991), 240–48.

Anderson, O. S., *The English Hundred Names*, 3 vols (Lund, 1934–39).

Bailey, K. A., 'The Hidation of Middlesex', *Transactions of the London and Middlesex Archaeological Society*, 39 (1988), 165–86.

——, 'The Hidation of Buckinghamshire: Part 1 Domesday', *Records of Buckinghamshire*, 32 (1990), 1–34.

——, 'The Hidation of Buckinghamshire: Part 2 Before Domesday', *Records of Buckinghamshire*, 34 (1992), 87–96.

——, 'Buckinghamshire Slavery in 1086', *Records of Buckinghamshire*, 37 (1995), 67–78.

——, 'Mills in Domesday Buckinghamshire', *Records of Buckinghamshire*, 39 (1997), 67–72.

Bailey, M., 'Introduction', *Little Domesday, Suffolk*, eds A. Williams and G. H. Martin (London, 2000), 9–30.

Balkwill, C. J., 'Old English Wic and the Origin of the Hundred', *Landscape History*, 15 (1993), 5–12.

Ballard, A., *The Domesday Inquest* (London, 1906).

Baring, F. H., 'Domesday Book and the Burton Cartulary', *EHR*, 11 (1896), 98–102.

——, 'The Conqueror's Footprints in Domesday', *EHR*, 13 (1898), 17–25.

——, 'The Exeter Domesday', *EHR*, 27 (1912), 309–18.

——, *Domesday Tables for the Counties of Surrey, Berkshire, Middlesex, Hertford, Buckingham and Bedford and the New Forest* (London, 1909).

Barlow, F., 'Domesday Book: A Letter of Lanfranc', *EHR*, 78 (1963), 284–9.

——, 'An Introduction to the Devon Domesday', *The Devon Domesday*, eds A. Williams and R. W. H. Erskine (London, 1991), 1–25.

——, *William Rufus* (London, 1983).

Bassett, S., 'Lincoln and the Anglo-Saxon See of Lindsey', *Anglo-Saxon England*, 18 (1989), 1–32.

Bates, D., *Normandy before 1066* (London, 1982).

——, *A Bibliography of Domesday Book* (Woodbridge, 1985).

——, 'Two Ramsey Writs and the Domesday Survey', *Historical Research*, 63 (1990), 337–9.

——, 'The Conqueror's Charters', *England in the Eleventh Century*, ed. C. Hicks, Harlaxton Medieval Studies, 2 (1992), 1–15.

——, 'England and the "Feudal Revolution"', *Il Feudalesimo Nell'Alto Medioevo*, Settimane de Studio del Centro Italiano di Studi Sull'Alto Medioevo (Spoleto, 2000), 611–49.

Baxter, S., 'The Representation of Lordship and Land Tenure in Domesday Book', *Domesday Book*, eds E. Hallam and D. Bates (Stroud, 2001), 73–102.

Baxter, S. and Blair, J., 'Land Tenure and Royal Patronage in the Early English Kingdom: A Model and a Case Study', *ANS*, 28 (2005), 19–46.

Beresford, M., and Hurst, J., *Wharram Percy: Deserted Medieval Village* (London, 1990).

Biddle, M. (ed.), *Winchester in the Early Middle Ages: An Edition and Discussion of the Winton Domesday*, Winchester Studies, i (Oxford, 1976).

Birss, R., and Wheeler, H., 'Roman Derby: Excavations 1968–83', *Derbyshire Archaeological Journal*, 105 (1985), 7–14.

Bishop, M. W., 'Multiple Estates in Late Anglo-Saxon Nottinghamshire', *Transactions of the Thoroton Society*, 85 (1981), 37–47.

Bishop, T. A. M., 'The Norman Settlement of Yorkshire', *Studies in Medieval History Presented to Frederick Maurice Powicke*, eds R. W. Hunt, W. A. Pantin, and R. W. Southern (Oxford, 1948), 1–14.

Blackstone, W., *Commentaries on the Laws of England*, 4 vols (Oxford, 1770).

Blair, J., 'Secular Minster Churches in Domesday Book', *Domesday Book: A Reassessment*, ed. P. H. Sawyer (London, 1985), 164–74.

——, 'Local Churches in Domesday Book and Before', *Domesday Studies*, ed. J. C. Holt (Woodbridge, 1987), 276–8.

——, 'An Introduction to the Surrey Domesday', *The Surrey Domesday*, eds A. Williams and R. W. H. Erskine (London, 1989), 1–17.

——, 'An Introduction to the Oxfordshire Domesday', *The Oxfordshire Domesday*, eds A. Williams and R. W. H. Erskine (London, 1990), 1–19.

——, *Anglo-Saxon Oxfordshire* (Stroud, 1994).

——, 'Debate: Ecclesiastical Organization and Pastoral Care in Anglo-Saxon England', *Early Medieval Europe*, 4 (1995), 193–212.

——, 'Estate Memoranda of c.1070 from the See of Dorchester-on-Thames', *EHR*, 116 (2001), 114–23.

Blomefield, F., *An Essay towards a Topographical History of the County of Norfolk*, 2nd edn, 11 vols, 1805–10 (London, 1808).

Bolland, W. C., *The General Eyre* (Cambridge, 1922).

Boyle, J. R., 'The Dings in York', *Notes and Queries*, 9th series, 4 (1899), 181–2.

Bradbury, J., 'Introduction to the Buckinghamshire Domesday', *The Buckinghamshire Domesday*, eds A. Williams and R. W. H. Erskine (London, 1988), 1–36.

Bridbury, A. R. 'Domesday Book: A Re-interpretation', *EHR*, 105 (1990), 284–309.

——, *The English Economy from Bede to the Reformation* (Woodbridge, 1992).

Brooke, C. N. L., *London 800–1216: The Shaping of a City* (London, 1975).

Brooke, C. N. L., and Keir, G., 'Streets and Wards', *London 800–1216* (London, 1972), 149–82.

Brooks, N. P., 'The Development of Military Obligations in Eighth- and Ninth-Century England', *England before the Conquest*, eds P. Clemoes and K. Hughes (Cambridge, 1971), 69–84.

Brown, R. A., *The Normans* (London, 1984).

Bryant, G. F., *Domesday Book: How to read it and what its text means* (Waltham, 1985).

Caenigem, R. C. Van, *Royal Writs in England from the Conquest to Glanvill: Studies in the Early History of the Common Law*, Selden Society, 77 (1959).

Cain, T., 'Introduction to the Rutland Domesday', *The Northamptonshire and Rutland Domesday*, eds A. Williams and R. W. H. Erskine (London, 1987), 18–34.

——, 'An Introduction to the Leicestershire Domesday', *The Leicestershire Domesday*, eds A. Williams and G. H. Martin (London, 1991), 1–21.

Cam, H. M., *Studies in the Hundred Rolls* (Oxford, 1921).

——, *The Hundred and the Hundred Rolls* (London, 1930).

——, '*Manerium cum Hundredo*: The Hundred and the Hundredal Manor', *EHR*, 47 (1932), 353–76.

Cambridge, E., and Rollason, D. W., 'Debate: The Pastoral Organization of the Anglo-Saxon Church: A Review of the "Minster Hypothesis"', *Early Medieval Europe*, 4 (1995), 87–104.

Cameron, K., *The Place-Names of Derbyshire*, English Place-Name Society, 27–9 (1959).

Campbell, J., 'Observations on English Government from the Tenth to the Twelfth Century', *TRHS*, 5th ser., 25 (1975), 39–54.

——, *The Anglo-Saxons* (London, 1982).

——, 'Some Agents and Agencies of the Late Anglo-Saxon State', *Domesday Studies*, ed. J. C. Holt (Woodbridge, 1987), 201–218.

Carpenter, D. A., 'The Decline of the Curial Sheriff in England 1194–1258', *EHR*, 91 (1976), 1–32.

Chaplais, P., 'William of Saint-Calais and the Domesday Survey', *Domesday Studies*, ed. J. Holt (Woodbridge, 1987), 65–78.

Chibnall, M., *Anglo-Norman England 1066–1166* (Oxford, 1986).

——, *The Debate on the Norman Conquest* (Manchester, 1999).

Clanchy, M. T., *From Memory to Written Record* (London, 1979).

Clark, C., 'English Personal Names *ca* 650–1300: Some Prosopographical Bearings', *Medieval Prosopography*, 8 (1987), 31–60.

——, 'Domesday Book – a Great Red-herring; Thoughts on some Eleventh-Century Orthographies', *England in the Eleventh Century*, ed. C. Hicks, Harlaxton Medieval Studies, 2 (1992), 317–31.

——, *Words, Names, and History: Selected Papers of Cecily Clark*, ed. P. Jackson (Woodbridge, 1995).

Clarke, H., 'Agriculture in Late Anglo-Saxon England', *Domesday Studies*, eds A. Williams and R. W. H. Erskine (London, 1987), 43–7.

Clarke, H. B., 'The Early Surveys of Evesham Abbey: An Investigation into the Problem of Continuity in Anglo-Norman England', unpublished PhD thesis, Birmingham 1977.

——, 'The Domesday Satellites', *Domesday Book: A Reassessment*, ed. P. H. Sawyer (London, 1985), 50–70.

Clarke, P. A., *The English Nobility under Edward the Confessor* (Oxford, 1994).

Clay, C., and Greenway, D. E., *Early Yorkshire Families* (Wakefield, 1973).

Clementi, D., 'Notes on Norman Sicilian Surveys', in Galbraith, *The Making of Domesday Book*, 55–8.

Condon, M. M. and Hallam, E., 'Government Printing of the Public Records in the Eighteenth Century', *Journal of the Society of Archivists*, 7 (1984), 348–88.

Cooper, A., 'Extraordinary Privilege: The Trial of Penenden Heath and the Domesday Inquest', *EHR*, 116 (2001), 1167–92.

——, 'Protestations of Ignorance in Domesday Book', *The Experience of Power in Medieval Europe, 950–1350*, eds R. Berkhofer, A. Cooper, and A. Kosto (Aldershot, 2005), 169–82.

Corbett, W. J., 'The Development of the Duchy of Normandy and the Norman Conquest of England', *The Cambridge Medieval History*, ed. J. R. Tanner, 5 (Cambridge, 1926), 481–520, 885–94.

Costen, M., *The Origins of Somerset* (Manchester, 1992).

Coulson, C., 'Cultural Realities and Reappraisals in English Castle Study', *Journal of Medieval History*, 22 (1996), 171–208.

——, 'Peaceable Power in English Castles', *ANS*, 23 (2000), 69–95.

Courtney, P., 'Saxon and Medieval Leicester: The Making of an Urban Landscape', *Transactions of the Leicestershire Archaeological and Historical Society*, 72 (1998), 110–45.

Cownie, E., 'The Normans as Patrons of English Religious Houses, 1066–1135', *ANS*, 18 (1995), 47–62.

——, *Religious Patronage in Anglo-Norman England, 1066–1135*, Royal Historical Society, Studies in History, new series (Woodbridge, 1998).

Creighton, O. H., 'Early Castles in the Medieval Landscape of Wiltshire', *Wiltshire Archaeological and Natural History Magazine*, 93 (2000), 105–19.

——, 'Early Castles and Rural Settlement Patterns: Insights from Yorkshire and the East Midlands', *Medieval Settlement Research Group Annual Report*, 14 (1999), 29–33.

——, 'Early Castles in the Medieval Landscape of Rutland', *Transactions of the Leicestershire Archaeological and Historical Society*, 73 (1999), 19–33.

——, 'Early Leicestershire Castles: Archaeology and Landscape History', *Transactions of the Leicestershire Archaeological and Historical Society*, 71 (1997), 21–36.

Crook, D., *Records of the General Eyre* (London, 1982).

Dalton, P., *Conquest, Anarchy and Lordship: Yorkshire, 1066–1154* (Cambridge, 1994).

Darby, H. C., 'Domesday Woodland in Huntingdonshire', *Transactions of the Cambridge-shire and Huntingdonshire Archaeological Society*, 5 (1931–6), 269–73.

——, 'Domesday Woodland in East Anglia', *Antiquity*, 8 (1934), 211–15.

——, 'The Domesday Geography of Cambridgeshire', *Proceedings of the Cambridge Antiquarian Society*, 36 (1934–5), 35–57.

——, *Domesday England* (Cambridge, 1977).

——, 'Domesday Book and the Geographer', *Domesday Studies*, ed. J. C. Holt (Woodbridge, 1987), 101–19.

——, *The Domesday Geography of Eastern England* (Cambridge, 1952; 2nd edn, 1957; 3rd edn, 1971).

Darby, H. C., and Campbell, E. M. J., *The Domesday Geography of South-East England* (Cambridge, 1962).

Darby, H. C. and Maxwell, I. S., *The Domesday Geography of Northern England* (Cambridge, 1962).

Darby, H. C., and Terrett, L. B., *The Domesday Geography of Midland England* (Cambridge, 1954; 2nd edn, 1971).

Darby, H. C. and Versey, G. R., *A Domesday Gazetteer* (Cambridge, 1975).

Darby, H. C., and Welldon Finn, R., *The Domesday Geography of South-West England* (Cambridge, 1967).

Darlington, R. R., 'Aethelwig, Abbot of Evesham', *EHR*, 48 (1933), 1–22, 177–98.

——, 'Wiltshire Geld Rolls', *Victoria County History of Wiltshire*, ii, eds R. B. Pugh and E. Crittall (Oxford, 1955), 169–221.

Davies, W., and Vierck, H., 'The Contexts of the Tribal Hidage: Social Aggregates and Settlement Patterns', *Frühmittelalterlichestudien*, 8 (1974), 223–93.

Davis, R. H. C., 'Domesday Book: Continental Parallels', *Domesday Studies*, ed. J. C. Holt (Woodbridge, 1987), 15–39.

Demarest, E. B., 'The Hundred-Pennies', *EHR*, 33 (1918), 62–72.

——, 'The *Firma Unius Noctis*', *EHR*, 35 (1920), 78–89.

——, 'The *Consuetudo Regis* in Essex, Norfolk and Suffolk', *EHR*, 42 (1927), 161–79.

Denton, J. H., *English Royal Free Chapels 1100–1300* (Manchester, 1970).

Desborough, D., 'An Introduction to the Staffordshire Domesday', *The Staffordshire Domesday*, eds A. Williams and G. H. Martin (London, 1991), 1–20.

——, 'An Introduction to the Warwickshire Domesday', *The Warwickshire Domesday*, eds A. Williams and G. H. Martin (London, 1991), 1–21.

Dickens, A. G., 'The Shire and Privileges of the Archbishop in Eleventh Century York', *Yorkshire Archaeological Journal*, 38 (1953), 131–47.

Dodgson, J. McN., 'Domesday Book: Place-names and Personal Names', *Domesday Studies*, ed. J. C. Holt (Woodbridge, 1987), 121–38.

Dodgson, J. McN. and Palmer, J. J. N., *Domesday Book: Index of Places* (Chichester, 1992).

——, *Domesday Book: Index of Persons* (Chichester, 1992).

Dodwell, B., 'The Honour of the Bishop of Thetford/Norwich in the Late Eleventh and Early Twelfth Centuries', *Norfolk Archaeology*, 33 (1965), 185–99.

——, 'The Making of the Domesday Survey in Norfolk: The Hundred and a Half of Clackclose', *EHR*, 84 (1969), 79–84.

Doree, S., *Domesday Book and the Origins of Edmonton Hundred* (Enfield, 1986).

Douglas, D. C., *The Social Structure of Medieval East Anglia* (Oxford, 1927).

——, 'Some Early Surveys from the Abbey of Abingdon', *EHR*, 44 (1929), 618–25.

——, 'Fragments of an Anglo-Saxon Survey from Bury St Edmunds', *EHR*, 43 (1928), 376–83.

Dove, P. E. (ed.), *Domesday Studies: being the Papers Read at the Meetings of the Domesday Commemoration 1886*, 2 vols (London, 1888–91).

Downer, L. J. (ed.), *Leges Henrici Primi* (Oxford, 1972).

Drage, C., 'Urban Castles', in J. Schofield and R. Leech (eds), *Urban Archaeology in Britain*, CBA Research Report, 61 (1987), 117–32.

Du Boulay, F. R. H., *The Lordship of Canterbury: An Essay on Medieval Society* (London, 1966).

Dugdale, W., *The Antiquities of Warwickshire*, 2 vols (London, 1656).

Dyer, C., 'A Note on Calculating GDP in 1086 and 1399', *The Commercialisation of English Society, 1000–1300*, eds R. H. Britnell and B. M. S. Campbell (Manchester, 1993), Appendix 3.

Eales, R., 'An Introduction to the Kent Domesday', *The Kent Domesday*, eds A. Williams and G. H. Martin (London, 1992), 1–49.

Ekwall, E., *The Concise Oxford Dictionary of English Place-Names*, 4th edn (Oxford, 1959).

Ellis, H., *A General Introduction to Domesday Book*, 2 vols (London, 1833).

English, B., *The Lords of Holderness 1086–1200* (Oxford, 1979).

——, 'Towns, Mottes and Ring-works of the Conquest', *The Medieval Military Revolution*, eds A. Ayton and J. L. Price (London, 1995), 45–61.

——, 'The Government of Thirteenth-Century Yorkshire', *Government, Religion and Society in Northern England 1000–1700*, eds J. C. Appleby and P. Dalton (Gloucester, 1997), 90–103.

Everson, P., Taylor, C. C., and Dunn, C. J., *Change and Continuity: Rural Settlement in North-West Lincolnshire* (London, 1991).

Eyton, R. W., *A Key to Domesday: The Dorset Survey* (Dorchester, 1878).

——, *Domesday Studies: An Analysis and Digest of the Somerset Survey and of the Somerset Gheld Inquest of AD 1084*, 2 vols (London, 1880).

——, *Domesday Studies: An Analysis and Digest of the Staffordshire Survey* (London, 1881).

Faith, R., *The English Peasantry and the Growth of Lordship* (London and Washington, 1997).

——, 'The Topography and Social Structure of a Small Soke in the Middle Ages: The Sokens, Essex', *Essex Archaeology and History*, 27 (1997), 202–13.

Faull, M. F., Moorhouse, S. A., Michelmore, D., *West Yorkshire: An Archaeological Survey to A.D. 1500* (Wakefield, 1981).

Feilitzen, O. von, *Pre-Conquest Personal Names of Domesday Book* (Uppsala, 1937).

Fellows-Jensen, G., *Scandinavian Personal Names in Lincolnshire and Yorkshire* (Copenhagen, 1968).

Fenoaltea, S., 'Review of *Domesday Economy*', *Speculum*, 63 (1988).

Finberg, H. P. R., *The Early Charters of Wessex* (Leicester, 1964).

Fleming, D. F., 'Landholding by *Milites* in Domesday Book: A Revision', *ANS*, 13 (1991), 83–98.

Fleming, R., 'Domesday Book and the Tenurial Revolution', *ANS*, 9 (1986), 87–102.

——, *Kings and Lords in Conquest England* (Cambridge, 1991).

——, 'Rural Elites and Urban Communities in Late Anglo-Saxon England', *Past and Present*, 141 (1993), 3–37.

——, 'Oral Testimony and the Domesday Inquest', *ANS*, 17 (1994), 101–22.

——, *Domesday Book and the Law: Society and Legal Custom in Early Medieval England* (Cambridge, 1998).

——, 'The New Wealth, the New Rich and the New Political Style in Late Anglo-Saxon England', *ANS*, 23 (2000), 1–22.

Flight, C., *The Survey of the Whole of England: Studies of the Documentation Resulting from the Survey Conducted in 1086*, British Archaeological Reports, British series, 405 (Oxford, 2006).

Foard, G., 'The Great Replanning?', *The Origins of the Midland Village*, Department of English Local History, University of Leicester (Leicester, 1992), 1–10.

——, 'The Early Topography of Northampton and its Suburbs', *Northamptonshire Archaeology*, 26 (1995), 109–22.

Ford, W. J., 'Some Settlement Patterns in the Central Region of the Warwickshire Avon', *Medieval Settlement*, ed. P. H. Sawyer (London, 1976), 274–94.

Fowler, G. H., 'The Devastation of Bedfordshire and the Neighbouring Counties in 1065 and 1066', *Archaeologia*, 72 (1922), 41–50.

——, 'An Early Cambridgeshire Feodary', *EHR*, 46 (1931), 422–3.

Fox, H. S. A. (ed.), *The Origins of the Midland Village*, Department of English Local History, University of Leicester (Leicester, 1992).

——, *The Evolution of the Fishing Village: Landscape and Society along the South Devon Coast, 1086–1550*, Leicester Explorations in Local History, 1 (Oxford, 2001).

Foy, J. D., *Domesday Book: Index of Subjects* (Chichester, 1992).

Frantzen, A. J., and Niles, J. D. (eds), *Anglo-Saxonism and the Construction of Social Identity* (Gainesville, 1997).

Freason, A., 'Domesday Book: The Evidence Reviewed', *History*, 71 (1986), 375–93.

Freeman, A., *The Moneyer and the Mint in the Reign of Edward the Confessor 1042–1066* (Oxford, 1985).

Friedman, R. E., *Who Wrote the Bible?* (London, 1988).

Galbraith, V. H., 'Royal Charters to Winchester', *EHR*, 35 (1920), 383–400.

——, 'An Episcopal Land-Grant of 1085', *EHR*, 44 (1929), 353–72.

——, 'Making of Domesday Book', *EHR*, 57 (1942), 161–77.

——, *The Making of Domesday Book* (London, 1961).

——, 'Notes on the Career of Samson, Bishop of Worcester (1096–1112)', *EHR*, 82 (1967), 86–101.

——, *Domesday Book: its Place in Administrative History* (Oxford, 1974).

Gardiner, M., 'Shipping and Trade between England and the Continent during the Eleventh Century', *ANS*, 22 (1999), 71–94.

Garnett, G., 'Coronation and Propaganda: Some Implications of the Norman Claim to the Throne of England in 1066', *TRHS*, 5th series, 36 (1986), 91–116.

——, review of A. Williams, *The English and the Norman Conquest*, *EHR*, 112 (1997), 1236–7.

Gelling, M., *Signposts to the Past: Place-Names and the History of England*, 3rd edn (Chichester, 1997).

Gelling, M. and Cole, A., *The Landscape of Place-Names* (Stamford, 2000).

Gillingham, J., 'The Introduction of Knight Service into England', *ANS*, 4 (1981), 53–64, 181–7 (notes).

——, 'The Most Precious Jewel in the English Crown: Levels of Danegeld and Heregeld in the Early Eleventh Century', *EHR*, 104 (1989), 373–84.

——, '1066 and the Introduction of Chivalry into England', in *Law and Government in England and Normandy: Essays in Honour of J. C. Holt*, eds G. Garnett and J. Hudson (Cambridge, 1994), 31–55.

——, 'Thegns and Knights in Eleventh-Century England: Who was then the Gentleman?', *TRHS*, 6th series, 5 (1995), 129–53.

Gilmour, B. J. J., and Roffe, D. R., 'Medieval and Later Occupation of the South-Western Part of the Lower City: Archaeological and Historical Evidence', *The Defences of the Lower City: Excavations at The Park and West Parade 1970–1972 and a Discussion of the Other Sites Excavated up to 1994*, ed. M. J. Jones, The Archaeology of Lincoln VII–2, Council for British Archaeology for the City of Lincoln Archaeology Unit (York, 1999), 262–7.

Glénisson, J., 'Les Enquêtes Administratives en Europe Occidentale aux XIIIe et XIVe Siècles', *Histoire Comparée de l'Administration*, eds W. Paravicini and K. F. Werner (Munich, 1980), 17–25.

Godfrey, A., and Hooper, K., 'Accountability and Decision-Making in Feudal England: Domesday Book Revisited', *Accounting History*, 1 (1996), 35–54.

Golding, B. J., 'An Introduction to the Hampshire Domesday', *The Hampshire Domesday*, eds A. Williams and R. W. H. Erskine (London, 1989), 1–27.

Golob, P. E., 'The Ferrers earls of Derby: A Study of the Honour of Tutbury 1066–1279', University of Cambridge, PhD, 1985.

Gover, J. E. B., *The Place-Names of Northamptonshire* (Cambridge, 1933).

Grassi, J. L., 'The Lands and Revenues of Edward the Confessor', *EHR*, 117 (2002), 251–83.

Green, J. A., 'The Last Century of Danegeld', *EHR*, 96 (1981), 241–58.

——, *English Sheriffs to 1154*, Public Record Office Handbooks no. 24 (London, 1990).

——, 'The Sheriffs of William the Conqueror', *Proceedings of the Battle Conference [ANS]*, 5 (1982), 129–45.

——, 'David I and Henry I', *Scottish Historical Review*, 75 (1996), 1–19.

——, *The Aristocracy of Norman England* (Cambridge, 1997).

Greenway, D. E., 'A Newly Discovered Fragment of the Hundred Rolls of 1279–80', *Journal of the Society of Archivists*, 7 (1982), 73–8.

Gregson, N., 'The Multiple Estate Model: Some Critical Questions', *Journal of Historical Geography*, 11 (1985), 339–51.

Grierson, P., 'Weights and Measures', *Domesday Studies*, eds A. Williams and R. W. H. Erskine (London, 1987), 80–5.

Gullick, M., 'The Great and Little Domesday Manuscripts', *Domesday Book: Studies*, eds A. Williams and R. W. H. Erskine (London, 1987), 93–112.

Gullick, M., and Thorn, C., 'The Scribes of Great Domesday Book', *Journal of the Society of Archivists*, 8 (1986), 78–80.

Hadley, D. M., 'Multiple Estates and the Origins of the Manorial Structure in the Northern Danelaw', *Journal of Historical Geography*, 22 (1996), 3–15.

——, *The Northern Danelaw: Its Social Structure, c.800–1100* (London and New York, 2000).

Hall, D., 'Fieldwork and Field Books: Studies in Early Layout', *Villages, Fields and Frontiers: Studies in European Rural Settlement in the Medieval and Early Modern Period*, eds B. K. Roberts and R. E. Glasscock, British Archaeological Reports, International Series, 185 (Oxford, 1983), 115–32.

——, 'An Introduction to the Northamptonshire Domesday', *The Northamptonshire and Rutland Domesday*, eds A. Williams and R. W. H. Erskine (London, 1987), 1–17.

——, *The Open Fields of Northamptonshire*, Northamptonshire Record Society, 38 (1995).

Hall, H., *Studies in English Official Historical Documents* (Oxford, 1908).

Hall, R., 'The Making of Domesday York', *Anglo-Saxon Settlements*, ed. D. Hooke (Oxford, 1988), 233–47.

Hallam, E. M., *Domesday Book through Nine Centuries* (London, 1986).

Hallam, H. E., *The New Lands of Elloe* (Leicester, 1954).

——, 'Some Thirteenth-Century Censuses', *EcHR*, 2nd series, 10 (1958), 340–61.

Hamshere, J. D., 'The Structure and Exploitation of the Domesday Book Estate of the Church of Worcester', *Landscape History*, 7 (1985), 41–52.

——, 'Regressing Domesday Book: Tax Assessments in Norman England', *EcHR*, 2nd ser., 40 (1987), 247–51.

——, 'Domesday Book, Cliometric Analysis and Taxation Assessments', *EcHR*, 2nd ser., 40 (1987), 262–6.

Harding, A., 'Plaints and Bills in the History of English Law, mainly in the period 1250–1350', *Legal History Studies 1972*, ed. D. Jenkins (Cardiff, 1975), 65–86.

Harfield, C. G., 'A Handlist of Castles Recorded in the Domesday Book', *EHR*, 106 (1991), 371–92.

Hart, C. R., *The Early Charters of Eastern England* (Leicester, 1966).

——, 'Hidation of Huntingdonshire', *Proceedings of the Cambridge Antiquarian Society*, 61 (1968), 55–66.

——, *The Hidation of Northamptonshire*, Department of English Local History, University of Leicester, Occasional Papers, 2nd series, 3 (Leicester, 1970).

——, *The Hidation of Cambridgeshire* Department of English Local History, University of Leicester, Occasional Papers, 2nd series, 6 (Leicester, 1974).

——, *Early Charters of Northern England and the North Midlands* (Leicester, 1975).

——, 'Land Tenure in Cambridgeshire on the Eve of the Norman Conquest', *Proceedings of the Cambridge Antiquarian Society*, 84 (1996 for 1995), 59–90.

——, *The Danelaw* (London, 1992).

Harvey, P. D. A., 'Rectitudines Singularum Personarum and Gerefa', *EHR*, 108 (1993), 1–22.

Harvey, S. P. J., 'The Knight and the Knight's Fee in England', *Past and Present*, 49 (1970), 3–43.

——, 'Domesday Book and its Predecessors', *EHR*, 86 (1971), 753–73.

——, 'Domesday Book and Anglo-Norman Governance', *TRHS*, 5th series, 25 (1975), 175–93.

——, 'Evidence for Settlement: Domesday Book', *Medieval Settlement*, ed. P. H. Sawyer (London, 1976), 197–9.

——, 'The Extent and Profitability of Demesne Agriculture in England in the Later Eleventh Century', *Social Relations and Ideas: Essays in Honour of R. H. Hilton*, eds T. H. Aston, P. R. Coss, C. Dyer, and J. Thirsk (Cambridge, 1983), 45–72.

——, 'Taxation and the Economy', *Domesday Studies*, ed. J. C. Holt (Woodbridge, 1987), 249–64.

——, 'Domesday England', *The Agrarian History of England and Wales*, ii, ed. H. E. Hallam (Cambridge, 1988), 45–136.

——, 'Taxation and the Ploughland in Domesday Book', *Domesday Book: A Reassessment*, ed. P. H. Sawyer (London, 1985), 86–103.

——, 'Taxation and the Economy', *Domesday Studies*, ed. J. C. Holt (Woodbridge, 1987), 249–64.

Hesse, M., 'Domesday Land Measures in Suffolk', *Landscape History*, 22 (2002), 21–36.

——, 'Domesday Settlement in Suffolk,' *Landscape History*, 25 (2003), 45–57.

Higham, N. J., 'Settlement, Land Use and Domesday Ploughlands', *Landscape History*, 12 (1990), 33–44.

——, *The Origins of Cheshire* (Manchester, 1993).

——, 'The Domesday Survey: Context and Purpose', *History*, 78 (1993), 7–21.

——, 'Patterns of Patronage and Power: The Governance of Late Anglo-Saxon Cheshire', *Government, Religion and Society in Northern England 1000–1700*, eds J. C. Appleby and P. Dalton (Gloucester, 1997), 1–13.

Hill, D., and A. R. (eds), *The Defence of Wessex: The Burghal Hidage and Anglo-Saxon Fortification* (Manchester, 1996).

Hill, J. W. F., *Medieval Lincoln* (Cambridge, 1948).

Hodgson, J. C., *History of Northumberland*, vi (Newcastle, 1902).

Holdsworth, C., 'The Church at Domesday', *Domesday Essays*, ed. C. Holdsworth, Exeter Studies in History, 14 (1986), 51–64.

Hollings, M., 'The Survival of the Five Hide Unit in the Western Midlands', *EHR*, 68 (1948), 453–87.

Hollister, C. W., *The Military Organization of Norman England* (Oxford, 1965).

Holt, J. C., 'The Prehistory of Parliament', *The English Parliament in the Middle Ages*, eds R. G. Davies and J. H. Denton (Manchester, 1981), 1–28.

——, '1086', *Domesday Studies*, ed. J. C. Holt (Woodbridge, 1987), 41–64, revised in J. C. Holt, *Colonial England, 1066–1215* (London, 1997), 31–57.

——, 'Domesday Studies 2000', *Domesday*, eds E. Hallam and D. Bates (Stroud, 2001), 19–24.

Holt, R. A., *The Mills of Medieval England* (Oxford, 1988).

——, 'Whose were the Profits of Milling? An Aspect of the Changing Relationship between the Abbots of Glastonbury and their Tenants, 1066–1350', *Past and Present*, 116 (1987), 3–23.

Hooke, D., 'The Droitwich Salt Industry: An Examination of the West Midland Charter Evidence', *Anglo-Saxon Studies in Archaeology and History*, 2 (1981), 123–70.

——, *The Anglo-Saxon Landscape: The Kingdom of the Hwicce* (Manchester, 1985).

Hooper, N., 'The Housecarls in England in the Eleventh Century', *ANS*, 7 (1984), 161–76.

——, 'An Introduction to the Berkshire Domesday', *The Berkshire Domesday*, eds A. Williams and R. W. H. Erskine (London, 1988), 1–28.

——, 'The Anglo-Saxons at War', *Weapons and Warfare in Anglo-Saxon England*, ed. S. C. Hawkes (Oxford, 1989), 191–201.

Hoyt, R. S., 'A Pre-Domesday Kentish Assessment List', *A Medieval Miscellany for Doris Mary Stenton*, eds P. M. Barnes and C. F. Slade, Pipe Roll Society, new series, 36 (1962 for 1960).

——, *The Royal Demesne in English Constitutional History, 1066–1272* (Cornell, 1950).

Hudson, J., 'Life Grants of Land and the Development of Inheritance', *ANS*, 5 (1983), 67–80.

——, *The Formation of the English Common Law: Law and Society in England from the Norman Conquest to Magna Carta* (London, 1996).

——, 'Court Cases and Legal Arguments in England, c. 1066–1166' *TRHS*, 6th series, 10 (2000), 91–115.

Hurnard, N. D., 'The Anglo-Norman Franchises', *EHR*, 64 (1949), 316–27.

Hyams, P., '"No Register of Title": The Domesday Inquest and Land Adjudication', *ANS*, 9 (1986), 127–41.

Jacob, E. F., *Studies in the Period of Baronial Reform and Rebellion, 1258–1267*, Oxford Studies in Social and Legal History, 8 (Oxford, 1925).

John, E., *Land Tenure in Early England* (Leicester, 1964).

Johnson, C., 'Introduction to the Norfolk Domesday', *Victoria History of the County of Norfolk*, ii, ed. W. Page (London, 1906), 1–38.

Jolliffe, J. E. A., 'Northumbrian Institutions', *EHR*, 41 (1926), 1–42.

——, *Pre-Feudal England: The Jutes* (Oxford, 1933).

——, 'A Survey of Fiscal Tenements', *EcHR*, 1st series, 6 (1935–6), 157–71.

Jones, G. R. J., 'Multiple Estates and Early Settlement', *Medieval Settlement*, ed. P. H. Sawyer (London, 1976), 15–40.

——, 'The Portrayal of Land Settlement in Domesday Book', *Domesday Studies*, ed. J. C. Holt, (Woodbridge, 1987) 183–200.

Joy, C. A., 'Sokeright', unpublished MA thesis, University of Leeds (1974).

Kapelle, W. E., *The Norman Conquest of the North: The Region and its Transformation 1000–1135* (London, 1979).

——, 'Domesday Book: F. W. Maitland and his Successors', *Speculum*, 64 (1989), 620–40.

——, 'The Purpose of Domesday Book: A Quandary', *Essays in Medieval Studies*, Proceedings of the Illinois Medieval Association, 9 (1992), 55–65.

Keats-Rohan, K. S. B., 'The Devolution of the Honour of Wallingford', *Oxoniensia*, 54 (1989), 311–18.

——, *Domesday People: A Prosopography of Persons Occurring in English Documents, 1066–1166: I. Domesday Book* (Woodbridge, 1998).

——, 'William I and the Breton Contingent in the non-Norman Conquest 1060–1087', *ANS*, 13 (1991), 157–72.

——, 'The Bretons and Normans of England: The Family, the Fief, and the Feudal Monarchy', *Nottingham Medieval Studies*, 36 (1992), 42–78.

——, *The Continental Origins of English Landholders 1066–1166 database and the COEL Database System on CD-ROM*, Coel Enterprises Ltd, 2002.

Keen, L., 'Coastal Salt Production in Norman England', *ANS*, 11 (1988), 133–80.

——, 'An Introduction to the Dorset Domesday', *The Dorset Domesday*, eds A. Williams and G. H. Martin (London, 1991), 1–26.

Kenyon, D., *The Origins of Lancashire* (Manchester, 1991).

Ker, N. R., 'Hemming's Cartulary: A Description of the Two Worcester Cartularies in Cotton Tiberius A. xiii', *Studies in Medieval History Presented to Frederick Maurice Powicke*, eds R. W. Hunt, W. A. Pantin, and R. W. Southern (Oxford, 1948), 49–75.

——, 'The Beginnings of Salisbury Cathedral Library', *Medieval Learning and Literature: Essays Presented to Richard Hunt*, eds J. J. G. Alexander and M. T. Gibson (Oxford, 1976).

——, *Medieval Manuscripts in British Libraries II, Abbotsford-Keele* (Oxford, 1977).

King, E., 'The Peterborough "Descriptio Militum" (Henry I)', *EHR*, 84 (1969), 84–101.

Kristensen, A. K. G., 'Danelaw Institutions and Danish Society in the Viking Age: Sochemanni, Liberi Homines and Königsfreie', *Medieval Scandinavia*, 8 (1975), 27–85.

Landon, J., 'Watermills and Windmills in the West Midlands, 1086–1500', *EcHR*, 2nd ser., 44 (1991), 424–44.

Latham, R. E., *Revised Medieval Latin Word List from British and Irish Sources* (London, 1965).

Lavelle, R., 'The "Farm of One Night" and the Organization of Estates in Late Anglo-Saxon Wessex', *Haskins Society Journal*, 14 (2005 for 2003), 54–82.

——, 'All the King's Men? Land and Royal Service in Eleventh-Century England', *Southern History*, 26 (2005 for 2004), 1–37.

Lawson, M. K., 'Those Stories Look True: Levels of Taxation in the Reigns of Aethelred II and Cnut', *EHR*, 104 (1989), 385–406.

——, 'The Collection of Danegeld and Heregeld in the Reigns of Aethelred II and Cnut', *EHR*, 99 (1984), 721–38.

Leaver, R. A., 'Five Hides in Ten Counties: A Contribution to the Domesday Regression Debate', *EcHR*, 2nd ser., 41 (1988), 525–42.

Lees, B. A., 'Introduction to the Suffolk Domesday', *Victoria History of the County of Suffolk*, i, ed. W. Page (London, 1911), 356–416.

——, 'The Statute of Winchester and the *Villa Integra*', *EHR*, 41 (1926), 98–103.

Lennard, R., 'A Neglected DB Satellite', *EHR*, 58 (1943), 32–41.

——, *Rural England 1086–1135: A Study of Social and Agrarian Conditions* (Oxford, 1959).

——, 'The Composition of the Domesday Caruca', *EHR*, 81 (1966), 770–5.

Lewis, C., Mitchell-Fox, P., and Dyer, C., *Village, Hamlet, and Field: Changing Medieval Settlements in Central England*, 2nd edn (Macclesfield, 2000).

Lewis, C. P., 'An Introduction to the Herefordshire Domesday', *The Herefordshire Domesday*, eds A. Williams and R. W. H. Erskine (London, 1988), 1–22.

——, 'The Early Earls of Norman England', *ANS*, 13 (1990), 207–23.

——, 'An Introduction to the Shropshire Domesday', *The Shropshire Domesday*, eds A. Williams and R. W. H. Erskine (London, 1990), 1–27.

——, 'The Earldom of Surrey and the Date of Domesday Book', *Historical Research*, 63 (1990), 327–36.

——, 'An Introduction to the Cheshire Domesday', *The Cheshire Domesday*, eds A. Williams and R. W. H. Erskine (London, 1991), 1–25.

——, 'An Introduction to the Lancashire Domesday', *The Lancashire Domesday*, eds A. Williams and R. W. H. Erskine (London, 1991), 1–41.

——, 'The Formation of the Honor of Chester, 1066–1100', *The Earldom of Chester and its Charters: A Tribute to Geoffrey Barraclough*, ed. A. T. Thacker, *Journal of the Chester Archaeological Society*, 71 (1991), 37–68.

——, 'Domesday Jurors', *The Haskins Society Journal*, 5 (1993), 17–44.

——, 'The French in England before the Norman Conquest', *ANS*, 17 (1994), 123–44.

——, 'Joining the Dots: A Methodology for Identifying the English in Domesday Book', *Family Trees and the Roots of Politics: The Prosopography of Britain and France from the Tenth to the Twelfth Century*, ed. K. S. B. Keats-Rohan (Woodbridge, 1997), 69–87.

Liddiard, R., 'Castle Rising, Norfolk: A "Landscape of Lordship"?', *ANS*, 22 (1999), 169–86.

——, 'The Deer Parks of Domesday Book', *Landscapes*, 4:1 (2003), 4–23.

Liebermann F., and Peacock, M. H., 'An English Document of about 1080', *Yorkshire Archaeological Journal*, 18 (1905), 412–16.

Loud, G. A., 'An Introduction to the Somerset Domesday', *The Somerset Domesday*, eds A. Williams and R. W. H. Erskine (London, 1989), 1–31.

Loyn, H. R., *The Governance of Anglo-Saxon England 500–1087* (London, 1984).

——, 'The Beyond of Domesday', *Domesday Studies*, ed. J. C. Holt (Woodbridge, 1987), 1–13.

——, 'A General Introduction to Domesday Book', *Domesday Book Studies*, eds A. Williams and R. W. H. Erskine (London, 1987), 1–21.

——, 'William's Bishops: Some Further Thoughts', *ANS*, 10 (1988), 223–35.

Mack, K., 'Changing Thegns: Cnut's Conquest and the English Aristocracy', *Albion*, 16 (1984), 375–87.

Maddicott, J. R., 'Edward I and the Lessons of Baronial Reform: Local Government 1258–93', *Thirteenth Century England, i: Proceedings of the Newcastle upon Tyne Conference*, eds P. R. Coss and S. D. Lloyd (Woodbridge, 1986), 1–30.

Mahany, C. M., and Roffe, D. R., 'Stamford: the Development of an Anglo-Scandinavian Borough', *ANS*, 5 (1983), 197–219.

Maitland, F. W., *Domesday Book and Beyond* (Cambridge, 1897).

——, *Township and Borough* (Cambridge, 1898).

Marten, L., 'The Impact of Rebellion on Little Domesday', *ANS*, 27 (2005), 132–50.

Martin, G. H., 'Domesday Book and the Boroughs', *Domesday Book: A Reassessment*, ed. P. H. Sawyer (London, 1985), 143–63.

——, 'Abraham Farley's Transcription of Domesday Book', *The Digital Domesday*.

——, 'An Introduction to the London Domesday', *The Middlesex and London Domesday*, eds A. Williams and G. H. Martin (London, 1991), 1–21.

Mason, J. F. A., 'The Date of the Geld Rolls', *EHR*, 69 (1954), 283–9.

——, *William the First and the Sussex Rapes*, Historical Association (1966).

Matthews, J. S., 'William the Conqueror's Campaign in Cheshire in 1069–70: Resistance in the North-West', *Northern History*, 40 (2003), 53–70.

Mayhew, N., 'Modelling Medieval Monetisation', *The Commercialisation of English Society, 1000–1300*, eds R. H. Britnell and B. M. S. Campbell (Manchester, 1993).

——, 'Appendix 2: The Calculation of GDP from Domesday Book', *The Commercialisation of English Society, 1000–1300*, eds R. H. Britnell and B. M. S. Campbell (Manchester, 1993), 195–6.

Mawer, A., and Stenton, F. M., *The Place-Names of Bedfordshire and Huntingdonshire* (Cambridge, 1926).

McDonald, J., *Production Efficiency in Domesday England, 1086* (London and New York, 1998).

——, 'Tax Fairness in Eleventh-Century England', *The Accounting Historians Journal*, 29 (2002), 173–94.

——, 'Using William the Conqueror's Accounting Record to Assess Manorial Efficiency', *Accounting History*, 10 (2005), 125–45.

McDonald, J., and Snooks, G. D., 'The Determinants of Manorial Income in Domesday England: Evidence from Essex', *Journal of Economic History*, 45 (1985), 541–56.

——, *Domesday Economy: A New Approach to Anglo-Norman History* (Oxford, 1986).

——, 'Were the Tax Assessments of Domesday England Artificial? The Case of Essex', *EcHR*, 2nd ser., 38 (1985), 353–73.

——, 'The Suitability of Domesday Book for Cliometric Analysis', *EcHR*, 2nd ser., 40 (1987), 252–61.

Meaney, A. L., 'Gazetteer of Hundred and Wapentake Meeting-Places of the Cambridge Region', *Proceedings of the Cambridge Antiquarian Society*, 82 (1994), 67–92.

Metcalf, D. M., 'The Taxation of Moneyers under Edward the Confessor', *Domesday Studies*, ed. J. Holt (London, 1987), 279–93.

Mew, K., 'The Dynamics of Lordship and Landscape as Revealed in a Domesday Study of the *Nova Foresta*', *ANS*, 23 (2000), 155–66.

Meyer, M., 'Women's Estates in Later Anglo-Saxon England', *Haskins Society Journal*, 3 (1991), 111–29.

——, 'The Queen's Demesne in Later Anglo-Saxon England', *The Culture of Christendom: Essays in Medieval History in Commemoration of Denis T. Bethell* ed. M. Meyer (London and Rio Grande, 1993), 75–113.

Miller, E., *The Abbey and Bishopric of Ely* (Cambridge, 1951).

Mills, A. D., *A Dictionary of English Place-Names* (Oxford, 1995).

Moore, J. S., 'The Domesday Teamland: A Reconsideration', *TRHS*, 5th series, 14 (1964), 109–30.

——, 'The Gloucestershire Section of Domesday Book: Geographical Problems of the Text, Part I', *Transactions of the Bristol and Gloucestershire Archaeological Society*, 105 (1987), 109–32.

——, 'Domesday Slavery', *ANS*, 11 (1989), 191–220.

——, '"Quot homines?": The Population of Domesday England', *ANS*, 19 (1996), 307–34.

——, *From Anglo-Saxon to Anglo-Norman: North Gloucestershire in Domesday Book*, Deerhurst Lecture 1998, The Friends of Deerhurst Church (Bristol, 2000).

Morris, W. A., *The Medieval English Sheriff to 1300* (Oxford, 1927).

Nash, A., 'The Population of Southern England in 1086: A New Look at the Evidence of Domesday Book', *Southern History*, 10 (1988), 1–28.

Newman, P. R., 'The Domesday Inquest and the Norman Land Settlement in the Yorkshire Wapentake of Ainsty', *Nottingham Mediaeval Studies*, 46 (2002), 1–24.

O'Brien, B. R., 'From *Morðor* to *Murdrum*: The Pre-Conquest Origin and Norman Revival of the Murder Fine', *Speculum*, 71 (1996), 321–57.

——, *God's Peace and King's Peace: the Laws of Edward the Confessor* (Philadelphia, 1999).

Oosthuizen, S., 'Sokemen and Freemen: Tenure, Status, and Landscape Conservatism in Eleventh-Century Cambridgeshire', *Anglo-Saxons: Studies Presented to Cyril Roy Hart*, eds S. Keynes and A. P. Smyth (Dublin, 2005), 186–207.

Owen, D. M., 'The Norman Cathedral at Lincoln', *ANS*, 6 (1983), 189–99.

——, 'The Beginnings of the Port of Boston', *A Prospect of Lincolnshire*, eds N. Field and A. White (Lincoln, 1984), 42–5.

——, *The Making of King's Lynn*, British Academy, Records of Social and Economic History, new series, 9 (1984).

Painter, S., 'Castle Guard', *The American Historical Review*, 40 (1935), 450–9.

Palliser, D. M., *Domesday York*, Borthwick Paper no. 78, University of York (York, 1990).

——, 'An Introduction to the Yorkshire Domesday', *The Yorkshire Domesday*, eds A. Williams and G. H. Martin (London, 1992), 1–38.

——, 'Domesday Book and the Harrying of the North', *Northern History*, 29 (1993), 1–23.

Palliser, D. M., Slater, T. R., and Dennison, E. P., 'The Topography of Towns 600–1300', in D. M. Palliser (ed.), *The Cambridge Urban History of Britain, vol. 1: 600–1540* (Cambridge, 2000), 153–86.

Palmer, J. J. N., 'The Domesday Manor', *Domesday Studies*, ed. J. Holt (Woodbridge, 1987), 139–54.

——, 'The Conqueror's Footprints in Domesday Book', *The Medieval Military Revolution: State, Society and Military Change in Medieval and Early Modern Europe*, eds A. C. Ayton and J. L. Price (London and New York, 1995), 23–44.

——, 'War and Domesday Waste', in *Armies, Chivalry and Warfare in Medieval Britain and France*, ed. M. Strickland (Stamford, 1998), 256–75.

——, 'The Wealth of the Secular Aristocracy in 1086', *ANS*, 22 (2000), 279–91.

—, 'Great Domesday on CD-ROM', *Domesday Book*, eds E. Hallam and D. Bates (Stroud, 2001), 141–50.

Parker, M. S., 'Some Notes on the Pre-Norman History of Doncaster', *Yorkshire Archaeological Journal*, 59 (1987), 29–43.

—, 'The Province of Hatfield', *Northern History*, 28 (1992), 42–69.

Parsons, D. N., Styles, T., and Hough, C., *The Vocabulary of English Place-Names (Á-Box)*, Centre for English Names Studies (Nottingham, 1997).

Parsons, D. N., and Styles, T., *The Vocabulary of English Place-Names (Brace-Cæster)*, Centre for English Names Studies (Nottingham, 2000).

Pearson, H., 'The Alecto Domesday Project', *Domesday Book*, eds E. Hallam and D. Bates (Stroud, 2001), 151–8.

Pelteret, D. A. E., *Slavery in Early Medieval England* (Woodbridge, 1995).

Percival, J., 'The Precursors of Domesday: Roman and Carolingian Land Registers', *Domesday Book: A Reassessment*, ed. P. H. Sawyer (London, 1985), 5–27.

Phythian-Adams, C., 'Rutland Reconsidered', *Mercian Studies*, ed. A. Dornier (Leicester, 1977), 63–86.

—, 'The Emergence of Rutland', *Rutland Record*, 1 (1980), 5–12.

—, *The Norman Conquest of Leicestershire and Rutland: A Regional Introduction to Domesday Book* (Leicester, 1986).

Pollock, F., and Maitland, F. W., *The History of English Law*, 2nd edn, 2 vols (Cambridge, 1923).

Poole, A. L., *The Obligations of Society in the Twelfth and Thirteenth Centuries* (Oxford, 1946).

Postan, M. M., *The Medieval Economy and Society: An Economic History of Britain in the Middle Ages* (London, 1972).

Postles, D., 'The Bordars of Domesday Derbyshire', *Derbyshire Archaeological Journal*, 106 (1986), 123–6.

Powell, W. R., *John Horace Round, Historian and Gentleman of Essex*, Essex Record Office Publications (Chelmsford, 2001).

Prescott, A., 'Sir Henry Ellis and Domesday Book', *Domesday Book*, eds E. Hallam and D. Bates (Stroud, 2001), 159–90.

Prestwich, J. O., 'The Career of Ranulf Flambard', *Anglo-Norman Durham, 1093–1193*, eds D. Rollason, M. Harvey, and M. Prestwich (Woodbridge, 1994), 299–310.

Public Record Office, *Domesday Book Rebound* (London, 1954).

Purser, T. S., 'The Origins of English Feudalism? An Episcopal Land-Grant Revisited', *Historical Research*, 73 (2000), 80–92.

Raban, S., 'The Making of the 1279–80 Hundred Rolls', *Historical Research*, 70 (1997), 123–45.

—, *A Second Domesday? The Hundred Rolls of 1279–80* (Oxford, 2004).

Rackham, O., *The History of the Countryside* (London, 1986).

Raftis, J. A., *The Estates of Ramsey Abbey* (Toronto, 1957).

Rahtz, P. A., and Bullough, D. A., 'The Parts of an Anglo-Saxon Mill', *Anglo-Saxon England*, 6 (1977), 15–37.

Rees Jones, S. R., 'Property, Tenure and Rents: Some Aspects of the Topography and Economy of Medieval York', unpublished D.Phil. thesis, University of York, 1987.

Reid, R. R., 'Barony and Thanage', *EHR*, 35 (1920), 161–99.

Reynolds, S., *Kingdoms and Communities in Western Europe 900–1300* (Oxford, 1984).

—, 'Towns in Domesday', *Domesday Studies*, ed. J. C. Holt (Woodbridge, 1987), 295–309.

——, 'Bookland, Folkland and Fief', *ANS*, 14 (1991), 211–27.

——, *Fiefs and Vassals: The Medieval Evidence Reinterpreted* (Oxford, 1994).

Riden, P., 'The Origin of the New Market of Chesterfield', *Derbyshire Archaeological Journal*, 97 (1978 for 1977), 5–15.

Roffe, D. R., 'Rural Manors and Stamford', *South Lincolnshire Archaeology*, i (Stamford, 1977), 12–13.

——, 'The Lincolnshire Hundred', *Landscape History*, 3 (1981), 27–36.

——, 'Norman Tenants-in-Chief and their Pre-Conquest Predecessors in Nottinghamshire', *History in the Making*, ed. S. N. Mastoris (Nottingham, 1985), 3–7.

——, *The Derbyshire Domesday* (Darley Dale, 1986).

——, 'The Origins of Derbyshire', *The Derbyshire Archaeological Journal*, 106 (1986), 102–22.

——, 'Nottinghamshire and the North: A Domesday Study', unpublished PhD thesis, Nottingham, 1987, online at http://www.roffe.co.uk/phdframe.htm.

——, 'Walter Dragun's Town? Lord and Burghal Community in Thirteenth-Century Stamford', *Lincolnshire History and Archaeology*, 22 (1987), 43–6.

——, 'An Introduction to the Huntingdonshire Domesday', *The Huntingdonshire Domesday*, eds A. Williams and R. W. H. Erskine (London, 1989), 1–23.

——, 'Domesday Book and Northern Society: A Reassessment', *EHR*, 105 (1990), 310–36.

——, 'An Introduction to the Derbyshire Domesday', *The Derbyshire Domesday*, eds A. Williams and R. H. W. Erskine (London, 1990), 1–27.

——, 'From Thegnage to Barony: Sake and Soke, Title, and Tenants-in-Chief', *ANS*, 12 (1990), 157–76.

——, 'Place-Naming in Domesday Book: Settlements, Estates and Communities', *Nomina*, 14 (1990–91), 47–60.

——, 'The Yorkshire Summary: A Domesday Satellite', *Northern History*, 27 (1991), 242–60.

——, 'An Introduction to the Lincolnshire Domesday', *The Lincolnshire Domesday*, eds A. Williams and G. H. Martin (London, 1992), 1–31.

——, 'Castles', *An Historical Atlas of Lincolnshire*, eds S. Bennett and N. Bennett (Hull, 1992), 34–43.

——, 'Hundreds and Wapentakes', *The Lincolnshire Domesday*, eds A. Williams and G. H. Martin (London, 1992), 33–9.

——, '*On Middan Gyrwan Fenne*: Intercommoning around the Island of Crowland', *Fenland Research*, 8 (1993), 80–6.

——, *Stamford in the Thirteenth Century: Two Inquisitions from the Reign of Edward I* (Stamford, 1994).

——, 'The Making of Domesday Book Reconsidered', *Haskins Society Journal*, 6 (1994), 153–66.

——, 'Hereward "the Wake" and the Barony of Bourne: A Reassessment of a Fenland Legend', *Lincolnshire History and Archaeology*, 29 (1994), 7–10.

——, 'The Historia Croylandensis: A Plea for Reassessment', *EHR*, 110 (1995), 93–108.

——, 'The Hundred Rolls and their Antecedents: Some Thoughts on the Inquisition in Thirteenth-Century England', *Haskins Society Journal*, 7 (1995), 179–87.

——, 'Great Bowden and its Soke', *Anglo-Saxon Landscapes in the East Midlands*, ed. J. Bourne (Leicester, 1996), 107–20.

——, 'The Hundred Rolls of 1255', *Historical Research*, 69 (1996), 201–10.

——, 'The Anglo-Saxon Town and the Norman Conquest', *Centenary History of Nottingham*, ed. J. V. Beckett (Manchester, 1997), 24–42.

——, 'Welbourn Castle, Lincolnshire', *Nottingham Medieval Studies*, 41 (1997), 54–6.

——, *Domesday: The Inquest and the Book* (Oxford, 2000).

——, 'Introduction', *Little Domesday, Norfolk*, eds A. Williams and G. H. Martin (London, 2000), 9–43.

——, 'The Early History of Wharram Percy', *The South Manor Area, Wharram: A Study of Settlement on the Yorkshire Wolds 8*, eds P. A. Stamper and R. A. Croft, York University Archaeological Publications, 10 (York, 2000), 1–16.

——, 'Domesday: The Inquest and the Book', *Domesday*, eds E. Hallam and D. Bates (Stroud, 2001), 25–36.

——, 'The Continental Origins of English Landholders 1066–1166 database and the COEL Database System on CD-ROM', *Nottingham Medieval Studies*, 45 (2001), 234–7.

——, 'The Historical Context', *Anglo-Saxon Settlement on the Siltland of Eastern England*, eds A. Crowson, T. Lane, K. Penn, and D. Trimble, Lincolnshire Archaeology and Heritage Reports Series, 7 (2005), 264–88.

——, 'Talking to Others: The Domesday Inquest', *Worlds Apart Together: Documents and Society in Medieval England and Japan*, eds H. Tsurushima and D. R. Roffe (forthcoming).

Roffe, D. R. and Mahany, C. M., 'Stamford and the Norman Conquest', *Lincolnshire History and Archaeology*, 21 (1986) 5–9.

Rollason, D. W., 'The Ecclesiastical Context', *The Origins of the Midland Village*, ed. H. S. A. Fox (Leicester, 1992), 73–90.

——, *Sources for York History to AD 1100*, The Archaeology of York, i (1998).

——, 'Monasteries and Society in Early Northumbria', *Monasteries and Society in Medieval Britain*, ed. B. Thompson, Harlaxton Medieval Studies, 6 (Stamford, 1999), 59–74.

Round, J. H., 'The Great Carucage of 1198', *EHR*, 3 (1888), 501–10.

——, *Geoffrey de Mandeville* (London, 1892).

——, *Feudal England* (London, 1895).

——, 'The Domesday Manor', *EHR*, 15 (1900), 293–302.

——, 'Introduction to the Hampshire Domesday', *Victoria County History of Hampshire*, I, ed. H. A. Doubleday (London, 1900), 399–447.

——, 'The Hidation of Northamptonshire', *EHR*, 15 (1900), 78–86.

——, 'Introduction to the Essex Domesday', *Victoria History of the County of Essex*, i, ed. H. A. Doubleday (London, 1903), 333–426.

Rumble, A. R., 'The Palaeography of the Domesday Manuscripts', *Domesday Book: A Reassessment*, ed. P. H. Sawyer (London, 1985), 28–49.

——, 'The Domesday Manuscripts: Scribes and *Scriptoria*', *Domesday Studies*, ed. J. C. Holt (Woodbridge, 1987), 79–100.

——, An Edition and Translation of the Burghal Hidage', *The Defence of Wessex: The Burghal Hidage and Anglo-Saxon Fortification*, eds D. Hill and A. R. Rumble (Manchester, 1996), 14–35.

Sawyer, P. H., 'The "Original Returns" and Domesday Book', *EHR*, 70 (1955), 177–97.

——, 'The Place-Names of the Domesday Manuscripts', *Bulletin of the John Rylands Library*, 38 (1955–6), 483–506.

——, 'Evesham A, a Domesday Text', *Worcestershire Historical Society Miscellany I* (Worcester and London, 1960), 3–36.

——, 'The Wealth of England in the Eleventh Century', *TRHS*, 5th series, 15 (1965), 145–64.

——, 'The Charters of Burton Abbey and the Unification of England', *Northern History*, 10 (1975), 28–39.

—— (ed.), *Medieval Settlement* (London, 1976).

——, '1066–1086: A Tenurial Revolution?' *Domesday Book: A Reassessment*, ed. P. H. Sawyer (London, 1985), 71–85.

——, *Anglo-Saxon Lincolnshire* (Lincoln, 1998).

Scales, L. E., 'The Cambridgeshire Ragman Rolls', *EHR*, 113 (1998), 553–79.

Schofield, J., and Vince, A., *Medieval Towns* (London, 1994).

Searle, E., 'Hides, Virgates and Settlement at Battle Abbey', *EcHR*, 2nd series, 16 (1963–64), 290–300.

Sheppard, J. A., 'Pre-Conquest Yorkshire: Fiscal Carucates as an Index of Land Exploitation', *Institute of British Geographers Transactions,* 65 (1975), 67–78.

Silvester R. J., 'West Walton: The Development of a Siltland Parish', *Norfolk Archaeology*, 39 (1987), 1101–17.

Slade, C. F., *The Leicestershire Survey c. A.D. 1130*, Department of English Local History, University of Leicester, Occasional Papers, 7 (Leicester, 1956).

Slater, T. R., 'English Medieval New Towns with Composite Plans: Evidence from the Midlands', *The Built Form of Western Cities: Essays for M.R.G. Conzen on the Occasion of his 80th Birthday*, ed. T. R. Slater (Leicester, 1990), 60–82.

——, 'English Medieval Town Planning', *Urban Historical Geography: Recent Progress in Britain and Germany,* eds D. Denecke and G. Shaw (Cambridge, 1988), 93–105.

Smith, A. H., *English Place-Name Elements*, English Place-Name Society, 25 and 26 (1956).

Snooks, G. D., 'The Dynamic Role of the Market in the Anglo-Norman Economy and Beyond, 1086–1300', *The Commercialisation of English Society, 1000–1300*, eds R. H. Britnell and B. M. S. Campbell (Manchester, 1993), 27–54.

——, 'A Note on the Calculation of GDP and GDP per capita in 1086 and 1300', *A Commercialising Society*, eds R. H. Britnell and B. M. S. Campbell (Manchester, 1995), appendix 1.

Soulsby, I. N., 'An Introduction to the Cornwall Domesday', *The Cornwall Domesday*, eds A. Williams and R. W. H. Erskine (London, 1988), 1–17.

Spoerry, P., 'The Topography of Anglo-Saxon Huntingdon: A Survey of the Archaeological and Historical Evidence', *Proceedings of the Cambridge Antiquarian Society*, 89 (2001), 35–47.

Stafford, P., 'Women in Domesday', *Reading Medieval Studies*, 15 (1989), 75–94.

——, 'The "Farm of One Night" and the Organisation of King Edward's Estates in Domesday', *EcHR*, 2nd series, 33 (1980), 491–502.

Stenton, D. M. (ed.), *The Great Roll of the Pipe for the Sixth Year of the Reign of King Richard the First, Michaelmas 1194*, Pipe Roll Society, 43 (1928).

Stenton, F. M., 'Domesday Survey', *Victoria History of the County of Derby*, i, ed. W. Page (London, 1905), 293–326.

——, 'Domesday Survey', *Victoria History of the County of Nottingham*, i, ed. W. Page (London, 1906), 207–46.

——, *Types of Manorial Structure in the Northern Danelaw* (Oxford, 1910).

——, 'Introduction', *The Lincolnshire Domesday and Lindsey Survey*, eds C. W. Foster and T. Longley, Lincoln Record Society, 19 (1921), ix–xlvi.

——, *The First Century of English Feudalism 1066–1166* (Oxford, 1932).

——, 'English Families and the Norman Conquest', *TRHS*, 4th series, 26 (1944), 1–12.

——, *The Free Peasantry of the Northern Danelaw* (Oxford, 1969).

——, 'The Danes in England', *Preparatory to Anglo-Saxon England*, ed. D. M. Stenton (Oxford, 1970), 136–65.

——, *Anglo-Saxon England*, 3rd edn (Oxford, 1971).

Stephenson, C., 'The Firma Unius Noctis and the Customs of the Hundred', *EHR*, 39 (1924), 161–74.

——, *Borough and Town: A Study of Urban Origins in England* (Cambridge, Mass., 1933).

——, 'Commendation and Related Problems in Domesday Book', *EHR*, 59 (1944), 289–310.

——, 'Notes on the Composition and Interpretation of Domesday', *Speculum*, 22 (1947), 1–15.

Stevenson, W. H., 'Land Tenures in Nottinghamshire', *Old Nottinghamshire*, 1st series, ed. S. P. Briscoe (Nottingham, 1881), 66–71.

——, 'A Contemporary Description of the Domesday Survey', *EHR*, 22 (1907), 72–84.

Strickland, M., *Anglo-Norman Warfare* (Woodbridge, 1992).

Stubbs, W., *The Constitutional History of England in its Origin and Development*, 3rd edn, 3 vols (Oxford, 1880).

——, *Select Charters and Other Illustrations of English Constitutional History from the Earliest Times to the Reign of Edward the First*, 9th edn (Oxford, 1913).

Swan, V. G., Jones, B. E. A., and Grady, D., 'Bolesford, North of Yorkshire: A Lost Wapentake Centre and its Landscape', *Landscape History*, 15 (1993), 13–28.

Swanson, H., *Medieval British Towns* (New York, 1999).

Swedberg, R., *The Max Weber Dictionary: Key Words and Central Concepts* (Stanford, 2005).

Tait, J., Review of *Domesday Book and Beyond*, *EHR*, 12 (1897), 768–77.

——, *The Medieval English Borough* (Manchester, 1936).

Taylor, C., *Fields in the English Landscape* (Stroud, 2000).

Taylor, P., 'The Endowment and Military Obligations of the See of London: A Reassessment of Three Sources', *ANS*, 14 (1991), 285–312.

——, 'Boundaries and Margins: Barnet, Finchley, and Totteridge', *Medieval Ecclesiastical Studies in Honour of Dorothy M. Owen*, eds M. J. Franklin and C. Harper-Bill (Woodbridge, 1995), 259–79.

——, 'Introduction', *Little Domesday Book, Essex*, eds A. Williams and G. H. Martin (London, 2000), 9–32.

Thacker, A. T., 'The Early Medieval City and its Buildings', *Medieval Archaeology, Art and Architecture at Chester*, ed. A. T. Thacker, British Archaeological Association, Conference Transactions, 22 (Leeds, 2000), 16–30.

Thacker, A. T. and Sawyer, P. H., 'Domesday Survey', *Victoria History of the County of Chester*, i, ed. B. E. Harris (London, 1987), 293–341.

Thomas, H. M., 'The Significance and Fate of the Native English Landholders of 1086', *EHR*, 118 (2003), 303–33.

Thorn, C., 'Marginal Notes and Signs in Domesday Book', *Domesday Book Studies*, eds A. Williams and R. W. H. Erskine (London, 1987), 113–35.

Thorn, F. R., 'The Identification of Domesday Places in the South-Western Counties of England', *Nomina*, 10 (1986), 41–59.

——, 'Hundreds and Wapentakes', *The Buckinghamshire Domesday*, eds A. Williams and R. W. H. Erskine (London, 1988), 37–41.

——, 'Hundreds and Wapentakes', *The Hampshire Domesday*, eds A. Williams and R. W. H. Erskine (London, 1989), 28–39.

——, 'Hundreds and Wapentakes', *The Sussex Domesday*, eds A. Williams and R. W. H. Erskine (London, 1990), 26–42.

——, '"Another Seaborough", "The Other Dinnaton": Some Manorial Affixes in Domesday Book', *Names, Places, and People: An Onomastic Miscellany for John McNeal Dodgson*, eds A. R. Rumble and A. D. Mills (Stamford, 1997), 345–77.

Thorn, F. R., and Thorn, C., 'The Writing of Great Domesday Book', *Domesday*, eds E. M. Hallam and D. Bates (Stroud, 2001), 37–73.

Tsurushima, H., 'Feodum in Kent c.1066–1215', *Journal of Medieval History*, 21 (1995), 97–115.

——, 'Domesday Interpreters', *ANS*, 18 (1996), 201–22.

Tudor, T. L., 'Repton, Northworthy (Derby), and Wirksworth', *Journal of the Derbyshire Archaeological and Natural History Society*, 44 (1922), 44–57.

Urry, W., *Canterbury under the Angevin Kings* (London, 1967).

Vinogradoff, P., *English Society in the Eleventh Century* (Oxford, 1908).

Walmsley, J. F. R., 'The "Censarii" of Burton Abbey and the Domesday Population', *North Staffordshire Journal of Field Studies*, 8 (1968), 73–80.

——, 'Another Domesday Text', *Medieval Studies*, 39 (1977), 109–20.

Wareham, A., 'The "Feudal Revolution" in Eleventh-Century East Anglia', *ANS*, 22 (2000), 293–321.

Warner, P., *The Origins of Suffolk* (Manchester, 1996).

Warren, W. L., *The Governance of Norman and Angevin England, 1086–1272* (London, 1987).

——, 'The Myth of Norman Administrative Efficiency', *TRHS*, 5th series, 34 (1984), 113–32.

Webber, T., 'Salisbury and the Exon Domesday: Some Observations Concerning the Origins of Exeter Cathedral MS 3500', *English Manuscript Studies 1100–1700*, I, eds P. Beal and J. Griffiths (Oxford, 1989), 1–18.

Welldon Finn, R., 'The Evolution of Successive Versions of Domesday Book', *EHR*, 66 (1951), 561–4.

——, 'The Exeter Domesday and its Construction', *Bulletin of the John Rylands Library*, 41 (1958–9), 360–87.

——, 'Some Reflections on the Cambridgeshire Domesday', *Proceedings of the Cambridge Antiquarian Society*, 53 (1960), 29–38.

——, 'The *Inquisitio Eliensis* Reconsidered', *EHR*, 75 (1960), 385–409.

——, *The Domesday Inquest and the Making of Domesday Book* (London, 1961).

——, *Domesday Studies: The Liber Exoniensis* (London, 1964).

——, *Domesday Studies: The Eastern Counties* (London, 1967).

——, 'Hampshire', *The Domesday Geography of South-East England*, eds H. C. Darby and E. M. J. Campbell (Cambridge, 1971).

——, *The Norman Conquest and its Effects on the Economy 1066–1086* (London, 1971).

Whalley, P., *The History and Antiquities of Northamptonshire, Compiled from the Manuscript Collection of John Bridges* (Oxford, 1791).

Wightman, W. E., *The Lacy Family in England and Normandy, 1066–1194* (Oxford, 1966).

——, 'The Significance of "Waste" in the Yorkshire Domesday', *Northern History*, 10 (1975), 55–71.

Williams, A., '*Princeps Merciorum Gentis*: The Family, Career and Connections of Ælfhere, Ealdorman of Mercia 956–83', *Anglo-Saxon England*, 10 (1982), 143–72.

——, 'How Land was Held Before and After the Conquest', *Domesday Book Studies*, eds A. Williams and R. W. H. Erskine (London, 1987), 37–8.

——, 'Apparent Repetitions in Domesday Book', *Domesday Book Studies*, eds A. Williams and R. W. H. Erskine (London, 1987), 90–2.

——, 'An Introduction to the Worcestershire Domesday', *The Worcestershire Domesday*, eds A. Williams and R. W. H. Erskine (London, 1988), 1–39.

——, 'The King's Nephew: The Family, Career, and Connections of Ralph, Earl of Hereford', *Studies in Medieval History Presented to R. Allen Brown*, eds C. Harper-Bill and J. L. Nelson (Woodbridge, 1989), 327–43.

——, 'An Introduction to the Gloucestershire Domesday', *The Gloucestershire Domesday*, eds A. Williams and R. W. H. Erskine (London, 1989), 1–39.

——, 'A Bell-House and a Burh-geat: Lordly Residence before the Norman Conquest', *The Ideals and Practice of Medieval Knighthood*, 4 (Woodbridge, 1992), 221–40.

——, *The English and the Norman Conquest* (Woodbridge, 1995).

——, 'The Spoliation of Worcester', *ANS*, 19 (1996), 383–408.

——, 'A West Country Magnate of the Eleventh Century: The Family, Estates and Patronage of Beorhtric son of Ælgar', *Family Trees and the Roots of Politics*, ed. K. S. B. Keats-Rohan (Woodbridge, 1997), 41–68.

——, *Kingship and Government in Pre-Conquest England c.500–1066* (London, 1999).

——, 'The Abbey Tenants and Servants in the 12th Century', *Studies in the Early History of Shaftesbury Abbey*, ed. L. Keen (Dorchester, 1999), 1131–60.

——, 'Little Domesday and the English: The Hundred of Colneis in Suffolk', *Domesday Book*, eds E. M. Hallam and D. Bates (Stroud, 2001), 103–290.

——, 'Meet the *Antecessores*: Lords and Land in Eleventh-Century Suffolk', *Anglo-Saxons: Studies Presented to Cyril Roy Hart*, eds S. Keynes and A. P. Smyth (Dublin, 2005), 275–87.

Williamson, T., *The Origins of Norfolk* (Manchester, 1993).

Witney, K. P., *The Jutist Forest: A Study of the Weald of Kent from 450 to 1380 AD* (London, 1976).

Wormald, P., 'Ethelred the Lawmaker', *Ethelred the Unready*, ed. D. Hill (Oxford, 1978), 47–80.

——, 'Domesday Lawsuits: A Provisional List and Preliminary Comments', *England in the Eleventh Century*, ed. C. Hicks, Harlaxton Medieval Studies, 2 (Stamford, 1992), 61–102.

——, 'Oswaldslow: an "Immunity"?', *St Oswald of Worcester: Life and Influence*, eds N. P. Brooks and C. Cubitt (Leicester and New York, 1996), 117–28.

——, *The Making of English Law: King Alfred to the Twelfth Century – Volume I, Legislation and its Limits* (Oxford, 1999).

Wright, M., *Introduction to the Laws of Tenure* (London, 1730).

Wyatt, D., 'The Significance of Slavery: Alternative Approaches to Anglo-Saxon Slavery', *ANS*, 23 (2000), 327–47.

Index

Martinsley Wapentake (Rutl), 43 n60, 92, 244, 245 n167, 296 n79
Martley (Suff), 89
Marton (Lancs), 247
Mashbury (Essex), 274 n92
Massingham (Norf), 49, 298
Matilda, Queen, wife of Henry I, 25
Matilda, Queen, wife of William I, 55
Matthew Paris, 4
Mayhew, N., 211
McDonald, J., 20
Medbourne (Leics), 302
median thegn, 150, 153, 157–8, 159, 163, 164–5, 170, 219, 223
Melling (Lancs), 247
Melsham Hundred (Wilts), 78
Membury (Devon), 75
Meols (Lancs), 247
Meon, West (Hants), 242 n149
mercenaries, 8, 14, 15, 181, 309
Merset Hundred (Salop), 92
Merton (Norf), 290
metastructures of lordship, 291–304
Meulan, Count of, Robert de Beaumont, 130
Mew, K., 199 n76
Mickleover (Derby), 247
Middleton (Derby), 295
Middleton (Norf), 49, 266, 270, 297, 298
Middleton, Stonely (Derby), 295
miles, 164, 219–20
milites inquisitores, 71. *See also* knights of the shire
Miles Crispin, 96, 171 n146, 172
Miles the porter, 119
military service, 9 n27, 128, 145–6, 152, 153 n48, 167 n100, 180, 181, 267, 287, 310
  boroughs, 124
  geld, 145, 183–4, 193–7, 267, 310–12
  pre-Conquest, 193
miller, 51
mill, 210, 230, 237–8, 242, 248, 315
  millstones, 230 n91
  value of, 238 n131, 242 n152
minster hypothesis, 237, 284
mint tax, 120
Mintlyn (Norf), 49, 266
Mitford Hundred (Norf), 48

moneyer, 121–2, 129, 130, 138 n142
Monksilver (Soms), 268
Monmouthshire, 131
Monnow, River, 131
Moore, J. S., 229, 230, 231
Morcar, Earl, 159 n80, 276 n102
  mother of, 117 n41
Morris, John, 32
Mortlake (Surrey), 243
Morton (Notts), 159, 263
Moulton (Lincs), 84
Moulton St Mary (Norf), 262
Muchelney (Soms), 202
multiple estates, 281–7, 304–5
multiple lord entries, 149–50
multiple manor entries, 83, 150 n32, 159 n85, 160, 252, 289 n41, 290
Mumby (Lincs), 83 n118
  hundred, 83 n118
Munby, Julian, 199 n76
Murton (Yorks), 260

Nafford (Worcs), 294
Nash, A., 230
National Archives, 1
Naunton (Worcs), 294
Netheravon (Wilts), 251
New Forest, 166, 199 and note
Newark Wapentake (Notts), 266
Newbold, place-name, 288
Newbold (Derby), 289 n40
Newbold Astbury (Ches), 289 n40
Newport Pagnell (Bucks), 202, 230
Newthorpe (Notts), 263
Newton Harcourt (Leics), 303
Newton, West, (Norf), 49, 298
Nigel the physician, 251
Nomina Villarum, 263
Norfolk, hundreds of, 48, 76
Norman Crassus, 80
Normancross Hundreds (Hunts), 297
Normanton (Derby), 263 n20
Normanton, Frieston, and West Willoughby (Lincs)
  three hundreds of, 225 n72
Northallerton (Yorks), 50 n90
Northampton (Northants), 115, 117, 118, 126, 141
  new borough, 133

Pensham (Worcs), 294
Pentateuch, 52
Pentney (Norf), 49, 297, 298
Peopleton (Worcs), 294
Perching (Sussex), 149 n30, 160 n90
Pershore (Worcs), 294, 296
  hundred (Worcs), 270, 293
Pershore Abbey, 294
personal names, 147–9, 163–6
Peter de Valognes, 79, 215 n22
Peterborough Abbey, 45, 84, 157, 173, 201,
    230, 232 n100, 246, 314
  abbot of, 79, 80, 112 n20
  cartulary of, 24
  lands, 212 n11, 232
Petherton, South (Soms), 267
Pevensey (Sussex), 114, 140
Pevensey Rape of (Sussex), 166
Peverel, honour of, 127 n102, 175
Phillimore edition of Domesday, 32–6
photozincography, 35
Pickering (Yorks), 207
Pickworth (Lincs), 262
Picot, sheriff of Cambridge, 69 n34, 71
    n50, 96
  Cambs breve, 95 n170
Piddle (Worcs), 294
Piddle, River (Dorset), 186
pigs, 6, 10, 25, 230, 233–4
Pilsey (Notts), 159
Pilsley (Derby), 295
Pinchbeck (Lincs), 84
  hundred, 84
Pirton (Worcs), 294
place-names, referents of, 184–90, 286
pleas, 97, 128, 257, 264, 277, 308
  in Kent, 277 n103
  shire and hundred, 130, 242
plough, 217–19, 233, 249, 309–10
  additional, 218
  could be restored, restaurari, 205 n99,
    207 n114, 218
  count of, 193, 207
  in Bath A, 217
  on inland, 209, 313
  plough shear, 233 n105
  slaves and, 227
  TRE, 51, 207
  supply to demesne, 15

See also overstocking
ploughland, 15, 44 n66, 51, 102, 106, 107
    n215, 131 n109, 198, 203–9, 217 n32,
    231, 249, 250, 252, 253, 260, 262,
    309–10, 315
  in East Anglia, 80 n101, 205
  meadow measured in, 72 n57
  new assessment, 15
ploughman, 227
Pollock, F., 65
population figures, 229–33
Postan, M. M., 229
Potterne (Wilts), 146 n14, 220
Powick (Worcs), 294
Prestgrave (Leics), 302
priest, 11, 60, 64, 77, 92, 229
pro manerio, 40, 53, 91 n159, 177, 179–80,
    311
  See also manor
productive efficiency, 21
Puddle, Little (Dors), 235
Pyrford (Surrey), 56
Pyrton Hundred (Oxon), 25

quando invenit, 50, 90
  See also value
Quarndon (Derby), 126
Quarrington (Lincs), 291, 292
querele, 69, 80, 308
quire signatures, 41
quotas, see geld

Ralph, Earl, 223 n64
r', require, 276 n101
Rackham, Oliver, 237
Rada, 174 n153
Radford (Notts), 263
radknight, radman, 51, 222, 224, 267. See
    also escort
Ragman inquest, see inquest
Raisthorpe (Yorks), 285
Ralf de Mortimer, 96, 119
Ralph, earl of Hereford, 150
Ralph Baynard, 47, 290
Ralph de Bapaume, 80
Ralph de la Pommeraye, 75
Ralph de Tosny, 47
Ralph Paynel, 80
Ralph Taillebois, 156, 194 n61

stratigraphy, textual, 32, 36–7, 43–7, 50
n90, 92, 104 n203, 148 n23, 269
Street (Kent), 131 n108
Strelley (Notts), 263
Stretton (Leics), 302, 303
Stretton (Rutl), 92
Stretton (Staffs), 209
Stuppington (Kent), 45 n71
sub, holding under, 162 n98
Sudborough (Northants), 240 n141
Sudbury (Suff), 114, 117 n41, 140
suit of court, 151, 156, 201, 216, 273
hundred, 25, 267, 271
seigneurial, 124
shire, 67, 271–3
See also jury
sulingland, 201
sulung, 190–1
summaries, 29, 30, 95–6, 178, 205, 213, 217,
241, 249, 260, 309, 311, 315, 316
Sunridge (Kent), 180 n186
Surrey
rate of aassessment, 192
sheriff of, 116 n34
Sussex, rate of assessment, 192
Swanscombe (Kent), 238 n130
Swarkestone (Derby), 263 n20
Swein of Essex, 124 n83
Swein, Earl, 145 n8
Swineshead (Beds), 267
Symeon, abbot of Ely, 95

taillia, tallagium, 47, 242
taini regis, 118 n42, 158, 158 n77, 163, 164,
289
Tait, James, 110
Tarrant, River (Dorset), 186
Taunton (Soms), 98, 154, 200 n83
customs of, 264–5
hundred, 264–5
Taverham Hundred (Norf), 48
Tavistock, abbot of, 274 n92
Tawton, South (Devon), 267
taxonomy, 54–61
Teigh (Rutl), 92, 188 n20
Templecombe (Soms), 107
tenant
TRE and TRW, 289–90
TRW, 163–5. *See also* honorial barony

tenuit, 102, 160, 161 n96, 162, 171, 172, 289,
290, 300
tenuit cum soca et saca, 161 n92
tenet de rege, 180 n185
tenuit libere, 161
terra, 152, 153, 170–1, 177, 315
terra regis, outside quotas, 194–5, 262–4
terra villanorum, 225
terre occupate, 29, 96, 99, 167, 275, 276,
278
Terrington (Norf), 49, 297, 298, 300 n93
territorialization of lordship, 318. *See also*
manorialization
Tewkesbury (Gloucs), 224, 282
Textus Roffensis, 24, 307
Thacker, A. T., 71–2
Thame Hundred (Oxon), 270
Thames Ditton (Surrey), 180 n186
Thaxted (Essex), 243
Theddingworth (Leics), 303
Thedwestrey Hunded (Suff), 261
thegnage, 155, 178, 223, 285
thegnland, 95 n172, 274 n92
thegns of the shire, 273 n87
Theodbert, 79
Thetford (Norf), 114, 118, 123 n75, 139, 140
burgesses, 123 n75
hundred, 48, 124
Thetford, bishop of, 47, 51, 85, 173 n150.
See also William
Thingoe Hunded (Suff), 261
third penny, 126. *See also* two pennies
Thistleton (Rutland), 92, 242 n153
Thixendale (Yorks), 285
Thomas, archbishop of York, 119
Thompson, John, 17
Thor, 159 n80
Thorbiorn, 123
Thorfinnr, 159 n80
Thorgot, 172
Thorgot Lag, 159 n80
Thorir, 173
Thorkil of Warwick, 164
Thorn, 290
Thorn, Caroline, 35, 36, 45, 46 n77, 57,
100
Thorn, Frank, 35, 36, 50, 57, 100, 189, 284
n17
Thorney (Cambs), 202